PENGUIN BOOKS

THE NORMANS IN SICILY

John Julius Norwich was born in 1929. He was educated at Upper Canada College, Toronto, at Eton, at the University of Strasbourg and, after a spell of National Service in the Navy, at New College, Oxford, where he took a degree in French and Russian. In 1952 he joined the Foreign Service and remained in it for twelve years, serving at the embassies in Belgrade and Beirut and with the British Delegation to the Disarmament Conference at Geneva. In 1964 he resigned from the service in order to write.

He has published two books on the medieval Norman Kingdom in Sicily, *The Normans in the South* and *The Kingdom in the Sun*, published in Penguin in one volume entitled *The Normans in Sicily*; two travel books, *Mount Athos* (with Reresby Sitwell) and *Sahara*; books on *The Architecture of Southern England* and *Glyndebourne*; and two anthologies of poetry and prose, *Christmas Crackers* and *More Christmas Crackers*. He is the author of *A History of Venice*, which was originally published in two volumes, and of *Byzantium: The Early Centuries* and *Byzantium: The Apogee*, the first two volumes of a projected three volume history of the Byzantine Empire. Many of his books are published by Penguin. In addition he has written and presented some thirty historical documentaries for television and is a regular lecturer on Venice and numerous other subjects.

Lord Norwich is chairman of the Venice in Peril Fund, Co-chairman of the World Monument Fund and a member of the Executive Committee of the National Trust. He is a Fellow of the Royal Society of Literature, the Royal Geographical Society and the Society of Antiquaries, and a Commendatore of the Ordine al Merito della Repubblica Italiana. He was awarded a CVO in 1993.

John Julius Norwich

———

THE NORMANS IN SICILY

THE NORMANS IN THE SOUTH
1016–1130
and
THE KINGDOM IN THE SUN
1130–1194

PENGUIN BOOKS

PENGUIN BOOKS

Published by the Penguin Group
Penguin Books Ltd, 27 Wrights Lane, London w8 5tz, England
Penguin Books USA Inc., 375 Hudson Street, New York, New York 10014, USA
Penguin Books Australia Ltd, Ringwood, Victoria, Australia
Penguin Books Canada Ltd, 10 Alcorn Avenue, Toronto, Ontario, Canada m4v 3b2
Penguin Books (NZ) Ltd, 182–190 Wairau Road, Auckland 10, New Zealand

Penguin Books Ltd, Registered Offices: Harmondsworth, Middlesex, England

The Normans in the South first published by Longmans, Green and Co. 1967
The Kingdom in the Sun first published by Longman Group Ltd 1970
This omnibus edition first published in Penguin Books 1992

3 5 7 9 10 8 6 4 2

Copyright © John Julius Norwich, 1967, 1970
All rights reserved

Made and printed in England by Clays Ltd, St Ives plc

CONTENTS

THE NORMANS IN
THE SOUTH

1016–1130

For Anne

CONTENTS

LIST OF ILLUSTRATIONS

LIST OF ILLUSTRATIONS

Genealogical trees

Maps

No chapter of history more resembles a romance than that which records the sudden rise and brief splendour of the house of Hauteville. In one generation the sons of Tancred passed from the condition of squires in the Norman vale of Cotentin, to kinghood in the richest island of the southern sea. The Norse adventurers became Sultans of an Oriental capital. The sea-robbers assumed together with the sceptre the culture of an Arabian court. The marauders whose armies burned Rome received at papal hands the mitre and dalmatic as symbols of ecclesiastical jurisdiction.

JOHN ADDINGTON SYMONDS,
Sketches in Italy and Greece

INTRODUCTION

In October 1961 my wife and I went on a holiday to Sicily. I think I was vaguely aware that the Normans had ruled there some time in the Middle Ages, but I certainly knew very little else. At any rate I was totally unprepared for what I found. Here were cathedrals, churches and palaces which seemed to combine, without effort or strain, all that was loveliest in the art and architecture of the three leading civilisations of the time—the North European, the Byzantine and the Saracen. Here, in the dead centre of the Mediterranean, was the bridge between North and South, East and West, Latin and Teuton, Christian and Muslim; superb, unanswerable testimony to an age of tolerance and enlightenment on a scale unknown anywhere else in mediaeval Europe and, even in succeeding centuries, seldom equalled. I became very over-excited and longed to know more. The holidays over, I took the only sensible course and made straight for the London Library.

I was in for a sad surprise. A few works, mostly in French or German, of formidable nineteenth-century scholarship and paralysing dullness, lurked on an upper shelf; but for the ordinary English reader, seeking merely a general account of Norman Sicily, there was practically nothing. For a moment I almost wondered whether that most invaluable and trustworthy of all English institutions had let me down at last; at the same time, I knew perfectly well that it hadn't. If the London Library did not possess the sort of book I wanted, it could only be because no such book was in existence. And so it was that I first came face to face with a question which, after five years, still has me baffled: why is it that one of the most extraordinary and fascinating epics of European history between the ages of Julius Caesar and Napoleon should be so little known to the world at large? Even in France any reference to the subject is apt to be greeted by a blank expression and a faintly embarrassed silence; while in England, which after all suffered a similar—though far less exciting—Norman conquest of its own at almost exactly the same time and was later to provide Sicily with several statesmen and even a queen, the general bewilderment seems to be yet greater. M. Ferdinand Chalandon, author of the still definitive work on the period, included in his monumental bibliography of well over six hundred items only one English author, Gibbon; and though in the sixty intervening years this country has produced a number of scholars, magnificently led by Miss Evelyn Jamison, who have hacked out many a clearing and planted their flags in the darker corners of the forest, to this day I know of only two non-specialist works in English which tell even part of the story in any detail: E. Curtis's *Roger of Sicily*, written with a conscientious if somewhat heavy hand shortly before the First World War, and *The Greatest Norman Conquest*—there's a give-away title if you like—by Mr J. Van Wyck Osborne, whose thoughtful scholarship is endlessly sabotaged by the exuberance of his imagination. Both these books, incidentally, were published in New York; both are long out of print; and neither covers the whole period.

The conclusion was inescapable: if I wanted a complete history of Norman Sicily in English for the average reader, I should have to write it myself. And that is how it comes about that I now put forward, gingerly and with much diffidence, the first of two volumes which will together carry the story through from the first day, in 1016, when a party of Norman pilgrims was accosted in the shrine of the Archangel Michael on Monte Gargano, to the last, a hundred and seventy-eight years later, when the brightest crown of the Mediterranean passed to one of the blackest of the German Emperors. The present volume covers the first hundred and fourteen of those years and closes on Christmas Day 1130, when Sicily at last became a kingdom, and Roger II her king. They are the epic years, the years of endeavour and conquest, dominated by the sons and grandsons of Tancred de Hauteville and, above all, by the towering bulk of Robert Guiscard, one of history's few military adventurers of genius to have started from nothing and died undefeated. Thereafter the mood changes; northern harshness softens in the sun; and the clash of steel slowly dies away, giving place to the whisper of fountains in a shaded patio and the ripple of plucked strings. Thus the second volume will tell of the golden age of Norman Sicily, the age of Cefalu, of Monreale and the Palatine Chapel at Palermo; and then, sadly, of its decline and collapse. True, its spirit was to live on for another half-century in Frederick II, *Stupor Mundi*, the greatest of Renaissance princes two hundred years before his time, and in his lovely son Manfred. But Frederick, though a Hauteville on his mother's side and by his upbringing, was also a Hohenstaufen and an Emperor. His is a glorious, tragic story; but it is not ours.

This book makes no claim to original scholarship. Apart from anything else, I am no scholar. Despite eight years of what is still optimistically known as a classical education and a recent agonising refresher course, my Latin remains poor and my Greek worse. Though I have all too often had to struggle through contemporary sources in the original, I have gratefully seized on translations wherever they have been available and duly noted them in the bibliography; and though I have tried to read as widely as possible around the subject so as to fit the story into the general European context, I do not pretend to have unearthed any new material or to have put forward any startlingly original conclusions. The same goes for fieldwork. I think I have visited every site of importance mentioned in this book (many of them in unspeakably adverse weather) but my researches in local libraries and archives have been brief and—except in the Vatican—largely unfruitful. No matter. My purpose was simply, as I have said, to provide ordinary readers with the sort of book I wished I had had on my first visit to Sicily—something that would explain how the Normans got there in the first place, what sort of a country they made of it, and how they managed to imbue it with a culture at once so beautiful and so unique. Pausing now for breath, I only wish that I could do them greater justice.

ACKNOWLEDGEMENTS

Among the many friends in Italy who have helped and advised me with this book, I should like in particular to thank Dr and Mrs Milton Gendel for all their hospitality as well as for much historical expertise; Miss Georgina Masson, whose deep knowledge of mediaeval Italy and many bibliographical suggestions were invaluable; the Duchessa Lante della Rovere for immensely useful research; Dom Angelo Mifsud, O.S.B., archivist of the Badia della Cava, Salerno; Conte Dr Sigmund Fago Golfarelli, head of the Press Department of the Ente Nazionale Italiano per il Turismo; and the late Father Guy Ferrari, whose recent untimely death is a sad blow for the Vatican Library and for all who work there.

In England I am especially grateful to Dr Jonathan Riley-Smith, whose kindness and erudition have saved me from many a nasty slip. Sir Steven Runciman and Mr Sacheverell Sitwell and their publishers, the Clarendon Press and Messrs Gerald Duckworth & Co., Ltd, have kindly allowed me to quote from their work; and I am also indebted to Messrs Routledge and Kegan Paul Ltd and to Messrs Thomas Nelson & Sons Ltd for their permission to reproduce material from Miss E. Dawes's translation of *The Alexiad* and Professor R. W. Southern's translation of Eadmer's *Vita Anselmi*. Professor Nancy Lambton of London University took endless trouble to track down the Iqbal poem which provides the epigraph for Chapter 13. The translation from the original Urdu was made specially for me by her late colleague, Mr G. D. Gaur—a spontaneous gesture to an unknown enquirer for which I fear I did not thank him adequately in his lifetime. My thanks are also due to Mr C. R. Ligota of the Warburg Institute and to several, alas anonymous, members of the staff of the Bibliothèque Nationale in Paris.

But my deepest gratitude goes to my cousin, Mr Rupert

Hart-Davis. No one understands better than he how a book should be written: no one could have given more generously of his time, experience and wisdom. My debt to him is enormous—and is shared, more than they know, by my readers, for if this book is found to be at all readable, it is due in large measure to him. Here is a debt which can be acknowledged, but never repaid.

Virtually every word of what follows has been written in the Reading Room of the London Library; and it only remains for me to echo the words of so many thousand authors before me—that without the Library's inexhaustible resources, supplemented by the patience, sympathy and good humour of every member of its staff, I do not see how my work could ever, possibly, have been done.

London, 1966   J. J. N.

Note: Translations, except where otherwise indicated, are my own.

PART ONE

THE CONQUEST

I

BEGINNINGS

His starrie Holme unbuckl'd shew'd him prime
In manhood where youth ended; by his side
As in a glistering *Zodiac* hung the Sword,
Satan's dire dread, and in his hand the Spear.

Paradise Lost, Book XI

To the traveller, heading eastwards from Foggia to the sea, the gaunt grey shadow of Monte Gargano looms over the plain like a thunder-cloud. It is a curious excrescence, this dark limestone mass rising so unexpectedly from the fields of Apulia and, heedless of the gentle sweep of the coastline, jutting forty miles or so into the Adriatic—curious and somehow awesome. For centuries it has been known as the 'spur' of Italy—not a very good name even from the pictorial point of view, since it is much too far up the boot and seems to have been fixed on backwards. It is more like a hard callus, accidental, unlooked-for and basically unwelcome. Even the land-scape, with its thick beech-forests, more Germanic than Italian; even the climate, raw and torn by winds; even the population, sombre, black-swathed and old (in contradistinction to anywhere else in Apulia, where the average age of the urban population, to all appearances exclusively male, seems to be about seven), bespeak a strange foreignness. Monte Gargano, to visitors and natives alike, is different. It does not really belong.

This feeling has always existed among the Apulians, and they have always reacted to it in the same way. Since the days of remotest antiquity an aura of holiness has hung over the mountain. Already in classical times it possessed at least two important shrines, one to Podaleirius—an ancient warrior-hero of small achievement and less

3

interest—and one to old Calchas, the soothsayer of the *Iliad*, where according to Strabo 'those who consult the oracle sacrifice to his shade a black ram and then sleep in the hide'. With the advent of Christianity these devotions continued, as frequently happened after the minimum of adjustment necessary to keep up with the times; so that by the fifth century, with a thousand years or so of uninterrupted sanctity behind it, the mountain was fully ripe for the miracle which then occurred. On 5 May in the year 493 a local cattle-owner, looking for a fine bull which he had lost, eventually found the animal in a dark cave, deep in the mountain-side. Repeated attempts to entice it out having proved unsuccessful, he at last in despair shot an arrow in its direction. To his astonishment, the arrow halted in mid-course, turned sharply back and embedded itself in his own thigh, where it inflicted an unpleasant flesh-wound. Hastening homeward as best he could, he reported the incident to Laurentius, Bishop of nearby Siponto, who ordered a three-day fast throughout the diocese. On the third day Laurentius himself visited the scene of the miracle. Scarcely had he arrived before the Archangel Michael appeared in full armour, announcing that the cave was henceforth to be a shrine to himself and to all the angels. He then vanished, leaving behind as a sign his great iron spur. When Laurentius returned with a party of followers a few days later, he found that the angels had been busy in his absence; the grotto had been transformed into a chapel, its walls hung with purple; everything was bathed in a soft, warm light. Murmuring praises, the bishop commanded that a church be built upon the rock above the entrance; and four months later, on 29 September, he consecrated it to the Archangel.[1]

In the little town of Monte Sant' Angelo Laurentius's church has long since disappeared, but the Archangel Michael is not forgotten. The entrance to his cave is now proclaimed by an octagonal thirteenth-century bell-tower and a rather ponderous porch built a hundred years ago in the romanesque style. Within, flight after flight of steps lead down into the bowels of the rock. On each side the walls are festooned with votive offerings—crutches, trusses, artificial limbs; eyes, noses, legs, breasts, inexpertly stamped on sheets

[1] The story is told in the Roman Breviary, Proper Office of the Saints for 8 May.

of tin; pictures, genuine peasant primitives, of highway collisions, runaway horses, overturning saucepans and other unpleasant accidents in which the victim owed his salvation to the miraculous intervention of the Archangel; and, most touching of all, fancy dress costumes which have been worn by small children in his honour—once again in gratitude for services rendered—tiny wooden swords, tinfoil wings and biscuit-tin breastplates, accompanied as often as not by a photograph of the wearer, all now gradually decaying against the dark, damp stone. At the bottom, guarded by a magnificent pair of Byzantine bronze doors—gift of a rich Amalfitan in 1076—lies the cave itself, in essence much as Laurentius must have left it. The air within it is still loud with the muttered devotions and heavy with the incense of fifteen hundred years, just as it is damp with the moisture that drips remorselessly from the glistening roof of rock and is subsequently dispensed to the faithful in little plastic beakers. The principal altar, ablaze with light and crowned with a glutinously emasculate statue of the Archangel which could not possibly be by Sansovino, takes up one corner; the rest is given over to crumbling columns, to long-abandoned altars in deep recesses, to darkness and to time.

It was not long before Monte Sant' Angelo became one of the great pilgrim shrines of Europe. It was visited by saints, like St Gregory the Great at the end of the sixth century, or like St Francis in the middle of the thirteenth, who set a poor example to the faithful by carving an initial on the altar just inside the entrance; by emperors, like the Saxon Otto II, who came with his lovely young Byzantine wife, Theophano, in 981, or their mystic, megalomaniac son Otto III who, in an excess of zeal, walked all the way barefoot from Rome; and also perhaps, on a somewhat humbler level in the year 1016, by a band of Norman pilgrims whose conversation with a curiously-dressed stranger in that very cave changed the course of history and led to the foundation of one of the most powerful and magnificent kingdoms of the Middle Ages.

By the beginning of the eleventh century the Normans had virtually completed the process by which, in barely a hundred years, they had transformed themselves from a collection of almost illiterate heathen barbarians into a civilised, if unscrupulous, semi-independent Christian state. It was, even for so energetic and gifted a race, a stupendous achievement. Men were still alive whose fathers could have remembered Rollo, the fair-haired viking who led his long-boats up the Seine and was enfeoffed with most of the eastern half of modern Normandy by the French king Charles the Simple in 911. To be sure, Rollo was not the earliest of the Norman invaders; the first wave had descended from the forests and the fjords over half a century before, and since then the migration had persisted at a fairly steady rate. But it was he who focused the energies and aspirations of his countrymen and set them on the path of amalgamation and identification with their new homeland. Already in 912 a considerable number of them, led by Rollo himself, received Christian baptism. Some indeed, according to Gibbon, received it 'ten or twelve times, for the sake of the white garment usually given at this ceremony', while the fact that 'at the funeral of Rollo, the gifts to monasteries for the repose of his soul were accompanied by a sacrifice of one hundred captives' suggests that in these early years political expediency may have been no less strong a motive for conversion than was spiritual enlightenment, and that Thor and Odin did not give way without a struggle before the feathery on-slaught of the Holy Ghost. But within a generation or two, as Gibbon himself admits, 'the national change was pure and general'. The same was true of language. By 940 the old Norse tongue, while still spoken at Bayeux and on the coast (where the newer immigrants presumably kept it alive), was already forgotten at Rouen; before the end of the century it had died out altogether, leaving hardly a trace behind. One last great institution remained for the Normans to adopt before they could become Frenchmen—an institution that in the years to come was to exert a perennial fascination over them and their descendants and was soon to form the cornerstone of two of the most efficiently run states the world has ever seen. This was the rapidly rising edifice of French law; and they adopted it with open arms.

A pre-occupation with law was a hallmark of most mediaeval societies of the West; but it remains one of the paradoxes of Norman history that it should have persisted so strongly among a race notorious for its lawlessness throughout Europe. Piracy, perjury, robbery, rape, blackmail, murder—such crimes as these were being committed, cheerfully and continually, on every level from the personal to the national, by Norman kings, dukes and barons, long before the Crusades came still further to debase the moral standards of the civilised world. The explanation is that the Normans were above all pragmatists. They saw the law, quite simply, as a magnificent and firmly rooted structure on which a state could be built, and which could be used as a bulwark to strengthen their position in any enterprise they might undertake. As such, it was not their master but their slave, and they sought to uphold it merely because a strong slave is more useful than a weak one. This attitude prevailed among all the Norman rulers, whether in the north or the south. It explains why even the most unscrupulous among them nearly always managed to produce some ingenious legal justification for everything they did; and why the greatest Norman architects of statehood, King Henry II of England and King Roger of Sicily, were to concentrate above all on building up a massive legal system throughout their realms. None of them ever looked upon the law that they created as an abstract ideal; still less did they make the mistake of confusing it with justice.

This pragmatic approach and preoccupation with outward form were also evident in the Norman attitude to religion. They seem to have been genuinely God-fearing—as everybody was in the Middle Ages—and like most people they clung to the simple, selfish mediaeval belief that the primary object of religion was to enable one, after death, to avoid the fires of hell and ascend to heaven as promptly and as painlessly as possible. The smoothness of this journey could, it was generally believed, best be assured by the straightforward means prescribed by the Church—regular attendance at Mass, the requisite amount of fasting, a little penance when necessary, an occasional pilgrimage and, if possible, generous endowments to religious foundations. So long as these formalities were observed, everyday life in the outside world was largely one's own affair and would not be too harshly judged. Similarly, there was no vital need to submit to the dictates of the Church in temporal matters. As we shall see, the genuine religious sentiments of a

Guiscard or a Roger never stopped them fighting tooth and nail against what they considered unwarrantable encroachments by the Papacy, any more than those of Henry Plantagenet prevented his battle with Becket. Excommunication was indeed a severe penalty, not lightly to be incurred; yet incurred it was, often enough, and at least so far as the Normans were concerned it seems to have had little effect on their policy; they were usually able to get it lifted again before long.

Materialistic, quick-witted, adaptable, eclectic, still blessed with the inexhaustible energy of their Viking forebears and a superb self-confidence that was all their own, the early Norman adventurers were admirably equipped for the role they were to play. To these qualities they added two others, not perhaps in themselves particularly praiseworthy, yet qualities without which their great kingdom of the south could never have been born. First or all they were enormously prolific, which meant a continually exploding population. It was this fact more than anything else that had brought the first immigrants from Scandinavia; and two hundred years later it was the same phenomenon that sent swarms of land-hungry younger sons still further south in their quest for *Lebensraum*. Secondly, they were natural wanderers—not just of necessity but by temperament as well. They showed, as an early chronicler noted, little loyalty to any of the countries which at various moments they called their own. The fastnesses of the north, the hills of Normandy, the broad meadows of England, the orange-groves of Sicily, the deserts of Syria, all were in turn forsaken by fearless, footloose young men looking for somewhere else, where the pickings would be better still.

And what better excuse to leave for such a search, what better framework in which to conduct it, than a pilgrimage? It was not surprising, at the dawn of the second millennium, when the world had not after all come to an end as had been predicted, and a wave of relief and gratitude was still sweeping across Europe, that of the thousands who thronged the great pilgrim roads so large a proportion should have been Normans. Their destinations were various; four in particular, however, enjoyed such sanctity that visits to them were sufficient to earn pilgrims total absolution—Rome, Compostela, Monte Gargano and, above all the rest, the Holy Land. At that period the city of Jerusalem had been for some four hundred years under Muslim domination, but Christian pilgrims were welcomed—one of their hostels had been founded by Charlemagne himself—and the undertaking presented no insuperable obstacle to anyone with time and energy enough; least of all to young Normans, who looked upon the journey as an adventure and a challenge and doubtless enjoyed it for its own sake, quite apart from the lasting— indeed eternal—benefit which it conferred upon their souls. For them, too, it had a particular appeal; on their return from Palestine they could disembark at Brindisi or Bari and from there follow the coast up to the shrine of the Archangel, who was not only the guardian of all seafarers and thus in any case presumably due for some expression of gratitude, but who also occupied a special place in their affections in his capacity as patron of their own great abbey at Mont-Saint-Michel.

Such appears to have been the course taken by the forty-odd Norman pilgrims who paid their fateful visit to Monte Sant' Angelo in 1016—according, at least, to the testimony of a certain William of Apulia who, at the request of Pope Urban II, produced his *Historical Poem Concerning the Deeds of the Normans in Sicily, Apulia and Calabria* just before the close of the eleventh century. William's account, in elegant Latin hexameters, begins with a description of how the pilgrims were approached in the cave by a strange figure dressed 'in the Grecian style' in a long flowing robe and bonnet. They found him unprepossessing, and his clothes frankly effeminate; but they listened to his story. His name, it appeared, was Melus, and he was a noble Lombard from Bari now driven into exile after leading an unsuccessful insurrection against the Byzantine Empire, which at that time held most of South Italy in its power. His life was dedicated to the cause of Lombard independence—which, he maintained, could easily be achieved; all that was needed was the help of a few stalwart young Normans like themselves. Against a combined Lombard-Norman army the Greeks would stand no chance; and the Lombards would not forget their allies.

It is hard to believe that piety was the dominant emotion in the hearts of the pilgrims, as they stepped out into the sunlight and gazed at the wide plain of Apulia lying beckoning at their feet. They cannot at this stage have foreseen how magnificent an epic lay ahead, nor how far-reaching would be its effects; but they cannot either have failed to realise the huge possibilities inherent in the words of Melus. Here was the chance they had been waiting for—a rich fertile land which they were being invited, implored almost, to enter, which offered them boundless opportunities for proving their worth and for making their fortune. Moreover, an operation of the kind proposed could be amply justified on both legal and religious grounds, aiming as it did at the liberation of a subject people from foreign oppression, and at the restoration of the Roman Church throughout South Italy in place of the despised mumbo-jumbo of Constantinople. It would be some years yet before these vague vistas of glory were focused into a clear ambition for conquest, and longer still before this ambition was so dazzlingly fulfilled; meanwhile the important thing was to hack out a firm foothold in the country, and for this the battle-cry of Lombard independence would do as well as any other.

So they told Melus that they would willingly give him the help he needed. At present their numbers were inadequate; in any case they had come to Apulia as pilgrims and were hardly equipped to embark immediately on a campaign. They must therefore return to Normandy, but only for so long as was necessary to make the proper preparations and to recruit companions-in-arms. In the following year they would be back to join their new Lombard friends, and the great enterprise would begin.

The patriotism of Melus was the more understandable since already by this time the Lombards could boast a long and distinguished history in Italy. Starting as just another bunch of semi-barbarian invaders from North Germany, they had settled around the middle of the sixth century in the territory that still bears their name, and had founded there a prosperous kingdom with its capital at Pavia. Meanwhile others of their compatriots had pressed farther south and had set up semi-independent dukedoms at Spoleto and Benevento. For two hundred years all had gone well; but in 774 Charlemagne swept down into Italy and captured Pavia, and the kingdom was at an end. The focus of Lombard civilisation now shifted to the dukedoms, especially to that of Benevento, which soon promoted itself to a principality and—although it was technically under papal suzerainty by virtue of a deed of gift from Charlemagne—continued to maintain the old Lombard traditions untarnished. There, where Trajan's magnificent triumphal arch still stands to mark the junction of the two principal Roman roads of the South, the Via Appia and the Via Trajana, the Lombard aristocracy grew steadily in influence and wealth, and by A.D. 1000 the three great princes of Benevento, Capua and Salerno were among the most powerful rulers in the peninsula, surrounded by courts ablaze with Byzantinesque splendour and endlessly conspiring to achieve their perennial dream—a united and independent Lombard state that would embrace the whole of southern Italy. With this object in view they deliberately did their utmost to obscure their own feudal position, acknowledging the suzerainty now of the Latin Empire of the West, now of the Byzantine Empire of the East (Benevento occasionally also paying lip-service to the claims of the Pope), for ever playing one off against the other. And naturally they never lost an opportunity of encouraging the various groups of Lombard separatists · in the territories of their Byzantine neighbour.

The Byzantine Empire, for its part, had had a sad record in Italy. Hardly had the armies of Justinian and his successor driven the Ostrogoths from the peninsula in the sixth century when they found it occupied by their erstwhile Lombard allies. Quick action might yet have saved the situation, but at that moment Constantinople was paralysed by palace intrigues and nothing was done. Meanwhile the Lombards dug themselves in. In 751 they were strong enough to expel the Byzantine Exarch of Ravenna, after which Greek influence was limited to Calabria, the heel of Italy around Otranto, and a few isolated merchant cities on the west coast, of which Naples, Gaeta and Amalfi were the most important. At first these cities were little more than prosperous colonies of the Empire, but as time went on they evolved into hereditary dukedoms, still fundamentally Greek in language and culture, acknowledging Byzantine suzerainty and bound to Constantinople by close ties of friendship and commerce, but for all practical purposes independent.

The advent of Charlemagne and his Franks, though disastrous to the Lombards, brought no corresponding advantages to the Greeks, serving only to introduce a rival claimant to the overlordship of southern Italy; and it was not until the ninth century, when the great dynasty of the Macedonians assumed power in Constantinople, that Basil I and his successor Leo VI the Wise were able to halt the decline and partially to restore Byzantine fortunes. As a result of their efforts the Theme of Langobardia—or, as it was usually called, the Capitanata—consisting of Apulia, Calabria and the Otranto region, was by the year 1000 a powerful and profitable province of the Empire, which in its turn had once again become the greatest single force in the peninsula. Meanwhile it continued to claim suzerainty over all the land south of a line drawn from Terracina in the west to Termoli on the Adriatic, and thus consistently refused to recognise the independence either of the Greek city-states or of the Lombard principalities.

Government of the Capitanata was beset with problems. First of all the whole territory lay wide open to the ravages of Saracen pirates from North Africa, who now dominated the entire western Mediterranean. Already in 846 they had raided Rome and pillaged St Peter's, and little more than twenty years later an uneasy and mutually painful alliance between the Eastern and Western Emperors had been necessary before they could be dislodged from Bari. A monk named Bernard, on a pilgrimage to Jerusalem in 870, wrote of how he had seen thousands of Christian captives being herded on to galleys at Taranto for shipment to Africa as slaves. Thirty years later—by which time, having gained effective control of Sicily, they had vastly improved their own strategic position—the Saracens annihilated Reggio and soon afterwards became so serious a menace that the Byzantine Emperor agreed to pay them an annual sum in protection money. In 953, however, this payment was stopped and the raids became worse than ever. In the last quarter of the tenth century, hardly a year went by without at least one major outrage.

Then there was the Western Empire to be watched. The general relapse that followed the extinction of Charlemagne's family with the death in 888 of Charles the Fat had afforded a welcome respite from its south Italian claims; but with the appearance of Otto the Great in 951 the dispute had flared up again more violently than ever. Otto had devoted his immense energies to the task of delivering Italy from the contagion of Greeks and Saracens alike, and for nearly twenty years the land had been torn by heavy and entirely inconclusive fighting. Peace seemed to have come in 970, when friendship between the two Empires was theoretically cemented by the marriage of Otto's son—later Otto II—to the Greek princess Theophano; but this only gave young Otto the opportunity, on his accession, of formally claiming the 'restitution' of all Byzantine possessions in Italy as part of his wife's dowry. His demands were naturally refused, and the war began again. Then, in 981, Otto descended into Apulia, his wrath on this occasion principally directed against the Saracens. In Constantinople the Emperor Basil saw his chance: of the two evils, Otto represented by far the greater long-term danger. Messengers sped to the Saracen leader and a temporary alliance was hastily arranged, as a result of which, after certain initial successes, Otto was soundly defeated near Stilo in Calabria; only an ignominious flight in disguise saved him from capture. He never recovered from the humiliation and died in Rome the following year, aged twenty-eight.[1] He was succeeded by a child of three and since then, not surprisingly, the Western Empire had given little trouble; but vigilance could never be relaxed for long.

Internally too there were grave difficulties. In Calabria and the heel, government was straightforward enough, since these regions had suffered relatively little penetration by the Lombards. On the other hand they had provided a refuge for large numbers of Greek monks, fleeing in the eighth century from Iconoclast excesses of Constantinople and in the tenth from the depredations of the Sicilian Saracens; and the resulting Greek influence, political, religious and cultural, was still everywhere supreme. Calabria in particular was to remain, throughout the Renaissance, one of the principal centres of Greek learning. But in Apulia the situation was more delicate.

[1] Otto is the only German Emperor to be buried in Rome. His tomb can still be seen in the *Grotte Vaticane*—minus its porphyry cover which, having originally been removed from the Mausoleum of Hadrian, now serves as the font of St Peter's.

The population was for the most part of Italo-Lombard stock and needed careful handling by the Catapan—the local Byzantine governor—who was compelled to allow a considerable degree of freedom. Thus the Lombard system of government was largely retained; Lombard judges and officials administered Lombard law, Greek procedures being prescribed only for cases of assassination (hypothetical) of the Emperor or (less hypothetical) of the Catapan. Latin was recognised as an official language. In most areas church administration was in the hands of Latin bishops appointed by the Pope; only in a few cities where there was a substantial Greek population were Greek bishops to be found.

Such a generous measure of autonomy was unparalleled anywhere else in the Byzantine Empire; yet the Lombards of Apulia were never content to live under Greek rule. They had always maintained a strong sense of nationality—after five hundred years they were still quite unassimilated into the Italian population —and this nationalist flame was for ever being fanned by the great principalities to the north and west. Besides, Byzantine taxation was notoriously heavy and, more serious still, recent years had shown that even with compulsory military service—always an unpopular institution—the Empire was incapable of guaranteeing the security of the Apulian towns, particularly those along the coast, from the Saracens. The Lombard populations of these towns had no choice but to organise their own defence. Standing militias accordingly sprang up, many of them equipped with enough ships to enable them to engage the pirates before they could make a landfall. Inevitably these militias constituted in their turn a serious danger to the Byzantine authorities, but in the circumstances they could hardly be disbanded. They also built up Lombard self-reliance, so that by the end of the tenth century an active and well-armed resistance movement had come into being. There had been a minor revolt in Bari in 987 and another far more serious one a decade later which took three years to stamp out. Meanwhile, an important Byzantine official had been assassinated. Then, in 1009, Melus had taken up arms. With his brother-in-law Dattus and a sizable following he had quickly gained possession of Bari, followed in 1010 by Ascoli and Trani; but in the spring of 1011 the newly-appointed Catapan gathered all available forces to besiege Bari and managed to bribe certain of the Greek inhabitants to open the city gates to his men. On 11 June Bari fell; Melus escaped and fled to Salerno. His wife and children were less fortunate. They were captured and sent as hostages to imprisonment at Constantinople.

High on a hill overlooking the modern *autostrada* that links Naples with Rome, the monastery of Monte Cassino looks, from a distance, much the same as it must have looked a thousand years ago. Its appearance is deceptive; during the desperate fighting of February and March 1944 virtually the entire abbey was reduced, by relentless Allied bombardment, to a pile of rubble, and the existing buildings are almost all post-war reconstructions. But, for all that, the life of the monastery has continued uninterrupted since the year 529 when St Benedict came to that hilltop and built, over the ruins of a pagan temple to Apollo, the huge mother-abbey that was the first of his foundations and the birthplace of the Benedictine Order.

In the history of the Normans in the South, Monte Cassino plays a continuous and vital part. As the greatest of Italian monasteries, it had been one of the chief centres of European learning throughout the Dark Ages. It had preserved for posterity the works of many classical writers which would otherwise have perished, including those of Apuleius and Tacitus; and it had somehow survived, with this precious heritage, a devastating Saracen raid in 881 in the course of which its church and other buildings had been largely destroyed. Now, at the time our story opens, it was entering upon its golden age. In the next two hundred years its power was to increase to the point where the monastery functioned almost as an independent state, in turn defying Franks, Greeks, Lombards, Normans, even on occasion the Pope himself; and twice seeing its own Abbot, always one of the most influential figures in the Latin hierarchy, raised to the throne of St Peter.

During the latter half of the eleventh century there lived at Monte Cassino a monk called Amatus—or, as he is sometimes called, Aimé —who between about 1075 and 1080 composed a history of the Normans in the South. Unlike William of Apulia who, one suspects, was primarily concerned to show off his mastery of Latin versification,

Amatus wrote in uncluttered prose; and he has left a pains-
taking and reasonably accurate account of events of which he was
a contemporary and often, possibly, an eye-witness. Unfortunately his original Latin text has been lost; all we possess is a
translation into an Italianate Old French made in the fourteenth
century and now surviving as an endearingly illustrated manuscript
at the Bibliothèque Nationale in Paris. For scholars, since Amatus
is unquestionably the most reliable source for the subject and period
he covers, this loss must be a sad blow; but for the rest of us it
means that his work, of which no modern English translation
exists, has been delivered from the heartbreaking convolutions of
mediaeval Latin and is not only for the most part comprehensible
but also, with its liveliness, naïveté and unending orthographical
charm, a joy to read.

Amatus tells us another story of Norman pilgrims which it is
tempting to relate to William's. According to his account a similar
group of some forty young Normans, returning in 999 on an
Amalfitan ship from Palestine, called at Salerno where they were
hospitably received by the reigning prince, Gaimar IV.[1] Their stay
was, however, rudely interrupted by Saracen pirates, to whose appalling brutalities the local populace was too frightened to offer
resistance. Disgusted at so craven an attitude, the Normans seized
their arms and descended to the attack. Their example gave new
courage to the Salernitans, many of whom now joined them; and
the Saracens, whom this delayed opposition had taken completely
off their guard, were all slaughtered or put to flight. Such spirit
was rare in the South. The delighted Gaimar at once offered these
paragons of valour rich rewards if they would only remain at his
court, but they refused; after so long an absence they must be
getting back to Normandy. On the other hand they would be quite
ready to discuss the matter with their friends at home, many of
whom would certainly be interested in the idea and whose courage
would be no whit inferior to their own. And so they departed,
accompanied by envoys from Gaimar laden with all those gifts

[1] Gaimar, who reigned in Salerno from 999 to 1027, is sometimes referred to as
Gaimar III. The numbering of Lombard dukes and princes was never properly stan-
dardised and constitutes a hideous pitfall to the unwary.

best calculated to attract intrepid northern adventurers—'lemons, almonds, pickled nuts, fine vestments and iron instruments chased with gold; and thus they tempted them to come to this land that flows with milk and honey and so many beautiful things.'

Now the year 1016, which saw Melus at Monte Sant' Angelo, also saw the only large-scale Saracen attack on Salerno; whereas in 999, the date which Amatus gives to his story, no such raid is known to have occurred. It may therefore be that, even if the story remains true in its essentials, the author has made at this point one of his rare chronological blunders, and that the two pilgrim visits were roughly contemporaneous. If this were so, might it not be that the two parties of pilgrims were one and the same? Could not the meeting with Melus at the shrine, ostensibly so fortuitous, have been deliberately engineered by himself and Gaimar, who had recently given him refuge and was one of the principal clandestine supporters of Lombard separatism? It is possible. On the other hand it is possible too, as a recent historian has cogently argued,[1] that both stories are legendary and that the earliest Norman arrivals were in fact simple refugees from their homeland who were subsequently pressed into the Lombard cause by Pope Benedict VIII as part of his anti Byzantine policy. We shall never know. But whether the persuader was prince, patriot or Pope, whether the persuaded were fugitives or pilgrims, of one thing we can be sure: the work was well done. By the spring of 1017 the first young Normans were already on their way.

[1] E. Joranson, 'The Inception of the Career of the Normans in Italy'.

2

ARRIVAL

Et en tant estoit cressute la multitude de lo pueple, que li champ ne li arbre non suffisoit a tant de gent de porter lor necessaires dont peussent vivre. . . . Et se partirent ceste gent, et laisserent petite choze pour acquester assez, et non firent secont la costumance de molt qui vont par lo monde, liquel se metent a servir autre; mes simillance de li antique chevalier, et voilloient avoir toute gent en lor subjettion et en lor seignorie. Et pristrent l'arme, et rompirent la ligature de paiz, et firent grant exercit et grant chevalerie.

(And the people had increased so exceedingly that the fields and forests were no longer sufficient to provide for them . . . and so these men departed, forsaking what was meagre in search of what was plentiful. Nor were they content, as are so many who go out into the world, to serve others; but, like the knights of old, they determined that all men should be subject to them, acknowledging them as overlords. And so they took up arms, and broke the bonds of peace, and did great deeds of war and chivalry.)

Amatus, I, 1, 2

IT was perhaps just as well that the Lombard leaders had demanded no references from the warriors whose aid they were seeking, and had imposed no criteria but courage. Word of their invitation had spread quickly through the towns and manors of Normandy, and the stories of the delights which the South could offer, the effeteness of its present inhabitants and the rewards which awaited any Norman prepared to make the journey, doubtless lost nothing in the telling. Such stories have always a particular appeal for the more unreliable sections of any population, and it was therefore hardly surprising that the earliest contingents of Norman immigrants into Italy, despite possible outward similarities with Amatus's *antique chevalier*, should have had little enough in common with the knights of Carolingian

legend whose exploits they so raucously sang. They seem to have
been largely composed of knights' and squires' younger sons who,
possessing no patrimony of their own, had little to attach them to
their former homes; but there was also a distinctly less reputable
element of professional fighters, gamblers and adventurers respond-
ing to the call of easy money. These were soon joined by the usual
riff-raff of hangers-on, increasing in numbers as the party rode
southwards through Burgundy and Provence. In the summer of
1017 they crossed the river Garigliano, which marked the southern
frontier of the Papal States, and made direct for Capua. There,
probably by previous arrangement, they found Melus impatiently
awaiting them with a sizable contingent of his own, all eager for
immediate battle.

The best chance of Lombard success clearly lay in attacking the
Byzantines before they had time to assess the new situation and
summon reinforcements; Melus was therefore right to impress
upon his new allies that there was no time to be lost, and to lead
them at once across the frontier into Apulia. As a result, they seem
to have taken the enemy entirely by surprise. By the approach of
winter and the end of the first year's campaign they could already
boast of several significant victories and could well afford to indulge
in their favourite joke about the effeminacy of the Greeks; and by
September 1018 they had driven the Byzantines from the whole
region between the Fortore in the north and Trani in the south. In
October, however, the tide suddenly turned.

On the right bank of the Ofanto river, about four miles from the
Adriatic, a great rock still casts its shadow over the field of Cannae
where, in 216 B.C., the Carthaginian army under Hannibal had inflicted on the Romans one of the bloodiest and most disastrous
defeats in their history. Here it was, twelve hundred and thirty-four
years later, that the Lombard and Norman forces under Melus
suffered a still greater catastrophe at the hands of the imperial
Byzantine army led by the greatest of all the Catapans, Basil
Boioannes. They were from the start hopelessly outnumbered. At
the insistence of Boioannes the Emperor Basil II had sent massive
reinforcements from Constantinople; Amatus writes that the Greeks
swarmed over the battlefield like bees from a hive and that their

lances stood straight and thick as a field of cane. But there was yet another, if only contributory, reason for the defeat: Norman military prowess was already famous in the Byzantine capital and Basil had accordingly stiffened his army with some northern warriors of his own—a detachment of his Varangian Guard, that great Viking regiment which had been sent him, in return for his sister, by Prince Vladimir of Kiev thirty years before. The Lombards fought bravely, but in vain; all but a handful were slaughtered, and with them collapsed Melus's last hopes of Lombard independence in Apulia. He himself managed to escape, and after months of aimless wandering through the duchies and the Papal States finally found refuge at the court of the Western Emperor Henry II at Bamberg. Here he died two years later, a broken and disappointed man. Henry, who as the chief rival of Byzantium for the domination of South Italy had often supported him in the past, gave him a superb funeral and a magnificent tomb in his new cathedral; but neither the skill of the monumental masons nor the hollow title of Duke of Apulia that Henry had conferred upon him shortly before his death could alter the fact that Melus had failed—and, worse still, that in his determination to bring freedom to his people he had unwittingly done the one thing that rendered that freedom for ever unattainable. He had given the Normans a taste of blood.

They too had fought bravely and suffered severe losses at Cannae. Their leader, one Gilbert, had fallen on the field, and it was a sadly depleted force that regrouped itself after the battle and elected his brother Rainulf as his successor. Now that Melus was gone they must fend for themselves, at least until they could find new paymasters. Dispiritedly they rode away into the hills to look for a place in which to entrench themselves—somewhere that would serve them as a permanent headquarters and would provide a rallying-point for the new immigrants who were still trickling steadily down from the north. Their first choice of site was unfortunate; during the construction of their stronghold they suffered a defeat far more humiliating than that of Cannae. William of Apulia tells us that they were suddenly beset by a plague of frogs, which appeared in such numbers that they were unable to continue the work. After they had beaten an ignominious retreat before the croaking chorus, they found a second location which fortunately proved more suitable; but even here they did not remain for long. Thanks to the constant stream of new arrivals their numbers were soon greater than they had ever been. Besides, despite the severity of their first defeat, their reputation as fighters was still unequalled; and their services were in demand on all sides.

The great cauldron of South Italy was never altogether off the boil. In a land surrounded and pervaded by the constant clashing of the four greatest powers of the time, torn apart by the warring claims of four races, three religions and an ever-varying number of independent, semi-independent or rebellious states and cities, a strong arm and a sharp sword could never lack employment. Many young Normans gravitated towards Gaimar in Salerno; others turned to his brother-in-law and rival, Prince Pandulf of Capua—'the Wolf of the Abruzzi'—whose energy and ambition were already causing his neighbours serious concern. Yet others preferred Naples, Amalfi or Gaeta. Meanwhile the Catapan Boioannes was consolidating his victory by building a new stronghold to defend his Apulian frontier—the fortress town of Troia at the mouth of the pass leading through the Apennines and out on to the plain. Having no forces available to provide a permanent garrison—the Varangians having by now returned in triumph to Constantinople—he had to look elsewhere; and, since they were after all merely mercenaries and the Catapan knew a good fighter when he saw one, there can have been little surprise when, only a year or so after Cannae, a well-equipped force of Normans rode off to Apulia to defend the lawful dominions of Byzantium against the continued dastardly attacks of Lombard trouble-makers.

Such an atmosphere of shifting loyalties and easy realignments might well have seemed injurious to Norman interests. Surely, it might be thought, if they were aiming to increase their power to the point where they would ultimately dominate the peninsula, the Normans should have remained united and not scattered so aimlessly among the countless factions that sought their aid. But at this early stage thoughts of dominion were still unformulated, nor was there much unity to be preserved. Self-interest was the first consideration; national aspirations came a poor second, if indeed they figured at all. Norman good fortune lay in the fact that the two so often coincided; and, paradoxically, it was their apparent disunity that prepared the way for their ultimate conquest. Had they maintained their cohesion they could not have failed to upset the balance of power in South Italy, since they were still too few to prevail alone yet already too numerous not to strengthen dangerously any faction to whom they might have given their undivided allegiance. By splitting up, constantly changing their alliances and contriving, in all the petty struggles in which they were involved, to emerge almost invariably on the winning side, they were able to prevent any single interest from becoming too powerful; by championing all causes they succeeded in championing none; and by selling their swords not just to the highest but to every bidder, they maintained their freedom of action.

The Normans were not the only people who had to reconsider their position after Cannae. At one stroke Byzantine power had been re-established throughout Apulia, and Byzantine prestige immeasurably increased all over Italy. The effect on the Lombard duchies was, as might have been expected, considerable. Early in 1019 Pandulf of Capua frankly transferred his allegiance to the Greeks, even going so far as to send the keys of his capital to the Emperor Basil. In Salerno Gaimar, while avoiding such expansive gestures, similarly made no secret of where his sympathies now lay. Most surprising of all—at least at first sight—was the attitude of Monte Cassino. The great monastery had always been considered the champion of the Latin cause in South Italy as represented by the Pope and the Western Emperor. As such it had supported Melus and his Lombards and had even offered his brother-in-law Dattus after Cannae the same place of refuge that he had occupied for a while after the earlier Lombard defeat of 1011—a fortified tower which it owned on the banks of the Garigliano. Then, only a few months later, it too declared itself in support of the claims of Constantinople. Only the Prince of Benevento remained loyal.

All this was bad news indeed for the Emperor Henry, and worse news still for the Pope. Benedict VIII, though upright and morally irreproachable,[1] was not a particularly religious figure. Member of a noble family of Tusculum, it seems doubtful that he had even taken holy orders at the time of his election in 1012; and throughout his twelve-year occupancy of the throne of St Peter he showed himself to be primarily a politician and a man of action, dedicated to the close association of the Papacy with the Western Empire and to the deliverance of Italy from all other influences. Thus in 1016 he had personally led an army against the Saracens; while against the Greeks he had given Melus and Dattus all the support he could, twice arranging with the authorities of Monte Cassino for the refuge of the latter in the Garigliano tower. Now he saw all his efforts brought to nothing and a sudden explosion by Byzantine power to a point beyond anything he had seen in his lifetime. The defection of Monte Cassino must have been a particular blow—though perhaps more understandable when he remembered that its abbot, Atenulf, was the brother of Pandulf of Capua and had recently acquired in somewhat mysterious conditions a large estate near Trani in Byzantine Apulia. Most serious of all, however, was the danger of continued Greek expansion. After the completeness of their recent triumph why should the Byzantines be content with the Capitanata? The Balkan wars that had so long occupied the formidable energies of Basil II and earned him the title of *Bulgaroctonus*—the Bulgar-Slayer—were now over; and the Papal States represented a rich prize which he might well believe to be in his grasp. Once Boioannes crossed the Garigliano there would be nothing between him and the gates of Rome itself; and the sinister family of the Crescentii, longtime enemies of the Counts of Tusculum, would know just how to turn such a catastrophe to their advantage. It was a hundred and fifty years since a Pope had journeyed north of the Alps, but after the news of Monte Cassino was brought to him Benedict hesitated no longer. Early in 1020 he set off to discuss the situation with his old friend and ally Henry II at Bamberg.

It is impossible to read about Benedict and Henry without reflecting how much more suitable it would have been if the Pope

---

[1] Irreproachable, that is, according to his lights. He must bear the stigma of having ordered the first official (though, alas, not the last) persecution of the Jews in the history of mediaeval Rome—as the result of a minor earthquake in 1020.

had been the Emperor and the Emperor the Pope. Henry the Holy fully deserved his nickname. Although perhaps hardly worthy of the canonisation he was to receive in the following century—an honour which appears to have been conferred largely in recognition of the dismal chastity in which he lived with his wife Cunégonde of Luxemburg—and although his piety was liberally laced with superstition, he remained a deeply religious man whose two main passions in life were the building of churches and ecclesiastical reform. These spiritual preoccupations did not, however, prevent him from ruling over his unwieldy empire with surprising efficiency. Despite his perpetual interference in church affairs he and Benedict had been friends ever since 1012 when Henry, still only King in Germany,[1] had supported Benedict in the papal election against his Crescentius rival; and their friendship, strengthened when Benedict intervened similarly for Henry and officiated at his and Cunégonde's imperial coronation in 1014, had been further cemented by Henry's religious and Benedict's political views. The horizon as yet showed no prospect of that long and agonising struggle between Empire and Papacy which was so soon to begin and would reach its apogee only with Frederick II more than two centuries later; for the moment the two still worked in harmony. A threat to the one was a threat to the other.

Benedict arrived in Bamberg just before Easter 1020; and after celebrating the feast with great pomp in Henry's new cathedral he and the Emperor at once settled down to business. At the start they had Melus to give them the benefit of his expertise on the South Italian political scene and Byzantine strengths and weaknesses; but a week after the Pope's arrival the 'Duke of Apulia' suddenly expired and the two had to continue alone. For Benedict, always incisive, the necessary course of action was clear: Henry himself must lead a full-scale expeditionary force into Italy. The purpose of this force, which would be joined at a suitable moment by the Pope himself, would not be to oust Byzantium altogether—there would be time for that later—but to show that the Western Empire and the Papacy

---

[1] The title of Emperor could be adopted only after the elected German king had been crowned by the Pope in Rome. Henry was first to call himself King of the Romans when Emperor-elect.

were powers to be reckoned with, ready to defend their rights. It would thus put new heart into any of the smaller cities or petty Lombard barons who might be wavering in their allegiance, while leaving Boioannes in no doubt that any further Greek advances would be made at his peril.

Henry, though sympathetic, was not immediately persuaded. Delicate as the situation was, the Greeks had not in fact moved beyond their own borders; and even though he did not technically recognise those borders, recent Byzantine actions had after all come about only as a result of Lombard insurrection and could hardly be classed as aggressive. The attitude of the Lombard duchies and of Monte Cassino was indeed a cause for anxiety but, as Henry well knew, they all valued their independence far too much to allow themselves to become Byzantine satellites. They alone would certainly not merit an expedition of the size which Benedict was proposing. When the Pope returned to Italy in June, the Emperor had still not finally committed himself.

For a year he hesitated, and for a year all was quiet. Then, in June 1021, Boioannes struck. By previous financial arrangement with Pandulf, a Greek detachment entered Capuan territory and swept down the Garigliano to the tower which Dattus, with a group of Lombard followers and a still faithful band of Normans, had by now made his headquarters and in which—trusting, presumably, in papal protection—he had decided to remain even after the *volte-face* of Capua and Monte Cassino. (Neither at this time nor at any other in his history does Dattus betray signs of marked intelligence.) The tower had originally been built and fortified as a protection against Saracen raiders. For such a purpose it was on the whole adequate, but it could not hold out for long against the well-equipped Greek force. Dattus and his men fought valiantly for two days, but on the third they were compelled to surrender. The Normans were spared but the Lombards were all put to the sword. Dattus himself was taken to Bari where, in chains, he was paraded on a donkey through the streets; then, on the evening of 15 June 1021, he was sewn into a sack together with a cock, a monkey and a snake and cast into the sea.

News of the outrage travelled swiftly to Rome and Bamberg.

Benedict, of whom Dattus had been a personal friend, was scandalised at this new treachery on the part of Pandulf and Abbot Atenulf,
who were known to have received a large reward for handing over
their compatriot—the last man still capable of raising the banner of
Lombard independence and openly committed to driving the Greeks
out of Italy. Moreover, it was the Pope who had advised Dattus to
take refuge in the tower and had arranged with Monte Cassino that
it should be made available for him. The honour of the Papacy had
thus been betrayed, a crime that Benedict could never forgive. His
letters to Henry in Bamberg, by which he had kept up a steady
pressure ever since his return to Italy, now took on a more urgent
note. The fate of Dattus was only the beginning; the success of this
operation would encourage the Greeks to acts of still wilder audacity.
It was imperative to take strong action while time yet remained. Henry
prevaricated no longer. At the Diet of Nijmegen in July 1021 it was
resolved that he should lead his imperial armies into Italy as soon as
possible. The rest of the summer and all autumn were spent in
preparations, and in the following December the immense host
began to march.

The expedition was intended primarily as a show of strength;
and a show of strength it unquestionably was. For the outward
journey it was split up into three separate divisions, the command
of which Henry typically gave to himself and two of his archbishops
—Pilgrim of Cologne and Poppo of Aquileia. The first division,
under Pilgrim, had orders to march down the west side of Italy
through the Papal States to Monte Cassino and Capua, there to arrest
Atenulf and Pandulf in the Emperor's name. It consisted, we are
told—though all such figures must be treated with suspicion—of
twenty thousand men. The second, estimated at eleven thousand,
would be led by Poppo through Lombardy and the Apennines to
the border of Apulia. Here, at a pre-arranged rendezvous, it would
link up with the main body of the army under Henry—more
numerous than the other two divisions put together—which would
have followed the eastern road down the Adriatic coast. The
combined force would then march inland to besiege and eradicate
Troia, that proud new Byzantine stronghold built by Boioannes

and manned by Normans, of which it had been agreed that a public example should be made.

Pilgrim marched straight to Monte Cassino as instructed, but he arrived too late. The Abbot had not underestimated the wrath of Benedict and knew that he could expect no mercy; on hearing of the approach of the imperial army he at once fled to Otranto and there hastily embarked for Constantinople. But retribution overtook him. Shortly before his departure from the monastery a furious St Benedict had appeared to him in a vision to inform him of the heavenly displeasure he had incurred and to remind him about the wages of sin; and indeed, hardly had his ship put out of harbour when a mighty tempest arose. On 30 March 1022 the vessel went down with all hands and Atenulf was drowned with the rest. Meanwhile Pilgrim continued to Capua. Pandulf was not disposed to give in without a struggle and at once called upon the inhabitants to defend the city walls; but he was so much disliked by his subjects that he found himself no longer able to command their loyalty in the face of the Archbishop's troops. Encouraged by certain Normans in his retinue, who also had no love for their erstwhile paymaster and correctly judged where their own advantage lay, a group of citizens stealthily opened the gates to the imperial army. Pilgrim was thus able to enter Capua, there to receive the submission of its fuming Prince.

The original plan now provided for Pilgrim to turn eastwards to rejoin the rest of the army. Before doing so, however, he decided to move on to Salerno where Gaimar, although his behaviour had been a good deal less reprehensible than that of his brother-in-law, still continued openly to profess pro-Byzantine sympathies and was clearly capable of causing trouble in the future if he were not discouraged. But as Pilgrim soon discovered, Salerno was a very different proposition from Capua. Its defences were considerably stronger and much more determinedly manned, for Gaimar was as popular as Pandulf was hated and his Norman guard was undismayed by the archiepiscopal cohorts. The city was besieged for over a month but, although hard pressed, obviously had no intention of surrendering. Meanwhile time was passing and Pilgrim still had a long hard road through the mountains between himself and his

Emperor. At last a truce was called and he agreed to raise the siege in return for an adequate number of hostages. Having thus protected his rear he turned away from Salerno and headed inland.

Henry also had marched swiftly. Despite the unwieldiness of his army and the rigours of the Alpine winter he and Archbishop Poppo, whose journey had been equally uneventful, had joined up as planned by mid-February 1022. Together they then proceeded inland to a point near Benevento where the Pope was awaiting them, and on 3 March Benedict and Henry made their formal entrance into the city. There they stayed for four weeks, resting and catching up with their correspondence—and, presumably, hoping for news of Pilgrim. Meanwhile the army prepared for action. At the end of the month they decided to delay no longer for the Archbishop and set off for Troia.

Boioannes had, as usual, done his work well. To the imperial troops emerging from the mountain passes on to the plain of Apulia, the immense spur on which Troia stands must have looked virtually impregnable; and the town itself, poised over the very edge of the frontier between Byzantine territory and the Duchy of Benevento, distinctly menacing. But the stern determination of the Pope and the pious fortitude of the Emperor set the required example, and on 12 April the siege began. For nearly three months it was to drag on as the weather grew steadily hotter, its grim monotony broken only by the arrival of Pilgrim with the news from Campania, and Pandulf, still seething, in his train. The news of Atenulf's fate left Henry unmoved; he is said to have merely muttered a verse from the seventh psalm[1] and turned away. Pandulf he condemned to death on the spot but owing to the intercession of the Archbishop, who had grown rather fond of his prisoner during their journey through the mountains, he was persuaded to commute the sentence to one of imprisonment beyond the Alps—an exercise of mercy which many people were before long to have cause to regret. The Wolf of the Abruzzi was led away in chains and the siege continued.

Unlike her famous Anatolian namesake, Troia held out to the end. Certain pro-German chroniclers have tried to maintain that Henry eventually managed to take the town by storm; one, the notoriously

[1] *He made a pit, and digged it, and is fallen into the ditch which he made.*

unreliable monk Radulph Glaber (the wildness of whose imagination was rivalled only by that of his private life, which gives him a fair claim to have been expelled from more monasteries than any other *littérateur* of the eleventh century), tells a typically far-fetched story of how Henry's heart was melted by the sight of a long procession of all its inhabitants, led by an elderly hermit carrying a cross. But if Troia had in fact surrendered it is inconceivable that some mention of it would not appear in any of the contemporary South Italian records —and scarcely more probable that Boioannes should have immediately afterwards granted the town new privileges as a reward for its fidelity.

So Henry was deprived of his triumph. He could not continue the siege indefinitely. The heat was taking its toll, and malaria, which remained the scourge of Apulia until well into the twentieth century, was rife in his army. At the end of June he decided to give up. The camp was struck, and the Emperor, who was by now in considerable pain from a gall-stone, rode slowly away into the mountains at the head of his huge but dispirited army. It was not the first time that the South Italian summer had conquered the greatest military forces of Europe; nor, as we shall see, was it to be the last. Henry met the Pope, who had preceded him, at Monte Cassino and here they remained for a few days, Benedict occupying himself with the induction of a new abbot and Henry seeking—successfully, we are told—miraculous relief from his stone. Then, after a short visit to Capua, where another Pandulf, Count of Teano, was installed in the palace of his disgraced namesake, Pope and Emperor left via Rome for Pavia, to attend an important council which Benedict had summoned on Church reform. To Henry such a gathering constituted an irresistible temptation, and it was not until August that he left for Germany.

His expedition had been only a very qualified success. Pilgrim admittedly had done his work well; with Pandulf and Atenulf removed from the scene there should be no more difficulties in Capua or Monte Cassino, while the hostages from Salerno and Naples (the latter had offered them of its own accord rather than face the possibility of a siege by the Archbishop's army) were a guarantee against trouble along that part of the coast. The Apulian

29

campaign, on the other hand, had been a fiasco. Troia's stubborn stand had shown up the fundamental impotence of imperial arms in Italy. Some sixty thousand men had been completely unable to subdue a small hill-town which had not even existed four years earlier. To make matters worse, they had been under the personal command of the Emperor, whose own reputation had thus suffered a heavy blow—while that of Boioannes, who had conceived, built, fortified and populated Troia, had acquired proportionately greater lustre. And the Catapan had yet another advantage, of which Henry was all too well aware; being resident in Apulia, he was able continually to maintain and consolidate his position and to seize without delay every opportunity for improving it. The Western Emperor, in contrast, could work only through his feudal vassals who, as had so recently been demonstrated, were apt to remain loyal only so long as it suited them. While he was on the spot in all his splendour, holding courts, dispensing justice and with a generous hand distributing his imperial largesse, these vassals were only too ready to offer their submission and to pay their homage. Once he was gone, the field was left open to malcontents and agitators; laws would be disobeyed, morale undermined, injunctions forgotten; Boioannes would miss no chances; and what then was to prevent the whole painfully rebuilt imperial structure from crumbling again?

For the Byzantines, as they watched the imperial host lumbering away into the mountains, the prevailing sentiment must have been one of relief. Had Henry taken Troia, all Apulia might have lain at his mercy. Following the reverses already sustained in the west, this would have meant the undoing of all that had been achieved in the past four years. Even as things were, there was much to be rebuilt; but thanks to Troia the foundations had remained secure. Greek diplomacy could get to work again. No wonder Boioannes rewarded the Troians so handsomely.

Thus, for the two protagonists, the campaign of 1022 had been inconclusive. Gains and losses seemed evenly balanced and it was hard to see where the advantage lay. Among the minor participants, Capua had suffered disaster, Salerno and Naples had been severely chastened. For one group only had the events of the year been entirely profitable. The Normans, by their stand at Troia, had saved Apulia for the Greeks and had earned the lasting gratitude of Boioannes. In the west, the part they had played in obtaining the submission of Capua was rewarded by Henry's engagement of a substantial Norman force to maintain and support Pandulf of Teano. Further contingents had been placed by the Emperor along the Byzantine frontier and at various places along the coast to guard against Saracen attacks. The Normans had in fact already mastered the art of being on the winning side, cashing in on all victories and somehow avoiding involvement in all defeats. On both sides of the peninsula they had strengthened their position; to both empires they had become indispensable. They were doing very well indeed.

3

ESTABLISHMENT

the five fair brothers,
Who attempted the world and shared it with themselves,
Coming out of Normandy from the fresh, green land
To this soil of marble and of broken sherds.

Sacheverell Sitwell,
'Bohemund, Prince of Antioch'

HENRY the Holy may have had no delusions about the difficulty of maintaining his influence in Italy after his return home, but not even he could have foreseen the speed with which his work would be destroyed. He had tried hard and he must have felt that in the west at least he had left a relatively stable situation. So, in a way, he had; but there was one eventuality for which he had made no provision. The improvement in his health which had followed the miraculous intercession of St Benedict at Monte Cassino proved, alas, as ephemeral as everything else he achieved in Italy. In July 1024 he died. He was buried not far from Melus in Bamberg Cathedral.

Henry left, as might have been expected, no issue; and with him the Saxon house came to an end. He was succeeded by a distant cousin, Conrad II the Salic. Conrad, both in character and outlook, was quite unlike Henry—he was sublimely uninterested, for example, in the affairs of the Church, except when they affected his political decisions—and there was no particular reason why he should have pursued his predecessor's policies; neither, however, was there any excuse for the act of blatant idiocy which he now committed. At the request of Gaimar of Salerno, who sent a smooth-tongued embassy, well laden with presents, to congratulate him on his accession, the new Emperor at once released Pandulf of Capua from his chains and left him free to return to Italy. Pope Benedict would never for a moment have countenanced such folly; but Pope Benedict was dead. He had preceded Henry to the grave by only a few weeks and had been succeeded, with unseemly haste, by his brother Romanus, who had immediately installed himself at the Lateran under the name of John XIX. Corrupt and utterly self-seeking, John had neither the energy nor the interest to remonstrate with Conrad. So it was that the Wolf of the Abruzzi returned to his old habitat and began once again to justify his name.

His first objective was to recover Capua and to avenge himself on all those of his subjects who had so recently betrayed him. For this he needed allies. On arrival in Italy, therefore, he at once sent out appeals for assistance—to Gaimar in Salerno, to the Catapan Boioannes and lastly to Rainulf the Norman, who was called upon to send as many of his compatriots as he could muster. Gaimar, who as Pandulf's brother-in-law had everything to gain from a restoration of the *status quo* in Capua, complied at once and had no difficulty in persuading Rainulf, who recognised another wide-open opportunity for Norman advancement, to do the same. Only the Greeks were disappointing in their response, although they had an admirable excuse. The Emperor Basil was preparing a military expedition of enormous size against the Saracens, who had by now achieved the complete domination of Sicily. By the time he received Pandulf's appeal the bulk of his army—Greeks, Varangians, Vlachs and Turks —had already arrived in Calabria, and Boioannes was even leading an advance-guard across the straits to occupy Messina in the Emperor's name. Pandulf, however, was not particularly worried at the lack of imperial support. Rainulf had now appeared with a gratifyingly large number of Norman cut-throats to stiffen Gaimar's force, and Capua was unlikely to offer serious resistance. Furthermore a small Greek contingent, somehow detached from the Sicilian expeditionary force, had turned up unexpectedly at the last moment and was now awaiting orders. (If Pandulf were to return to power Boioannes would not have wished it to be without some Byzantine assistance.) There was no point in delaying further. Accordingly, in November 1024, the siege of Capua began.

It lasted a good deal longer than Pandulf had expected. The river Volturno provides the city with a superb natural defence on three sides. Thanks to this, to the immensely strong land-walls which covered the fourth side and, doubtless, to the Capuans' determination to postpone for as long as possible the return of their detested lord, they held out for eighteen months and would indeed probably have continued longer but for an unexpected catastrophe. On 15 December 1025, just as he was about to leave Constantinople for Sicily, the Emperor Basil died. His sixty-five-year-old brother Constantine VIII, who succeeded him, was an irresponsible voluptuary who, despite having technically shared the throne for the past half-century, was quite unfitted to pursue Basil's majestic designs. He therefore called off the Sicilian expedition just as it was gathering momentum, and Boioannes was now able to direct the whole weight of his huge army against Capua.

From that moment the defenders had no chance. In May 1026 the Count of Teano decided that the Capuan throne had become too hot for him and accepted Boioannes's offer of safe conduct to Naples in return for his surrender. The gates of the city were opened and almost exactly four years after his disgrace the Wolf was back where, at least in his own view, he belonged. The chroniclers spare us the details of his vengeance on the Capuans, many of whom might well have preferred to maintain their resistance to the end and then go down fighting. As for the Norman garrison, it probably emerged none the worse; the victorious prince owed much to Rainulf, and in any battle in which Normans had fought on both sides it had already become the regular practice for those on the winning side to seek clemency for their less fortunate compatriots.

And yet Pandulf was still not satisfied. Naples, in particular, worried him. Duke Sergius IV, though nominally a vassal of Byzantium, had behaved with remarkable fecklessness at the time of Archbishop Pilgrim's campaign, putting up no resistance of any kind and offering hostages before he was even threatened. He had not lifted a finger to help Pandulf regain his rightful patrimony; and now he was actually giving refuge to the ridiculous Count of Teano. The fact that this refuge had been arranged by Boioannes did nothing to reassure Pandulf; he merely suspected, not without reason, that this was a deliberate move on the part of the Catapan, to whom the continued availability of a rival claimant to the throne of Capua might well prove useful in the future. In any case Sergius was an untrustworthy neighbour and as such must be dealt with. The only obstacle was Boioannes, who was on excellent terms with Sergius and would certainly come to his assistance against Pandulf should the need arise.

Then, in 1027, the Catapan was recalled. For the Eastern Empire this was an error almost as great as Conrad's liberation of Pandulf three years before. As Basil II's right hand in Italy, Boioannes had by a superb combination of diplomatic and military skill restored Byzantine supremacy in the South and raised it to its highest level for three hundred years. Now, with the Emperor and the Catapan both gone, the decline was beginning. It began in the classic tradition, with insubordination allowed to go unpunished.

If Boioannes had been in Italy, or if Basil had been alive, Pandulf would never have dared to attack Naples; but the Capitanata was now without a governor, and in Constantinople the doddering old hedonist Constantine was incapable of seeing further than the Hippodrome. The Wolf—*le fortissime lupe* as Amatus calls him—seized his chance. Some time during the winter of 1027–28 he swept down on Naples and, thanks as usual to treachery from within, took possession of it after the shortest of struggles. Sergius went into hiding and the terrified Count of Teano sought refuge in Rome, where he died soon after.

Pandulf's position must now have appeared almost unassailable. He was master not only of Capua and Naples but also in effect of Salerno, since Gaimar had died in 1027 and his widow, Pandulf's sister, had assumed the regency for her sixteen-year-old son. With neither the Eastern nor the Western Emperors making the slightest effort to stop him—Conrad had actually travelled to Italy for his coronation a few months before and had docilely accepted Pandulf's homage as Prince of Capua—and the Pope equally ineffectual, he could allow his ambitions free rein. He was still only forty-two; given a modicum of luck and whole-hearted Norman support, he should have little difficulty in taking Benevento and the cities along the coast. Then, if the present state of apathy continued to prevail in Constantinople, there would be nothing to prevent his marching into the Capitanata, and the old Lombard dream of a unified South Italian empire would be realised at last.

Such a prospect could not be expected to appeal to Amalfi, Gaeta and their smaller neighbours. They valued their independence and their close commercial and cultural links with Constantinople; they had no particular affection for the Lombards; and, like everybody else, they disliked Pandulf intensely. Meanwhile the citizens of Naples, few of whom had ever wanted the Prince of Capua in the first place, were beginning to suffer from his harshness and rapacity and to plan his overthrow.

The key to the situation lay with Rainulf. Of all the Norman bands that were now disseminated through the peninsula, his was the largest and most influential; and its numbers were constantly being increased as fresh recruits arrived at his invitation from the north. If Pandulf could enlist his support there would be little hope for the rest of southern Italy. Fortunately, however, the sudden rise of Capua was as unwelcome to Rainulf as to anyone else. He was a born politician, one of the very few Normans at this stage to realise the full measure of the stakes for which he was playing, and he saw far enough ahead to understand that Pandulf's continued success might prove disastrous to Norman interests. He had supported the Prince of Capua long enough; the time had now come to change sides. He knew perfectly well how indispensable his support would be to the city-states, and when messengers arrived—as he knew they would—from Sergius of Naples and the Duke of Gaeta with proposals for an alliance, he was in a position to make his own terms.

The negotiations were successful, and led to plans; the plans were successful, and led to action; the action was successful and in 1029, less than two years after his expulsion, Sergius had returned to Naples and the Wolf was back in his Capuan lair, licking his wounds. The Normans had won again. This time, however, they obtained a more lasting reward for their services. Whether it was granted at their insistence or whether Sergius was himself only too anxious to provide for his future security we cannot be sure; but whatever the reason, early in 1030 Rainulf was formally presented with the town and territory of Aversa—receiving, as an additional token of gratitude and respect, the hand in marriage of Sergius's own sister, the widow of the Duke of Gaeta.

It was, for the Normans, the greatest day since their arrival in Italy. After thirteen years they at last had a fief of their own. Henceforth they would no longer be a race of foreign mercenaries or vagabonds. The land they occupied was theirs by right, legally conferred upon them according to the age-old feudal tradition. They were tenants of their own freely-elected leader, one of their own kind yet now himself a member of the South Italian aristocracy, brother-in-law of the Duke of Naples. To a people so conscious of due form and legality, such an advance in status was of inestimable significance. It had little effect at first on their general behaviour; all the old activities continued—the playing of one side against another, the fomentation of discord among the squabbling Greek and Lombard barons, the selling of their swords to any who would buy. But they now had a clear long-term object in view—the acquisition of land for themselves in Italy. Many rootless groups of Normans still roamed the hills and the highways leading a life of freebooting and brigandage; yet more and more of their leaders would, after 1030, set themselves up in fixed and fortified settlements in imitation of Rainulf, and devote their energies to the carving out of a permanent territory of their own. From the moment that the Normans become landowners their whole attitude begins to change —not only towards their neighbours but towards the country itself. Italy is no longer just a battlefield and a bran-tub, no longer a land to be plundered and despoiled; but one to be appropriated, developed and enriched. It is, in fact, their home.

For a while, Rainulf seems to have occupied himself principally with the task of strengthening and consolidating his new fief.[1]

[1] There has long persisted a popular legend, probably originating with the English chronicler Ordericus Vitalis, according to which Aversa took its name from the Latin *Adversa*, i.e. the place of those who were hostile to the other inhabitants of the country. It is, alas, unfounded. The name already exists in records dating from the very first years of the century, before Rainulf and his followers left Normandy. Aversa, though its cathedral still bears traces of Norman work, is now a curiously uninteresting town, chiefly notable for being the birthplace of Cimarosa and for its enormous lunatic asylum.

Aversa lies on the open Campanian plain between Capua and Naples and was thus bound to receive the attentions of Pandulf before long. So indeed it did; but not altogether in the way that had been expected. In 1034 Rainulf's wife, the sister of Duke Sergius, suddenly died. Pandulf had a niece, whose father had recently succeeded to the throne of Amalfi; and her hand he now offered to the sorrowing widower. The promise of such consolation, with all that it involved—alliance with Pandulf and the inevitable ruin of Sergius, his erstwhile brother-in-law and greatest benefactor—was more than Rainulf could resist. He accepted. Sergius had only recently sustained the loss of Sorrento, which at Pandulf's instigation had revolted against him and established itself as an independent city-state under Capuan protection; he now had to suffer the incomparably heavier blow of the defection of Aversa, and with it the loss of the Norman support on which he most depended. On the personal level the shock was equally shattering; the sister he loved was dead, the brother-in-law he respected had betrayed him. There was no justice, no loyalty, no gratitude. He did not care to go on. Broken in spirit, he left Naples and entered a monastery where, shortly afterwards, he died.

This was probably the most treacherous act in Rainulf's life; but if he felt any remorse he certainly did not show it. He had, as always, but one object—the strengthening of his own position—and in the pursuit of this end he flung himself with enthusiasm into his new alliance. Thus there began a period during which the Prince of Capua, supported by the lord of Aversa and the Dukes of Sorrento, Salerno and Amalfi, showed himself to be unquestionably the greatest power in the land. Only a few years before, Rainulf had been devoting all his energies to curbing Pandulf's ambitions, but since his own advancement the situation had been transformed. The strength of Capua, great as it was, now depended entirely on the Norman alliance, and in any case Rainulf was no longer just an ally; he was a potential rival.

For the time being, however, he was prepared to let Pandulf enjoy his glory. And the Prince of Capua was doing so to the full when the first of the sons of Tancred de Hauteville rode down into Italy.

Some eight miles to the north-east of Coutances in Normandy

lies the little village of Hauteville-la-Guichard. Nothing but its name now remains to connect it with that strange, gifted clan whose reputation and influence once bestrode the civilised world from London to Antioch. At the beginning of the last century, however, the remains of an old castle could still be seen beside a running stream, and a French historian, Gauttier du Lys d'Arc, writing of a visit there in 1827, proudly quotes the words of a local peasant who lived there: '*Chest ichin, mes bons messeus, qu'est né l'incomparable Tancrède, et Robert Guiscard, qui veut dire prudent; ils ont baillé des trésors immenses d'or au bienheureux Geoffroy pour bâtir notre cathédrale, pour remercier Dieu des graces qu'il leur avait faites d'avoir si bien réussi dans leurs guerres de Sicile et d'Egypte.*'[1]

Tancred himself is fortunate in having had thrust upon him an immortality which he did little to deserve. There was nothing incomparable about this petty provincial baron, commander of a modest group of ten knights in the militia of Duke Robert of Normandy; indeed, from the little we know of him, he does not even appear to have been particularly remarkable—unless it was for his determined and persistent fecundity. Writing towards the turn of the century Geoffrey Malaterra, a Benedictine monk whose *Historia Sicula* is our principal source for the early beginnings of the Hautevilles, tells us that Tancred's first wife was a certain Muriella, a lady 'splendid in morals and birth', by whom he had five sons—William, Drogo, Humphrey, Geoffrey and Serlo. On her death he married again, for reasons which Malaterra finds it necessary to explain in some detail:

Since he was not yet old and could not therefore maintain continence but, being an upright man, found dishonourable intercourse abhorrent, he took to him a second wife. For, mindful of the apostolic words; *to avoid fornication, let every man have his own wife*, and further: *but whoremongers and adulterers God will judge*, he preferred rather to be content with one legitimate wife than to pollute himself with the embraces of concubines.

The eager Tancred now therefore married the lady Fressenda

---

[1] 'Here it was, good sirs, that the incomparable Tancred was born, and Robert Guiscard—that is, the crafty one. They gave our blessed Geoffrey great loads of golden treasure to build our Cathedral, in thanks to God for bringing them such victories in their wars in Sicily and Egypt.'

'in generosity and morals not inferior to the first', who presented him in swift and apparently effortless succession with seven more sons—Robert, Mauger, another William, Aubrey, Tancred, Humbert and Roger—and at least three daughters. For this formidable brood the family fief was clearly inadequate. Owing, however, to Rainulf's repeated appeals for reinforcements, the opportunities offered to young Normans in South Italy were well known; and in about 1035 the first three of the Hauteville boys decided to seek their fortunes there. Over the Alps they rode, William, Drogo and Humphrey, and made straight for Aversa; and so it was that they soon found themselves members of Rainulf's army in service with the Prince of Capua.

Pandulf was not long to hold the loyalty of the Hautevilles. Within a year or two, as might have been expected, he had antagonised all his allies. They were shocked by his compulsive double-dealing, insulted by his high-handedness, revolted by his cruelty. Even by eleventh-century standards his behaviour was insufferable—most of all towards the Church. He had already cast the Archbishop of Capua into chains and replaced him with his own bastard son; and now he was deliberately intensifying his persecution of Monte Cassino. Ever since the hasty departure and death of his brother he had borne a grudge against the great monastery, over which he had determined to regain control; in particular he hated Atenulf's successor, the Abbot Theobald. Thus, at the first opportunity, he lured Theobald to Capua and flung him into gaol. A new abbot was immediately elected, but Pandulf took no notice; setting up one of his henchmen as 'general administrator', he seized control of all the monastery revenues, expropriated the land and parcelled it out as a reward for those Normans who had served him best. The poor monks were powerless; they could offer no resistance, even when they saw all their precious treasure and plate being carried away to Capua. They were kept half-starved—on the day of the Assumption there was not even any wine to celebrate the Mass— and Amatus, who was probably there at the time, reports that before long most of the brothers had left the monastery in despair, the abbot included—'and those that remained were wretchedly treated'.[1]

[1] et cil qui remainstrent estoient vilanement traitié.

The standard of revolt was raised by the young Prince of Salerno, Gaimar V,[1] who had now grown to manhood and was determined to assert himself against his uncle's tyranny. He had all the makings of a worthy antagonist. 'This Gaimar', writes Amatus, 'was more courageous than his father, more generous and more courteous; indeed he possessed all the qualities a layman should have—except that he took an excessive delight in women.'[2] This pardonable weakness did not, however, mitigate the anger of young Gaimar when in 1036 he heard that his own niece had been the victim of an attempted rape by the Prince of Capua. For him it was the last straw; but it was also just the sort of excuse he had been waiting for. The other cities and duchies were, for the most part, only too pleased to give him their support; Rainulf switched his allegiance with the effortlessness born of long practice, and within a few weeks the whole land was once again in arms.

Pandulf had been somehow able to retain the loyalties of one or two of his old allies, including that fair sized contingent of Normans whose support he had purchased with lands from Monte Cassino. The defection to Gaimar of Rainulf and his followers consequently meant that the active forces on both sides were now largely composed of Normans—a fact which explains the somewhat indecisive nature of the fighting which followed. Gaimar would, as he himself knew, ultimately prove the stronger; but he knew also how quickly the pendulum could swing, and with a wisdom beyond his years he realised that no lasting victory could be achieved without imperial ratification. The only problem was—which Empire? In the past fifteen years both the Eastern and the Western had sent armies to assert their power in South Italy; this was perhaps a moment to play one against the other. The Prince of Salerno therefore sent appeals to both Emperors for their intervention and arbitration, justifying his recent actions by a long and detailed rehearsal of his uncle's crimes.

Conrad II, already in North Italy, was well aware of the chaotic

---

[1] Or IV. See p. 16 n.

[2] *Cestui Gamérie estoit plus vaillant que le père et plus libéral et cortois à donner, liquel estoit aorné de toutes les vertus que home sécular doit avoir fors de tant que moult se délictoit de avoir moult de fames.*

situation prevailing in the south, for which, by his thoughtless release of Pandulf twelve years before, he bore the indirect responsibility. During those years, however, Conrad had learned much; he had also built up a reputation for strength and, above all, for justice. He could not ignore Gaimar's appeal—particularly after he heard that a similar one had already been addressed to Constantinople. His own authority must be maintained over his vassals, and the supremacy of the Western Empire over the Eastern in the peninsula must be clearly demonstrated. In the first months of 1038, at the head of his army, he marched down to restore order.

He went straight to Monte Cassino. Several of the fugitive monks had already made their way to his court and laid their complaints before him; but on arrival at the monastery he found the situation even worse than he had feared. Messengers were at once sent to Pandulf ordering him in the Emperor's name to restore all the monastic lands and property that he had filched and, at the same time, to release the countless political prisoners who were languishing in Capuan gaols.

Pandulf was in a hopelessly untenable position. He had no allies of consequence and no means of opposing the Emperor. At first he adopted the tactics of penitence, offering substantial sums of money and his own children as hostages for his future good behaviour. Conrad accepted; but before long Pandulf's son escaped from his custodians and the Wolf reverted to his old form. Trusting to ride out the storm till the Emperor was safely back in Germany, he fled to one of his outlying castles at Sant' Agata dei Goti (its ruins still stand) and barricaded himself in. It was no use. The Emperor, ably assisted by Rainulf and his Normans, dealt with Pandulf's few remaining adherents in a swift mopping-up campaign and then returned to Capua where he solemnly installed Gaimar on the throne, to the plaudits of a populace heavily bribed with Salernitan gold. The game was up—Pandulf had one course only open to him. He fled to his old friends in Constantinople. But even here he was unlucky. On his arrival, to his intense surprise and for reasons which he could not understand, he was immediately clapped into prison.

Conrad returned the same summer to Germany. His expedition

had been short, but entirely successful. He had dealt with Pandulf, restored Monte Cassino to its old prosperity, and demonstrated once again the power and efficacy of imperial justice. Equally important, he had left supreme in South Italy a strong, energetic and remarkably virile young man who respected him and owed him a debt of considerable gratitude. Within a year the Emperor would be dead, aged barely fifty; but he would leave his southern dominions far healthier and more stable than poor Henry, his predecessor, had been able to do.

The real triumph was Gaimar's. While still only at the threshold of manhood he had raised himself to a position higher than ever his father or uncle had attained. In doing so he had incurred no enmities, broken no promises. He had not only the approval, but the active support and friendship of the Emperor of the West. He was generally popular in Italy. He had intelligence and health, and was outstandingly handsome. For him indeed the future seemed to smile.

But the Normans too had cause for satisfaction. Rainulf and his men had ended up as usual on the winning side. They had fought for Gaimar, and they had fought for Conrad. Their losses has been small, their numbers were still increasing. Most important of all, Gaimar had arranged that the Emperor, before leaving Italy, should confirm Rainulf's possession of Aversa by granting him a title of nobility and simultaneously transferring his vassalage from Naples to Salerno. And so it came about that in the summer of 1038 Conrad II formally invested Rainulf the Norman with the lance and gonfalon of the County of Aversa. As the new Count rose from his knees, no one knew better than he did why this investiture had been performed—simply to ensure that he, as sworn vassal to the Prince of Capua and Salerno, would be obliged to defend his suzerain as and when necessary from all his enemies. But at the moment this was of little consequence. The important fact was that Rainulf was now not only a major landowner, a local aristocrat and one of the most powerful military leaders in Italy; he was also a member of the imperial nobility, possessor of rights and a title which could be withdrawn from him only by the Emperor himself. Another vital and essential step had been taken towards his by now clearly-beheld objective—the Norman domination of the South.

As for the three young Hautevilles, their introduction into Italian politics had taught them much. They had seen how tumultuous was the land of their choice, how quickly an intelligent youth could scale the heights of power, how easily a prince could be brought low. They had learnt, too, that in a land of such shifting currents and brittle alliances diplomacy was as important as courage, that a sharp sword was valuable but a sharp mind more valuable still. They had witnessed both the strength of the imperial hand when it was imminent and its ineffectiveness when it was remote. And they had before them the example of a leader who, playing his cards with subtlety and care, had in twenty years achieved wealth, influence and nobility.

These were lessons that they would not forget.

4

SICILY

There's Sicily, for instance,—granted me
And taken back, some years since . . .

Browning, King Victor and King Charles

THE Prince of Salerno's appeal for assistance, to which Conrad II had reacted so promptly and effectively in 1038, had met with a disappointing lack of response from Constantinople, whither it had also been addressed. Since the removal of Boioannes in 1027 Greek influence in Italy had steadily declined. Pandulf was not the only one to have taken advantage of the weakness of Constantine VIII. In Apulia the Lombards were again growing restive under a succession of ineffectual Catapans; while the Saracens, who had seen in the death of Basil II the merciful hand of Allah, had redoubled the violence of their attacks and were extending the radius of their operations dangerously near to Constantinople itself.

If only the Bulgar-Slayer had left a son all might have been well. As things were, the problem of the succession was becoming increasingly confused. Constantine died in 1028, leaving no sons either—only three daughters, of whom the eldest, badly disfigured by smallpox, had long ago been packed off to a convent. The other two, Zoë and Theodora, were almost equally ill-favoured, both unmarried and well past their prime. It was typical of Constantine that he did nothing to remedy this situation until he was on his deathbed; he then picked on the elderly Mayor of Constantinople, Romanus Argyrus, and hurriedly married him off to Zoë. Three days later he died, and Romanus and Zoë jointly ascended the throne. Romanus, however, was not to enjoy it for long. He soon fell victim to a disagreeable wasting disease which caused his hair and beard to fall out—a condition ascribed by some to the prodigious quantity of aphrodisiacs he had vainly consumed in the hopes of begetting a son on the fifty-year-old Zoë, and by others to slow poison. The latter is not unlikely; for the Empress having at last awakened to the realisation of the joys she had been missing, was clearly determined to make up for lost time and had taken a lover— a handsome though epileptic young Paphlagonian money-changer called Michael. This youth was in fact the brother of the most powerful eunuch of the court, a certain John the Orphanotrophos, who had become the virtual administrator of the Empire and, being determined that his family should found a dynasty—he himself being regrettably disqualified from doing so—had purposely introduced Michael to Zoë with this end in view. The plot was successful; the Empress fell besottedly in love and soon was making no secret of her eagerness to be rid of her useless husband. On Good Friday 1034 Romanus expired in his bath. That same evening Michael married his elderly mistress and became Emperor.

For the beginning of a new reign, such circumstances were hardly auspicious; but Michael IV, with his brother's help, proved a notable improvement on his predecessor. Before long he started to develop plans for continuing the work begun by Basil II and driving the Saracens from Sicily. Their continual raids were no longer merely an annoyance; they were rapidly becoming a threat to Byzantine security. And it was not only the coastal towns that were suffering from their depredations. The city merchants complained that the high seas were alive with pirates, prices of imports were rising accordingly and foreign trade was beginning to suffer. To all Greeks, Sicily remained part of the Byzantine birthright; it still possessed a considerable Greek population. That it should still be occupied by the heathen was therefore an affront to both national security and national pride. The Arabs must go.

The chances of launching a successful campaign were in some ways more favourable for Michael than they had been for Basil ten years earlier. Civil war had now broken out among the Arab rulers in the island. The Emir of Palermo, al-Akhal, had suddenly found himself confronted with an insurgent army led by his brother Abu Hafs and stiffened by six thousand warriors from Africa under the command of Abdullah, son of the Zirid Caliph of Kairouan; and, in 1035, growing desperate, he appealed to Byzantium for help. Michael agreed—such an opportunity, he knew, might never be repeated. Before he could send more than a token force, news of al-Akhal's assassination removed this useful pretext for a Sicilian landing; but the revolt was now rapidly spreading through Sicily, and the Saracens, more and more hopelessly divided, seemed unlikely to be able to offer much resistance to a concerted Byzantine attack. Moreover, a major pirate raid on the Thracian coast had recently aroused alarm in the capital, which was beginning to feel itself threatened. And so preparations for the expedition continued as before, more slowly—since time now seemed to be on the side of the Greeks—but with all the care and thoroughness of which the Emperor and his sinister, efficient brother were capable. Only the avowed object was changed: there was no longer any question of honouring an alliance. The Greeks were out to reconquer Sicily.

When, therefore, in 1036 Gaimar appealed to Constantinople for military assistance in South Italy, prior commitments in Sicily furnished as valid an excuse as when Pandulf had made a similar appeal a dozen years before. Even without such an excuse, it is far from certain whether Michael would have taken decisive action; Pandulf had been a useful ally to Byzantium in the past and his cause was still by no means hopeless; why should the Eastern Empire bestir itself to eliminate the man who for twenty years had been one of the greatest thorns in the flesh of its western rival? Two years later, however, the situation had changed. Pandulf had been soundly beaten and his position was destroyed, apparently beyond hope of recovery. Gaimar on the other hand was powerful, and he was ambitious. If ever he were to turn against Byzantium, he could make serious trouble in the Capitanata. Besides, the Sicilian plans were taking shape and it was hoped that the Prince of Salerno-Capua and his fellow-rulers, who had suffered as much as anyone from the Arab raids, would make generous contributions in men and money. If Pandulf had had time to reflect a little, his imprisonment on arrival at Constantinople might have come as less of a shock.

The Sicilian expedition sailed in the early summer of 1038. It had been put under the command of the greatest of living Byzantine generals, the gigantic George Maniakes, still glorious from a series of Syrian triumphs six years before. Maniakes was, in character and achievement as in physique, well over life-size—one of those colourful near-geniuses thrown up at intervals through history who seem to have the world at their feet, only to lose it again through some compensatory defect which betrays them in a moment of crisis. The historian Michael Psellus has left us a fearsome description:

I myself saw the man, and marvelled at him; for nature had combined in his person all the qualities necessary for a military commander. He stood to the height of ten feet, so that to look at him men would tilt back their heads as if towards the top of a hill or a high mountain. His countenance was neither gentle nor pleasing, but put one in mind of a tempest; his voice was like thunder and his hands seemed made for tearing down walls or for smashing doors of bronze. He could spring like a lion and his frown was terrible. And every thing else about him was in proportion. Those who saw him for the first time discovered that every description they had heard of him was but an understatement.

The army which this magnificent ogre was to command was as usual heterogeneous. Its strongest element was an impressive Varangian contingent under the almost legendary Norse hero Harald Hardrada, returning from a pilgrimage to Jerusalem; its weakest a body of grumbling Lombards and Italians from Apulia who made no secret of their disgust at having been forced into Byzantine service. In between came the great bulk of Maniakes's force, composed principally of Greeks and Bulgarians. They were transported by a fleet of galleys commanded by a certain Stephen, an erstwhile ship-caulker whose only distinction was to have long ago married the sister of the Orphanotrophos and so to have woken up one morning to find himself the Emperor's brother-in-law—an event which had led to his rapid elevation to several positions of high responsibility, all well beyond his powers to fulfil.[1]

The expedition did not go at once to Sicily but first headed round to Salerno, there to collect a contribution from Gaimar. They found the young prince more than ready to help. The growth of his power

---

[1] Of Stephen, Psellus writes: 'I saw him after the metamorphosis. . . . It was as if a pygmy wanted to play Hercules and was trying to make himself look like the demi-god. The more such a person tries, the more his appearance belies him—clothed in the lion's skin but weighed down by the club' (tr. E. R. A. Sewter).

had led to an unwontedly peaceful political climate, and the increasing numbers of idle Norman adventurers, bored, predatory and totally unprincipled, looking for trouble and constrained to live off the land, were proving a grave embarrassment to him. He retained, naturally, the Count of Aversa and his more trustworthy followers, who would be indispensable if an emergency should arise; but from the remainder, three hundred of the youngest and most headstrong were given their marching orders for Sicily and, encouraged by promises of large rewards, were embarked together with a number of Italians and Lombards on Stephen's ships. They included, inevitably, the Hautevilles.

The island of Sicily is the largest in the Mediterranean. It has also proved, over the centuries, to be the most unhappy. The stepping-stone between Europe and Africa, the gateway between the East and the West, the link between the Latin world and the Greek, at once a stronghold, observation-point and clearing-house, it has been fought over and occupied in turn by all the great powers that have at various times striven to extend their dominion across the Middle Sea. It has belonged to them all—and yet has properly been part of none; for the number and variety of its conquerors, while preventing the development of any strong national individuality of its own, have endowed it with a kaleidoscopic heritage of experience which can never allow it to become completely assimilated. Even today, despite the beauty of its landscape, the fertility of its fields and the perpetual benediction of its climate, there lingers everywhere some dark, brooding quality—some underlying sorrow of which poverty, Church influence, the Mafia and all the other popular modern scapegoats may be the manifestations but are certainly not the cause. It is the sorrow of long, unhappy experience, of opportunity lost and promise unfulfilled; the sorrow, perhaps, of a beautiful woman who has been raped too often and betrayed too often and is no longer fit for love or marriage. Phoenicians, Greeks, Carthaginians, Romans, Goths, Byzantines, Arabs, Normans, Germans, Spaniards, French —all have left their mark. Today, a century after being received into her Italian home, Sicily is probably less unhappy than she has been for many centuries; but though no longer lost she still seems

49

lonely, seeking always an identity which she can never entirely find.

The Greeks first reached Sicily in the eighth century before Christ. Dislodging the indigenous inhabitants and a few Phoenician trading posts, they introduced the vine and the olive and built up a flourishing colony. This soon became one of the major cultural centres of the civilised world, the home of poets such as Stesichorus of Himera—whom the gods struck blind for composing invectives against Helen of Troy—and philosophers such as the great Empedocles of Acragas, who did much valuable work on the transmigration of souls and, having already served a long and tedious apprenticeship as a shrub, suddenly relinquished his mortal clay for higher things one morning in 440, when another branch of scientific enquiry led him too far into the crater of Mount Etna. But the golden age did not last long. The Peloponnesian War and the famous Athenian expedition brought the island into the thick of European affairs and opened the way to the first inroads by Carthage which, together with various Greek tyrants in individual cities (of whom Dionysius of Syracuse is the most celebrated), maintained its power until the third century B.C. Finally in 241, as a result of the First Punic War which stained the whole island red, Sicily was established as a Roman Province.

During the age of the Republic, the Romans treated Sicily with little respect. That monstrous inferiority complex to which they always gave way when confronted with Greek culture led to further destruction and exploitation on a colossal scale. A few free Greek cities managed to retain their independence, but over much of the island liberty was almost extinguished as the slave-gangs toiled naked in the fields, sowing and harvesting the corn for Rome. From time to time a serious slave revolt or a scandal such as the corrupt governorship of Verres—made notorious by the castigations of Cicero—casts a harsh though fleeting light on the prevailing conditions, but for most of this period Sicily bore her sufferings in silence. With the Empire the situation improved a little; Hadrian, that indefatigable traveller, paid a visit in A.D. 126 and climbed Etna, but at no time was the island considered more than the principal granary of Rome. As such it was taken for granted. No serious attempt was made to impose Roman civilisation, and despite a certain influx of Latin-speaking settlers it remained essentially Greek in language and outlook.

By the middle of the fifth century the Roman Empire in the West was on the threshold of extinction, and more and more of the provinces and colonies were slipping from its grasp. In A.D. 440 Sicily fell to the Vandals, who shortly afterwards passed it by treaty to the Ostrogoths; and for a time the island was ruled by Gothic counts. The Sicilians were treated with consideration, but they always resented their barbarian overlords. They therefore gave an enthusiastic welcome to the 'liberating' forces of the Emperor Justinian in 535. The Goths withdrew without showing any sign of fight except at Panormus—the present Palermo, but then a small port of very secondary importance.[1] Here the local governor attempted a stand; but Belisarius, most brilliant of Justinian's generals, ordered the Byzantine fleet to sail into the harbour, so close inshore that the masts of the ships rose above the town walls. He then had boats full of soldiers hoisted to the yard-arms, whence they were able to shoot down on the defenders. The Goths gave in.

Sicily was once again an imperial province. At one moment, indeed, it almost became a good deal more. In the middle of the seventh century the Byzantine Emperor Constans II, understandably concerned for the future of his western provinces under the whirl-wind surge of Islam, took the immense decision to shift the balance of the Empire westwards and to transfer his capital accordingly. Rome was the obvious choice; but after a depressing twelve-day visit there in 663—he was the first Emperor for nearly three hundred years to set foot in the Mother City—he gave up the idea and settled instead in the infinitely more congenial Greek atmosphere of Syracuse. It is fascinating to speculate how the history of Europe would have been changed if the capital had remained in Sicily; but the palace and court officials never became reconciled to the change, and five years later one of them, in a fit of uncontrollable nostalgia,

[1] Despite its superb geographical position, Palermo became the metropolis only under Saracen occupation. This explains why the city possesses virtually no classical antiquities—temples, theatres, even ruins—on the scale of those to be found elsewhere on the island. Almost the sole exceptions are a beautiful mosaic pavement of Orpheus and the animals and another representing the Four Seasons, now to be seen at the National Museum.

attacked the Emperor in his bath and felled him with the soap-dish. By now the Arabs were directing their main offensive towards Asia Minor and Constantinople itself, and so Constans's son and successor, Constantine IV the Bearded, had no choice but to return at once to the Bosphorus. Sicily was left in peace again.

This peace continued, generally speaking, throughout the eighth century, during which Sicily, like Calabria, became a haven for refugees from that *'calvinisme anticipé'*,[1] the iconoclast movement in Constantinople; but in the ninth it was shattered. The Muslims had waited long enough. They had by now overrun the whole of the North African coast, and had in fact already been harassing the island for some time with sporadic raids. In 827 they saw their chance of achieving permanent occupation: the local Byzantine governor, Euphemius by name, was dismissed from his post after an unseemly elopement with a local nun. His reply was to rise in revolt and pro-claim himself Emperor, appealing to the Arabs for aid. They landed in strength, rapidly entrenched themselves, took little notice of Euphemius (who in any case soon came to a violent end) and three years later stormed Palermo which they made their capital. Subse-quent progress was slow: Messina fell in 843 and Syracuse, after a long and arduous siege during which the defenders were finally reduced to cannibalism, surrendered only in 878. But after this the Byzantines seem to have admitted defeat. A few isolated outposts in the eastern part of the island held out a little longer—the last, Rometta, even into the middle of the tenth century—but on that June day when the banner of the Prophet was raised over Syracuse, Sicily became, to all intents and purposes, a part of the Muslim world.

Once the wars of conquest were over and the country had settled again, life continued pleasantly enough for most of the Christian communities. They were normally allowed to keep their freedom, on payment of an annual tribute which many must have preferred to the military service that had always been compulsory under Byzantine rule; and the Saracens displayed, as nearly always through-out their history, a degree of religious toleration which permitted the churches and monasteries and the long tradition of Hellenistic

[1] Lenormant.

scholarship to flourish as much as ever they had done.[1] In other ways too the island benefited from its conquerors. The Arabs brought with them a whole new system of agriculture based on such innovations as terracing and syphon aqueducts for irrigation. They introduced cotton and papyrus, citrus and date-palm and enough sugar-cane to make possible, within a very few years, a substantial export trade. Under the Byzantines Sicily had never played an important part in European commerce, but with the Saracen conquest it soon became one of the major trading centres of the Mediterranean, with Christian, Muslim and Jewish merchants thronging the bazaars of Palermo.

And yet, among the many blessings conferred upon Sicily by her Arab conquerors, that of stability was conspicuously absent. As the links of loyalty which at first held the Emir of Palermo and his fellow-chieftains to the North African caliphate grew ever more tenuous, the emirs themselves lost their only cohesive force; they became increasingly divided against each other and so the island found itself once again a battleground of warring factions. And it was this steady political decline, culminating in the Zirid invasion under Abdullah referred to above, that in 1038 brought the Greeks —and their Norman allies—to Sicily.

Some time during the late summer the Greek army landed on Sicilian soil. At first they carried all before them. Courageously as the divided Saracens fought, they could do little to stem the tide. Messina fell almost at once and was followed, after heavy fighting, by Rometta, the key fortress that commanded the pass linking Messina with the northern coastal road to Palermo. Of the next stage of the campaign we know little—the chroniclers are silent or

---

[1] Towards the end of the tenth century St Nilus, the famous Calabrian abbot, sent the Emir of Palermo a sum of money with which he hoped to ransom three of his monks, captured by Saracen raiders. He supported his request with a letter to the Emir's chief notary, a Christian, but can hardly have expected as cordial a response as he in fact received. The Emir liberated the monks and returned the ransom under cover of a letter saying that he would have provided the monastery with a grant of immunity from raids, if the Abbot had only requested it. He went on to invite Nilus to settle in Sicily, promising him that he would enjoy there all the honour and veneration that were his due.

impossibly vague.[1] There seems, however, to have been a slow but steady advance on Syracuse where, in 1040, we find Maniakes and his troops laying siege to the city. The Muslim garrison resisted fiercely, and held their assailants long enough to allow Abdullah to muster a relief force in the mountains behind Syracuse with the object of swooping down on Maniakes's rear. Word of this plan reached the Greeks just in time; wheeling round, Maniakes surprised Abdullah's men near Troina and immediately attacked. The defeat was absolute. The Muslims fled in disorder and the garrison of Syracuse, realising that they could no longer hope for relief, surrendered without more ado. The exultant Greek population lost no time in arranging thanksgiving services, and disinterred from their hiding-places all their most treasured religious relics to do greater honour to their glorious liberator; though they cannot have been best pleased when Maniakes had the body of St Lucia removed from its coffin and, finding the saint (as Amatus describes her) 'as whole and sweet-smelling as the first day she was put there', sent her with his compliments to the Emperor.

It is hard to estimate how much of this early success was due to the Norman contingent in Maniakes's army. The Norman chroniclers, from whom most of our information comes, stress the valour of their compatriots to the point where the Greeks often appear to have had nothing to do but pick up the spoils when the battles were over. Certainly the Normans fought hard and well; and it was during the siege of Syracuse that William de Hauteville, catching sight of the redoubtable Emir of the city as he rode out on a sortie, made a sudden charge, unhorsed him and left him dead on the ground. For this exploit he was ever afterwards known as *Bras-de-Fer*, the Iron-Arm; and the glory which he won before the walls of Syracuse was to serve him in good stead on his return to the mainland.

Yet the main credit for the success of the expedition up to this point must go to Maniakes. What might have been a disastrous

[1] One of the few clues remaining is the abbey church of S. Maria di Maniace near Maletto, built on the site of one of Maniakes's victories by the local Greek population soon after the battle, enlarged and restored by Count Roger I and Countess Adelaide towards the end of the century. This was the church around which, in about 1170, Queen Margaret was to found the large and richly-endowed Benedictine abbey of Maniace, last of the great Norman foundations in Sicily.

defeat by Abdullah's forces was turned to victory by the effectiveness of his intelligence and the speed and energy of his generalship. He himself had suffered negligible losses, except possibly at Rometta, and in less than two years had restored the eastern half of the island to Christian hands.[1] It was a tragedy, not only for him but for the whole Byzantine Empire, that at this of all moments he should have been recalled, in disgrace, to Constantinople.

The demoralisation of the Byzantine forces and their collapse after the victory of Syracuse were so sudden and so complete that one can readily understand the Saracens' contention that Allah had again intervened on their behalf. Everything seemed to go wrong at once. And just as he takes the credit for the victories, so now some at least of the blame must fall on the personality of Maniakes. Superb general as he was, he cannot have been an easy colleague. He had never attempted to hide his contempt of Stephen, and when he heard after Troina that Abdullah had somehow managed to escape by sea through the naval blockade, he forgot himself so far as to lay hands upon the admiral physically. Stephen—for whom, in view of his assailant's size, the experience must have been not only humiliating but also alarming in the extreme—determined on revenge and sent an urgent message to his imperial brother-in-law denouncing Maniakes for treasonable activity. Maniakes was summoned to the capital where, without being given any opportunity to answer to charges made against him, he was cast unceremoniously into prison. His successor, a eunuch called Basil, proved as incapable as was Stephen; the Greeks lost their momentum and their morale; and the retreat began.

Meanwhile the Normans had left in disgust. Once again Maniakes seems to have been at fault. Many an inspired general has proved intolerable off the battlefield, and Maniakes's undoubted propensities towards violence could not fail to lead him into trouble with his men. Soon after the capture of Syracuse a dispute arose over the distribution of spoils, of which the Normans had decided that they

[1] The Castello Maniace which now stands on the southernmost tip of the Syracuse peninsula dates only from the thirteenth century. But even though it has no direct historical association with the great George, it remains a magnificent memorial to his name.

were receiving less than their fair share. This claim may have been justified; a Greek city, liberated by a Greek army, clearly provided no opportunity for plunder or pillage and it is doubtful if these self-confessed mercenaries had received much recompense for the best part of two years' campaigning. At all events the Normans persuaded the leader of the Salerno contingent, a Greek-speaking Lombard called Arduin, to remonstrate with Maniakes on their behalf. Amatus's story that Arduin had himself refused to surrender a captured Arab horse to the Commander-in-Chief may or may not be true; if so, the fact must have inflamed the general's wrath still further. What is virtually certain is that Arduin was stripped and beaten for his presumption, and that he, the Normans and their Salternitan comrades left the Greek army forthwith and returned to the mainland, taking the Scandinavian brigade with them.

With the departure of all their best fighting men, followed by that of their only capable general, there was little hope left for the Greeks. But more trouble was to come. For several years dissatisfaction had been growing in Apulia. Young Argyrus, the son of Melus who had recently returned to Italy after years of imprisonment in Constantinople, had inherited all his father's rebellious spirit; and he had little difficulty, particularly after the Greek press-gangs had begun their forcible recruiting for the Sicilian expedition, in working up the Italians and Lombards in Apulia against their Byzantine masters. Already in 1038 several Greek officials had been murdered; in 1039 the situation was near flash-point; and in 1040 Argyrus gave the signal for revolt. The Catapan was assassinated, and all the local militias along the Apulian coast rose up in a mutiny which the local Greek garrisons, themselves seriously depleted, were unable to contain.

5

INSURRECTION

Et lo matin li Normant s'en aloient solachant par li camp, et par li jardin lo menoit à Vénoze laquelle estoit de près de Melfe, liez et joians sur lor chevaux, et vont corrant çà et là: et li citadin de la cité virent cil chevalier liquel non cognoissoient, si s'en merveilloient et orent paour. Et li Normant a une proie grandissime et sanz nulle brigue la menoient ad Melfe. . . . Et d'iluec s'en vont à la belle Puille, et celles choses qui lor plaisoit prenoient, et celle qui ne lor plaisoient leissoient. . . .

Il firent lor conte Guillerme fil de Tancrède, home vaillantissime en armes et aorné de toutes bonnes costumes, et beauz et gentil et jovène.

(And in the morning the Normans rode gaily off through the meadows and gardens towards Venosa, which is not far from Melfi, happy and joyful on their horses, cavorting hither and thither; and the citizens of the town saw these unknown knights, and wondered at them and were afraid. And the Normans returned with immense plunder and brought it back without trouble to Melfi . . . And from there they set off for lovely Apulia, and what they liked they took, and what they did not like they left. . . .

And William, Tancred's son, they made their Count, a man most courageous in war, and possessed of all good qualities; handsome, and noble, and young.)

Amatus, II

By the time the news of the insurrection reached Constantinople, the Emperor Michael was obviously dying. His epilepsy now made it necessary for his throne to be placed so that purple curtains could be drawn at a moment's notice in the event of a sudden seizure, while most of his failing energies were taken up with ascetic practices and charities—in particular the asylum for reformed prostitutes which he had recently founded in the capital. His brother the Orphanotrophos, however, acted swiftly and appointed an able young general, Michael Doukeianos, as the new Catapan with instructions to restore order in Apulia at any cost. Doukeianos left at once and, summoning all available men, by the end of 1040 had managed to damp down—though not by any means entirely to extinguish—the flames of revolt. He was a man of energy and imagination and, but for one mistake, he might easily have succeeded in restoring Byzantine fortunes in Italy. By that one mistake he destroyed them for ever.

Soon after his arrival the new Catapan found it necessary to pay a hurried visit to Sicily—presumably to hasten the departure of the remnants of the Greek army, whose help was urgently needed in Apulia. On his return journey—he may have taken ship to Salerno—he met Arduin, who had returned with the Normans to Gaimar's court. From the start the two seem to have been on excellent terms; Arduin spoke perfect Greek; he was an experienced soldier who could call on a large number of Normans to fight with him; and his recent quarrel with the disgraced Maniakes may well have been an additional point in his favour. At all events it was not long before Arduin, a Lombard, accepted the Catapan's offer of the post of *topoterites*, or military commander, of Melfi, one of the principal hill-towns along the Byzantine frontier.

Should Doukeianos have known better? His gullibility certainly proved his undoing, but it must not be too hastily condemned. A strong commander was required for Melfi, and strong commanders were rare among the Greeks in Italy. Arduin could boast an excellent record and had in the past fought well for the Byzantine cause. His departure from Sicily could not possibly be held against him— continued service with Maniakes would have been impossible after what had happened at Syracuse. In language and cultural background he seemed more Greek than the Greeks, and even if he was of Lombard origin, this did not necessarily imply disloyalty; Lombards had often held high positions in the Capitanata. Besides, the need was urgent and Doukeianos could not afford to be too particular. He little knew how hugely he would be betrayed.

Arduin's motives can only be guessed. Ambition certainly played the major part. He was a Lombard; the Lombards were in revolt. Here was an opportunity, and he suddenly found himself with the

means to seize it. To command a body of three hundred fearless
Norman knights on a victorious campaign must have been an
exhilarating experience, and he knew that those same knights, if it
was made worth their while, would be ready to leap into action
again at his command. His support for the Lombard cause at this
moment might therefore tip the scales and make all the difference
between the independence and the subjection of his race. Moreover
he was still smarting from the treatment he had suffered from
Maniakes and was bent on avenging himself on the Greeks. As soon
as he reached Melfi, therefore, he began quietly subverting the local
populace. Amatus writes in breathless admiration of his technique:

He gave frequent feasts, to which he invited well-born and lowly alike,
offering them choice meats; and when they had eaten he would speak to
them in gentle words . . . feigning sympathy for the hardships they
suffered from their Greek overlords and the insults endured by their
womenfolk. . . . Ah, with what wise subtlety did he stir up gentry and
people against those who ill-treated them![1]

In March 1041, as soon as he was sure of support within the town,
Arduin travelled secretly to Aversa. There, with the covert support
of Rainulf, he found his three hundred Norman stalwarts, gathered
under twelve chiefs who included William and Drogo de Hauteville. His proposition was simple enough; he would give them
Melfi as their headquarters and from there the Lombards and
Normans together would drive the Greeks once and for all from
South Italy, dividing the conquered territory equally between them.
The Normans did not need much persuading, and Arduin's exhortation, if Amatus's account of it is accurate, was nothing short of
masterly—working first on their pride, then on their ambition, next
arousing their contempt for the enemy and finally appealing directly
to their covetousness:

You still occupy this land which was given to you, yet you live in it like
mice in the skirting . . . now it is time to reach out with a strong hand, and
in this I will be your leader. Follow me; I will go before, you will follow;

[1] *Faisoit sovent convit, li gentilhome et li non gentil envitoit a son convit, et lor donoit délicioses
viandez; et puiz quant avoient mengié parloit de amicables paroles . . . et feingnoit qu'il estoit
dolent de la grevance qu'il souffroient de la seignorie de li Grex, et l'injure qu'il faisoient à lor
moilliers et à lor fames. . . . Ha! quel sage soutillesces pour lever la seignorie à li seignor qui lui
firent injure, et émut lo puple contre eaux!* [II, 16].

and let me tell you why—because I will lead you against men who are as women, and who live in a rich and spacious land.[1]

The *topoterites* had left his post under cover of darkness, alone; he returned with an army. The inhabitants of Melfi at first hesitated when they saw it; but Arduin's ever-agile tongue persuaded them that this was the means of their deliverance. They opened the gates. It was a momentous decision. From that day Melfi became the spearhead of the revolt. Already heavily fortified by the Greeks and now almost impregnable on its Apennine hill-top, it constituted the perfect mountain stronghold. From it the Norman knights, still highwaymen at heart, could spread out in all directions, raiding and pillaging to their hearts' content; to it they could return with their plunder, confident in its security and in their own immunity from reprisals.[2]

Within days Venosa fell; then Lavello, then Ascoli. The Catapan, bitterly conscious of his own responsibility for what had happened—though he may not yet have realised the full dimensions of the catastrophe—hastened up from Bari with all the forces he could muster, and on 16 March he sighted the main body of the Norman army, now swelled by large numbers of Lombards, near the banks of the Olivento, a little stream running just below Venosa. Calling a halt, he sent a mesenger across to them, offering them the choice: either they could leave Byzantine territory peaceably and at once, or they must meet his own army in battle on the morrow.

The Normans had heard communications of that sort before, and knew how to deal with them. During the harangue one of the twelve chiefs, Hugh Tuboeuf, had approached the messenger's horse and had been stroking it approvingly; now, as the man finished, he suddenly turned and struck it one mighty blow between the eyes with his bare fist, laying the luckless animal unconscious on the ground. At this, according to Malaterra, the messenger in a paroxysm

---

[1] *Vouz encoire estes en ceste terre qui vouz a été donée et vouz i habitez comme la sorice qui est en lo partus. . . . entre il convient que faille estende vostre main forte et dont je vouz menerai; venez apres moi, et je irai devant et vous apres; et vouz dirai pourquoi je voiz devant, que sachiez que je vouz menerai a homes comme fames, liquel demorent en molt ricche et espaciouse terre* [II, 17].

[2] The hill of Melfi is still crowned by the ruins of its Norman castle. It was, however, largely rebuilt in 1281 and suffered severely in the earthquake of 1851. Little of the original structure now remains.

of fear fainted dead away; but the Normans, having with some difficulty restored him to his senses, gave him a new horse, better than the first, on which they sent him back to the Catapan with the message that they were ready.

The battle was fought the next morning. It ended in a total defeat of the Greeks. Many of them were killed, including nearly all the contingent of Varangians that Doukeianos had brought up from Bari; and a large number were drowned as they tried to cross the swollen waters of the Olivento. The Catapan could only withdraw his battered remnants; more soldiers would have to be found before he met the Normans a second time.

Again the press-gangs scoured the towns and villages of Apulia. They moved quickly and at the beginning of May their work was done. This time it was the river Ofanto that saw the confrontation of the two armies—at Montemaggiore, on that same field of Cannae that Greeks, Lombards and Normans had drenched with their blood twenty-three years before. Though the dispositions were similar, the outcome was radically different from that of 1018. The Normans were again outnumbered, but now it was their turn to sweep their adversaries from the field. Their general was William de Hauteville, the Iron-Arm. He was suffering from a high fever and had not intended to take part in the battle, but as he watched from a nearby hill the temptation suddenly became too great. Jumping from his litter, he charged down the slope into the thick of the fray and led his men to victory.

News of these two consecutive defeats caused grave concern in Constantinople. Doukeianos was transferred to Sicily, where he was given the ungrateful task of salvaging what was left of the expedition; he was succeeded in Apulia by another Boioannes, son of the great Basil. But if there had been any hopes that this young man's ability might match that of his brilliant father, they were soon disappointed. The new Catapan, who had brought no reinforcements with him, rightly decided to avoid pitched battles if he could, and resolved instead to besiege the Normans and the Lombards in Melfi; but they were too quick for him. Streaming from the town before the Greek army had reached it they encamped near by at Monte Siricolo, near Montepeloso. Here, on 3 September 1041, they inflicted their third defeat on the hapless Byzantines and took prisoner the Catapan. Boioannes was handed over to Atenulf, brother of the reigning Prince of Benevento, who had recently been given the titular leadership of the rising. Lashed to his horse, he was paraded in triumph through the streets of the city. Meanwhile the cumulative effect of the three Lombard victories had been to undermine what was left of Byzantine prestige in Apulia; Bari, Monopoli, Giovinazzo, Matera, all declared themselves openly for the insurgents. The revolt was fast gathering momentum.

But now dissension broke out. The Lombards of Apulia were not prepared to be dictated to by Arduin, nor to accept, even as a figurehead, the colourless Atenulf of Benevento, both of whom they rightly suspected of being the unconscious tools of the Normans. In this they were supported by Gaimar, since 1038 the Prince of Capua as well as Salerno, who, being himself by far the most powerful of Lombard princes, deeply resented the choice of Atenulf as leader. A similar split appeared in the Norman ranks. The little colony which had been installed in Troia twenty years before had now, like its counterpart in Aversa, grown in numbers and influence and saw no cause to take orders from a group of freebooting upstarts in Melfi. These Apulian Normans therefore joined with their Lombard neighbours in demanding as their chief young Argyrus, who had after all been the instigator of the revolt and who, as Melus's son, was better qualified by blood for the leadership than was any Beneventan princeling. It was in vain for Arduin and his supporters to point out that they, and not the Apulians, had done all the fighting; the ground was cut from under their feet by Atenulf himself, who was discovered to have sold Boioannes back to the Greeks and to have kept all the ransom money for himself. Their candidate disgraced, the Melfi faction capitulated. In February 1042 Argyrus was formally acclaimed by the Normans and Lombards together in the Church of S. Apollinare at Bari.

This rivalry between Argyrus and Atenulf makes it clear that, whatever the Norman chroniclers may imply, there was still no overt question of a seizure of power by the Normans for themselves; this was still essentially a revolt by Lombards against Byzantines and was generally regarded as such. The possibility of electing a Norman as leader is never suggested, for the Normans are still theoretically mercenaries, fighting for territorial rewards perhaps, but not for political domination. And yet it is not so simple as that. From about 1040 one is conscious of a slow change in the atmosphere. Norman prestige now stems from something deeper than military prowess; Norman views are sought on questions unrelated to strategy and warfare, while they themselves take decisions which affect not only their own position but the future of the peninsula as a whole. Their place in Italy is no longer questioned, and their attitude to the land has something proprietary about it which was not there before. Their future is growing clearer to them all the time, and they seem to be waiting only for a leader who will focus their aspirations and translate them into action.

That leader was not long in coming.

The quarrels among the Normans and the Lombards were as nothing compared to the events which now took place in Constantinople. On 10 December 1041 Michael IV died. The Orphanotrophos was ready. Determined as ever that his own family should continue to occupy the imperial throne, he had already induced Zoë to adopt his nephew—son of the admiral Stephen—as heir-presumptive. This step, however, proved his undoing. Michael V, surnamed Calaphates—the caulker—after his father's early profession, had scarcely assumed power before he banished his uncle, to whom he owed everything, to a distant place of exile. A few weeks later it was the turn of Zoë herself; the old empress's head was shaved and she was unceremoniously packed off to end her days on an island in the Sea of Marmora. The departure of the Orphanotrophos was lamented by no one; but Zoë was an anointed empress of the great Macedonian house, and the news of her exile caused furious rioting throughout the capital. When Michael appeared in the imperial box at the Hippodrome he was pelted with arrows and stones; and within a few hours a mob was marching on the Palace. Zoë was hastily retrieved and displayed on the balcony; but it was too late. The citizens, now backed by the Church and the aristocracy, refused to submit any longer to the misrule of the upstart Paphlagonians. Zoë's younger sister Theodora, whom she had forced to take the veil and who had now for many years led the life of a recluse, was carried protesting from her house to Santa Sophia, where she was acclaimed as Empress; and Michael, who had sought sanctuary in the Monastery of the Studion, was dragged to a public square of the city where, in the presence of his subjects, his eyes were put out. So it was that Zoë and Theodora, cordially detesting one another and both manifestly unfitted to rule, together assumed the supreme executive power of the Byzantine Empire.

This uneasy tandem did not last long. As Michael Psellus, who knew her well, was later to point out, Zoë would have been quite willing to see a stable-boy on the imperial throne rather than let her sister share power with herself; and within two months, though now sixty-four, she flung herself with undiminished eagerness into the arms of her third husband, Constantine Monomachus, an agreeable and attractive roué to whom, as the Emperor Constantine IX, poor Theodora was only too pleased to surrender her share of the throne. Meanwhile the disappearance from the capital of the last of the Orphanotrophos's dreadful family meant the liberation of Maniakes. Restored once again to favour, he was immediately appointed Catapan and sent to redress the ever-worsening situation in Italy. Within a month of Michael V's deposition he had landed at Taranto to find that, with the single exception of Trani, the whole of Apulia north of a line drawn from Taranto to Brindisi had declared for Argyrus.

The horrors of that summer of 1042 were long remembered in Apulia. Maniakes advanced up the coast magnificent in his wrath, burning the towns, massacring their inhabitants—men and women, the aged and the children, monks and nuns alike. Some were strung from the trees, others—including many children—buried alive. Monopoli, Matera, Giovinazzo, or what was left of them, all capitulated, begging for mercy.

At this rate the whole of the Capitanata might have been regained; but once again the Byzantines were betrayed by their own corruption. Constantine Monomachus openly cherished a mistress whose brother, Romanus Skleros, had some time before seduced Maniakes's wife. In consequence a bitter feud had arisen; and when Constantine assumed the throne it was an easy matter for this Skleros to arrange for the Catapan's recall. For the second time in little more than two years Maniakes had fallen victim to palace intrigue; he had no intention of submitting again. This time it was he himself who revolted. Refusing to recognise Constantine, he allowed his army to proclaim him emperor. He seized his successor on his arrival in Italy, stuffed his ears, nose and mouth with dung and tortured him to death; then, leaving the Capitanata to look after itself, he hurriedly crossed the Adriatic—whose storms, according to William of Apulia, he first tried to assuage by human sacrifice. Marching on Thessalonica, he met and defeated an imperial army at Ostrovo in Bulgaria, but fell, mortally wounded, at the moment of victory. His head was carried back to Constantinople and exhibited, impaled on a spear, at the Hippodrome. To a glorious, tempestuous, ill-starred life it was perhaps a not altogether unfitting end.

Meanwhile the Lombards, as usual with Norman support, had fought back, and at the time of Maniakes's second recall were besieging Trani, the one city of northern Apulia which had throughout the hostilities remained unflinchingly loyal to Byzantium. With their enormous wooden siege-engine, the largest that had ever been seen in South Italy and the admiration of all eyes, they were confident that they would soon force the city to capitulate. So, indeed, they would have, but for the bitter and unexpected blow that now struck them. Argyrus, their elected leader, son of the venerated Melus and himself now the living embodiment of Lombard nationalism, went over to the enemy. Before doing so he caused the great siege tower to be burned, and his erstwhile followers had no choice but to retire from Trani, humiliated and bewildered.

Argyrus's defection is hard to explain. That he received heavy bribes from the Greeks is certain; Maniakes's ill-fated successor had brought him letters from Constantine offering him wealth and high rank in return for his allegiance to the Empire. But why were such offers accepted? Argyrus had lived, fought and suffered imprisonment for his beliefs; his sincerity and integrity had never been questioned, nor had his patriotism. Particularly after the departure of Maniakes Lombard chances of success were excellent, and as elected leader of the revolt he stood to gain far more than even Constantine IX could offer. Perhaps there were other factors of which we know nothing; perhaps, for example, he suddenly perceived that the Normans constituted a greater long-term threat to the Lombard cause than the Greeks. We can only hope so, and be thankful that it was not given to Melus, lying in his over-decorated tomb at Bamberg, to know of his son's dishonour.

The insurgents now found themselves once again without a leader. Of the two Lombards who had first been picked, one had been guilty of sharp practice and the other of arrant treachery, and among their demoralised compatriots no further candidates could be found of sufficient calibre to assume the command. The Normans, moreover, tired of this Lombard double-dealing, had now determined to elect a supreme chief of their own. Since the victories of Syracuse, Montemaggiore and Montepeloso, there was one obvious choice—William Bras-de-Fer; and so, in September 1042, Tancred's eldest son was unanimously proclaimed leader of all the Normans in Apulia with the title of Count.

But counts, in those feudal days, could not exist independently. They could only form part of that continuous chain of vassalage which connected the Emperor, through the princes, the dukes and the lesser baronage, to the humblest of the peasantry. William was therefore obliged to seek a suzerain, and he found one ready to hand. Gaimar of Salerno, who as we have seen was by now only too anxious to associate himself with the insurrection, willingly agreed to William's proposals. At the end of 1042 he rode with Rainulf of Aversa to Melfi, and there he was acclaimed as 'Duke of Apulia and Calabria' by the assembled Normans. Bestowing upon William, as a gage of friendship, the hand in marriage of his niece, the daughter of Duke Guy of Sorrento, Gaimar then shared out among the twelve chiefs all the lands *acquestées et à acquester*—not only those territories which had already been conquered, but also all those that might in future fall into their hands. There could have been no more forth-right declaration of intention—the fighting would continue until the last Greek had been driven from the peninsula. Meanwhile the Iron-Arm, confirmed as Count of Apulia under Gaimar's suzerainty with authority to found new baronies as new land was conquered, was allotted Ascoli as his particular fief; his brother Drogo received

Venosa; while Rainulf of Aversa, not one of the twelve but too powerful to be ignored, was granted Siponto and part of Monte Gargano. Melfi itself remained the common property of all the chiefs, their supreme headquarters in Apulia and, as Gibbon puts it, 'the metropolis and citadel of the republic'.

South Italy had suffered a radical change. From now on we hear little more about Lombard nationalism. Gaimar, as Duke of Apulia and Calabria, had a nation of his own which he was resolved to extend at the expense of Greek and Lombard alike; while in 'liberated' Apulia the effective power lay exclusively with the Normans, whose tenure had been legalised at Melfi and who would relinquish their land to no one. They were now entrenched in Apulia even more firmly and widely than in Campania; and they were there to stay.

What, it may be asked, had become of Arduin—he who had brought the Normans to Apulia, installed them in Melfi and who, more than anyone, had been responsible for their success? His bargain with the chiefs at Aversa had been that all conquests should be shared equally between himself and them; but of the original sources only Amatus—without much conviction—suggests that the Normans kept their word. None of the other chroniclers mention Arduin after this time. Perhaps he died, killed in one of the early battles or victim of the fury of Maniakes; perhaps, like Argyrus, he was bought off by the Greeks; or perhaps, as is most likely, the Normans, fearing that his continued presence might create an embarrassment, cast him aside like an old cloak that has served its purpose and is of use no more.

6

THE NEWCOMERS

Cognomen Guiscardus erat, quia calliditatis
Non Cicero tantae fuit, aut versutus Ulysses.

(Guiscard he came to be called; for not cunning Cicero even
Could ever have matched him in craft; nor yet the wily Ulysses.)
William of Apulia, Book II

As the power of Normans increased and news of each succeeding
triumph found its way back to France, so the tide of immigration
swelled; and some time in 1046, a little more than three years after
the dispositions of Melfi, two young men appeared in South Italy
within a few months of each other. Each was, in his own way, to
achieve greatness; each was to found a dynasty; and one was
destined to shake the very foundations of Christendom, to hold one
of the strongest Popes in history within the hollow of his hand, and
to cause the imperial thrones of East and West alike to tremble at
his name. They were Richard, son of Asclettin, later to become
Prince of Capua, and Robert de Hauteville, shortly to win the
surname of Guiscard—the Cunning.[1]

Both started with certain advantages over their fellow-immigrants.
Richard was the nephew of Rainulf of Aversa. His father, Rainulf's
younger brother Asclettin, had been awarded the County of Acerenza at Melfi. His elder brother, also called Asclettin, had been one
of Rainulf's most brilliant lieutenants and, when Rainulf died in
1045, had himself briefly ruled in Aversa until his own death a

[1] The name seems first to have been given to Robert by his wife's nephew, Girard of
Buonalbergo. The word itself, in Latin often *Viscardus* and in Old French *Viscart*,
comes from the same root as the German word *Wissen* and our own *Wise*, *Wisdom*.
Gibbon connects it more closely with *Wiseacre*.

few months later. Richard had been brought up in Normandy, but when he reached the peninsula with his impressive following of forty mounted knights he was confident of a glorious future. His hopes were not to be disappointed. Amatus, not perhaps altogether unmindful of the generous endowments which Richard later bestowed on his monastery, has left us a charming description of him:

At this time there arrived Richard, Asclettin's son, well-formed and of fine lordly stature, young, fresh-faced and of radiant beauty, so that all who saw him loved him; and he was followed by many knights and attendants. It was his habit to ride a horse so small that his feet nearly touched the ground.[1]

Robert, on the other hand, travelled alone. Born in 1016, the sixth of Tancred's sons though the eldest by his second marriage, he was unable to afford a suite and could put his trust only in the generosity of his half-brothers. It was unfortunate for him that William Bras-de-Fer should have died just about the time of his arrival, but William was succeeded as Count of Apulia by his brother Drogo, so Robert's future prospects seemed bright enough. In fact, as he would soon learn, his own right arm and the supple intelligence that won him his nickname would prove more effective aids to advancement than any number of family connexions.

The chroniclers of the time left us plenty of descriptions of this extraordinary man, 'a fair, blue-eyed giant, who was perhaps the most gifted soldier and statesman of his age'.[2] The best is by Anna Comnena whose father, Alexius I Comnenus, was afterwards to find himself settled on the imperial throne of Constantinople just in time to defend it against Robert's advancing armies. Anna, it should be remembered, is writing of a time many years later, when the Guiscard was at the summit of his power but no longer young. Her description fascinatingly combines the contempt of one born in the purple for a comparative upstart, the hatred of a loyal daughter for her father's arch-enemy, the admiration

[1] *En celui temps vint Ricchart fill de Asclitine, bel de forme et de belle estature de seignor, jovène home et clère face et resplendissant de bellesce, liquel estoit amé de toute persone qui lo véoit; liquel estoit sécute de moult de chevaliers et de pueple. Cestui par industrie chevauchoit un petit cheval, si que petit s'en failloit que li pié ne féroient à terre* [II, 43].

[2] *Shorter Cambridge Mediaeval History.*

of any intelligent observer for an unquestionably great man, and an element of that uncomplicated sexual attraction to which Anna remained all her life deeply and unashamedly susceptible:

This Robert was Norman by descent, of insignificant origin, in temper tyrannical, in mind most cunning, brave in action, very clever in attacking the wealth and substance of magnates, most obstinate in achievement, for he did not allow any obstacle to prevent his executing his desire. His stature was so lofty that he surpassed even the tallest, his complexion was ruddy, his hair flaxen, his shoulders were broad, his eyes all but emitted sparks of fire, and in frame he was well-built where nature required breadth, and was neatly and gracefully formed where less width was necessary. So from tip to toe this man was well-proportioned, as I have repeatedly heard many say. Now Homer says of Achilles that when he shouted his voice gave his hearers the impression of a multitude in an uproar, but this man's cry is said to have put thousands to flight. Thus equipped by fortune, physique and character, he was naturally indomitable, and subordinate to nobody in the world. Powerful natures are ever like this, people say, even though they be of somewhat obscure descent.[1]

The two young adventurers found their new home in a state of what was, even by mediaeval Italian standards, unparalleled political confusion. In Apulia the war between the Normans of Melfi—now, despite their technical vassalage to Gaimar, fighting openly for their own self-aggrandisement—and the Byzantines based on Bari had been raging indecisively up and down the coast; it was now spreading to Greek Calabria. The turncoat Argyrus, soon after his defection, had been made Catapan—an appointment which can only be satisfactorily explained if it formed part of his bribe—and for three years had proved as able and energetic a champion of the Greek cause as he had ever been of the Lombard. Byzantine power in Italy was now seriously imperilled and the Greeks were everywhere on the defensive, but it was thanks to Argyrus that the Normans found their advance so costly and so slow. In the west the chaos was greater still. The Emperor Michael, determined to punish Gaimar for his part in the insurrection, had shortly before his own downfall released Pandulf of Capua from prison, and early in 1042 the old Wolf had returned in fury to Italy, thirsting for Gaimar's blood and determined to prove that his fangs were as sharp as ever. He managed

[1] *The Alexiad*, I, 10 (tr. Dawes).

to secure the alliance of certain of his old followers, but neither he nor Gaimar was strong enough to win a clear victory.

In June 1045 Rainulf of Aversa died. He alone had been the architect of Norman expansion in Italy; his foresight had recognised the magnitude of what might be achieved, his political sense and subtlety had guided his more headstrong compatriots towards its realisation. Though he had never hesitated to change sides when Norman interests demanded it, he had remained for nine years loyal to Gaimar and continued so until his death. A few months later, after his successor Asclettin had followed him prematurely to the grave, a brief and ultimately unimportant quarrel over the succession led to a break with the Prince of Salerno and a consequent swing of the Normans of Aversa towards Pandulf; but in 1046 Gaimar invested Drogo de Hauteville as Count of Apulia and gave him his daughter's hand in marriage; Drogo mediated between Aversa and Salerno; and the former harmony was restored.

Allies of Gaimar though they were, the Normans were not, however, prepared—nor even altogether able—to devote their entire energies to the overthrow of Pandulf. They had more important business of their own. For some years many of the largest and most profitable of the castles and estates belonging to Monte Cassino had been in Norman hands, some illegally granted them by Pandulf in return for military support, others freely leased them by the monastery for the protection that it hoped to enjoy in return. In both cases the results had been disastrous. Normans were never desirable neighbours; and the monastery's tenants had everywhere used their holdings as centres for brigandage, from which they would issue forth only to ravage and plunder the surrounding country. For miles round Monte Cassino not a farm, not a vineyard, not a household was safe from their attacks; the land was racked and desolated. At one moment matters reached such a point that the Abbot, having appealed unsuccessfully to the powerless Gaimar, resolved to travel to Germany and lay the matter before the Emperor himself; he would doubtless have done so if he had not been shipwrecked off Ostia. With the return of Pandulf the situation became graver still, and it was more than ever necessary to eliminate these Norman bandits who would be bound to abet the renewed attacks and depredations which the monastery confidently expected from its old enemy.

Now, for the first time, the Normans discovered what it was like to be on the other side of an insurrection. Monks, peasants, towns-folk, villagers, whole neighbourhoods resorted to out-and-out guerrilla warfare. They were desperate and could no longer afford to be scrupulous. Amatus tells how a young Norman baron called Rodolf came one day to the monastery with a band of followers. They entered the church to pray—leaving, as was the custom, their swords outside. No sooner had they done so than the monastery servants seized the pile of weapons and the horses, slammed the church doors shut and began ringing the bells for all they were worth. Assuming that the monastery was being attacked, all the country folk within earshot came hurrying to the rescue, burst open the doors of the basilica and hurled themselves upon the astonished Normans, who had only their short daggers with which to defend themselves. They fought bravely, but had no chance. Soon they surrendered, asking only that out of respect for the house of God their lives should be spared; but their prayers went unheeded. By the time the monks arrived Rodolf was a prisoner and his fifteen Normans lay dead on the church floor. From that day the Normans round Monte Cassino seem to have given less trouble, though we are told that Gaimar was hard put to prevent those of Aversa from rising *en masse* against the monastery to avenge their compatriots.

*   *   *

Una Sunamitis[1]	A Shulamite woman
Nupsit tribus maritis.	Has three husbands.
Rex Henrice,	O King Henry,
Omnipotentis vice,	Regent of the Almighty,
Solve connubium	Dissolve this marriage
Triforme dubium.	Triple and doubtful.

Lines addressed to Henry III by Wiprecht the Hermit

[1] *Sunamitis* is an interesting word. It comes from one of the several Vulgate translations of the *Song of Solomon* in which it replaced the more usual version *Sulamitis*. The English text in the 1611 Bible reads: 'Return, return, O Shulamite; return, return, that we may look upon thee' (*Song of Solomon*, vi, 13). The Song of Songs is so patently erotic that it is nowadays hard to believe that the allegorical interpretation—according

72

Meanwhile in Rome the Papacy had sunk to a level of decadence which was never surpassed—if occasionally equalled—before or since. Three men were circling, as in the closing stage of some grisly game of musical chairs, round the throne of St Peter; no one could tell on whose head the tiara properly belonged. Benedict IX, nephew of Benedict VIII and John XIX, may or may not have been only twelve years old when, after gigantic bribery, he succeeded his uncles in 1033. But he was certainly a wild profligate—his success with women is said to have been such that he was generally suspected of witchcraft—and was so thoroughly despised in Rome that in 1044 the citizens, who had already on one occasion tried to assassinate him at the high altar, hounded him from the city and forced him to abdicate. His place was taken by a creature of the Crescentii, Sylvester III. Less than two months later Benedict managed to evict Sylvester and to return to St Peter's, but he did not stay for long. His debauches were too much even for eleventh-century Rome; he had also set his heart on marriage. He therefore abdicated again, this time in favour of his godfather, John Gratian, who under the name of Gregory VI set himself in all sincerity to restore the self-respect of his office and of the Church. For a time things looked better; but soon Benedict, thwarted of his marriage by the understandable resistance of his intended father-in-law, set himself up once again as Pope; while Gregory, whose election for all his reforming spirit had been deeply stained with simony, had his back to the wall. The Roman clergy, confronted now with three Popes, one at St Peter's, one at the Lateran and a third at S. Maria Maggiore, turned in despair to Henry III, King of Germany, son and successor of the Emperor Conrad.

Henry was twenty-two years old when Conrad died in 1039, but he had been trained for kingship from his infancy and had been King of Germany since the age of eleven. He was a serious, deeply conscientious young man with a clear concept of his responsibilities

to which it describes the relationship between Jehovah and Israel and, by extension, Christ and the Church as represented by a passionate lover and a Shulamite woman—was almost universally accepted from the days of the early fathers until the sixteenth century, when it was vigorously denied by the Anabaptists. In Wiprecht's time it would have been unquestioned.

as a Christian ruler, and he looked upon this undignified wrangling in Rome as an insult to Christendom. Accordingly in the autumn of 1046 he descended into Italy, where, at two separate synods in Sutri and in Rome, all three rival Popes were deposed. In their place he nominated his trusted friend and compatriot Suidger, Bishop of Bamberg, who as Clement II performed the imperial coronation of Henry and his second wife,[1] Agnes of Guienne, on Christmas Day. The new Emperor and the new Pope then continued their southward journey.

The most important point to be settled was the future of Capua. Here, on 3 February 1047, Henry held a conference attended by Gaimar, Pandulf, Drogo de Hauteville and Rainulf II Trincanocte, nephew of the old Rainulf, who had lately in his turn been elected Count of Aversa. The increasing power of Gaimar had for some time been causing the Empire anxiety and it was not altogether a surprise, particularly after substantial sums of money had changed hands, when Henry restored Capua to a triumphant Pandulf. The fury of the Prince of Salerno, who had occupied the principality for nine years, was however also to be expected; and the fighting, which had recently given way to an uneasy truce, flared up again.

The other important result of the Capua meeting can have done little to improve Gaimar's temper. From the imperial point of view his own position and that of the Normans were both highly irregular. His title of 'Duke of Apulia and Calabria' had been conferred upon him by Norman acclamation, and this in its turn was the only authority by which he had invested Drogo and the rest with their titles and fiefs. Neither party, in fact, had any support except the other. It was now for Henry to put the situation on a sound feudal footing. He gave Drogo a full imperial investiture as *Dux et Magister Italiae Comesque Normannorum totius Apuliae et Calabriae*,[2] and at the same time formally confirmed Rainulf in his County of Aversa. Gaimar probably retained his overall suzerainty, though even this is uncertain; but his spurious dukedom was now taken from him, and he never used the title again.

The Emperor now moved on to Benevento, where he received

---

[1] Henry had previously been married to Gunhilda, daughter of King Canute.
[2] Duke and Master of Italy and Count of the Normans of all Apulia and Calabria.

an unpleasant shock. The city closed its gates and refused to admit him. For some years—ever since the replacement of Prince Atenulf by Argyrus at the head of the Lombard insurrection—the Beneventans had been on bad terms with the Normans and with Gaimar; and they seem also to have had a guilty conscience over their extremely ungracious reception a little time before of Henry's mother-in-law, returning from a pilgrimage to Monte Gargano. Henry could not spare the time for a siege; his presence was needed in Germany. Without further fuss he handed the whole duchy over to Drogo and Rainulf, and ordered the always amenable Clement to follow up with a general sentence of excommunication. The two then rode away to the north, leaving the Normans to settle the matter as they saw fit.

In the general turmoil of these years the two newcomers, Robert and Richard, found plenty of employment for their swords. For Robert, however, the first welcome which awaited him at the court of his half-brother was distinctly lukewarm. Drogo was prepared to accept him on equal footing with any other young Norman knight, but he refused to ennoble him or to give him any territory of his own. Available land in Apulia was still scarce and far outstripped by the demand; there must by now have been many Norman captains with long years of Italian campaigning behind them, waiting for promised fiefs which they considered they had richly earned but which, thanks to the dogged resistance of the Byzantines, remained in enemy hands. Drogo's full brother Humphrey had himself had to wait till 1045 before he received his county of Lavello, and even this came to him only on the death of the previous incumbent; to discriminate in favour of Robert, young, inexperienced and untried, would have been to invite rebellion. Furious, Robert rode off for other fields where his qualities might be better appreciated. He fought under various colours in those interminable skirmishes which filled the lives of the petty barons of the day until, some time in 1048, he joined Pandulf of Capua, now despite his sixty-two years once more in full cry against his old enemy Gaimar and, as usual, making life intolerable for all who lived within the increasing radius of his activities.

Robert doubtless learned a lot from Pandulf, but their association did not last long. Whether or not Amatus is right in suggesting that they parted after Pandulf broke his promise to give Robert his daughter and a castle we do not know. The point is academic, because in 1049 came the day so long awaited and fervently wished-for throughout Campania. On 19 February Pandulf of Capua died. A French historian[1] writes that: 'Even if we make allowance for exaggeration and legend [in the chronicles of Monte Cassino] . . . it remains true that, of all the many detestable bandits of the eleventh century, Pandulf was one of the vilest.' It is impossible not to agree with him. Only once more in the chronicles does the Wolf of the Abruzzi show his face: another, slightly later writer from Monte Cassino, Leo of Ostia, tells us how, some time after his death, his shade was seen by a certain Pythagoras, page to the Duke of Naples, in a wood. Returning alone after a hunting expedition with his master, Pythagoras encountered two monks 'of extremely reverend appearance' who led him to 'a certain pond, most muddy and horrible of aspect'. Here they found Pandulf 'lately dead, bound with chains of iron and miserably immersed up to the neck in the mud of that same pond. Meanwhile two excessively black spirits, making cords of wild vine-shoots, tied them round his neck and plunged him into the very depths of the pond and pulled him up again.'[2] The image is worthy of Dante, though Leo of Ostia was writing two hundred years before the *Inferno* was thought of. The punishment reserved for Pandulf as he reports it was certainly unpleasant, but it was not undeserved.

Robert returned to Drogo, to find him as adamant as ever about a fief. Drogo, had, however, recently returned from an expedition to Calabria where he had left a number of garrisons to guard the mountain passes. Largely to get him out of the way, he now offered his tempestuous half-brother the command of one of these, at Scribla near Cosenza. Calabria was a desolate land, mountainous, hostile and distinctly uninviting. Until Gaimar and the Iron-Arm first began to open it up in 1044 and built an important castle at Squillace, it had been largely ignored by Normans and Lombards alike. Technically it was still part of the Greek Empire, to which

[1] O. Delarc, *Les Normands en Italie*, p. 185 n.   [2] Leo of Ostia, II, 61.

those of its inhabitants who possessed any political consciousness
—mostly Basilian monks[1] and their disciples—remained theoretically loyal; but Byzantine power was on the wane throughout Italy,
and Calabria, for all its grimness, seemed to offer greater long-term
advantages to an ambitious young man than either Campania or
Apulia. Robert accepted.

Scribla was a hell-hole. Lying deep in the valley of the Crati, hot,
airless and rank with malaria, it offered little prospect of continued
life, let alone of material advancement. Robert soon left it and, with a
picked company of companions-in-arms, set himself up in the time-
honoured Norman tradition of freebooting brigandage on higher,
healthier and more easily defensible ground at S. Marco Argentano.
Even there life was hard. After years of Saracen raids the few towns
in the neighbourhood, mostly grouped together along the coast,
were too well fortified for Robert to attack them. There was no
choice but to live off the land. Scattered farms and monasteries and
the few Byzantine administrative outposts in the area all suffered in
their turn, but so did the Normans. Amatus fancifully compares their
plight with that of the children of Israel in the wilderness, and tells us
that when Robert next saw Drogo he 'confessed his poverty, and what
his lips said his appearance confirmed, for he was exceeding thin'.[2]

Such conditions, however, were an ideal proving-ground for his
wits, and it was during his time at S. Marco that Robert acquired
the sobriquet which he was to keep for the rest of his life. Many
stories are told of his trickery; they redound much to his ingenuity
but little to his credit. Perhaps the most enjoyable, though possibly
apocryphal, of these stories is told by William of Apulia. A certain
hill-top monastery (probably Malvito, near Monte Pareta) was
coveted by the Guiscard for its commanding position, which made
it virtually unassailable. One day a solemn funeral procession was
seen winding its way up the path; the Normans indicated a draped
coffin and asked the Abbot for a requiem mass, in honour of their
dead comrade, to be said in the chapel. Their request was granted.

---

[1] i.e. monks following the Orthodox rite. They take their name from St Basil, the
principal founder of Orthodox monasticism in the fourth century. The Eastern Church
knows no proliferation of monastic orders of the kind familiar in the West.

[2] *'lui dist sa poureté, et cellui dist de sa bouche moustra par la face, quar estoit moult
maigre'* (Amatus, III, 9).

Unarmed as was usual on such occasions, they filed into the building and laid the coffin reverently before the altar. The service began. Suddenly the pall was flung back, the corpse leaped to its feet, disclosing the pile of swords on which it had been lying, and the mourners, seizing them, started laying about the astonished monks. The monastery was theirs—though the Apulian is careful to point out that once a Norman garrison had been installed the monks were permitted to continue in residence.

It would be unwise to put too much faith in this report, which crops up in various guises on several other occasions in Norman history. A far better documented story, equally illustrative of Robert's methods and almost certainly true in its essentials, concerns the misfortune which befell a certain Peter, Greek governor of the town of Bisignano near S. Marco. One day the two met for a parley, and Robert, as he approached the appointed place, ordered his escort to halt and rode forward alone. Peter, seeing this, did likewise. As the two drew together Peter leaned a little out of his saddle towards Robert in the customary gesture of salutation. In a flash Robert seized him by the neck and pulled him to the ground. Then, before the Greeks could come to their chief's rescue, he half-carried, half-dragged him back to the waiting Normans, who bore him triumphantly off to S. Marco and later obtained a huge ransom.

Anna Comnena tells another version of this story,[1] but she confuses the names and suggests that Guiscard's victim at this time was in fact his father-in-law. Typically she adds a further gloss of her own. 'When he had once got him in his power, he first pulled out all his teeth, at each tooth demanding a colossal sum of money, and enquired where this money was stored. And he did not stop pulling them until he had taken them all, for both teeth and money gave out simultaneously.'

Although Anna is wrong in referring to Robert's father-in-law in this connexion, the Guiscard certainly contracted his first marriage at about this time. His bride was a certain Alberada, who appears to have been the aunt of an influential Apulian baron, Girard of Buonalbergo—although she can still have been little more than a child at the time, since we find her still alive some seventy years

[1] *Alexiad,* I, xi.

and two husbands later, making an important donation in 1122 to the Benedictine Monastery of La Cava, near Salerno. Her age at her death is unknown; but in the much-restored church of the Abbey of the Santissima Trinità, just outside Venosa, her grave may still be seen.

While Robert was thus forced to live on his courage and his wits, Richard was fast fulfilling his highest ambitions. His initial welcome at Aversa had been chillier, if anything, than Robert's at Melfi; Rainulf II saw in the arrival of his predecessor's brother a threat to his own position and thought only of getting rid of him as quickly as possible. Richard accordingly rode off eastward into the mountains, and after a short period of service with Humphrey de Hauteville joined up with another footloose baron, Sarule of Genzano. With Sarule's help and by methods at once predatory and totally unscrupulous, he soon became powerful enough to challenge Rainulf, who was forced to buy him off with a grant of land previously owned by his brother Asclettin. Next he came to grips with Drogo; but here he was less fortunate, for Drogo captured him and threw him into prison. Richard's career was thus at Drogo's mercy; it was saved only by the death in 1048 of Rainulf, whose infant son Herman needed a regent to govern on his behalf. The first appointment, an undistinguished baron embarrassingly named Bellebouche, having proved unsatisfactory, the choice now fell on Richard. He was still languishing in Drogo's dungeons, but the intervention of Gaimar soon procured his release. According to Amatus, Gaimar then clothed him in silk and brought him to Aversa where, by the will of a joyful people, he was acclaimed Count. To begin with Richard seems to have governed in Herman's name, but within a year or two that name is heard no more. By what seems almost like a tacit agreement, the chroniclers all draw a discreet veil over what happened to the boy. We are left to draw our own conclusions.

7

CIVITATE

S'el s'aunasse ancor tutta la gente
  Che già, in su la fortunata terra
  Di Puglia, fu del suo sangue dolente . . .
Con quella che sentío di colpi doglie
  Per contrastare a Ruberto Guiscardo. . . .

(Nay, if there once again together stood
  All those, who on Apulia's fateful soil
  Bewailed the dark effusion of their blood . . .
With those who felt the body-rending blows
  Delivered by the Guiscard's mighty sword. . . .)
                              Dante, *Inferno*, XXVIII

POPE Clement II lasted less than a year. His body was taken back from Italy to his old see of Bamberg—he is the only Pope to have been buried in Germany—and the odious Benedict IX, who was widely rumoured to have poisoned him, re-established himself for the next eight months at St Peter's. In July 1048 the Emperor Henry's next appointee arrived in Rome. He ruled, under the title of Damasus II, for exactly twenty-three days before expiring at Palestrina. Whether, as some said, the heat had proved too much for him or whether Benedict was simply becoming more expert has never been properly established; but to most of the great church-men of the time his death made the Papacy seem a less desirable prize than ever, and Henry, called upon to fill the vacancy for the third time in less than two years, was finding the task increasingly difficult. Finally, at a great council held at Worms in December 1048, German and Italian bishops called unanimously for the Emperor's second cousin, a man of tried ability and undoubted saintliness, Bruno, Bishop of Toul.

Bruno's reluctance to accept this invitation was unfeigned, and indeed hardly surprising. He agreed only on condition that his appointment would be spontaneously ratified by the clergy and people of Rome on his arrival, and accordingly set out for the Eternal City in January 1049, dressed as a simple pilgrim. Once there, however, he was immediately acclaimed and consecrated under the name of Leo IX, and for the next six years until his death at fifty-one this tall, red-haired, military-looking Alsatian—he had in fact commanded an army in the field during one of Conrad II's punitive expeditions into Italy—proved himself to be one of the greatest Popes of the middle ages. Like John XXIII in our own day, he did not live to see the culmination of the great work which he began; but though others still greater than he were to carry it forward to a point beyond any he can have dreamed of, it was St Leo IX who first broke the dreadful spell which had for so long paralysed and degraded the Church of Rome, and who laid the foundations for a reformed and resurgent Papacy—foundations on which St Gregory VII and his successors were later so majestically to build.

Scarcely had Leo assumed the papal power when affairs in South Italy thrust themselves on his attention. Nowhere in Christendom was the state of the Church so deplorable. Simony had reached a pitch where the highest ecclesiastical appointments were being trafficked about and put up to auction like so much dead merchandise. The prevailing strictures against marriage were occasionally honoured so far as to stop priests from actually marrying their concubines, but seldom prevented them from raising large families. Church tithes went unpaid and many religious houses considered themselves lucky if they managed to keep the treasures and estates they already possessed. Such was the burden of every despatch that Leo received from the South; and these official reports were confirmed by countless letters of complaint from monks, travellers and even ordinary pilgrims, for whom the journey to Monte Gargano was now an open invitation to assault, robbery and abduction by Norman brigands. The monk Wilbert, Leo's earliest biographer, writes that the Normans, 'welcomed as liberators, soon became oppressors'; to many they were worse than the Saracens, who at least confined themselves to isolated raids, while the Normans kept up an unrelenting pressure on all who were weaker than themselves. Vines were slashed, whole harvests burnt; meanwhile reprisals by the local populace added to the unrest. John, Abbot of Fécamp, who had narrowly escaped with his life after a recent pilgrimage, wrote to Leo at this time: 'Italian hatred of the Normans has now become so great that it is near impossible for a Norman, even if he be a pilgrim, to travel through the cities of Italy without being set upon, abducted, stripped of all he has, beaten and tied with chains—all this if he does not give up the ghost in a foetid prison.'

Such a state of affairs would have amply justified strong action in South Italy; but there were other, political, considerations which made Leo's intervention more necessary still. The Normans were steadily extending their dominion, approaching ever closer to the papal frontiers, and their position had been vastly strengthened when Henry III, two years before, had not only invested them as imperial vassals but had also allowed his anger so to cloud his better judgment as to concede to them the insubordinate Benevento. In doing so he had clearly forgotten—and Pope Clement had been too feckless to remind him—that for some two and a half centuries Benevento had remained, in theory at any rate, papal territory. Though the See of St Peter had never been able to exert full temporal authority over the principality, Leo could not allow it to fall into Norman hands.

No one shared this view more wholeheartedly than the Beneventans themselves. Thanks to the feebleness of their princes, their power and influence had continued to decline since the beginning of the century, and they knew that they could not possibly defend themselves against an all-out attack by the Normans, who already held such key-points on the mountain passes as Bovino and Troia. But to whom could they turn for help? Certainly not to Henry, nor yet to Gaimar, whose own position now entirely depended on the continuation of the Norman alliance; while Byzantium was a spent force in Italy, fighting a rearguard action for its own survival. Their only hope was Rome; and certain Beneventan ambassadors who had come to congratulate Leo on his accession and to request him to lift Clement's excommunication had already hinted that the

city might wish, in certain circumstances, to place itself uncon-
ditionally under papal protection.

Before reaching any final decisions, however, Leo determined
to examine the situation at first hand. For several months in 1049
and again in 1050 we find him travelling through the peninsula,
calling at all the principal cities and religious foundations. The
ostensible reason for his first visit was a pilgrimage to Monte
Gargano, and on his second it was given out that the Pope was
travelling on 'Church affairs'; but the greatest authority on the
period[1] hints darkly that '*la politique ne fut pas étrangère à ce déplacement
de Léon IX*', and indeed the Pope's true preoccupations must have
been an open secret. He found the situation even worse than he
feared. It was presumably on the basis of what he saw at this time
that he shortly afterwards wrote to the Emperor Constantine complaining of how the Normans, 'with an impiety which exceeds that of
pagans, rise up against the Church of God, causing Christians to
perish by new and hideous tortures, sparing neither women, children
nor the aged, making no distinction between what is sacred and
what is profane, despoiling churches, burning them and razing them
to the ground'.[2] Strong measures would have to be taken, and taken
quickly, against the Normans if anything were to be salvaged of the
Church in South Italy and if the Patrimony of Peter itself were to be
preserved.

In the winter of 1050–51 Leo travelled to Germany to discuss
matters with the Western Emperor, and on his return to Rome in
March found awaiting him another delegation from Benevento
with the news that the nobles of the city had swept away their
erstwhile rulers and had decided to surrender themselves entirely
into his hands. It was an offer the Pope had fully expected, and one he
could not refuse. A synod in Rome prevented him from leaving
immediately but he was in Benevento at the beginning of July, when
he found the principality entirely submissive to the Holy See. The
next problem was to ensure its protection, and for this purpose Leo
invited Drogo and Gaimar to a council. They came at once, and
readily gave the Pope all the guarantees he sought—too readily as it

[1] F. Chalandon, *Histoire de la Domination Normande.*
[2] Migne, *M.P.L.*, 143, Col. 777 begins.

turned out. Drogo's authority as Count of Apulia was far from complete, and hardly had he left Benevento to return to Melfi when messengers arrived at Salerno, whither the Pope had continued with Gaimar, to tell of further Norman outrages on Beneventan territory. Leo was furious, and was only slightly pacified by Gaimar's explanations that Drogo was undoubtedly doing his best, but had not yet had a chance of bringing his wilder compatriots under control. Still fuming, he at once dictated a letter to Drogo demanding his further immediate intervention, the speedy restoration of order and whatever reparations might be thought appropriate.

This letter never reached its destination, for the messenger to whom it was entrusted heard news on the way which sent him back at full speed to Salerno. Drogo de Hauteville had been assassinated.

As the Normans' unpopularity grew, so the opposition to them had crystallised into three separate factions—the pro-Byzantines, encouraged and subsidised by Argyrus, who were working for the restoration of Greek power in the peninsula; the Papalists, who would have liked the whole region to follow the recent example of Benevento; and the independents, who saw no reason why the South of Italy should not be left to itself and governed by the old Italo-Lombard aristocracy that could already boast five centuries' experience. Though the pro-Byzantine party must bear the lion's share of suspicion, we shall never know for sure which of these three factions was responsible for Drogo's death. All we can be certain about is that on St Lawrence's Day, 10 August, 1051, the Count of Apulia went to the chapel of his castle at Monte Ilaro (now Montella) to attend a celebratory mass. As he entered the building he was set upon by a certain Risus, who had been lying in wait behind the door, and killed instantly. Risus was presumably not alone, for we are told that several of Drogo's followers perished with him; and since a number of other Norman chiefs throughout Apulia met their deaths on the same day and in similar circumstances we can only conclude that his assassination was part of a vast conspiracy to rid the land once and for all of its oppressors.

If such a conspiracy in fact existed, it was a sad failure. The Normans' hold on the country was not appreciably weakened; they

had merely been roused to anger. Moreover, they had lost their
leader and, showing little eagerness to elect another, were meanwhile able to take their vengeance free from all control. Drogo had
been a moderate man—*sage chevalier*, Amatus calls him—God-
fearing and fundamentally honest; and though he may have lacked
that last ounce of steel necessary for the full enforcement of his
authority, he was well aware of the need for discipline. In spite of
the recent events at Benevento, his death therefore marked a further
worsening of the situation from Leo's point of view. Drogo had at
least been willing to discuss matters reasonably and respectfully
and had shown himself amenable if not always effective. Now there
was no longer even a spokesman empowered to speak for the
Normans as a whole, and the land was declining fast into anarchy.
If order and tranquillity were to be restored, it would have to be by
force. The Pope had masses said on Ascension Day for Drogo's
soul and began to raise an army.

The task proved harder than he had expected. Henry III, though
he had been partly responsible for the present situation, was probably still nettled at the Pope's take-over of Benevento; he was
also involved in a war with Hungary and various internal problems.
He refused all military support. So too did the King of France, who
was having quite enough trouble with the Normans at home. Help
came, however, from the one quarter whence Leo had least expected
it—Constantinople. Argyrus, recently ennobled as a reward for his
past services with the empty title of Duke of Italy, Calabria, Sicily
and—surprisingly—Paphlagonia, was still his Emperor's principal
expert and adviser on Italian policy; and he had recently returned
from the capital where he had managed to convince Constantine—
in face of furious opposition from the Greek Patriarch—of the
necessity of a *rapprochement* with the Latins. The Normans, he argued,
were now a far greater menace to Byzantine interests than the
Western Emperor, the Lombards or the Pope had ever been, and
there was no other way of breaking their power over the peninsula.
Argyrus's own Lombard origins may have lent additional feeling
to his words; his counsels prevailed and before the year 1051 drew
to a close he had reached full agreement with Leo on joint military
action.

In Italy itself most of the petty barons of the south and centre answered the Pope's call readily enough. Many had already suffered from Norman raids and were beginning to fear for their own survival, while others simply saw the tide approaching and were anxious to stem it while there was still time. When, however, Leo appealed to Gaimar (whom he had deliberately left till last) he met with a point-blank refusal. It can hardly have surprised him. Drogo had married Gaimar's sister; the Norman-Salernitan alliance had been virtually uninterrupted for fifteen years, to the immeasurable benefit of both sides. If Gaimar were now to desert his allies—and incidentally his vassals—they might well topple his own throne before Leo or anyone else could come to his assistance. Moreover, if things went according to the Pope's plan and the Normans were driven from Italy, there would be nothing to protect the Prince of Salerno from the triumphant Byzantine–Papal alliance; and Gaimar's past record was hardly such as to endear him to the Greeks. He therefore returned to Leo a message, polite but firm, pointing out not only that he could never join any league against the Normans but also that he would find it impossible to stand aside and allow them to be attacked.

The second part of the message came as a blow to the Pope. Though he cannot have expected Gaimar's support, he may well have had hopes for his neutrality. Meanwhile the Prince of Salerno had taken care that his message should be publicised as widely as possible, and news of the position adopted by the mightiest of all the southern rulers was having a dangerously demoralising effect on the Italian and Lombard elements of the army now beginning to assemble. Their despondency was being still further increased by hideous stories, now being spread by Salernitan agents, of the Normans' military prowess, and by warnings of the dire revenge that they would exact, after their inevitable victory, on all those who had dared to take up arms against them.

But there were darker portents than these in the air. Amatus tells us in detail of the many '*signez merveillouz*' which now appeared, both in Salerno and also, apparently, in Jerusalem. A Cyclopean child was born with one eye in the middle of its forehead and with the hoofs and tail of a bull. Another appeared with two heads. A river

—we are not told which—ran red with blood, and an oil lamp in the Church of St Benedict was found filled with milk. All these things, Amatus assures us, foretold the death of Gaimar.

And now indeed the Prince of Salerno came in his turn to a violent end. A pro-Byzantine party had seized power in Amalfi and had at once risen against the domination of Salerno, refusing to pay the usual tribute. Somehow the insurgents had managed to secure the support of part of Gaimar's own family; and so it was that on 2 June 1052 Gaimar V of Salerno was struck down in the harbour of his capital by his four brothers-in-law, sons of the Count of Teano, the eldest of whom now proclaimed himself as successor. Both the principal enemies of Byzantium had thus been murdered within a year, and although the Greeks do not seem to have been as directly responsible on this occasion as they do for the death of Drogo, it is hard to absolve them altogether from guilt.

Of that section of Gaimar's family which had remained loyal, one member only escaped capture and imprisonment by the insurgents. This was the prince's brother, Duke Guy of Sorrento, who at once galloped off to fetch help from his Norman friends. For them the situation was as serious as it was for Salerno. Gaimar had been their only ally; if Salerno should fall under Byzantine influence they would be surrounded and, with Leo in his present mood, probably doomed as well. Fortunately Guy found them already mobilised between Melfi and Benevento. Fortunately too he found that, after nearly a year of chaotic interregnum, they had at last elected a chief —his own sister's husband, Humphrey de Hauteville. It was typical of the Normans that before agreeing to help they should have negotiated with Guy a high price for their assistance; but the distracted Duke was prepared to agree to anything, and only four days after Gaimar's death the Norman army was encamped before the walls of Salerno.

Against the massed Norman force the four brothers of Teano had no chance at all. Taking Gaimar's young son Gisulf with them, they barricaded themselves in the citadel; but their own families had fallen into Norman hands and Guy was therefore able to negotiate for the return of his nephew, before whom, as legal heir and successor of Gaimar, he immediately did homage. The Normans would have preferred to see Guy himself assume the throne of Salerno at such a moment, but they were impressed by his selflessness. They too then declared themselves for Gisulf, who confirmed them in all their existing territorial possessions. It only remained to deal with the rebels, and these within a day or two were forced to capitulate. Gisulf and Guy, showing once again a moral sense rare for their time and position, had promised that their lives should be spared; but as the prisoners left the citadel the Normans, pointing out that they for their part had promised nothing, fell upon them with their swords. They killed not only the four ringleaders but, in grisly reprisal, thirty-six others as well—one for every wound that had been found on Gaimar's body.

Gaimar V of Salerno was the last of the great Lombard princes of South Italy. At the peak of his power his domains extended over the wide territories of Capua, Sorrento, Amalfi and Gaeta, and his suzerainty over the Normans of Aversa and Apulia. His influence was felt through the length and breadth of the peninsula, as he proved when, by the prestige of his name alone, he almost effortlessly sabotaged the military preparations of the Pope of Rome himself. Only sixteen when he came to the throne, having then and throughout his life to contend with the unscrupulous ambitions of Pandulf of Capua on the one hand and the Normans on the other, he proved a match for both, and he did so without once breaking his word or betraying a trust. Up to the day he died his honour and good faith had never once been called in question. He was then forty-one years old. Under his son Gisulf the principality of Salerno was to survive for one more generation, but it never regained its former glory, and in 1075 it lost its independence for ever. The Normans saw to that.

To Leo IX, watching from Benevento, these developments can have afforded little comfort. The murder of Gaimar, much as it must have shocked and revolted him, had momentarily strengthened his position; but in the events which followed, the Normans and Salernitans had given unmistakable proof of how quickly and devastatingly they could act in unison, and the lesson had not been lost on the already apprehensive papal troops. Many of these had discreetly deserted and the remainder, if they were to be persuaded to fight at all, would have to be heavily reinforced. Back went Leo to Germany, to make a second, more urgent appeal to Henry III. His journey was not entirely in vain; while celebrating the Christmas of 1052 with the Emperor at Worms he managed to obtain formal imperial recognition of the papal title to Benevento and certain other South Italian territories. But thanks to the machinations of Leo's old enemy, Bishop Gebhard of Eichstätt, the army which Henry had at last reluctantly put at his disposal was recalled before it reached the frontiers of Italy, and the Pope found himself with no alternative but to do his own recruiting. Fortunately he had with him his chancellor and librarian, Frederick, brother of the Duke of Lorraine; and this warlike priest—later to become Pope Stephen IX —was able to procure a body of some seven hundred trained Swabian infantry which was to prove the mainstay of the army. Around this solid nucleus there quickly gathered a motley and undisciplined collection of mercenaries and adventurers, most of whom had apparently thought it wise to leave Germany—'à la suite', as a French historian[1] puts it, 'de fâcheuses aventures'.

As it deceded through Italy in the spring of 1053, the army continued its snowball growth. As Gibbon describes it:

In his long progress from Mantua to Beneventum, a vile and promiscuous multitude of Italians was enlisted under the holy standard: the priest and the robber slept in the same tent; the pikes and crosses were intermingled in the front; and the martial saint repeated the lessons of his youth in the order of march, of encampment, and of combat.[2]

Although few of the new adherents may have been persons of unblemished moral character, Gibbon's description is exaggerated; it is unlikely that the Papal forces were much more tatterdemalion than most of the other armies of the Middle Ages. But by the time that they reached Benevento at the beginning of June they were numerically more than a match for anything the Normans could put into the field, and nearly all the non-Norman barons of South Italy had rallied again to Leo's standard. The Duke of Gaeta, the Counts of Aquino and Teano were there, and Peter, Archbishop of Amalfi; there too were detachments from Rome and the Sabine hills, from Campania and Apulia, from the Marsi, Ancona and

---

[1] Chalandon.   [2] Gibbon, ch. LVI.

Spoleto, all drawing new courage from each others' presence and, most of all, from that of their solemn, white-robed leader, who had now assumed personal command of the army and was steadily infusing them with his own serene confidence.

Leo had been in contact with Argyrus during the journey south and had arranged to join the Byzantines near Siponto in northern Apulia. Since, however, the main road east from Benevento was dominated by the Norman-held fortresses of Troia and Bovino, he now led his army along a more circuitous northern route, through the valley of the Biferno and thence east behind Monte Gargano. The Normans watched his progress carefully. Their own situation, they now knew, was more serious than at any time since the first of their number had arrived in Italy thirty-six years before. On the results of the fighting that lay ahead depended their whole future in the peninsula; if they lost, there would be no second chance. And victory looked a good deal less certain than it had in 1052. They were outnumbered and without allies; even the Salernitans, who owed their city and probably their lives to Norman valour, had let them down in their hour of need. Ranged against them were not only two armies, the Papal and the Byzantine, but also the entire indigenous population of Apulia, who looked upon them with unconcealed loathing and were determined to do all they could to ensure their destruction. On their side they had only their formidable military reputation; courage, cohesion and discipline; and their own sharp swords.

Richard of Aversa had already joined Humphrey with all the warriors he could muster; Robert Guiscard had arrived from the depths of Calabria with a sizable force of his own; and the combined army which must by now have comprised, apart from certain essential garrisons, virtually the entire adult male Norman population of South Italy, threaded its way through the mountains and down on to the Apulian plain. Its first task was, obviously, to prevent Leo from linking up with the Byzantines. Once reaching Troia, therefore, it turned north and, on 17 June 1053, on the bank of the river Fortore near Civitate, found itself face to face with the papal army.

The story of the battle of Civitate is one of the best-documented chapters in the whole history of the Normans in the South. All the principal chroniclers on the Norman side recount it in detail, and their accounts agree. More surprising is the extent to which these versions are confirmed by German and papal sources—including a letter to the Emperor Constantine from Leo IX himself.[1] Naturally some allowance for personal or political bias has to be made; but in general the different versions resemble each other so closely that we can piece together what is probably a fairly accurate picture of the course of events.

Neither side was eager for immediate battle. The Pope wished to wait for the arrival of the Byzantines, while the Normans, who, for all their unscrupulousness in the affairs in this world, suffered genuine misgivings at the prospect of raising their swords against the Vicar of Christ, still hoped to reach a peaceful settlement. No sooner were they encamped, therefore, than they sent a deputation to Leo, humbly putting their case before him and offering him their homage. William of Apulia adds that they admitted their past wrongs and promised their loyalty and obedience. But it was no use.

The tall, long-haired Teutons jeered at these Normans of shorter stature. . . . They surrounded the Pope and arrogantly addressed him: 'Command the Normans to leave Italy, to lay down their arms here and to return to the land whence they came. If they refuse this, then accept not their peaceful proposals.' The Normans departed, sorrowful that they had failed to make peace, and carried back the haughty replies of the Germans.[2]

And so the following morning, on the little plain that extends before the confluence of the Fortore and its tributary, the Staina, battle began. Pope Leo maintains—and his word cannot be doubted —that the first Norman onslaught was made while negotiations were still in progress; but it must be remembered that he was deliberately playing for time, hoping every moment for the arrival of Argyrus, while the Normans, equally conscious of the approach of the Greek army, were keen for the battle to begin—if begin it must—as soon as possible. They also had another even more urgent reason for haste; they were starving. The local peasantry refused them all provisions, and to deprive them further had already begun to gather in the harvest, even though much of the corn was still green. The

---

[1] Already quoted on p. 83.　　　[2] William of Apulia, II, 80 ff.

Norman soldiers often had nothing with which to sustain themselves but a handful or two of grain, dried before the fire. Their sudden attack may have been the only means of forcing the issue.

It came from the Norman right flank and was led by Richard of Aversa. Facing him were the Italians and Lombards of the Papal army. The Apulian notes that this heterogeneous group was drawn up without any attempt at military order, the soldiers having no idea of how to dispose themselves in war; and Richard went through them like butter. At the first shock of impact, they broke in confusion and without further ado fled from the field, with the Count of Aversa and his men in hot pursuit. Meanwhile, however, Humphrey de Hauteville, who was commanding the centre, had found Leo's Swabians a very different kind of adversary. Successive Norman charges failed utterly to disrupt their ranks, and in the fighting which followed they wielded their two-handed swords with a courage and determination that the Normans had never encountered since they came to Italy.

The left wing of the Norman army had been placed under Robert Guiscard and included the contingent that he had brought with him from Calabria. Their orders were to remain in reserve and then to enter the fray at whatever point their presence seemed most to be required. Here is William of Apulia again, in a translation which, while keeping as closely as possible to the sense of the original, tries to recapture something of his own racy Latin hexameters:

> Then Robert, perceiving his brother enmeshed in a furious struggle,
> Beset by a desperate foe who would never bow down in surrender,
> Called up the troops of his ally Girard, Lord of bright Buonalbergo,
> With those who obeyed him alone, his devoted Calabrian cut-throats,
> And splendid in courage and strength, he flung himself into the battle.
> Some were despatched by his lance; there were others whose heads were sent spinning
> With a blow of his sword—while even his hands wrought dire mutilations.
> The lance in his left hand, the sword in his right, ambidextrously flashing,
> Turning aside every blow, confounding all those who attacked him,
> Dashed three times from his horse, three times he leaped back to the saddle;

Inspired by unquenchable fire in his heart, that would lead him to
                                                        triumph.
Just as the ravening lion, that falls on inferior creatures,
Grows more wildly enraged if he finds his authority challenged,
Rising huge and superb in his wrath and, admitting no quarter,
Tears and devours every beast in his path, as he scatters the others,
So the great Robert dealt death to the Swabian hordes who opposed
                                                        him.
Varied the means he employed; some had feet lopped off at the ankles,
Others were shorn of their hands, or their heads were sliced from their
                                                        shoulders;
Here was a body split open, from the breast to the base of the stomach,
Here was another transfixed through the ribs, though headless already.
Thus the tall bodies, truncated, were equalled in size with the smaller;
Enabling all to behold how the glorious palm of the victor
Goes not to overgrown giants, but to those of more moderate stature.

What, however, eventually decided the day was not so much the
courage of Robert and Humphrey as the arrival of Richard of
Aversa, returned from his murderous pursuit of the Italians and
Lombards. He and his followers now plunged once again into the
fray, and this further addition to the Norman ranks destroyed the
last hopes of the papalists. Even now, however, the German contingents refused to surrender; those same tall, long-haired Teutons,
who had laughed at the stockiness of the Normans and persuaded
the Pope to reject their proposals of peace, fought on and were
killed to the last man.

Standing high on the ramparts of Civitate, Pope Leo had watched
the battle. He had seen half his army put to ignominious flight,
the other half remorselessly butchered. His Byzantine allies had
let him down; had they arrived in time the battle might have
ended very differently, but they would never dare to take on the
Normans alone. And now he had to face yet another humiliation;
for the citizens of the town, anxious to ingratiate themselves with
the Normans, refused his request for asylum and handed him over
to his enemies. But the Normans, though victorious, were not
triumphant. In the past few hours they had been too occupied with
the Swabians to remember their supreme antagonist; now, as they
gazed on the proud, melancholy man standing before them, they
seem to have been genuinely overcome. Falling on their knees,

they implored his forgiveness. Then after two days of solemn obsequies for the dead, who were buried where they lay, they escorted the Pope back to Benevento.

Leo was in an ambiguous position. He was not, in the strictest sense of the word, a prisoner. Contrary to his expectations, he and his retinue were being treated by the Normans with the utmost consideration and courtesy. As Amatus puts it:

The Pope was afraid and the clergy trembled. But the victorious Normans reassured them and offered the Pope safe conduct, and then brought him with all his retinue to Benevento, furnishing him continually with bread and wine and all that he might need.[1]

On the other hand, though he was able to transact day-to-day papal business, he was certainly not a free agent; and it soon became clear to him that the Normans, for all their solicitude, had no intention of allowing him to leave Benevento until an acceptable *modus vivendi* had been established.

The negotiations dragged on for the next nine months. They cannot have been easy. For most of this time Leo seems to have remained intractable. As late as January 1054, in his letter written from Benevento to the Emperor Constantine (of which there will be more to say in the next chapter), he makes it clear that as far as he is concerned the struggle will continue. 'We shall remain faithful to our mission to deliver Christendom, and we shall lay down our arms only when the danger is past,' he writes, and looks forward to the day when, by the Eastern and Western Emperors together, 'this enemy nation will be expelled from the Church of Christ and Christianity will be avenged'. But as the months wore on, his health grew worse; and when Henry, whose arrival with an army he had been confidently awaiting, still showed no signs of coming to his aid, he saw that he had no choice but to make terms. We have no means of telling what was eventually agreed, nor are there any surviving papal bulls to attest formal investitures; but we can safely assume that Leo eventually gave his *de facto* recognition to all the Norman conquests to date, including very probably certain terri-

---

[1] '*Li pape avoit paour et li clerc trembloient. Et li Normant vinceor lui donnerent sperance et proierent que securement venist lo pape, liquel meneront o tout sa gent jusque a Bonvenic, et lui aministroient continuelment pain et vin et toute choze necessaire*'. (III, 38).

tories within the principality of Benevento—though not the city itself, which retained its papal allegiance. Once this agreement had been reached there was no longer any reason to prevent his return to Rome, and he accordingly left on 12 March 1054—with Humphrey, courteous as ever, accompanying him as far as Capua.

For the unhappy Pope, whose five hard years of papacy had been spent in almost continuous travel through Germany and Italy, this was the last journey; and he who had been accustomed to pass many hours of every day in the saddle now made his final entry into Rome on a litter. Worn out by his exertions, disillusioned by the betrayal of his Emperor and cousin, broken by his shattering defeat at Civitate and deeply wounded by the fulminations of Peter Damian and others, who attributed this defeat to the wrath of God against a militarist Pope, he had succumbed during the long months of mental anguish at Benevento to a wasting disease which caused him constant pain.[1] On his arrival at the Lateran, he knew that his end was near. He gave instructions that a grave should be quickly prepared in St Peter's and that his litter should be laid alongside it; and there on 19 April 1054, the date which he himself had predicted, he died surrounded by the clergy and people of Rome. His death was serene and peaceful, but clouded by the consciousness of failure. No Pope had worked harder for the reform of the Church in Italy; few of those who had tried had been more totally unsuccessful in their own lifetime. During those last days he is said to have been granted several heavenly visions; but he could hardly have seen how superbly the work he had begun would be carried on after him, nor how quickly the seeds he had sown would ripen and bear fruit. Least of all could he have suspected that within only thirty years of his death those same Normans, against whom he had staked all and lost, would emerge as the sole friends and preservers of the resurrected Papacy.

Meanwhile for the Normans a new chapter had begun in their

---

[1] There is no reason to believe the subsequent inevitable rumours that Leo, like his two predecessors, was a victim of slow poison administered at the instigation of Benedict IX. Such rumours had by now become little more than a conditioned reflex after the death of a Pope; the principal proponent of the theory, Cardinal Benno, goes so far as to accuse the incorrigible Benedict of the murders of six Popes within thirteen years.

great Italian adventure. The battle of Civitate had been as decisive for them as that which was to be fought thirteen years later at Hastings would be for their brothers and cousins. Never again would their basic rights in South Italy be questioned; never again would their wholesale eviction from the peninsula be seriously contemplated. They had shown themselves to be something more than just another ingredient in the Italian stewpot, a sparring-partner for Capuans, Neapolitans or a few half-hearted Byzantine provincials. This time, without a friend or ally, they had taken on the Vicar of Christ and with him the best fighters, German and Italian, that he could put into the field. And they had won. Their possessions, already ratified by the Emperor, had now been confirmed by the Pope. Their reputation for invincibility stood at its highest. The attitude of the outside world towards them would now be tinged with a new respect.

All this, and much more besides as yet undreamed of, had been won in a few nightmare hours on the banks of the Fortore. Not many travellers pass that way nowadays; but those who do may still see, a mile or two to the north-west of the modern village of San Paolo di Civitate, the ruins of an old cathedral; and they may still trace the line of the ramparts from which Pope Leo watched the destruction of his army and his hopes. Of the city itself that treated him so basely, nothing remains; it was totally annihilated, as if by some divine if belated retribution, at the beginning of the fifteenth century. But excavations of the site in 1820 revealed, just outside the walls, several huge piles of skeletons. All were male, all bore the marks of dreadful wounds, and a large number were found to be of men well over six feet tall.

8

SCHISM

Upon Michael, neophyte and false Patriarch, brought only by mortal fear to assume the monkish habit, and now for his abominable crimes notorious; upon Leo, so-called Bishop of Ochrid; upon Constantine, chancellor of that same Michael, who has publicly trampled the liturgy of the Latins beneath his feet; and upon all those who follow them in their aforesaid errors and presumptions, except that they repent, let there be Anathema Maranatha as upon the Simoniacs, Valesians, Arians, Donatists, Nicolaitans, Severians, Pneumatomachi, Manichaeans, Nazarenes, as upon all heretics and finally upon the Devil and all his angels. Amen, Amen, Amen.

Last paragraph of Humbert's Bull of Excommunication.

DURING his honourable captivity in Benevento Pope Leo had set himself to learn Greek. His biographer, Wibert, suggests that he did so because he wished to be able to read the Holy Scriptures in that language. Such a desire was praiseworthy, and may have been genuine enough; but it seems likely that his real purpose was to be at less of a disadvantage in his dealings with Constantinople, which were growing steadily more complicated.

From the political point of view it was clear to the Pope, to Argyrus, and through Argyrus to the Emperor Constantine, that the Papal–Byzantine alliance was essential if the Normans were ever to be eliminated from Italy. Even after the *débâcle* of Civitate—which might well have ended differently if the two armies had managed to join up as planned—it could have done much to check the Norman advance. Instead, within thirteen months of the battle, it came to an abrupt and painful conclusion, stained with mutual recriminations and abuse; so that before the end of the decade the Papacy had openly and enthusiastically espoused the cause of Norman expansion.

The reason for this immense reversal is not hard to trace; it is to be found in one of the greatest disasters ever to have befallen Christendom—the great schism between the Eastern and Western Churches. Looking back over their past history with all the advantage of hindsight, we can see that this rupture was, sooner or later, inevitable; but the fact that it occurred when it did was largely due to the stresses and strains resulting from the Norman presence in South Italy.

The two Churches had been growing apart for centuries. Their slow estrangement was in essence a reflexion of the old rivalry between Latin and Greek, Rome and Constantinople; and the first and fundamental reason for the schism was in fact the steadily increasing authority of the Roman Pontificate, which led to arrogance on the one side and resentment on the other. The old Greek love of discussion and theological speculation was repugnant, even shocking, to the dogmatic and legalistic minds of Rome; while for the Byzantines, whose Emperor bore the title of *Equal of the Apostles* and for whom matters of dogma could be settled only by the Holy Ghost speaking through an Oecumenical Council, the Pope was merely *primus inter pares* among the Patriarchs, and his claims to supremacy seemed arrogant and unjustified. Already in the ninth century matters had very nearly come to a head; beginning with a purely administrative dispute over the Archbishopric of Syracuse, the quarrel soon spread—first to personalities, when Pope Nicholas I questioned the suitability of the Byzantine Patriarch Photius for his office, and thence to dogma when Photius publicly (and truthfully) claimed that a Roman bishop, Formosus of Porto, was in Bulgaria delivering himself of violent attacks against the Orthodox Church and insisting on the inclusion of the word *Filioque* in the Nicene Creed. This word, by which the Holy Ghost is said to proceed not only from the Father but also from the Son, had for some time been slowly gaining acceptance in the West, where, however, it was generally considered to have little theological importance. The Byzantines, on the other hand, considered it destructive of the whole balance of the Trinity, so carefully formulated by the early Fathers at Nicaea over five centuries before; and they bitterly resented the arrogance of Rome in presuming to amend the word of God as revealed to a Council of the Church. After the death of Pope

Nicholas, thanks to the goodwill of his successors and of Photius himself, friendly relations were outwardly restored; but the problems remained unsolved, the *Filioque* continued to gain adherents in the West, and in Constantinople the Emperor maintained his claim to rule as the Vice-Regent of Christ on earth. It was only a question of time before the quarrel broke out again.

The Papal–Byzantine alliance by which Leo IX and Argyrus set such store had from its inception been violently opposed by Michael Cerularius, Patriarch of Constantinople. An ex-civil servant, more of an administrator than a churchman, he had ordered the blinding of John the Orphanotrophos in prison in 1043; intransigent, ambitious and narrow-minded, he both disliked and distrusted the Latins; above all, he hated the idea of papal supremacy. Although, thanks to the influence of Argyrus, he had been unable to prevent the alliance, he had determined to sabotage it in whatever way he could. His first opportunity came over the question of ritual, when he learned that the Normans, with papal approval, were enforcing Latin customs—in particular the use of unleavened bread for the sacrament—on the Greek churches of South Italy. Immediately he ordered the Latin churches in Constantinople to adopt Greek usages, and when they refused he closed them down. Next, and still more disastrous, he induced the head of the Bulgarian Church, Archbishop Leo of Ochrid, to write to the Orthodox Bishop John of Trani in Apulia a letter violently attacking certain practices of the Western Church which he considered sinful and 'Judaistic'.

This letter, which contained a specific injunction to John that he should pass it on to 'all the bishops of the Franks, to the monks and the people and to the most venerable Pope himself', reached Trani in the summer of 1053—just at the time when the principal Papal Secretary, Humbert of Mourmoutiers, Cardinal of Silva Candida, was passing through Apulia on his way to join Leo in his captivity. John at once handed it to Humbert, who paused only to make a rough Latin translation and, on his arrival at Benevento, laid both documents before the Pope. To Leo, who already felt bitter about the non-appearance of the Byzantine army at the one moment when its presence had been most needed, this gratuitous insult came as the last straw. Furious, he ordered Humbert to draft a detailed reply setting out the arguments for papal supremacy and defending all the Latin usages which had been called in question. Humbert did not mince his words; both Pope and Cardinal were determined to give as good as they got—the very form of address they chose, 'To Michael of Constantinople and Leo of Ochrid, Bishops', was calculated to hit the Patriarch where it would hurt most—and it was perhaps just as well that, before the letter could be despatched, another missive arrived in Benevento, this time bearing at its foot the huge purple scrawl of the Emperor Constantine himself. He had clearly been horrified to learn, rather belatedly, of the patriarchal machinations, and was now doing his utmost to set matters right. His letter is lost, but is unlikely to have contained anything very remarkable; Leo's reply suggests that it simply expressed condolences for Civitate and made vague proposals for a further strengthening of the alliance. Far more surprising was a second letter, accompanying the Emperor's. This, apart from one or two infelicities of phrasing, seemed to radiate good-will and conciliation; it prayed for closer unity between the Churches, and contained no reference whatever to the disputed Latin rites. And it was signed by Michael Cerularius, Patriarch of Constantinople.

Cerularius, having at last been persuaded by the Emperor or—more probably—by Bishop John of Trani how much was at stake, seems, however reluctantly, to have made a genuine effort to heal the breach; and Leo would have been well-advised to overlook being addressed as 'Brother' instead of 'Father' and other similar little pinpricks and let the matter rest. But he was tired and ill; and encouraged by Cardinal Humbert, who throughout the events which were to follow showed himself to be every bit as waspish and bigoted as the Patriarch, he determined to make no concessions. He therefore agreed that papal legates should be sent to Constantinople to thrash the whole question out once and for all, and allowed Humbert to draft two more letters in his name for these legates to deliver. The first of these, to Cerularius, addressed him as 'Archbishop', which was at least one degree politer than before; but it was otherwise quite as aggressive as its predecessor, being concerned less to defend the Latin usages themselves than to attack the Patriarch's presumption in questioning them in the first place. It also reprimanded him

for having pretensions to oecumenical authority—which was probably due to a mistake in the Latin translation of his letter—and
suggested that his election had been uncanonical, an accusation
which was not remotely justified. Leo's second letter was to the
Emperor and was, as we have seen, largely devoted to political
affairs, in particular his determination to continue his war against the
Normans. Nevertheless it carried a sting in its tail; the last paragraph
contained a vehement protest against the Orthodox Patriarch's 'many
and intolerable presumptions . . . in which if, as Heaven forbid, he
persist, he will in no wise retain our peaceful regard'. Perhaps to
soften the effect of this veiled threat, the Pope concluded with a
commendation of the legates whom he would shortly be sending to
Constantinople. He hoped that they would be given every assistance
in their mission, and that they would find the Patriarch suitably
repentant.

Such tactics were a grave miscalculation. If the Pope valued the
Byzantine alliance—and the Byzantines were, after all, the only allies
he had against the Norman menace—it was foolish of him to reject
the opportunity of conciliation with the Orthodox Church; and if
he had been a little better informed about affairs in Constantinople
he would have known that the personal goodwill of the Emperor
would never suffice to override the Patriarch, who was not only a
far stronger character than Constantine—by now a sick man, almost
crippled with paralysis—but who also had the full weight of public
opinion behind him. Finally it was hardly tactful to choose as legates
on this particularly delicate mission Humbert himself, narrow-
minded and rabidly anti-Greek, and two others, Frederick of
Lorraine, the papal chancellor, and Archbishop Peter of Amalfi,
both of whom had fought at Civitate and might be expected to
share Leo's resentment at the Byzantines for letting them down.

This tight-lipped trio set off in the early spring of 1054 and
arrived in Constantinople at the beginning of April. From the outset
things went badly. They called at once on the Patriarch, but took
offence at the manner in which they were received and stomped
unceremoniously from the Palace without any of the customary
civilities, leaving the Pope's letter behind them. Their own anger
was, however, nothing to that of Cerularius when he read this latest

document. It confirmed his worst suspicions. Against his better judgment he had been induced to make a gesture of conciliation, and here it was flung back in his face. Worse was to follow: for the legates, who had since been received by the Emperor with his usual courtesy, had been encouraged by this reception to publish in Greek translation the full text of the Pope's earlier, still undespatched, letter to the Patriarch and Leo of Ochrid, together with a detailed memorandum on the disputed usages.

To the Patriarch this was the final insult. Despite the fact that the earlier letter had been addressed, however disrespectfully, to him, he had not even heard of its existence until now, when it was being angrily discussed all over the city. Meanwhile a closer examination of the second letter—which had at least, after a fashion, been delivered—revealed that the seals on it had been tampered with. Immediately he thought of his old enemy Argyrus. Was it not more than probable that Humbert and his friends had called, on their way to Constantinople, at his Apulian headquarters and shown him the letter? And if he had seen it, might he not even have altered the text? Forgetting, in his anger, that Argyrus's interest was to heal the breach between the two Churches rather than to open it further, Cerularius decided that the so-called legates were not only discourteous; they were dishonest as well. He therefore refused to recognise their legatine authority or to accept from them any further communications.

A state of affairs in which a fully accredited Papal legation, cordially welcomed by the Emperor, remained unrecognised and totally ignored by his Patriarch could not continue for long; and it was lucky for Cerularius that news of Pope Leo's death, which reached Constantinople within a few weeks of the legates' arrival, to some extent solved the problem for him. Humbert and his colleagues had been Leo's personal representatives; his death thus deprived them of all official standing. The Patriarch's grim satisfaction at this development can easily be surmised; it may, however, have been somewhat mitigated by the absence of any corresponding discomfiture on the part of the legates. Seemingly unabashed by this blow to their status, they now became more arrogant than ever.

The publication of the draft reply to Leo of Ochrid's letter had provoked a firm riposte from one Nicetas Stethatus, monk at the monastery of Studium, criticising in particular the Latins' use of unleavened bread, their habit of fasting on Saturdays and their attempts to impose celibacy on their clergy. This document, though outspoken and occasionally clumsy, was couched in polite and respectful language; but it drew from Humbert, instead of a reasoned reply, a torrent of shrill, almost hysterical invective. Ranting on for page after page, describing Stethatus as a 'pestiferous pimp' and a 'disciple of the malignant Mahomet', suggesting that he must have emerged from the theatre or the brothel rather than from a monastery, and finally pronouncing anathema upon him and all who shared in his 'perverse doctrine'—which, however, it made no attempt to refute—this extraordinary diatribe can only have confirmed the average Byzantine in his opinion that the Church of Rome now consisted of little more than a bunch of crude barbarians with whom no agreement could ever be possible.

Cerularius, delighted to see his enemies not only shorn of their authority but making fools of themselves as well, continued to hold his peace. Even when the Emperor, now fearing with good reason for the future of the papal alliance on which he had set his heart, forced the luckless Stethatus to retract and apologise to the legates; even when Humbert went on to raise with Constantine the whole question of the *Filioque*, detestation of which was by now a cornerstone of Byzantine theology, no word issued from the Patriarchal Palace, no sign that the high Orthodox authorities took any cognizance of the undignified wrangle which was now the talk of the city. At last—as Cerularius knew it would—this imperturbability had its effect. Humbert lost the last shreds of his patience. At three o'clock in the afternoon of Saturday, 16 July 1054, in presence of all the clergy assembled for the Eucharist, the three ex-legates of Rome, a cardinal, an archbishop and a papal chancellor, all in their full ecclesiastical regalia, strode into the church of Santa Sophia and up to the High Altar, on which they formally laid their solemn Bull of Excommunication. Then, turning on their heel, they marched from the building, pausing only to shake the dust ceremonially from their feet. Two days later they left for Rome.

Even apart from the fact that the legates were without any papal authority and that the Bull itself was therefore invalid by all the standards of Canon Law, it remains an extraordinary document. Here is Sir Steven Runciman on the subject:

Few important documents have been so full of demonstrable errors. It is indeed extraordinary that a man of Humbert's learning could have penned so lamentable a manifesto. It began by refusing to Cerularius, both personally and as Bishop of Constantinople, the title of Patriarch. It declared that there was nothing to be said against the citizens of the Empire or of Constantinople, but that all those who supported Cerularius were guilty of simony (which, as Humbert well knew, was the dominant vice at the time of his own Church), of encouraging castration (a practice that was also followed at Rome), of insisting on rebaptising Latins (which, at that time, was untrue), of allowing priests to marry (which was incorrect; a married man could become a priest but no one who was already ordained could marry), of baptising women in labour, even if they were dying (a good early Christian practice), of jettisoning the Mosaic Law (which was untrue), of refusing communion to men who had shaved their beards (which again was untrue, though the Greeks disapproved of shaven priests), and, finally, of omitting a clause in the Creed (which was the exact reverse of the truth). After such accusations, complaints about the closing of the Latin churches at Constantinople and of disobedience to the Papacy lost their effect.[1]

In Constantinople, where the narrow-minded arrogance of Humbert and his friends had already made them thoroughly disliked, the news of the excommunication spread quickly. Demonstrations in support of the Patriarch were held throughout the city. They were first directed principally against the Latins, but it was not long before the mob found a new target for its resentment—the Emperor himself, whose evident sympathy for the legates was rightly thought to have encouraged them in their excesses. Luckily for Constantine, he had a scapegoat ready to hand. Argyrus himself was in Italy, as yet unaware of what had happened and still working for the papal alliance; but those of his family who chanced to be in the capital were instantly arrested. This assuaged popular feeling to some extent, but it was only when the Bull had been publicly burnt and the three legates themselves formally anathematised that peace returned to the capital.

[1] *The Eastern Schism.*

Such is the sequence of the events, at Constantinople in the early summer of 1054, which resulted in the lasting separation of the Eastern and the Western Churches. It is a sad, unedifying story because, however inevitable the breach may have been, the events themselves should never, and need never, have occurred. More strength of will on the part of the dying Pope or the senile Emperor, less bigotry on the part of the ambitious Patriarch or the pig-headed Cardinal, and the situation could have been saved. The fatal blow was struck by a disempowered legate of a dead Pope, representing a headless Church—since the new Pontiff had not yet been elected—and using an instrument at once uncanonical and inaccurate. Both the Latin and the Greek excommunications were directed personally at the offending dignitaries rather than at the Churches for which they stood; both could later have been rescinded, and neither was at the time recognised as introducing a permanent schism. Technically indeed they did not do so, since twice in succeeding centuries—in the thirteenth at Lyons and in the fifteenth at Florence—was the Eastern Church compelled, for political reasons, to acknowledge the supremacy of Rome. But though a temporary bandage may cover an open wound it cannot heal it; and, despite even the balm applied by the Oecumenical Council in 1965, the wound which was jointly inflicted on the Christian Church by Cardinal Humbert and Patriarch Cerularius nine centuries ago still bleeds today.

9

CONSOLIDATION

Roger, the youngest of the brothers, whom youth and filial devotion had heretofore kept at home, now followed his brothers to Apulia; and the Guiscard rejoiced greatly at his coming and received him with the honour which was his due. For he was a youth of great beauty, tall of stature and of elegant proportion . . . He remained ever friendly and cheerful. He was gifted also with great strength of body and courage in battle. And by these qualities he soon won the favour of all.

Malaterra, I, 19

In the general exhilaration that followed their victory at Civitate, the Normans little suspected the magnitude of the events in Constantinople for which they had unwittingly provided the spark, nor the fact that in doing so they had probably saved themselves from extinction. They were on the other hand fully aware that the defeat of a massed papal army had added immeasurably to their reputation. Through the towns and villages of the peninsula there were now many who believed them to be genuinely invincible, as a result of some sinister contract with the powers of darkness; while even those who continued to suspect that they might yet succumb to a superior force were compelled to admit that for the moment no such force appeared to exist. This prevailing mood of defeatism offered them an advantage which the Norman leaders were quick to seize; and the records for the next few years tell of an almost unbroken succession of minor victories as one town after another fell, with hardly a struggle, to their attacks. Their principal target was what remained of Byzantine Apulia, where the demoralised Greeks, already deprived of papal support, unsuccessful in their attempted negotiations with Henry III and soon temporarily to lose the leadership of Argyrus, were incapable of prolonged resistance.

By the end of 1055 Oria, Nardo and Lecce had all capitulated, while Robert Guiscard, plunging deep into the heel of Italy, had taken Minervino, Otranto and Gallipoli in one gigantic stride and was building up his power and reputation at such a rate that Count Humphrey, fearing for his own position, hastily despatched him back to his old stamping-ground in Calabria.

By this time Robert had attracted a considerable following, and his second term of occupation of San Marco must have been even more terrifying for the local inhabitants than his first. Fortunately for them he did not stay long. A highly satisfactory expedition against the southern territories of Gisulf of Salerno, during which Cosenza and certain other neighbouring towns fell to the Normans, occupied a few months, and soon after his return to the camp messengers arrived with an urgent summons for him to return to Melfi. Count Humphrey was dying. The two half-brothers had never been close—William of Apulia reports that on one occasion Robert so angered the Count that he found himself cast into a dungeon— but Humphrey seems to have understood that there was no other possible successor and he therefore appointed Robert guardian and protector of his infant son Abelard, and administrator of all his lands during Abelard's minority. Then, in the spring of 1057, he died. He had been a hard, jealous, vengeful man, with a streak of cruelty that had showed itself in the savage tortures inflicted on the murderers of his brother Drogo, and again on certain chiefs who had failed him at Civitate; but even if he lacked Drogo's fundamental goodness of heart and the gay panache of William the Iron-Arm, even if already before his death he was beginning himself to feel outshone by the brilliance of the young Guiscard, he had yet proved himself a strong and courageous leader, fully endowed with all those qualities which had already, in barely twenty years, made the name of Hauteville famous through half Europe.

When he saw Humphrey buried next to William and Drogo in the monastery of the Santissima Trinità at Venosa, Robert can have shed few tears. Geoffrey, his only surviving elder brother in Italy, had failed to achieve any particular distinction; William, Count of the Principate, and Mauger, Count of the Capitanata, two younger brothers recently arrived, were doing well for themselves—especially

William, who had already wrested a castle from the Prince of Salerno at San Nicandro, near Eboli—but neither they nor any other Norman barons could approach the Guiscard in power or prestige. As Humphrey had foreseen, the succession was incontestably his. Even before his election, he had characteristically seized all the lands of his nephew and ward Abelard and had added them to his own extensive possessions; and when, in August 1057, he was formally acclaimed as his brother's successor by the Normans assembled at Melfi, and all Humphrey's personal estates devolved upon him also, he became the greatest landowner and the most powerful figure in all South Italy. It had taken him just eleven years.

But though Robert Guiscard was now supreme, his chief rival, Richard of Aversa, was not far behind. The Normans of Melfi and those of Aversa still retained their separate identities, and Richard had consequently not been a contender for the Apulian succession —he had anyway been fully occupied elsewhere. Young Gisulf of Salerno, despite the efforts of his uncle Guy of Sorrento to restrain him, had almost from the day of his accession determined to oppose the Normans in every way he could. It was a short-sighted policy, since, especially after Civitate (where the Salernitans had been noticeable by their absence), the Lombard princes of South Italy could no longer hope to stem the Norman tide, and the policy of co-operation which had served his father Gaimar in such good stead was now even more vital if an independent Salerno was to be maintained; yet Gisulf quickly drew upon himself the armed hostility of Richard of Aversa and managed to keep his throne only by means of a last-minute alliance with Amalfi; while Richard in the north and Robert and William de Hauteville in the south relentlessly harried his borders, paring away the outlying Salernitan territory bit by bit until he was at last left with little more than the city itself.

The days of Salerno were obviously numbered, but it was not the first of the Lombard principalities to fall to Norman arms. Since 1052 Richard had had his eye on Capua, where the young prince Pandulf, son of the 'Wolf of the Abruzzi', showed little of the military vigour or political sense of his odious father. Once already the Count of Aversa had beaten the Capuans to their knees and forced the wretched inhabitants to pay seven thousand gold bezants to preserve their liberty; and when in 1057 Pandulf died, Richard struck again. Within days he had ringed Capua with fortified watch-towers, cutting off the citizens from the fields and farms on which they depended for subsistence. They defended themselves valiantly; 'the women carried the stones to the men and brought comfort to their husbands, and the fathers taught their daughters the arts of war; and so they fought side by side, and comforted each other together'.[1] But the city was unprepared for a siege and before long the threat of starvation forced it to sue for peace. This time there was no question of a ransom; Richard was determined on conquest. The only concession he would allow was that the keys to the gates and the citadel should remain technically in Capuan hands—which, for four more years, they did. Meanwhile Richard the Norman became Prince of Capua, and the hereditary Lombard rule which had lasted for more than two centuries was extinguished.

For Salerno the situation now became more desperate than ever; but Richard was in no hurry to finish it off when easier, quicker returns seemed to be promised elsewhere. In nearby Gaeta he had recently arranged for the marriage of his daughter with the son of the ruling Duke, Atenulf, but the boy had died in the early autumn of 1058, shortly before the wedding ceremony. The occasion should have been one for condolences from the intended father-in-law; instead the new Prince of Capua addressed to Duke Atenulf a demand for the *Morgengab*, by which according to Lombard law one quarter of the husband's fortune became the property of the wife after the marriage. In this Richard had not one shred of justi-fication; as its name clearly implied, the *Morgengab* was payable only on the day following the nuptials, as a mark of their successful and satisfactory consummation.[2] Atenulf naturally refused. This gave Richard all the pretext he needed. Among the modest appanages of Gaeta at this time was the little county of Aquino, a short distance over the mountains to the north; within a few days this innocent, unsuspecting town found itself under siege and its outlying farms

[1] Amatus, IV, 28.

[2] 'This famous gift, the reward of virginity, might equal the fourth part of the husband's substance. Some cautious maidens, indeed, were wise enough to stipulate beforehand a present which they were too sure of not deserving.' (Gibbon, ch. XXXI.)

and villages overrun with Normans, burning and pillaging as they went.

Here was a typical example of Norman methods at their worst: the trumping-up of some legalistic excuse, however shaky; a half-hearted attempt to pin the blame on the intended victim; and then the attack itself, whenever possible with a vastly superior force, pursued without regard for decency or humanity. Such techniques are all too familiar in our own day; what was more characteristic of the people and the time was the fact that while the siege of Aquino was still in progress the Prince of Capua took the opportunity of making his first official visit to Monte Cassino, only a few miles away, and there received a hero's welcome. The monastery, which had always formed part of Capuan territory, had as we have seen suffered long and bitterly from Richard's predecessors; and the last of the Pandulfs, while in most respects but a pale shadow of his father, had continued the old tradition of oppression and persecution with unabated vigour. Any conqueror, even a Norman, who would deliver Monte Cassino from this hated régime could be sure of an enthusiastic reception. Amatus, a probable eye-witness, has left us his own account of the scene:

And afterwards the Prince, with a few of his men, ascended to Monte Cassino to give thanks to St Benedict. He was received with royal pomp; the church was decorated as if for Easter, the lamps were lit, the court-yard was loud with singing and rang with the prince's praise. . . . And the abbot washed his feet with his own hands, and the care and defence of the monastery were entrusted to his keeping. . . . And he vowed that he would never make peace with those who might seek to deprive the Church of its goods.[1]

But there was another, deeper reason for the warmth of the welcome given to the Prince of Capua. Until the spring of 1058 the monastery had been under the control of Frederick of Lorraine, a veteran of Civitate and of the fateful legation at Constantinople and still rabidly anti-Norman, who had been appointed abbot the previous year and had technically retained this position throughout his eight months' papacy as Pope Stephen IX.[2] On 29 March of

[1] Amatus, IV, 13.

[2] There is some confusion among historians over the numbering of the various Stephens who have occupied the papal throne, depending on whether or not they

that year, however, Pope Stephen died, and the monks elected as their new abbot the thirty-one-year-old Desiderius of Benevento. The career of Desiderius provides an admirable illustration of the doctrine of *noblesse oblige* as it existed in eleventh-century Italy. A member of the ruling dynasty of Benevento, he had seen his father killed by the Normans during one of the skirmishes of 1047 and had thereupon decided to renounce the world. For a Lombard prince this was not easy. Twice before he was twenty-five he escaped to a monastic cell; twice he was tracked down and forcibly returned to Benevento. After his family was expelled from the city in 1050 the situation became a little easier and he fled again, first to the island of Tremiti in the Adriatic and later to the desolation of the Majella, but soon he was recalled once more—this time by Pope Leo IX, who had just taken over Benevento and saw how greatly his hand would be strengthened against the loyalists if the young prince, who had by now been received into the Benedictine Order, were a member of his entourage. Desiderius served Leo well, but life in the Curia failed to attract him and as soon as the Pope died he settled at Monte Cassino, there to resume—he hoped—the contemplative life. For four years he seems to have succeeded, but early in 1058 we find him nominated as member of a new papal legation to Constantinople, from which he was saved by news awaiting him at Bari of the death of Pope Stephen. Thanks to a gift of three horses and a safe-conduct from Robert Guiscard he was able to take the direct route, through Norman territory, back to Monte Cassino; and there, on the day after his arrival, he was installed as abbot.

Always reluctantly, Desiderius was fated to play an important part in state affairs, both ecclesiastical and secular, for the next quarter of a century until his own papacy as Victor III. Soon after Civitate and certainly before any other leading churchman, he brought himself to accept the one unassailable fact of South Italian politics—that the Normans were in Italy to stay, and that opposition to them

recognise a doubtful Stephen II, who was elected to succeed Pope Zachary in 752 but died four days later, before his consecration. For this reason Frederick of Lorraine is sometimes known as Stephen X. Most authors, however, prefer to call him Stephen IX; this is, moreover, the title that appears on the inscription of his tomb as ordained by his brother Godfrey the Bearded—who should have known if anyone did.

was therefore not only futile but self-destructive. Only by maintaining their good-will at all costs could the monastery hope to survive. Events proved him triumphantly right. Amatus has already told us of the promise by the Prince of Capua—doubtless the direct result of Desiderius's reception of him—to protect monastic property, and within a week or two this promise had been reinforced by a formal charter confirming the great abbey in all its lands and possessions.

However well-advised Desiderius may have been in his new policy, the fact that he should first have made it manifest at a moment when nearby Aquino was fighting for its life against immense Norman odds must have appeared somewhat heartless; and it was probably in an attempt to retain some favour with Aquino that he took advantage of Richard's presence and generally benevolent mood to suggest that his demand for the *Morgengab* might be reduced, and that the Duke Atenulf might be asked for only four thousand *sous* instead of five thousand—'because he was poor', as Amatus explains. For once, the Prince of Capua made a concession; and the luckless Atenulf, after a few more weeks of hopeless resistance during which Aquino reached starvation-point, was at last compelled furiously to pay up.

To the population of South Italy the progeny of old Tancred de Hauteville must have seemed interminable. Already no fewer than seven of his sons had made their mark in the peninsula, four having risen to the supreme leadership and the remaining three firmly established in the first rank of the Norman baronage. And still this remarkable source showed no sign of exhaustion, for there now appeared on the scene an eighth brother, Roger. He was at this time some twenty-six years old, but though the youngest of the Hautevilles he was soon to prove himself a match for any; while to the devotee of the Norman Kingdom in Sicily he is the greatest and most important of them all.[1]

Like the majority of young Normans on their first arrival in Italy,

[1] Roger is sometimes surnamed Bosso; but as the name is neither frequent, necessary or melodious it can be ignored. It tends also to create confusion with Roger's nephew, Roger Borsa, whom we shall meet anon.

Roger made straight for Melfi; but he cannot have stayed there long, for already in the autumn of 1057 we find him in Calabria with Robert Guiscard, who had returned there as soon as his investiture was over. The new Count of Apulia apparently saw nothing in his former freebooting life that was incompatible with his recently-acquired dignities, and it was to this profitable if precarious existence that he now introduced his young brother. Roger proved an apt pupil. Camped near Cape Vaticano, on the summit of the highest mountain in the district so that the local population should remain ever conscious—and fearful—of his presence, he and his men soon subdued much of western Calabria. Such was his success that when, a few months later, the Guiscard had to return in haste to quell a local rising in Apulia—an emergency that was to become ever more familiar in the years to come—he had no hesitation in leaving Roger in charge; and when this rising, despite his efforts, assumed such dangerous proportions that Melfi itself was captured and Robert's leadership seriously imperilled, it was to Roger in Calabria that he called for help. His brother's arrival proved decisive and the revolt was quashed.

It was a happy partnership, but it did not last. The rupture seems to have been Robert's fault. He had always been famous for his generosity towards his followers; now, in his dealings with his brother, he suddenly began to display a parsimoniousness as inflexible as it was uncharacteristic—until Roger, who had in the first months of their association dutifully forwarded to Robert in Apulia much of the plunder resulting from his first Calabrian campaign, now found himself unable even to pay his own retinue. Such at least is the story given us by Malaterra. His chronicle, which was written some years later at Roger's request, may well be tendentious at this point, but it is not altogether improbable. Could it not, perhaps, indicate a new aspect of the Guiscard's character now appearing for the first time—jealousy of his brother, many years younger and possessed of ambitions and qualities in no way inferior to his own? Was there in fact room in Italy for both of them?

At all events, some time at the beginning of 1058 Roger angrily left Robert Guiscard's service. One of the advantages of his late arrival in the peninsula was that he had plenty of brothers already established to whom he could turn, and he now accepted the invitation of William de Hauteville, Count of the Principate, who in the four years since his arrival in Italy had captured nearly all the territory of Salerno south of the city itself and who had sent Roger a message offering him an equal share of all that he possessed—'excepting only', as Malaterra is careful to point out, 'his wife and children'. Thus it was that Roger soon found himself ensconced in a castle towering high over the sea at Scalea, an admirable vantage-point from which to make regular inroads, largely for the purposes of horse-stealing and highway robbery, into the Guiscard's territories. It must have been a profitable time; Malaterra tells us of one single *coup*—the ambush of a group of wealthy merchants on their way to Amalfi—with the profits from which, in plunder and ransom money, Roger engaged a hundred more soldiers for his growing army.

But the young man was destined for greater things than a life of brigandage, and looking back at him down the perspectives of history we can see that the decisive turning-point of his life in Italy came in 1058, when Calabria was overtaken by a terrible famine. The Normans had brought the trouble on themselves; their deliberate scorched-earth policy had left, over an immense area, not an olive-tree standing, not a cornfield to harvest.

Even those who had money found nothing to buy, others were forced to sell their own children into slavery. . . . Those who had no wine were reduced to drinking water, which led to widespread dysentery and often an affection of the spleen. Others on the contrary sought to maintain their strength by an excessive consumption of wine, but succeeded only in so increasing the natural heat of the body as to affect the heart, already weakened for want of bread, and thus to produce further internal fermentations. The holy observance of Quadragesima, so strongly upheld by the holy and reverend fathers, was set aside so that there was much eating not only of milk and cheese but even of meat—and that, moreover, by persons who had some pretensions to respectability.

This last sentence of Malaterra suggests that in the early part of the year at any rate the situation may not have been too acute, but the unfortunate Calabrians were soon reduced to more drastic extremities.

They sought to make bread with weed from the rivers, with bark from certain trees, with chestnuts or acorns which were normally kept for pigs; these were first dried, then ground up and mixed with a little millet. Some fell on raw roots, eaten with a sprinkling of salt, but these obstructed the vitals, producing pallor of the face and swelling of the stomach, so that pious mothers preferred to snatch such food away from the very mouths of their children rather than allow it to be eaten.

After months of such conditions, followed by a harvest scarcely less meagre than that of the previous year, the desperate populace rose against its Norman oppressors. The revolt began with local refusals to pay taxes or report for military service, continued with the massacre of the sixty-strong Norman garrison at Nicastro and rapidly spread through Calabria. Robert Guiscard, already over-extended and still actively defending his Apulian possessions, was growing used to local uprisings, but these were usually confined to small groups of discontented nobles. This time, with the whole native population up in arms over a steadily increasing area, the situation was more serious. Clearly he could no longer afford the unnecessary internecine squabbles which not only sapped his strength but, as events in Calabria and elsewhere had made plain, also encouraged insubordination among his subjects. Messengers sped to Roger at Scalea; and this time he could not accuse the Guiscard of any lack of generosity in the terms he offered. If Roger would now settle the Calabrian insurrection, half the affected terri-tory, plus all that remained for future conquest between Squillace and Reggio, would be his. He and Robert would enjoy equal rights and privileges in every city and town.

For the Count of Apulia it was the only possible course. He had bitten off more than he could at present chew. In so wild and mountainous a country, with its inhabitants so restless and its lines of communication so slender, no prince however strong could maintain his domination single-handed. Roger seized his chance. Down the coast he rode, at the head of all the soldiers he could muster. Whether he was able to do anything to alleviate the hard-ships of his future subjects is not recorded; we do not even know whether he tried very hard. Nor do the chroniclers tell us what action he took against the insurgents—but they never mention the Calabrian insurrection again.

While his young brother was settling affairs in the South, Robert Guiscard was thinking—reluctantly, one suspects—about consolidation. His instincts were always towards acquisition rather than the maintenance of what he had already won, and his long-term ambitions were fixed, as ever, on aggrandisement and conquest. But it was clear that he could not hope to extend his dominions any further until his Apulian vassals could be kept in more effective control. The Lombards in particular, though no longer in themselves a danger to his authority, were proving a constant irritant and a brake on his progress. As their political power had waned, their national solidarity seemed if anything to have increased. Feeling—with good reason—that the Normans, their erstwhile allies, had betrayed their trust, they remained sullen and unco-operative and made no effort to hide their resentment.

Some means must therefore be found of reconciling the Lombards, even partially, to their Norman overlords. The traditional method of solving such problems was by a marriage alliance, but here there were difficulties. Only one Lombard family of sufficient prestige and distinction was now left in Italy—the ruling family of Salerno. Prince Gisulf had a sister, Sichelgaita; but unfortunately the Count of Apulia's only child, Bohemund, son of his wife Alberada of Buonalbergo, was still little more than a baby and even by mediaeval standards hardly of marriageable age. Possible combinations were thus limited. Robert Guiscard, however, was never afraid of taking the plunge. He now discovered, with much display of consternation, that his marriage to Alberada fell within the prohibited degrees of kinship. He was therefore legally still a bachelor, and Bohemund a bastard. Why should he himself not marry Sichelgaita, thus uniting the Norman and Lombard ruling families over his great South Italian dominion?[1]

Gisulf does not appear to have been any too keen on the idea. He had always hated the Normans, who had already shorn him of almost all he possessed and whom, according to William of

[1] Both Delarc and Osborne have argued that Robert Guiscard's wedding to Sichelgaita did not take place till 1059, after the Council of Melfi. It is certainly true that Nicholas II strengthened the consanguinity laws in April 1059, and that Robert might therefore have been in a stronger position after that time. If his first marriage was in fact uncanonical, this might explain why Alberada seems to have borne him no ill-will;

Apulia, he and his compatriots considered 'a savage, barbarous and abominable race'.[1] On the other hand Pope Stephen, from whom he had been hoping for active support against them, had just died; and Gisulf desperately needed an ally who would be able to hold Richard of Capua and William de Hauteville in check. If the Guiscard could not control his own brother, then no one could. And so, with reluctance, the Prince of Salerno gave his consent—on condition, however, that William were first brought to heel. Robert asked nothing better. He already bore William a grudge for having led his brother Roger astray and encouraged his escapades from Scalea, and was only too pleased to get his own back. His knights and vassals were by now gathering round him for the marriage festivities, and he at once called upon them all to join him in an immediate punitive thrust to the south. The response was, as usual, virtually unanimous. 'No Norman knight refused to accompany him, except only Richard [of Capua], for the loving harmony which formerly existed between Robert and Richard was a little strained.'[2]

Once William had been put in his place, Gisulf made no further objection to the proposed marriage. Readers, if such there be, of Walter Scott's *Count Robert of Paris* may remember the excessively unpleasant Countess Bremhilde, for whom the new Countess of Apulia served as a model. It is a portrait at once unkind and unfair. Sichelgaita was cast in a Wagnerian mould and must be appreciated as such. In her we come face to face with the closest approximation history has ever dared to produce of a Valkyrie. A woman of immense build and colossal physical strength, she was to prove a perfect wife for Robert, and from the day of their wedding to that of his death she scarcely ever left her husband's side—least of all in battle, one of her favourite occupations. Anna Comnena who, as Gibbon points out, 'admires, with some degree of terror, her masculine virtues', reports that 'when dressed in full armour the

after his death she was to have masses said for the repose of his soul and she was eventually buried near him at Venosa. But it does not explain how, soon after the annulment, she came to marry Robert's nephew Richard, son of Drogo. Moreover Malaterra clearly states that the Salernitan marriage was in 1058, and Amatus bears him out. It looks as though we shall have to accept their opinion.

[1] '*Esse videbantur gens effera, barbara, dira.*'
[2] Amatus, IV, 20.

woman was a fearsome sight',[1] and we shall see how, many years afterwards at Durazzo, she saved a dangerous if not desperate situation by her courage and example. At such moments, charging magnificently into the fray, her long hair streaming from beneath her helmet, deafening the Norman armies with huge shouts of encouragement or imprecation, she must have looked—even if she did not altogether sound—worthy to take her place among the daughters of Wotan; beside Waltraute, or Grimgerda, or even Brünnhilde herself.

But however much he may have gained by his wife's alarming ferocity on campaign, Robert had married Sichelgaita for reasons which were diplomatic rather than military; and in this field the union brought him far more lasting advantage. The Guiscard now acquired in Lombard eyes a prestige well beyond that which even his immense natural abilities could have brought him. As William of Apulia puts it, 'this alliance with so noble a family lent new brilliance to Robert's already celebrated name. Those who had heretofore obeyed him only through compulsion now did so out of respect for the ancient law, remembering that the Lombard race had long been subject to the ancestors of Sichelgaita.'

Robert doubtless intended that his future offspring should also benefit from the strain of Lombard nobility which they would inherit from their mother. That they largely failed to do so was not Sichelgaita's fault. In the course of time she presented him with at least ten children, including three sons; none, however, was to show in any significant degree the qualities that earned for their parents their places in history. The Lombard blood attenuated the Norman, and the only one of Robert's progeny to prove himself a worthy son of his father was young Bohemund—now cast out with his mother Alberada to grow up a disinherited bastard, but later to become the first Frankish prince of Outremer and one of the foremost Crusaders of his time. The Guiscard's heir and successor, for all the Lombard loyalties he believed he could command, was to show throughout his life a weakness and timidity which his father would have despised and from the consequences of which only his uncle Roger, a Norman through and through, was able—in part—to redeem him.

[1] *The Alexiad*, I, 15.

10

RECONCILIATION

The acquisition of the ducal title by Robert Guiscard is a nice and obscure business.

Gibbon, ch. LVI

THE death of Leo IX in April 1054 threw the Church once again into a state of deep confusion. Determined as his reforms had been, they had had little time to take root in the stony ground of Rome; the Pope's enforced absence in Benevento had allowed the old aristocratic families to regroup themselves, and the moment he died the Counts of Tusculum, the Crescentii and the rest were back again at their old intrigues. The party of reform still had strength enough to prevent a snap election—which would almost certainly have brought to power the most open-handed of the reactionary candidates—but their two strongest leaders, Cardinal Humbert and Archdeacon Hildebrand, were both abroad and they needed some higher power to support them if their will was to prevail.

The interregnum lasted a year. At last, after both sides had appealed to Henry III for a decision, the reformers proved triumphant and Henry nominated his own principal counsellor, Gebhard, Bishop of Eichstätt, who was duly enthroned at St Peter's on 13 April 1055, under the title of Pope Victor II. It is hard to believe that any immediate successor of Pope Leo—let alone a politician of Gebhard's ability and experience—coming to power less than two years after Civitate, could have had no interest in the Norman problem; yet this was the case. We have seen him earlier in Germany, doggedly obstructing all Leo's efforts to raise an army;

and subsequent events had apparently produced no change in his views. His mind was fully occupied with Church administration and imperial affairs, and when he came to Rome he was still unprepared to give much detailed consideration to the problems of the South. By the spring of 1056, however, the flood of complaints against new Norman outrages forced him to accept the fact that he had underrated them. Leo had been right; such a state of affairs could not be allowed to continue. In August he travelled back to Germany to confer with Henry—perhaps a little sheepishly—on what action was necessary. The Emperor trusted his old adviser implicitly; if the Pope considered that a campaign was called for, then a campaign there would have to be. But as so often happened when action was planned against the Normans, fate intervened on their behalf. Henry was thirty-nine years old and had known hardly a day's illness in his life. At the end of September he was suddenly struck down by fever, and within a week he was dead.

It was lucky for the Empire that Pope Victor was in Germany at the time. Henry was succeeded as King by his five-year-old son, Henry IV, under the nominal regency of his mother, the Empress Agnes of Guienne; but as none of the advisers round the throne possessed half the Pope's knowledge or understanding of imperial affairs, Victor found himself during the next six months wielding the power not only of the Papacy but of the whole Empire of the West. Now once again there were more immediate problems to be faced than that of the Normans and, doubtless with relief, he banished them from his mind. It was not until the spring of 1057 that he returned to Italy; and before the misfortunes of the South could reclaim his undivided attention, he too fell victim to a fever. On 28 July he died at Arezzo. The escort party returning his body to Germany was ambushed and robbed at Ravenna, and he was hastily buried in Theodoric's Mausoleum, then doing service as a Church.

This time the succession was easier. There was no Emperor to consult, the King of Germany was only six and Archdeacon Hildebrand, by far the most powerful and influential member of the Curia, was in Rome and ready to act swiftly. He it was who had persuaded Henry III to appoint Victor two years before, and he now had no difficulty in imposing on the cardinals his new candidate—Frederick of Lorraine, once Pope Leo's chief lieutenant, at present filling in time as Abbot of Monte Cassino and henceforth to be known as Pope Stephen IX.[1] For the Normans Stephen's election seemed to spell catastrophe. Long ago he had boasted to Leo that he could exterminate them with a hundred knights; they had proved him wrong at Civitate and he had not forgiven them. They knew him, then, to be their implacable enemy; they also knew that his elder brother, Duke Godfrey the Bearded of Lorraine, had recently married the widowed Marchioness Beatrice of Tuscany and had thus assumed the control of the strongest and best-organised power in North Italy; and they cannot have failed to hear the universal rumours of how Pope Stephen was planning to take advantage of Henry IV's minority by transferring the Imperial Crown from the House of Franconia to that of Lorraine. Once Godfrey was Emperor, and the combined imperial and papal force was to march down at full strength into South Italy, they would have little chance of survival. The Pope's first actions after his consecration seemed to confirm their worst fears. Still titular Abbot of Monte Cassino, he sent orders to the monastery that it should at once forward to him all its gold and silver plate, promising later repayment at high interest. (The monks complied, but with such bad grace that Stephen regretfully decided not to accept the plate after all.) Next, as we have seen, he decided to send a new legation to Constantinople with instructions to revive the delicate project of a Byzantine alliance.

In the circumstances it was only to be expected that when Stephen died in his turn after less than eight months on the throne of St Peter some degree of suspicion should have fallen on the Norman leaders. Their motives were certainly strong. But they had little experience of the tortuous intriguing that provided a full-time occupation for so many of the inhabitants of the Eternal City, and it is doutful whether at this stage they possessed the technique or the contacts necessary for a *coup* of such magnitude. In the later years in Sicily they were to show themselves a match for any of their oriental subjects in the slippery arts of antechamber or alcove; for the moment, however, they were still very much men of the North, and poison occupied no place in their usual armoury. More likely

[1] See p. 110, n. 2.

suspects—if indeed there was any foul play at all—were, as usual, the Roman nobles, who much preferred the distant, nebulous authority of the Empire to the prospect of domination by the nearer and considerably more powerful House of Lorraine. But Stephen had long been a sick man, and it is a more probable, if duller, hypothesis that, like most people even in the Middle Ages, he died a natural death. It claimed him in Florence at the end of March 1058; and, as the Pope expired, the Normans breathed again.

The reformist leaders were once again absent from Rome—Humbert in Florence and Hildebrand not yet back from Germany, whither he had gone rather belatedly to announce Pope Stephen's election; and once again the reactionaries saw their chance. Experience over the past few years had taught them that on occasions of this kind everything depended on speed. A *coup d'état* was hastily arranged by a Tusculan-Crescentian alliance, and within a few days John Mincio, Bishop of Velletri, was enthroned as Pope under the inauspicious title of Benedict X. From the point of view of Hildebrand and his friends, the choice could have been a lot worse; the new Pope may have been weak-willed, but Leo IX had made him a cardinal and Stephen had considered him as a possible alternative candidate to himself. They could not, however, accept the manner of his election, which they considered uncanonical and corrupt. Leaving Rome in a body, they met Hildebrand in Tuscany and settled down to decide on a Pope for themselves.

The choice fell on Gerard, Bishop of Florence, an irreproachably sound Burgundian who in December 1058, once he was assured of the support of the Empress Agnes and—equally important—of Duke Godfrey of Lorraine, allowed himself to be consecrated as Pope Nicholas II. He and his cardinals, supported by Duke Godfrey with a small military contingent, then advanced upon Rome, where their partisans, led by a certain baptised Jew named Leo di Benedicto Christiano, opened the gates of Trastevere. Quickly they occupied the Tiber Island, which they made their headquarters. Several days of street-fighting followed, but at last the Lateran was stormed, Benedict barely managing to escape to Galeria.[1]

[1] The city of Galeria was abandoned in 1809, but its ruins may still be seen just off the Viterbo road about twenty miles from Rome.

The reform party had won again, but the cost had been considerable. Benedict X was still at large, and he had retained a loyal following; many Romans who had been forced to swear allegiance to Nicholas raised their left hand to do so, pointing out that with their right they had already taken an oath of fidelity to his rival. More disturbing still was the knowledge that victory could not even now have been achieved without the military support provided by Duke Godfrey. In short, after all the efforts of the past decade, the Papacy was once again where it had been when Pope Leo had found it—caught fast between the Roman aristocracy and the Empire, able sometimes to play one off against the other but never sufficiently strong to assert its independence of either. The task of reform could not possibly be accomplished in such conditions. Somehow the Church must stand on its own feet.

First came the problem of Benedict. Only thirteen years before, his odious namesake had demonstrated just how much harm could be done by a renegade anti-Pope; Benedict X was a far more popular figure than Benedict IX, and this time there was no Emperor ready to sweep down into Italy and restore order, as Henry III had done. Duke Godfrey had returned to Tuscany—though this was perhaps just as well, since he had recently displayed a curious half-heartedness that had led to suspicions of a secret intrigue with the Romans. And so the Church took a surprising, fateful step. It called upon the Normans for aid.

Though he may have taken earlier advice from Abbot Desiderius, the final decision can only have been Hildebrand's. No other member of the Curia, not even Nicholas himself, would have had the combination of courage and prestige it demanded. Throughout Italy, and above all among the churchmen of Rome, the Normans were still considered—not unreasonably—as a collection of barbarian bandits, no better than the Saracens who had terrorised the South before them. For many of the cardinals the thought of an alliance with such men, whose record of sacrilege and desecration was notorious and who had dared, only five years before, to take arms against the Holy Father himself and hold him nine months a captive, must have seemed more appalling by far than any accommodation with the Roman nobility, or even with Benedict himself. But this ugly, unprepossessing little Tuscan, of obscure, possibly Jewish origins and a standard of learning and culture well below that of most of his colleagues, knew that he was right. Pope and Cardinals bowed, as nearly always, before his will; and in February 1059 he set off in person for Capua.

Richard of Capua was naturally delighted by Hildebrand's approach, and gave him a warm welcome. A year ago Pope Stephen had seemed to threaten him and his compatriots with extinction; now Stephen's successor had sent his most distinguished cardinal to seek Norman aid. It was a sign, moreover, that his recent reception at Monte Cassino was not, as he had feared, an isolated phenomenon but was indicative of a radical change in papal thinking. Such a change was rich in promise. Instantly he put three hundred men at Hildebrand's disposal, and the cardinal returned hurriedly to Rome with his new escort. By mid-March he and Nicholas were together encamped before Galeria, watching their army lay siege to the town. The Normans, employing their usual tactics, inflicted appalling devastation upon the entire region, burning and pillaging in all directions; the Galerians resisted with great courage, beating back repeated attempts to storm the walls, but at last they were forced to surrender. Benedict was captured, publicly unfrocked, and imprisoned in the church of Sant' Agnese in Rome; and the era of Norman-Papal friendship had begun.

The fate of Benedict X came as a profound shock to the reactionary group in Rome. They had expected neither the degree of resolution and unity of purpose with which the cardinals had opposed his election, nor the vigour with which he had subsequently been swept aside. And now, before they were able to recover, Hildebrand dealt them a second blow, still more paralysing in its long-term effects. The procedure governing papal elections had always been vague; at this time it was based on a settlement, originated by the Emperor Lothair I in 824 and renewed by Otto the Great in the following century, according to which the election was carried out by the entire clergy and nobility of the Roman people, but the new Pontiff was to be consecrated only after he had taken the oath to the Emperor. Such a decree, loose enough in its original conception and looser still in its interpretation through well over two hundred years, was bound to lead to abuses. Apart from the power which it gave to the Roman aristocracy, it also implied a measure of dependence on the Empire which, though counter-balanced by the need for every Emperor to submit to a papal coronation in Rome, by no means accorded with Hildebrand's ideas of papal supremacy. Now, with the Romans in disarray, a child on the throne of Germany and the assurance of armed Norman support if the need should arise, it could at last be scrapped.

In April 1059 Pope Nicholas held a synod at the Lateran; and there, in the presence of a hundred and thirteen bishops and with Hildebrand as always at his side, he promulgated the decree which, with one or two later amendments, continues to regulate papal elections to the present day. For the first time the responsibility for electing a new Pope was placed squarely on the cardinals, while to prevent simony the cardinal-bishops were also required to super-intend the election itself. Only after a Pontiff had been elected was the assent of the rest of the clergy and people to be sought. Lip-service was still paid to the imperial connexion by a deliberately vague stipulation that the electors should have regard for 'the honour and respect due to Henry, at present king and, it is hoped, future emperor' and to such of his successors as should personally have obtained similar rights from the Apostolic See, but the meaning was plain; in future the Church would run its own affairs and take orders from no one.

It was a brave decision; and not even Hildebrand would have dared to take it but for the Normans. To both the Empire and the nobility of Rome it amounted to a slap in the face, however diplo-matically delivered, and either side might be expected now or later to seek the restitution of its former privileges by force of arms. But Hildebrand's conversations with the Prince of Capua, to say nothing of recent events at Galeria, had given him—and through him the Church as a whole—new confidence. With the aid of a mere three hundred Normans from Capua he had thrown the foremost of his enemies back in confusion; how much more might not be accomplished if the entire Norman strength from Apulia and Calabria could also be mobilised behind the papal banners? Such support would enable the Church to shake off once and for all the last shreds of its political dependence, and allow the most far-reaching measures of reform to be enacted without fear of the consequences. Besides, the events of 1054 had produced a climate between Rome and Constantinople in which there was clearly no hope of an early reconciliation in the theological field; the sooner, therefore, that the perverted doctrines of the Greeks could be swept altogether from South Italy, the better. The Normans, having at last established tolerable relations with their Lombard subjects, were at this moment forcing the Byzantines back into a few isolated positions in Apulia —notably Bari—and into the toe of Calabria. Left to themselves they would soon finish the job; then, in all likelihood, they would start on the Sicilian infidels. They were by far the most efficient race on the entire peninsula and, for all their faults, they were at least Latins. Should they not therefore be encouraged rather than opposed?

Richard and Robert, for their part, asked nothing better than an alliance with the Church of Rome. However much they and their countrymen may have victimised individual religious foundations in the past, they had always—even at Civitate—shown respect for the Pope, and had taken arms against him in self-defence only after all attempts at a peaceful settlement had failed. They were not so strong that they did not welcome a guarantee against the threat of a combined onslaught by Empire and Papacy, or an ally against any other enemy—Byzantine, Tuscan or Saracen—with whom they might on occasion be faced. On the other hand they were quite powerful enough to negotiate with the Pope on an equal political footing. Their hopes were therefore high when Nicholas II left Rome in June 1059 with an impressive retinue of cardinals, bishops and clergy and—possibly at Robert Guiscard's invitation—headed south-west towards Melfi.

Slowly and magnificently the papal train passed through Campania. It stopped at Monte Cassino where it was joined by Desiderius, now the Pope's official representative in the South and thus in effect his ambassador to the Normans; it wound its way through the mountains to Benevento, where Nicholas held a synod; to Venosa, where he ostentatiously consecrated the new church of the Santissima Trinità, burial-place of the first three Hautevilles and thus the foremost Norman shrine in Italy; and finally to Melfi, where he arrived towards the end of August and found, waiting at the gates of the town to receive him, a huge assemblage of Norman barons headed by Richard of Capua and Robert Guiscard, hastily returned from Calabrian campaigning to welcome his illustrious guests.

The synod of Melfi which was ostensibly the reason for the Pope's visit has largely been forgotten. Its principal object was to try to reimpose chastity, or at least celibacy, on the South Italian clergy—an undertaking in which, despite the unfrocking of the Bishop of Trani in the presence of over a hundred of his peers, later records show it to have been remarkably unsuccessful. Nicholas's presence proved, however, the occasion of an event of immense historical importance to the Normans and the Papacy alike—their formal reconciliation. It began with the Pope's confirmation of Richard as Prince of Capua, and continued with his ceremonial investiture of Robert, first with the Duchy of Apulia, next with Calabria and finally—though the Guiscard had never yet set foot in the island—with Sicily.

By just what title the Pope so munificently bestowed on the Normans territories which had never before been claimed by him or his predecessors is a matter open to doubt. Where the mainland of Italy was concerned, documentary evidence suggests that he was basing himself on Charlemagne's gift to the Papacy of the Duchy of Benevento two and a half centuries before. The frontiers of this territory were then ill-defined and had since proved elastic; at one moment they could have been said to comprise all the peninsula south of the city itself, though they did not by any means do so in the eleventh century. And it was after all only twelve years before that Henry III, restoring Capua to Pandulf in the presence of Pope Clement, had made it quite clear that he considered the principality an imperial fief. With regard to Sicily Nicholas was on still shakier ground; the island had never been subject to Papal control, and his only authority seems to have been the so-called Donation of

Constantine—a document by which the Emperor Constantine I was held to have conferred upon Pope Sylvester and his successors the temporal dominion over 'Rome and all the provinces, places and cities of Italy and the western regions'. This had long been a favourite weapon used in support of Papal claims; it was not until the fifteenth century that, to much ecclesiastical embarrassment, it was exposed as a forgery, shamelessly concocted in the papal Curia some seven hundred years earlier.[1]

But none of those present in Melfi on that August day was likely to raise embarrassing issues of this sort. In any event Nicholas could afford to be expansive; he was getting so much in return. He was admittedly lending papal support to the most dangerous and potentially disruptive of all the political elements in South Italy; but by investing both its leaders, whose relations were known to be strained, he was carefully keeping this element divided. Furthermore Robert Guiscard and Richard of Capua now swore him an oath which changed, radically and completely, the whole position of the Papacy. By a lucky chance the complete text of Robert's oath—though not, unfortunately, Richard's—has come down to us in the Vatican archives—one of the earliest of such texts still extant. The first part, concerning an annual rent to be paid to Rome of twelve pence of Pavia for each yoke of oxen in his domains, is of relatively little importance; the second, however, is vital:

I, Robert, by the Grace of God and of St Peter Duke of Apulia and of Calabria and, if either aid me, future Duke of Sicily, shall be from this time forth faithful to the Roman Church and to you, Pope Nicholas, my lord. Never shall I be party to a conspiracy or undertaking by which your life might be taken, your body injured or your liberty removed. Nor shall I reveal to any man any secret which you may confide to me, pledging me to keep it, lest this should cause you harm. Everywhere and against all adversaries I shall remain, insofar as it is in my power to be so, the ally of the holy Roman Church, that she may preserve and acquire the revenues and domains of St Peter. I shall afford to you all assistance that may be necessary that you may occupy, in all honour and security, the papal

---

[1] The earliest extant copy of this document is to be found at the Bibliothèque Nationale in Paris (M.S. Latin, No. 2777) and dates from the ninth century. The relevant passage reads: *'quamque Romae urbis et omnes Italiae seu occidentalium regionum provincias loca et civitates'*.

throne in Rome. As for the territories of St Peter, and those of the
Principality [of Benevento], I shall not attempt to invade them nor even
to ravage them [sic] without the express permission of yourself or your
successors, clothed with the honours of the blessed Peter. I shall con-
scientiously pay, every year, to the Roman Church the agreed rent for the
territories of St Peter which I do or shall possess. I shall surrender to you
the churches which are at present in my hands, with all their property,
and shall maintain them in their obedience to the holy Roman Church.
Should you or any of your successors depart this life before me I shall,
having taken the advice of the foremost cardinals as of the clergy and
laity of Rome, work to ensure that the Pope shall be elected and installed
according to the honour due to St Peter. I shall faithfully observe, with
regard both to the Roman Church and to yourself, the obligations which
I have just undertaken, and shall do likewise with regard to your successors who will ascend to the honour of the blessed Peter and who will
confirm me in the investiture which you have performed. So help me
God and his Holy Gospels.

The ceremonies over, Nicholas returned to Rome, his retinue
now further increased by a substantial Norman force. Richard, whose
oath was presumably on similar lines, headed for Capua while
Robert hastened back to rejoin his army in Calabria, where it was
besieging the little town of Cariati. All three could be well satisfied
with what they had done.

Others, however, did not share their satisfaction. Gisulf of
Salerno had suffered yet another blow to his power and his pride.
His last hopes of mobilising papal support against the hated Normans
had crumbled, and he could now look forward to nothing but an
unglamorous decline in his dwindling domain, for ever at the mercy
of the Prince of Capua and sustained only by occasional reflected
rays from his brother-in-law Robert Guiscard. The Roman aristocracy retreated into its musty palaces, furious and frightened. The
Byzantines saw that they had lost their last chance of preserving
what was left of their Italian possessions. And in the Western
Empire, shorn of its privileges at Papal elections, faced with a new
alliance as formidable militarily as it was politically, and now, as a
crowning insult, forced to watch in impotent silence while immense
tracts of imperial territory were calmly conferred on Norman
brigands, the reaction to Nicholas's behaviour need not be described.
It was lucky for Italy that Henry IV was still a child; had he been a

few years older, he would never have taken such treatment lying down. As it was, the Pope's name was thenceforth ostentatiously omitted from the intercessions in all the imperial chapels and churches; but we may wonder whether Nicholas—or Hildebrand—greatly cared.

11

INVASION

Italien ohne Sizilien macht gar kein Bild in der Seele: hier ist der Schlüssel zu allem.

(Italy without Sicily cannot be conceived: here is the key to everything.)

Goethe, writing from Palermo
in April 1787. (*Italienische Reise*)

The terms of Robert Guiscard's investiture at Melfi and of his subsequent oath of allegiance to Pope Nicholas left no doubt as to the direction of his future ambitions. Sicily, lying green and fertile a mere three or four miles from the mainland, was not only the obvious target, the natural extension of that great southward sweep of conquest that had brought the Normans down from Aversa to the furthermost tip of Calabria; it was also the lair of the Saracen pirates—recently, thanks to the continual internecine warfare within the island, less audacious and well-equipped than in former times, but still a perennial menace to the coastal towns of the south and west. While Sicily remained in the hands of the heathen, how could the Duke of Apulia ever ensure the security of his newly-ratified dominions? In any case he was now a loyal servant of the Pope, and had not Nicholas himself charged him to purge papal lands of the infidel oppressors? Like most of his compatriots, Robert was fundamentally a religious man; and among other less commendable motives there was certainly a spark of the genuine crusader spirit in his heart as he threaded his way south from Melfi, through Calabria and over the high Aspromonte from which he could gaze down

131

across the straits to Sicily, warm and inviting in the September sun, with only the plume of Etna a snow-white warning on the horizon.

But before the Guiscard could spread out the map of Sicily, he must roll up that of Calabria. One or two towns in the region still remained occupied by Greek garrisons; if these were not quickly eliminated they might create serious problems with his lines of communication and supply once the Sicilian venture was properly under way. He rode straight to Cariati. His men had already been besieging it for many weeks without success, but on Robert's arrival it surrendered almost at once; and before he returned to Apulia for the winter Rossano and Gerace had in their turn capitulated. Now only Reggio remained in Byzantine hands. Early in 1060, after a brief excursion to the south-east during which the Greeks were chased from Taranto and Brindisi, the Guiscard was back with his army beneath its walls. There he was met by Roger, whom he left in charge during his absence and who had foresightedly spent the winter constructing massive siege-engines. It was the first time since the Normans came to Italy that they—as opposed to their Lombard allies—had had recourse to weapons of this kind; but Reggio was the capital of Byzantine Calabria and the Greeks were expected to sell it dearly. So indeed they did. At last, however, they were forced to surrender, and the Duke of Apulia rode in triumphal procession through the city, between the long rows of marble villas and palaces for which it was famous. The garrison, to whom Robert had offered generous terms, fled to a nearby fortress on the rock of Scilla[1] where they held out for a little while longer; but they soon realised that their cause was hopeless and, one moonless summer night, all embarked secretly for Constantinople. On that night Greek political rule in Calabria came to an end. It never returned.

Now at last Robert and Roger were ready for Sicily. The chief obstacles had been overcome. The Greeks had been eliminated from all Italy except the city of Bari, where, though possibly hard to evict, they should prove easy enough to contain; and Bari was in

---

[1] Opposite the legendary Charybdis, on the Sicilian shore. Chalandon translates Malaterra's *Scillacium* as Squillace, but is surely wrong. To reach Squillace, which is some seventy miles from Reggio even as the crow flies, the Greeks would have had to cross the whole Aspromonte massif, passing through Norman-held territory the whole way.

any case far away. Everywhere else the phrase *Magna Graecia,* so
long used to describe Byzantine Italy, could be discounted as a
quaint historical expression. The Pope had given the expedition his
blessing. The Western Empire was powerless to intervene. Even in
Sicily itself conditions seemed relatively favourable. In many areas
the local population was still Christian and could be expected to
welcome the Normans as liberators, giving them all the help and
support they needed. As for the Saracens, they were certainly brave
fighters—no one questioned that—but they were by now more
divided among themselves than they had ever been and were hardly
likely to prove a match for a cohesive and well-disciplined Norman
army. The island was at this time being squabbled over by three
independent emirs. First there was a certain Ibn-at-Timnah, who
controlled much of the south-east, with major garrisons at Catania
and Syracuse; then there was Abdullah Ibn Haukal, dominating
the north-western corner from his palaces at Trapani and Mazara;
finally, between the two, was the Emir Ibn al-Hawas with his seat
at Enna.[1] All three princes had by now shaken off their earlier
allegiance to the Zirid Caliph of Kairouan, who had himself been
dislodged from his capital a year or two previously and was now
fighting for his life among the tribal factions of North Africa;
and all were at constant loggerheads with each other. It did not look
as though the Norman conquest of Sicily would take very long.

   In fact, from first to last, it took thirty-one years, longer than
most of the Normans concerned had been in Italy—longer indeed
than many had been alive. For they had reckoned without Apulia,
where Robert Guiscard's by now traditional enemies stubbornly
refused to lie down, dividing his energies and—more important—
his resources at the one time when he desperately needed all he had
for the Sicilian operation. The details of his Apulian campaigns
against a new Byzantine army and his own rebellious subjects need
not in themselves trouble us very much; their importance lies in the
effect which they had on the course of events in Sicily. This was not
wholly bad. That the continual necessity of fighting on two fronts

---

   [1] Until 1927 this fortress-city was known as Castrogiovanni, a corruption of the
Arabic Kasr Janni. In that year Mussolini restored its original name of Enna, by which
it had been known throughout antiquity.

delayed and impeded the Sicilian success, rendering it infinitely more hazardous and expensive than it would otherwise have been, is a point which hardly needs emphasis; the Norman expeditionary force was chronically, sometimes disastrously, undermanned and ill-supplied. And yet, paradoxically, it was the Guiscard's Apulian preoccupations during this period that made Sicily the brilliant and superbly-organised kingdom it later became. As Robert found himself compelled to spend more and more of his time dealing with his enemies on the mainland, so the army in Sicily, nominally under his command, fell increasingly under the control of Roger, until the younger brother could at last assume effective supremacy. This, as we shall see, later led to the division of Robert's domains and so allowed Roger, freed of Apulian responsibilities, to devote to the island the attention it deserved.

Roger must have been well aware that, by the terms of the Melfi investiture, all Sicily when conquered would be held by Robert, and that, whatever his own achievements, he could in theory expect only such rewards as his capricious brother might choose to offer him; yet he must also in some degree have foreseen the future pattern of events, and he probably suspected that his opportunities might prove greater than they at present appeared. Certainly he showed himself from the outset to be every whit as eager and enthusiastic as the Duke of Apulia himself. A few weeks after the capture of Reggio he had made an experimental foray across the straits, landing one night with some fifty or sixty chosen followers near Messina and advancing on the town; but the Saracens had emerged in strength and driven the raiders back to their boats. Meanwhile preparations began for the full-scale invasion.

They were painfully slow. Already Apulia was stirring, and in October 1060 Robert Guiscard was summoned back in all urgency. The Emperor Constantine X Ducas, who had the year before assumed the throne of Constantinople, had despatched a new army to Italy in a final effort to save what was left of his Langobardian Theme. It was not a particularly large force, but it took the Normans by surprise at a moment when the Guiscard was away in Calabria and at first met with little resistance. Even when Robert and his brother, Mauger, appeared with a hastily-assembled army of their own they were not immediately able to check the Greek advance, and by the end of the year much of the east coast had been recaptured and Melfi itself was under siege. By January 1061 the situation was so serious that Roger and the rest of the troops in Calabria were sent for. The Sicilian operation looked like being indefinitely postponed.

But Roger was not put off so easily. By mid-February he was back again in Calabria, just in time to seize a new opportunity which suddenly and unexpectedly presented itself. The feuding which had so long continued between two of the Sicilian emirs, Ibn at-Timnah and Ibn al-Hawas, had now flared up into open warfare. Some time before, in a disastrous attempt to patch up their quarrel, Ibn at-Timnah had married the sister of Ibn al-Hawas, but the latter was now holding her in his eagle's-nest fortress at Enna and refusing to return her to her husband. His reluctance was readily understandable and doubtless shared by the lady herself, since she had recently had an argument with Ibn at-Timnah in the course of which he had called in a drunken fury to his slaves and ordered them to open her veins; fortunately her son, in the nick of time, had summoned the doctors and saved her life. Soon after her flight her husband, probably more anxious to preserve his self-respect than his marriage, had marched on Enna to recover his rightful property; but he had been unable to make any impression on the most impregnable stronghold in all Sicily and had instead suffered an inglorious defeat in the valley below. He and the remnants of his army had then retreated in disorder to Catania, and there his spies soon informed him that Ibn al-Hawas was preparing a punitive force with which he had openly sworn to finish him off once and for all.

Roger was at Mileto when, in the second week of February 1061, Ibn at-Timnah arrived in person to seek his aid and to offer him—according to the Arab historian Ibn al-Athir—no less a prize in return for the liquidation of his enemy than the domination of the whole of Sicily. It was not the sort of proposition that he could possibly ignore. Quickly he assembled a force of a hundred and sixty knights and several hundred foot-soldiers, together with a small fleet under Geoffrey Ridel, one of the Guiscard's most able commanders, and landed a few days later in the extreme north-eastern corner of the island. Previous experience warned him against arousing the garrison of Messina; his plan this time, approved by Ibn at-Timnah who was with him, was to follow the north coast along to Milazzo, making sorties inland wherever they seemed indicated and ravaging as much as possible of Ibn al-Hawas's territory on the way. Then, although none of the chroniclers is entirely explicit on the point, his intention seems to have been to secure the Milazzo promontory as a permanent Norman bridgehead in Sicily which could be used for the landing of stores, reinforcements and, ultimately, the main body of the army.[1] At first all went well. Milazzo was taken and so, with hardly a struggle, was Rometta. The plunder was considerable—it included, apparently, a large quantity of cattle—and, to make sure of getting it safely back to Reggio, the entire army returned to Cape Farò, where the fleet was lying at anchor. Meanwhile, however, the alarm had been raised in Messina. The garrison had hurried up the coast and was now drawn up on the hillside just out of sight of the beach. More cautious this time—for the Norman force was far larger than that which they had so effortlessly repulsed the year before—the Saracens planned to wait until the loading operations were in full swing and then attack when the Normans were divided between the beach and the ships. It was a good idea, and it might well have succeeded; fortunately for the Normans, however, contrary winds made embarkation difficult, and before the work could begin Roger learned of the enemy's presence. His half-brother Serlo—one of the four Hautevilles who had not come to seek his fortune in Italy—had a son of the same name who had recently joined his uncle in Calabria and was already showing unusual promise. This boy Roger now sent to attack the Saracens' flank, enjoining him above all to prevent their possible retreat along the narrow coastal strip leading back to Messina. The plan worked; and the Arabs, instead of taking the invaders by surprise, suddenly found themselves surrounded. Few survived.

Roger hastened to follow up his advantage. With any luck Messina

[1]The Allies used the Cherbourg peninsula in much the same way during the Normandy landings of June 1944.

would have been left almost defenceless. He and his men reached the city the same evening, and at dawn on the following day the attack began. But now it was the Normans' turn to be surprised. Despite their losses the people of Messina, men and women together, leaped to the defence of their city. Roger saw that he had miscalculated. There would be no quick victory after all. Moreover, his tiny army would be easy prey for any relief force which Ibn al-Hawas might send out from the interior. He gave the order to retire. It was, for the Saracens, just the encouragement they needed, and it turned the scale of battle. A few minutes later the Norman retreat had turned to flight, with the Messinans in hot pursuit. Here was disaster; but still worse was to come. The contrary winds of the previous day had been the prelude to a great storm which was tearing at the ships lying at anchor off Farò. Embarkation, which had been difficult before, was now impossible. For three days the Normans waited, huddled on the open beach, blocked by the Saracens from any natural shelter and defending themselves as best they could from their repeated attacks. As Amatus frankly reports, 'What with fear and cold together, they were in a most miserable state.' Finally the sea calmed and they managed to get away, but they had not gone far before they were intercepted by a Saracen fleet from Messina, and the ensuing naval battle continued to the very entrance of Reggio harbour. One Norman ship was lost; the others, battered but still afloat, struggled into port to discharge their exhausted and shivering passengers. The expedition, after so promising a start, had ended in something suspiciously like a fiasco.

The blame lay squarely on the shoulders of Roger. Brave as he was, he had not yet learnt that in the art of war prudence is as valuable a quality as courage. Their successes of the last forty years had been largely due to the fact that the Normans, except occasionally in their mercenary days, had never sought a battle that they could not be reasonably certain of winning; nor, since they still depended largely on immigration for their fighting strength, did they ever unnecessarily risk the lives of their men. Twice in the past year Roger had done both. The fate of the Maniakes expedition in 1040—in which several of the older knights in his entourage had probably participated—should have made it clear enough that the

Saracens, divided or not, would fight hard and bitterly to preserve their island; and this self-evident fact had been further confirmed by Roger himself only a year before. To have launched yet another madcap expedition, carelessly planned and inadequately equipped, at a few days' notice and on behalf of an unbalanced and treacherous Emir, was an act of irresponsible folly whose consequences were entirely deserved.

It is to be hoped that Robert Guiscard spoke seriously to his brother on these lines when he joined Roger in Calabria early the following May. He had brought with him as much of his army as he could spare. The spring campaign in Apulia had been highly successful; Melfi had been relieved, Brindisi and Oria recaptured. A few towns in the heel were still in Byzantine hands, but the bulk of the Greek army had retreated to Bari and was unlikely to contemplate any further offensives for the time being. Six clear months of good campaigning weather lay ahead—time, perhaps, to get a firm grip on Sicily before winter closed in. There were other reasons too—apart from his natural impatience—which made Robert anxious to invade the island as soon as possible. Ibn al-Hawas, fully aware of Norman intentions, was already strengthening Messina with eight hundred knights and a fleet of twenty-four ships, and it was plain that the longer the Normans waited, the tougher would be the resistance that they would eventually have to face. Robert was worried, too, about his Apulian vassals. The Byzantine invasion had kept them busy for the past few months, but now that the Greeks had retreated they were beginning to grow restless again. What they needed was a long-term task to perform, a bold and exciting new programme of conquest that would unite them under his leadership against a common enemy. Roger also was chafing; in no way deterred by his earlier reverses, he had spent the spring preparing and planning the main expedition. If it did not start soon he would be off on his own again.

Within a few days of the Guiscard's arrival at Reggio, the armies were ready to embark. Even by the standards of the time they did not amount to a very sizeable force—perhaps some two thousand all told, with knights and foot-soldiers in roughly equal proportions.

They were in fact considerably fewer than Robert had hoped, but
the Apulian situation made it unlikely that he would be able to raise
more in the foreseeable future. Given good generalship, they should
suffice. After the February *débâcle*, however, one thing was plain.
No expedition could succeed without securing its lines of communication with the mainland. This meant control of the straits, which
in its turn involved the possession of Messina; not, as Roger at
least knew to his cost, an easy proposition, but one to which there
was no alternative, especially now that the Saracen fleet had been
so drastically reinforced. The best chance lay in surprise.

In the middle of May 1061 the nights were dark and still. The
new moon appeared on the twentieth, and it was probably on about
the eighteenth at dusk that the Norman spearhead of some two
hundred and seventy horsemen under the command of Roger de
Hauteville slipped out of the little harbour of S. Maria del Farò in
thirteen ships, and landed a few hours later on a deserted beach
some five miles south of Messina.[1] Their crossing was comparatively
long—some ten miles or so farther than would have been necessary
if Robert Guiscard had chosen the shortest distance over the straits
—but it proved a wise choice. The Saracens were expecting the
invading force, whose arrival they knew to be imminent, to take
the most direct route and to land, as Roger had done in February,
some way to the north of the city; and their land and sea patrols
were ceaselessly sweeping the coastline between Messina and Cape
Farò. Such a concentration left the southern entrance to the straits
totally without defence; Roger and his men passed across unmolested
and before daybreak the fleet was back again in Calabria, ready to
take the second wave of troops on board.

The purpose of the advance party was primarily reconnaissance,
but Roger was not one to err on the side of caution. Moving off
from the beach-head towards Messina soon after dawn, he almost at
once came upon a Saracen mule-train, laden with money and supplies

[1] In an interesting article, '"Combined Operations" in Sicily, A.D. 1060–78' D. P.
Waley suggests that the Normans had learnt the art of transporting horses across the
sea from the Byzantines, and that the experience gained in 1061 proved of value five
years later at Hastings, where it is known that Duke William's invasion force included
knights from South Italy and Sicily.

for the Messina garrison. It was a providential opportunity. The Saracens were taken entirely by surprise and within a few minutes had been slaughtered to the last man; and hardly had the Normans regrouped themselves before a flurry of white sails off the coast announced the arrival of the next section of the invading army.

Roger now found himself with a force of nearly five hundred men. It was still no larger than that which had fared so disastrously on his previous expedition, but this time he knew that another 1500 under Robert Guiscard were on their way. Furthermore the Saracens of Messina had as yet given no indication that they knew of the Norman landings; there was consequently a good chance of taking them unawares. Messina was only a mile or two distant; the sun had hardly risen. Cautiously the Normans advanced. Outside the city they waited, watching; the ramparts, to which three months before the citizens had so magnificently rallied, were now deserted and quiet. For the second time that morning Providence had aligned herself on the Norman side. What was the use of waiting for Robert? Roger could handle this operation by himself. He attacked.

It was over almost as soon as it had begun. Long before the Duke of Apulia had sailed, with the bulk of his army, over a friendly and tranquil sea to his new domain, the city of Messina was in Norman hands. The Saracens had fallen victims to their own caution. In their anxiety to block the Norman's passage across the straits they had left not only the southern approaches to Messina but even the city itself undefended. The garrison, patrolling the coast to the north, never learnt what had happened until too late; and then, rightly concluding that return meant instant capture, fled to the interior. Those on the ships found themselves in a similar situation; once the port of Messina was in enemy control, to sail south into the narrows was to invite disaster. Turning about, they hastily rounded Cape Farò and headed westward to safety.

On his arrival, the Duke of Apulia rode in triumph through a largely deserted city. There had been the inevitable looting, but relatively little carnage. Malaterra tells in shocked admiration of a young Saracen noble who ran his beloved sister through with his own sword rather than allow her to fall into the lascivious clutches of the infidel; but most of the Muslim population managed to escape, unharmed and without much difficulty, into the hinterland. The Guiscard was only too pleased to see them go. Above all, he must ensure the security of Messina; the last thing he wanted was a large untrustworthy element in the population. There remained, in consequence, only the Christian—largely Greek—minority to extend to him a bewildered and cautious welcome and to arrange at his command a service of thanksgiving in their church. Robert was now more than ever at pains to stress the divinely-appointed nature of his expedition; not only was he in any case convinced of it himself—and the circumstances of the city's capture certainly seemed to argue some degree of celestial favour—but it would clearly have a salutary effect if the local Christians could be persuaded to look at the Norman invasion from a religious point of view.

Robert's next task was to transform Messina into the impregnable bridgehead he needed. For a week without respite, day and night, his army worked on the defences. Walls were rebuilt and extended, ramparts raised, towers fortified, new earthworks dug. When all was ready, a contingent of cavalry was installed as permanent garrison. It entailed a grave depletion of his military strength in the the field, but where Messina was concerned he could afford to take no chances. Meanwhile, quick as always to turn Norman ambitions to his own advantage, there reappeared on the scene the sinister figure of Ibn at-Timnah to ingratiate himself once again into Norman counsels. As soon as Roger's earlier expedition had run into difficulties he had removed himself hastily out of harm's way to his castle at Catania; now, more plausible and subservient than ever, he returned to find a new and ready audience in the Guiscard himself. His proposals were unchanged; if the Normans would help him against Ibn al-Hawas, supreme control over Sicily would be theirs.

Whatever Robert's private feelings may have been about Ibn at-Timnah, he could not afford to dismiss him. This man was, with Ibn al-Hawas, the most powerful of the Sicilian Emirs. Now that Messina was secure, his friendship would give the Normans effective control of all eastern Sicily, with the whole length of vital coastline facing the mainland. He could provide guides, interpreters, weapons, food and all the various forms of expertise which Europeans in Muslim lands so conspicuously lacked. Here, it

seemed, was yet another manifestation of divine benevolence—
though Robert may well have reflected that in this case the Almighty
could scarcely have selected a more unlikely vehicle for His purposes.
And so it was that a week or so later, as soon as the defences of
Messina had been completed to his satisfaction, the Guiscard led
his army forth again, with Roger and Ibn at-Timnah riding at his
side, on the next stage of his Sicilian adventure.

From Messina there were two ways of approaching the domains
of Ibn al-Hawas. The shortest was to follow the coast southwards
to a point near Taormina and then, turning inland, to follow the
Alcántara valley round the northern slopes of Etna and on to the
central plateau. Ibn at-Timnah preferred, however, to lead his
Norman friends by the alternative route, passing through territory
which, though theoretically loyal to him, had recently shown signs
of falling away and would doubtless benefit from a sight of the
Norman army at close quarters. This would have an additional
advantage in that it would allow Robert to secure the formal
allegiance of Rometta, without which the mountain passes commanding the approach to Messina from the west could never be
properly secured.

Rometta was then, as it is today, a superb natural stronghold; in
addition it had been heavily fortified by the Saracens. To George
Maniakes in 1038 it had proved a formidable obstacle, and might
easily have done the same in 1061 to Robert Guiscard: fortunately,
however, the governor had remained loyal to Ibn at-Timnah.
Now, for the second time in only four months, he greeted the
Normans' arrival with every sign of pleasure. Presenting himself
without delay at their camp, he knelt at Robert's feet, swore
allegiance to him on the Koran and offered him, among a host of
other gifts, the keys to the citadel and the town. This was the final
link in the defensive chain which the Guiscard had flung round
Messina; now at last he could proceed in confidence.

Though irritated as always by the slowness of the infantry—
Amatus tells us that he was always galloping on ahead with his
horsemen and then having to wait while the foot-soldiers caught up
—the Duke managed to maintain a remarkable speed. Two days'

journey from Rometta brought him to Frazzanò, at the foot of the pass leading up to the so-called *pianura di Maniace*, the plateau on which the gigantic George and the first of the young Hautevilles had distinguished themselves twenty-one years before. Here Robert drew his breathless army to a halt. Till now there had been no serious opposition anywhere along the route; the region through which they had passed was largely Christian, and the local populations had welcomed them with real—though, as they were soon to learn, misplaced—enthusiasm. But once they reached the Simeto river the Normans would be on hostile territory; and spies were already bringing in reports of the mighty army which Ibn al-Hawas was preparing to lead against them from his fortress at Enna. The advance continued, but now the Guiscard was more wary. At Centuripe he suffered his first check. His attack on the town met with heavy resistance and, rather than risk losses he could ill afford, he raised the siege almost at once, leaving the town untaken. A short excursion eastwards was more successful; Paternò fell without a struggle, the Muslims melting away before the Norman advance 'like wax before a fire', as Amatus puts it. And then, since the much-vaunted Saracen army was still many miles distant and not apparently over-anxious to show itself, Robert wheeled his troops to the right and advanced along the valley of the Dittaino, plunging ever deeper into the enemy's heartland until he pitched his camp among the watermills immediately beneath the great crag of Enna itself.

Of all the mountain-fortresses of Sicily, Enna was among the highest and the most forbidding. Two centuries before, the Saracens themselves had been able to capture it from the Greeks only by crawling one by one up the main sewer. It could clearly never be taken by storm, and Robert, conscious of the shortage of time before winter would force his retreat, was anxious to avoid a siege. He therefore deliberately trailed his coat, challenging Ibn al-Hawas on his very threshold to come out and fight and to give the Normans a taste of that formidable reception he was said to have prepared. Yet the Saracens still held back, and for four days the Normans waited in a mood of mounting frustration, laying waste the surrounding countryside and doing their impatient worst to needle the Emir into action. On the fifth day they succeeded.

It is impossible, as so often in the history of this period, to give any reliable estimate of the numbers involved in the battle that followed. We learn from Malaterra that the Saracen army comprised fifteen thousand; it may be an exaggeration, but there is nothing inherently improbable about it. One thing, at all events, is clear; the Normans were outnumbered many times over. Robert Guiscard had at the start only some two thousand men. He had left a strong garrison at Messina, and possibly others at Rometta and elsewhere. Ibn at-Timnah may have supplemented the Norman army with a few Saracen turncoats, but these are not likely to have been many since they are nowhere mentioned in the chronicles. When Malaterra estimates Robert's strength at about seven hundred he may not, therefore, be very far out.

And yet the battle of Enna was an overwhelming victory for the Normans. Geography, as well as numbers, was against them; they had no strong places into which they could retire for rest or consolidation, no well-stocked magazines of arms or supplies. But courage and, above all, discipline—these they had in plenty, and of a kind which the Saracens had never before encountered. To them they added a new and powerful religious fervour to drive them forward when, newly confessed and shriven and with Robert's huge voice still thundering in their ears, they charged into battle. And so the first major engagement, on Sicilian soil or anywhere else, fought between properly constituted armies of Normans and Saracens ended in rout. Five thousand of Ibn al-Hawas's men managed to reach the safety of their fortress; the remainder, by nightfall, lay dead or dying along the river bank. Norman losses were negligible.

Plunder apart, the results of the victory were largely indirect. Ibn al-Hawas with the rump of his army—and, presumably, Ibn at-Timnah's wife—was safe in his citadel, whence the Normans were as far as ever from dislodging him; and although a siege was ordered even before the Norman wounded had been carried from the field, it was plain to all that to capture such a place would be a long and arduous task. Meanwhile, however, news of the battle was spreading quickly through the valleys, where few of the local chieftains shared their Emir's determination. Before long the first of them had appeared at the Guiscard's camp; and in the weeks that followed they came by the score, heads bowed and arms folded across their chests, their mules piled high with gifts and tribute. Such eagerness to make formal submission was hardly surprising; they were now defenceless while the Normans, true to their old habits during siege warfare, were despatching daily raiding-parties to terrorise and lay waste the countryside as only they knew how. Harvest-time was approaching, but the Muslim farmers could expect little from their burnt-out fields and devastated vineyards. Ibn al-Hawas, peering out during those summer nights from his beleaguered stronghold, must have seen the flames from the neighbouring homesteads blazing even more brightly than the Norman campfires directly below him. The sight may not have caused him much distress; his own losses had been far greater. But he must have suspected that for him and for his people this was the beginning of the end; Sicily would never be the same again.

In the short term, however, time was on the Emir's side. Robert Guiscard could not in his present circumstances undertake a winter campaign; he was already dangerously extended and would need to consolidate his gains before he could safely return to the mainland. After two months of siege in the remorseless Sicilian summer, Enna showed no signs of weakening, but Norman patience was beginning to wear thin. Already Roger, impetuous as always, had grown tired of the inactivity and had galloped off with three hundred men on another of his so-called reconnaissance expeditions, leaving a trail of pillage and devastation all the way to Agrigento and returning with enough plunder to reward the entire army. This doutbless proved a valuable sweetener, but it was by now clear that the siege would soon have to be raised. Some time in July or early August Robert gave the signal and, to the relief of the besiegers almost as much as the besieged, led his men away down the valley whence they had come.

With so small an army at his disposal and so many of his men now bent on returning to their Apulian homes, the Guiscard could not hope to secure any part of Ibn al-Hawas's territory. Farther north, however, in that no-man's-land which, though technically within the domains of Ibn at-Timnah, was never safe for long against the incursions of his rival, the Greek Christian inhabitants implored him to leave a permanent garrison and easily persuaded some of the more rootless Norman knights to settle on Sicilian soil. And so, in the autumn of 1061, there arose a few miles from the north coast, near the ruins of the classical Aluntium, the first Norman fortress to be built on the island. Perched among the foothills of the Nébrodi, and commanding the passes which provided the principal channel for Saracen attacks, it constituted for the local inhabitants both an effective defence and an ever-present reminder of Norman strength. In the following years this isolated stronghold was to grow into a prosperous little town. Such it remains today; and of Robert Guiscard's work it still retains not only a ruined castle but also the name, S. Marco d'Alunzio, which he gave it in memory of that other S. Marco in Calabria where his career had begun only fifteen short years before.

Back at Messina, Robert Guiscard was joined by Sichelgaita who, after a brief tour of inspection of her husbands's new domains, bore him triumphantly off to Apulia for Christmas. Roger accompanied them as far as Mileto in Calabria, which he had made his mainland headquarters; but he could not rest. Sicily continued to beckon. There was still too much work to be done—or rather, perhaps, too many opportunities to be seized. By early December he was back in the island with two hundred and fifty of his followers. After a second tornado-like progress through the Agrigento region he turned back north again to Troina, a higher and more commanding fortress even than Enna. Fortunately it was populated main' y by Greeks, who at once opened their gates to Roger's army. Here he spent Christmas; here, too, he learned to his joy that his old love from early days in Normandy had arrived in Calabria, where she was awaiting his return and hoping, as she had always hoped, to become his wife.

Judith of Evreux was the daughter of a first cousin of William the Conqueror. When she and Roger had first known each other, any idea of her marrying the youngest and poorest of the relatively humble Hautevilles must have been out of the question; but since then many things had changed. A violent quarrel had broken out between Duke William and Robert de Grantmesnil, Judith's half-brother and guardian, abbot of the important Norman monastery of St Evroul-sur-Ouche. In consequence Robert had fled, with Judith, her brother and sister and eleven faithful monks, first to Rome, where he tried to seek redress from the Pope, and then on to his countrymen in the south. Robert Guiscard had received them well. Anxious to weaken the hold of the Greek monasteries in Calabria, he was already encouraging the settlement of Latin monks wherever possible, and had at once founded, with a handsome endowment, the abbey of S. Eufemia in Calabria where the celebrated liturgical and musical traditions of St Evroul could be maintained.[1] But Roger also had his plans. By now he had achieved in Italy a degree of power and influence second only to that of the Guiscard himself. Few non-ruling families in Europe would any longer consider him an unworthy bridegroom. The moment he heard of Judith's arrival he hurried to Calabria to meet her, and found her waiting for him at the little town of S. Martino d'Agri. They were married on the spot. Roger then led his bride to Mileto, where the union was officially celebrated—with the assistance, in good St Evroul style, of a large concourse of musicians. It was undoubtedly a love match, and the young couple seem to have been very happy; but their honeymoon was all too short. Roger had serious work to do; early in the new year, 'in no way moved by his wife's tearful entreaties', he left her in Mileto and returned to Sicily.

The year 1062 had started well, but it failed to live up to its early promise. After little more than a month's campaigning during which the town of Petralia was the only gain of any importance, Roger returned to the mainland, determined to settle once and for all a domestic issue which had been worrying him for some time. The Duke of Apulia was back again at his old tricks. Already in 1058 he had undertaken to share his Calabrian conquests equally with his brother; since then, however, disturbed by Roger's increasing influence and fearing for his own position, he had refused to honour his promises. While Roger's attention had been focused on Sicily he had grudgingly accepted the money which Robert offered him

---

[1] S. Eufemia was in its turn the mother-abbey of many Sicilian foundations, including that of S. Agata at Catania, now the Cathedral.

instead of the stipulated territories, but now that he was married the position was different. The *Morgengab* tradition which had proved so useful to the Prince of Capua some years before was universally upheld in Norman Italy, and it was unthinkable that any great baron, least of all a Hauteville, should be unable to enfeoff his wife and her family in a manner befitting their rank and station. Messengers were accordingly despatched to the Duke in Melfi carrying Roger's formal demands, together with a warning that if these were not fully met within forty days, he would be compelled to obtain his rights by force.

Thus, for the second time in four years, the whole momentum of the Norman advance was checked while its two greatest architects squabbled over the spoils. As on the previous occasion, it was less the ambition of the junior brother than the jealousy of the senior that provided the spark; Roger was too much of a Hauteville to prove an easy subordinate, but neither in 1058 nor in 1062 do his demands seem to have been unreasonable. The fault was Robert's. Sure as was his political instinct in most situations, he was apt to lose all sense of proportion whenever he suspected that his own supremacy was being challenged or eroded by his younger brother. On this occasion in particular he could ill afford to antagonise Roger. The Byzantine army was still entrenched at Bari and doubtless preparing new offensives; if Robert hoped to hold it in check while at the same time following up the advantages so far gained in Sicily he must have a lieutenant on whose courage and resourcefulness he could rely. And now the situation became even more serious; for during the forty days set by Roger before the expiry of his ultimatum, word came from Sicily that Ibn at-Timnah, who was meanwhile continuing the spring campaign along the north coast, had been led into an ambush and murdered. His death had had an immediately tonic effect on the morale of his enemies, to the point where the Norman garrisons of Petralia and Troina, fearing for their lives, had deserted their posts in panic and fled back to Messina.

At this moment it would still have been possible for the Duke of Apulia to acknowledge his obligations and settle the argument before it was too late. Instead he marched furiously down into Calabria and besieged Roger in Mileto. The story that follows seems to belong to that ridiculous half-way world which lies between musical comedy and melodrama. It is recorded in fascinating detail by Malaterra and is worth summarising here less for its intrinsic historical importance than for the light which it sheds on the characters of two extraordinary men and on the way in which affairs of state were occasionally conducted nine centuries ago.

One night during the siege of Mileto, Roger stole secretly from the city to seek help from the neighbouring town of Gerace, whither he was shortly afterwards pursued by a furious Guiscard. The inhabitants of Gerace, faithful to Roger, slammed their gates on the Duke as he arrived; later, however, disguising himself under a heavy cowl, he managed to slip in unobserved. Once inside the town, he made his way to the house of a certain Basil, whom he knew to be loyal, and with whom he wanted to discuss ways of re-establishing his authority. Basil and his wife Melita, regardless of the risks they were running, asked their distinguished guest to stay to dinner but, unfortunately for Robert, while they were waiting for their meal he was recognised by a servant, who at once gave the alarm. Within minutes the house was surrounded by an angry crowd. Basil, panicking, fled to the nearest church for asylum, but was caught and struck down by the mob before he reached it; Melita was also captured and suffered an even more terrible fate; she was impaled on a stake and died in agony. Robert, on the other hand, the cause of all the trouble, kept his head. His call for silence was obeyed, and his powers of oratory were equal to the crisis. For his enemies, he declared, he had but a single message; let them not, for their own sakes, get carried away by the pleasure of finding the Duke of Apulia in their power. Today fortune frowned on him, but all that ever came to pass did so by the will of God, and tomorrow their respective positions might easily be reversed. He had come among them freely, of his own accord and without any hostile intent; they, for their part, had sworn fidelity to him and he had never played them false. It would be shameful indeed if a whole city, heedless of its oath, should now hurl itself pointlessly against a single, unarmed man. They should remember, too, that his death would earn them the lasting hostility of the Normans, whose friendship they were at present fortunate enough to enjoy. It would be avenged, implacably and without mercy, by his followers, whose anger would be almost as dreadful as the dishonour which would fall upon themselves and their children for having caused the death of their innocent, beloved and devoted leader.

The people of Gerace cannot have been altogether taken in. For fifteen years the name of Robert Guiscard had been enough to send peasants stumbling from the fields to barricade their homes, monks burrowing under the monastery cellars to bury their treasure and plate; it was a little late for him to start playing the injured lamb. And yet his words had their effect. Slowly, as he spoke, the crowd grew calmer. Perhaps after all it might be better not to take too precipitate a decision. The Duke was moved to a place of safety, and all Gerace deliberated what was to be done.

Robert's followers, waiting outside the walls of the town, soon learnt of the turn events had taken. Only one course was open to them. Choking back their pride they sought out Roger, who was encamped a few miles away, and begged for his help. Roger was now enjoying himself. He knew that he no longer had any cause to fear for his own safety; his brother's life was in his hands and he could make whatever terms he liked. Naturally he could not allow Robert to come to any serious harm. For all their quarrelling, he loved him after a fashion; he respected his genius; above all, he needed him for the Sicilian operation. But he saw no reason not to make the most of the present state of affairs. Riding in full state to Gerace, he summoned all the elders to meet him in an open space outside the gates. They arrived to find him purple with rage. Why, he demanded, had the town not immediately handed his brother over to him? It was he, not they, who had suffered from the Guiscard's duplicity; he only had the right to inflict the punishment such conduct deserved. Let the so-called Duke he delivered up to him at once; otherwise, let the citizens of Gerace bid farewell to their town, and to the farms and vineyards with which it was surrounded, for by morning all would be razed to the ground.

The poor burghers were probably only too pleased to comply. Roger's threats offered them a means of escape from an impossible position. Robert was sent for, and hastily handed over; and all waited breathlessly to see what chastisement had been reserved for him. They were due for a surprise. Roger dropped his mask of anger and strode forward, arms outstretched, to greet his brother; and within a moment the two were embracing each other like Joseph and Benjamin—the phrase is Malaterra's—and weeping tears of joy at their reconciliation. Robert immediately promised full satisfaction of all Roger's territorial demands and, still beaming, the brothers rode off together to Mileto. As subsequent events were to prove, the quarrel was even now not entirely over; once the Duke found himself reunited with his wife and the main body of his army he began to regret his too easy acquiescence, and for a short while the fighting broke out anew; but his heart was no longer in it and before long the two greatest of the Hautevilles were friends again.

The manner in which, after this unlovely wrangle, Calabria was finally divided between Robert and Roger is still not altogether clear. It seems to have been based on a scheme according to which each town and castle was individually divided into two separate areas of influence, being thus prevented from giving active support to either brother against his rival. Such a system suggests that the degree of mutual trust now established between the two still fell some way short of the ideal; in practice it must have been so complicated and cumbersome that we can only wonder that it worked at all. And yet both brothers seem to have found it satisfactory enough. Certainly it must somehow have enabled Roger to bestow upon Judith the *Morgengab* she deserved, and upon her family such estates as befitted their new dignity. For Robert Guiscard it had been an expensive lesson, but he had learnt it well.

For Roger, too, the quarrel with his brother had been expensive. It had cost him several valuable campaigning months which should have been spent in Sicily, and it was not until the high summer of 1062 that he was able to return to the island. This time, no doubt remembering the tears which she had shed when he had left her behind in the spring, he took Judith with him. They landed, with an army of three hundred, in early August and went straight to Troina. Despite the ignominious flight of the Norman garrison after Ibn at-Timnah's assassination, the town had suffered no Saracen attacks in Roger's absence, and if he noticed that the welcome which the

Greek inhabitants now extended to himself and his young wife seemed rather cooler than on his first arrival, he attached no particular importance to the point. Everything seemed peaceable enough. After a week or two spent putting the fortifications in order Roger left Judith in the care of the new garrison and set off on his long-delayed campaign.

This was the moment for which the Greeks of Troina had been waiting. As so many of their compatriots and co-religionists were to find during the early years of Norman domination, their new masters were often worse than the old. They were more demanding than the Saracens, tougher and more unscrupulous in getting what they wanted. Even their Christianity was incomprehensible, crude in its practices, barbaric in its language; and their free and easy ways with the local women were already notorious throughout the island. The Troinans had suffered particularly in this last respect. The hasty departure of their first Norman garrison had seemed to them a deliverance; but now it had been replaced, and by a still larger body of troops than before. They laid their plans carefully; and so soon as Roger and his army were a safe distance away, they struck. Their primary objective was the person of Judith. Once they had her in their power they could hold her hostage until the Normans agreed to withdraw from the town. But they had reckoned without the new garrison, who now fought back with all the courage and determination that their predecessors had lacked. All day long the battle continued, up and down the precipitous streets, while messengers sped to Roger with the alarm.

Roger, who had been besieging Nicosia, returned at full gallop, and arrived to find the situation worse than he had feared. Seeing a chance to rid themselves for ever of their Norman oppressors, several thousand Saracens from the neighbouring country had poured into Troiana and had made common cause with the Greeks. Against such numbers the Normans could not hope to defend the whole town; Roger at once ordered a general retreat to the few streets immediately surrounding the citadel. Barricades were hastily erected, look-outs stationed, outposts manned. This time it was the Normans' turn to be besieged. And so they were, for four months—perhaps the most testing period in the entire history of Norman

Sicily. They had been caught completely by surprise; provisions were already dangerously low and, worst of all, Sicily was soon in the grip of the earliest and most merciless winter in living memory. Troina stands nearly four thousand feet above sea level; the Normans were without warm clothing or blankets, and the area behind their roughly-improvised fortifications possessed little, short of the buildings themselves, that could be used as fuel. Somehow morale remained high; Malaterra reports that despite their hunger, toil and lack of sleep, the besieged Normans kept up each other's spirits, 'hiding their sorrow and feigning a sort of hilarity in countenance and speech'. Poor Judith, too, sharing a single woollen cloak with her husband by day and huddling with him under it by night, put on as brave a face as she could; and yet 'she had only her own tears with which to quench her thirst, only sleep to palliate the hunger that tormented her'. Somehow one feels that, for all her courage, she was no Sichelgaita.

By the beginning of 1063 Roger knew that he could not hold out much longer. There was hardly any food left, and his soldiers were too undernourished to support the cold as stoically as they had at the outset. Fortunately there were signs that the Saracens who kept the night watch beyond the barricades were also feeling the strain. These men had one defence against the cold which was denied to the Normans—the rough red wine of the region, forbidden by the Prophet but now temporarily hallowed in Muslim eyes for its calorific properties. It did indeed keep them warm; but, as the Norman look-outs were quick to report, they were consuming it in larger and larger quantities with other more dangerous effects. Roger saw his chance. One January night, with the wind whistling colder than ever down the narrow streets, he prepared his men for a final offensive. Waiting till silence descended on the Saracen watch-posts, he stole silently over the barricades. All was as he had suspected. The sentries had surrendered to the effects of their potations, and were sleeping like children. Quickly he beckoned to his followers. Their footsteps made no sound in the deep snow; the Greek and Saracen forward positions were taken before their defenders knew what had happened, and by morning Troina was once again in Norman hands.

Roger's vengeance was swift. The ringleaders of the insurrection were hanged instantly, and the penalties reserved for their accomplices were probably hardly less severe. Malaterra spares us the details, preferring to tell us instead of the great feast with which the Normans celebrated the end of their ordeal. They had deserved it. In the past four months Roger, Judith and their followers had been subjected to hardships greater than those which any Norman leader had been called upon to face since the first of their number appeared in the South. They had come through magnificently, thanks to their courage, their initiative and, above all, their endurance. But they had seen, too, just how precarious still was their Sicilian foothold.

12

CONQUEST

Dextera Domini fecit virtutem.
Dextera Domini exaltavit me.

(The right hand of God gave me courage.
The right hand of God raised me up.)

> Roger's motto, inscribed on his
> shield after the battle of Cerami

THERE was no denying it; Sicily was proving a more formidable proposition than Roger—or anyone else—had expected. His fundamental problem was the same as it had always been, the chronic shortage of manpower. This was not of overriding importance in pitched battles; the Normans had shown at Enna and elsewhere that, at least in mountainous terrain, their superior discipline and military technique would prove decisive over sheer weight of numbers. But a few hundred men could not be everywhere at once, and the advantages of victory were soon lost if political domination could not be maintained. At present their strength was inadequate to keep effective control even in the north-east. Moreover it was now nearly two years since the start of the Sicilian operation, and the element of surprise, one of the most valuable of all weapons to a numerically inferior army, had long since been forfeited. The Norman presence in Sicily had by now had the inevitable catalytic effect on the Saracens, who, once rid of the baleful influence of Ibn at-Timnah, had set aside their differences in the face of a common enemy. The Zirid Sultan Temim had sent his two sons Ayub and Ali, each at the head of an army, to help their Sicilian brethren stem the Christian tide; while Roger had been fighting for survival at Troina, these two young princes had landed at Palermo and Agrigento respectively and had at once begun preparations for a concerted attack.

Roger still had only three or four hundred men; and it was unlikely that Robert Guiscard, fully occupied with the Byzantines in Apulia, would be able to spare him many more. To make matters worse, he had lost all his horses at Troina—where they had probably provided the staple diet for four months—and he now had to make a hurried journey back to the mainland for replacements. It says much for the thoroughness with which he had crushed the revolt that he should have been willing, once again, to leave Judith in the town during his absence; but she had learnt a lot in the past few months, and Malaterra writes approvingly of the way in which she now assumed command of the defences, making regular daily and nightly rounds of the garrison to ensure that all the soldiers were awake and on the alert. After nine centuries it would perhaps be unchivalrous to suggest that these tours of inspection were prompted more by nervousness than by conscience; but in view of what had happened the last time she was left behind, the poor girl could hardly be blamed for feeling a little uneasy.

Her husband, however, was soon back again, with horses and supplies in abundance—though still with very few men. Throughout the spring of 1063, working out from Troina, he and his young nephew Serlo—already the ablest of his commanders and a Hauteville to his fingertips—engaged the Saracens in a quantity of minor skirmishes from Butera in the south to Caltavuturo in the north. Plunder was good and the store-rooms at Troina began to fill up nicely again, but it was not until midsummer that the Normans were able to get to grips with the main Saracen army, now tempered with the newly-arrived Africans, which had recently left Palermo and was now heading east, under the green banner of the Prophet, towards the Christian strongholds.

Eight miles or so to the west of Troina lies the little town of Cerami, in a fold of the hills above the river that shares its name. Rivers seemed to bring the Normans luck; on the mainland the Olivento, the Ofanto and above all the Fortore had run red with the blood of their enemies, and in Sicily the Dittaino had already

witnessed a similar triumph. After the events of the previous
winter Roger wished at all costs to avoid another siege; the Cerami,
on the other hand, provided an admirable rallying-point for his
tiny army, together with plenty of good look-out positions from
which he could survey the enemy assembling on the hills opposite.
Once again, as at Enna, the Normans were heavily—it seemed
hopelessly—outnumbered. The size of the Saracen army is unknown;
Malaterra estimates it at 'thirty thousand, not counting the foot-
soldiers, whose numbers were infinite'. As usual he exaggerates;
but a major force of this kind, gathered from all over Sicily and
reinforced with important detachments from North Africa, must
certainly have run into thousands. Against them Roger could muster
only a hundred knights, with another thirty under Serlo; assuming
proportionate numbers of infantry, the Norman army in its entirety
cannot have been more than five or six hundred strong.

For three days Normans and Saracens watched each other; on the
fourth Malaterra tells us that 'our men, no longer able to tolerate
seeing the enemy so close without attacking him, confessed themselves with the utmost piety, made their penances and then, trusting
in God's mercy and certain of His help, rode off into battle'. Hearing
that the Saracens were already besieging Cerami, Roger quickly
despatched Serlo with his thirty knights to hold the town as best
he could; and once again his brilliant young nephew proved equal
to the task. When Roger arrived with the bulk of the army a short
time later he found that the first wave of the attackers had already
fled. Cerami was still his.

All this, however, as Roger well knew, was but a preliminary. The
enemy was regrouping for the main attack, and the Normans barely
had time to draw themselves up in line of battle before the Saracen
army charged. Ignoring Serlo on the flank, they directed the whole
weight of the onslaught against the centre, where Roger himself
was commanding, in one enormous and concerted effort to smash
the Norman force by sheer impetus and force of numbers. They
nearly succeeded, but somehow the Norman line held. Meanwhile
Serlo galloped to his uncle's aid. All day the battle continued, until
the mangled, trampled bodies lay thick over the field, Then suddenly,
as evening drew on, the Saracens turned in flight, Roger and his

men close on their heels. The pursuit led ultimately to the Saracen camp.

Loaded down with booty, the Normans now installed themselves in the tents of the Mahommedans, seizing their camels and all else that they found there. Then, on the morrow, they left to seek out those twenty thousand foot-soldiers who had fled to the mountains for refuge. Many of these they killed, the remainder they took captive and sold as slaves, receiving for each a great price. But after a little time, the contagion which arose from the rotting corpses on the battlefield drove them away and they returned to Troina.[1]

To Roger the battle of Cerami was of vital importance. Now at last Norman mastery of the whole region between Troina and Messina was assured. Though sporadic revolts in isolated areas would still occur, it would never again be seriously contested. Once again a Norman force had inflicted an annihilating defeat on a Saracen army many times its own strength; this time the battle had been greater, its result more significant and decisive, than that of Enna two years before. But the Normans had prevailed for the same reasons as always—by a combination of courage and discipline which was then unknown in the Muslim world, shot through with a religious enthusiasm born of their still growing belief in divine guidance. By now this belief had reached the point where Malaterra is able to record without apparent surprise how, just before the Normans rode into battle at Cerami, their ranks were joined by a fair young knight, mounted on a snow-white stallion and armed *cap-à-pie*, in his hand a lance from which there streamed a white pennant bearing a shining cross. It was not long before he was recognised as St George himself, come to lead the soldiers of Christ to victory; and many later testified to having seen his emblem flying also from the point of Roger's own lance at the height of the battle. In recognition of these signs, Roger ordered a sumptuous present to be sent to Pope Alexander II; and so it was that a week or two after the battle the citizens of Rome stood agape while a procession of four camels—the finest of the Saracens' military stable —shambled slowly through the streets.

Pope Alexander must have been delighted with his present; quite

[1] Malaterra, II, 53.

apart from their exotic character and zoological interest, and more important than either, those camels were a living indication to him that Roger was on his side and that he could probably look to the Hautevilles for support as and when necessary. The Pope was having a trying time. The electoral reforms of Nicholas II had had the very effect that they had been specifically designed to avoid. They made a disputed papal succession inevitable, for how could the Empress-Regent Agnes accept any candidate canonically elected in Rome without giving implicit approval to the new dispensations? Nicholas's death in 1061 thus created a situation even more hopelessly confused than usual. Once again there were two Popes struggling for the possession of St Peter's. Alexander's was the stronger claim, since his election by the Cardinal-Bishops—led, as always, by Hildebrand—had been canonically impeccable. On the other hand his rival, the anti-Pope Honorius II, chosen by Agnes and supported by the Lombard bishops—who, as St Peter Damian uncharitably remarked, were better fitted to pronounce upon the beauty of a woman than the suitability of a Pope—had influential partisans in Rome and plenty of money with which to nourish their enthusiasm; and it was only with the military assistance of Richard of Capua—provided now for the second time at Hildebrand's request— that Alexander had been enabled to take possession of his see. Even then Honorius had not given up. As late as May 1063, after Agnes had been removed and an imperial council had declared for his rival, he had even managed to recapture the Leonine City[1] for a short time— and though he was formally deposed in the following year he was to uphold his claims until the day of his death. Throughout this period Alexander needed all the support he could find. In return for his camels he sent Roger a papal banner to go before him and inspire his army in its future campaigns. More significant still, he proclaimed absolution for all those who joined Robert and Roger in their holy task of delivering a Christian land from the domination of the heathen. Henceforth, not only in the hearts of the Normans but in the eyes of Christendom, the conquest of Sicily was a Crusade.

[1] That part of Rome on the right bank of the Tiber, including the Vatican and the Castel Sant' Angelo, which was fortified in the ninth century by Pope Leo IV immediately after the sack of the city by the Saracens.

It is a characteristic of wars that they are apt to last considerably longer than the combatants expect. Roger and his men, slipping across the straits of Messina on that moonless May night in 1061, were neither the first nor the last warriors to embark on their troop-ships in the probable hope that it would all be over by Christmas. As we have seen, by the Christmas of that year the Normans had secured little more than a bridgehead, while at the end of 1062 such celebrations as the unfortunates in Troina may have permitted themselves can have been anything but festive. In 1063 some progress had been achieved but, as the days began to draw in towards the third autumn since the launching of the expedition, Roger must have been conscious of a growing atmosphere of frustration and disappointment among his countrymen. Admittedly their three seasons in Sicily had won them the control of perhaps a quarter of the island, but even this moderate success had been due to a remarkable early run of luck and to a combination of special circumstances which could never be repeated. If they had not managed to take Messina by surprise there was no reason to suppose that a siege of the city would have been any more successful than their attempts on Enna or Agrigento. Most of their advance had been through largely Christian territory where they had become more accustomed to deputations of welcome than to armed resistance; and they had throughout enjoyed the protection of Ibn at-Timnah, who had been able to guarantee them against attacks from the south and south-east while they advanced towards the centre. By contrast, the unconquered land that lay before them was Muslim through and through. Ibn at-Timnah was dead; his enemy Ibn al-Hawas, despite heavy losses, was still holding out at Enna, and the Saracens were now more united than they had been for a century. As the Normans advanced, their supply-lines would grow steadily longer and more vulnerable, and recent experience had proved that not even the native Christians could be trusted to support them once their backs were turned. Finally, as always, they were pitiably few—a factor which might enhance the glory of their victories but, for practical reasons, augured ill for the future. With their present numbers they might conquer, but they could never control.

When the exhilaration of Cerami had passed, these must have been the gloomy reflections that occupied Roger's mind and led him, among other considerations, to reject outright the next opportunity which was put in his way. It came, suddenly and unexpectedly, from Pisa. Whether the Pisans were merely enraged by the incessant incursions of Sicilian-based Saracen pirates or whether, with their well-known eye to the main chance, they were deliberately trying to associate themselves with the Normans in anticipation of their eventual victory is not known. Pisan contemporary records, how-ever, confirm Malaterra's report that in August 1063 the city sent a fleet to Sicily, where it sought Roger's co-operation in a combined land and sea attack on Palermo. Roger's reply was disappointing. He had other unfinished business and could take on no further commitments. Later, perhaps, something of the kind might be arranged; for the moment the Pisans would have to wait. The Pisan admiral argued with him, but it was in vain; Roger merely repeated that he was not ready, and that he could not risk his men in such conditions. At last, despairing of any help from the Normans, the admiral sailed off in dudgeon to attack Palermo by himself. Without any shore support, the attempt was doomed to failure, and the Pisans were lucky to escape more or less unscathed. According to Malaterra their only prize was the great chain with which the Palermitans had blocked their harbour mouth. This, he tells us, they seized; and then 'believing, like true Pisans, that they had achieved some great matter, they returned forthwith to their homes'.[1]

It cannot have been an easy decision for Roger to take. He had no particular love for the Pisans and may well have resented their intervention; at the same time the offer of a fully-equipped fleet for such an operation must have been tempting for an ambitious and

[1] An inscription in Pisa Cathedral claims that the Pisans did in fact manage to land a small force near the mouth of the Oreto, where they laid waste the villas and gardens in the neighbourhood. It also records the capture of six Saracen ships—five of which, however, they burned. All this may well be true; Malaterra probably had no first-hand knowledge of what took place and anyway tends to minimise their achievements as much as he can. What is certainly false is the passage in the *Chronica Pisana* (Muratori *R.I.S.*, vol. VI, p. 167), according to which the Pisans captured Palermo and returned with so much plunder that they were able to start construction of their Cathedral. This was indeed begun in 1063, but Palermo stood until the Normans captured it nine years later.

impatient leader. But by now he had probably received advance information of the new campaign which Robert Guiscard was already planning for the following year. The situation had recently improved in Apulia; Brindisi, Oria and Taranto were back in Norman hands, and the Duke was once again able to turn his attention towards Sicily. Knowing this, Roger would naturally have been reluctant to risk his own meagre resources for the sake of Pisa; better far to husband them in preparation for a grand new all-Norman offensive with his brother.

And so he bided his time until, early in 1064, Robert appeared in Calabria with an army of some five hundred knights and a thousand-odd foot-soldiers. Roger met him at Cosenza to plan the campaign. This time the strategy would be different; they would waste no more energy on Enna or the interior, but would head straight along the north coast of the island to Palermo itself. Once they had the capital, the rest—even in so decentralised a land as Sicily—would surely follow. As always when Hautevilles were in command, the army moved fast. No opposition was encountered, and only a few days after crossing the straits Robert drew up his troops on what seemed a suitable site for their encampment on one of the hilltops overlooking Palermo. His choice nearly proved disastrous. Forty-six years previously the remnants of the first Norman army to appear in Italy, retreating after Cannae, had been driven from their chosen headquarters by a plague of frogs. It had been a humiliating experience, but not a harmful one. The new natural hazard which awaited them proved to be both.

The tarantula spider had long been the scourge of Southern Italy, and particularly of that region around Taranto which gave it its name; but nowhere can it have been more plentiful or malevolent than on the hill now selected by Robert Guiscard. The bite of this Sicilian variety was fortunately not followed by that wild and hysterical agitation of the body which later became famous as both the principal symptom and the only remedy for its poison—and, in the tarantella, accounted for the only dance in Europe to have been developed for purely medicinal purposes. The consequences as related by Malaterra seem, none the less, to have been unpleasant in the extreme:

This *taranta* is a worm which has the appearance of a spider but possesses a cruel and envenomed sting, such that those whom it attacks are forthwith filled with a most poisonous wind. Their distress increases till they are no longer able to contain this same wind, which comes forth noisily and indelicately from their backsides so that unless a hot compress or some other still more powerful calorific is at once applied, it is said that their very lives are in peril.

It was not an auspicious beginning. The camp was hastily transferred to a more salubrious site, but Norman nerve had clearly been shaken. The impetus was gone. The Conca d'Oro, that huge chain of mountains that enfolds the city of Palermo, provided a superb landward defence. Not a movement by an attacking army could pass unobserved from its fortresses and watchtowers, and even when Robert reached the city walls, he was able to make little impression on them. For three months his sorry siege continued, but to no avail. Saracen shipping continued to pass freely through the harbour mouth, and the Palermitans seemed scarcely even inconvenienced. It was like Enna all over again, only this time there was not even a pitched battle by which the Normans could redeem their pride. And so the Guiscard found himself, for the second time in three years, leading a dispirited army back to Italy, where the situation was again deteriorating and from which he could never be absent for long. Apart from the capture of one insignificant little town (Bugamo, now long since disappeared) he had accomplished nothing; even Agrigento, with which he attempted rather halfheartedly to console himself on the return journey, withstood his attack. He now had to face the fact that in the Muslims of western Sicily he was faced with a stronger and more determined enemy than any that he or his family had yet encountered—Lombard, Frankish or Byzantine. As 1064 drew to a close it began to look as if the Norman advance had at last reached its limit.

For four years, like a ship becalmed, the Norman army in Sicily lay isolated and powerless, all its momentum gone. No pitched battles are recorded, no new conquests, no significant advance. For tales of Norman achievement over this period we must look to Northern Europe, to the beaches of Kent and the field of Hastings;

where the Normans in Sicily were concerned, the years around 1066 were among the dullest in their history.

For Roger it must have been a time of maddening frustration. He never relaxed his pressure on the enemy; but with an army as diminutive as his the only possible tactics could be those of attrition, wearing the Saracens down by constant guerrilla activity and playing endlessly on their nerves so that they never felt safe from the danger of sudden raid or ambush. With this end in view he moved his temporary capital forward to Petralia, a town which he had captured already in 1062 but which now, its rocky escarpments newly fortified, provided an admirable advance headquarters from which all the country round Palermo was within easy range. Working out from here to the north, south and west, he was able to keep the Saracens on the defensive; but that was all. There was only one consolation; his opponents were now again hopelessly divided. Ibn al-Hawas had at first welcomed the arrival of the North African armies under Ayub and Ali; not long after Cerami, however, he had grown suspicious of the increasing power of the young princes, and the consequent dissension had quickly ripened into civil war. Even though Roger was himself still too weak to inflict any major defeat on the Saracens, he could at least watch with satisfaction while they did their utmost to destroy each other.

For Robert Guiscard too these were unprofitable years. He had stepped ashore in Calabria after the abortive expedition of 1064 only to find himself faced with a new revolt of his Apulian vassals. This, the most serious uprising with which he had yet had to contend, was led by Jocelin, Lord of Molfetta, and three of his own nephews; the brothers Geoffrey of Conversano and Robert of Montescaglioso and their cousin Abelard, whom the Guiscard had brazenly robbed of his inheritance after the death of Abelard's father, Duke Humphrey, seven years before. These three young men, making common cause with Byzantium through the agency of Perenos, Duke of Durazzo —who kept them well supplied with money and equipment from across the Adriatic—had rebelled in April 1064, soon after the Guiscard's departure for Sicily, and during the months of his absence had carried all before them. Robert's return in the late summer slowed their progress to some extent, but despite his efforts the revolt continued to spread. In 1066 it was further strengthened by a new contingent of Varangians from Constantinople, and by the end of that year not only Bari but the two other principal Apulian ports of Brindisi and Taranto were firmly in Greek hands.

The year 1067 marked a general stalemate, both in Apulia and Sicily. Then, in 1068, almost simultaneously for Robert and for Roger, came relief. At least where the Guiscard was concerned, it sprang from an unexpected quarter. For some years past the Byzantine Empire had been watching with mounting anxiety the steady westward advance of the Seljuk Turks. In little more than a generation these tribesmen from beyond the Oxus had subdued Persia and Mesopotamia. Baghdad, seat of the Arab Caliphate, had fallen to them in 1055; Armenia and Cilicia had followed; and now they were driving inexorably up through Asia Minor towards Constantinople itself. After the death of Constantine X Ducas in 1067 the Byzantines were left without an Emperor, imperial power having passed to his widow, the Empress Eudoxia; but it was clear that in the face of the Seljuk threat a leader must immediately be found, and so it was that Eudoxia was persuaded into a hasty if reluctant marriage with a certain Romanus Diogenes—so called, according to William of Apulia, because of his forked beard— a Cappadocian commander of long experience and undoubted bravery who, on 1 January 1068, was acclaimed Emperor. With the accession of Romanus and his immediate concentration on a desperate military effort against the Turks, the Greek initiative in Italy was halted; and, deprived from one moment to the next of all outside support, the rebellious vassals lost their nerve. One after another they capitulated, until by mid-February only Geoffrey of Conversano remained. Entrenched in his mountain fortress of Montepeloso he held out for several months, deserted by all his former allies, Greek and Norman alike. Then in June the Guiscard managed to suborn one of Geoffrey's officers, who, tempted by the promise of a fief of his own, secretly opened the gates. Robert's army poured in; Geoffrey, taken by surprise, had no course but surrender; the traitor duly received his fief; and the revolt was over.

The satisfaction which Robert Guiscard must have felt as he saw the Apulian opposition crumble and his own authority re-established would have been still greater had he known that, just about the time that he was besieging Montepeloso, his brother was dealing the final death-blow to all organised military resistance in Sicily. In the previous year the Saracen forces had been brought once again under a unified command. The Zirid troops under Ayub had met the army of Ibn al-Hawas in a last pitched battle, during which the redoubtable old Emir had been killed. Ayub had at once laid claim to the succession and had been formally recognised at Agrigento, Enna and Palermo. This gave him the degree of authority he needed to assume command of the entire Saracen forces. No longer hamstrung by internecine disputes, he now determined to take the first favourable opportunity of drawing the Normans out into an open conflict of the very kind which, since the defeat at Cerami, he and his compatriots had always sought to avoid; and so on a summer morning in 1068 the Norman army, out on one of its regular forays in the countryside south of Palermo, found its way blocked by a great Saracen host before the little town of Misilmeri.[1]

Roger must have been surprised at so radical a change in the enemy's tactics, but he does not seem to have been unduly disconcerted. Malaterra has left us a report of the speech which he made to his troops just before the battle. Smiling, he told them that they had nothing to fear; this was only the enemy that they had already beaten several times before. What if the Saracen leader had changed? Their own God remained constant, and if they put the same trust in Him as they had in the past He would accord them a similar victory. It is doubtful whether the Normans even needed these words of encouragement. Familiarity with Saracen military methods was fast breeding contempt; they themselves were, after all, soldiers of God, fulfilling His purpose; and the spoils once again promised to be excellent. All they awaited was Roger's signal; when he gave it, they charged.

It was soon over. According to Malaterra, hardly a single Saracen remained alive to carry the dreadful news back to Palermo. As things turned out, however, this proved unnecessary. Among the prizes of battle, and just as intriguing to Roger as the camels seized

[1] Known in Arab times as Menzil el Emir, 'the Emir's village'.

at Cerami, the Normans had carried off several baskets of carrier pigeons. The use of these birds had been well-known in classical antiquity but seems to have died out during the Dark Ages until, like so many other ancient arts and sciences, it was revived by the Saracens. It is unlikely that Roger had ever had any in his possession before, but the idea of using them at once for his own purposes was more than he could resist. He ordered that to the leg of each bird should be attached a scrap of material dipped in Saracen blood; the pigeons were then released, to fly back to Palermo with their macabre message. It was, in its way, the culmination of the psychological warfare that Roger had been carrying on for the past four years; and the effect that it had in the capital seems to have been all that he could have wished. 'The air,' writes Malaterra, 'was loud with the lamentations of women and children, and sorrow was great among them as the Normans rejoiced in their victory.'

The battle of Misilmeri broke the back of Saracen resistance in Sicily. Ayub had staked not only his army but his whole political and military reputation on its outcome, and he had lost. With what remained of his following he fled back to Africa, never to return. He left the island in total confusion, its Muslim population in despair. Their army shattered, their leaders gone, they could no longer hope to withstand Norman pressure. Palermo itself lay only ten miles or so from Misilmeri; they would defend it as best they could, but the truth could no longer be doubted—their capital was doomed. And once it had fallen to the Christians, the few Arab strongholds left remaining in the island would soon follow.

But Roger was not ready for the capital. Its inhabitants could not be expected to submit without a struggle; and his own forces, though adequate for pitched battles in mountainous terrain, were hardly sufficient for a siege. Besides, the capture of Palermo would be tantamount to the subjection of the whole island, and this in its turn would entail problems of control and administration which, with only a few hundred men at his disposal, he could not possibly envisage. There was fortunately no cause to hurry; the Saracens were far too demoralised to regroup themselves quickly. Better to wait, to suspend all further offensive operations until Robert had settled affairs in Apulia. Then the two could tackle the Sicilian problem together and in earnest.

The insurrection quashed, Robert Guiscard had treated his rebellious vassals with surprising clemency. Certain of them had had property confiscated, but a large number—including even Geoffrey of Conversano, who bore as much of the original responsibility as anyone—seem to have escaped scot-free. There was, as always with the Guiscard, a good reason for his attitude; he now needed every ally he could find for a last all-out drive against the Greeks. Current Byzantine preoccupations with the Seljuk menace offered him a magnificent and long-awaited opportunity for stamping out the final vestiges of imperial power from the peninsula, and now that his own internal difficulties had been settled he was free to seize it. His first step was to issue a general appeal to all Normans and Lombards in Italy to join him; the Greeks were deeply entrenched after their five centuries of occupation, and even without reinforcements from Constantinople they would be hard to dislodge. Then, hardly waiting for a response to his call, he marched with his full army to Bari.

Capital of Byzantine Langobardia, headquarters of the Greek army of the peninsula, the largest, richest and best defended of all the Apulian cities, Bari was the only possible target for the Guiscard's great offensive. He was, however, well aware that the successful siege of such a place would involve the greatest single military operation the Normans had undertaken in the fifty years since their arrival in Italy. The old city stands on a narrow promontory, jutting out northwards into the Adriatic; Robert was thus faced with the necessity of combining orthodox siege measures against the massive land walls with an immense naval blockade. Herein, apparently, lay his greatest disadvantage. The Normans had little experience of naval warfare. Such ships as they possessed had been used principally as transports, and even for these they were largely dependent on Greek crews from Calabria. For the Greek populations of Apulia, on the other hand, the sea was an integral part of their existence. Upon it they depended for their prosperity, their food, their defence, their communications, even their language and culture; and in consequence they had become known throughout the Mediterranean for the sureness of their seamanship and the accuracy of their navigation. Bari was well-supplied with ships of all kinds, and Perenos of Durazzo would probably be able to provide more if required. With such overwhelming advantages its inhabitants felt that they had little to fear.

And they showed it. Parading to and fro along the ramparts, brandishing aloft all the richest treasures they and their city could boast, using their gold and silver plate to reflect the sunlight into the eyes of the Normans uncomfortably clustered in the newly-dug ditches below, they mocked at the Guiscard's notorious rapacity, challenging him to come up and help himself to what he saw. But Robert, Malaterra tells us, was fully equal to this sort of thing, shouting gleefully back his thanks to the good citizens for keeping his property for him so carefully, and assuring them that they would not have charge of it much longer.

The Duke of Apulia was frequently thus underestimated, but never for very long. The first surprise for the Bariots came with the sudden appearance off their shores of a Norman fleet. Robert's Sicilian experiences, and in particular the abortive attempt on Palermo four years earlier, had taught him a lot about the value of sea power. Ever since then he had been collecting a navy from up and down the Adriatic coast; and though this had been originally intended for use against Saracens rather than Greeks, he had recently summoned every available vessel to Bari. Even now his sea force was embryonic in comparison with what it was to become a few years later; but it was adequate for his purpose. Drawing the ships into line abreast, and harnessing each one to its neighbours with great iron chains forged specially for the occasion, he formed them into a single, solid barrier encircling the entire promontory on which the city stood. The last ship at each end was moored to a heavily-fortified jetty; it could thus be easily boarded by the land forces who, crossing from ship to ship, could hasten to the relief of any part of the line that might be attacked. Meanwhile the army proper had disposed itself along the walls and was already blocking all approaches from the landward side. To the intense surprise of its citizens, Bari was surrounded. The taunts from the ramparts stopped abruptly. On 5 August 1068 the great siege began.

It was long and costly for both sides. The Greek leader Byzantius soon managed to slip through the Norman lines and, somehow evading his pursuers, to reach Constantinople, where he persuaded the Empress to agree to a relief expedition. (Luckily for him, he arrived after the departure of the Emperor for Asia Minor; Romanus, for whom the Normans seven hundred miles away were of little importance compared with the Seljuk hordes on his doorstep, might have shown less sympathy.) Early in 1069 the Greek ships appeared in the Adriatic. The Normans intercepted them and, after an early reverse, eventually sank twelve supply transports off Monopoli; but their cordon around Bari failed to stand up to a direct attack and several of the relief vessels, including that carrying Byzantius together with the new Catapan and a distinguished military commander, Stephen Pateranos, broke through into the harbour with arms and supplies for the beleaguered city. To the Normans their failure must have been not only humiliating but demoralising too; if they could not maintain their blockade Bari might hold out for ever. But the Duke of Apulia refused to give up. All through 1069 the siege dragged on and, despite the assassination of Byzantius in July, all through 1070 as well. Some time during the autumn Pateranos, growing worried by the threat of famine as well as by an increasingly vocal pro-Norman faction within the city, planned to have the Guiscard murdered in his turn. One evening when Robert was sitting at dinner in the wood-and-wattle hut which he occupied near the foot of the ramparts a hired assassin crept up and hurled a poisoned javelin at him through a chink in the wall; if we are to believe William of Apulia it was only Robert's severe catarrh, which prompted him at that precise moment to duck his head under the table to spit, that saved his life. Thanks to this happy chance he escaped unharmed; but on the following morning the Normans began work on a building of stone, without chinks, where their leader could live safe from any repetitions of the incident.

The winter of 1070–71 was hard for besiegers and besieged alike, both physically and in the toll it took of their morale. The stalemate had continued without remission for two and a half years. The city had been relieved before and might be relieved again; meanwhile, however, food supplies were dangerously low. Pateranos decided on a last appeal. The Turkish threat was, he knew, still grave. On the other hand he himself was not without influence in the capital and there was just a chance that he might now be able to persuade the Emperor Romanus, who had had some success in his recent campaigns, to devote part of his resources to the salvation of Apulia before it was too late. The Norman blockade once again proved inadequate; soon Pateranos was speeding on his way to Constantinople.

Robert Guiscard was equally determined to break the deadlock. His *cordon sanitaire*, however formidable its appearance, had not proved conspicuously successful, while on the landward side his army had failed to make the slightest impression on the city walls. Moreover, his enormous siege-towers were being burnt down with depressing regularity every time they were trundled into position. He had made more progress, to be sure, in the diplomatic field; his chief agent within the city, Argirizzo, was using his regular handsome subventions of Norman money to make free food distributions to the poor, and by this and other means converting most of the non-Greek inhabitants to pro-Norman sympathies; even among the Greeks themselves there was a growing feeling that continued resistance was useless and that the time had now come to negotiate. But such opinions carried no weight with the commanders of the city; the die-hards were still all-powerful, and a further Byzantine relief force, if it were to get through, could restore morale overnight. Robert, too, felt the need of some fresh blood, some injection of imagination and new ideas to restore impetus to his army. He sent for Roger.

Roger arrived from Sicily, bringing what men and ships he could, at the beginning of 1071. His appearance was perfectly timed. The Emperor Romanus, despite his preoccupation with the Seljuks, had been moved by Pateranos's appeal and had ordered that a relief force be immediately prepared at Durazzo, under the command of the Guiscard's arch-enemy Jocelin, the Norman lord of Molfetta, who had been a main instigator of the recent insurrection and had subsequently taken refuge in the imperial dominions, where he had been ennobled with the dukedom of Corinth. Pateranos had meanwhile returned to Bari with the news; he had also instructed the citizens to keep a close watch for the approach of the Byzantine ships and, as soon as they sighted them, to set flares along the walls of the city so that their rescuers might be guided safely and speedily into port. But the promise of relief, after so long a siege, went to the Bariots' heads. As Malaterra reminds us, 'nothing comes quickly enough for those who wait', and that same night, though the horizon remained dark, the air was loud with celebration and the ramparts seemed ablaze with flaming torches. To the besiegers below, such signs could mean only one thing: quickly Roger strengthened the watch on the sea side. Some time passed; then, one night, his lookouts reported the lights of many lanterns, 'shining like stars at the mast-tops'. At once he gave the order to embark, and the Norman ships sailed out to meet the enemy.

Malaterra maintains—though it seems unlikely—that the Greeks mistook the Norman ships for those of their compatriots coming out to welcome them, and were consequently caught off their guard. At all events the sea-battle that followed, though fierce, was one-sided. Even a major disaster which befell the Normans when a hundred and fifty of them, all in their heavy cuirasses, ran to the same side of their ship, capsized it and were drowned, failed to restore Byzantine fortunes. The main force of the attack had been directed on the Greek flagship—recognisable from its double mast-lights— and before long the wretched Jocelin found himself a prisoner on board Roger's own vessel, speeding back to the Norman camp where Robert Guiscard was waiting. Robert, Malaterra goes on,

had been in great fear for Roger's safety . . . and when he heard that the Count was returned safe and victorious, he still could not believe it until he saw him with his own eyes; but then he wept for joy, assuring himself that his brother had suffered no hurt. Roger now clothed Jocelin magnificently in the Greek style and offered him captive to the Duke.

The Normans had paid dearly enough for their first great naval victory, but it was decisive and complete. Of the twenty Byzantine ships involved, nine were sunk and not one was able to penetrate into the harbour of Bari. After a few more weeks of increasing despair the commanders within the city saw that they could hold out no longer. Argirizzo and his followers seized one of the principal towers, which, despite the entreaties of that section of the population that feared Norman vengeance more than starvation itself, they delivered up to Robert Guiscard; and on 16 April 1071 the Duke, with Roger at his side, rode triumphantly through the streets of Bari. Much to their surprise, he treated the Bariots well. Peace terms were reasonable and he even restored to the citizens certain lands outside the walls where the Normans had recently been in occupation. But then he could afford to be magnanimous. Since the time of Justinian Bari had been Greek—sometimes capital of a great and prosperous province, sometimes merely the centre of a tiny enclave from which the banners of Byzantium fluttered alone in a turbulent and hostile land; but on that day, the Saturday before Palm Sunday, those banners were struck for the last time.

13

PALERMO

Weep as you will your tears of blood,
O grave of Arabian civilisation.
Once this place was alive with the people of the desert,
And the ocean was a playground for their boats. . . .
O Sicily you are the glory of the ocean. . . .
You were the cradle of this nation's culture,
Whose fire like beauty burnt the world;
Sadi the nightingale of Shiraz wept for the destruction of Baghdad;
Dag shed tears of blood for the ruination of Delhi;
When the heavens destroyed Granada
It was the sorrowing heart of Ibn Badrun who lamented it;
Unhappy Iqbal is fated to write your elegy. . . .
Tell me your pains, I too am immersed in pain,
I am the dust of that caravan of which you were the destination.
Fill the colours in the pictures of the past and show them to me;
Make me sad by telling the tales of past days.

Iqbal, *Bāng-i Dara*. Tr. G. D. Gaur

THE core of the Norman army had now been fighting without interruption for more than three years. They had had no respite between the end of the vassals' rebellion with the capture of Montepeloso and the beginning, at Bari, of the last victorious round against the Byzantines. Now, after one of the hardest sieges of Italian history, and one moreover which led to the elimination of their oldest and stubbornest enemy, they might have expected a chance to rest. If so, they were disappointed. Summer was approaching; and summer, for Robert Guiscard, meant only one thing—the season for campaigning and conquest. South Italy was safe at last, and the Sicilian operation had been hanging fire too long. He had dealt with the Greeks; now it was the Saracens' turn.

One of Robert's greatest gifts as a leader was his ability to infect those under his command with his own energy and enthusiasm. Preparations began at once. They were different, both in scale and in kind, from those he had made for his last Sicilian expedition seven years previously; for in the interval the Normans had become a naval power. A curious aspect of their forebears' transformation, in the preceding century, from Vikings into Frenchmen was the speed with which they had blotted out their Scandinavian maritime traditions. Even in Normandy they seem to have shown little awareness of the potentialities of a strong navy; those who had come to settle in Italy had all arrived on foot or on horseback over the mountains, and for the first fifty years in their new homeland seem never to have taken to the sea except when, as in the short passage across the straits of Messina, it was unavoidable. Suddenly all this was changed. In Sicily Robert and Roger had together learnt that without an effective naval force, raised to the same standards of training and discipline as the army, there could be no further conquests. At Bari they had proved the corollary, that with such a force they could undertake and succeed in ventures hitherto unthinkable. In this knowledge, and the new, broader political outlook which it engendered, was to lie the greatness of the Kingdom of Sicily, so soon now to be established.

After the capture of Bari Robert sent his brother back at once to Sicily, while he himself hurried south along the coast to Otranto. Here his fleet had already begun to assemble—causing, incidentally, widespread alarm across the Adriatic in Durazzo, where Duke Perenos hastily ordered the strengthening of his own maritime defences—and here the Guiscard remained until, in late July, no fewer than fifty-eight fully-equipped ships, manned as usual by Greeks, set sail for Calabria. He did not travel with them; by taking the land route with the army he could settle some minor disaffection at Squillace on the way. But he met them a week or two later at Reggio and from there, in the first days of August 1071, the combined force crossed to Sicily.

Roger was waiting at Messina to discuss plans. The primary Norman objective was naturally a co-ordinated land and sea attack on Palermo, but as a preliminary to this he had an idea of his own in which he thought his brother might be interested. It involved Catania. Here was a strategically important harbour, roughly half-way down the east coast of the island and thus, while Norman strength was concentrated at Messina, within easy striking distance; moreover, having recently been the seat of Ibn at-Timnah, it was still fundamentally well-disposed to the Normans and might consequently be taken easily and cheaply. Roger's plan was simple. He would go to Catania, where he was sure of a courteous reception, and would seek permission for certain Norman ships to put in at the harbour there on their way to Malta. Such a request the Catanians could hardly refuse. Robert would then arrive with the fleet and enter without opposition. Once within the harbour, he and his men would have no difficulty in occupying the city.

It was not perhaps the most honourable of proposals but, as Roger knew, it was just the kind of idea that appealed to the Guiscard. And it worked perfectly. The Catanians were taken completely by surprise, realising how they had been tricked only when resistance was already hopeless. They fought courageously, but after four days were obliged to surrender. The Normans refortified the city and, leaving behind a strong garrison to ensure its future obedience, departed for Palermo. Roger, who was anxious to see Judith at Troina, travelled by land with the bulk of the army; Robert did not accompany him. Though as strong and energetic as ever, he was now in his middle fifties; and the way from Catania to Palermo was long and arduous, particularly in the full blaze of a Sicilian August. Memories of his last land approach were still painful. Besides, someone had to command his new fleet. This time he resolved to go by sea.

In the middle of the eleventh century Palermo was one of the greatest commercial and cultural centres of the Muslim world. Cairo doubtless exceeded it in size; Cordova may have outshone it in magnificence; but for beauty of situation, perfection of climate and all the broad range of amenities which together constituted the characteristic Arab *douceur de vivre*, Palermo was supreme. There are no detailed descriptions of the city at the time of its capture by the Normans, but change was slow in the Middle Ages and it must have been substantially the same as when it was visited by the Arab geographer Ibn Haukal just a century before. He has left us with a picture of a busy commercial metropolis boasting no less than three hundred mosques—in the largest of which, formerly a Christian church, were said to be preserved the mortal remains of Aristotle, suspended in a casket from the roof—countless markets, exchanges, streets of craftsmen and artisans and one of the first paper-mills in Europe.[1] The whole was surrounded by parks and pleasure-gardens, murmurous with fountains and running streams of the kind that the Muslim world understands so well. We can only guess at the size of its population; but the assiduous Abbé Delarc, basing himself on Ibn-Haukal's assurance that the butchers' guild alone numbered seven thousand members, has calculated that eleventh-century Palermo must have sheltered some quarter of a million inhabitants.

It was about the middle of August when Roger arrived with the bulk of the Norman army outside the capital. He had met with no serious opposition on his way from Catania, and now pitched his camp a mile or two to the east of the city, where the little river Oreto ran down to the sea. It was a district of rich palaces and pleasure-domes, of gardens and orange-groves where the great merchants sought solace from the heat and hubbub of the capital—very different from that verminous hilltop where the Normans had encamped seven years before. Still there was no opposition; Roger and his men simply helped themselves, and Amatus writes delightedly of how they shared out 'the palaces and all that they found outside the city, and gave to the nobles the pleasure-gardens full of fruit and watercourses; while even the knights were royally provided for in what was veritably an earthly paradise'.[2]

The Norman army had, however, little enough time to enjoy their idyllic surroundings. Here was a foretaste of the pleasures that

---

[1] Paper had been invented by the Chinese some time in the fourth century A.D. The technique was learnt by the Arabs after the capture of Samarkand in 707 and was introduced into Spain by the Moors in the first half of the eleventh century. From there it soon spread to Sicily. A deed signed by Roger in 1102 is still extant, and is the oldest dated European paper document yet discovered.

[2] 'Lo palaiz et les chozes qu'il troverent fors de la cité, donnent a li prince li jardin delectoz pleins de frutte et de eaue, et pour soi li chevalier avoient choses royals et paradis terrestre li.' (VI. 16)

awaited them, a material incentive to greater effort; but meanwhile there was work to be done. Robert Guiscard and the fleet were expected almost hourly; a suitable landing-place must be found and made safe for his disembarkation. At the mouth of the Oreto stood a small fortress known as the Castle of Yahya, which served the dual purpose of protecting the eastward approach to Palermo and of barring the river itself to hostile ships. It gave little trouble. The garrison, goaded by Roger's taunts, emerged to fight; within minutes fifteen of its soldiers had been killed and thirty more taken prisoner. The castle, renamed after St John, became a Norman stronghold and was soon afterwards converted by Roger, as a thank-offering for his success, into a church.[1]

The Duke of Apulia soon arrived with his fleet, and gave orders for an immediate attack. As the galleys sailed forward to block the harbour entrance the army, now forming a great arc with Roger on the left advancing north-west and Robert on the right pressing westwards along the coast, moved slowly up towards the bastions of the city. The Palermitans were ready. By now they can have had little if any hope of victory, but they knew that on their resistance depended the whole future of Islam in Sicily. Their fight was not just for Palermo but for the glory of the Prophet; if they were to perish in the attempt, had he not promised them the rewards of Paradise? For years they had been expecting this moment, strengthening their fortifications, walling up all but two or three of the city gates. The Norman vanguard, advancing to the ramparts, were greeted with a deluge of arrows and stones.

And so, a bare four months after the fall of Bari, the Normans found themselves engaged on another siege—this time for the greatest prize of all. It was considerably more eventful than its predecessor; the Saracens were bolder and more adventurous than the Greeks had been, making constant sorties and often deliberately opening one gate or another to entice the besiegers forward into hand-to-hand fighting. But their courage was of little avail. Nor did they have better fortune by sea. Robert Guiscard had abandoned

---

[1] In 1150 it became a leper hospital. The church, now known as S. Giovanni dei Lebbrosi, still stands, with a few traces of the old Saracen fortress remaining in the garden to the east of it.

his old tactics of throwing a permanent barrage of ships across the harbour; the idea had not been much of a success at Bari and would in any case have been impracticable, for topographical reasons, at Palermo. Instead he kept the bulk of his fleet at the mouth of the Oreto, ready for quick action as necessary. It proved to be a wise decision. William of Apulia tell us in his relentless hexameters of how one day—it must have been in the late autumn of 1071—a combined Sicilian and African fleet appeared off Palermo. Robert at once ordered all those under his command, Normans, Calabrians, Bariots and captive Greeks, to take Holy Communion; only then did they set sail to meet the enemy. At first they were hard pressed, and there were moments when it even seemed as though the Muslims, who had tented their ships with great lengths of red felt as a protection against missiles, were about to achieve at sea that victory which on land had always eluded them. Slowly, however, the Normans gained the upper hand, until by the end of the day the surviving remnants of the Saracen fleet were scuttling towards Palermo with all the speed of which their exhausted oarsmen were capable. Just in time the Palermitans ran their great chain—successor to that which the Pisans had carried off eight years before—across the harbour-mouth; but the Guiscard refused to be baulked of his prey. Somehow the Norman ships crashed through, and it was in the port of Palermo itself that their blazing firebrands completed the destruction of the Sicilian navy.

During the Middle Ages the greatest danger to any town undergoing a protracted siege was that of famine; and in Palermo famine was now spreading swiftly. The mountains of the Conca d'Oro, which had so often protected the capital in the past, had now become a liability, since they enabled the Norman army—larger than any of its predecessors though still probably less than ten thousand strong—to cover a far greater area than would otherwise have been possible. All the main approaches to the south and east were blocked by Roger's troops, while to the west his mobile patrols were just as effective at intercepting relief supplies as were Robert's pinnaces in the roadstead to the north. In the circumstances the Normans might have been content to wait patiently for the city's inevitable surrender; but they too were pressed. In December

messengers arrived with grave news for Robert; once again his
vassals had betrayed him. His nephew Abelard, still nursing the old
grievance, had taken advantage of the Guiscard's prolonged absence
to revolt for the second time, abetted by his younger brother
Herman and the lords of Giovinazzo and Trani. Together they had
won the support of Richard of Capua, now at the zenith of his
power, of Gisulf of Salerno and, quite probably, of the Byzantines.
The insurrection, having begun in Apulia, was now rapidly spreading through Calabria also. Robert was faced with a cruel decision;
should he return at once, letting Palermo slip once again from his
grasp, or should he remain to capture and consolidate, at the possible risk of his Italian domains? He decided to stay in Sicily,
but no longer to wait while disease and famine in the besieged city
slowly sapped its resistance. He would now have to force the issue.

In the heart of the old city of Palermo lay the district of Al-Qasr
—the Fortress—a quarter of crowded markets and *souks*, clustered
around the great Friday Mosque and ringed by its own nine-gated
wall. Here, at dawn on 5 January 1072, Roger's infantry attacked.[1]
The battle that followed was long and bloody. Fighting with all the
determination of their despair, the defenders poured out from the
gates and hurled themselves against their assailants. At first, by
sheer force of numbers and momentum, they put the Norman
infantry to rout, but just in time Robert Guiscard flung in his
waiting cavalry and with one mighty charge saved the situation.
Now it was the Saracens' turn to flee, the Normans hard on their
heels. They might have escaped with their lives, but the watchers
on the walls, knowing that they could not receive them back into
safety without also admitting their pursuers, slammed the gates in
their faces. Thus the bravest of Palermo's defenders found themselves trapped between the Norman cavalry and the unyielding
bastions of their own city. They went down fighting.

Now seven of the Guiscard's huge siege-ladders were slowly
nudged into position. To the Normans below, who had already
tried the temper of Saracen steel, they must have seemed to lead to

[1] Al-Qasr covered the area which now lies roughly between the Palazzo Reale and
the Quattro Canti, bounded by the Via Porta di Castro on one side and the Via del
Celso on the other.

certain death, and there was a general reluctance to take the first step. Finally, inspired by one of Robert's magnificent exhortations, a certain Archifrede began to climb. Two others followed. They reached the top unharmed, but in the ensuing struggle on the battlements their shields were smashed and they could go no farther. Somehow they managed to scramble back down the walls and lived to enjoy their glory, Archifrede at least having carved his name in a little corner of history. But Al-Qasr was still unconquered.

The Guiscard saw that he would have to change his tactics. By now the number of turbaned figures milling on the ramparts above him suggested that elsewhere in the city the defences might be under-manned. Telling Roger to maintain the pressure as strongly as ever, he slipped away with three hundred picked troops towards the north-east. Here, between Al-Qasr and the sea, lay the more modern quarter of Al-Khalesa, the administrative hub of Palermo, composed largely of public buildings—the arsenal and the prison, the *divan* and the government offices, the Emir's palace rising importantly from their midst. This district too was fortified, but less forbiddingly than its neighbours;[1] and, as the Guiscard had foreseen, it was now practically undefended. Up went the ladders and soon the Norman scaling-party, buoyant if a little blood-stained, was within the city and opening the gate to Robert and the rest of his men.[2] Their possession did not go undisputed. The defenders of the Fortress, panic-stricken at the news of their entry and furious at having been tricked, came charging down upon them. Another bitter struggle followed; the Saracens were powerless against the Norman swords, but it was nightfall before their last survivors picked their way back along the narrow corpse-strewn streets to the still defiant shadows of Al-Qasr.

That night the defenders of Palermo knew that they had lost. Some even now wished to continue the fight for the honour of their

[1] The walls extended along the sides of the square now formed by the Piazza della Kalsa (still preserving its old Arabic name), the Porta Felice, the church of S. Franceso d'Assisi and the Piazza Magione.

[2] Until a few years ago, the gate through which Robert is said to have entered could still be seen. It lay behind the first altar on the right in the little church of S. Maria della Vittoria, just off the Piazza dello Spasimo. But the Church—for no good reason that I have been able to discover—has now been demolished.

Faith, but counsels of prudence prevailed and early the following morning a delegation of notables called on the Duke of Apulia to discuss terms for the surrender of their city. Once again Robert showed himself generous in victory. There were to be no reprisals, he promised, and no further looting. All Saracen lives and property would be respected. He desired their friendship and asked only their allegiance and an annual tribute, in return for which the Normans would undertake to interfere neither with the practice of the Muslim religion nor with the application of the Islamic law.

Despite the crusading character of the whole Sicilian expedition —which the Guiscard had felt and stressed from its very outset— his toleration and amenability at this moment need cause us no surprise. He had no cause to foster the Saracens' hostility to their new overlords. Besides, he had to be free to return to the mainland as soon as possible and therefore wished to avoid protracted negotiations; Al-Qasr had still not surrendered and was quite capable of making trouble for days, even weeks, to come. In any case he was not naturally vindictive—Geoffrey of Conversano and the whole Greek population of Bari could vouch for that—and the rights which he was now granting to the Muslims were only those which they had always allowed in the past to the Christian communities under their domination. Nevertheless, such toleration was becoming increasingly rare—it was only twenty-seven years later that the soldiers of the First Crusade, entering Jerusalem, massacred every Muslim in the city and burned all the Jews in the great central synagogue—and the Saracens had expected harsher treatment. Great must have been their relief when, after protracting the negotiations for a couple of days so that face might be saved and due decorum preserved, they could give their final acceptance to the Norman terms. Even then, neither they nor Robert Guiscard himself can have understood the full significance of their agreement. For the Saracens of Sicily it marked the end of their political independence, but also the beginning of an age of unprecedented order and peace during which, under a strong but benevolent central government such as they themselves had never been able to achieve, their artistic and scientific gifts would be encouraged and appreciated as never before. For the Normans it became the foundation-stone of their new political philosophy, enabling them to build up a state that for the next hundred years would stand to the world as an example of culture and enlightenment, giving them an understanding and breadth of outlook which was to be the envy of civilised Europe.

On 10 January 1072 the Duke of Apulia made his formal entry into Palermo. He was followed by his brother Roger, his wife Sichelgaita, his brother-in-law Guy 'of Salerno and then by all the Norman chiefs who had fought with him in the campaign. They rode through the city to the ancient basilica of S. Maria, now hastily reconsecrated after two hundred and forty years' service as a mosque.[1] Here the service of thanksgiving was performed, according to the Greek rite, by the old Archbishop of Palermo—who, says that staunch Latin Malaterra, 'although a timid Greek, had continued to follow the Christian religion as best he could'—and, if we are to believe Amatus, the very angels of heaven added their voices to those of the congregation.

Their greatest objective now at last attained, the Normans had indeed good reason for rejoicing; the more so since news of the fall of Palermo had led to the spontaneous capitulation of several other regions, notably that of Mazara in the south-west. Subjection of the island was not yet complete; independent emirates still struggled on at Trapani and Syracuse, to say nothing of Enna where young Serlo had been conducting a guerrilla campaign for the past six months, harassing the local authorities and successfully preventing any relief expeditions from being sent to Palermo. But henceforth final pacification was only a matter of time. Meanwhile there was the question of feudal tenure to be settled. It created no difficulties. Robert Guiscard, already provisionally invested as Duke of Sicily by Pope Nicholas thirteen years before, claimed general suzerainty over the whole island. He reserved, however, for his own direct tenure only Palermo, half Messina and half of the Val Demone—the mountainous region of the north-east in whose conquest he had himself participated. The rest was to be held

[1] Traces of this original basilica still survive in the Chapel of the Incoronata attached to the present Cathedral.

by his tenant-in-chief Roger, now Great Count of Sicily, who would also keep all that he might personally acquire in the future, as would his two principal lieutenants, Serlo de Hauteville and Arisgot of Pozzuoli.

Serlo, alas, did not live to claim his fief. Some time during the summer of 1072 he and a handful of his men were tricked into an ambush near Nicosia, close by the confluence of the Cerami and the Salso. Outnumbered many times over by the Saracen cavalry, he knew that he was doomed; but leaping on to a huge rock, he and his followers fought magnificently to the end and sold their lives dearly. Malaterra maintains that those who slew him tore out his heart and ate it, hoping that his heroism might thus be transferred to themselves, and that his head was sent as a token of homage to 'the king in Africa'. When the sad news was brought back to Palermo Roger, who knew his nephew best and haf fought so often by his side, was inconsolable; Robert, we are told, 'made a manly show of hiding his own tears, not wishing to add to his brother's grief'. Serlo had been the best-loved, as well as the bravest, of all the young Norman knights. He had no chance to fulfil his bright promise; and now he faces a far unworthier adversary. As this book goes to press, a firm of contractors is at work methodically demolishing the rock on which he died—the *Pietra di Serlone* which, carved with a great cross, has stood for nine centuries in his memory, rising stark and sheer from the fields.

It was autumn before Robert Guiscard returned to the mainland. The most likely explanation is that he had by now learnt through his agents that the situation in Apulia and Calabria was less serious than he had previously feared, and that it was not expected to deteriorate further—a theory which appears more probable still in the light of the speed with which he was to restore order early the following year. At all events he stayed in Palermo throughout the summer of 1072, working with his brother on the construction of two strong citadels—one in Al-Qasr and the other, smaller, commanding the harbour entrance in Al-Khalesa—and on the establishment of a Norman administration to supplement the already existing Saracen institutions. At the head of this, as Governor of Palermo in his name, he appointed one of his principal lieutenants with the title of Emir. It was the first Sicilian example of that characteristic Norman readiness to adopt local forms and customs, and of that easy eclecticism which was to give their new country so much of its character and strength.

A day or two before his departure the Duke called a meeting of all the Saracen notables. The siege and capture of Palermo had, he explained, been a long and expensive operation, one that had cost him much money and, in particular, a very large number of horses. His hearers took the point. Hastily forestalling the specific demands which they knew would follow, they showered upon him presents of every kind, including all the horses and gold he needed; several, indeed, went even further, sending their sons to join his suite as an earnest of their fidelity and allegiance. And so, as 1072 drew to its close, loaded with the riches of his new dukedom and followed by his victorious army which already comprised most of the races of southern Europe and was now further adorned by the flower of young Saracen manhood, Robert Guiscard rode proudly back to Italy. In a life of uninterrupted achievement this had been his greatest triumph. Since the first half of the ninth century Sicily had been wholly or largely in Muslim hands, constituting the most forward outpost of Islam, from which raiders, pirates and expeditionary forces had maintained an unremitting pressure against the southern bastions of Christendom. The task of subduing them, a task which had baffled the two greatest Empires in the world, separately and in combination, for some two hundred and fifty years, had been left for him to perform; and he had performed it— apart from a few isolated pockets of resistance which would trouble him little and Europe not at all—with a handful of men in barely a decade. His satisfaction must indeed have been great; it would have been greater still had he been able to see into the future and so understand the tremendous historical implications of what he had done. For the Norman conquest of Sicily was, together with the contemporary beginnings of the *Reconquista* in Spain, the first step in the immense Christian reaction against the Muslim-held lands of the southern Mediterranean—that reaction which was one of the hallmarks of the later Middle Ages and which was shortly to develop into the colossal, if ultimately empty, epic of the Crusades.

PART TWO

THE BUILDING OF THE KINGDOM

14

POLARISATION

The Eastern Church has fallen away from the Faith and is now assailed on every side by infidels. Wherever I turn my eyes . . . I find bishops who have obtained office irregularly, whose lives and conversation are strangely at variance with their sacred calling. . . . There are no longer princes who set God's honour before their own selfish ends . . . and those among whom I live—Romans, Lombards and Normans—are, as I have often told them, worse than Jews or pagans.

> Letter from Gregory VII to Hugh of Cluny,
> 22 January 1075

ROBERT GUISCARD never returned to Sicily. His talents were those of a soldier rather than an administrator, and once a territory was safely in his hands it seemed to lose its attraction for him. In point of fact, the island when he left it towards the end of 1072 was by no means conquered. The Saracen Emirs at Trapani in the west and Taormina in the east still showed no sign of submission; the death of Serlo had given new impetus to the resistance in the centre; while south of a line drawn between Agrigento and Catania the Normans had scarcely even begun to penetrate. But for Robert such considerations were of little importance. Palermo was his: he was now Duke of Sicily in fact as well as in name. It was time to look to his mainland dominions and, once order there had been restored, to return to his rightful place on the European stage. Fortunately Roger seemed content to remain on the island. He could complete the task of pacification at his leisure. It would keep him occupied.

Roger asked nothing better. Though he lacked the Guiscard's superb *panache*, he was if anything more intelligent and certainly far more sensitive than his brother. Sicily had captured his imagination from the start and for ten years had continuously fascinated him. He had probably fallen under that curious spell with which the Islamic world so frequently beguiles unsuspecting northerners; but there was more to it than that. What Robert had seen merely as a bright new jewel in his crown, a territorial extension of the Italian peninsula inconveniently cut off by a strip of water, Roger recognised as a challenge. Those narrow straits, by protecting the island from the eternal squabbles of South Italy, offered Sicily possibilities of greatness far beyond anything that could be hoped for on the mainland. They also afforded him the chance of escaping, once and for all, from his brother's shadow.

Of all the tasks that lay ahead, the most important was to extend Norman authority throughout the island. This, he knew, would take time. After the Guiscard's departure reliable manpower was shorter than ever; with only a few hundred knights under his command Roger could not hope to do much more than consolidate his past conquests. For the rest, he could only trust in his diplomatic skill to sap the Saracen resistance until it died of inanition or at least grew weak enough for him to deal with by military methods. In other words, the Muslims must whenever possible be persuaded voluntary to accept the new dispensations. They must be treated with tolerance and understanding. And so they were. Norman Douglas, in *Old Calabria*, has monstrously slandered his namesakes by claiming that 'immediately on their occupation of the country they razed to the ground thousands of Arab temples and sanctuaries. Of several hundred in Palermo alone, not a single one was left standing.' Nothing could be more at variance with Roger's policy. Although from the early days of the conquest he did all he could to encourage Italian and Lombard colonisation from the mainland, his Saracen subjects still far outnumbered their Christian neighbours and it would have been folly for him to antagonise them unnecessarily; nor thus could he and his successors ever have created that atmosphere of interracial harmony and mutual respect which so characterised the Kingdom of Sicily in the following century.

Naturally the dictates of security came first. Taxation was high for Christian and Saracen alike, and more efficiently imposed than in former times. Roger also introduced, in an attempt to increase his military strength, an annual period of conscription which was doubtless no more popular than such measures ever are with those directly affected. In the outlying villages and the countryside there were also the inevitable odd cases where local governors victimised in varying degrees the populations under their authority. But for the most part—and certainly in Palermo and the major towns—the Saracens seem to have found little cause for complaint. Such of the mosques as they had originally converted from Christian churches were now reconsecrated, but all others were open, as they had always been, for the prayers of the Faithful. The law of Islam was still dispensed from the local courts. Arabic was declared an official language, on equal footing with Latin, Greek and Norman French. In local government, too, many provincial Emirs were retained at their posts. Others, potential troublemakers, were removed; but frequently the removal took the acceptable form of a bribe, perhaps of a free grant of land, to move to some other region where they would have less of a following. Nowhere on the island did the Normans show any of that brutality which was so unpleasant a feature of their conquest of England during this period. In consequence, the sullen resentment so much in evidence among the Saracens in the early days after the fall of Palermo was gradually overcome as Roger won their confidence; and many of those who had fled to Africa or Spain came back within a year or two to Sicily and resumed their former lives.

His new Christian subjects presented the Count with a different problem. Here he had to contend with a growing feeling of disillusion. The enthusiasm with which the Sicilian Greeks had first welcomed the Normans as liberators of their island from the infidel yoke was now wearing thin. The Frankish knights might emblazon the Cross on their banners, but most of them seemed a good deal more brutish and uncivilised than the Muslims. Besides, they followed the despised Latin liturgy; they crossed themselves with four fingers and from left to right; and, worst of all, their installation in Palermo had led to a hideous influx of Latin priests and monks, who were even appropriating some of the newly-recovered Greek churches for their own use. All over Europe the old antipathy between Greek and Latin, sharpened now by a generation of schism, had been growing steadily worse; in Sicily it was assuming unprecedented and ominous proportions.

Roger was fully aware of the danger. He had not forgotten that fearful winter at Troina ten years before, when the Greeks had made common cause with the Saracens against his army, and he and Judith had nearly died of cold and starvation. It had taught him, as nothing else could have done, that their loyalty was not to be taken for granted. Already he had given them full guarantees that their language, culture and traditions would be respected, but this was clearly not enough. He must now give them material help in the reconstitution of their Church. Apart from the aged Archbishop of Palermo, who after his eviction from the capital had been carrying on to the best of his tremulous ability from the neighbouring village of Santa Ciriaca, the Orthodox hierarchy of Sicily had completely collapsed. Such Basilian[1] monasteries as remained were moribund and penniless.

With his usual perspicacity Roger saw that this was the field in which he might most easily regain Greek support. Funds were put at the disposal of the Orthodox community for the reconstruction of their churches, and before long the Count had personally endowed a new Basilian foundation—the first of the fourteen that he was to establish or restore during the remainder of his life. Staffing of the new houses presented no problem. Life had been growing progressively more difficult for the Greek monks of Calabria, where both Robert Guiscard and the Pope—and Roger himself, in those areas under his control—were anxious to complete the process of Latinisation as quickly as possible. Many of them were doubtless only too pleased to be brought to Sicily, where they were welcomed not only by their co-religionists but also by the Government as a desirable reinforcement of the Christian population. One condition only did Roger make: there could no longer be any question of the Sicilian Greeks considering themselves ecclesiastically subject to the Patriarch in Constantinople, nor of their owing any allegiance to the Byzantine Emperor. Administratively they must be subordinated to the Latin hierarchy which was quickly taking shape in the island. Although the links between Sicily and Constanti-

[1] See p. 77 n.

nople had in practice long ceased to exist, the acceptance of Roman supremacy must have seemed to many Greeks a bitter pill to swallow; but Roger was careful to sugar it with gifts and privileges —even an occasional special exemption from the jurisdiction of the local bishops[1]—and they soon accepted the inevitable.

And so, from those earliest days in Palermo after Robert Guiscard had left all Norman-held Sicily in his effective control, the Great Count began to lay the foundations of a multiracial and polyglot state in which Norman, Greek and Saracen would, under a firmly-centralised administration, follow their own cultural traditions in freedom and concord. It was, in the circumstances, the only possible policy; but Roger's remarkable success in pursuing it could have been achieved only by a combination of his outstanding administrative gifts with a breadth of vision and eclectic intellectual appreciation rare in the eleventh century. He genuinely admired what he had seen of Muslim civilisation, and particularly Islamic architecture; while his apparent interest in the Greek Church was such that at one period the new Orthodox bishops were seriously discussing the possibility of converting him. Sicily was fortunate, at this crucial point in her history, in having a ruler whose own personal inclinations so closely corresponded with the island's needs.

These inclinations certainly made Roger's task easier than it might otherwise have been, but there were other factors which rendered it infinitely more complicated. One was the constant guerrilla warfare along the borders of Norman territory, a nagging reminder that there could be no peace or any major economic development while a good third of the land remained unsubdued. The other was Robert Guiscard. His powers, formidable as they were, could never quite keep pace with his ambitions; and time and again in the years to come Roger was to find himself obliged to lay aside his work in Sicily and hasten across the straits to his brother's aid.

As we have seen, the Duke of Apulia had been in no hurry to return to the mainland. The revolt of his nephews and their allies

[1] Similar exemptions had long been known in the Orthodox world. The monasteries of Mt Athos, for example, were originally independent of the Patriarch of Constantinople and subject only to the Emperor himself; and that of St Catherine on Mt Sinai was later to be elevated still further to the rank of a separate autocephalous Church.

had proved less dangerous than he had at first believed, and he had never doubted his ability to deal with it. Events proved him right. He rode straight to Melfi, where all the loyal vassals were summoned to meet him; then, as the year 1073 opened, he led his army eastward to the Adriatic coast. Trani fell on 2 February; Corato, Giovinazzo, Bisceglie and Andria followed in swift succession; the rebel leaders Herman and Peter of Trani were captured and imprisoned. In March Robert turned his attention to the little town of Cisternino. At first it seemed disposed to offer rather more serious resistance, but the Guiscard was in a hurry. Cisternino belonged, as he well knew, to his prisoner, Peter of Trani. A great wattle screen was hastily prepared, and the unfortunate Peter lashed to it. Behind this cover the Normans advanced. The defenders could not counter-attack without killing their liege-lord, and Peter himself could only cry out to them to surrender. They obeyed.

With the capture of Cisternino the Apulian rising was effectively at an end. It had been stamped out in less than three months. One hostile garrison still remained in Canosa,[1] where it had been stationed by Richard of Capua some time before; but the town was already short of water when Robert's army arrived, and it surrendered with scarcely a struggle. The Guiscard returned in triumph to Trani, where he again showed that sudden impetuous magnaminity which was one of his most endearing characteristics. It would not have been his way to feel any twinges of remorse for what he had done to Peter of Trani at Cisternino; his actions had had the desired effect, and for him the end always justified the means. But he clearly felt that his miserable prisoner had suffered enough. Excepting only the city of Trani itself, he now restored to him all the lands and castles he had previously confiscated.

Robert's clemency did not however extend to all his other erst-while enemies. With a minor Apulian baron he could afford to be generous, but Richard of Capua presented a more serious long-term threat to his position. For fourteen years, ever since the two chief-tains had together received their papal investitures at Melfi, Richard had been building up his influence in the west. He was now supreme

---

[1] Canosa di Puglia, between Melfi and Barletta, is not to be confused with Canossa in Tuscany, so soon to win its own memorable place in history.

in Campania and even as far north as Rome, where he had made himself indispensable to Pope Alexander—and to Hildebrand—during their trial of strength with the anti-Pope Honorius. Since then, however, he had broken his oath of vassalage and in 1066 had actually marched on Rome; and though on that occasion he had been driven back by Tuscan forces he was known still to have his eye on the Patriciate of the City. Like the Duke of Apulia, he had had his difficulties in the past with insubordinate vassals; and when, only a year or two before, he had gone so far as to appeal to his rival for help in putting down a revolt, Robert had obliged with a detachment of troops that he could ill afford to spare. More recently still, when the Guiscard had asked him for a contribution towards the Palermo expedition, Richard had promised a hundred and fifty knights, but they had never turned up—instead, they had presumably been sent to reinforce the Apulian rebels. It seemed a curious way for a brother-in-law to repay past kindnesses. The Prince of Capua was in short too strong, too slippery and too dangerous. He would have to be dealt with.

But the momentum of the past three months could not continue for ever. While busying himself in Trani with preparations for his great march against Capua, Robert—whose gigantic frame normally shrugged off fevers and distempers like so many drops of rain—was struck down by a grave illness. Hoping that a change of air might restore him, he had himself carried to Bari; but his condition steadily worsened. Sichelgaita, as always at his side, could no longer hope for his life. Hastily she summoned his vassals and as many Norman knights as she could muster and forced them to elect, as her husband's successor, her eldest son Roger—nicknamed Borsa, the purse, from his early-ingrained habit of counting and recounting his money. He was a weak and hesitant thirteen-year-old who gave the impression that a childhood spent with Robert and Sichelgaita had been too much for him. This would indeed have been understandable enough; but it did not make him a good choice as future Duke of Apulia, particularly since his elder half-brother Bohemund—the Guiscard's son by his cast-off wife Alberada of Buonalbergo—had already distinguished himself in the field and was clearly the only one of his father's sons to have inherited any of the Hauteville qualities. On the other hand, Bohemund does not seem to have been present at Bari, and Sichelgaita was. Her son, she pointed out, being half a Lombard, would be more acceptable to the Lombard populations of Apulia than any full-blooded Norman; and her personality was not such as to invite contradiction. And so Roger Borsa was elected with only one dissentient voice—that of his cousin Abelard, still nursing his old grievance and claiming that he, as Duke Humphrey's son, was the rightful heir to the dukedom. When the vassals, their duty done, took leave of the mighty leader with whom, in one way or another, they had fought for so long, not all hearts may have been equally heavy; but in each there must have been a consciousness that things could never be the same again— that Apulia itself would in future be a diminished place. And indeed, within a few days of their return to their homes, the news was spreading like wildfire the length and breadth of the peninsula: Robert Guiscard was dead.

Word reached Rome towards the end of April, just as the city was mourning another loss—that of Pope Alexander. This time, at least, there was to be no trouble over the succession: the choice was too obvious. Archdeacon Hildebrand had already wielded effective power in the Curia for some twenty years, during many of which he had been supreme in all but name. When, according to a carefully prearranged plan, the crowd seized him during Alexander's funeral service, carried him to the Church of St Peter in Vinculis and there exultantly acclaimed him Pope, they were doing little more than regularising the existing state of affairs; and the canonical election that followed was the purest formality. Hastily he was ordained a priest—a desirable qualification to the Papacy which seems to have been overlooked during the earlier stages of his career—and was immediately afterwards enthroned as Supreme Pontiff in the name of Gregory VII.

Of the three great Popes of the eleventh century—Leo IX, Gregory VII and Urban II—Gregory was at once the least attractive and the most remarkable. Whereas the other two were aristocrats, secure in the possession of all that noble birth and a first-class education could bestow, he was a Tuscan peasant's son, Lombard

by race, whose every word and gesture betrayed his humble origins.[1]
They assumed the Papacy almost as of right; he achieved it only
after a long and arduous—though increasingly influential—apprenticeship in the Curia, and for no other reason than his immense
ability and the power of his will. They were both tall, and of out
standingly distinguished appearance; he was short and swarthy,
with a pronounced paunch and a voice so weak that, even making
allowance for his heavy regional accent, his Roman colleagues often
found it difficult to understand what he said. He had none of Leo's
obvious saintliness, nor any of Urban's adroit political instinct or
diplomatic flair. He was neither a scholar nor a theologian. And yet
there was in his character something so compelling that he almost
invariably dominated, automatically and effortlessly, any group of
which he found himself a member.

His strength lay, above all, in the singleness of his purpose.
Throughout his life he was guided by one overmastering ideal—the
subjection of all Christendom, from the Emperors down, to the
authority of the Church of Rome. But just as the Church must be
supreme upon earth, so too must the Pope be supreme in the Church.
He was the judge of all men, himself responsible only to God; his
word was not only law, it was the Divine Law. Disobedience to
him was therefore something very close to mortal sin. Never before
had the concept of ecclesiastical autocracy been carried to such an
extreme; never before had it been pursued with such unflinching
determination. And yet this very extremism was to prove ultimately
self-destructive. Confronted by adversaries of the calibre of Henry
IV and Robert Guiscard, as determined as himself but infinitely
more flexible, Gregory was to learn to his cost that his persistent
refusal to compromise, even when his principles were not directly
involved, could only bring about his downfall.

One of the Pope's first official acts on his accession was to write
his condolences to Sichelgaita. The letter is not included among his
collected correspondence, but the version given by Amatus so

---

[1] Hildebrand, or Hildeprand, was a common Lombard name. His father's name,
Bonizo, is an abbreviation of Bonipart, which seven centuries later we find again in the
form of Buonaparte. Napoleon was also of Lombard stock. He and Hildebrand had
much in common.

precisely expresses what we know of Gregory's thinking that it may well have been based on an authentic text. It runs as follows:

The death of Duke Robert, that dearest son of the Holy Church of Rome, has left the Church in deep and irremediable sorrow. The Cardinals and all the Roman Senate do greatly grieve at his death, seeing themselves thereby brought low. . . . But in order that Your Grace should know of Our goodwill and of the perfect love which we bore your husband, We now request you to inform your son that it is the pleasure of the Holy Church that he should receive at her hands all those things which his father held from the Pope Our Predecessor.

It was, by any standards, a profoundly hypocritical letter. Gregory had no cause to love Robert. The Duke had not lifted a finger to help the Papacy in its recent tribulations, while his brother Geoffrey and Geoffrey's son Robert of Loritello were even now ravaging valuable Church lands in the Abruzzi. On the other hand, the Pope was genuinely anxious that the Guiscard's successor should receive a proper investiture for his lands and titles; the Hautevilles were papal vassals, and he had no intention of allowing them to forget it. Roger Borsa was by all accounts a gentle and pious young man; he should prove a lot more amenable than his tempestuous father. In the circumstances, therefore, it can hardly have been a happy surprise for Pope Gregory when a week or two later he received a reply to his letter, not from a sorrowing widow but from Robert Guiscard himself, now well on his way to complete recovery. He was happy to inform the Pope—and through him, doubtless, the Cardinals and the Senate—that the reports of his death had been without foundation. However, he continued cheerfully, he had been most touched by the kind things the Pope had said about him, and asked nothing more than to be allowed to remain His Holiness's most obedient servant.

Robert must have enjoyed dictating his letter; but he too was anxious for a formal reinvestiture. During his Sicilian campaigns the Pope's blessing had been of little significance except as a means of boosting his army's morale; but now that he was concentrating once again on his Italian possessions—and perhaps already beginning to nurse plans for vast enterprises beyond them—a renewed compact with Gregory could only strengthen his hand. It would have a psychological effect on the more obstreperous of his vassals and, more important still, would make it harder for the Pope to withhold his support if Robert should ask it. And so, through the good offices of Abbot Desiderius of Monte Cassino, an interview was arranged between Gregory and the Guiscard, to take place at Benevento on 10 August 1073.

The occasion proved a total fiasco. Indeed it seems possible that the two never even met. There were, for a start, serious difficulties over protocol. The Pope wished to receive Robert in his Benevento palace; the Duke, on the other hand, who may have had some advance warning of an assassination attempt, refused to set foot within the city and proposed that the meeting should take place outside the walls—a solution which Gregory found inconsonant with his papal dignity. Poor Desiderius must have had a thankless task, shuttling backwards and forwards between these two determined and mutually suspicious characters, arguing and cajoling with each in turn in the relentless heat of a Campanian August; but even if his efforts were successful and Duke and Pontiff were at last brought face to face, their confrontation seems to have done more harm than good. The only result was a complete rupture of relations between them—and a recognition by both parties that alliance was impossible and that alternative arrangements would have to be made.

There is something mysterious about the whole Benevento affair. The recent correspondence between the two parties may not have been notable for its sincerity, but it was outwardly cordial—even fulsome—and it revealed on both sides a genuine desire for discussions. What could have happened to alter the situation so radically? The breakdown cannot be ascribed entirely to the Guiscard's suspicions, nor to Gregory's pride. It may be that the Pope had insisted, as an essential preliminary to any agreement, that Robert put a stop to the continual incursions of his brother and nephew into the Abruzzi, and that the Duke had declared himself unable or unwilling to take the necessary action. Certainly Gregory felt very strongly on the matter: he was soon afterwards to send to the affected area a bishop, notorious for his strong-arm methods, whom he had applauded two years earlier for having deprived a number of rebellious monks of their eyes and tongues. But there is no evidence that the Abruzzi question was even raised at Benevento. All we know is that the Pope, on leaving the city, made straight for Capua; that he there confirmed Prince Richard in all his possessions; and that the two of them forthwith concluded a military alliance against the Duke of Apulia.

Back in Rome in the autumn of 1073, Pope Gregory was worried. Some months earlier, shortly after his accession, he had received a secret and urgent appeal from the new Byzantine Emperor, Michael VII, in Constantinople. The Empire of the East was facing the gravest crisis in its history. Two years before, at the very moment when Robert Guiscard was eliminating, by the capture of Bari, the last vestiges of Greek power in Italy, the Byzantine army under the Emperor Romanus IV Diogenes had suffered total annihilation by the Seljuk Turks near the Armenian town of Mantzikert. The whole of Asia Minor now lay open to the invaders, and from Asia Minor it was but a short leap to the capital itself. Romanus was taken prisoner by the Seljuks; their leader, Alp Arslan, soon gave him back his liberty, but on his return to Constantinople Romanus found that his stepson Michael had replaced him on the imperial throne. After a brief and futile attempt at a restoration, he had surrendered to the new government on receiving guarantees of his personal safety. With his long experience of Constantinople, he should have known better. The guarantees were forgotten; the old ex-Emperor's eyes were put out with red-hot irons, and five weeks later he was dead. Michael himself had played little active part in these events. He was a scholarly recluse with no appetite for political intrigue, content to be led by his chief mentor and minister, the brilliant but odious Michael Psellus.[1] And it may well have been on Psellus' advice that he had written to the Pope imploring him to raise a Crusading army by which Eastern Christendom might finally be delivered from the fearful shadow of the infidel.

Gregory was deeply affected by the appeal. The two Churches

---

[1] The character of Psellus is nicely illustrated by the letter which he wrote at this time to the dying Romanus. Himself the principal author of the old man's downfall, he now congratulated him on the fortunate martyrdom by which, he argued, the Almighty had deprived him of his eyes because He had found him worthy of a higher light.

might be in schism, but he still considered himself responsible before God for the entire Christian world. Besides, this was a heaven-sent opportunity to bring the Byzantines back once again into the Roman fold, and he was determined not to let it pass him by. On the other hand he could not possibly launch an effective Crusade in the east while he was under a constant threat at home from Robert Guiscard and his Normans. They must be eliminated, once and for all. But how? He had few expectations of his new alliance with Richard of Capua, which he had concluded largely to prevent the two Norman leaders from joining forces themselves. Robert Guiscard was unquestionably the stronger of the two, but it was plain from their years of intermittent warfare that neither would ever be able to achieve a decisive victory over the other. The Pope's only remaining southern ally, Gisulf of Salerno, was an even more hopeless case. The Normans had already relieved him of nearly all the territory that had once made his principality the most powerful in the peninsula; and now, as the winter of 1073 drew near, came the news of another serious blow to his fortunes: Amalfi had voluntarily placed herself under the protection of the Duke of Apulia. It was Gisulf's own fault. He had never forgiven the Amalfitans for the part they had played in the assassination of his father twenty-one years before. Though never strong enough to capture the city by force of arms, he had always made life as unpleasant as he could for its people; and many hair-raising tales were told of the sufferings endured by such luckless Amalfitan merchants as from time to time fell into his clutches.[1] When in 1073 Duke Sergius of Amalfi died, leaving only a child to succeed him, his subjects had therefore taken the one sensible course open to them. Robert had naturally accepted their offer. He loathed his brother-in-law Gisulf and had long had his eye on Salerno—which, but for the family feelings of Sichelgaita, he would probably have attacked long before. The possession of Amalfi would make his task much easier when the moment came.

[1] Amatus speaks of one unfortunate victim whom Gisulf kept in an icy dungeon, removing first his right eye and then every day one more of his fingers and toes. He adds that the Empress Agnes—who was now spending much of her time in South Italy—personally offered a hundred pounds of gold and one of her own fingers in ransom, but her prayers went unheard.

This new and unexpected success for the Guiscard disturbed Pope Gregory more than ever. At once he set to work to raise an army. As 1074 opened, papal messengers were already speeding north from Rome—to Beatrice of Tuscany and her daughter Matilda, and to Matilda's husband, Godfrey the Hunchback of Lorraine,[1] to Azzo, Marquis of Este and William, Count of Burgundy, who was further instructed to pass the appeal on to Counts Raymond of Toulouse and Amadeus of Savoy. The Pope left them in no doubt of his intentions, nor of the order of priority in which he had determined to carry them out. He was not, as he was careful to emphasise, gathering this great host together simply to shed Christian blood; indeed he hoped that its very existence might prove an adequate deterrent to his enemies. 'Furthermore,' he added, 'we trust that yet further good may emerge in that, once the Normans are subdued, we may continue to Constantinople to the aid of those Christians who, beset by most frequent Saracen attacks, do insistently implore our aid.'

The replies to these letters seem to have been prompt and favourable. By March the Pope was able to announce at the Lenten Synod that his army would assemble the following June at a point near

---

[1] At this point the family relationships between the House of Tuscany and Lorraine have become rather involved, since Beatrice's stepson was also her son-in-law. Thus the position was as follows:

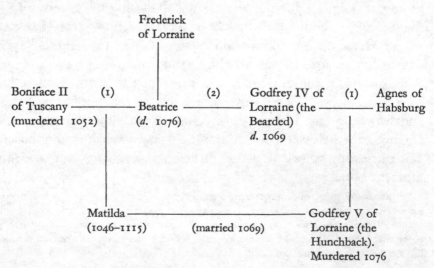

Viterbo, whence it would march against the Duke of Apulia and his followers—whom, for good measure, he now excommunicated. As the weeks went by and more and more troops gathered at the appointed place his spirits began to rise again, until at the beginning of June he felt strong enough to give his enemy one more chance Peremptory as always, he summoned Robert to meet him at Benevento for a final conference.

Now it was the Guiscard's turn to feel alarm. A generation ago, at Civitate, he and his brothers and Richard of Aversa had successfully routed a papal army, but in those days the Normans were united. This time they were split, the Prince of Capua firmly aligned with the Pope. Robert and his men, fighting without allies, would have to proceed with caution. But perhaps after all there was still a chance of agreement. The reply he returned to Gregory was unctuously humble. His conscience was clear; he had never given the Pope cause for offence or disobeyed him in any way; and he would of course be honoured, anywhere and at any time, to present himself before His Holiness. And so, accompanied by a heavy escort —for he still did not trust Gregory an inch—he rode back to Benevento.

In his long and rampageous career Robert Guiscard had often been astonishingly lucky; but never had Fortune smiled on him more kindly than at this moment. Three days he waited at the gates of the city; the Pope never appeared. Just as all Gregory's plans had been laid and his army stood in readiness for the assault, dissension had broken out in its ranks. Once again the fault lay with Gisulf of Salerno. In recent years the conduct of his ships on the high seas had come dangerously close to piracy. The Amalfitans had probably suffered most, but many Pisan merchantmen had fared little better. When, therefore, the Pisan contingent among the troops provided by the Countess Matilda found themselves face to face with Gisulf in person, they made no secret of their feelings towards him. As soon as Gregory saw what was happening, he hastily packed the Prince of Salerno off to Rome; but it was too late. Sides had been taken up and the whole army was split. Within days it had broken up in confusion.

For the Pope this was disaster—and, where his relations with the

Guiscard were concerned, an intense personal humiliation. Everything seemed to conspire against him. The army in which he had
put his trust had disintegrated without taking a step into Norman
territory; the Crusade which he had as good as promised the Byzantine Emperor and on which he had staked his reputation was more
remote than ever; the opportunity for reuniting the Churches under
his authority was slipping once again from his grasp. Worst of all,
he—the Vicar of Christ on earth—had been made to look a fool in
front of his enemies. And even this was not the end of his tribulations. A party of the Roman aristocracy—disaffected as always—
was now actively plotting to get rid of him. He did not know that
one of his own cardinals, a member of this group, had recently
approached Robert Guiscard and offered him the imperial crown in
return for his assistance; or that Robert, seeing that the whole plan
was hopelessly unrealistic, had refused to become involved. Even
if he had, the knowledge would hardly have given him much consolation.

On Christmas Eve 1075 his enemies struck. The Pope was
dragged from the altar in the crypt of S. Maria Maggiore when he
was saying Mass, and carried off to a secret prison. He was soon
found and released by an indignant populace, and had the satisfaction
of personally saving his erstwhile captor from being lynched; but
not before the world had seen just how shaky were the foundations
on which his throne rested.

And now, when he was least ready to sustain it, Gregory received
his first intimation of the greatest blow of all—that from which he
would never altogether recover. Young Henry IV, King of the
Romans and Western Emperor-elect, was preparing to descend into
Italy, to dethrone the Pope and to have himself crowned Emperor.

15

EXCOMMUNICATIONS AND
INVESTITURES

Henry, not by usurpation but by God's holy will King, to Hildebrand, not Pope but false monk.

This salutation thou hast deserved, upraiser of strife, thou who art cursed instead of blessed by every order in the Church. . . . The archbishops, bishops and priests thou hast trodden under thy foot like slaves devoid of will. . . . Christ has called us to the Empire but not thee to the Papacy. Thou didst acquire it by craft and fraud; in scorn of thy monastic cowl thou didst obtain by gold favour, by favour arms, and by arms the throne of peace, from which thou hast destroyed peace. . . .

I, Henry, by God's grace King, with all our bishops call on thee: Descend, descend!

Letter from Henry IV to Pope Gregory,
Worms, 24 January 1076

HENRY IV had come to the throne of Germany shortly before his sixth birthday. He was now twenty-five. He had not made a particularly auspicious start to his reign; his mother, the Empress-Regent Agnes, had been totally unable to control him, and after a wild boyhood and a deeply disreputable adolescence he had acquired, by the time he assumed power at the age of sixteen, a reputation for viciousness and profligacy which augured ill for the future. This reputation he was at last beginning to live down, but throughout his unhappy life he remained hot-tempered, passionate and intensely autocratic. Thus as he grew to manhood he became ever more resentful of the increasing arrogance of the Roman Church and, in particular, of those reformist measures by which it was seeking to cast off the last vestiges of imperial control. Henry had been too young to oppose Nicholas II's decree regulating papal elections, but he was determined that this separatist trend should go no further. Even before the elevation of Hildebrand to the Papacy it was plain that a clash between Church and Empire was inevitable. It was not long in coming.

The scene was Milan. Nowhere in Italy did the spirit of ecclesiastical independence from the dictates of Rome burn more brightly than in this old capital of the North, where an individual liturgical tradition had been jealously preserved since the days of St Ambrose seven centuries before; nowhere were the new Roman reforms, especially those relating to simony and clerical celibacy, more bitterly resented by the diehards. On the other hand the government of the city was now dominated by a radical left-wing party known as the Patarines, who, partly through genuine religious fervour and partly through hatred of the wealth and privilege that the Church had so long enjoyed, had become fanatical supporters of reform. Such a situation would have been explosive enough without imperial intervention; but in 1072, during a dispute over the vacant archbishopric of Milan, Henry had aggravated matters by giving formal investiture to the anti-reform candidate while fully aware that Alexander II had already approved the canonical election of a Patarine. Here was an act of open defiance that the Church could not ignore; and at his Lenten Synod of 1075 Hildebrand—now Pope Gregory VII—categorically condemned all ecclesiastical investitures by laymen, on pain of anathema. Henry, furious, immediately invested two more German bishops with Italian sees and added for good measure a further Archbishop of Milan, although his former nominee was still alive. Refusing a papal summons to Rome to answer for his actions, he then called a general council of all the German bishops and, at Worms on 24 January 1076 formally deposed Gregory from the Papacy.

The King had long been eager to come to Rome for his imperial coronation, but his quarrel with successive Popes over investitures had prevented him. After the Council of Worms, however, he saw that his journey could no longer be postponed. Gregory had not reacted to his deposition with the savagery that was already rumoured,[1] but he was clearly not going to accept it lying down. If

---

[1] Writing at a time when castration and mutilation were commonplaces in Constantinople, Anna Comnena harps on the subject with morbid fascination. 'He vented

therefore the Council were not to be held up to ridicule, he would have to be removed by force and a successor installed. The need was for a swift, smooth military operation; and while it was being prepared, steps must be taken to deprive the Pope as far as possible of local Italian support. North of Rome this would be difficult; the formidable Countess Matilda of Tuscany was a devout champion of the Church, her loyalty to Gregory unwavering. To the South, however, the prospects looked more hopeful. The Duke of Apulia in particular seemed to have no great love for the Pope. He might well overlook his feudal responsibilities if it were made worth his while to do so. Once he and his men could be persuaded to participate in a combined attack on Rome, Gregory would not stand a chance.

The importance which Henry attached to the Guiscard's friendship can be judged from his choice of ambassadors—Gregory, Bishop of Vercelli, one of his staunchest supporters against papal claims, and Eberhard, his Chancellor for Italy. They reached Robert, probably at Melfi, early in 1076 and formally offered him an imperial investiture of all his possessions; they may even have mentioned the possibility of a royal crown. But the Duke was unimpressed. His own position was for the moment secure—more so than it had been for a considerable time. He now enjoyed complete freedom of action throughout his domains, and he saw no reason to jeopardise this by giving Henry further excuses to meddle in South Italian politics. His reply was firm, if a trifle sanctimonious. God had given him his conquests; they had been won from the Greeks and Saracens, and dearly paid for in Norman blood. For what little land he possessed that had ever been imperial, he would consent to be the Emperor's vassal, 'saving always his duty to the Church'—a proviso

his rage on Henry's ambassadors; first he tortured them inhumanly, then clipped their hair with scissors . . . and finally committed a most indecent outrage upon them, which transcended even the insolence of barbarians, and so sent them away. My womanly and princely dignity forbids my naming the outrage inflicted on them, for it was not only unworthy of a high priest, but of anyone who bears the name of a Christian. I abhor this barbarian's idea, and still more the deed, and I should have defiled both my pen and my paper had I described it explicitly. But as a display of barbaric insolence, and a proof that time in its flow produces men with shameless morals, ripe for any wickedness, this will alone suffice if I say that I could not bear to disclose or relate even the tiniest word about what he did. And this was the work of a high priest. Oh, justice!' (*The Alexiad*, Bk I, 13, tr. Dawes).

which, as he well knew, would make his allegiance valueless from Henry's point of view. The rest he would continue to hold, as he had always held it, from the Almighty.

It is hard to believe that the ambassadors took the Guiscard's protestations of loyalty to the Church at their face value, but they returned laden with gifts and well pleased by their reception. Even if Robert was not prepared to compromise his own position to oblige King Henry, the last thing he wanted was to antagonise him at such a moment. The stage was being set for the direct confrontation of the two most powerful figures of Western Europe. Its outcome was still impossible to predict, but one thing was certain— the ensuing upheaval would create opportunities for Norman advancement which must not be missed. Hurriedly the Guiscard sent a message to Richard of Capua. Their constant skirmishing had always been indecisive and ineffectual; it was unworthy of them both. All Normans must stand together if they were to profit by the coming crisis. Could not the two leaders now meet to discuss an end to the hostilities between them?

On his way to Capua, the messenger encountered one of Richard's men, bound for Melfi with a similar proposal. A conference was arranged—probably on neutral ground at Monte Cassino, since we know that Abbot Desiderius was present as mediator. He was tired of seeing his monastery lands used as a perpetual battleground, and had long worked for such a reconciliation.[1] In fact the interview gave him little trouble—far less than those nightmare days with Guiscard and the Pope at Benevento three years before. Neither side had made any significant conquests at the expense of the other and both were genuinely anxious to reach an understanding, so the terms were simple enough. Each leader agreed to return what he had won and revert to former frontiers. Once this had been arranged, there was no obstacle to a treaty of alliance.

Meanwhile Pope Gregory had acted with his usual vigour. At his Lenten Synod of February 1076 he deposed all the rebellious

---

[1] Chalandon believes (I, 243) that Desiderius was acting on the Pope's instructions. This seems unlikely. Gregory would not have been pleased to see the Normans reunited at such a moment; nor would he have encouraged leading members of his hierarchy to negotiate with excommunicates.

bishops and thundered out his sentence of excommunication on King Henry himself. The effect in Germany was cataclysmic. No reigning monarch had incurred the ban of the Church since Theodosius the Great seven centuries before. It had brought that Emperor to his knees and it now threatened to do the same for Henry. The purely spiritual aspect did not worry him unduly—that problem could always easily be solved by a well-timed repentance—but the political consequences were serious indeed. In theory the ban not only absolved all the King's subjects from their allegiance to the Crown, but it also rendered them in their turn excommunicate if they had any dealings with him or showed him obedience. If it were strictly observed, therefore, Henry's government would disintegrate and he would be unable to continue any longer on the throne. Suddenly he found himself isolated. He had badly overplayed his hand.

The Pope's grim satisfaction can well be imagined as he watched his adversary struggling to retain the loyalties of those around him; but it must have been tempered by the news reaching Rome from the South. With Robert and Richard now once more a united force, his own position in Italy was gravely endangered. There was still a chance that Henry might extricate himself from his present difficulties and march on the Eternal City, and if this were to occur it was essential that the Norman army should be firmly aligned on the papal side. The situation was, however, complicated by the uncomfortable fact that the Duke of Apulia also lay under sentence of excommunication. Gregory's highly developed sense of his own prestige would never allow him to make the first move towards lifting it, but he could at least arrange for a few hints to be dropped. Already in March 1076 we find him writing to the Bishop of Acerenza, instructing him to give absolution to Count Roger and his men before their return to Sicily and adding—what was probably the real point of the letter—that if Roger were to raise the subject of his brother's position he should be reminded that the doors of the Church were always open to the truly repentant, Robert included. The Pope was ready 'to receive him with a father's love . . . to loose him from the bonds of excommunication and to number him once again among his divine sheep'.

But as spring came to South Italy, and with it the fine campaigning weather, such consoling reflections as these were far from Robert's mind. King Henry would clearly have to delay his journey until he could restore his position among his own vassals; meanwhile the Norman army was once more united and it seemed a pity not to take full advantage of the fact. The time had come for the Duke of Apulia and the Prince of Capua to turn their combined attention towards Salerno, where Prince Gisulf was growing daily more insufferable. Knowledge of his powerlessness against his detested brother-in-law had only increased his tendency to arrogance and bluster. His behaviour had alienated his allies one by one; and his few remaining friends—including Abbot Desiderius and even the Pope, who had no wish to see his last South Italian supporter swallowed up—had vainly begged him, in his own interest, to show a little moderation. Eventually Sichelgaita herself, knowing that Robert's patience could not be much longer restrained, made a final attempt to bring her brother to his senses; but Amatus— admittedly a biased reporter where Gisulf is concerned—writes that the Prince merely flew into one of his rages and warned his sister that she would soon find herself in widow's weeds.

It was his last chance, and he had thrown it away. In the early summer of 1076 Norman tents sprang up before the walls of the city and a Norman fleet drew up in line across the harbour-mouth. The siege of Salerno had begun.

Gisulf's position was hopeless from the outset. In mediaeval siege warfare the besieged normally put their faith in one or more of three possibilities. They might be saved by a relief force despatched by a foreign ally; they might hold out until such moment as the besiegers were forced, through shortage of food or time, to give up the attempt and take themselves off elsewhere; or they might themselves stage a break-out and defeat the enemy in pitched battle. But at Salerno in 1076 there was no chance of any of these. All the other Lombard states of South Italy had already been absorbed by the Normans, and Gisulf had long ago alienated his Italian neigh-bours. Only the Pope retained some sympathy for him; but the Pope had no army, and even if he had he would not have dreamed of setting himself up against the Normans at such a moment. The second possibility was equally remote, since the surrounding land was rich and fertile—besides, the Norman army was being continuously revictualled by its own fleet. Finally, there was no hope of a successful *sortie*. The besieging force contained not only the most experienced and highly-trained Norman troops in the whole peninsula; it also comprised important contingents of Apulian and Calabrian Greeks and of Saracens from Sicily—the latter henceforth to form an integral part of the Guiscard's army in all his operations. Faced with such a host, the Salernitan soldiery was overwhelmingly outnumbered; and before long it was also starving.

For years Gisulf had been one of the most hated figures in South Italy; but it was only now, in the last disastrous year of his power, that he revealed the full blackness of his character. Foreseeing the Norman attack some time in advance, he had ordered every inhabitant of Salerno to lay in a two-year stock of provisions, on pain of expulsion from the city. It was not an oustandingly sagacious move —anyone could have seen that if Gisulf were to persist in his rabid anti-Norman policy, such an attack was inevitable—but it should at least have spared Salerno any problems about food once the siege had begun. Instead, soon after the enemy had taken up their positions under the walls, the Prince seized one-third of every household's supply for his own granaries. Later, finding even this insufficient, he sent his men round the city requisitioning what little remained. The result was famine. At first, Amatus tells us, the citizens ate their horses, dogs and cats; but soon these too were gone. As winter approached, the death-rate steadily increased. Gisulf opened his granary, but his motives seem to have been mercenary rather than humanitarian, since—once again according to Amatus— measures of wheat bought for three bezants were soon being offered for resale at forty-four. Emaciated corpses lay where they had fallen in the streets, 'but the Prince did not spare them so much as a glance, passing cheerfully by just as if he were not to blame.' Few people complained, for it was universally known that complaints were punished by blinding or by one or more of Gisulf's favourite forms of amputation. If his people were to die anyway, it was better to do so quietly.

In such conditions prolonged resistance was impossible. Salerno held out for some six months. Then, on 13 December 1076 through treason from within, the gates of the city were opened. The undernourished garrison, probably only too pleased to see an end to its sufferings, capitulated without a fight; and the last of the great Lombard principalities of South Italy was no more. Gisulf and one of his brothers, who had clearly had no difficulty in keeping up their own strength, retreated with a few followers to the citadel—whose ruins, inaccurately known as the Castello Normanno, still dominate the city from the north-western heights. There they held out till May 1077, but at last they too had to submit.

Robert was not prepared to negotiate terms. He had decided that henceforth Salerno should be his capital. Here was the greatest and most populous Italian city south of Rome, a proud principality for two hundred years and seat of Europe's most renowned school of medicine for longer still. He would restore its ancient glory and usher in a new period of power and magnificence, to be symbolised by the superb cathedral which he was even now planning to build. He therefore demanded, quite simply, the territorial possessions *in toto* of the Prince of Salerno and of his two brothers, Landulf and Gaimar—and one thing more besides. Among Salerno's most treasured relics was one of St Matthew's teeth, a holy if unattractive object which the Duke of Apulia had long coveted and which he knew Gisulf to have kept with him in the citadel. This too he now ordered the Prince to surrender; but the desiccated fang which Gisulf, faithless to the last, now forwarded to his conqueror, reverently wrapped in a silken cloth, was the former property not of the Evangelist but of a recently-deceased Jew of the city. It was a clumsy deception. Robert at once sent for a priest who had been familiar with the original relic and who now unhesitatingly proclaimed his new acquisition as spurious. A message was returned to Gisulf forthwith: if the genuine tooth were not despatched by the following day, every one of his own would be forfeit. There were no more prevarications. We can only hope, as we shuffle through the cathedral treasuries of Europe, that all the other relics presented for our veneration have been as scrupulously authenticated.

When Gisulf left Salerno he rode straight to Capua. Robert

Guiscard had treated him with his usual generosity, giving him not only his freedom but also money, horses and pack-animals with which to make the best of it; but the Prince's temper was not so easily assuaged. He now hoped to undermine the Norman unity that had been his undoing by sowing new dissension between the two leaders. He was disappointed. Richard of Capua in no way resented the fact that Salerno had passed into the domains of the Duke of Apulia; this had been understood from the beginning. Richard was not even particularly interested in Salerno. What he wanted was Naples—the one city, tightly wedged between his territories and Robert Guiscard's, that had somehow managed to maintain its independence. Robert had promised, in return for his assistance against Gisulf, to help him besiege it; and the Apulian fleet had indeed already arrived off the coast and started the usual blockade. The Prince of Capua was, in short, well satisfied with the alliance, and he gave his visitor short shrift. Gisulf had no alternative but to continue his journey north-west to his last remaining friend, the Pope.

Gregory VII was still away in Tuscany, where he had achieved the greatest—indeed almost the only—triumph of his unhappy pontificate. His sentence of excommunication against Henry had been more successful than even he had dared to hope. The German princes, meeting at Tribur in October 1076, had agreed to give their King a year and a day from the date of his sentence in which to obtain papal absolution. They had already called a diet at Augsburg for the following February. If by the 22nd of that month the ban had not been lifted, they would formally renounce their allegiance and elect another King in his place. Henry could only bow to their decision. From his point of view it might have been worse. It called, quite simply, for his own abject self-abasement before the Pope. If this was to be the price of his kingdom, he was ready to pay it. Fortunately there was still one alpine pass—the Mont-Cenis—unblocked by snow. Crossing it in the depth of winter with his wife and baby son, he hastened through Lombardy and at last found the Pope at the fortress of Canossa, where he was staying as guest of his friend the Countess Matilda pending the arrival of an escort to conduct him to Augsburg. For three days the King waited as a humble penitent for an audience, while Gregory—perhaps uncertain of what to do for the best but doubtless savouring every instant of his adversary's discomfiture—refused him admission. Finally the Pope saw that he had no alternative but to relent and to give Henry the absolution he needed.

The story of Canossa, usually enlivened by an oleaginous illustration of the King, barefoot and dressed in sackcloth, shivering in the snow before the locked doors of the castle, has always been a favourite with the writers of children's history books, where it is apt to appear as an improving object-lesson in the vanity of temporal ambition. In fact Gregory's triumph was empty and ephemeral, and Henry knew it. His humiliation had nothing to do with repentance. It was a cold-blooded political manœuvre which was necessary to secure his crown, and he had no intention of keeping his promises after they had served their purpose. The Pope, too, can have had few delusions about the King's sincerity. Had his Christian conscience permitted him to withhold absolution he would doubtless have been only too happy to do so. As it was, he had won an unquestionable moral victory; but of what use was a victory after which the vanquished returned unabashed to his kingdom, there to launch a bloody civil war against his still rebellious vassals, while the victor remained cooped up in a Tuscan castle, blocked from Germany by the savage hostility of the Lombard cities and powerless to intervene? His triumph had been sweet enough while it lasted, but he found the aftertaste singularly unpleasant.

Not until September did the Pope return to Rome. As usual, bad news awaited him. First there was Gisulf, to tell him of the fall of Salerno. Next came grave reports from Naples, where Richard's army and Robert's navy were mercilessly maintaining their siege. More serious still was the situation to the east, where two Norman armies, under the Guiscard's nephew Robert of Loritello and Richard's son Jordan, were pressing ever deeper into the Church lands of the Abruzzi. But the worst shock of all was still to come. On 19 December the Duke of Apulia attacked Benevento. The Pope was outraged. Technically, the town had been papal territory since the days of Charlemagne, whose gift had been confirmed when the Beneventans had ousted their worthless rulers and voluntarily placed themselves under the protection of Gregory's old master Leo IX twenty-seven years before. Since then it had become the principal bastion of the Papacy in South Italy, with its own papal palace where he himself had held court. This unprovoked attack was far worse than a renewed declaration of war, it was a gratuitous insult to the throne of St Peter itself.

And even that was not everything. Besides showing his contempt for the Papacy Robert Guiscard, by laying siege to Benevento, was holding the Pope's own sentence of excommunication up to ridicule. That same sentence that had brought Henry IV, heir to the Roman Empire of the West, cringing to Canossa less than a year before had been directed against this upstart Norman brigand with no adverse effect whatever. If anything, it seemed to have acted on him like a tonic. Certainly the populations of Salerno, Naples, the Abruzzi— for Robert of Loritello and his followers had all been implicitly included in the ban—and now Benevento itself would be revising their earlier opinions about the power and authority of the Church. And they would be right. The Pope had no army, and apparently no prestige either. There was only one thing he could do. Perhaps the Guiscard and his odious compatriots had not heard him the first time. On 3 March 1078 he excommunicated them again.

In normal conditions the new sentence would probably have passed as unheeded as its predecessor, but the Pope had timed it better than he knew. A few days after its official publication in Capua, Prince Richard fell ill; a month later, after an eleventh-hour reconciliation with the Church, he was dead; and the whole pattern of South Italian politics was changed overnight. Richard, like Robert Guiscard, had been a vassal of the Pope, and his son Jordan saw at once that there could be no question of succeeding to his father's throne while he remained under sentence of excommunication. Hastily calling off both the siege of Naples and his own operations in the Abruzzi, he hastened to Rome to make his peace with his suzerain and to assure him of his undying fidelity.

Robert Guiscard was not by nature a sentimental man, but the news of his brother-in-law's death cannot have left him entirely unmoved. The two had arrived from Normandy at the same time

over thirty years before, and their rise to power had been rapid.
For as long as many of their subjects could remember they had
together dominated the two great Norman communities of the
South, building up the early settlements at Aversa and Melfi into the
rich and powerful states they had now become. Like all good Norman barons, they had been at war for most of the time; but they had
fought side by side as often as face to face, and if on occasion
promises had been broken or friendship betrayed, that was all in
the game—an integral part of life as they knew it. Neither bore any
lasting grudge; each had a healthy respect for the capacities of the
other; and for the past two years they had worked in a happy, easy
partnership that was proving highly profitable to them both. The
Guiscard was now sixty-two; for him Richard's death must have
meant the passing of an era.

He himself felt his ambitions and energies undiminished; and
plans for conquests more daring and far-flung than any he had yet
undertaken were already beginning to crystallise in his mind. But
he saw that for the moment he would have to draw in his horns.
Young Jordan, by his ridiculous decision to go and grovel in Rome
just as they were all doing so well, had destroyed the whole momentum of the Norman advance and made himself a willing tool of the
Pope. What was to prevent Gregory from forcing him to march
his army, now once more unemployed, to the relief of Benevento?
It was not worth the risk. Robert gave his own troops the order
to withdraw. Benevento would have to wait.

His fears were justified. At last the Pope had found an ally—and,
what was more, an ally with an army—and he was determined to
make full use of him. Barely three months after Richard's death, we
find Gregory staying at Capua. He can have had no difficulty in
imposing his formidable will on the young Prince, alone, inexperienced and pitifully conscious of his exposed position against
an angry and predatory Duke of Apulia. Nor had the Pope yet
performed that all-important investiture. Jordan may not have liked
the proposals which Gregory now put to him, but he was poorly
placed to argue.

Fortunately for them both, Robert Guiscard had bitterly antagonised all his principal vassals earlier in the year, when he had forced

them to meet the cost of the elaborate celebrations which had attended the wedding of one of his daughters to Hugh, son of the Marquis Azzo of Este. Such exactions were a recognised obligation of vassals in the feudal societies of the North; but to the Norman barons in Apulia, many of whom remembered the Guiscard's beginnings and considered him to be no whit superior in birth or breeding to themselves, his demands had seemed unpardonable arrogance. They paid up because they had no choice; but when Jordan, certainly at the Pope's instigation and probably at his expense, allowed himself to become the focus for a new revolt against the Duke of Apulia, they were ready to answer his call.

The revolt was well-organised and widespread, beginning in the autumn of 1078 simultaneously at several points in Calabria and Apulia and extending rapidly through all Robert Guiscard's mainland dominions. There is no need to trace it in detail. Rebellion was endemic in South Italy; Robert was never secure enough to prevent it altogether, never so weak that he could not deal with it effectively when it came. For this reason one insurrection tended to be very like another. Even the ring-leaders—men such as Abelard, Geoffrey of Conversano or Peter of Trani—changed little, thanks largely to Robert's lack of vindictiveness, between one outbreak and the next. On this occasion nine months sufficed for the Guiscard to reassert his authority to the point where he was able to bring Jordan— through that eternal mediator Desiderius—to a separate peace. Jordan had in fact taken suprisingly little active part in the rebellion he had launched; it may be that his heart was never really in it and that he soon regretted his easy submission to papal pressure. Robert was now able to concentrate on Apulia where, after a whirlwind campaign through the winter of 1078–79, not the least remarkable feature of which was the successful siege of Trani by Sichelgaita while her husband was occupied with Taranto, he soon mopped up the remaining rebels. By the following summer the task of pacification was complete.

Away in Rome, Pope Gregory had watched his hopes crumble. Ill fortune continued to dog him. He, who had devoted his entire life to the service of God, had in the seven years of his pontificate been blocked at every turn by the forces of iniquity. The renewed excommunication which he had hurled at Henry IV, now a very different figure from the grovelling penitent of Canossa, was proving a good deal less effective than the first. His threatened descent into Italy to claim the Imperial Crown could not, it seemed, be very much longer postponed. Once again the Papacy was in grave danger; and once again—since Jordan was clearly a broken reed—the key to the situation appeared to lie with Robert Guiscard. He, like Henry, was a double-excommunicate—except that in his case both sentences were running concurrently—but the fact had not prevented him from reimposing his authority wherever it had been called in question. He was now more firmly entrenched than ever. When, in the past, the Pope had considered trying to regain his allegiance, pride and his old fear of losing face had always held him back. He could not afford such scruples now. If he did not come to terms with the Duke of Apulia—and quickly—Henry IV would do so on his own account and Gregory would soon find himself a Pope without a throne. Already in March 1080 we find his tone softening slightly towards the Normans; at the Lenten Synod of that year he issued a further warning to all 'invaders and pillagers' of Church lands, but this time added a conciliatory note: that if any of these had just cause for complaint against the inhabitants of the territories concerned, they should lay the case before the local governors; and that if justice was still denied them they might themselves take steps to recover what was rightfully theirs—'not in a thieving manner, but in a spirit befitting a Christian'.

The Pope, for once, was trimming his sails. Some time during the spring he instructed Desiderius to begin serious negotiations with Robert Guiscard. They were successful; and on 29 June 1080 at Ceprano, the Duke of Apulia at last knelt before Gregory VII and swore his fealty for all those lands that he had previously held from Popes Nicholas and Alexander. The more recently—and questionably—acquired territories of Amalfi, Salerno and the March of Fermo were left in suspense for the time being, but this was not a point to worry Robert unduly: it was enough for him that Gregory should have implied, in the words of his investiture, his effective *de facto* recognition of the new conquests. The legal technicalities could be settled later. Meanwhile the meeting at Ceprano had been another diplomatic victory for the Guiscard, and both parties were well aware of the fact. Gregory must at last have understood how ill-advised he had been to stand on his dignity at Benevento seven years before, while his own position was still comparatively strong. But it was too late now for self-recriminations of that kind. He needed Robert's support, and he must pay the price demanded. It was his only hope if he were to survive the oncoming storm.

And indeed, as the Duke of Apulia laid his huge hands between those of his Pope and thunderously pledged his loyalty and allegiance, the clouds were gathering faster than either of them knew. Four days earlier, in the little town of Brixen—now Bressanone—just south of the Brenner Pass, Henry IV had presided over a great council of his German and Lombard bishops. There, by common consent, Gregory VII had once again been deposed; and Archbishop Guibert of Ravenna, under the title of Clement III, had been proclaimed Pope in his stead.

16

AGAINST BYZANTIUM

O wisest and most learned of all men. . . . Those who have conversed with you and know you well speak highly of your intelligence and of the piety which you show not only in your religious faith but in the management of all your affairs. You are reputed to be a man of great prudence and at the same time a lover of action, with a spirit at once simple and lively. Thus, both in your character and your habits, do I recognise myself in you; and so I offer you the cup of friendship. . . .

The Emperor Michael VII to
Robert Guiscard

To Robert Guiscard, riding south from Ceprano to his new capital at Salerno during those July days of 1080, life must have looked as rich and radiant as the countryside around him. All his domains were tranquil, all his enemies subdued. His Apulian and Calabrian vassals were licking their wounds. After their last outbreak he had dealt with them rather more harshly than usual; he expected no more trouble for the moment from that quarter. The Pope and the Prince of Capua were likewise on their best behaviour. Admittedly King Henry might soon be making his long-threatened appearance in Rome; but Robert was not afraid of King Henry, who by his very existence was already serving a most useful purpose in keeping the Pope in order. Anyway the Duke's recent oath to Gregory did not oblige him to sit around twiddling his thumbs and waiting for a German army that might never come. He had more important things to do; and at sixty-four he could not afford to waste time.

He had long dreamed—and over the past two years his dreams had gradually ripened into plans—of a great concerted Norman attack on the Byzantine Empire. The Greeks were his oldest and most persistent enemies. He had ousted them from Italy, but even now they had not given up the struggle. Any of his Apulian vassals contemplating revolt could always count on sympathy and support from Constantinople, while the Byzantine province of Illyria just across the Adriatic was the recognised gathering-place for all Norman and Lombard exiles from Italy—his incorrigible nephew Abelard now among them. This alone in Robert's eyes would more than justify a punitive campaign—but his real reasons lay deeper.

Virtually all the Duke's mainland possessions had been conquered from the Greeks, and were thus impregnated with the heady fragrance of Byzantine civilisation. As a result of this the Normans had suddenly found themselves surrounded by the language and religion, the art and architecture and all the other outward manifestations of a culture more sophisticated and insistently pervasive than any other then known to Europe. Always acutely susceptible to foreign influences, they had not been slow to respond. In Apulia, where the population in general was overwhelmingly Lombard, both impact and response were less; but in Calabria, where the dominant cultural flavour had always been Greek, the Norman overlords had preserved nearly all the old administrative forms and customs and had generally been far more inclined to adopt Byzantine ways than to impose their own. After his investiture by Pope Nicholas with the Duchy of Calabria, Robert Guiscard had gone still further in this direction, deliberately presenting himself to his new subjects as successor to the Basileus, slavishly copying the imperial insignia on his own seals and even wearing, on formal occasions, careful models of the Emperor's own robes of state. It has not been unusual for peoples finding themselves in close proximity to the Greeks to develop, on the cultural level, a marked inferiority complex; it happened to the Romans and, later, to most of the Slavs; the Turks have not recovered from it to this day; and the Normans, even the invincible, confident Normans, were no exception. They knew only one remedy—conquest.

In the last decade Byzantium herself had sunk deeper and deeper into chaos. Around her frontiers her enemies—Hungarians and Russians to the North and West, Seljuk Turks to the South and East—maintained a relentless pressure; while, at her very heart, a succession of incompetent rulers and corrupt officials had brought her to the brink of political and economic collapse. Her ancient glory remained, but her greatness was gone. Never in her seven and a half centuries of history had her condition been more desperate than in the summer of 1080. Robert Guiscard, by a fortunate coincidence, had never been stronger. Constantinople lay, apparently powerless, before him. His army was in need of employment; so too was his fleet. Its novelty still fascinated him, but he was tired of using it for those interminable blockades. The time had come to cast it in a more active role and to find out just how much it could really do. Thirty-five years earlier he had arrived in Italy, the sixth son of an obscure and impoverished Norman knight. The throne of the Eastern Empire would make a fitting end to his career.

Events in Constantinople during the last few years had provided him, if not with an adequate reason for intervention, at least with an excuse. When, in the early summer of 1073, the Emperor Michael had appealed to the Pope for aid against the infidel, he had not thought it necessary to add that he was already in correspondence with the Duke of Apulia. He had in fact written Robert a letter some months before, couched in a style which, if typically Byzantine in all its verbose convolutions, is at least refreshingly devoid of false modesty. Other princes, the Emperor explained, counted themselves sufficiently honoured if they merely received occasional assurances of his peaceful intentions towards them; but the Duke, whom he knew to be similarly endowed with deep religious faith, must not be surprised to find himself singled out for a greater token of imperial regard. What better token could there be than a military alliance, sealed by a loving marriage? He therefore proposed that Robert, after a seemly pause for self-congratulation, should forthwith take upon himself all the enviable duties of an ally of the Empire—defending its frontiers, protecting its vassals and battling ceaselessly with its enemies. In return, one of his daughters would be received with all honour at Constantinople and given to the Emperor's own brother as his bride.

The Guiscard must on the whole have been gratified to receive the letter. Despite its tone, which he probably found more amusing than offensive, it was a further testimonial to his growing reputation. Even with Byzantium in its present plight, imperial marriages of the kind that Michael was now proposing were not carelessly undertaken. On the other hand, he cordially disliked the Greeks—he always had—and he saw no reason to involve himself with them unnecessarily. He therefore sent no reply. The Emperor, clearly astonished at such a display of indifference, tried again. This time his manner was a good deal less patronising; he even resorted to flattery, and actually went so far as to compare the Duke of Apulia with himself. There followed a prolonged encomium of his brother who was, it appeared, outstanding in his wisdom and virtue and 'so handsome, if one must talk of such qualities, that he might be a statue of the Empire itself', born in the purple and thus in every respect an ideal bridegroom for one—the most beautiful, he was now careful to specify—of Robert's daughters.

As a letter it was even more entertaining than its predecessor; but still the Guiscard refused to answer. Only when a third missive arrived towards the end of 1074 did he begin to show interest. Michael had meanwhile improved his proposal. He now suggested his young son Constantine as the Duke's prospective son-in-law, and went on to offer Robert no less than forty-four high Byzantine honours for distribution among his family and friends, carrying with them a total annual grant of two hundred pounds in gold. Robert hesitated no longer. The imperial succession was always a tricky business in Constantinople; there was however no doubt that the son, born in the purple,[1] of the ruling Emperor had a better chance than most, and the opportunity of seeing his own daughter on the throne of Byzantium was not one that he was prepared to miss. The offer of the honours, which would effectively put all his principal lieutenants in receipt of open bribes from Constantinople, was probably less welcome; but it was a risk worth taking. He accepted Michael's proposal, and shortly afterwards the unhappy bride-to-be was bundled off to Constantinople, there to pursue her studies in the imperial *gynoecoeum* until her fiancé should be of marriageable age. Anna Comnena, writing some years later, rather bitchily suggests[2] that young Helena—she had been re-baptised

[1] i.e. Born to an Emperor during his reign. To be born in the purple (*porphyrogenitus*) was a far greater distinction than that of primogeniture.

[2] *Alexiad*, I, 12.

with the Greek name on being received into the Orthodox Church soon after her arrival—proved to be considerably less well-favoured than the Emperor had hoped, and that her intended husband was as terrified of the thought of marriage to her 'as a baby is of a bogeyman'. Anna was herself subsequently betrothed to Constantine, with whom she was to fall passionately in love; she can therefore hardly be considered an impartial judge. But we are left, none the less, with an uncomfortable suspicion that Helena had inherited the fearsome build of her parents.

For the next few years Robert Guiscard, busy in Italy, could give little serious thought to Byzantine affairs. Then, in 1078, Michael VII was in his turn overthrown. More fortunate than his predecessor, he was allowed to retire unharmed to a monastery—a welcome translation from his point of view, since the cloister suited his bookish temperament far better than the palace had ever done; within a few years, through sheer ability, he rose to become Archbishop of Ephesus. His dethronement, however, put paid to the Norman alliance, and the unfortunate Helena found herself immured in a convent of her own with which she was, in all probability, rather less well pleased. Her father heard the news with mixed feelings. His immediate hopes of an imperial son-in-law had been dashed; on the other hand his daughter's former position and subsequent treatment gave him an admirable pretext for intervention. Unfortunately Jordan's revolt had broken out before he could take any effective steps; but by the summer of 1080, with order once again restored in his own dominions, he was able to begin preparations in earnest. As it happened, he had lost nothing by the delay. In Constantinople the situation was going from bad to worse. Michael's successor, the elderly general Nicephorus Botaneiates, had failed miserably to halt the decline, and the whole Empire was now in a turmoil of civil war, with the various provincial military commanders in desperate competition for supreme control. Meanwhile the Turks, by playing one off against the other, were rapidly building up their own position, and had recently established the so-called Sultanate of Rum, embracing nearly the whole of Asia Minor. In such conditions it looked as though a well-planned Norman offensive would have excellent chances of success.

He collected all, under age and over age, from all over Lombardy and Apulia, and pressed them into his service. There you could see children and boys and pitiable old men who had never, even in their dreams, seen a weapon; but were now clad in breastplates, carrying shields and drawing their bows most unskilfully and clumsily, and usually falling on their faces when ordered to march. . . . This behaviour of Robert's was a counterpart of Herod's madness, or even worse; for the latter only vented his rage on babes, whilst Robert did so against boys and old men.[1]

Thus Anna Comnena describes the Guiscard's preparations for the campaign; and all through the autumn and winter the work went on. The fleet was refitted, the army increased in numbers—though not as drastically as Anna suggests—and provided with new weapons and equipment. Pope Gregory, obviously remembering his humiliating failure to answer Michael's appeal seven years before, gave it his blessing and sent instructions to all the South Italian bishops to assist the enterprise in whatever way they could. In a mighty effort to stir up enthusiasm among his Greek subjects, Robert had even managed to produce a disreputable and transparently bogus Orthodox monk, who appeared in Salerno at the height of the preparations and gave himself out to be none other than the Emperor Michael in person, escaped from his monastery and trusting in his gallant Norman allies to replace him on his rightful throne. Nobody believed him much; but the Guiscard, professing to be entirely convinced by his claims, persisted in treating him with exaggerated deference throughout the months that followed.

Then, in December, Robert decided to send an ambassador to Constantinople. A certain Count Radulf was accordingly despatched, with instructions to demand satisfaction from Botaneiates for the treatment accorded to the Lady Helena and, if possible, to win the adherence of the large number of Normans who were at that time in the imperial service. His mission was not a success. Whilst in the city he fell under the spell of the most brilliant of all the young Byzantine generals and the one outstanding politician of his generation—Alexius Comnenus, at that time Grand Domestic and Commander of the Armies of the West; and at some point on his homeward journey he heard the news that he had probably been

[1] *The Alexiad*, I, 14 (tr. Dawes).

expecting: Alexius had forced the unhappy old Botaneiates to abdicate, packed him off uncomplaining[1] to a monastery, and on Easter Day 1081 had himself been crowned Emperor.

Radulf found his master at Brindisi. The Guiscard was not in a good temper. Understandably fearful lest he be left defenceless against King Henry, Pope Gregory was repenting of his former attitude and making difficulties again. He had already persuaded Robert to leave him a few troops and was now trying to stop the whole enterprise. Robert had put his foot down. He felt himself in a fairly strong position. The Pope knew that he had recently received a suggestion from Henry, similar to that made by Michael a few years before, for a marriage alliance between Henry's son Conrad and another of the Guiscard's daughters; he would not risk driving his vassal into the enemy camp by a further excommunication. Neither, however, would he take no for an answer; and Robert was still being pestered to draw back just at the time when he needed all his energy and concentration for the coming campaign.

Radulf's report was not calculated to improve matters. Now that the usurper Botaneiates had himself been overthrown there was, he pointed out, no longer any reason for the expedition. The new Emperor, Alexius, had been a good friend of Michael and had in fact long served as guardian to young Constantine, to whom he had even offered a share in his government. Alexius himself wanted nothing but friendship with the Normans; as for the Lady Helena, she would be as safe with him as if she were back in Salerno. Moreover, Radulf went on, it was his duty to inform his master that he had with his own eyes seen the ex-Emperor in his monastery; he thus had proof positive that the pretender to the throne whom Robert kept at his side and by whose claims he set so much store was in fact a cheat and an impostor. Robert had only to send him packing and make overtures of peace and friendship to Alexius. Then Helena might still marry Constantine or, alternatively, return to the bosom of her family; much bloodshed might be averted; and the army and navy could disperse to their homes.

[1] Some time afterwards Botaneiates was asked by an old acquaintance whether he minded the change in his fortunes. He replied: 'Abstinence from meat is the only thing that bothers me: for the rest I care very little.' (*The Alexiad*, III, 1.)

Robert Guiscard was famous for the violence of his rages; and his fury with the ingenuous Radulf was fearful to behold. No news could conceivably have been more unwelcome to him. The last thing he wanted now was peace with Constantinople. His superbly equipped expeditionary force was lying at Brindisi and Otranto ready to sail; the grandest prize in Europe lay within his grasp. He was no longer remotely interested in the imperial marriage, which, even it it were to take place, would no longer be so imperial anyway. Still less did he want his daughter back in Italy—he had six others, and she was serving a much more useful purpose where she was. So far as he was concerned the disreputable pretender was still Michael—though it was a pity that he was not a better actor—and Michael was still the legitimate Emperor. The only important thing now was to embark before Alexius cut the ground from under his feet by returning Helena to him or—worse still—King Henry's appearance in Rome made his departure impossible. Fortunately he had already despatched his eldest son Bohemund with an advance party across the Adriatic. The sooner he could join them the better.

Bohemund was now twenty-seven. He was cast in his father's mould, with broad shoulders surmounting an immense barrel-chest, a fresh complexion and thick fair hair which he kept close-cropped, after the fashion of the younger generation of his compatriots. The most striking thing about him, however, was his enormous height, which a slight stoop did nothing to conceal. It was another inheritance from his father: Normans and Greeks were inclined to be stocky, and when Robert was not around Bohemund seemed to tower above all the other knights and their associates. Of his early life we know little. He had been a child of four when the Guiscard had cast off his mother Alberada, but she had brought him up as everything that a Norman knight should be, and he had fought loyally and courageously—if without any conspicuous successes— for his father during the 1079 insurrection. Now that he had been given his first independent command, he was resolved to show his true worth. He had already captured the port of Valona, immediately opposite the heel of Apulia where the straits of Otranto are at their narrowest, whose sheltered bay would provide a superb natural bridgehead for the main body of the fleet when it arrived. From there he had headed south to Corfu; but a preliminary attack on the island had shown him that the local garrison would be more than a match for his small force, and he had wisely withdrawn to Butrinto where he was now awaiting his father's arrival.

The great fleet sailed in the second half of May 1081. It carried, apart from the ships' crews, about thirteen hundred Norman knights supported by a large body of Saracens, some rather dubious Greeks and an unknown quantity of heterogeneous foot-soldiers who must certainly have numbered several thousand. At Valona it was joined by a few Ragusan vessels—the Ragusans, like so many other Balkan peoples, were always glad of the opportunity for a crack at the Byzantines—and then moved slowly down the coast to Corfu where the garrison, seeing now that resistance was useless, surrendered almost at once. Having thus assured his bridgehead, and with it the free passage of reinforcements from Italy, the Guiscard could begin fighting in earnest. His first target was Durazzo—the old Roman Dyrrachium—capital and chief port of Illyria, from which the eight-hundred-year-old Via Egnatia ran east across the Balkan peninsula, through Macedonia and Thrace to Constantinople itself.

But soon it became clear that progress was not going to be so easy. Heading northward round the Acroceraunian promontory— respectfully avoided by the ancients as the seat from which Jupiter Fulminans was wont to launch his thunderbolts—the Norman fleet was overtaken by one of those sudden tempests to which the Eastern Mediterranean is so dramatically subject in the summer months. Several of the vessels were lost, and no sooner had the battered remainder hove to, a few days later, in the roadstead off Durazzo than they saw, looming on the northern horizon, a long and menacing line of high-masted ships. By their curious rig, half-way between the Greek and the Italian, they were all too easily identifiable as Venetians. Their city was not only technically part of the Byzantine Empire, it also had important commercial links with Constantinople; and to protect both these and their manifold other trading interests the Venetians had appointed themselves keepers of the peace throughout the Adriatic and beyond. It was lucky for the Greeks that they had, for the Byzantine navy had been allowed to deteriorate to an even more dangerous degree than the army and no longer possessed any means of itself enforcing imperial authority. That was why Alexius, hearing of the Apulian landings on his coast, had sent the Doge an urgent appeal which he knew would not go unheeded. The Venetians had arrived only just in time, but under the pretext of negotiations they managed to obtain from the Normans a short period of grace during which they prepared for the coming battle. Then, under cover of darkness, they bore down upon the Apulian fleet.

The Guiscard's men fought with courage and determination, but their inexperience of naval warfare betrayed them. The Venetians had taken advantage of the preliminary truce to adopt the old Byzantine trick, used by Belisarius at Palermo five and a half centuries before, of hoisting manned dinghies to the mastheads, from which their soldiers could shoot down on to the enemy below; they had also apparently learned the old Byzantine secret of Greek fire, since Malaterra writes of how 'they blew that fire, which is called Greek and is not extinguished by water, through submerged pipes, and thus cunningly burned one of our ships under the very waves of the sea'. Faced with such tactics, the Normans found themselves at a hopeless disadvantage. After a long battle which cost them dear in ships and men, their line was shattered and the Venetians were able to beat their way to safety in the harbour of Durazzo.

But it took more than this to discourage the Duke of Apulia, who now settled down to besiege the city. The Emperor had put George Palaeologus, his own brother-in-law and one of the bravest of his generals, in personal command of the garrison with instructions to keep the Guiscard occupied while he himself raised an army against the invaders; and the garrison, knowing that relief was on the way, fought stoutly. All summer long the siege continued, enlivened by frequent sorties by the defenders—in one of which Palaeologus fought magnificently throughout a sweltering day with an arrow-head embedded in his skull. Then, on 15 October, the Byzantine army appeared, the Emperor Alexius himself riding at its head.

Alexius Comnenus came of an old and distinguished Byzantine family which had already produced one Emperor—his uncle, Isaac I—and was proud of its long military traditions. When, in his thirty-third year, he so brilliantly manœuvred his own way to the throne, he already had well over a decade's experience in the field, fighting in Epirus and Thrace as well as nearer his home in Asia Minor. In particular he had gained a useful foretaste of his enemy's methods. Among the raffish crowd of Normans who had drifted into Byzantine service at that time was an extraordinary adventurer called Roussel of Bailleul. Roussel's military record was not unblemished, since already in 1071 at Mantzikert, seeing that the Greek position was hopeless, he had refused to lead his men into battle; but he had somehow charmed his way back into imperial favour—seasoned soldiers were hard to find—and had soon afterwards been sent by the Emperor Michael to lead a mixed force of Norman and Frankish cavalry against Turkish marauders in Anatolia. Once deep in enemy-held territory he had again betrayed his trust and, with his three hundred loyal followers, set up a self-declared independent Norman state on the South Italian pattern. It had not lasted long— the Emperor easily persuaded the Seljuks themselves to liquidate it, in return for the formal cession of territories they already held— but Roussel had managed to escape, and Alexius had been sent to hunt him down. He had found him in Amasea, where the outlaw had cheerfully set himself up as governor and had so endeared himself to the local population that they agreed to his removal only on being told, untruthfully, by Alexius that he had been blinded. A period of imprisonment at Constantinople had followed, but in 1077, with the army of Botaneiates marching on the capital, the desperate Michael had given his captive one more chance; and Roussel, now reinvested with a new regiment, had inflicted a crushing defeat on the rebels before turning traitor for the third time and declaring for the usurper.

On their way from Amasea to Constantinople Alexius had in his turn fallen victim to Roussel's fascination; and later, when the Norman was starving in prison, he had even secretly brought him food. But he had also learnt never to underestimate Norman intelligence, cunning or military skill. Roussel had probably often spoken to him of Robert Guiscard, in whose army he had formerly served; and from the day when the spies first warned him of Robert's intentions Alexius had known that it would take all the Empire's remaining strength to survive the expected onslaught. He had worked hard and fast to raise an adequate defence force, and as far as numbers were concerned he had been remarkably successful. But too many of his followers were insufficiently trained or of doubtful loyalty, and it cannot have been with any great feelings of confidence that he led them through the tortuous Macedonian passes and out on to the plain before Durazzo.

The first problem was one of strategy. Should the Byzantine army attempt to besiege the Normans in their own camp, or should they draw them out into a pitched battle? Certain of his advisers favoured the former course, but Alexius decided to fight. Winter would soon be approaching and he simply could not trust his men through a protracted siege. On 18 October, three days after his arrival, he attacked. By this time Robert Guiscard had moved a little to the north of the city and had drawn up his own battle-line, stretching inward from the coast and facing towards Durazzo. He himself had assumed command of the centre, with Sichelgaita, fully armed and mailed, beside him and Bohemund on his left, inland, flank.

As was the invariable rule when the Emperor took the field in person, his imperial Varangian bodyguard was present in strength. At this time it consisted largely of Englishmen, Anglo-Saxons who had left their country in disgust after Hastings and taken service with Byzantium. Many of them had been waiting fifteen years for the chance of avenging themselves on the detested Normans, and they attacked with all the strength and vigour of which they were capable. They fought on foot, since the huge two-handed axes that were their principal weapon were far too heavy to be wielded from the saddle. Swinging these round their heads and then slamming them at horses and riders alike, they struck terror in the hearts of the Apulian knights, few of whom had ever come across a line of foot-soldiers who did not at once break in the face of a charge of cavalry. The horses too soon began to panic, and before long the Norman right had turned in confusion, many galloping straight into the sea to escape what seemed to them certain massacre.

But now, if contemporary reports are to be believed, the day was saved by Sichelgaita. The story is perhaps best told in the words of Anna Comnena:

Directly Gaita, Robert's wife (who was riding at his side and was a second Pallas, if not an Athene) saw these soldiers running away, she looked fiercely after them and in a very powerful voice called out to them in her own language an equivalent to Homer's words 'How far will ye flee? Stand, and quit you like men!' And when she saw that they continued to run, she grasped a long spear and at full gallop rushed after the fugitives; and on seeing this they recovered themselves and returned to the fight.[1]

Now, too, Bohemund's left flank had wheeled to the rescue, with a detachment of cross-bowmen against whom the Varangians, unable to approach within axe-range, found themselves defenceless. Having advanced too far beyond the main body of the Greek army, they were unable to retire to safety and could only fight where they stood. At last the few exhausted Englishmen remaining alive turned and sought refuge in a nearby chapel of the Archangel Michael; but the Apulians immediately set it on fire—they were a long way now from Monte Gargano—and the last of the Varangians perished in the flames.

Meanwhile, in the centre, the Emperor was still fighting bravely; but the cream of the Byzantine army had been destroyed at Mantzikert, and the motley collection of barbarian mercenaries on whom he now had to rely possessed, as he had feared, neither the discipline nor the devotion to prevail against the Normans of Apulia. A sortie from Durazzo under George Palaeologus had failed to save the situation, and to make matters worse Alexius suddenly saw that he had been betrayed by his vassal, the Serbian King Constantine Bodin of Zeta, and by a whole regiment of Turkish auxiliaries of whom he had had high hopes. His last chance of victory was gone; his army was everywhere in full retreat. He turned from the field. Cut off from his men, weak from exhaustion and loss of blood and in considerable pain from a wound on his forehead, he rode slowly and without escort back over the mountains to Ochrid, where he might recover and regroup what he could of his shattered forces.

After this victory the fall of Durazzo could only be a question of time; but despite the fact that the city was now without a governor —George Palaeologus having been unable to re-enter it quickly enough after his sortie—it somehow held out for another four

[1] *The Alexiad*, IV, 6 (tr. Dawes).

months. Not till 21 February 1082 were the Apulians able to burst
open the gates, and then only through the treachery of a Venetian
resident who, according to Malaterra, demanded as his reward the
hand of one of Robert's nieces in marriage. But, from Durazzo on,
the tempo of conquest quickened; the local populations, aware of
their Emperor's defeat and the absence of any nearby imperial army
to which they could look for relief or salvation—many of them felt
no particular loyalty to Byzantium in any case—offered no resistance
to the advancing Normans; and within a few weeks the whole of
Illyria was in the Guiscard's hands. He then marched east to Kastoria,
which also surrendered instantly. It was the most important town
he had taken since leaving Durazzo; its capitulation seemed a good
augury for the future—and a still better one when the garrison, to
whose charge it had been personally consigned by the Emperor,
was found to consist of three hundred more of the Varangian
Guard. If not even the crack troops of the Empire were any longer
prepared to oppose the Norman advance, then surely Constantinople
was as good as won.

But the following April, while Robert Guiscard was still at
Kastoria, messengers reached him from Italy. All over the peninsula,
they reported, Alexius's agents had been busy. Once again Apulia
and Calabria were up in arms, and much of Campania as well. They
also brought a letter from Pope Gregory. Henry was at his gates.
The Duke's presence was urgently required at Rome.

17

FROM ROME TO VENOSA

Remember therefore the holy Roman Church your Mother, who loves you above all other Princes and has singled you out for her special trust. Remember, for her you have sworn an oath; and in what you have sworn —that which, even had you not done so, would still be your Christian duty to perform—you will not fail. For you are not unaware of how much strife has been stirred up against the Church by Henry, the so-called king, and of how urgently she needs your aid. Wherefore act now; for just as the son will desire to fight against iniquity, so will the Church his Mother be grateful for his devotion and succour.

We hesitate to place on this letter our leaden seal, lest it fall into the hands of our enemies and they turn it to fraudulent use.

Gregory VII's letter to Robert Guiscard, 1082

ROBERT GUISCARD had launched his Byzantine expedition only just in time. Within a week of his departure from Otranto in 1081 Henry IV had appeared on the outskirts of Rome, the new anti-Pope Clement in his train. Fortunately for Gregory, he had underestimated the degree of resistance that he would encounter and had brought very few troops with him; so that when, somewhat to his surprise, he found that the Romans intended to remain loyal to their own Pontiff, he had had no option but to retire into Lombardy. The following spring, however, he made a second attempt; and although it too was to end in failure, by this time the mood in South Italy had changed. Henry's continued successes in Germany, where he had now eliminated virtually all serious opposition, and in Lombardy where he personified the most militant forces of separatism and reaction, had increased his prestige everywhere; and with Robert Guiscard already far away and—if the reports were to be believed— advancing steadily in the opposite direction, there was a growing feeling among Normans, Italians and Lombards alike that their future lay with the Western Empire. Jordan of Capua was among the first to transfer his allegiance; shrugging off the inevitable excommunication, he now swore fealty to Henry and received from him in return a formal investiture of his principality; and most of the minor Campanian barons followed suit. So, even, did Abbot Desiderius of Monte Cassino who, as the years wore on, was beginning to show an alarming deterioration of moral fibre that boded ill for the future. Away in Apulia poor Roger Borsa, to whom the Guiscard had entrusted the care of his mainland dominions during his absence, was powerless to reassert his father's authority—particularly since Abelard and Herman and their ever-restless friends, many of whom had taken advantage of the changed circumstances to return from exile, were now once again in full revolt.

When, in April 1082—less than a year after his departure—all this news reached the Duke of Apulia at Kastoria, he saw that he had no time to lose. Leaving the command of the expedition to Bohemund, and swearing by the soul of his father Tancred to remain unbathed and unshaven until he could return to Greece, he hurried back with a small escort to the coast where his ships were waiting and crossed at once to Otranto; from there, pausing only to collect what troops he could from Roger Borsa, he made for Rome. He arrived to find the immediate danger past; Henry had withdrawn again from the city—this time to Tuscany, there to ravage the estates of the Pope's staunchest ally, the Countess Matilda. Though he had left his anti-Pope Clement at Tivoli with a regiment of Germans, Clement would give no serious trouble while his protector was away. The Guiscard was able to return to Apulia and put his own house in order.

But Rome was not to be left in peace for long. At the beginning of 1083 Henry reappeared with a larger army than on either of the previous occasions and settled down in earnest to besiege the Leonine City.[1] It was his third attempt, and it was successful. The defenders had grown tired of these annual attacks, and their loyalty had been dangerously undermined by Byzantine bribes, distributed both directly by Alexius's agents within the city and indirectly

[1] See p. 159 n.

by Henry's. Through the spring and early summer they held out, but on 2 June a mixed party of Milanese and Saxons scaled the walls, overcame the guards and finally took possession of one of the towers. Within an hour or two Henry's soldiers had swept into the city and were fighting a furious battle in and around St Peter's. Pope Gregory, however, had been too quick for them. He had no intention of surrendering. Hurrying to the Castel Sant' Angelo, he barricaded himself in and prepared for a new siege.

It would have been easy now for Henry to proceed to his imperial coronation, which anti-Pope Clement would have been only too happy to perform; but he still held only the Leonine City, on the right bank of the Tiber. The rest of Rome remained faithful to Gregory, and he knew that such a ceremony would never be generally accepted while the true Pope remained alive and in the capital. Could not the Romans themselves, who surely stood to gain everything from a reconciliation, somehow mediate between himself and the Pope and so bring about a compromise? It was their duty to try, he told them; and try they did. But again Henry had underestimated. Gregory was not to be moved an inch. Utterly convinced of the justice of his cause and consequently of divine support, he seems to have been equally certain that, sooner or later, he would prevail. If Henry wanted his coronation, he must remember—and observe— the oath he had sworn at Canossa. A general synod would be called the following November and would doubtless discuss the matter further. Meanwhile there was nothing more to be said. Silently, with patience and dignity, he settled down in his stronghold to wait for the Duke of Apulia to come to his relief.

The Guiscard, however, showed no immediate sign of doing so. It was not altogether his fault. Throughout the autumn and winter of 1082 and the first half of 1083 he had been fully occupied with the rebels in Apulia; it was only on 10 June—a week after the imperial troops had entered the Leonine City—that he had recaptured the last stronghold, Canosa, from his nephew Herman and so brought the insurrection to an end. The campaign had been harder than he had expected—Byzantine money had obviously had a lot to do with it—and if he had not been able to appeal to his brother Roger to bring much-needed reinforcements over from Sicily, it would have

Norman Knights. Three eleventh-century chessmen from Southern Italy (Cabinet des Médailles, Paris)

Monte Sant'Angelo: The cave of the Archangel as it is today

Venosa: ruins of the SS. Trinità

Cerami: the battlefield

A battle against the Saracens, as depicted on a Sicilian peasant cart

Mazara Cathedral: Roger I strikes down a Saracen. (Stone-carving of 1584)

Serlo's rock

Mazara: ruins of the castle built by Roger I in 1073

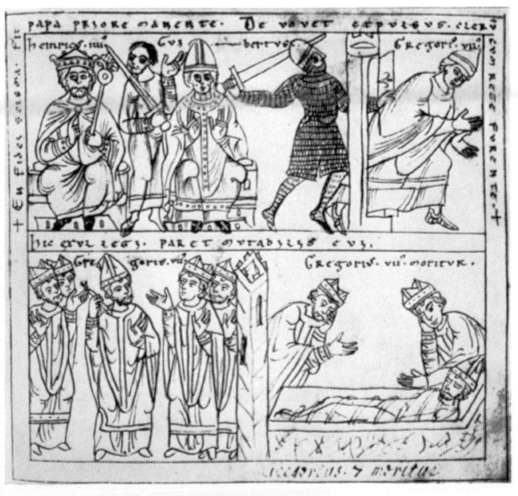

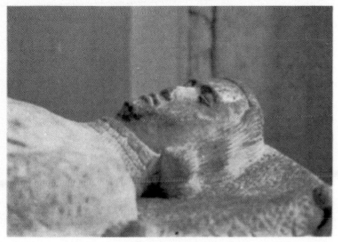

Henry IV and the Anti-Pope Clement III watch while Gregory VII escapes from Rome and dies at Salerno.

(Chronicle of Otto of Freising, 1156, University of Jena)

Salerno Cathedral: Tomb of Roger Borsa

Sant'Angelo in Formis, near Capua. Desiderius's church, built about 1075

The Tiber Island, Rome. The tower by the bridge is the Torre della Contessa, part of the Countess Matilda's fortress in which Popes Victor III and Urban II both took refuge

Canosa di Puglia:
Bohemund's Tomb

The Sarcophagus
of Count Roger I
(Archaeological
Museum, Naples)

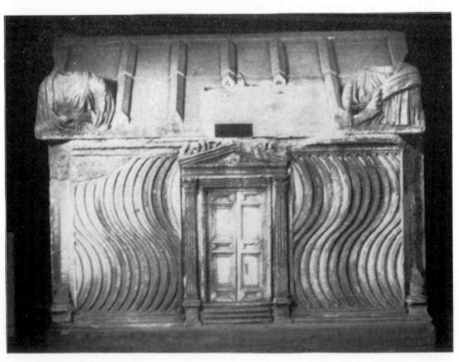

Cefalù: a distant prospect from the west

Cefalù Cathedral: the west front

Cefalù Cathedral: Christ Pantocrator

Bari: the church of St Nicholas

Troia: the Cathedral

continued a great deal longer than it did. As soon as it was safe for
them to leave Apulia he and Roger had in fact set off in the direction
of Rome for a short preliminary campaign against Jordan of Capua;
but at this moment the Great Count was urgently recalled to Sicily
with his men by a sudden emergency, and Robert, knowing that
he had not the necessary forces to take on Henry single-handed,
retired to prepare a major expedition for the following year. From
his point of view there was plenty of time. His oath, sworn at
Ceprano, bound him to render assistance to the Pope—and Popes
apart, his own position in Italy would be seriously threatened if
Henry, once crowned Emperor and supported by an obedient
Clement III, were allowed to have his own way in South Italy. But
Henry was at present back in Tuscany, wasting his energies in vain
attempts to subdue the Countess Matilda; and his army, Robert
knew, was small and not particularly efficient. In six months or so it
should be possible for the Duke to get together a new army of his
own which he could lead against the King of the Romans without
any fear as to the outcome. Then at his leisure he could deliver the
Pope—and, perhaps, name his own conditions. Meanwhile Gregory
would just have to wait. Safely ensconced in the Castel Sant' Angelo,
he seemed to be in no immediate danger. A few months' more
discomfort—and even a little more humiliation—would do him no
harm.

The projected synod was duly held in November. It proved a
farce. The King had sworn that he would not prevent any of the
hierarchy faithful to Gregory from attending; but as the appointed
day drew near he saw that the Pope on his side had no intention of
admitting any of those imperialist bishops whom he had excommunicated and that, in consequence, to keep the oath would be
simply to play into his hands. Henry never allowed his promises to
interfere with his policies. All Gregory's most fervent supporters,
including the Archbishop of Lyons and the Bishops of Como and
Lucca, found themselves barred from Rome; and a papal legate,
the Cardinal-Bishop Odo of Ostia, was actually imprisoned. In vain
did the furious Pope hurl fresh excommunications and anathemas
from behind the walls of his fortress; Henry took no notice. The
Synod ended, and such few bishops as had managed to attend

dispersed to their sees; a ludicrous suggestion by some of the Roman nobles for a compromise, by which Gregory would not actually perform Henry's coronation but would pass him down the imperial diadem on a stick from the battlements of Sant' Angelo, met with the contempt it deserved. The stalemate continued.

And still Robert Guiscard failed to appear.

At the first approach of spring in the year 1084 Henry decided to force the issue. He would never be able to bring his inflexible adversary to terms as long as the Pope could look forward to eventual relief by Robert Guiscard. If, on the other hand, he could take the Normans by surprise while they were still unready for him, he might be able to prevent their ever reaching Rome. That should make Gregory much more amenable. Early in March, leaving only a small garrison in the Leonine City, he accordingly set off for Apulia with his army. He had not gone very far before he was overtaken by messengers from the capital. The Romans, it appeared, had at last grown tired of the struggle and had sent to tell him that they would offer no more resistance; their city was his for the taking.

To surrender at that precise moment to the imperial forces was an act of utter folly; and it sealed the fate, not only of Pope Gregory, but of Rome itself. Had Henry been allowed to continue his advance against the Duke of Apulia, he would either have been beaten by an overwhelmingly superior force or, more likely, would have retreated hastily to the North. In either event the Normans would have subsequently made short work of the German garrison remaining in Rome and would have entered the city as deliverers rather than as conquerors. By changing sides at a time when they knew that the most powerful ruler in Italy, if not in Europe, was preparing to march, the people of Rome made disaster inevitable. They were to pay dearly for their mistake, but they had only themselves to blame.

Hurrying back with all the speed his army could muster, Henry entered Rome in triumph on 21 March and—accompanied by his wife, the long-suffering Queen Bertha of Turin, and his anti-Pope Clement—took up residence in the Lateran. Three days later, on Palm Sunday, Pope Gregory was formally deposed by the Lombard bishops, and Clement consecrated as his successor; and on Easter Day, 31 March, Henry and Bertha were crowned with the imperial crown in St Peter's. For Gregory the situation was now desperate. Parts of Rome still remained loyal to him—the Coelian and the Palatine, for example, both held by his nephew Rusticus, and the Tiber Island, burial-place of St Bartholomew, which remained in the faithful hands of the Pierleoni. The Capitol itself was also holding out. But all these strongholds were already under attack; unless help came quickly they would not last long. Where was Robert Guiscard? A group of the Pope's most trusted cardinals was sent south to find him at all costs and pass on his suzerain's last appeal.

When Robert heard of the Romans' surrender he needed no further persuading. His own future as well as the Pope's was at stake. Those long months of delay, however, had not been wasted, and it was with a formidable army—William of Apulia's estimate of six thousand horse and thirty thousand foot-soldiers may not be far out—that he set off for the capital at the beginning of May. Ahead of him, to give the Pope courage, he sent Abbot Desiderius; and at last, on 24 May 1084, he rode up the Via Latina and, roughly on the site of the present Piazza di Porta Capena, pitched his camp beneath the walls of Rome.

Henry had not waited for him. Desiderius—sitting, as always, firmly on the fence—had no sooner informed the Pope of Robert's impending arrival than he had gone straight to the Emperor with the same message; and his description of the size and strength of the Guiscard's new army had been more than enough to make up Henry's mind. Summoning a council of the leading citizens of Rome, he explained to them that his presence was urgently required in Lombardy. He would of course be back as soon as circumstances permitted; meanwhile, he trusted them to fight gallantly against all attackers and so to prove themselves worthy subjects of the Empire which bore their name. Then, three days before the Duke of Apulia appeared at the gates of the city, he fled with his wife and the greater part of his army, the terrified anti-Pope scurrying behind.

The Romans, already deeply regretting their change of heart two months before, were left in an impossible position. Having first traduced their Pope to the Emperor, they in their turn had found themselves betrayed. And now the presence of the Norman army on their very threshold seemed to paralyse them. It was clearly useless to try to withstand such an army, particularly with Gregory's supporters still so numerous within the city; at the same time, as if possessing some ghastly foreknowledge of what lay ahead, they could not bring themselves to open the gates. For three more days the Duke of Apulia waited in his camp, uncertain perhaps whether Henry's flight was genuine, and meanwhile laying careful plans with the Pope's representatives. Then, on the night of 27 May, under cover of darkness, he silently moved his army round to the north of the city. At dawn he attacked, and within minutes the first of his shock-troops had burst through the Flaminian Gate. They met with a stiff resistance: the whole area of the Campus Martius—that quarter lying immediately across the river from the Castel Sant' Angelo—became a blazing holocaust. But it was not long before the Normans had beaten the defenders back over the bridge, released the Pope from his fortress and borne him back in triumph through the smoking ruins to the Lateran.

For Robert Guiscard that day marked the pinnacle of his glory and his power. The year 1084 had already seen the two greatest potentates of Europe, the Emperors of the East and of the West, fleeing at his approach; it now saw him extend a gracious—if slightly bloodstained—hand to one of the most redoubtable Popes of the Middle Ages and raise him up once again to his rightful throne. At the High Mass of thanksgiving held to celebrate Gregory's deliverance, the mind of both Duke and Pontiff must have gone back to that distant day in 1053 when, on the plain of Civitate, the Hautevilles and their followers had defended against the forces of the Roman Church their right to remain in Italy. Thirty-one years later they had collected several more excommunications, but they had also saved Rome more than once. Not for the first time, the Pope must have been glad that their defence had proved so effective.

But his triumph was short-lived. Although Rome was already but a poor despoiled shadow of what it had once been, it yet remained richer and more populous than any other city in the centre or south of the peninsula, and to the Guiscard's men it offered possibilities of plunder on a scale such as few of them had ever

before experienced. They were making the best of it; and the whole
capital was now given over to scenes of rapine and pillage in which
the several brigades of Sicilian Saracens were not conspicuous for
their restraint. To the Romans these Saracens were the forces of
Antichrist. Refractory children were still silenced with gruesome
tales of the outrages of the infidel—of their hideous habits and
unspeakable appetites, and of those lightning raids when they
would sweep down like falcons out of a clear sky, giving no quarter,
selling women and girls—and boys too—by their thousands into
slavery; raids which culminated in that dreaful day when, in 846,
their galleys had sailed up the Tiber, sacked the Borgo and wrenched
the silver plate from the very doors of St Peter's itself. But even then
their depredations had been confined to the right bank of the river;
this time no district was safe, and the Christians were no better than
the Saracens. On the third day, with bestiality and bloodshed still
continuing unabated, the people of Rome could bear it no longer:
suddenly, in desperation, the whole city rose against its oppressors.
Robert Guiscard, for once taken by surprise, found himself surrounded. He was saved in the nick of time by Roger Borsa who, in
a rare burst of activity, smashed his way through the crowds with a
thousand men-at-arms to his father's rescue—but not before the
Normans, fighting for their lives, had set fire to the city.

Here, for Rome, was disaster—disaster unparalleled in its history
since the barbarian invasions six centuries before. Churches, palaces,
ancient temples came crashing down before the advancing flames.
The Capitol and the Palatine were gutted; in the whole area between
the Colosseum and the Lateran hardly a single building escaped the
inferno. Many of the inhabitants perished in their dwellings; others,
fleeing for their lives, were cut down by the Normans as they ran,
or else were captured and sold into slavery. When at last the smoke
cleared away and such Roman leaders as remained alive had
prostrated themselves before the Guiscard, a naked sword roped
round their necks in token of surrender, their city lay empty, a
picture of desolation and despair.

And what thoughts now, one wonders, must have occupied the
mind of Pope Gregory as he surveyed the blackened ruins around
him, the streets impassable with piles of fallen masonry, the corpses

already putrefying in the heat of a Roman June? He had won his battle—after a fashion—but at what a price? The heroic Popes of the past had saved their city from the invaders—Leo I from Attila's Huns, his own namesake Gregory the Great from the conquering Lombards; he, though in many ways greater than either, had delivered it up to destruction. And yet neither in his own letters nor in the chronicles of the time is there any suggestion of remorse for the evil he had brought upon Rome. His conscience seems to have been astonishingly clear. As he saw it, he had been fighting for a principle; it was a great principle and a vital one, and thanks to his own strength and courage it had been upheld. The present sufferings of his people were simply the inevitable retribution which by their faithlessness they had brought upon themselves. God's will had been done.

So, with that sublime arrogance which was one of his chief and most unattractive characteristics, must Gregory have reasoned. But for him too there was to be retribution. The Roman populace, who had acclaimed him with such enthusiasm eleven years before and had endured the hardships of siege and civil war on his behalf, now saw him—and not without good reason—as the cause of all their misery and loss; and they were hungry for revenge. Only the presence of Robert Guiscard and his army prevented them from tearing their once-adored Pope limb from limb. But Robert had no desire to stay in Rome longer than was absolutely necessary; apart from the danger of further outbreaks, he was anxious to resume his Byzantine campaign. During his ill-starred pontificate Gregory had been called upon to suffer many humiliations; but the greatest of all, he now saw, had been saved till the last. When the Normans left Rome, he would have to leave with them. And so he made ready to depart, and a few days later accompanied his deliverer on a brief and largely inconclusive expedition against the anti-Pope Clement, who had dug himself in at Tivoli. They returned on 28 June; and at the beginning of July, escorted by Robert Guiscard and the mighty host of Normans and Saracens that had been at once his salvation and his undoing, he turned his back on Rome for the last time—the proudest of pontiffs, now little better than a fugitive from the city that hated him. Southward they rode, first to Monte

Cassino, then on to Benevento—where news awaited them that Clement III had taken advantage of Gregory's departure to reoccupy St Peter's—and so, finally, to Salerno. There the Pope was settled in a palace befitting his dignity; and there, on 25 May 1085, he died. He was buried in the south-east apse of the new cathedral—built, according to the inscription which runs to this day across the façade, by 'Duke Robert, greatest of conquerors, with his own money'—which the Pope had consecrated only a few weeks before and where his tomb may still be seen.

In spite of the discredit which he had unwittingly brought upon the Papacy in his last years, the body of his achievement was greater than he knew. He had gone a long way towards establishing papal supremacy over the hierarchy of the Church—the practice of lay investitures was rapidly losing ground and was to die out altogether in the following century—and even if he had not won a similar victory over the Empire, he had at least asserted his claims in such a way that they could never again be ignored. The Church had shown her teeth; future Emperors would defy her at their peril. And yet, although he never relinquished his plans to return to Rome at the head of an army and to regain his throne, Gregory died if not a broken, at least a disappointed, disillusioned man; and his last words—'I have loved righteousness and hated iniquity, therefore I die in exile'—were a bitter valediction.

The previous autumn, with a new fleet of a hundred and fifty ships, the Duke of Apulia had returned to Greece. Bereft of his leadership, the Norman expeditionary force had suffered near-disaster. For a year Bohemund had managed to maintain the momentum and, after two important victories at Yanina and Arta, had pressed the Byzantines back until all Macedonia and much of Thessaly lay under his control; but in the spring of 1083 Alexius outsmarted him at Larissa and turned the tide. Dispirited, homesick, its pay long overdue and now still further demoralised by the immense rewards which Alexius was offering to all deserters, the Norman army fell away. Bohemund was forced to return to Italy to raise more money, and his principal lieutenants surrendered as soon as his back was turned; next, a Venetian fleet recaptured

Durazzo and Corfu; and by the year's end Norman-held territory was once again confined to one or two offshore islands and a short strip of the coast.

The arrival of Robert, accompanied by all three of his sons, Bohemund, Roger Borsa and Guy, and bearing money, supplies and substantial reinforcements, put new heart into the broken remnants of his army. Although now sixty-eight, he seems to have been in no way cast down at the prospect of waging his campaign all over again from the beginning, and immediately settled down to plan the recapture of Corfu. Bad weather delayed his ships at Butrinto until November, and when at last they were able to cross the straits they were set upon by a combined Greek and Venetian fleet and soundly beaten in pitched battle twice in three days. So severe were the Norman losses that the Venetians sent their pinnaces flying homeward to announce the victory. Now, however, it was their turn to pay the price for underestimating the Guiscard. After the preceding encounters, few of Robert's ships were in condition to sail at all, let alone to venture a third battle; but, seeing the pinnaces disappear over the horizon and realising that this was his opportunity of taking the enemy by surprise, he quickly summoned every vessel he possessed that was still afloat, and flung this battered fleet forward in one more onslaught. He had calculated it perfectly. Not only were the Venetians unprepared and depleted, but the heavier galleys, according to Anna Comnena, had been emptied of ballast and provisions and were consequently so high in the water that when, in the heat of the battle, their entire complements of soldiers and crew dashed to the same side of the deck, many of them capsized. (Anna assesses the Venetian dead at thirteen thousand and dwells—perhaps with more morbid pleasure than strict historical accuracy—on the mutilations inflicted by the Guiscard on his 2500 prisoners.) Corfu fell; and it was a generally happier and more hopeful army that settled down in its winter quarters on the mainland to repair the ships and make ready for the following year's campaign.[1]

[1] Anna goes on to describe a fourth battle in which she maintains that the Venetians got their revenge, but there is nothing in Venetian records to substantiate her story; and Dandolo's *Chronicon Venetum* (Muratori, *R.I.S.,* vol. XII) states that the Doge was deposed as a result of the Corfu catastrophe. It looks as though the Princess is guilty of a particularly unscrupulous piece of wishful thinking.

But in the course of the winter a new enemy appeared—one more deadly than the Venetians and the Byzantines together, and one which was destined to bring to an end not only the expedition but what Chalandon calls 'the first, heroic, period of the history of the Normans of Italy'. It was a raging epidemic, probably typhoid, and it struck without mercy. Even when it did not kill, it left its victims in a state of utter exhaustion from which they needed many weeks to recover, and by spring five hundred knights were dead and a large proportion of Robert's army effectively incapacitated. Yet even now the Guiscard remained cheerful and confident. Of his immediate family only Bohemund had succumbed—in conformity with that strange tendency of epidemics to attack the apparently strongest—and had been sent back to Bari to recuperate; and in the early summer, determined to get his men once again on the move, he despatched Roger Borsa with an advance force to occupy Cephalonia.

A few weeks later the Guiscard himself set out to join his son; but now, as he sailed southward, he felt the dreaded sickness upon him. By the time his ship reached Cape Ather, the northernmost tip of the island, he was desperately ill. There was no time to sail down the coast to where his son was waiting; the vessel put in at the first safe anchorage, a little sheltered bay still called, in his memory, by the name of Phiscardo. Here, six days later, on 17 July 1085, he died, his faithful Sichelgaita at his side. He had outlived Pope Gregory by less than two months.

Anna Comnena tells a curious story of how, as Robert lay dying, he looked over the sea to Ithaca and learned from a local inhabitant of a ruined town on the island, which had once been known as Jerusalem; and of how he suddenly remembered the words of a soothsayer who years before had prophesied that: 'As far as Ather you shall bring all countries under your sway, but from there you shall depart for Jerusalem and pay your debt to nature.' The story is presumably apocryphal,[1] but it is of a certain interest in relation to what is certainly the most surprising of all the Guiscard's achievements—his subsequent reputation in legend as a Crusader. The several biblical place-names in north-western Greece—Anna also

[1] Holinshed tells a very similar story of the death of Henry IV of England in 1413.

mentions the little harbour of Jericho, formerly Orikos, which Robert had captured during his first Balkan campaign—would naturally have been seized upon, and subsequently misinterpreted, by the minstrels and *jongleurs* who were soon to sing of his exploits; and it has been convincingly demonstrated how various incidents in his Byzantine expedition at last found their way into the *Chanson de Roland*.[1] Robert was indeed a perfect example of the *chevalier sans peur*; but even his most enthusiastic admirers would have been hard put to describe him as *sans reproche*, and it comes as something of a surprise to find him numbered among the stainless paladins of legend. But even this is not all.

> Poscia trasse Guglielmo, e Rinoardo
> E il duca Gottifredi la mia vista
> Per quella croce, e Roberto Guiscardo.[2]

The old ruffian had, specifically reserved for him though still two centuries away in the future, a crown sublimer still—the ultimate accolade of a place in Dante's Paradise.

Despite the claims of his glorious new cathedral at Salerno, Robert Guiscard had always wished to be buried with his brothers in the Abbey Church of the Santissima Trinità at Venosa; his body was therefore packed in salt and a ship made ready to return it, with Sichelgaita and Roger Borsa, to Italy. But the turbulence which had so characterised Robert's life did not, even in his death, desert him. On its way across the Adriatic the vessel, overtaken by a sudden tempest, almost foundered off Otranto and the coffin was swept overboard. It was eventually retrieved, but prolonged contract with the sea water had not improved its contents. In the condition in which it was found, the corpse could clearly travel no farther. The heart and entrails were removed, reverently jarred, and left at

---

[1] See the fascinating article by H. Gregoire and R. de Keyser in *Byzantion*, vol. XIV, 1939.

[2] Thereafter William and Rainouart, and then
Duke Godfrey to the Cross compelled mine eye;
Last, Robert Guiscard flashed across my ken.

Dante, *Paradiso*, XVIII, 46–48,
tr. G. Bickersteth.

Otranto; the remainder, embalmed in the nick of time, then proceeded on its last journey.

Venosa, says Gibbon, is 'a place more illustrious for the birth of Horace than for the burial of the Norman heroes'. Whether we agree with him or not, we have to admit that the little town nowadays contains more to interest the classical scholar than the mediaevalist. Of the abbey buildings of the SS. Trinità there is little left save a wall or two and a few sad and broken colonnades. The church—transformed by Robert's brother, Drogo, while still Count of Venosa, from a modest Lombard basilica into an edifice worthy to serve as the family shrine of the Hautevilles—still stands, together with the wall of another which Drogo began and Robert continued but neither lived to finish. Unfortunately, however, Baedeker's comment in 1883 that 'it has recently undergone restoration in questionable taste' is all too true; not much remains to tell us of how it must have looked when Pope Nicholas consecrated it in 1058 or when one Hauteville after another was laid to rest in its shade. The vaguely classicising and obviously refurbished tomb of Robert's first wife Alberada, with its self-effacing epitaph to the effect that if anyone is looking for her son Bohemund they will find his tomb at Canosa, is plain enough, somewhat awkwardly set in the north aisle; and we may even with an effort persuade ourselves to accept Norman Douglas's suggestion that one of the poor patches of fresco left on the walls is in fact a portrait of Sichelgaita. But the Guiscard himself is even less worthily commemorated. His original tomb has long since disappeared; only its epitaph, preserved by William of Malmesbury, has come down to us.[1] Gone, too, are the tombs of William, Drogo and Humphrey. Some time in the sixteenth century the remains of all four brothers were united in one simple monument

[1] *Hic terror mundi Guiscardus; hic expulit urbe*
Quem Ligures regem, Roma, Lemannus habent.
Parthus, Arabs, Macedumque phalanx non texit Alexin,
At fuga; sed Venetum nec fuga nec pelagus.

(Here lies the Guiscard, terror of the world; by his hand, he whom the Germans, the Ligurians and even Rome itself called King was driven from the City. From his wrath neither the Parthians not the Arabs, nor even the forces of Macedon, could save Alexius, whose only hope lay in flight; while for Venice, neither flight nor the protection of the ocean were of any avail.)

which may yet be seen. It carries no inscription. The only clue to its contents is a line from William of Apulia, still legible in the fresco on the wall above: '*Urbs Venusina nitet tantis decorata sepulchris.*'[1]

Now Robert, as rumour insisted and many said, was a most exceptional leader, quick-witted, good-looking, courteous in conversation, ready too in repartee, loud-voiced, easily accessible, very tall in stature, his hair always close-cut, long-bearded, always anxious to maintain the ancient customs of his race. He preserved the perfect comeliness of his counten-ance and figure until the end, and of these he was very proud, as his appearance was considered worthy of kingship; he showed respect to all his subordinates, more especially to those who were well-disposed towards him. On the other hand he was very thrifty and fond of money, very business-like and greedy of gain and, in addition to all this, most ambi-tious; and since he was a slave to these desires, he has incurred the serious censure of mankind.[2]

Such are the flowers which, in Gibbon's phrase, 'the joyful Anna Comnena scatters over the grave of an enemy'. Her description is probably accurate enough as far as it goes, but Anna is too chauvin-istic and tendentious an observer to recognise the measure of the Guiscard's greatness. A man who began his career as a penniless brigand and horse-thief and who ended it with both Emperors simultanteously on the run and the greatest of mediaeval Popes in his power deserves a mightier tribute than this. Robert had found South Italy a confusion of races and religions, of principalities, duchies and petty baronies, all of them endlessly, pointlessly at loggerheads; he left it welded together into a single state. He has been taken to task[3] for failing to provide any form of administration to check the power of the Norman barons on the one hand and the Lombard nationalists on the other, and it is true that his talents lay more in the direction of war than of civil government; but the persistent rebelliousness of his vassals—a characteristic which was to endure as long as Norman domination itself—increases rather than diminishes the immensity of his achievement. He began with one advantage only: the supremacy, among the Norman barons of

[1] 'The city of Venosa shines with the glory of such sepulchres.'
[2] Tr. Dawes.
[3] E. Jamison, 'The Norman Administration of Apulia and Capua', *Papers of the British School at Rome*, VI, 1913.

Apulia, of his three brothers before him. For the rest he had to rely
solely on his natural gifts—his faultless generalship allied with a
superb diplomatic sense; his toughness and resolution in war, his
mercy and generosity in peace; his genuine piety on the one hand,
which he somehow managed to keep above and apart from his
brilliant handling of successive Popes, and, on the other, that easy
tolerance and eclecticism which often kept him on better terms with
his Italian, Greek, Lombard and even his Saracen subjects than with
his Norman vassals. He also possessed, to an extraordinary degree,
those two qualities of temperament which, perhaps more than any
others, are indispensable to political greatness—the superb self-
confidence that melts away doubts and difficulties and allows
ambition to keep pace with imagination, and the inexhaustible
energy that never failed until, in his seventieth year, death overtook
him. As for his personal valour, the most revealing proof is given
by William of Malmesbury, who tells of how Duke William of
Normandy—the Conqueror—used to screw up his own courage by
reminding himself of the Guiscard's; and indeed in their achievements the two greatest Normans of their time had more than a little
in common. But in their characters there was one all-important,
fundamental difference. The Conqueror, whatever his other qualities,
remained throughout his life mean, gloomy and austere. Robert, by
contrast, never lost that streak of cheerful irresponsibility with which
he began. He was that rarest of combinations, a genius and an
extrovert; and, as the chronicles close on his life, they leave us with
the picture of a gigantic blond buccaneer who not only carved out
for himself the most extraordinary career of the Middle Ages but
who also, quite shamelessly, enjoyed it.

With Robert Guiscard dead and Bohemund, its only other able
commander, convalescing in Apulia, the Byzantine expedition was
at an end. At Sichelgaita's insistence, Roger Borsa had once again
been designated by his father as successor to the Dukedom, and had
apathetically been recognised as such by what was left of the army;
but he had never had much stomach for this—or indeed for any other
—campaign, and he certainly had no intention of continuing it now.
Neither did he like the idea of leaving Bohemund, even in his

present state of health, to his own devices in Italy, where he would be bound to take advantage of his half-brother's absence and make a bid for power. Leaving his men to find their way home as best they could, he therefore returned at once with his mother to take formal possession of his new dominions; while the once-mighty army, hopelessly demoralised by the Guiscard's death and heartily sick of the Balkans in any case, followed in a general *sauve-qui-peut* as discreditable as it was undignified.

Roger Borsa's fears were not ill-founded. Bohemund, as we shall see, did indeed contest his right of succession and, even after being bought off with the best part of southern Apulia, was to remain a painful thorn in his half-brother's flesh for another ten years until he sailed away to win richer prizes still—and, incidentally, immortality—on the First Crusade. After he was gone, other rebellions followed, both Norman and Lombard; and though the anaemic young Duke somehow managed to retain his throne throughout his miserable life, the decline of the Duchy of Apulia which began with the Guiscard's death was to continue uninterruptedly until and even beyond that day in 1111 when his son followed him to the grave. So, mercifully, the spotlight shifts back to Sicily; but before we follow it we must briefly take leave of two other characters who now fade from our story.

First Sichelgaita. History has dealt harshly with her. Her ferocity on the battlefield—a quality which in national heroines like Boadicea or Joan of Arc evokes the rapturous applause of historians—has earned her more ridicule than approbation; while the contemporary Anglo-Norman chroniclers—Ordericus Vitalis, William of Malmesbury and the rest—almost unanimously accuse her of poisoning her husband and Bohemund as well. This ludicrous theory, for which they offer not a shred of evidence, must presumably have its roots in her persistent championing of her own son, Roger Borsa, in preference to the full-blooded Norman Bohemund, as her husband's successor—an attitude which, though it proved to be in the ultimate interests both of Norman Sicily and of Bohemund himself, was finally to destroy the Duchy of Apulia as a separate state. In fact, while her influence on Robert Guiscard was always considerable, she seems to have remained utterly devoted to him throughout the quarter-century and more of their married life; and the poisoning story, like the countless similar rumours that so frequently attended the deaths of mediaeval princes, can be dismissed as nonsense. Sichelgaita was to survive another five years, largely devoted to helping her son to preserve his tottering throne against Bohemund's machinations. She died in 1090 in her native city, and was buried at Monte Cassino.

Finally we must spare a parting thought for her daughter Helena, left disconsolate in a Byzantine convent, serving first as an unwilling pretext for her father's ambitions and later as a pathetic hostage whom he had not the faintest desire to redeem. If we are to believe Ordericus Vitalis—and there is no particular reason why we should —she was joined at some stage by a sister, and the two princesses lived for almost twenty years in the imperial palace at Constantinople, where 'their office was, every morning, when the Emperor had risen from his bed and was washing his hands, to present him with a towel, and, holding an ivory comb, to dress the Emperor's beard'. This assertion has been rejected by a later commentator as 'indelicate and improbable', and indeed it is. A safer, sadder guess would be that the poor girl was left—an unwanted bird in an inadequately gilded cage—to the mercies of some grisly abbess until her father was dead and her mother forgotten. Then and only then did Alexius return her, as he should have done on his accession, to what remained of her family. By then her chances of finding a husband were slim, and there is no record of her ever having married. Eventually she settled down at Roger's Sicilian court. He was the only one of the Hautevilles to have shown her any real sympathy; and though she cannot have cherished any very warm feelings for his Greek subjects, to her uncle her knowledge of their language and customs must have been invaluable. Perhaps this was some consolation to her; but for one who might have been an Empress it was a poor substitute.

18

VICTORS AND VANQUISHED

O Sea! You conceal beyond your further shores a veritable Paradise. In
my own country I knew only joy, never misfortune.

There, in the dawn of my life, I saw the sun in his glory. Now, in exile
and in tears, I witness his decline. . . .

O that I could embark on the crescent moon, fly to the shores of Sicily
and there crush myself against the breast of the sun!

> Ibn Hamdis, refugee from Syracuse
> after its capture by the Normans

At the moment that death came to Robert Guiscard on the island of
Cephalonia, his brother Roger was laying siege to Syracuse. In the
thirteen years that had elapsed since the capture of Palermo he had
maintained his pressure on the Saracen resistance until it was now
confined to the centre and south-east of the island; but it had been a
hard struggle, against odds that varied only between the disproportionate and the overwhelming. There were few pitched battles; this
was a war of sudden sorties and ambuscades, in which a handful of
knights would sweep down from some mountain citadel on to an unsuspecting town, ravage it, annihilate the garrison and disappear once
again into their fastness. It was a war, too, which offered immense
opportunities for deeds of individual daring, a war which is still
fought along the sides of Sicilian peasant carts and, amid the clatter-
ing of tin armour and the thudding of turbaned heads, in the traditional puppet-shows of Palermo.

Gradually the enemy was pushed back. The year 1077 saw the
collapse of the last two Saracen strongholds in the west. The siege
of Trapani was brought to an abrupt end when Roger's bastard son
Jordan led a surprise raid on the grassy promontory where the

defenders grazed their sheep and cattle, and at one stroke deprived them of their principal food supply; the neighbouring stronghold of Erice, on the other hand, perched up on its dizzy pinnacle a mile or two to the east, surrendered only after the unsportsmanlike intervention of St Julian, who suddenly appeared with a pack of voracious hounds and released them upon the infidels.[1] Two years later, in August 1079, Taormina followed. The Emir had long considered his position to be impregnable, but on finding it ringed with no fewer than twenty-two Norman fortresses supported by a naval blockade, he saw that continued resistance was in vain. His surrender was followed by the capitulation of the whole Etna massif, and by the end of 1079 all Sicily north of the Agrigento-Catania line, save only the still indomitable Enna, had accepted the Normans as its overlords.

But now the advance was halted again. Minor revolts among the Saracens of Giato[2] and Cinisi accounted for the rest of 1079 and much of 1080, and in 1081 Roger was needed elsewhere. He was never allowed to forget that however heavily occupied he might be in Sicily he was still, first and foremost, his brother's vassal. If Robert Guiscard called for his assistance on the mainland it was his duty to obey. There was, admittedly, something further to be considered, beyond the narrow issue of feudal obligation: the Count knew perfectly well that he depended on Robert's Italian dominions for his own lines of communication and supply, and that should there occur a catastrophe in Apulia or—worse still—in Calabria, his position in Sicily might well become untenable. All the same, it must have been galling to sacrifice, time after time, a hard-won initiative to answer the Guiscard's call. He had already lost the best part of a year that way in 1075—during which his son-in-law Hugh of Jersey had been killed and his army soundly defeated in a battle undertaken, in defiance of Roger's strict instructions, against

[1] For eight and a half centuries from that day the place was known as Monte San Giuliano; only in 1934, with Mussolini's attempt to revive the old imperial past, did it revert to its earlier name. Throughout this period it was noted not only for the steepness of its precipices but also for the beauty of its women. 'They are said to be the loveliest of the whole island—may Allah deliver them into the hands of the Faithful!' notes Ibn Jubair piously.

[2] Now S. Giuseppe Iato.

the Emir of Syracuse—and now, in the spring of 1081, the summons came again. Robert, about to launch his ill-fated expedition against the Byzantine Empire and understandably doubtful about Roger Borsa's reliability in moments of stress, needed his brother in Italy during his absence. Roger cannot have had much enthusiasm for the prospect; responsible now for all three dukedoms—for he himself had even fewer delusions about his nephew—he must have recognised that with the Guiscard's best troops away in Greece he would be hopelessly over-extended in the event of serious trouble.

And the next few weeks proved him right. Almost at once the Count found himself faced with two simultaneous emergencies. One was at Gerace, in Calabria, where a Norman baron had allied himself with the local Greek population and raised the standard of revolt; the other arose in Sicily where Bernavert,[1] Emir of Syracuse, managed to regain possession of Catania. Roger was still occupied at Gerace; without waiting for his return, his son Jordan with two other leaders, Robert de Sourval and Elias Cartomi—the latter almost certainly a converted Saracen—led a force of a hundred and sixty knights against Bernavert and recaptured the city. Thus, when the Count was at last able to return to the island, all was quiet again; but he knew that next time he might not be so lucky.

That winter saw a further strengthening of the fortifications of Messina—which Roger rightly considered the key to Sicily. Then, with the coming of spring in 1082, the same considerations that brought Robert Guiscard hurrying back from Kastoria led him once again to summon his brother to his aid. Leaving Sicily in Jordan's charge, the Count set off at once. This time he knew that his presence was essential, for the Guiscard was faced with one of the most desperate crises of his career. The story of that crisis has already been told. It was more than a year before Roger returned to Sicily, and even then he would probably not have done so for a lesser cause than that which, in the summer of 1083, so urgently called him home. Jordan, his own son—he who had shown such initiative

---

[1] This version—Malaterra's—of the Emir's name is obviously corrupt, but the Saracen sources tell us nothing. The most likely guess is that his name was really Ibn al-Wardi; but Amari, the greatest authority on the Saracens in Sicily, remains unconvinced. See his *Storia dei Musulmani di Sicilia*, vol. III, p. 149 n.

at Trapani and such courage only two years before at Catania—had allied himself with a few discontented knights and rebelled against his father's authority. Already he had taken possession of Mistretta and of S. Marco d'Alunzio, the first Norman castle ever to be built on Sicilian soil; and he was now marching on Troina, where his father's treasure was stored.

Roger sped back to Sicily. His arrival seemed to stop the rebels in their tracks; and he soon saw that the danger was no longer one of a quickly spreading revolt, but rather that Jordan and his friends, out of sheer despair, might take refuge among the Muslims. And so, once order had been restored, he pretended to shrug off the whole matter. The ringleaders, beguiled into thinking that a free pardon would be theirs for the asking, gave themselves up. Only then did the Count reveal his determination. His son's twelve principal accomplices were condemned to be blinded, while Jordan himself languished for several days in hourly expectation of a similar fate. At last he received his father's pardon, and thenceforth served him loyally until his death. Never again in Sicily was Count Roger's authority questioned.

When, in 1081, Jordan had recaptured Catania, he had unfortunately failed to lay his hands on Bernavert himself, who had escaped back to his stronghold at Syracuse. Since then the Emir had lain low; but suddenly, in the summer of 1084—just about the time that Robert Guiscard was marching on Rome—he returned to the attack. This time his objective was not Norman-held Sicily, but the towns and villages along the Calabrian coast. Nicotera suffered particularly severely at his hands as did the suburbs of Reggio, where the Saracens desecrated and despoiled two churches before making their getaway. But the worst atrocity of all was yet to come; at the beginning of autumn Bernavert's ships descended upon the Convent of the Mother of God at Rocca d'Asino[1] and carried all the nuns back in triumph to the Emiral harem.

These last outrages introduced a new and sinister element into the struggle. Although, largely for reasons of morale, Robert Guiscard and Roger had both stressed the crusading aspect of the Sicilian

---

[1] The village can no longer be identified.

conquest during its early years, from the moment that Roger began building up a multiracial society and administration he had been careful to show respect and, later, his genuine admiration for the traditions of Islam. No one knew better than he that a viable Sicilian state could be constructed only on a basis of complete religious toleration, and he was always at pains to emphasise to his Saracen subjects that such military measures as might still be necessary were being undertaken—often with Muslim contingents fighting on the Norman side—for the sole purpose of political unification. Freedom of religion would always be granted to the conquered. As time went on, the majority of Saracens in Norman-held territory had grown to accept these assurances and, mellowed by the return of an ordered and efficient government and the promise of further prosperity to come, had been ready to give Roger their loyalty. Now, suddenly, there came a deliberate attempt by the Emir of Syracuse to reawaken religious animosities. Already in Calabria Christian opinion had hardened once more against the Muslims; if Bernavert were not quickly eliminated, confessional strife would flare up again throughout Sicily also, and all Roger's work would come crashing down in ruins.[1]

Immediately Roger began to prepare for a major campaign, on a scale unequalled since that which he had led against Taormina five years before. Throughout the winter and spring he worked, until in mid-May 1085 all was ready. On Wednesday the 20th his fleet set sail from Messina.[2] That night it reached Taormina; on Thursday it was near Catania; and on Friday evening the ships anchored off Cape S. Croce, some fifteen miles north of Syracuse, where Jordan—now fully restored to his father's favour—was waiting with the cavalry. Before going farther, Roger decided on a reconnaissance.

[1] Chalandon infers, from accounts of the religious ceremonies which accompanied the military preparations for the Syracuse expedition, that Roger deliberately set out to inflame the passions of his Christian subjects against the Infidel. He underestimates the Count. It was normal to say masses, give alms and perform sundry special acts of devotion before embarking on any military enterprise; but to stoke confessional fires at such a moment would have been contrary to his whole Sicilian policy and might well have proved disastrous.

[2] Amari, who puts the expedition a year later, in 1086, has got his chronology a little confused. I follow Chalandon, whose reasoning (vol. I, p. 338) seems incontrovertible.

A certain Philip was sent forward in a light pinnace manned by twelve Arabic-speaking Sicilians—the greater part presumably Saracens themselves—and managed, under cover of darkness, not only to enter the enemy harbour but by passing his ship off as a local vessel to sail right through the middle of Bernavert's fleet. By Sunday he was back with full information about its size and strength. The Count laid his plans accordingly. On a lonely stretch of coast the army and navy assembled together to hear mass; then at nightfall, confessed and newly shriven, they set off on the last stage of their journey.

The battle was fought at daybreak the following morning, in those same waters outside the harbour where the ships of Syracuse had destroyed the Athenian fleet almost exactly fifteen centuries before. Now they were not so fortunate. The Norman crossbowmen, lining the decks and perched at the mastheads, could shoot accurately from a far greater range than Bernavert's archers could hope to command; and the Emir soon saw that his only chance was to move in close and come to grips with his attackers. Giving the order for a general advance and directing his own helmsman to head straight for Roger's flagship, he led his fleet through a hail of arrows into the thick of the Norman line; then, as he came alongside, without waiting for grappling-irons, he leaped for the enemy deck. It was an act of immense courage, but it failed. Whether through miscalculation or exhaustion—for he had already been seriously wounded by a Norman javelin—he jumped short. Into the sea he fell; the weight of his armour did the rest.

Seeing their leader drowned, the Syracusan sailors quickly lost heart. Most of the ships were captured then and there; others fled back into harbour, only to find Jordan and his men already entrenching themselves along the land-walls of the city. The ensuing siege lasted all through the heat of the summer. In vain the defenders tried to appease the Normans by setting free all their Christian prisoners—including, presumably, the luckless nuns of Rocca d'Asino; Roger would accept nothing but unconditional surrender. At last, in October, Bernavert's chief widow, with her son and the leading notables of the town, secretly took ship and, slipping unperceived through the Norman blockade, escaped south to Noto. Their departure settled the issue. Deserted now by their own leaders, the Syracusans gave in.

With the death of Bernavert on 25 May 1085—the very day on which Pope Gregory finally turned his face to the wall at Salerno— Saracen resistance to the Normans was broken. The Emir, even though he possessed little real authority beyond the immediate neighbourhood of Syracuse, had had sufficient force of personality to capture the imagination and fire the enthusiasm of all those of his co-religionists who felt as he did; after him there was no one. The Saracens lost hope: their spirit was gone. Syracuse, as we have seen, held out for a few more months, but only in the hope of gaining more favourable terms. Such other pockets as remained unpacified were to last only for as long as Roger, after his brother's death once again temporally preoccupied with mainland affairs, allowed them to do so.

Some time in September 1085, a week or two after he had laid what was left of his father in his tomb at Venosa, Roger Borsa called a meeting of his chief vassals to receive their formal recognition and homage as Duke of Apulia. Their acclaim was, if anything, even more half-hearted than that of the army in Greece two months before. The rise of the Hautevilles was still resented by nearly all the Norman barons of South Italy. They had given a certain amount of reluctant loyalty to Robert Guiscard, first because they had had little choice and secondly because they had grudgingly recognised his courage and his superb gifts of leadership; even then they had never hesitated to take up arms against him when they got the chance. For his son, who possessed none of Robert's genius and whose very blood was tainted with that of the subject Lombard race, they had little affection and less respect.

But Sichelgaita had done her work well. Key vassals had been approached in advance and bribed as necessary. Out for themselves as always, they were probably only too pleased to give their assent; if they must acknowledge an overlord, then surely the weaker the better. One only remained implacably opposed to Roger Borsa's succession—Bohemund, as impetuous and consumed with ambition as the Guiscard had been before him, knowing himself more justly entitled in law and infinitely better qualified in character and ability to inherit his father's dominions. Unable to find any adherents among his fellow-vassals, Bohemund had looked farther afield and had acquired the support of Jordan of Capua, who naturally leaped at the chance of encouraging dissension among his greatest rivals. Backed by the Capuan army, fresh and well-equipped—in contrast to the debilitated skeletons who had limped home from Greece with Roger Borsa—these two together constituted a formidable opposition; but Sichelgaita had gained for her son what she knew would be the decisive advantage—the championship of his uncle, unquestionably the most powerful figure in South Italy since the Guiscard's death.

Roger's support for his nephew and namesake was no more altruistic than that of the Apulian vassals. Although in recent years he had been the effective ruler of all Sicily, his brother had always retained direct tenure of the Val Demone in the north-east, of the city of Palermo and of half Messina, as well as general suzerainty over the whole island. These possessions would be passed to his successor, and Roger had no wish to find himself hamstrung by a new overlord who would try to take an active part in Sicilian affairs. On the other hand he had his lines of communication to consider. The future of Calabria must be assured and, with Bohemund and the Prince of Capua both out for his blood, it hardly looked as though Roger Borsa would be the best man to assure it. And so the Count too had asked his price. In return for his support, he had demanded from his nephew the immediate cession to him of all the Calabrian castles that had in the past been held jointly by Robert Guiscard and himself. It was the first of many agreements by which, while remaining a loyal vassal, a wise counsellor and an indispensable ally, Roger would over the next fifteen years steadily increase his own power, on both sides of the straits, at his nephew's expense.

The Count had left the siege of Syracuse for Salerno, to pay homage to Roger Borsa after his installation. The ceremony was concluded without incident, but no sooner had the vassals dispersed than Bohemund launched his attack. He struck at the farthest and, probably, the most inadequately defended corner of his half-brother's domains—the heel of Apulia. Sweeping southward from his own castle at Taranto, he had seized Oria and Otranto almost before Roger Borsa knew what was happening. Now he was in a position to dictate his own terms, and the new Duke had little alternative but to accept them. Peace was not restored until he had ceded to Bohemund not only the conquered cities but also Gallipoli, Taranto and Brindisi and most of the territories between Brindisi and Conversano, with the title of Prince of Taranto. Thus, within a few months of the Guiscard's death, the first and greatest of his dukedoms had been irreparably split. Roger Borsa had not started well.

His uncle, on the other hand, was rapidly building up his strength. By the spring of 1086, with Calabria at last under his effective control and an uneasy peace patched up between his nephews, Count Roger felt ready to devote his attention again to Sicily. On 1 April his army laid siege to Agrigento. The town fell on 25 July, and among those taken prisoner were the wife and children of a certain Ibn Hamud, who had succeeded old Ibn al-Hawas as Emir of Enna. Ibn Hamud was the last of the leading Saracens to remain unsubdued—largely because the Normans had never until now made any effort to subdue him; and Roger, remembering the towering impregnability of his citadel and the fruitless siege of a quarter of a century before, was anxious at all costs to bring him to terms. He therefore gave orders that his distinguished captives should be treated with honour and due deference, and began forthwith to plan his approach to the Emir.

The rest of the year was taken up with entertaining Roger Borsa —now making his first visit to Sicily as its Duke—rebuilding the fortifications of Agrigento, and generally consolidating Norman control over the newly-won territory. Meanwhile, Roger felt, he could profitably leave Ibn Hamud to reflect on his situation. Apart from Enna, only two small pockets of resistance now remained in all Sicily—Butera and Noto, neither of which was equipped to withstand a concerted attack. Final pacification of the island was, therefore, imminent and inevitable. The Emir could no longer expect aid from outside; with his wife and family already in Norman hands, he would be well-advised to come to terms.

Early in 1087, with a hundred lancers as his escort, Roger rode from Agrigento to the foot of the great pinnacle on which Enna stands and invited Ibn Hamud, under a promise of safe-conduct, down for a parley. He found the Emir in entire agreement with everything he had to say, perfectly prepared to capitulate and exercised only by the problem of how best to do so without losing face. By now the Count had lived too long among the Muslims to underestimate the importance of such a question; he too wanted the surrender to pass off as smoothly as possible, and was more than willing to co-operate in whatever way Ibn Hamud might suggest. A solution was soon found, and it was with a good deal of quiet satisfaction that Roger rode back with his men to Agrigento. Some days later Ibn Hamud descended again from his castle, this time at the head of his troops and accompanied by a number of his principal advisers. Their route took them through a narrow defile; just as they entered it they were set upon by a vastly superior Norman force and surrounded. In such circumstances resistance was out of the question. Their captors then moved on to Enna itself which, deprived of Emir, army and notables, also gave in at once. Ibn Hamud, his family restored to him, had himself baptised—the fact that his wife now fell within the prohibited degrees of kinship was discreetly overlooked—and retired to Calabria where Roger, in accordance with his usual practice, had provided him with an extensive estate. There he lived out his remaining years, far removed from his old spheres of influence, but happily and in the style to which he was accustomed, like any other Christian gentleman.

Meanwhile, on the mainland, a new and pressing problem had arisen. It was now more than a year since Pope Gregory had died, and the perennial difficulties over the succession were looming larger than ever. The anti-Pope Clement, having failed to ingratiate himself with the Romans, had been expelled from the city, and the throne of St Peter lay once again untenanted. Not that there was any dearth of candidates; Gregory himself had named four on his deathbed—Archbishop Hugh of Lyons, Bishops Odo of Ostia and Anselm of Lucca, and Desiderius of Monte Cassino. Of these the majority of the Cardinals—as well as the people of Rome—favoured Desiderius. As abbot of one of the greatest and most venerable monasteries of Europe, he had influence and the control of enormous wealth; his talents as a diplomat were well known; he had long enjoyed the respect and trust of the Normans, having successfully mediated between Robert Guiscard and Richard of Capua in 1075 and having also been largely responsible for Robert's reconciliation with Pope Gregory at Ceprano five years later. Admittedly, by acting as broker between Richard's son Jordan and Henry IV in 1082, and in that same year himself coming to a separate agreement with the Emperor-to-be, Desiderius has been considered by many good churchmen to be carrying his peace-making activities too far, and had suffered a twelve-month papal ban for his pains; but Gregory had later forgiven him and, in the now more moderate climate of political opinion, it was thought that the abbot's excellent personal relations with the Emperor would prove, if anything, an advantage. Desiderius thus seemed to be in all respects an admirable candidate for the Papacy. There was only one drawback: he categorically refused to accept it.

His attitude is easy enough to understand. He was a natural recluse, a scholar and a contemplative. Forty years before, with considerable difficulty, he had succeeded in renouncing the palace of a Lombard prince in favour of a monk's cell; having eventually found his way to Monte Cassino, he had shown himself a great abbot, bringing the monastery the peace and tranquillity it needed after many years as a battleground, and securing for himself the way of life for which, he believed, God had intended him. All his political exertions, all his celebrated diplomacy, had been directed towards these two objects. As a result his abbey had grown and flourished, and with its ever-increasing wealth Desiderius had transformed it from a ramshackle collection of buildings, strife-torn and long-neglected, into the most magnificent architectural and artistic achievement in the South. He had done more; by bringing from centres as far afield as Constantinople skilled craftsmen in mosaics, fresco and *opus Alexandrinum*—that ornamental marble pavement-work which still glorifies so many churches in South Italy—he had become a patron and cultural influence unique in his country and his age.[1]

[1] Desiderius's basilica at Monte Cassino, dedicated in 1071 by Pope Alexander in the presence of Hildebrand, St Peter Damian and all the principal Norman and Lombard

Monte Cassino, then, was Desiderius's life, its adornment his pleasure, its greatness his ultimate ambition. He had no desire to exchange that most comfortable of cloisters for the intrigues and passions, the danger and heat and violence of papal Rome. He knew, too, that he was without the force of character or driving determination that was the most necessary qualification for the Papacy. A man of gentleness and peace, he possessed none of the Hildebrandine steel. Besides, his health was beginning to give way. He was only fifty-eight, but he may well have already suspected that he had not much longer to live. As soon as the anti-Pope had fled, he had therefore hastened to Rome in an effort to ensure the rapid election of some other suitable candidate, and he did his best to persuade Jordan of Capua and the Countess Matilda to support his efforts; but when he saw that they too were determined on his own succession he could only repeat his refusal and return hurriedly to his beloved monastery.

His champions, however, proved just as stubborn; they would not even consider an alternative candidate, and so the stalemate dragged on for nearly a year until, at Easter 1086, a body of cardinals and leading bishops assembled in Rome and sent Desiderius a formal summons to join them in their deliberations. Reluctantly he obeyed —and once again found himself deluged with entreaties to change his mind. Still he stood firm. At last, in desperation, the assembly agreed to accept whatever candidate he chose to name. Desiderius immediately proposed Odo of Ostia, adding with characteristic diffidence that if this choice did not meet with immediate approval in Rome he would willingly give the new Pope shelter at Monte Cassino for as long as was necessary. But it was no use. The more he spoke, the greater grew the determination to have him and no other. Odo's candidature was rejected on the grounds that it would

leaders in South Italy—excepting only Robert Guiscard and Roger, busy besieging Palermo—has, alas, been destroyed; his hand can, however, be clearly seen in the exterior of Robert Guiscard's cathedral of Salerno, built in the form of a Roman basilica with an atrium adorned with antique columns from Paestum, and mosaics of Byzantine style but Italian workmanship. More remarkable still, and one of the treasures of Italy, is the little church of S. Angelo in Formis, just outside Capua, whose frescoes still seem as brilliant as on the day they were painted, and show just how fresh and vigorous Italian romanesque painting could be.

contravene Canon Law, which everybody knew was nonsense; the
Roman populace, doubtless well-briefed in advance and anyway
trained to this sort of thing since the election of Hildebrand
thirteen years before, clamoured louder than ever for Desiderius;
and the reluctant abbot was carried, struggling, off to the nearby
church of S. Lucia where, to his despair, he heard himself joyously
proclaimed as Pope Victor III. The red cope was cast about his
shoulders before he could prevent it; but no amount of cajolery
could persuade him to don the rest of the papal insignia.

Four days later, riots broke out in the city. Roger Borsa had
chosen this moment to liberate the Imperial Prefect of Rome, whom
his father had taken prisoner two years before. Whether in doing so
he was deliberately spiking the guns of Jordan of Capua and the
papal Curia (who had recently refused ratification for his new
Archbishop of Salerno) or whether he was simply acting with his
usual cluelessness is not certain; at any rate it was a foolish move.
Desiderius, well-disposed and malleable, was the best possible
choice of Pope from the Norman point of view; but now the Prefect
went straight to Rome where, stirring up the old imperialist faction,
he successfully prevented the formal consecration in St Peter's. For
the new Pope this was confirmation of his worst fears. He seemed
almost to welcome the opportunity to prove that he was not of papal
calibre. Making no attempt at resistance, he left the city at once and
took ship to Terracina whence, having made a full and formal renunciation of his throne, he returned with all speed to Monte Cassino.

Now the situation was worse than ever. Now, too, the first voices
hostile to Desiderius began to be heard. Hugh of Lyons and Odo of
Ostia, both nominees of the dying Gregory and both considering
themselves eminently suitable candidates for the papal tiara, naturally
resented the manner in which it had been thrust on to the head of a
colleague who was at once unwilling and manifestly incapable. In
October these two disgruntled prelates, accompanied by several
others who had by now come round to their way of thinking, arrived
at Salerno; Roger Borsa, still thwarted over his Archbishop, gave
them a ready welcome; and though we cannot be sure just what took
place during their deliberations, from that time the abbot's popularity began to wane. Had he not made a separate treaty with Henry

IV when Henry was openly threatening not only the city of Rome
but even the person of the Pope himself? Had he not, indeed,
suffered a year's excommunication in consequence? Was such a man
truly the best that could be found to assume the Vicariate of Christ?

It was inevitable, sooner or later, that these rumblings from
Salerno should reach the ears of Desiderius, safely back in his abbey.
What was more surprising was the effect they had on him. For the
first time since Gregory's death he began to show signs of determination. Perhaps it was the thought of seeing one of his opponents on
the throne that goaded him into action. He had never liked Hugh of
Lyons, who had publicly expressed disapproval at his dealings with
the imperialists; while Odo, whom he himself had nominated only a
few months before, had chosen an odd way to express his gratitude.
But Desiderius was by nature neither jealous nor vindictive. For
more than thirty years his actions had been motivated by two considerations only—the good of his monastery and the peaceful
continuance of his own life within its walls—and it is here that we
must seek an explanation for the steps he now took. It may be that
Jordan, still his determined champion, suddenly hit upon the one
way to infuse him with a little spirit and suggested to him that the
elevation of either of his opponents might have unfavourable effects
on his own position as abbot; similar rumours may even have
reached him from other, better-placed sources. Whatever the reason,
Desiderius pulled himself together and, by virtue of his former
authority, summoned a council of the Church at Capua. There, in
March 1087, he solemnly announced his resumption of the Papacy.
His clerical opponents walked out forthwith, doubtless trusting that
their ally Roger Borsa would support them; but the Duke had been
summoned secretly by Desiderius the previous night and had come
to a very satisfactory arrangement about his Archbishop of Salerno.
Unreliable as always, he now proclaimed himself for the Pope.
Victor resumed, without further reluctance, the vestments he had
so eagerly cast off and started at once for Rome, the combined
Norman troops of Apulia and Capua in his train.

The atmosphere in the City had not improved during his absence.
The Imperial Prefect, whom his departure had left in undisputed
control, had summoned back anti-Pope Clement and reinstalled

him in the Vatican; and it was the Vatican, and in particular old St Peter's itself, that now received the full shock of the Norman attack. Its defenders did their best, but St Peter's was no St Angelo's; it could not be held for long. Clement withdrew to the Pantheon and barricaded himself in; and on 9 May the Bishop of Ostia, reconciled at last to the inevitable, consecrated Victor III in the basilica. Even now, however, the Pope's triumph was far from complete. Trastevere was his, but Rome itself remained in imperialist hands and the Normans, their primary purpose achieved, were understandably reluctant to venture once again into the old city, where memories of 1084 were still dangerously fresh. In the circumstances Victor had no difficulty in persuading himself that it was useless to remain in his see; within a fortnight he was back at Monte Cassino.

This time he felt safe from his enemies; but God, who had in other respects treated him with so much consideration, still refused to protect him from his friends. Now it was Countess Matilda of Tuscany who appeared at the gates of Rome, intent on expelling Clement and his supporters, insistent on Victor's presence at her side. Wearily the wretched pontiff dragged himself back to the city where, immured with his unwanted champion in the Pierleoni stronghold on the Tiber Island,[1] he had to face another two months' tribulation through the height of the Roman summer while the tide of battle swung back and forth, ever bloodier but always inconclusive. In July, by now seriously ill, he could bear it no longer and departed, via Benevento, for the monastery he should never have left; and there, on 16 September, he died. He was buried in the chapter-house; but the whole abbey, which he had reconceived and recreated, was his monument. For the monks of Monte Cassino his memory would be imperishable; for the rest of the world he had proved a disappointment and an anticlimax, whose story served only to corroborate two truths which should have been self-evident—that great abbots do not necessarily make great popes, and that, just as in the days of Gregory, the Papacy still depended for its survival on Norman steel.

[1] The mediaeval tower which still rises from the island just south of the Ponte Fabricio is part of the old fortress. It is still known as the Torre della Contessa, in memory of Matilda. The Pierleoni had further guarded the approach by fortifying the theatre of Marcellus, immediately opposite the island on the left bank.

19

THE GREAT COUNT

Lingua facundissimus, consilio callidus, in ordinatione agendarum rerum providens.

(Most ready of tongue, wise in counsel, far-sighted in the ordering of affairs.)

Malaterra on Roger, I, 19

SEVENTY-ONE years had passed since that day when Melus had approached the pilgrims in the Archangel's cave—seventy-one years during which the great tide that had swept across South Italy, carrying the Normans upon its crest and engulfing all others, had never once faltered in its career. It had carried them through Aversa, Melfi, and Civitate, through Messina, Bari and Palermo, and even to Rome itself; it had raised them, with each succeeding decade, to new heights of glory and power; and if occasionally for a year or two the impetus had seemed to diminish, it had always proved merely to be gathering strength for a still grander forward surge. Now, suddenly, in the last dozen years of the century, the pace slackens. The old momentum is lost. It is as if, no longer able to cope with so relentless an onrush of events, time itself has grown tired.

So, at least, it appears to the historian. To those of the Duke's subjects who lived in mainland Italy during those years, life probably continued much the same—except that it was perhaps a little duller since the Guiscard's death, for his energy and ebullience had made themselves felt far beyond the immediate sphere of his vassals, his soldiers and those whose lives were immediately affected by his policies. But dullness, alas, did not mean security. The old quarrel between Roger Borsa and Bohemund broke out again in the autumn of 1087, and during the next nine years few regions of the South were to escape the consequences of their rivalry. Civil wars tend inevitably to be sterile, exhausting a country physically and financially while offering no hope of expansion or conquest or economic gain; that which now spread across the peninsula was even more profitless than most since, though it enabled Bohemund to tighten his grip on his half-brother's dominions, its effects were largely to be nullified when, in 1096, he left on the First Crusade.

But it was not only the local populations that had cause to regret the passing of the old order. There were others, outside the Dukedom, who found themselves increasingly concerned over the anarchy into which it was slipping; and chief among these was Odo, the former Bishop of Ostia who, six months after the death of Pope Victor, had been elected to succeed him on the papal throne under the name of Urban II. This stately, scholarly aristocrat from Champagne, a zealous reformer who had been Prior of Cluny before coming south to join the Curia, had little in common with his pathetic predecessor. He was, instead, a staunch upholder of papal supremacy on the Gregorian model—except that he possessed all the polish and diplomatic finesse that his exemplar had so disastrously lacked. Since his city was now once again firmly in the hands of the anti-Pope Clement and the imperialists he had been elected and consecrated at Terracina, and he well knew that Norman help would be necessary if he were ever to return to Rome. At the beginning of his pontificate, with the Duke of Apulia fully occupied with the Prince of Taranto, such help was obviously out of the question; and it was only after a personal visit by Urban to Sicily that Count Roger was able to patch up another temporary peace between his nephews and so to make possible an armed expedition to Rome by which, in November 1088, the Pope entered the city. Even then he found himself, like Victor before him, confined to the tiny Tiber Island; and by the following autumn he was back in exile. Not until Easter 1094, and then by bribery, was he able to penetrate to the Lateran Palace and, six years after his consecration, to assume his rightful throne.

Most of those six years Urban had spent wandering through South Italy; and the more he wandered the more convinced he must have become that it was on Count Roger rather than his nephew that the mantle of Robert Guiscard had fallen. The new Duke of Apulia was a well-meaning but worthless cypher, despised by Normans and Lombards alike, struggling along as best he could but increasingly dependent on his uncle and more and more inclined to take refuge from his inadequacy in the churches and monasteries where, alone, his open-handedness and undoubted piety made him genuinely popular. Bohemund on the other hand, if he was already showing some of his father's genius, had also inherited his restlessness and irresponsibility. Although in the Pope's eyes he was an outlaw—having taken up arms against a papal vassal—his stength was rapidly increasing: in 1090 he had managed to annex Bari, as well as several towns in Northern Calabria, and he now exercised effective control, not only over the heel of Italy but also over the entire region between Melfi and the Gulf of Taranto. Even if he could be prevented from destroying the South, his influence in the peninsula would never be anything but disruptive. There was equally little hope to be drawn from the principality of Capua; Jordan had died in 1090 and his son Richard, still a minor, had been thrown out by the populace and was now living in exile.

In 1094 Count Roger was sixty-three years old, and at last the undisputed master of Sicily. Butera had yielded to him soon after Urban's visit in 1088 and Noto, the last bastion of Saracen independence, had followed voluntarily in 1091. That same year, as an additional protection against raids from the south, he had led an expedition to Malta, which had also surrendered without a struggle. Of those areas of Sicily which Robert Guiscard had retained for himself, half the cities of Palermo and Messina and much of the Val Demone remained technically the property of Roger Borsa—the other half of Palermo having been acquired by the Count the previous year in return for helping his nephew at the siege of Cosenza. But although he was deprived of their revenues, Roger's authority ran as firm here as everywhere else on the island.

The two decades that had elapsed since the fall of the Sicilian capital had had a deep effect on his character. During his youth he had shown as much hot-blooded impetuosity as any of his Hauteville brothers; but whereas the Guiscard had remained to the end of his life the adventurer and soldier of fortune he had always been, Roger had developed into a mature and responsible statesman. Moreover, despite his conquests, he had proved himself to be fundamentally a man of peace. Never during the slow extension of his authority over the island had he used military force to gain results which might have been achieved by negotiation; never, when war was inevitable, had he embarked on it until he could be confident of victory. The process, from first to last, had taken a long time—most of his adult life—but it had enabled him to consolidate as he went along, and it had eventually secured for him the respect and trust of the large majority of his subjects, whatever their religion or race. It was more than Robert Guiscard had ever been able to boast.

Robert, it must be admitted, had had to contend with one immense and perhaps ultimately insuperable handicap—his vassals. Jealous, insubordinate, ever resentful of his domination, they were the curse of the South, the supreme obstacle to its prosperity and cohesion. They had, however, an undoubted right to be where they were: many of their families had already settled in Italy before the the first of the sons of Tancred had left their father's manor. The Guiscard had been forced to accept them as a necessary evil and to deal with them as best he could. In Sicily, on the other hand, things were different. There the Hautevilles had arrived first in the field with full papal authority behind them; they constituted the only fount of honour; and they had taken care from the outset to prevent the establishment of any large fiefs that might subsequently jeopardise their own position.

Thus it was that Roger of Sicily had become, by the beginning of the last decade of the eleventh century, the greatest prince of the South, more powerful than any ruler on the Italian mainland. To Pope Urban, whose tenure of Rome was still by no means assured— the Castel S. Angelo was to remain in the hands of the anti-Pope's faction till 1098—it was clear that if the Papacy were once again seriously threatened only the Count would be able to provide the necessary southern support. Roger, to be sure, was not the easiest of allies. He knew his worth and, with the Pope just as with his nephew, he drove hard bargains. On the other hand he needed a strong Latin element in Sicily. Without it he would not only have found his present position difficult but would have had no religious backing on which to rely in time of crisis; and he well understood that three potentially opposing factions tend to be safer and easier to handle than two. Thus, while taking care never to offend or frighten the Greek and Islamic communities, he had from the outset given cautious encouragement to the vanguard of Latin churchmen who had arrived in Sicily in the early years of the conquest. By April 1073 a Latin Archbishopric had already been established in Palermo; during the next fifteen years, as the ecclesiastical immigration gathered strength, Frenchmen were installed as bishops in Troina, Mazara, Agrigento, Syracuse and Catania; and before 1085 the first Sicilian Benedictine abbey had been founded, at Roger's own expense, on the island of Lipari.

The Papacy, while obviously gratified to see the influence of the Mother Church so rapidly expanding in a land where it had been unknown only a few years before, at first viewed Roger's actions with some misgiving. Gregory VII, as we have seen, did not take kindly to the appointment of bishops by lay rulers; and though the Great Count never claimed the right of investiture as a matter of principle as Henry IV had done, he plainly had no intention of relinquishing his effective control of Church affairs. Fortunately Gregory had been too fully occupied elsewhere to bother overmuch with Sicily; and Urban, though his views on the subject were avowedly identical,[1] approached the problem with a degree of diplomacy of which his predecessor would never have been capable. It was not only a question of needing Roger as an ally. The Pope, who may have been already pondering the idea of a huge international Crusade to deliver the Holy Land from the Infidel, could hardly come out in active opposition against the one successful crusader in the West, who after two and a half centuries had restored much of Sicily to the Christian fold. Lurking, too, at the back of his mind there was possibly a further uneasy doubt: could he be alto-

---

[1] 'All that he [Gregory] rejected I reject, what he condemned I condemn, what he loved I embrace, what he regarded as Catholic I approve, and to whatever side he was attracted I incline' (from a circular letter written by Urban immediately after his election, March 1088).

gether sure of Roger's own devotion to the True Faith? Admittedly
the Count, for purposes of practical administration, had subordinated
the Orthodox churches in Sicily to his Latin hierarchy; but he had
taken this step more in self-defence against Byzantine influence than
in submission to Rome. He was, moreover, setting up Basilian
monasteries at an alarming rate, and rumours of a possible important
conversion had long been current in Palermo and elsewhere. Urban
could not afford to take any chances.

Neither, however, could he allow the Count to claim rights which
belonged properly to himself; and whatever may have been the
primary reason for his visit to Roger at Troina in 1088—whether it
was to seek help for a march on Rome or, as Malaterra suggests, to
discuss Byzantine proposals for an end to the schism—it seems
clear enough that the two reached a mutually satisfactory agreement
on the whole question of the Church in Sicily. Henceforth, in
return for his recognition of papal supremacy in ecclesiastical
affairs, we find Roger enjoying a large measure of autonomy, making
his own decisions in the Pope's name and only in the last resort—as
when Urban refused to elevate Lipari to a bishopric in 1091—
submitting to papal *force majeure*.

For a decade all went smoothly. In the interim Roger's daughter
Constance married Conrad, Henry IV's rebel son who had allied
himself with his father's enemies, and soon Sicily became known as
one of the leading champions of the papalist cause. Then, in 1097,
Urban miscalculated. Without giving the Count any prior warning,
he appointed Robert, Bishop of Troina and Messina, as his Apostolic
Legate in Sicily. For Roger such interference was unwarranted and
intolerable. The unfortunate Robert was seized in his own church
and put under instant arrest.

In other circumstances and with other protagonists such a crisis
might have spelt serious trouble between Sicily and the Papacy; but
Roger and Urban were both consummate diplomats, and, by a lucky
chance, an opportunity to settle the matter soon presented itself.
Some months before, Jordan of Capua's son Richard, now grown
to manhood, had appealed to both the Duke of Apulia and the
Count of Sicily for help in regaining his principality, from which
he and his family had been expelled soon after his father's death.

They had agreed—Roger Borsa in exchange for suzerainty over all Capuan lands, his uncle in return for the surrender of Capuan claims to Naples. The siege began in the middle of May 1098 and lasted forty days; and it was an easy matter for the Pope, on the pretext of an attempt at mediation, to travel down to the beleaguered city. Roger received him with every courtesy, putting, we are told, six tents at his disposal; and in the talks that followed—which were attended also by Bishop Robert as a proof of the Count's goodwill— he seems to have admitted that he had acted hastily and expressed suitable regret. While these talks were still in progress, Capua surrendered and its Prince was reinstated; Pope and Count accordingly withdrew to Salerno, and it was there that they decided upon a formula which has led to more speculation and heated controversy than any other incident in the whole history of Sicilian relations with Rome. This formula was enshrined in a letter, addressed by Urban on 5 July 1098 to 'his most dear son, Count of Calabria and Sicily', in which he undertook that no papal legate should be appointed in any part of Roger's dominions without the express permission of the Count himself or his immediate heirs, whom Urban now formally invested with legatine powers. The letter further granted Roger complete discretion in the choice of bishops whom he might send to future councils of the Church.

Several distinguished historians of the period[1] have argued that by acquiring the perpetual Apostolic Legation the Great Count was obtaining rights which far exceeded those enjoyed by any other lay potentate in the Christian West. Catholic apologists, on the other hand, anxious to refute the exaggerated claims of later Sicilian rulers down the centuries, have gone to immense pains to show that the Pope in fact gave away very little; and recent research seems to have proved them right. Certainly the legatine office was withdrawn from Bishop Robert; yet it is worth noting that Urban's letter is careful not to confer it formally on Roger but merely authorises him to act *instead* of a Legate ('*Legati vice*'). Moreover, the letter purports to be merely a written confirmation of an earlier verbal promise; and though the Pope may be referring to an undertaking given immedi-

---

[1] Chalandon, *Histoire de la Domination Normande*, and Caspar, *Die Legatengewalt der normannisch-sicilischen Herrscher*, to name but two.

ately beforehand at Capua or Salerno, an examination of Roger's handling of Church affairs during the previous ten years suggests that he had in fact considered himself empowered with legatine rights ever since Urban's visit of 1088. This would also explain his fury at the appointment of Robert—the only time in his career that he is known to have laid hands on the clergy.[1]

If, then, we accept this modern interpretation of the Pope's letter, it emerges simply as the record of a ten-year-old agreement from which both sides stood to gain. The powers it gave Roger were by no means absolute, nor were they long to remain unique: a few years later King Henry I was to acquire almost identical rights over the Church in England. But they should not be underestimated on that account. Roger now had written authority from Rome to take decisions on his own initiative which would have been impossible if the Pope had possessed full local representation, and which gave him an effective practical control of the Latin Church in his dominions such as he already enjoyed over the Orthodox and Muslim communities. It may not have been so brilliant a diplomatic victory as was previously supposed, but it was no mean achievement.

Pope Urban was not the only distinguished ecclesiastic to appear below the walls of Capua during those summer days of 1098. St Anselm, Archbishop of Canterbury, who was a Lombard by birth, had left England in despair the previous October—William Rufus, having, not for the first time, made his life intolerable—and was staying in the neighbourhood when he received a message from Roger Borsa inviting him on a short visit to the siege. According to Anselm's friend and biographer, the monk Eadmer (who was also present), the Archbishop accepted and remained outside Capua until the fall of the city, 'living in tents set well apart from the noise and tumult of the army'; and there, soon after his arrival, the Pope had joined him. The following story is best told in Eadmer's own words:

The Lord Pope and Anselm were neighbours at the siege . . . so that their households seemed rather to be one than two, nor did anyone willingly come to visit the Pope without turning aside to Anselm. . . . Indeed,

---

[1] This whole question is brilliantly discussed by E. Jordan, 'La politique ecclésiastique de Roger I et les origines de la "Légation Sicilienne"'.

many who were afraid to approach the Pope, hurried to come to Anselm, being led by that love which knows no fear. The majesty of the Pope gave access only to the rich: the humanity of Anselm received all without any exceptance of persons. And whom do I mean by *all*? Even pagans as well as Christians. There were indeed pagans, for the Count of Sicily, a vassal of Duke Roger, had brought many thousands of them with him on the expedition. Some of them, I say, were stirred, by the reports of Anselm's goodness which circulated among them, to frequent our lodging. They gratefully accepted offerings of food from Anselm and returned to their own people making known the wonderful kindness which they had experienced at his hands. As a result he was from this time held in such veneration among them, that when we passed through their camp —for they were all encamped together—a huge crowd of them, raising their hands to heaven, would call down blessings on his head; then, kissing their hands as they are wont, they would do him reverence on their bended knees, giving thanks for his kindness and liberality. Many of them even, as we discovered, would willingly have submitted themselves to his instruction and would have allowed the yoke of the Christian faith to be placed by him upon their shoulders, if they had not feared that the cruelty of their Count would have been let loose against them. For in truth he was unwilling to allow any of them to become Christian with impunity. With what policy—if one can use that word—he did this, is no concern of mine: that is between God and himself.   [tr. Southern.]

Eadmer was never the most objective of biographers, and it is difficult to believe that Count Roger's Saracen troops were either as numerous or as adulatory as he suggests. His account is interesting, however, for its reference to their master's refusal to allow their conversion. In years to come, succeeding rulers of Sicily were to incur much odium for the apparent coldbloodedness with which they used Muslim soldiers against their Christian enemies, and for the vigour with which they were wont to oppose all evangelical attempts. Such policies may well have seemed immoral to bigoted mediaeval minds, but they certainly justified themselves in practice. First of all, by establishing a crack force of Saracen troops, commanded by Saracen officers and maintaining their traditional fighting methods, Roger provided a useful outlet for the military instincts and talents of his Muslim subjects, preventing them from feeling second-class citizens and giving them a pride of participation in the new Sicilian state. Secondly, he knew how dangerously religious sanctions could affect the morale of any Christian fighting force. His relations with the Papacy were normally amicable enough, but there was no telling how long they might remain so. Only by preserving a strong Islamic contingent in his army could he be sure that, in the event of a brush with the Pope, he would still retain a body of first-class soldiers whose loyalties would continue undivided. Finally, the addition of the Saracen brigades made the Count's army supreme in the peninsula, stronger than that of Capua or even that of the Duke of Apulia himself.

Roger's growing respect for the Saracens as soldiers had its counterpart in his civil administration. As he slowly won their confidence they began to respond to his leadership; and as their qualities, particularly in commercial and financial affairs, became more apparent, so the governmental posts held by Muslim functionaries increased in number and importance. In Palermo itself the Governor was always a Christian—though even here he retained the Arabic title of Emir, which passed into the Latin language in the form of *ammiratus* and from which, through Norman Sicily, our own word *admiral* is derived; elsewhere, in nearly all regions of the island whose populations were wholly or predominantly Muslim, government was left in the hands of the local Saracen Emirs. And so, with the return of peace and security to the land, the old Arab artistic and intellectual traditions were reawakened; poets, scientists and craftsmen appeared anew and were greeted with admiration and encouragement; and the foundations were laid for the great cultural efflorescence of twelfth-century Sicily, to which the Arab contribution was to be the richest and brightest of all.

In these circumstances it is hardly surprising that when, at Clermont in November 1095, Pope Urban summoned the princes and peoples of Christendom to take up arms against the Saracen and deliver the Holy Places from heathen pollution, his words should have had little appeal for the Count of Sicily. Among the knights and barons of Apulia, in whose hearts the old Norman wanderlust still burned as fiercely as ever, the response had been enthusiastic and immediate—to such an extent that Roger Borsa, who was, as usual with his uncle's help, busy besieging a rebellious Amalfi when the news of the Crusade reached South Italy, suddenly found himself faced with the mass desertion of nearly half his troops and was obliged to raise the siege. A few months later the great Crusading army, marching down the peninsula to its ports of embarcation, was swelled beyond all estimates as Norman warriors in their hundreds joined its ranks, led by the gigantic Bohemund himself, with no fewer than five other grandsons and two great-grandsons of old Tancred de Hauteville in his train.

For the Duke of Apulia, despite the unfortunate depletion of his army, the general exodus must have come as a godsend, delivering him at one stroke of all the most dangerous and disruptive elements in his duchies. But the excitement and commotion of that summer seem to have left his uncle unmoved. Roger had had enough of crusading. The Arab historian Ibn al-Athir tells of how, at about this time, the Count was offered the assistance of a Frankish army if he would lead an expedition to Africa against Temim, the Zirid Sultan of Mahdia, in what is now Tunisia. He continues:

At these tidings Roger assembled his companions and asked their advice. All replied: 'By the Gospel, this is an excellent plan for us and for him; thus will all the country become Christian.' But Roger lifted his foot and made a great fart, saying 'By my faith, here is far better counsel than you have given.... When that army is here I shall have to provide a numerous fleet, and much else besides, to transport it across to Africa, it and my own troops too. If we conquer the country, the country will be theirs; meanwhile we shall have to send them provisions from Sicily and I shall lose the money I draw each year from the sale of my produce. If on the contrary the expedition is unsuccessful, they will return to Sicily and I shall have to suffer their presence. Moreover Temim will be able to accuse me of bad faith towards him, claiming that I have broken my word and that I have severed the links of friendship existing between our countries.

Ibn al-Athir was writing some hundred years after Roger's death. His facts are a little confused; the episode in question is most probably connected with Roger's known refusal to join a joint Pisan and Genoese expedition against Temim in 1086. The account is therefore less remarkable for its historical accuracy than for the light it sheds on the Count's reputation in the Arab world. It is also one of the few anecdotes to have come down to us that gives us a picture, however imprecise or fleeting, of Roger the man. About his personality and his private life we know infuriatingly little— save that he certainly seems to have possessed in full measure the philoprogenitiveness of the Hautevilles. Existing records testify to at least thirteen and probably seventeen children by various mothers, to three of whom—his beloved Judith of Evreux having died young—he was successively married; but the list may not be exhaustive. The rest of his character can only be deduced from what we know of his career.

But what a career it was. When Roger died, on 22 June 1101, in his mainland capital of Mileto, he was seventy years old. Forty-four of those years had been spent in the South, and forty had been largely devoted to the island of Sicily. The youngest of the Haute-villes, he had begun with even fewer advantages than his brothers; but by the time of his death, though still only a Count and remaining the faithful vassal of his nephew, he was generally reckoned as one of the foremost princes of Europe, one whom no less than three Kings—Philip of France, Conrad of Germany[1] (son of Henry IV) and Coloman of Hungary—had sought as a father-in-law. Sicily he had transformed. An island once despairing and demoralised, torn asunder by internecine wars, decaying after two centuries of misrule, had become a political entity, peaceful and prosperous, in which four races—since, as a result of Roger's efforts, several thriving Lombard colonies were now established round Catania—and three religions were living happily side by side in mutual respect and concord.

Here—with its significance extending in time and space far beyond the confines of the central Mediterranean—lies the cornerstone of Roger's achievement. In a feudal Europe almost entirely given over to bloodshed, loud with the tumult of a thousand petty struggles, rent by schism, and always overshadowed by the titanic conflict between Emperor and Pope, he left a land—not yet even a nation—in which no barons grew over-turbulent, and neither the Greek nor the Latin Churches strove against the lay authority or against each other. While the rest of the continent, with a ridiculous combination of cynical self-interest and woolly-headed idealism, exhausted and disgraced itself on a Crusade, he—who alone among European leaders had learnt from his own experience the vanity of the crusading spirit—had created a climate of enlightened political and reli-

---

[1] Conrad died before his father, having revolted against him; but he was acknowledged king in Italy.

gious thinking in which all races, creeds, languages and cultures were equally encouraged and favoured. Such a phenomenon, unparalleled in the Middle Ages, is rare enough at any time; and the example which Count Roger of Sicily set Europe in the eleventh century might still profitably be followed by most nations in the world today.

20

ADELAIDE

While all the other Christian princes of the world have always done their utmost, both personally and by their great generosity, to protect and nurture our kingdom like a tender shoot, this prince and his successors have never to this day addressed us one word of friendship—despite the fact that they are better and more conveniently placed than any other princes to offer us practical assistance or counsel. They seem to have kept this offence always green in their memory, and so do they unjustly visit upon a whole people a fault which should properly be imputed to one man only.

William of Tyre, Bk XI

NOTHING now remains of Count Roger's abbey of the SS. Trinità at Mileto. An earthquake destroyed it, with the rest of the town, in 1783, and all that could be salvaged of its founder's tomb was the antique sarcophagus itself, which now lies in the Archaeological Museum at Naples.[1] Its church was neither large nor particularly grandiose, but on that late June day in 1101 it must have offered the mourners physical as well as spiritual consolation; and it was from its cool shadows that, the funeral service over, a dark-haired young woman stepped out with her two little boys into the sunshine.

Countess Adelaide was the daughter of a certain Marquis Manfred, brother of the great Boniface del Vasto of Savona. She had married Roger as his third wife in 1089, when her husband was approaching sixty and, despite an undoubted virility to which his two sons and a dozen-odd daughters bore more than adequate testimony, still without any suitable male heir. Jordan, whom he loved and who had inherited all the Hauteville qualities, had been born out of wedlock;

---

[1] See photograph opposite p. 257.

while Geoffrey, his only legitimate son, was a leper who lived secluded in a remote monastery. For a time it had looked as though Adelaide were going to fail in her duty; and when, two years after the marriage and with the young Countess still as slim as ever, the news spread through Sicily that Jordan had died of a fever at Syracuse,[1] Roger's hopes of founding a dynasty seemed bleak indeed. At last, however, his prayers were answered. In 1093 Adelaide was brought to bed of a son, Simon; and two years later, on 22 December 1095, she presented him with another, whom, with justifiable pride —for he was now sixty-four—he called Roger.

The succession no longer gave cause for concern; but the future of Sicily still looked bleak, and many of the congregation that day in the SS. Trinita must have found their minds wandering from the words of the Requiem to dwell on the difficult years ahead. Simon was just eight years old, Roger barely five and a half; a long regency was inevitable. Adelaide was young and inexperienced, and a woman. A North Italian from Liguria, she had no deep hold on the loyalties of any of the peoples whom she was now asked to control —Normans, Greeks, Lombards or Saracens. Her knowledge of languages is unlikely to have stretched further than Italian, Latin and a smattering of Norman French. How could she possibly cope with the government of one of the most complex states of Europe?

The chronicles of this period are so lamentably thin that we have little means of telling how Adelaide overcame her difficulties. Ordericus Vitalis, a mine of misinformation in many respects but often surprisingly well-documented where South Italy and Sicily are concerned, tells us that she sent to Burgundy for a certain Robert, son of Duke Robert I, married him to her daughter—he presumably means one of her eleven step-daughters—and entrusted the government to him for the next ten years, after which she had him poisoned. As we saw in the case of Sichelgaita, Ordericus is all too ready to ascribe perfectly natural deaths to sinister causes, and this part of his account is almost certainly untrue. For the rest, it seems a little

---

[1] A stone recording Jordan's death and burial is still preserved in the exquisite little Norman Church of S. Maria at Mili S. Pietro, a few miles south of Messina. This was built by Count Roger in 1082 as one of his many Basilian foundations. Though sadly dilapidated and now part of a remarkably ramshackle farm, it is well worth a visit.

strange that Robert's name should not once be mentioned in contemporary local records, though these are too sketchy to allow us to draw any firm conclusions. Of the two greatest modern authorities on the subject, Amari dismisses Ordericus's story as a complete fabrication; Chalandon, with reservations, accepts it. We can take our choice.

However she managed, Adelaide was outstandingly successful. For her ministers she seems to have relied principally on native Sicilians of Greek or Arab extraction, while such Norman barons—always more trouble than Greeks and Saracens put together—who hoped to take advantage of her regency to increase their own rights and privileges soon discovered their mistake. Thus the Countess was able to devote much of her time to her chief responsibility, the bringing up of her two sons as worthy successors to their father. Here too she did her work well—in so far as fate permitted. But on 28 September 1105 her elder son Simon died; and it was young Roger, not yet ten years old, who now became Count of Sicily.

Of Roger's childhood we know next to nothing. There is an undocumented tradition to the effect that at the end of 1096 he was baptised by St Bruno, founder of the Carthusian Order, who was then living in a hermitage next to his monastery of La Torre, near Squillace; apart from this, we can only fall back on the equally unsatisfactory testimony of a certain Alexander, Abbot of S. Salvatore near Telese, who later produced a tendentious and extremely patchy account of the earlier part of his reign. Alexander tells of how, while their father was still alive, the two little princes used to fight together and how Roger, who always came out on top of his elder brother, would claim Sicily for himself, offering to compensate Simon with a bishopric or, if he preferred it, the Papacy. By this alone, the abbot suggests, he proved himself born to rule—a theory for which he finds additional confirmation in Roger's somewhat exaggerated charity; never, we are told, did the boy refuse alms to beggar or pilgrim, but would always empty his pockets of all that he had and then ask his mother for more. Unfortunately Alexander is writing at second-hand and his work, which was commissioned by Roger's sister Matilda, is often nauseatingly sycophantic. Later he becomes a useful and even fairly reliable source, but for this period he is neither informative nor trustworthy; and it is only in default of anything better that these two dreary little contributions to our knowledge—if such they are—have found their way into this book.

There occurred, however, in these cloudy but apparently un-eventful years one development of immeasurable significance both for the future of the state and for the shaping of its ruler. When in Sicily and not engaged on campaign, Roger I—as we must now call him—had based himself first at Troina and, latterly, at Messina, whence he could keep a closer eye on his Calabrian domains; but his personal preference was always for his old mainland castle at Mileto. Here it was that he normally kept his family and here, however frequent his absences, that he had made his home. Adelaide changed all that. In Calabria she doubtless felt herself hemmed in by the Norman barons, whom she disliked and distrusted. Messina was better, but it was still a small town and life there must have had little enough to offer. S. Marco d'Alunzio, where Roger also seems to have spent some of his childhood, was smaller still, though perhaps cooler and healthier in the summer months. There was only one real metropolis in Sicily, and that was Palermo—a city with a population now approaching three hundred thousand, and two centuries as a thriving capital already behind it; with flourishing craft centres and industries; with palaces, administrative offices, arsenals and even a mint.[1] The date at which Countess Adelaide finally fixed her capital at Palermo is uncertain. The process was probably a gradual one, but it was certainly complete by early 1112, when, in the old palace of the Emirs, the city witnessed the knight-ing of its young prince. It was a great day for Roger. Shortly afterwards, in June, when he and his mother together issued a grant of privileges to the Archbishop of Palermo, he could proudly style himself *Rogerius, jam miles, jam comes*.

The move to the metropolis was the last stage in the building-up of Sicilian, and especially Saracen, self-respect. Here was final proof that Sicily was no longer looked upon by her conquerors as a

[1] The Sicilian treasury and mint was to remain largely staffed by Muslims (though controlled by Greeks) throughout the Norman period. Many Norman coins continued to bear Arabic inscriptions and even Islamic ones—though they sometimes had a cross added, or the Byzantine legend 'Christ conquers'. The Italian word for mint, *zecca*, is a direct appropriation from the Arabic, dating from this time.

subordinate province. Adelaide and Roger, by coming to live permanently in Palermo, were showing that they not only trusted but depended on their Saracen subjects for the prosperity and smooth running of the state. More important still was the effect which it had on the formation of Roger himself. His father had grown up a Norman knight, and a Norman knight he had essentially remained throughout his life. The son, deprived of paternal influence from the age of five, was first and foremost a Sicilian. Apart from one or two close relations he knew few Normans; his Italian mother, whom he worshipped, infinitely preferred the Greeks, and thus the world in which he grew up was a Mediterranean-cosmopolitan one of Greek and Muslim tutors and secretaries, of studies pursued and state affairs conducted in three languages under cool marble colonnades, while outside the fountains splashed among the lemon-trees and the muezzin interminably summoned the faithful to prayer. It was all a far cry from Hauteville-la-Guichard; and it infused Roger's character with an exotic strain which cannot wholly be ascribed to his mother's Mediterranean blood. This was obvious enough in the darkness of his eyes and hair; but those in later years who came to know him well, and such of his fellow-princes as were to cross swords with him in the diplomatic field, soon learned to their cost that the Count of Sicily was not only a southerner; he was also an oriental.

The First Crusade had been a resounding, if undeserved, success. Its journey across Europe and Asia Minor had taken a heavy toll, and there had been anxious moments at Constantinople when the Emperor Alexius, understandably disturbed at the presence of a huge, heterogeneous and largely undisciplined army at his gates, had insisted that the Crusaders should swear fealty to him before continuing on their march. In the end, however, all the difficulties had been overcome. The Seljuks had been smashed at Dorylaeum in Anatolia; Frankish principalities had been set up at Edessa and Antioch; and on 15 July 1099 amid scenes of hideous atrocity and carnage, the soldiers of Christ had battered their way into Jerusalem, where, in the Church of the Holy Sepulchre, they had clasped together their bloodstained hands in prayer and thanksgiving.

Of all the Crusaders one man stood out head and shoulders above the rest. Bohemund, though no match in rank for such mighty princes as Godfrey of Bouillon or Raymond of Toulouse, had quickly shown his superiority as a soldier and a diplomat. He knew the Balkans well from his earlier campaigns; he spoke fluent Greek; he had been the hero of Dorylaeum and of the siege of Antioch. At Antioch he had stayed, and there he had established himself as the most powerful figure among all the Franks of Outremer. It was a magnificent performance, one that his father might have envied; it set the seal upon his greatness and assured him his place in history. But it did not last. In the summer of 1100 Bohemund had led an expedition against the Danishmends along the upper Euphrates, in the course of which he had been defeated and taken prisoner. Ransomed after three years' captivity, he had regained Antioch only to find that increasing pressures from the Saracens on the one hand and from Alexius and Count Raymond on the other had made its position almost untenable. Only massive reinforcements from Europe could save the situation. The year 1105, therefore, saw him back in Italy. There and in France, where the following year he married King Philip's daughter Constance, he managed to raise a new army; but his ambition led him astray and instead of returning directly to the East, he unwisely decided to march on Constantinople. Once again the Emperor, helped as usual by the Venetians, proved too strong for him, and in September 1108, in the gorges of the river Devol in what is now Albania, Bohemund was forced to seek terms. Alexius let him off lightly enough; he was allowed to remain in Antioch as an imperial vassal, though most of his Cilician and Syrian coastline was to be surrendered to the Emperor's direct control, and the Latin Patriarch of Antioch was to be replaced by a Greek. For Bohemund, however, the humiliation was too great to be borne. He never returned to the East but retired, broken, to Apulia where in 1111 he died. He was buried at Canosa; and visitors to its Cathedral can still see, huddled against the outside of the south wall, his curiously oriental-looking mausoleum—the earliest Norman tomb extant in South Italy.[1] Its beautiful bronze

[1] They should also take care not to miss the superb late eleventh-century Bishop's throne, supported on two marble elephants.

doors, engraved with Arabic designs and a eulogistic inscription, open to reveal an interior bare but for two little columns and the tombstone itself—on which is carved, in letters whose coarse magnificence still catches the breath, one word only: BOAMVNDVS.

But as Bohemund's star had waned, another had been steadily on the ascendant—that of Baldwin of Boulogne, formerly Count of Edessa, who on Christmas Day 1100, in the church of the Nativity at Bethlehem, had been crowned King of Jerusalem. In the first decade of his reign Baldwin, despite a youthful period in Holy Orders, had brilliantly maintained the supremacy of the lay power over that of the Church, and had already gone a long way towards converting the poor and scattered territories of his kingdom into a strong, cohesive state. Matrimonially, however, he had been less successful. He had always had an eye for a pretty girl, and the prevailing atmosphere of his court, though never undignified, could scarcely have been described as monastic; but the Armenian princess whom he had taken as his second wife was generally agreed to have gone too far. Her rumoured reception of certain Muslim pirates into whose clutches she had fallen—not, it was said, with as much reluctance as might have been supposed—on her way from Antioch to assume her throne had not endeared her to her husband; and after a few years in which she had done little to redeem her reputation he had dismissed her—first to a nunnery in Jerusalem and then, at her urgent request, to Constantinople, where she found the permissiveness of the capital a good deal more to her taste. Baldwin had meanwhile resumed with relief his bachelor life; and this he continued to enjoy until, at the end of 1112, he heard that Countess Adelaide of Sicily, having laid aside the cares of the Regency with the coming of age of her son, was looking for a second husband.

In spite of the profitable trade agreements which he had been able to conclude with the Italian mercantile republics, Baldwin's kingdom was chronically short of funds. On the other hand it was common knowledge that Adelaide had amassed enormous wealth during her years in Sicily, which was rapidly becoming one of the chief centres of the entrepôt trade between Europe and the Levant. There were other considerations as well. The Sicilian navy was already a force to be reckoned with; and its support would immeasurably strengthen the position of Jerusalem among her neighbour states, Christian and Saracen. Baldwin made up his mind. An embassy was immediately despatched to Palermo with a formal request for the Countess's hand in marriage.

And Adelaide accepted. She had never liked the Franks as a race, but how could anyone refuse an offer to be Queen of Jerusalem? Moreover she had no delusions about her worth and knew that she could name her own terms. If Baldwin stood to gain from the alliance, she would take good care that her son Roger would not be the loser. Her acceptance, therefore, was given on one condition; that, if the marriage was childless—and she was, after all, no longer in her first youth—the crown of Jerusalem should pass to the Count of Sicily. Baldwin, who had no children living, raised no objection; and so, in the summer of 1113, the Countess Adelaide sailed for the East.

Her journey was not without incident. An attack by pirates was successfully beaten off, but shortly before her arrival there arose so terrible a storm that the three ships sent out by Baldwin to escort her were driven far off course into the Bay of Ascalon, still in Saracen hands, and only with difficulty managed to fight their way out. But when at last the Sicilian galleys glided proudly into the harbour of Acre, the King and all those around him saw that here indeed was a bride worth waiting for. Albert of Aix, one of the most informative of the historians of the First Crusade, was not present on that August morning; but his account of the scene, written some twenty years later, is worth quoting for the picture it gives of a landfall probably unequalled in splendour since the days of Cleopatra.

She had with her two triremes, each with five hundred warriors, and seven ships carrying gold, silver, purple, and great quantities of precious stones and magnificent vestments, to say nothing of weapons, cuirasses, swords, helmets, shields blazing with gold, and all other accoutrements of war such as are employed by mighty princes for the service and defence of their ships. The vessel on which the great lady had elected to travel was ornamented with a mast gilded with the purest gold, which glinted from afar in the sunlight; and the prow and the poop of this vessel, similarly covered with gold and silver and worked by skilful craftsmen, were wonderful to behold. And on one of the seven ships were the Saracen archers, most stalwart men clothed in resplendent garments of great price, all destined as gifts to the King—such men as had no superiors in their art in the whole land of Jerusalem.

The effect of Adelaide's arrival was not lost on the knights of Outremer; few countries of the West would have been capable of such a display. But Baldwin had done his best to arrange a reception worthy of his Queen.

The King, informed of his illustrious lady's arrival, went down to the port with all the princes of his kingdom and the members of his court, magnificently and variously clothed; he was surrounded by all his royal pomp, followed by his horses and his mules covered with purple and gold, and accompanied by his musicians sounding trumpets and playing on all kinds of instruments to delight the ear. So the King received the Princess as she descended from the vessel. The open spaces were strewn with beautiful carpets of many colours, and the streets were swathed with purple in honour of the great lady, herself mistress of such abundance.[1]

A few days later the marriage was solemnised, amid scenes of comparable splendour, in the palace of Acre; and the royal couple proceeded in state, through towns and villages hung with flags, to Jerusalem. All too soon, however, rejoicing gave way to disillusion. Baldwin's army had not been paid for months; Frankish barons and knights had to be compensated and indemnified for lands recaptured by the Saracens; and by the time these and other outstanding debts had been settled there was little left of Adelaide's immense dowry. The Queen, for her part, found the Normans and Franks of Outremer no more congenial than their counterparts in South Italy. More serious still, Baldwin was soon forced to admit that although he had put away his previous wife he had never formally divorced her. Suddenly a great wave of popular feeling arose against Adelaide—and also against the Patriarch Arnulf of Jerusalem, to whose well-known simonies was now added the yet graver charge of conniving at a bigamous marriage.

For some time Baldwin prevaricated. Adelaide bored him and he had spent all her money, but the link with Sicily was still valuable to him and he hesitated to send her away. In the spring of 1117, however, he fell dangerously ill; and Arnulf, who had been deposed from his Patriarchate and then reinstated by the Pope in return for a

[1] Albert of Aix, Bk. XII.

promise to work for the Queen's dismissal, managed to persuade him that only by taking such a step could he avoid the pains of eternal damnation. The Patriarch's further injunction—that Baldwin should also summon his former, legitimate, wife back to Jerusalem—went unfulfilled; she was still living it up in Constantinople and enjoying herself far too much to contemplate a return. But as far as Adelaide was concerned, this was the end. Baldwin, restored to health, held firm to his decision; and the unhappy queen, despoiled and humiliated, was packed off home to Sicily with the minimum of ceremony or consideration. She had never particularly liked Baldwin, and she cannot have altogether regretted leaving the rigours of Palestine for the sophistication and comfort of Palermo; but she had sustained an insult which neither she nor her son ever forgave. She herself died the following year and was buried in the cathedral of Patti, where her tomb—not, alas, contemporary—may still be seen.[1] As for Roger, another historian of the Crusade—William of Tyre—was to report in about 1170 that this treatment of his mother 'imbued him for ever with a violent hatred of the Kingdom of Jerusalem and its people'. The humiliation of Adelaide, grave as it was, was not the only offence of which Baldwin had been guilty; by renouncing her he also broke the promise he had given in their marriage contract—that, in default of further children, the Crown of Jerusalem should pass on his death to Roger. Thus when, a decade or so later, the King of Sicily was to show his strength for the first time in the Eastern Mediterranean, he was acting not just as an aggrieved son avenging his mother's honour, but as a defrauded and ambitious monarch, in arms against the usurpers of his realm.

[1] The tomb itself is obviously Renaissance, though the recumbent effigy above it may be original. It will be found in the south transept of the Cathedral, set into the east wall. The inscription describes Adelaide as Roger's mother, but makes no mention of her period as Queen of Jerusalem—a chapter of her life which she, and Roger, doubtless preferred to forget.

21

THE FLEDGLING YEARS

O young son of Ali, O little lion of the holy garden of the Faith, for whom the lances form a living hedge! Thou didst show thy bared teeth, and the blue points of thy lances! Those blue-eyed Franks, surely they shall receive none of thy kisses!

Ibn Hamdis of Syracuse

THE good fortune that had attended the Countess Adelaide throughout her regency—only to desert her so shatteringly thereafter—remained true to her son during the first few crucial years of his personal rule. Roger was barely sixteen and a half when he assumed effective power, the untried ruler of a heterogeneous state which, though prosperous, was still potentially explosive. He desperately needed a period of peace in which to flex his muscles, to feel his own authority within him, not as a mere tool of government, but as an integral part of his being.

And it was granted to him. The great exodus to Outremer had drained off many of the most obstreperous of his mainland vassals and lowered the political temperature throughout South Italy. To Sicily, meanwhile, it had brought only increased affluence, and the island was now richer than at any time in its history. Even before the Crusade the volume of Levantine commerce—with cities like Tripoli, Alexandria and Antioch, as well as with Constantinople itself—had been steadily growing; and the Norman conquest of the South had now made the straits of Messina safe, for the first time in centuries, to Christian shipping. To the Italian mercantile republics of the west coast such a development was of enormous significance; we know, for example, that in September 1116 Roger granted a plot of land at Messina to the Genoese consul for the building of a hospital there, and it is safe to assume that Pisa, Naples, Amalfi and others had also staked their claims. In such conditions the Greeks and Arabs of Sicily—two races in which the commercial sense was, then as now, particularly highly developed—were in no mind to make trouble; they were far too busy making money instead. And so the young Count was able to settle himself comfortably on his throne, thanking God for the priceless gift of a Crusade, of which he himself, though not even a participant, was ultimately to prove the greatest beneficiary of all.

This new outburst of military and commercial activity in the Mediterranean fired Roger's imagination and awoke his ambition. He did not, he knew, possess his father's—still less his uncle's—military gifts. The warlike pursuits which played so large a part in the education of other young Norman knights had been largely absent from his own woman-dominated upbringing, a fact which reinforced that natural preference for diplomatic rather than military methods which he was to keep throughout his life. But Sicily was no longer the geographical backwater it had been when the conquest was launched half a century before. Its economic explosion had been meteoric and spectacular; Palermo, long a thriving metropolis, was now busier than ever in the past; Messina and Syracuse were boom-towns; the island had suddenly become the hub of a newly-expanded and fast-developing Latin world. Roger was determined that his own political influence should grow in due proportion; and that he himself, like Robert Guiscard before him, should make his presence and power felt among the princes of Europe—and of Africa and Asia too.

As a first step, wealth must be converted into strength; and strength for an island realm could mean only one thing—an invincible navy. The Sicilian fleet had been an important force ever since the Guiscard's day; Roger I had kept it up, enlarged it, and put it to good use at Syracuse, Malta and elsewhere; but only Roger II was to make it supreme. From his day until the extinction of Norman power in the island, nation and navy were one and inseparable; it is hardly possible to conceive of either without the other. The navy meant Sicily's prosperity in peace, her sword and her shield in time of war; and in the years to come the promise of its support or the threat of its opposition was to cause many a foreign power to think again.

Just as the navy was more than a navy, so was its admiral more than an admiral. At first, as we have seen, the word *ammiratus* had no nautical implications; it was merely a latinisation of the Arabic title of Emir which, after the change of capital, came to be applied in particular to the Emir of Palermo, since 1072 traditionally a Greek Christian. In the early days of Count Roger I this official had been merely a local governor. His responsibilities had been great, embracing every aspect of the administration of a city which had by now probably surpassed Cordova as the greatest Muslim metropolis of Europe; but his authority had been confined within narrow geographical limits. As time went on, however, and particularly during Adelaide's regency, his position grew in importance until it covered all the Count's dominions in Sicily and Calabria. The fixing of the court in Palermo was the first and most obvious reason for the change, but there was also another—the character and ability of the Emir himself. He was at this time a Greek Christian called Christodulus, known to the Muslim chroniclers as Abdul-Rahman al-Nasrani. These two names seem to be connected—the Greek means *Slave of Christ*, the Arabic *Slave of the All-Merciful, the Christian* —and thus he may well have been an Arab convert, or perhaps even, as Amari suggests, a member of one of those originally Christian but long apostatised families which had now returned to their original faith. At all events he seems to have been the outstanding figure of his time, who received in succession the titles of *proto-nobilissimus* and *protonotary*—innovations which reveal how the Norman court was consciously basing itself on Byzantine models— and before long found himself President of the Council of State. As such he was made responsible for the building-up of the fleet— of which, as a natural extension of his duties, he soon assumed the overall command. It may be that he was abler as an administrator than as a strategist; certainly, as we shall shortly see, he fails to emerge with any particular distinction from the one naval operation of which a full account has come down to us, and this probably explains why, from about 1123, he was gradually to fall under the shadow of his still more brilliant and dashing successor, George of

Antioch. But for some fifteen years before that, saving only the Count himself, Christodulus was supreme in Sicily—the first of that coruscating line of Sicilian Admirals who contributed so much to the glory of their country and bequeathed their title to the world.

For the historian these first years of Roger's reign are unutterably frustrating. The sources are so few, so barren of any significant or revealing information, that we cannot hope to build up an accurate picture. Just occasionally, as in the Jerusalem episode, when the external affairs of Sicily bring her into contact with other, better-documented societies, some narrow shaft of light manages to filter through the mist and allows us a glimpse of a prosperous and fast-developing state; for the rest of the time, until her local chroniclers resume a coherent tale, we can see this period of her history only in the light of one of those opaque but luminous summer mornings in which the early haze is finally dispelled to reveal a blazing, crystalline noon-day.

For the young Count, on the other hand, it must have been a happy and exhilarating time as he watched his power and wealth increase, learned how to wield and enjoy them, and gradually became aware of his own remarkable gifts. Inevitably there were problems; equally inevitably the Pope ranked high among them. Urban had died in 1099, a fortnight after the Crusaders entered Jerusalem, but—ironically enough—just before news of the victory reached Rome. He had been succeeded by a good-natured Tuscan monk, Paschal II. It is said that when William Rufus of England was told that the character of the new Pope was not unlike that of Archbishop Anselm, the King exclaimed: 'God's Face! Then he isn't much good'—a remark which, though quietly memorable in its way, is hardly fair to either ecclesiastic. Paschal may have been of gentle disposition; he may have lacked that last ounce of moral fibre which would have enabled him to stand firm after his two months' imprisonment, with sixteen of his cardinals, by the Western Emperor Henry V in 1111;[1] but he was no weakling, and he

---

[1] Ordericus Vitalis's bland statement that two thousand Normans from Apulia hurried to his rescue and drove Henry from Rome is without any kind of foundation. Prince Robert of Capua tried to send three hundred, but they were turned back half-way by the Count of Tusculum. Ordericus is probably confusing 1111 with 1084.

was certainly not prepared to remain silent while the young Count of Sicily arrogated to himself privileges which properly belonged to the See of St Peter.

Roger for his part had taken a high-handed line from the start. Already in 1114 he had deposed the Archbishop of Cosenza, and there is other evidence to suggest that he had largely forgotten his father's undertaking, made in return for the legatine privileges of 1098, that henceforth the Latin clergy of Sicily should be subject only to Canon Law. By 1117 his relations with the Pope had deteriorated still further, for it was Paschal who had insisted on his mother's removal from Jerusalem, and whom he therefore held to be equally responsible, with Baldwin, for her humiliation. There was certainly some acrimonious correspondence at this time between Palermo and Rome, in the course of which the Pope seems to have tried still further to limit the terms of the 1098 agreement. The letter which he wrote Roger on this occasion is however couched in language so deliberately ambiguous as to raise more problems than it solves, and to have inspired more learned speculation, even, than Urban's original. A detailed discussion of it falls mercifully outside the scope of a general history;[1] suffice it to say that there is no evidence, over the remaining twenty-seven years of his reign, to suggest that Roger took the slightest notice.

All too soon, however, the young Count found himself beset by a graver and more immediate problem, this time of his own making. Conscious of his growing strength, confident of his naval supremacy, he soon began to cast covetous eyes southward across the sea to the African coast. Sicilian relations with the Zirids of Africa had been excellent ever since his father's day; Roger I had been bound by treaty with Temim, Prince of Mahdia, and had refused on at least one occasion—that of the Pisan-Genoese expedition of 1086—to attack him. More recently, internal strife between the Zirids and the Berber tribe of the Beni-Hammad had led to the devastation of much of the fertile North African coastal strip, and Sicily had been able to export all her surplus grain to the famine-stricken areas on highly profitable terms. In return she had begun to accept increasing

[1] Such a discussion will be found in E. Jordan's article referred to above (p. 274 n).

quantities of Arab merchandise; and by the time Temim's son Yahya died in 1116 a Sicilian commercial mission was permanently established at Mahdia and there was a frequent, friendly traffic of Sicilian and Saracen ships in both directions across the narrow sea.

But trade was not enough for Roger; his thoughts were on conquest, for how else could he prove himself a ruler worthy of his father, his uncle and his Hauteville name? All he needed was a suitable excuse, and in 1118 it was offered. A certain Rafi ibn Makkan ibn Kamil, described by Amari as half-governor, half-usurper of the African city of Gabes, had recently built and equipped a great merchant galley with which he proposed to carry on a profitable trading business on his own account. Prince Yahya, during his lifetime, had raised no objection and had even gone so far as to provide Rafi with iron and timber for the work; but his son and successor Ali proved less easy-going. Claiming that the right to engage in merchant shipping was a prerogative of the Prince alone, he warned Rafi that his ship would be confiscated the moment it put out of harbour, and lent additional force to his threat by sending ten of his own vessels to Gabes. Rafi, outraged, appealed to Roger. He had intended, he wrote, that his ship's maiden voyage should take her to Palermo, with a cargo of gifts which would reflect the high esteem in which he had always held the Count of Sicily. Ali's attitude was thus not only an injustice to himself but an insult to Roger. Surely it would have to be avenged.

Roger doubtless treated the bit about his presents with the scepticism it deserved. He had lived too long among the Arabs to be taken in by that sort of thing. Anyway, he needed no such additional persuasions. Shortly afterwards some twenty-four of his best warships appeared off Gabes. Ali was ready for them and watched as they drew nearer. His timorous advisers urged him at all costs to preserve the Sicilian alliance, but he ignored them. This was a matter of principle and he had no intention of backing down. That night the Normans landed. Rafi received them well and held a great banquet in their honour; but no sooner had they settled down at the table than the doors were flung open and Ali's men burst, sword in hand, into the room. The Sicilians were taken completely by surprise; they could offer little resistance. They barely managed to regain their ships and, confused and humiliated, to beat their way home to Palermo. Ali had won the first round.[1]

Relations now quickly deteriorated on both sides. Ali first imprisoned all Sicilian commercial agents in his territories, confiscating their property, Soon after, in a rare gesture of conciliation, he released them again; but Roger immediately demanded further concessions which he probably knew to be unacceptable, and on Ali's refusal threatened a full-scale naval attack on Mahdia. Ali replied with dark hints about a combined onslaught against Sicily by himself and his Almoravid neighbours, who by this time controlled Southern Spain and Portugal, the Balearic Islands and all North Africa west of Algiers. War seemed inevitable, and preparations began in earnest. They were still continuing when, in July 1121, Ali suddenly died. His son Hassan was a boy of twelve; the cares of government were entrusted to his chief eunuch; and the resulting unrest—for Saracen Emirs tended to be no more amenable than Norman barons—led to general confusion on the lines already familiar in South Italy and elsewhere. Had Roger struck now, North Africa might have been his for the taking; but he missed his chance. For reasons which need not concern us at present, he had chosen this moment to make his first major foray into Apulia; and by the time he had regrouped his forces the situation in Mahdia had changed.

Roger's Apulian adventure was, as we shall see in the next chapter, by no means unsuccessful; and it would probably have distracted him for some years from the North African question but for a new and unexpected development which brought him abruptly down to earth. In the summer of 1122 a Saracen fleet commanded by a privateer named Abu Abdullah ibn Maimun, in service with the Almoravids, descended in force on the town of Nicotera and its neighbouring villages along the Calabrian coast. It was the first attack Roger had sustained on his own territory—the first from

[1] Such, at least, is the version of the story told by the Tunisian writer at-Tigani two hundred years later. Ibn al-Athir makes no mention of any engagement; according to him, the Sicilians simply saw that the opposition was too strong for them, and sailed away again without disembarking. The truth will never be known—though it seems unlikely that Roger's navy, outnumbering as it did Ali's ships by more than two to one, should have behaved quite so cravenly as either of the two chroniclers suggests.

Africa since his father's pact with Sultan Temim some forty years before. There must have been many in Nicotera who still remembered that fearful raid by Bernavert of Syracuse in 1084; but this was infinitely worse. The entire town was sacked; women and children were raped and carried off into slavery; and every object of value that could not be carted down to the waiting ships was burnt or otherwise destroyed.

Roger had paid little attention at the time to Ali's threats of an alliance with the Almoravids; but now, rightly or wrongly, he decided that this outrage had been inspired from Mahdia and he held young Hassan responsible. His military preparations, in suspense since Ali's death, were resumed with a new intensity and determination. This would no longer be a war of national aggrandisement; it would be a war of revenge. Additional ships and men were summoned from Italy; a security embargo was placed on all vessels bound for Arab ports in Africa or Spain; and by midsummer 1123 the fleet was ready. According to the official Saracen account subsequently compiled on Hassan's orders, it consisted of three hundred ships, carrying a total of a thousand and one mounted knights and thirty thousand footsoldiers. As usual, the numbers are probably exaggerated; but the expedition was almost certainly larger than anything seen in Sicily since the early days of the conquest.

The very scale on which it was conceived and launched makes it all the more surprising that Roger should not have led it in person. He was now twenty-seven, an age by which the average Norman knight usually had a good ten years of hard campaigning behind him. He had been married five years—to Elvira, daughter of King Alfonso VI of Castile—and had already at least two sons to succeed him. And this was the first important military undertaking of his career. There is no record of any major crisis elsewhere that might have retained him at home or even drawn him to Apulia; indeed, he seems to have spent most of the late summer and autumn of 1123 rather desultorily in Eastern Sicily and his Calabrian domains. And so, in the absence of any evidence to the contrary, we can only conclude that he did not accompany the expedition because, quite simply, he preferred not to. All his life he was more an intellectual than a soldier; war was the one art in which he never excelled. Though he did not recoil from it as an instrument of policy, he always saw himself primarily as a statesman and administrator and tended, when he could, to leave the fighting to others more suited by aptitude and inclination for the job. There would, to be sure, be periods of his life during which, like any other ruler of his time, he would be obliged to take the field in person. On these occasions he would normally acquit himself well enough. But there would also be times when it was clear that physical courage was never, as it was with his father or uncles, an inherent part of his character—that it could be summoned, when required, only by dint of a deliberate and conscious effort.

It was, therefore, under the command of Admiral Christodulus that the expedition set sail from Marsala in July 1123. Almost at once a storm arose—the Normans were always very unlucky with their weather—and the ships were forced ashore on Pantelleria, where the troops lost no time in practising all the things that they intended to do to the Arabs of Mahdia. But they were soon able to put to sea again, and on 21 July the fleet hove to off some little islets then known simply as the *Ahasi* (the sandy ones) some ten miles north of the town.[1] They seemed adequately protected from enemy attack by the narrow strait which separated them from the mainland; but this strait was itself dominated by a castle, known locally as ad-Dimas, which accordingly became the first Sicilian objective. Before moving to the attack, Christodulus needed more information about Saracen strength in Mahdia itself. A detachment of cavalry was put ashore under cover of darkness and headed south towards the town; and the following morning the admiral personally led twenty-three ships on a similar sortie to brief himself on the maritime defences.

He was not gone for long; the most cursory inspection was enough to convince him that, from the sea at any rate, Mahdia was virtually impregnable. To a commander who thought largely in

[1] There is some doubt as to which precisely these islands were. My own inclination is to identify them with the Kuria group; but the area is full of shallows and shoals, and the whole conformation may well have changed significantly in eight centuries.

terms of naval power, this was a serious blow; but worse was to
come, for he returned to the islands to find the Sicilian camp in
desolation. Somehow an Arab raiding party had managed to cross the
straits, liquidated such opposition as it had encountered, sacked the
commissariat and returned with a rich plunder of arms and equipment. Suddenly Christodulus saw his whole expedition threatened
with failure. That night, in what was left of the camp, Sicilian morale
was at a very low ebb indeed.

Meanwhile, however, the admiral's young lieutenant George of
Antioch had not been wasting his time. This extraordinary man,
whose imagination and initiative were soon to make him famous
throughout the Mediterranean, had been born in Antioch of Greek
parents; but at an early age he had accompanied his father to North
Africa where they had both taken service with Sultan Temim. On
Temim's death, George found himself on bad terms with his successor, Yahya; he probably also recognised that it was Palermo, and
not Mahdia, that held the key to future power in the Mediterranean.
One Friday morning in 1108, while his Muslim superiors were all at
prayer, he accordingly disguised himself as a sailor and slipped on to a
Sicilian ship that was lying in the harbour. It took him to Palermo,
where he went straight to the palace and presented himself for
government service. Within a few years, first in the revenue department and later on an official trade mission to Egypt, George
established himself as one of the ablest and most devoted servants
of the Sicilian state, and won the favour of Christodulus and of the
Count himself. It was not surprising; his qualifications alone made
him unique. Here was a skilled administrator, a Christian bilingual
in Greek and Arabic and a fine seaman whose knowledge of North
Africa's coastal waters matched his understanding of her political,
economic and diplomatic affairs. Thus, when Christodulus had
begun to plan his expedition against Mahdia, he had had no hesitation in appointing the brilliant young Levantine as his second-in-
command.

And George, for his part, had not been slow in justifying the
appointment. By means unknown he quickly succeeded in suborning
the garrison commanders of ad-Dimas, and on the third day after
their arrival the Sicilians gained possession of the fort without a

struggle and installed their own garrison—estimated by at-Tigani at a hundred men. Here was victory of a kind; but even this was to be turned, all too soon, to defeat. In the two years that had passed since the death of Ali, his son Hassan, though still only fourteen, had managed to assert his authority over most of the country; and this unprovoked invasion—for he appears to have had nothing to do with the Nicotera raid—was just what he needed to rally the waverers to his banner. At the first approach of the Sicilian fleet he had proclaimed a *jihad*—holy war on the infidel—and on 26 July, the fourth night after the landing, he struck. His army advanced quietly from the south, under cover of darkness; and then suddenly, with a great shout of '*Akbar Allah!*' which, the chroniclers tell us, caused the very earth to tremble, flung itself against ad-Dimas.

Once more we are forced to rely on later Arab sources for the story of the battle that followed, though at-Tigani reproduces the text of the official report circulated by Hassan immediately after his victory. We may therefore suspect, even though we cannot entirely discount, tales of the blind panic that seized the invading army, of the headlong rush to the ships, of the terrified cavalry pausing only to cut the throats of their horses rather than see them fall into Saracen hands. What seems certain is that Roger and his advisers had again miscalculated. Pride in their fleet had led them to neglect the land army and to underestimate the strength of the African opposition. It was their second humiliation in five years; and on this occasion, trounced by a child of fourteen, they had lost their honour and a good deal more besides.

Safely aboard their ships and out of range of Hassan's archers, the Sicilians regained a little of their morale—enough, at least, to enable them to assess the situation. Their main concern now was for the garrison still holding out at ad-Dimas. Christodulus was unwilling to leave them to their fate without making an attempt at rescue. For a week his galleys hovered off the coast awaiting their opportunity; but they waited in vain. The Muslims, well aware of Sicilian intentions, maintained ceaseless vigilance over the castle; and at last, with his own supplies beginning to run short, the admiral saw that the situation was hopeless. He gave the order to depart; and his fleet spread its sails to the wind and vanished over the northern horizon. In the whole unedifying campaign, it was now left to the garrison to show the first—and last—flicker of Sicilian spirit. All attempts to buy their lives from the Saracens having failed, they resolved to sell them dearly. They held out as long as they could; then on 10 August, their supplies of food and water alike exhausted, they burst out from ad-Dimas, sword in hand. They were slaughtered to a man. Meanwhile their returning comrades had once again run into bad weather; many ships were lost; and of the three hundred that had sailed so confidently from Marsala a month before, only a hundred—according to Hassan's claim—returned to Sicily.

Virtually overnight, young Hassan—whose appreciation of the value of publicity and whose technique in its handling marks him out as a ruler far in advance of his time—had become the hero of Islam, to be celebrated by poets from Cordova to Baghdad. Roger, on the other hand, had suffered a loss of prestige from which he would take long to recover. The first important military enterprise of his reign, his first venture into the international field to prove himself a major power in Europe, had ended in fiasco. He does not seem to have looked for scapegoats. Christodulus, who must be held largely responsible for the disaster, was to decline in influence from this time, but he was neither disgraced nor dismissed; while George of Antioch, whose initial capture of ad-Dimas was the only triumph —however shortlived—of the whole campaign, emerged with his reputation untarnished. But for all the Christians in Sicily it was a bitter blow; and a contemporary Arab historian[1] reports an eye-witness account of a 'Frankish knight' in Roger's audience-chamber, tearing at his beard until the blood streamed down his face and swearing revenge. The Count himself, though less demonstrative, must have felt much the same. There was a strong streak of vindictive-ness in his character, and he never forgot an injury. But he was also a patient man, and he had no intention of risking his reputation still further with a third attack—not, at least, for the moment. Hostilities with Hassan continued for some years, but only in a desultory way; an alliance which Roger was to form in 1128 with Count Raymond of Barcelona was directed principally against the Almoravids of Spain,

[1] Abu es-Salt, quoted by Amari, *Storia dei Musulmani di Sicilia*, vol. III, p. 387.

rather than the Zirids, and anyway it came to nothing. By then, however, he had preoccupations elsewhere. He was to experience many more triumphs and disasters before that day, just a quarter of a century later, when George of Antioch would carry his banner proudly into Mahdia and set the record straight at last.

22

REUNIFICATION

The ducal towns like Salerno, Troia, Melfi, Venosa, and others which were left without protection of their lord, were seized with tyrant force by this man or by that. And each man did that which seemed good in his own eyes, for there was no one to say him nay. And since none feared punishment in this life, so did men deliver themselves up more and more freely to evil deeds. Thus it was not only travellers who journeyed in fear of their lives, but the very peasants themselves, who could not even till their own fields in safety. What more can I say? If God had not kept alive a scion of the Guiscard's line to preserve the ducal power, the whole land would surely have perished of its own wickedness and cruelty.

Alexander of Telese, Bk I, ch. 1

DURING the forty-odd years that had elapsed since Robert Guiscard's death, the fortunes of the Duchy of Apulia had suffered a steep and steady decline. Roger Borsa, plodding miserably in his father's footsteps, had done his pathetic best to hold it together, and indeed after the submission of Capua in 1098[1] could even boast technical dominion over all South Italy—more than Robert had ever been able to achieve. But Capua, like most of his other successes, had been won only by courtesy of his uncle, the Count of Sicily, who always demanded territorial concessions in return; and when, after the Count's death, the poor Duke of Apulia found himself largely deprived of Sicilian help, his patrimony began to disintegrate faster than ever into anarchy. Roger Borsa died in February 1111, a week or so before his old enemy Bohemund and ten days after Pope Paschal had been carted off by an implacable Henry V into captivity, still pleading in vain for Norman assistance. He was laid to rest in his father's cathedral of Salerno, where his tomb —a somewhat unsuitable fourth-century sarcophagus carved with

[1] See p. 273.

figures of Dionysus and Ariadne, but covered with a contemporary representation of its present occupant in high relief—stands in the south aisle. For all his inadequacies as a ruler, he had been a good and upright man in his way; but his death was not widely mourned outside his immediate family and the churches and monasteries he had so loved to endow—as, in particular, the Abbey of La Cava near Salerno where prayers are still offered every evening after compline for the repose of his soul.[1]

He was succeeded by a child—William, the youngest and sole survivor of his three sons, whose mother, Alaine of Flanders, now assumed the regency. It was an unfortunate state of affairs to arise at such a moment, when a strong hand was more than ever needed; and it was made more unfortunate still by the death of Bohemund. If he had lived, he might have seized control and saved the dukedom; as things turned out, he left his widow, Constance of France, on the throne of Taranto, governing on behalf of their infant son Bohemund II. Thus, with the country in chaos, the Pope in prison and a strong-willed and determined Emperor encamped only a few miles from Rome, South Italy found itself under the titular authority of three women—Adelaide, Alaine and Constance—all of them foreigners and two without the slightest experience of politics or government. It was small wonder that, particularly among the Lombard populations, the general atmosphere of demoralisation and hopelessness should have developed into a great resurgent wave of anti-Norman feeling. What advantage, men asked, had these brigands ever brought to Italy? In the century since their arrival, hardly a year had passed without its quota of ravaged towns and devastated harvests, without its addition of further pages to the South's sad history of bloodshed and violence. Here were the destroyers of the old Lombard heritage; yet they had proved incapable of setting up anything lasting in its place. The country had only one chance of salvation—Henry the Emperor who, having just dealt so successfully with the Pope, would now doubtless turn his attention to the Normans themselves.

[1] In a letter dated St Valentine's Day 1966, the keeper of the monastic Archive, Dom Angelo Mifsud, O.S.B., writes that 'the gratitude of the monks of La Cava towards their illustrious benefactor has not ceased, nor has it ever been interrupted'.

But Henry did nothing of the sort. He marched his army north instead of south, leaving Paschal—by now free again and growing in confidence with every step the Emperor took away from Rome—more closely linked than ever to the Normans, his only southern allies. His dependence on them was to increase still further after the death, in 1115, of the seventy-year-old Matilda of Tuscany; and meanwhile the Duchy of Apulia continued on its mouldering course. The Regent Alaine, too, died in 1115. Her son William was described by Romuald, Archbishop of Salerno, as 'generous, kind, humble and patient, pious and merciful and much beloved by his people'; he also, it seems, was a great respecter of Church and clergy. Unfortunately the good archbishop had used almost exactly the same words when speaking of Roger Borsa; and William was soon revealed as being even more disastrously incompetent than his father had been before him. Whereas Roger Borsa had at least tried to make his presence felt—and, with his uncle's assistance, had occasionally even succeeded—William hardly seemed capable of making the effort. He never lifted a finger, when Henry V descended once again on Rome in 1117, to assist his papal suzerain who had confirmed him in his rank and titles only three years before; it was to Capua, not to Salerno, that the wretched Pope had to turn in his hour of need. Nor was he any more effectual within his own dominions. Throughout South Italy his vassals had taken the law into their own hands; all were perpetually at loggerheads; and even a long-drawn-out civil war in Bari, culminating in the murder of its Archbishop, the imprisonment of Princess Constance and the enthronement of a usurper, Grimoald, elicited only a token protest from the Guiscard's grandson.

Such was the chaos which prevailed when, in 1121, Roger of Sicily decided that the moment had come to intervene. The reasons for his timing are not altogether clear; nor do we have any certain knowledge of his area of operations, though these were presumably first directed against those regions of Calabria which had not already been acquired by his father in return for services rendered. But whatever the details, the expedition proved even more successful than Roger could have hoped. Ignoring the entreaties of the new Pope, Calixtus II, who was anxious to do all he could to buttress his ineffectual neighbour against the growing threat of Sicily, he manoeuvred his cousin during the next twelve months to no less than three separate treaties. It was not a difficult task. William was not only weak militarily; he was also desperately short of money, so that even when he could assemble an army in the field he usually found himself quite unable to pay it. Roger, for his part, always preferred to make his purchases with gold rather than blood; and thus it was that all three sets of negotiations seem to have been conducted on a largely financial basis. The last of them actually came about through an appeal from William for help; and the account by a local chronicler[1] of the incident reveals as much about the character of the Duke himself as it does about the state of his Dukedom.

And when [William] was come to the Count of Sicily, he wept, saying, 'Noble Count, I appeal to you now in the name of our kinship and because of your great riches and power. I come to bear witness against Count Jordan [of Ariano], and to seek your aid in avenging myself upon him. For recently, when I was entering the city of Nusco, Count Jordan rode out before the gates with a troop of knights, and showered threats and insults upon me crying, "I will cut your coat short for you"; after which he plundered all my territory of Nusco. Since I have not sufficient strength to prevail against him, I had perforce to endure his offences, but now I eagerly await my revenge.'

Roger, as usual, had asked his price; and by the summer of 1122 he had gained possession not only of all Calabria that was not already his—first pledged for a consideration of sixty thousand bezants, and subsequently surrendered to him outright—but of those halves of Palermo and Messina which had heretofore technically remained ducal property. Even now he kept up the pressure against his cousin—particularly around the territory of Montescaglioso in the instep, as it were, of the peninsula—but his initial object had been achieved. For the rest, he could afford to bide his time.

He had not very long to wait. The next two or three years made it plain that Duke William and his Lombard wife could expect no children, and William himself may have had intimations of an early death. At all events he accepted, in 1125, an invitation to meet the Count at Messina to discuss the future of his Duchy, and there it

[1] Falco of Benevento.

was that, in return for another heavy subsidy, he formally recognised Roger as his heir.

On 25 July 1127, at the age of thirty, Duke William of Apulia died in his turn at Salerno. His wife Gaitelgrima, who loved him, cut off her hair to cover his corpse; it was then laid, as his father's had been, in an antique sarcophagus and placed in the Cathedral.[1] Like Roger Borsa, William seems to have been popular enough as a man; Falco, the Lombard chronicler of Benevento who hated the Normans and all they stood for, has left us a moving account of how the people of Salerno flocked to the palace to look for the last time on a ruler 'who was lamented more than any duke or emperor, before him'. But William had shown himself unworthy of his name and of his throne, and with his death the once-great Duchy of Apulia flickered ingloriously to its end.

He died as incompetently as he had lived; for, while occupied to his last breath in making bequests to Monte Cassino, La Cava and other favoured foundations, he seems to have forgotten, deliberately or otherwise, to ratify his promise to Roger over the succession. Certainly no mention of the matter appeared in his will; worse, his disastrous anxiety to please everybody had apparently led him to make similar promises elsewhere. According to one report[2] the dying duke, in an access of piety, had crowned his other endowments by leaving his entire estate to the Holy See; while William of Tyre, the great historian of Outremer, speaks of an arrangement he had made with Bohemund II before his departure to the Holy Land in 1126, according to which the first to die, if he left no issue, should bequeath his dominions to the other. Thus, on his cousin's death, Roger found himself not, as he had expected, the sole and unquestioned heir to South Italy, but merely one of a number of rival claimants.

By this time young Bohemund was too far away to cause trouble,

[1] The sarcophagus, which is adorned with a frontal relief of Meleager and the boar, is Roman, and of the third century. It now stands beneath the arcade just outside the main entrance.

[2] Walter of Thérouanne in his life of Charles, Count of Flanders, to whose account Ordericus Vitalis, Bk XII, ch. 44, lends additional strength.

but Pope Honorius II[1] was very much harder to ignore. For more than sixty years, ever since Alexander II had discovered the advantages of playing Robert Guiscard and Richard of Capua off against each other, it had been papal policy to keep the Normans divided; Honorius, a man of humble origins but considerable ability, was well aware of the danger of allowing the Count of Sicily to seize his cousin's realm and thus bringing an influential, self-willed and ambitious ruler to the very threshold of the Papal States. Moreover, as suzerain of all South Italy, he had no need to assert his own claims to Duke William's inheritance; if he could merely show Roger's to be invalid, the Duchy of Apulia would revert to him by default. He believed, too, that he could count on the support of the Norman baronage. Several of its members had already taken advantage of Duke William's death to make formal declaration of the independence they had long enjoyed in practice, and many others were determined to prevent the Duchy from reconstituting itself in the firm, authoritative hands of the Count of Sicily.

Against such opposition, Roger knew that his best hope lay in being able to present the Pope and his allies with a *fait accompli*; and in the first days of August he sailed, with a hastily-gathered fleet of seven ships, to Salerno. His reception was frigid. The widespread grief at William's death had not apparently prevented an anti-Norman faction from immediately seizing control of the city; the gates were closed against him; and, to the protestations of his spokesmen that their Lord had come in peace, to take possession of his Duchy by a hereditary right confirmed in person by the late Duke, the Salernitans replied simply that they had suffered too much and too long from Norman occupation and that they could tolerate it no more. But the Count would not take no for an answer. Day after day, with quiet determination, he urged his claim. Tension gradually mounted; the city elders, courteous at first, grew hostile; but even after one of his chief negotiators was murdered by a Salernitan mob, Roger preserved his calm. And all the time his ships remained in full view, firmly anchored in the bay.

[1] Not to be confused with the anti-Pope, also styled Honorius II, who had so complicated the life of Alexander II some sixty years before.

At last his patience was rewarded. He soon managed to make secret contact with the pro-Norman party in the city led by Archbishop Romuald, and it was they who finally persuaded their recalcitrant fellow-citizens to submit to the inevitable. In existing circumstances Salerno would not in any case be able to maintain its independence; surely it was wiser to negotiate while the Count was still prepared to offer favourable conditions than to risk the sort of siege by which his uncle had captured the city half a century before. And so, on the tenth day, the Salernitans came to terms. They would accept Roger, they promised, as their Duke, on three conditions: first, that the fortifications and castle should remain in their hands; second, that they should never be conscripted into military service more than two days' march from Salerno; and thirdly, that no Salernitan should be imprisoned without proper trial. Roger had no time to waste; he accepted. The gates were opened, and he made his ceremonial entry into the city, where the Bishop of Cappaccio, traditional enthroner of Salernitan princes, anointed him Duke of Apulia. It was a near-bloodless victory, a victory of patience and diplomacy—the kind Roger liked best; and it was followed at once by the submission of Amalfi on similar lines.

Meanwhile Count Rainulf of Alife, husband of Roger's half-sister Matilda, had hurried south to greet his brother-in-law and pledge his support. All he asked in return was that the new Duke should grant him suzerainty over his neighbour the Count of Ariano. The request was well-timed; Count Jordan of Ariano, Duke William's persecutor, had been killed the previous week, and his son was hardly in a strong position to object. Roger had no wish to see Rainulf, whom with good reason he heartily mistrusted, any more powerful than he was already; but he needed his help. Once again he agreed. It was a decision he would live to regret.

The news of Roger's success reached Pope Honorius at Benevento, where he had gone to keep a closer watch on developments. It caught him largely unprepared; but now he too acted with decision, and sent a message to Roger at Salerno, formally forbidding him on pain of anathema to assume the ducal title. He might have saved himself the trouble; only two days after his own arrival a troop of

four hundred cavalry appeared outside the walls of Benevento
with Roger at their head. It was the second time in a week that he
had taken the Pope by surprise, but on this occasion he may well
have been equally surprised himself. His journey to Benevento seems
to have been made in response to a message he had received from
certain supporters in the city, congratulating him on his succession
and assuring him of their good will. It had probably encouraged
him to think that even this outpost of papal power in the South
might be his for the taking—in which case the presence of Honorius
in his palace must have come as something of a shock.

Roger was anxious not to antagonise the Pope unnecessarily
while there still remained a chance of obtaining his recognition;
but Honorius was not like the men of Salerno—arguments, promises
and bribes alike left him cold. In such circumstances to delay in
Benevento was pointless. Instructing the local barons, whom he
knew to be on his side, to keep the papal troops occupied by harrying
the city and its surroundings till further notice, the Count accordingly left with his own army for Troia. From here, the gateway to
Apulia and the scene of one of the earliest Norman triumphs in
Italy, he passed to Melfi, where his new dukedom had had its
first uncertain beginnings almost a century before; and, as he rode,
he must have gazed over the plain of Apulia to where the dark
massif of the Gargano crouched on the horizon—sheltering, somewhere in its depths, the cave of the Archangel. Roger would have
been brought up on Malaterra's history, and the first sight of a land
he knew so well by repute may have added still further to his
conviction that he and he alone was born to rule it. The people of
the towns and villages through which he passed seemed to share
this view; as he continued south-east along the foot of the mountains,
he was everywhere acclaimed with apparent rejoicing. The end of
August found him, with a great gathering of bishops, barons and
notables, including his Emirs Christodulus and George of Antioch,
at Montescaglioso; thence, moving slowly through loyal Calabria,
he at last reached Reggio where he received solemn recognition of
his Calabrian claims; and before the onset of winter he was back in
Sicily.

The unexpected warmth of his reception throughout the dukedom from the moment he had left Salerno had persuaded Roger that his position was already secure. Only the Pope was still holding out against him, but sooner or later even the Pope was bound to see reason. And if he did not, what harm could he do without a single powerful ally in the South? So at least Roger must have reckoned; never otherwise would he have taken the huge risk of returning at such a moment to Sicily and leaving the field free for his enemies.

Roger's lightning progress had certainly given him the advantage of surprise, but its very speed carried its own dangers. The towns at which he had stopped, the barons through whose fiefs he had passed, had had no opportunity to take stock of the situation or to consult one another. Thus, unprepared and undecided, they were virtually forced to pay lip-service to his claims—an obligation which they performed the more readily in the knowledge that these claims had no validity until they were recognised by the Pope. And Roger, in the exhilaration of his success, had believed them.

Honorius had been slower off the mark, and had been further obstructed by the gadfly tactics of Roger's partisans round Benevento. But he had lost no time in raising support, and by the end of October had rallied to his cause most of the leading barons of the South—Grimoald of Bari, Robert, Tancred, and Alexander of Conversano, Geoffrey of Andria, Roger of Ariano and, the moment his brother-in-law's back was turned, Rainulf of Alife, who had pledged his allegiance to the new Duke only two months before. Meanwhile the citizens of Troia, under the guidance of their bishop, William,[1] had also revised their opinions; and it was at Troia that Honorius's villainous crowd—all of whom had long histories of faithlessness and rebellion behind them—assembled in November and, in the presence of the Pope himself, bound themselves in solemn league against the usurper. A few weeks later they received a further addition to their strength—Prince Robert II of Capua, who had just succeeded his father and was crowned on 30 December.

---

[1] Bishop William's portrait can still be made out on the bronze doors of Troia Cathedral, which date from 1119. Near it is an adulatory inscription, describing him as 'Liberator Patriae' and adding that 'in the year of the death of Duke William of Salerno the people of Troia destroyed their citadel and fortified the city, in the cause of liberty, with walls and a palisade'.

He was, we are told by Falco, a puny creature; 'of delicate constitution, he could endure neither labour nor hardship'. But Honorius, overjoyed by this opportunity of reviving the old Apulia–Capua counterpoise, determined to take full advantage of the occasion. Having failed, Falco tersely points out, to achieve anything good or useful in Benevento, he rode to Capua to attend the ceremony in person; and there, before the assembled congregation of Robert's vassals, he delivered himself of a passionate oration in which, after dwelling at length on the atrocities committed by Roger's men against the Beneventans, he confirmed the Count as excommunicate and granted indulgences to all those who should take up arms against him. The movement was beginning to assume all the trappings of a Crusade.

Away in Palermo, Roger had recognised his mistake. Once again, just as in the North African affair three years before, he had underestimated the opposition. But this time he was less concerned. It was typical of him that even now, with the papal league already massing its forces, he should have tried to buy Honorius off with the surrender of two towns—Troia and Montefusco—and a substantial sum of money. Only when these attempts failed did he begin serious preparations for war, and still he seemed to be in no particular hurry. It was not until May 1128 that he returned, with an army estimated at two thousand knights and fifteen hundred archers, to the mainland. His plan of campaign was to assure himself of the southern half of the dukedom, where the forces of the league were at their weakest, before pitting himself against the main body of the opposition in the north. Hastening through Calabria, to which his title was unquestioned, he therefore struck straight across to those regions around the heel of Italy which his cousin Bohemund, before departing for the Holy Land, had left in the joint care of the Pope and Alexander of Conversano. It was a wise decision. Taranto, Otranto and Brindisi surrendered without demur, and by mid-June Roger was in undisputed control of all Italy south of the Brindisi-Salerno line.

The Pope, meanwhile, had been in serious difficulties. Rainulf of Alife and Robert of Capua—the first through self-interest, the second through pusillanimity—were threatening to withdraw from the league, while Roger's supporters had increased their pressure on

Benevento. It was already midsummer before Honorius made sure
of his allies and led them to the relief of his city; only then could
he concentrate his full attention on Roger in Apulia. Early July
found him and his forces in the region of Bari, still having encountered neither sight nor sound of the enemy; then, turning
towards the south-west, he advanced to a point on the Bradano,
no longer identifiable, where the shallow, stony river-bed provided
an easy ford; and it was here that he saw the Sicilians waiting for
him, strongly entrenched among the hills on the farther bank.

Roger had the advantage of position; his army was fresh and
rested, and his Saracen shocktroops were probably eager for the
fray. Yet, typically, he refused to attack. Alexander of Telese
sycophantically suggests that veneration for the Pope restrained
him; this seems highly improbable. Far likelier is it that the size of
the papal army, together with his own instinctive aversion from
unnecessary bloodshed, convinced the Count that there were other,
better ways of gaining his objective. He was right. For more than
a month the two armies faced each other, as one attempt after
another failed to lure the Sicilians down from their vantage-point.
Meanwhile Honorius's feudal levies, who could be conscripted
only for a limited period in any one year, grew increasingly restive;
quarrelling broke out, as it always did, among the various league
members; and the fierce July sun beat remorselessly down on the
unprotected papal camp. From his shady retreat on the opposite
hillside Roger could imagine the Pope's discomfiture; and he was
not surprised to receive a message one night informing him that
His Holiness might, after all, be prepared to negotiate.

And indeed Honorius had no choice. He was now beginning to
understand what Roger had perhaps known all along—that his
league was too fissile to last, its individual members too long
accustomed to independence and lawlessness to be able to sink
their differences in a common cause. Already they were at each
other's throats; soon they might well be at his; and Robert of Capua,
who had, predictably, fallen ill and was now lying groaning in his
tent, was not the only one to be speaking of giving up the struggle.
The Pope also saw that he was faced with an adversary too powerful
to be crushed, and with too much moral right on his side to be

dismissed out of hand. South Italy needed peace—so much was certain—and although the Count of Sicily could be trusted to disrupt that peace for as long as the dukedom were denied him, he might also be the one man capable of imposing it if he were given the chance. The danger of accepting so formidable a figure as a neighbour was still undeniable, but it was a risk which would have to be taken.

The negotiations, which were conducted on the papal side by the Papal Chancellor, Cardinal Aimeri of S. Maria Novella, and by Cencius Frangipani, took place at night in conditions of the utmost secrecy; for Honorius was understandably anxious that his allies should not hear of their betrayal until his dispositions were made. He was a proud man and now thought only of saving his own face; he seems to have made no effort to obtain terms for anyone else. Roger too knew just what he wanted—investiture as Duke of Apulia, under papal suzerainty as always but with no other strings attached. Granted this, and provided only that his own dignity were preserved, he was prepared to fall in with Honorius's wishes; he had no desire to humiliate him unnecessarily. And so it was agreed. Nothing would be done on the spot, but if Roger would come himself to Benevento and formally seek investiture, it would no longer be denied him. The barons of the league, informed of the cessation of hostilities and somehow dissuaded from taking their vengeance on the papal person, dispersed in fury; and Honorius set off for Benevento to await his distinguished visitor.

Roger arrived early on 20 August and set up his camp on Monte S. Felice, just outside the city. Three more days of negotiation followed on points of detail. There could, he explained, be no further question of surrendering to the Pope the towns of Troia and Monte-fusco which he had offered him some months before; but he would willingly swear to respect the papal status of Benevento and even— if His Holiness insisted—guarantee the continued independence of Capua. This last concession—a final, pathetic attempt on the part of Honorius to preserve that traditional balance of power by which he had always set so much store—must inwardly have irked him; certainly Robert of Capua had done little enough to deserve such consideration. For the moment, however, the matter was unimportant—it could always be renegotiated later if necessary.

By the evening of 22 August everything was settled. On one point, however, the Count had remained adamant: he refused to allow the ceremony to take place on papal territory. It had therefore been agreed that he should meet Honorius outside the walls of Benevento, on the bridge spanning the Sabato river. There, soon after sunset, by the light of countless flaming torches and in the presence, according to Falco, of twenty thousand spectators, the Pope invested Roger with lance and gonfalon, just as Pope Nicholas had invested Robert Guiscard nearly seventy years before; while the Duke of Apulia, secure at last in his title, placed his hands within those of his suzerain and swore him fealty. Once again, as in Robert's day, Apulia, Calabria and Sicily were united under the same ruler. And he was still only thirty-two. Only one more step remained to be taken.

23

CORONATION

And so, when the Duke was led in royal state to the Cathedral, and was there anointed with the holy oil and invested with the dignity of kingship, the splendour of his majesty and the magnificence of his apparel were beyond the power of words to express or imagination to conceive. Truly it seemed to those who saw him as if all the riches and honours of the world were there assembled.

Alexander of Telese, ch. IV

By granting Roger the investiture of all the territories previously held by Robert Guiscard, Pope Honorius had admitted himself beaten; but not all the southern barons were prepared to surrender so easily. The new Duke was clever—anyone could see that—and more cunning even than his uncle had been before him. His military reputation, on the other hand, was still extremely questionable. Ever since his first intrusion into mainland affairs he had displayed a suspicious reluctance to do any real fighting. His successive triumphs had all been won by bribery, diplomacy, speed of movement or slow attrition; it still remained for him to prove himself as a soldier against a determined enemy. Besides, even the Guiscard had failed to establish any permanent peace in his domains; and the Guiscard had not had Sicily to look after as well. With so large and so remote a dukedom under his direct control in addition to the mainland territories—and one, moreover, in which he apparently intended to retain his capital—the new Duke would find it still more difficult to impose his authority. Militarily his investiture was of little significance. Henceforth he might enjoy papal support, but recent events had shown just how little that was worth in terms of effective power. And though South Italy was full of fair-weather friends who would bow before him as he passed, there was still not one town or village throughout the peninsula on whose loyalty he could wholly rely in time of crisis. And so, once again, the barons and the cities of Apulia rose up against their lord; and Roger's new dominions, on that historic evening when Pope Honorius entrusted them to his care, were already in a state of armed and open rebellion.

Roger was beginning to grow accustomed to this state of affairs. Characteristically, he looked upon his dukedom with the eye of an administrator rather than that of a soldier; and he had always known that Apulia, with its enormous fiefs and its traditional hatred of centralised authority, would present a far greater administrative problem than he would ever encounter in Sicily. His task would be to succeed where his uncle had failed and to set up, for the first time in centuries, a strong and enforceable government all through the South, firmly based on the rule of law. Such a task would not be accomplished overnight. But Roger also knew that the very same spirit of independence which had created the problem would also make possible its solution, since it would ensure that his enemies remained divided. Even under the leadership of the Pope they had been unable to act together; now that they were deprived of it they would be more ineffectual still. The few weeks of summer that remained he spent trying to consolidate his position in the north; then, as winter approached, he returned via Salerno to Sicily.

In the spring of 1129 he was back, with an army of three thousand knights and twice that number of infantry, including archers and his regiment of Saracens. The ensuing campaign went much as he had planned. Brindisi, admittedly, under the able command of his own cousin, young Geoffrey of Conversano,[1] withstood his onslaught until the besiegers were forced by hunger to retire; but few other towns seemed disposed to offer much resistance. While Roger's army moved along the coast, mopping up the opposition as it went, sixty of his ships under George of Antioch blockaded Bari. Its self-styled prince, Grimoald, had been one of the most determined and

---

[1] This Geoffrey, described by the Abbot of Telese simply as the 'son of Count Alexander', may possibly have been of the family of Clermont rather than that of Conversano; but the latter is more likely.

powerful of the rebels; but early in August he too had to give in. His surrender led to the capitulation of Alexander, Tancred and Geoffrey of Conversano; and the revolt was over.

Or very nearly. One important city alone remained unsubdued. The people of Troia to whom, less than two years before, the Pope had granted a commune in return for their support, were reluctant to renounce so soon their newly-acquired privileges. Now that Honorius had betrayed them, they looked desperately round for other protectors. First they turned to Capua; but Prince Robert, as might have been expected, was unwilling to antagonise the new Duke of Apulia. Understandably most other barons felt much the same, and the Troians had given up hope of ever finding a champion when there suddenly appeared at their gates the one man who could never resist the chance of adding to his fiefs, whatever the attendant disadvantages—Roger's renegade brother-in-law, Rainulf of Alife. Eagerly they accepted his terms—protection in return for possession —and Rainulf moved in with his followers. But within a few days his new subjects saw how rash they had been. Roger was already on the march. He did not head straight for Troia—that was no longer necessary. An attack on one of the outlying castles was quite enough, as he knew it would be, to bring Rainulf hurrying to him with peace proposals, and a pact was quickly concluded. The Count of Alife might retain possession of Troia on condition that he held it in fief from his brother-in-law. It was an arrangement eminently satisfactory to both parties. Only the citizens of Troia, who now found themselves landed with two liege-lords instead of one, had any cause to complain. They had nobody but themselves to blame. Had they known Rainulf a little better they might have guessed that he never intended to hold out against the Duke, and that his one idea was to improve his own bargaining position. But it was too late now. Troia, twice betrayed, resisted a few days longer; then, inevitably, it too surrendered.

It may seem surprising that Roger should have allowed Rainulf to get away with so barefaced a *coup*—particularly after his record over the past two years. The truth is that the Count of Alife, slippery as he was, was no less trustworthy than most of his fellow-vassals— indeed, he may have been slightly more so, if family ties counted for anything—and those vassals had somehow to be persuaded to accept the ducal dominion. Roger's task was to win their support, not to antagonise them. His attitude towards his brother-in-law was, in fact, typical of that which he showed in his dealings with the defeated rebels. Outwardly at least—for no one ever knew what he was thinking—he bore them no malice. Once or twice, as at Brindisi or in the following year at Salerno, he manned the local citadel with a Sicilian garrison to prevent further outbreaks against his authority; but there as elsewhere the rebel lords were granted his full pardon and confirmed—even Grimoald of Bari—in their former possessions.

Only among deserters from his own ranks did the Duke show unyielding firmness. Some weeks previously another of his cousins, Robert of Grantmesnil,[1] had withdrawn with his men from the siege of Montalto, ostensibly on the grounds that his fief was too small and he himself too poor to support a long campaign. The length of the obligatory period of a vassal's service to his lord was a common ground for complaint and often a genuine cause of hardship; but it was also one of the cornerstones of the feudal system and could not be modified. Roger was not unsympathetic; he even went so far as to promise to increase his cousin's holding as soon as the revolt was crushed. But he was powerless to prevent Robert's defection. The moment peace was restored, he pursued him to his castle at Lagopesole and forced his submission. There, before the assembled knights, Robert was obliged to accept a public reprimand; Roger then granted his request for leave to return to Normandy, provided that he renounced all his southern fiefs. It took another year, and another campaign, before the troublesome count was finally banished from Italy; but he had served as a useful example to his fellows. A vassal, once he had sworn fealty to his lord, was bound to him by certain obligations. For as long as Roger II was Duke of Apulia, no refusal to acknowledge these obligations would be tolerated.

In September 1129 Duke Roger, his authority at last firmly

---

[1] The son of William de Grantmesnil and the Guiscard's daughter Mabilla. He is not to be confused with his namesake, the guardian of Roger I's first wife, Judith.

established, summoned all the bishops, abbots and counts of Apulia and Calabria to a solemn Court at Melfi. It was the first of a series of such Courts that would mark his reign; and its purpose was to lay the foundations of his future government in South Italy. Each of his vassals in turn was now required, in the presence of his assembled fellows, to swear a great oath not only confirming his feudal obligations but, in the interests of pacification, carrying them a stage further. The precise wording of this oath is, alas, lost to us, but it seems to have fallen into three main parts. It began with the normal swearing of fealty and obedience, first to the Duke himself and then to each of his two eldest sons who had accompanied him—young Roger, now about eleven years old, and Tancred, a year or two younger. There followed a specific undertaking to observe a ducal edict now promulgated forbidding all private war—that favourite pursuit among members of the knightly class, with which so much of their time and energy was normally occupied. Finally the counts were made to swear to uphold order and justice by with-holding their aid from thieves, robbers and all who sought to despoil the land, by surrendering them to the Duke's Courts wherever they might be established, and by promising their pro-tection to all feudal inferiors, clerical or lay, as well as to all pilgrims, travellers and merchants.

It was a compendious oath, and even more far-reaching than appears at first sight. The swearing of fealty was usual enough; though even here it is interesting that Roger should have specifically involved the two young princes, thereby strengthening their claims to the eventual succession—and, perhaps, giving a first hint of his future policy of setting up his sons as viceroys over the mainland. He also made it abundantly clear that what he was demanding of his vassals was something more than a formality. In the years to come we find him imposing this oath, time and time again, not only on the barons and knights but on all free classes of his subjects, as a constant reminder of their duty. Was he, by this continued insistence, already moving towards that exalted, semi-mystical concept of kingship on the Byzantine model, which so appealed to his oriental spirit and which, in his later years, he was so successfully to realise? It is possible. What is certain is that he was, deliberately or not, 'preparing the way for the extended theory of treason which was peculiar, in the twelfth century, to the Sicilian monarchy'.[1]

But the real significance of the Court of Melfi is to be found not in the first but in the second section of the vassals' oath. It had occasionally happened in the past that the South Italian barons had sworn—usually for a strictly limited period—to respect the rights and property of the non-knightly classes; but they had always preserved the right of feud, by which they could—and did—make war on each other to their hearts' content. Only when a Pope promulgated the so-called *Treuga Dei*, the Truce of God, could they sometimes be persuaded to suspend these activities. In recent years at least three Popes—Urban, Paschal and Calixtus—had tried by this means to halt the decline of Apulia into anarchy; but none of them had been conspicuously successful, if only because the maintenance of such a truce depended entirely on voluntary oaths sworn by the various parties concerned. This time it was different. The right of feud was abolished from above, at one stroke and for ever —an achievement at that time unparalleled in Europe outside England and Normandy. The oath accepting this abolition was sworn to Roger personally; and thus was brought into being the Duke's Peace, for which he himself assumed the ultimate responsibility, both in its maintenance and in the punishment of those by whom it should be disturbed—for the third part of the oath, with its reference to the surrender of malefactors to the Duke's Courts, made it clear that Roger had no intention, even now, of relying solely on the honour of his feudatories. This was the beginning of his penal code, and he intended to give it teeth.

The first great assembly of Melfi, at which in 1043 the pioneer generation of Norman barons, with Roger's uncle William the Iron-Arm at their head and Gaimar of Salerno as their suzerain, had divided their conquered territories into the twelve counties of Apulia, had long since passed into history. There may, however, have been a few old men in the little hill-town who still dimly remembered that August day just seventy years before when Robert Guiscard, colossal in his prime, had received his three duchies from Pope Nicholas II. Both of these occasions had marked

[1] Evelyn Jamison, 'The Norman Administration of Apulia and Capua'.

new chapters in the epic of the Norman domination of South Italy. Here, now, was a third. This time there were no investitures, no allocations of fiefs; but there was, for every Norman knight and baron present, the same unmistakable intimation that one era was past and another just beginning. It cannot have been an altogether welcome sensation. The old ways, the chaotic legacy of Roger Borsa and his son, might have proved disastrous for the security and prosperity of the land as a whole, but for the privileged classes they had often been agreeable—and profitable—enough. Now, for the first time in forty-five years, the South found at its head a strong man, able and determined to rule. Things would be different in future.

The year 1129, already an *annus mirabilis* for Roger, was to end with a further triumph. The position of Capua had been ambiguous ever since the death of its prince, Richard II, in 1106. Now Richard had, eight years before, recognised the suzerainty of the Duke of Apulia in return for help in his reinstatement; but his successors do not seem to have followed his example, and neither Roger Borsa nor Duke William was of the calibre to assert their claims. Thus, by default, Capua had once again become an independent state—the sovereignty of which Roger, by the terms of his Benevento investiture, had bound himself to respect. How long he would in fact have done so is an open question; Capua, though now but a poor shadow of its former self and constituting no conceivable military threat, remained an irritation and an obstacle to the complete unification of the South which sooner or later he would surely have found intolerable. Fortunately the matter was decided for him. The gutless young Robert, finding himself now entirely bereft of allies, decided to come to terms with his neighbour before it was too late, and voluntarily recognised the Duke as his lawful suzerain.

This unsolicited submission, which effectively reunited Capua with the Duchy of Apulia and so left Roger the undisputed master of the Norman South, marked the final frustration of all Honorius II's efforts to maintain the tenuous balance of power; and it might well have been expected to provoke angry reactions from Rome. But by the time the news of Prince Robert's capitulation reached the Lateran, Honorius was lying desperately ill; and in the months that followed—months that would bring the Duke of Apulia the greatest prize of his career—the Papal Curia would find itself saddled with other more urgent preoccupations.

The Jewish colony has existed in Rome uninterruptedly since the days of Pompey. Having first settled in Trastevere, by the Middle Ages it had already crossed the river and now occupied that same quarter on the left bank, just opposite the island, which Pope Paul IV was later to enclose as a ghetto and in which its synagogue still stands. Nowadays, as it slowly recovers from its recent sufferings, it presents little enough evidence of prosperity; but in the early twelfth century Roman Jewry enjoyed, by reason of its enormous wealth, both influence and prestige within the papal city. Pre-eminent among its leading families was that of the Pierleoni, whose close connexions with succeeding Popes had led them, the better part of a century before, to embrace the Christian faith; and since that time the continuance of the papal favour, assisted by the panoply and splendour with which they surrounded themselves, had raised them to a social and financial position at which they admitted no superiors among the most illustrious princely houses of Rome.

One distinction only was still lacking—but that the most important distinction of all. The Pierleonis had not yet themselves produced a Pope. The omission was understandable in the circumstances, but it would have to be rectified. For some years, therefore, their eyes had been hopefully fixed on the most brilliant of their scions, a certain Peter di Pierleoni who was rising rapidly in the hierarchy. His qualifications were excellent. His father had been a trusted lieutenant of Gregory VII, and he himself, after a period of study in Paris under the great Abelard himself, had become a monk at Cluny. Recalled to Rome in 1120, he had been appointed Cardinal by Paschal II at his father's request and had subsequently served as Papal Legate first in France and then in England, where he had appeared with a particularly splendid retinue at the Court of King Henry I. Henry seems to have been impressed: if we are to believe William of Malmesbury, the Cardinal returned to Rome so laden with rich presents as to cause raised eyebrows at the Curia. There is in fact no evidence to suggest that Pierleoni was more

venal or corrupt than any other of the contemporary princes of the
Church; on the contrary, his genuine piety and irreproachable
Cluniac background had made him a staunch upholder of many
aspects of Reform.[1] But he was capable, strong-willed and intensely
ambitious; and, like every potential candidate for the throne of
St Peter, he had enemies. Of these the most dangerous were the
Hildebrandine party—what might be called the left wing of the
Curia—who feared that a Pierleoni Pope would lead the Papacy
back into its bad old ways until it became once again the tool—or
even the plaything—of the Roman aristocracy; and his family's
most implacable rivals, that other formidable brood of fellow-
upstarts—the Frangipani.

By the beginning of February 1130 it was clear that Pope Honorius
was near his end; and Cardinal Pierleoni, who enjoyed the support
of many of the Sacred College, most of the nobility and practically
all the lower orders in Rome, among whom his carefully dispensed
generosity had become proverbial, was the obvious successor. But
the opposition was taking no chances. Led by the Chancellor of the
Curia, Cardinal Aimeri[2]—whom we last met, with Cencius Frangipani, negotiating with Roger II on the banks of the Bradano—they
seized the dying Pontiff and carried him off to the monastery of St
Andrew, safe in the centre of the Frangipani quarter, where they
would be able to conceal his death until suitable dispositions had
been made for the future.[3] Next, on 11 February, Aimeri summoned
to the monastery such cardinals as he felt he could trust and began
preparations for the new election. Now such a proceeding, apart
from being manifestly dishonest, was also a flagrant breach of Pope
Nicholas's decree of 1059, and it provoked an immediate reaction

---

[1] Other more outspoken accusations, by such robust prelates as Manfred of Mantua
or Arnulf of Lisieux (who actually wrote a book called *Invectives*) to the effect that the
cardinal seduced nuns, slept with his sister, etc., can be discounted as being simply
the normal, healthy Church polemic of the kind to be expected at times of schism.

[2] Aimeri was a Frenchman, and I have therefore preferred the French version of his
name. He is often called Almeric, or Haimeric, in the German fashion.

[3] This monastery was founded by Gregory the Great. The site is now part of the
Church of S. Gregorio Magno, to the left of which there stands among the cypresses a
chapel still dedicated to St Andrew, traditionally on the site of Gregory's original oratory. Opposite, at the end of the Circus Maximus, a ruined tower marks the site
of the old Frangipani fortress.

from the rest of the Curia. Hurling anathemas against 'all those who would proceed to the election before the funeral of Honorius', they thereupon nominated a commission of eight electors of all parties who, they decreed, should meet in the Church of St Adrian—not St Andrew—when, and only when, the Pope had been safely laid in his grave.

This refusal to countenance an election at St Andrew's was clearly due to the unwillingness of Cardinal Pierleoni and his adherents to put themselves at the mercy of the Frangipani, but when they arrived at St Adrian's they found the situation no better there. Aimeri's men had already taken possession of the whole place and had fortified it against them. Furious, they turned away and—accompanied now by several other cardinals who had no particular love for Pierleoni but were outraged by the conduct of the Chancellor—gathered instead at the old Church of S. Marco, where they settled down to await developments.

On 13 February the rumour swept through Rome that the Pope was dead at last, and that the news was being deliberately suppressed. An angry crowd gathered outside St Andrew's, and was dispersed only after poor Honorius had shown himself, trembling and haggard, on his balcony. It was his last public appearance. The strain had been too much for him, and by nightfall he was dead. In theory his body should have been allowed to lie for three days in state; but since the election of a new Pope could not take place before the burial of the old, Aimeri had no time for such niceties. Almost before the corpse was cold it was flung into a temporary grave in the courtyard of the monastery, and early the following morning the Chancellor and those who shared his views elected to the Papacy Gregory, Cardinal-deacon of S. Angelo. He was rushed to the Lateran and formally, if somewhat hastily, installed under the title of Innocent II; he then retreated to S. Maria in Palladio—now S. Sebastiano in Pallaria—where, thanks to the Frangipani, he could keep out of harm's way.

The lovely ninth-century basilica of S. Marco in Rome has suffered as grievously as most of it fellows from the indignities of baroque restoration; but its great apse mosaic still glows as glorious as ever, and the church itself offers a haven of silence and peace after the tumult of the Piazza Venezia outside. The atmosphere must have been very different on the morning of St Valentine's Day 1130, when the news of Honorius's death and Innocent's succession was brought to those assembled within its walls. Their numbers had been steadily growing, and they now comprised virtually all the high dignitaries of the Church—apart from those who had sided with Aimeri—including some two dozen Cardinals, together with most of the nobility and as many of the populace as could squeeze their way through the doors. With one accord the Cardinals declared the proceedings at St Andrew's and the Lateran uncanonical, and acclaimed Cardinal Pierleoni as their rightful Pope. He accepted at once, taking the name of Anacletus II. At dawn that morning there had been no Pope in Rome. By midday there were two.

Innocent or Anacletus—it is hard to say which candidate possessed the stronger claim to the Papacy. Anacletus, certainly, could boast more overall support, both among the Cardinals and within the Church as a whole. On the other hand those who had voted for Innocent, though fewer in number, had included the majority of the electoral commission of eight which had been set up by the Sacred College. The manner in which they had performed their duties was to say the least questionable, but then Anacletus's own election could scarcely have been described as orthodox. It had, moreover, taken place at a time when another Pope had already been elected and installed.

One thing was certain. In Rome itself, sweetened by years of bribery, the popularity of Anacletus was overwhelming. By 15 February he and his party were in control of the Lateran, and on the 16th they took St Peter's itself. Here, a week later, he received his formal consecration—while his rival, whose place of refuge had already been the object of armed attacks by Anacletus's partisans, had to be content with a similar but more modest ceremony at S. Maria Novella. Day by day Anacletus entrenched himself more firmly, while his agents dispensed subsidies with an ever more generous hand, until at last his gold—supplemented, according to his enemies, by the wholesale pillage of the principal churches of Rome —found its way into the Frangipani fortress itself. Deserted by his last remaining champions, Innocent had no choice but to flee.

Already by the beginning of April we find him dating his letters from Trastevere; a month later he had secretly hired two galleys, on which, accompanied by all his loyal cardinals except one, he escaped down the Tiber.

His flight proved his salvation. Anacletus might have bought Rome, but elsewhere in Italy popular feeling was firmly behind Innocent. In Pisa he was cheered to the echo, in Genoa the same; and while his rival lorded it in the Lateran he himself was now free to canvas support where it most mattered—beyond the Alps. From Genoa he took ship for France, and by the time he sailed into the little harbour of St Gilles in Provence much of his old confidence had returned. It was well justified. When he found, awaiting him at St Gilles, a deputation from Cluny with sixty horses and mules in its train ready to escort him the two hundred odd miles to the monastery he must have felt that, at least so far as France was concerned, his battle was as good as won. If the most influential of all French abbeys was prepared to give him its support in preference to one of its own sons, he had little to fear from other quarters; and when the Council of Etampes, summoned in the late summer to give a final ruling, formally declared in his favour, it did little more than confirm a foregone conclusion.

France then was sound; but what of the Empire? Here lay the key to Innocent's ultimate success; and here Lothair the Saxon, King of Germany, showed no particular eagerness to make up his mind. His inclinations and background should have predisposed him favourably enough; he had long upheld the ecclesiastical and papalist party among the German princes, and had received in return the support of Honorius II and Chancellor Aimeri. On the other hand, he was still engaged in a desperate struggle for power with Conrad of Hohenstaufen, who had been elected King in opposition to him three years before, and he had to weigh his actions with care. Besides, he had not yet been crowned Emperor in Rome. To antagonise the Pope who actually held the City was a step that might have dangerous implications.

Innocent, however, was not unduly worried; for his case was by now safely in the hands of the most powerful of all advocates and the outstanding spiritual force of the twelfth century—St Bernard of

Clairvaux. Later in this story we shall have to take a closer look at St Bernard, whose influence on European affairs in the next quarter-century was to be so immense and, in many respects, so disastrous. For the moment let it suffice to say that he had thrown all his formidable energies, all the weight of his moral and political prestige, into the scales on Innocent's behalf. With such a champion the Pope could afford to be patient and allow events to take their course.

The same, however, could not be said for Anacletus. He too was conscious of the need for international recognition, particularly in Northern Europe; but whereas Innocent was able to whip up support in person, he had had to rely on correspondence, and he had so far been singularly unsuccessful. In an effort to reassure King Lothair he had even gone so far as to excommunicate his rival Conrad, but the King had been unimpressed and had not even had the courtesy to answer his subsequent letters. In France, too, his Legates were snubbed; and now, as reports reached him of more and more declarations for Innocent, he began to grow seriously alarmed. The weight of the opposition was far greater than he had expected; and, more disturbing still, it was not only the ruling princes who appeared to favour his antagonist, but the Church itself. During the past fifty years, thanks largely to the Cluniac reforms and to the influence of Hildebrand, the Church had shaken off the shackles imposed on it by Roman aristocrats and German princelings, and had suddenly developed into a strong and cohesive international authority. Simultaneously the mushroom growth of the religious orders had given it a new efficiency and impetus. Cluny under Abbot Peter the Venerable, Prémontré under Norbert of Magdeburg (he who had persuaded Lothair to leave Anacletus's letters unanswered), Cîteaux under St Bernard—all were vital, positive forces. All three were united in favour of Innocent, and they carried the body of the Church with them.

And so Anacletus took the only course open to him: like many another desperate Pope in the past, he turned to the Normans. In September 1130, just about the time when the Council of Etampes was deciding in Innocent's favour, he left Rome via Benevento for Avellino, where Roger was waiting to receive him. The negotiations were soon completed. They may have been carefully prepared

in advance; on the other hand the main issues were simple enough
and can have called for little discussion. The Duke of Apulia would
give Anacletus his support; in return, he demanded one thing only
—a royal crown.

The request was prompted by something far deeper than personal
vanity. Roger's task was to weld together all the Norman dominions
of the South into one nation. The resulting state could be nothing
less than a Kingdom; to maintain the identities of three separate
duchies would be to invite disintegration. Moreover, if he were not
a King, how would he be able to treat on equal terms with the other
rulers of Europe and the East? Domestic considerations pointed in
the same direction. He must have a title that would set him above
his senior vassals, the Princes of Capua and Bari, one that would
bind all his feudatories to him with a loyalty deeper than that which
a mere Duke could command. Briefly, he needed kingship not just
for its own sake but for the sake of the mystique surrounding it.
But the Pope remained and would remain his suzerain, and he knew
that if he were to assume a crown without the papal blessing, his
prestige, far from being enhanced, would be gravely endangered.

Anacletus was sympathetic. If, as now seemed likely, the Duke of
Apulia was to be his only ally, it was plainly desirable that his
position should be strengthened to the utmost. And his claims were
incontrovertible. There was no reason for delay. On 27 September,
back at Benevento, he issued a Bull granting to Roger and his heirs
the Crown of Sicily, Calabria and Apulia, comprising all those
regions which the Dukes of Apulia had ever held of the Holy See,
together with the Principality of Capua, the 'honour' of Naples—a
deliberately ambiguous phrase, since Naples, still technically
independent and with vague Byzantine affiliations, was not the
Pope's to endow—and the assistance of the papal city of Benevento
in time of war. The seat of the Kingdom would be in Sicily, and the
coronation ceremony might be performed by the Sicilian archbishops. In return Roger pledged his homage and fealty to Anacletus
as Pope, together with an annual tribute of six hundred *schifati*—a
sum equivalent to about 160 ounces of gold.

It remained only for Roger to make similar dispositions with his
own vassals. He was determined that no one should be able, now or

in the future, to charge him with usurpation. Returning to Salerno, he therefore called another assembly, on an only slightly smaller scale than that which had met at Melfi the previous year, still comprising all the senior and most trustworthy nobles and clerics and probably including representatives of the chief cities and towns. To them he submitted proposals for his elevation, which they unanimously accepted. It may have been a formality, but similar formalities had been traditional preliminaries to coronations in England,[1] France and Germany for two centuries, and to Roger it was vital. However much his personal sympathies and upbringing might have inclined him towards the Byzantine concept of absolute rule, he knew that he could win the support of his Norman barons only by presenting them with an unexceptionable, legally-constituted monarchy as it was understood in the West. Now that he had been acclaimed at Salerno his legal and moral position was, he knew, as secure as he could possibly make it. He had the approval of both Church and State, of his suzerain and of his vassals. He was free to go ahead.

'It was,' wrote the Abbot of Telese, who was there, 'as if the whole city was being crowned.' The streets were spread with carpets, the balconies and terraces were festooned in every colour. Palermo was thronged with the King's vassals, great and small, from Apulia and Calabria, all of whom had received a royal summons to the capital for the great day, each trying to outdo his rivals in the magnificence of his train and the splendour of his entourage; with wealthy merchants, who saw in this huge concourse possibilities of gain that might never be paralleled in their lifetime; with craftsmen and artisans, townsmen and peasants from every corner of the Kingdom, drawn by curiosity and excitement and wonder; Italians, Germans, Normans, Greeks, Lombards, Spaniards, Saracens, all adding to the clamour and colour of what was already the most exotic and cosmopolitan city of Europe.

Through such crowds as these, on Christmas Day 1130, King Roger II of Sicily rode to his coronation. In the Cathedral there

---

[1] Acclamation of the monarch is still, eight hundred years later, an integral part of the English coronation service.

awaited him the Archbishop of Palermo and all the Latin hierarchy of his realm, together with representatives of the Greek Church to which he had always shown such favour. Anacletus's special envoy, the Cardinal of S. Sabina, first anointed him with the holy oil; then Prince Robert of Capua, his vassal-in-chief, laid the crown upon his head. Finally the great doors of the Cathedral were flung open and, for the first time in history, the people of Sicily gazed upon their King.

The crisp winter air was loud with the cheering of the populace, the pealing of the bells and the jangle of the gold and silver trappings on the seemingly endless cavalcade which escorted the King back to the Palace. Thither his guests followed him; and there, in a great hall that glowed red with scarlet and purple hangings, he presided at a banquet the like of which had never before been seen in Palermo. The abbot records with amazement how there was not one dish for the meats, not one cup for the wines, that was not of the purest gold or silver; while the servants, 'even those who waited at the tables', were resplendent in garments of silk. Now that Roger was at last a King, he found it both agreeable and politic to live like one.

Coronations are normally less likely to mark the ends of stories than their beginnings; that of King Roger does both. He was to reign for another twenty-three years, during the greater part of which his life would continue in much the same way as before—in building up his own position and that of his country, in playing off successive Popes and Emperors against one another, and in ceaselessly struggling, as his father and uncle had struggled before him, to keep his vassals under adequate control. But 25 December 1130 nevertheless represents something more than a convenient point at which to pause. On that day the object for which the Hautevilles had so long striven—subconsciously perhaps, but striven none the less—was achieved; henceforth Sicily seems to radiate a new confidence, a new awareness of her place in Europe and of the mission she has to fulfil. The chronicles become fuller and more informative; the characters recover their flesh and blood; and the cultural genius that was Norman Sicily's chief legacy to the world bursts at last into the fullness of its flower. The years of attainment are ended; the years of greatness begin.

THE HOUSE OF HAUTEVILLE

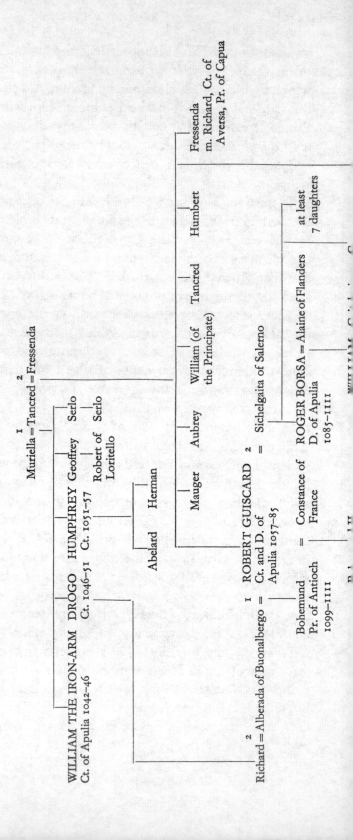

ROGER I
Great Count of Sicily

= 1. Judith of Grantmesnil
2. Eremberga, d. of William of Mortain
3. Adelaide, d. of Manfred of Savona

Jordan (illeg.) †1091

(1) Matilda m. Ct. of Tolouse

(1) 2 daughters

(1 or 2) Geoffrey

(1 or 2) Mauger

(1 or 2) Constance m. Conrad, s. of Henry IV

(1 or 2) Busilla m. Coloman K. of Hungary

(1 or 2) several other daughters

(2) Matilda m. Rainulf of Alife

(3) Simon b. 1093 Ct. under Regency of Adelaide 1101–05

(3) ROGER II b. 22 Dec. 1095 ct. 1105–28 D. of Apulia 1128–30 K. of Sicily 1130–54

THE NORMAN DYNASTY OF AVERSA AND CAPUA

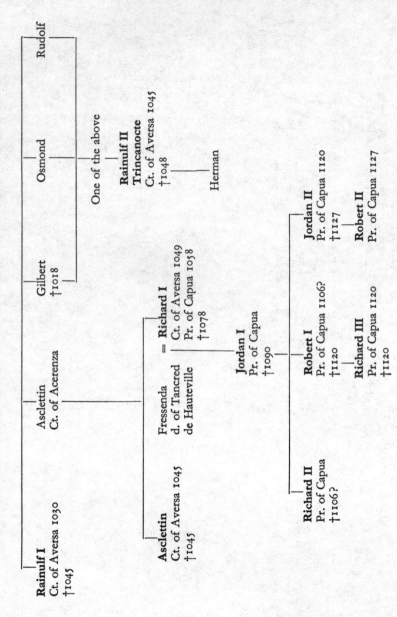

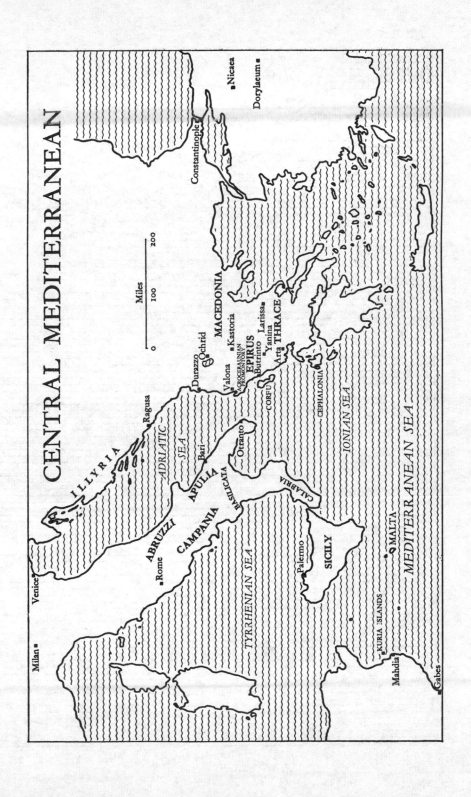

CENTRAL MEDITERRANEAN

Milan ■

Venice ■

ILLYRIA

Ragusa ■

ADRIATIC ~ SEA

ABRUZZI

Rome ■

CAMPANIA

APULIA

Bari ■

Otranto ■

BASILICATA

CALABRIA

TYRRHENIAN SEA

Palermo ■

SICILY

MALTA ◇

KURIA ISLANDS ■

Mahdia ◇

Gabes ■

MEDITERRANEAN SEA

IONIAN SEA

CEPHALONIA

CORFU ■

Durazzo ■

Ochrid ◇

Valona ■

ACROCERAUNIAN PROMONTORY

Butrinto ■

EPIRUS

Yanina ■

Arta ■

Kastoria ■

MACEDONIA

Larissa ■

THRACE

Constantinople ■

Nicaea ■

Dorylaeum ■

Miles

0   100   200

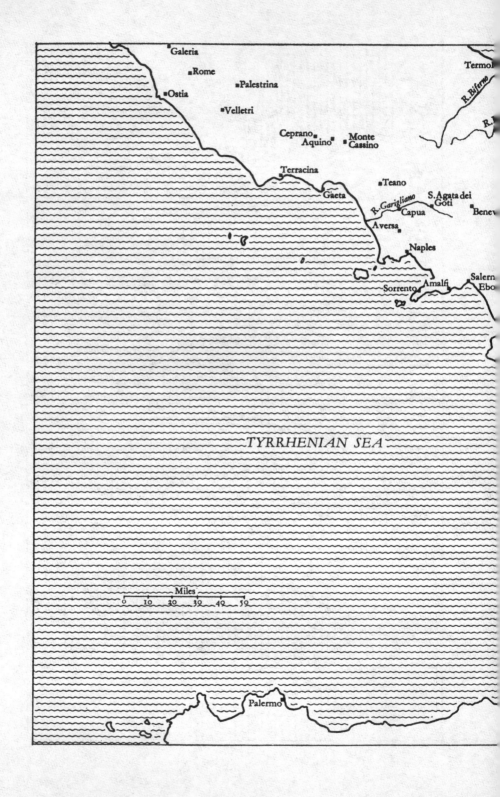

Galeria

Rome

Palestrina

Ostia

Velletri

Ceprano
Aquino   Monte
          Cassino

Terracina

Gaeta   Teano

        R. Garigliano   S. Agata dei
                         Goti
                Capua   Benev

        Aversa

                Naples

        Sorrento Amalfi   Salern
                           Ebo

Termol

R. Biferno

R.

TYRRHENIAN SEA

Miles
0   10   20   30   40   50

Palermo

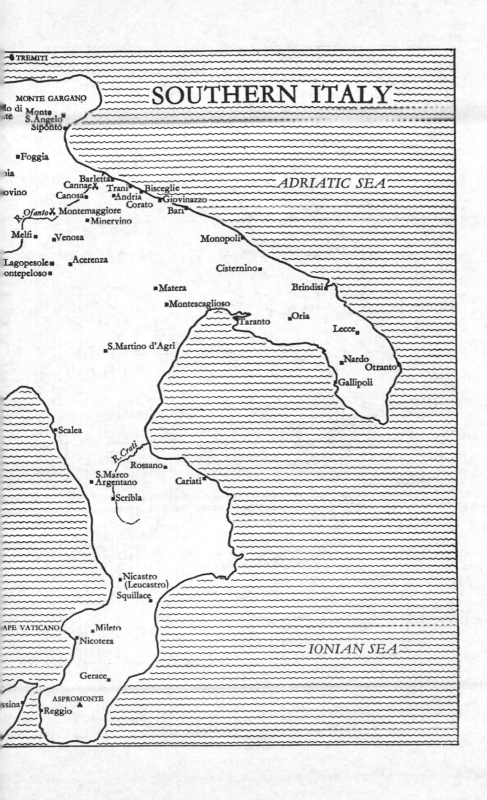

TREMITI

MONTE GARGANO

lo di Monte
S.Angelo
Siponto

Foggia

Barletta
Cannae
Canosa
Trani Bisceglie
Andria Giovinazzo
Corato
Bari
Montemaggiore
Minervino

R. Ofanto Montemaggiore
Minervino

Melfi Venosa

Lagopesole
ontepeloso Acerenza

Matera

Montescaglioso

S.Martino d'Agri Taranto

ADRIATIC SEA

Monopoli

Cisternino

Brindisi

Oria

Lecce

Nardo
Otranto

Gallipoli

Scalea

R. Crati
Rossano

S.Marco
Argentano
Cariati

Scribla

Nicastro
(Leucastro)
Squillace

APE VATICANO Mileto
Nicotera

IONIAN SEA

Gerace

ASPROMONTE

ssina Reggio

SOUTHERN ITALY

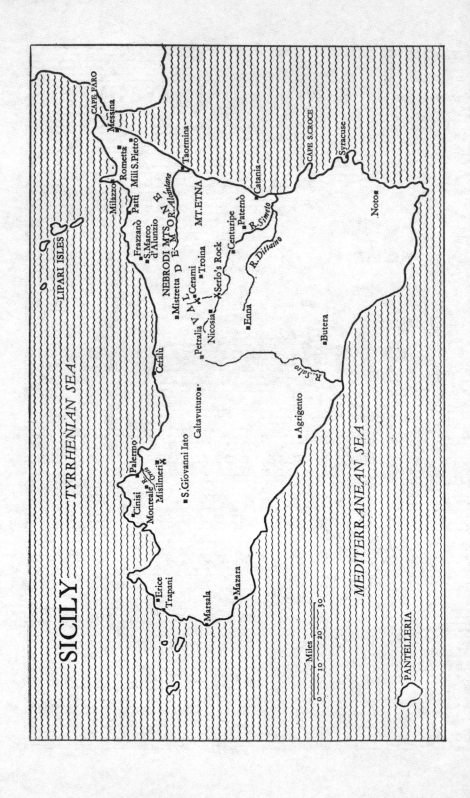

SICILY

TYRRHENIAN SEA

MEDITERRANEAN SEA

LIPARI ISLES

PANTELLERIA

CAPE FARO
Messina
Milazzo
Rometta
Patti Mili S.Pietro
Frazzanò
S.Marco d'Alunzio
NEBRODI MTS. N.
Mistretta D E
Alcàdana
M.OR.
Cerami
Petralia V A L
Troina
Nicosia
Serlo's Rock
Enna
Butera
Cefalù
Caltavuturo
Calatavuturo
S.Giovanni Iato
Palermo
Monreale
Misilmeri
Iato
Cinisi
Erice
Trapani
Marsala
Mazara
Agrigento
R.Salso
TAORMINA
MT.ETNA
Centuripe
Paternò
R.Simeto
R.Dittaino
Catania
CAPE S.CROCE
Syracuse
Noto

Miles
0 10 20 30

BIBLIOGRAPHY

NOTES ON THE PRINCIPAL SOURCES

Amatus (Aimé) of Monte Cassino

Amatus lived as a monk at the monastery of Monte Cassino during the second half of the eleventh century. He was thus presumably an eye-witness of many of the events he chronicles, and is consequently the best source for the early history of the Norman conquest of Italy, covering the period from its beginnings to 1080. His main object is avowedly to tell of the glories of Robert Guiscard and Richard of Capua, but his facts seem to be generally accurate.

The original Latin text of Amatus's work has been lost, but there exist at the Bibliothèque Nationale two early fourteenth-century copies of a translation into an Italianate Old French. A page from one of these (No. 688, *fonds français*) is reproduced opposite p. 49. The work has never to my knowledge been translated into English.

Geoffrey Malaterra

A Benedictine monk of Norman origin, Malaterra seems to have come to Apulia as a young man and later to have settled at Robert Guiscard's foundation of S. Eufemia, from which he eventually moved to its daughter house, S. Agata at Catania. At the outset he makes it clear that he is writing on the instructions of Count Roger I, and that his chronicle is based not on documents but on oral tradition and hearsay; it is therefore not surprising that the first part should be rather vague. After 1060, however, his narrative tightens. Apart from one longish digression about Robert Guiscard's Byzantine expedition, he is now dealing with Roger in Sicily to the exclusion of all else, and may well be recording on occasion the Count's own reminiscences; at any rate he is the best—indeed, practically the only—source for Roger's Sicilian wars and, in view of his semi-official standing, he is presumably fairly trustworthy. His chronicle stops in 1099. No English or French translations exist.

William of Apulia

William's epic poem was written at the instigation of Pope Urban II and is dedicated to Roger Borsa. It can be dated fairly accurately to the last few years of the eleventh century—probably between 1095 and 1099. It tells the story from the beginning until the death of Robert Guiscard in 1085, and the return of Roger Borsa and the army to Italy. Unlike other pro-Norman chroniclers of the period, William was an Italian; Chalandon suggests that he came from Giovinazzo, which certainly seems to get more than its share of favourable mentions. Relying largely on local sources, he is particularly useful where events in Apulia are concerned; he is less good on western Italy and Sicily. His work has two main themes—the providential succession of the Byzantines by the Normans, and the glorification of the House of Hauteville. There is a French translation by Marguérite Matthieu (see below).

Leo of Ostia

Leo Marsicanus came from a noble family of the Marsi and entered Monte Cassino in about 1061. Forty years later Paschal II created him Cardinal-Bishop of Ostia. He was a personal friend of Abbot Desiderius, at whose request he wrote his chronicle of the monastery and to whom it is dedicated. Although the work was begun only after 1098, Leo's first draft takes no note of Amatus and is based on archives and oral traditions; later, however, he seems to have come across his predecessor's work and rewrote much of his own in consequence, bringing his account up to the year 1075. It was subsequently continued by Peter the Deacon who, though he was to become librarian of the monastery and to play an important part in its affairs, proved an unscrupulous and untrustworthy chronicler: Chalandon, in a rare burst of feeling, speaks of his *détestable réputation*. Leo's own work, however, is well-informed and of considerable value. There is no English or French translation.

Falco of Benevento

Member of one of the leading families of Benevento, a Palace notary and scribe, Falco wrote a retrospective history of his own city and South Italy as a whole between 1102 and 1139. It is of interest not only for its own qualities—it is reliable, methodical, vivid, and contains much of which its author was an eyewitness—but also because it reflects the opinions of a Lombard patriot, for whom the Normans were little better than a bunch of uncivilised brigands. An Italian translation exists and is listed below.

Alexander of Telese

Alexander, Abbot of the monastery of S. Salvatore near Telese, wrote his chronicle at the request of the Countess Matilda, sister of Roger II. Though ostensibly a biography of Roger, the first part is sketchy in the extreme; we are told nothing about Adelaide's regency and the account becomes interesting only from 1127, with the events leading up to the establishment of the Sicilian Kingdom. From that point until 1136, when Alexander abruptly breaks off, he becomes a valuable source—though allowance must be made for his extreme tendentiousness. For him Roger was divinely appointed to bring peace and order to the South, after meting out just punishment for earlier iniquities. Despite his cloth, the Abbot has little respect for the Pope, and even chides Honorius II for his 'insolence'. There is an Italian translation listed below.

I. ORIGINAL SOURCES

1. Collections of Sources

(*The abbreviations used elsewhere in this bibliography and in the footnotes follow each entry in parentheses.*)

AMARI, M. *Biblioteca Arabo-Sicula*. Versione Italiana, 2 vols. Turin and Rome, 1880–81. (*B. A.S.*)

ARCHIVIO STORICO SICILIANO. (*A.S.S.*)

BOUQUET, M. *et al. Recueil des Historiens des Gaules et de la France*. 23 vols. Paris, 1738–1876. New Series, Paris 1899– (in progress). (*R.H.F.*)

Corpus Scriptorum Historiae Byzantinae. Bonn, 1828–97. (*C.S.H.B.*)

GUIZOT, F. *Collection des Mémoires Relatifs à l'Histoire de France*. 29 vols. Paris, 1823–27. (*G.M.H.F.*)

JAFFE, P. *Bibliotheca Rerum Germanicarum*. 6 vols. Berlin, 1864–73. (*J.B.R.G.*)

MIGNE, J. P. *Patrologia Latina*. 221 vols. Paris, 1844–55. (*M.P.L.*)

Monumenta Germaniae Historica, ed. G. H. Pertz, T. Mommsen *et al.* Hanover, 1826– (in progress). (*M.G.H.*)

Monumenta Gregoriana, ed. Jaffé. *J.B.R.G.*, vol. II.

MURATORI, L. A. *Rerum Italicarum Scriptores*. 25 vols. Milan, 1723–51. (*R.I.S.*)

RE, G. DEL. *Cronisti e Scrittori Sincroni della Dominazione Normanna nel Regno di Puglia e Sicilia*. 2 vols. Naples, 1845, 1868. (*R.C.S.S.*)

Recueil des Historiens des Croisades. Publ. Académie des Inscriptions et Belles Lettres, Paris, 1841–1906. *Historiens Occidentaux*, 5 vols (*R.H.C.Occ.*)

WATTERICH, J. M. *Pontificum Romanorum qui fuerunt inde ab exeunte saeculo IX usque finem saeculi XIII vitae ab aequalibus conscriptae*. Leipzig, 1862. 2 vols. (*W.P.R.*)

2. Individual Sources

ALBERT OF AIX. *Liber Christianae Expeditionis pro Ereptione, Emundatione et Restitutione Sanctae Hierosolymitanae Ecclesiae*. In *R.H.C.Occ.*, vol. IV.

ALEXANDER OF TELESE. *Rogerii Regis Siciliae Rerum Gestarum Libri IV*. In *R.C.S.S.*, vol. II (with Italian translation).

AMATUS OF MONTE CASSINO. *Ystoire de li Normant*, ed. V. de Bartholomaeis, Fonti per la Storia d'Italia, Scrittori, Rome, 1935.

ANNA COMNENA. *The Alexiad*, tr. E. Dawes, London 1928.

Annales Barenses. In *M.G.H. Scriptores*, vol. V.

ANNALES BENEVENTANI. In *M.G.H. Scriptores*, vol. III.

AN-NUWAYRI, ed. Amari, with Italian translation. *B.A.S.*, vol. II.

ANONYMUS VATICANUS. *Historia Sicula*. In *R.I.S.*, vol. VIII.

AT-TIGANI, ed. Amari, with Italian translation. *B.A.S.*, vol. II.

BERNARD OF CLAIRVAUX, ST. *Vita Prima*. In *M.P.L.*, vol. 185.

BRUNO. *Vita Sancti Leonis IX*. In *W.P.R.*, vol. II.

CEDRENUS, GEORGIUS. *Synopsis Historiarum*, ed. Bekker. In *C.S.H.B.* Bonn, 1839. 2 vols.

EADMER. *Historia Novarum in Anglia et de Vita Anselmi*, tr. R. W. Southern. London, 1962.

FALCO OF BENEVENTO. *Chronicon*. In *R.C.S.S.*, vol. II (with Italian translation).

GLABER, RADULF. *Historiarum Sui Temporis, Libri V*. In *R.H.F.*, vol. X.

IBN AL-ATHIR. *Kamel al Tawarikh*, ed. Amari, with Italian translation. *B.A.S.*, vol. I.

IBN HAMDIS OF SYRACUSE. Ed. Amari, with Italian translation. *B.A.S.*, vol. II.

IBN JUBAIR. *Account of a visit to Sicily*. French translation, with notes by M. Amari, *Journal Asiatique*, Series IV, vols 6 and 7, December. 1845, January/March 1846; Italian translation in *B.A.S.*, vol. I.

JOHN OF SALISBURY. *Historia Pontificalis*, ed. with translation by M. Chibnall. London, 1956.

LEO OF OSTIA (MARSICANUS). *Chronicon Monasterii Casinensis*. In *M.G.H. Scriptores*, vol. VII, and *M.P.L.*, vol. 173.

MALATERRA, GEOFFREY. *Historia Sicula*. In *M.P.L.*, vol. 149 and *R.I.S.*, vol. V.

ORDERICUS VITALIS. *The Ecclesiastical History of England and Normandy*, tr. with notes by T. Forester. London 1854. 4 vols.

PSELLUS, MICHAEL. *Chronographia*, tr. E. R. A. Sewter. London, 1953.

ROMUALD OF SALERNO. *Chronicon*. In *R.C.S.S.*, vol. I with Italian translation; also in *M.G.H., Scriptores*, vol. XIX or *R.I.S.*, vol. VII.

SKYLITZES, JOHN. ᾽Επιτομή ἱστοριῶν, ed. Bekker (Cedrenus's Copy of main section). In *C.S.H.B.*, vol. II.

WIBERT. *Vita Leonis IX*. In *W.P.R.*, Vol. I.

WILLIAM OF APULIA. *Gesta Roberti Wiscardi*. In *M.G.H., Scriptores*, vol. IX. For French translation see M. Mathieu, *Guillaume de Pouille: La Geste de Robert Guiscard*. (Istituto Siciliano di Studi Bizantini e Neoellenici. Palermo, 1961.)

WILLIAM OF MALMESBURY. *Gesta Regum Anglorum*. In *M.P.L.*, vol. 179 and *M.G.H., Scriptores*, vols X, XIII. English translation with notes by J. A. Giles, London, 1895.

WILLIAM OF TYRE. *Belli Sacri Historia and Historia Rerum in Partibus Transmarinis Gestarum*. *R.H.C.Occ.*, Vol. I. Also with French translation in *G.M.H.F.*, vols. 16–18.

II. MODERN WORKS

AMARI, M. *Storia dei Musulmani di Sicilia.* 3 vols. Florence, 1854–72.

Atti del Convegno Internazionale di Studi Ruggeriani (21–25 Aprile, 1945). Società Siciliana di Storia Patria, Palermo, 1954.

BARLOW, J. W. *A Short History of the Normans in South Europe.* London, 1886.

BIBICOU, H. 'Une page d'histoire diplomatique de Byzance au XIe. siècle: Michel VII Doukas, Robert Guiscard et la pension des dignitaires', *Byzantion,* 29–30, 1959/60.

Biblioteca Storica Principato, vol. XVI, *Il Regno Normanno.* Istituto Nazionale Fascista di Cultura, 1930.

BLOCH, H. 'The Schism of Anacletus II and the Glanfeuil Forgeries of Peter the Deacon of Monte Cassino', *Traditio,* VIII, 1952 (Fordham University).

BORDENACHE, R. 'La SS. Trinità di Venosa, Scambi ed Influssi architettonici ai tempi dei primi Normanni in Italia', *Ephemeris Dacoromana, Annuario della Scuola Romena di Roma,* VII, 1938.

BUCKLER, G. *Anna Comnena.* London, 1929.

BURY, J. B. *History of the Later Roman Empire.* London, 1889. 2 vols.

— *History of the Eastern Roman Empire.* London, 1912.

— 'The Roman Emperors from Basil II to Isaac Komnenos', *English Historical Review,* IV, 1889.

CAHEN, C. *Le Régime Féodal de l'Italie Normande.* Paris, 1940.

— 'Notes sur l'histoire des croisades et de l'orient latin', *Bulletin de la Faculté des Lettres de l'Université de Strasbourg,* XXIX, 1950–51.

Cambridge Medieval History. 8 vols. Cambridge, 1911–36.

CASPAR, E. *Roger II und die Gründung der normannisch-sicilischen Monarchie.* Innsbruck, 1904.

— *Die Legatengewalt der normannisch-sicilischen Herrscher im 12. Jahrhundert.* Rome, 1904.

Catholic Encyclopaedia, The, ed. C. G. Herbermann. 15 vols. London and New York, 1907–12.

CHALANDON, F. *Essai sur le Règne d'Alexis I Comnène.* Paris, 1900.

— *Histoire de la Domination Normande en Italie et en Sicile.* Paris, 1907. 2 vols.

COHN, W. *Die Geschichte der normannisch-sicilischen Flotte unter der Regierung Rogers I und Rogers II, 1060–1154.* Breslau, 1910.

CRONIN, V. *The Golden Honeycomb.* London, 1954.

CURTIS, E. *Roger of Sicily.* New York, 1912.

DELARC, O. *Les Normands en Italie.* Paris, 1883.

Dictionary of National Biography.

Dictionnaire de Théologie Catholique, ed. Vacant and Mangenot. 9 vols in 15. Paris, 1926–50.

Dictionnaire d'Histoire et de Géographie Ecclésiastiques, ed. Baudrillart. Paris, (in progress).

DIEHL, C. *Etudes Byzantines*. Paris, 1905. 2 vols.
— *L'Art byzantin dans l'Italie Méridionale*. Paris, 1894.

DOUGLAS, N. *Old Calabria*. London, 1920.

Enciclopedia Italiana.

Encyclopaedia Britannica. 11th edn.

FASOLI, G. 'Problemi di Storia medievale siciliana', *Siculorum Gymnasium* N.S.4. 1951.

FOORD, E. *The Byzantine Empire*. London, 1911.

FREEMAN, E. A. *A History of Sicily*. 4 vols. London, 1891–94.

FUAINO, M. 'La Battaglia di Civitate (1053)' in *Archivio Storico Pugliese*, II, fasc. 1–2, 1949.

GAUTTIER DU LYS D'ARC. *Histoire des Conquêtes des Normands en Italie, en Sicile et en Grèce*. Paris, 1830.

GAY, J. *L'Italie Méridionale et l'Empire Byzantin*. Paris, 1904.

GIBBON, E. *The Decline and Fall of the Roman Empire*, ed. J. B. Bury. London, 1896. 7 vols. (See especially Chap. LVI.)

GREGOIRE, H., and DE KEYSER, R. 'Le Chanson de Roland et Byzance', *Byzantion*, XIV, 1939.

GREGOROVIUS, F. *History of the City of Rome in the Middle Ages*, tr. A. Hamilton. 8 vols. in 13, London, 1894–1902.

HASKINS, C. H. *The Normans in European History*. London, 1916.
— 'England and Sicily in the twelfth century', *English Historical Review*, July and October, 1911.
— *Studies in the History of Mediaeval Science*. Cambridge, Mass., 1924.

JAMISON, E. 'The Sicilian Norman Kingdom in the Mind of Anglo-Norman Contemporaries', *Papers of the British Academy*, XXIV, 1938.
— 'The Norman Administration of Apulia and Capua, especially under Roger II and William I, 1127–66', *Papers of the British School at Rome*, VI, 1913.

JORANSON, E. 'The Inception of the Career of the Normans in Italy', *Speculum*, XXIII, July 1948.

JORDAN, E. 'La politique ecclésiastique de Roger I et les origines de la "Légation Sicilienne"', *Le Moyen Age*, 33/34, 1922–23.

LENORMANT, A. *La Grande Grèce*. 3 vols. Paris, 1881–84.

LA LUMIA, I. *Studi di storia siciliana*. Palermo, 1870. 2 vols.

MASSON, G. *The Companion Guide to Rome*. London, 1965.

MENAGER, L. R. 'L'Institution Monarchique dans les Etats Normands d'Italie', *Cahiers de Civilisation Médiévale*, II, 1959.
— 'Les Fondations Monastiques de Robert Guiscard, Duc de Pouille et de Calabre', *Quellen und Forschungen aus Italienischen Archiven und Bibliotheken*, 33, 1959.
— 'La "Byzantinisation" réligieuse de l'Italie Méridionale (IX–XIIe.

siècles) et la politique monastique des Normands d'Italie', *Revue d'Histoire Ecclésiastique*, 53/4, 1958–59.

MOR, C. G. 'Roger II et les assemblées du royaume normand dans l'Italie méridionale', *Revue historique de droit français et étranger*, Série IV, 36, 1958.

OSBORNE, J. VAN WYCK. *The Greatest Norman Conquest.* New York, 1937.

OSTROGORSKY, G. *History of the Byzantine State*, tr. Joan Hussey. Oxford. 1956.

PACE, B. *I barbari e i bizantini in Sicilia.* In *A.S.S.*, vols 35, 36. Palermo, 1911.

PARDI, G. 'Storia demografica della città di Palermo', *Nuova Rivista Storica*, 3, 1919. (Corrected by J. Beloch, *Bevölkerungsgeschichte Italiens*, I, Berlin, 1937.)

PONTIERI, E. *Tra i Normanni nell' Italia Meridionale.* Naples, 1948.

ROUSSET, P. *Les Origines et les Caractères de la Première Croisade.* Neuchâtel, 1945.

RUNCIMAN, S. *History of the Crusades.* Cambridge, 1954. 3 vols.

— *The Eastern Schism.* Oxford, 1955.

SCHLUMBERGER, G. *L'Epopée byzantine à la fin du Xe siècle.* Paris, 1896–1905. 3 vols.

STEFANO, G. DI. *Monumenti della Sicilia Normanna.*

STEINBERG, S. I Ritratti dei Re Normanni di Sicilia', *La Bibliofila*, XXXIX, 1937.

SYMONDS, J. A. *Sketches in Italy and Greece.* London, 1874.

WALEY, D. P. '"Combined Operations" in Sicily, 1060–78', *Papers of the British School at Rome*, XXII, 1954.

WHITE, L. T. *Latin Monasticism in Norman Sicily.* Pub. 31 (Monograph 13), Medieval Academy of America. Cambridge, Mass., 1938.

WILL, C. *Die Anfänge der Restauration der Kirche im 12. Jahrhundert.* Marburg, 1859–61.

WILLIAMS, W. *St Bernard of Clairvaux.* Manchester, 1953.

THE KINGDOM
IN THE SUN

1130–1194

For my mother

CONTENTS

CONTENTS

LIST OF ILLUSTRATIONS

353

Henry VI makes his triumphal entry into Palermo (Peter of
Eboli MS.) *Burgerbibliothek, Berne*

Genealogical trees

Maps

The maps and genealogical trees are drawn by John Messenger

In Sicily one might find, all within a few miles of each other, the castle of some newly-created baron, an Arab village, an ancient Greek or Roman city and a recent Lombard colony; in one and the same town, together with the native population, there might be one quarter of Saracens or Jews, another of Franks, Amalfitans or Pisans; and among all these various peoples, there would reign that peaceful tranquillity which is born of mutual respect. . . . The bells of a new church, the chanting of the monks in a new abbey, would mingle with the cry of the *muezzin* from the minaret, calling the faithful to prayer. Here was the Latin Mass, modified according to the Gallican liturgy; here, the rites and ceremonies of the Greeks; here, the rules and disciplines of the Mosaic Law. The streets, squares and markets revealed a marvellous variety of costume; the turbans of the orientals, the white robes of the Arabs, the iron mail of the Norman knights; differences of habits, inclinations, celebrations, practices, appearances: infinite and continuous contrasts, which yet came together in harmony.

I. LA LUMIA,
History of Sicily under William the Good, 1867

INTRODUCTION

Just over sixty years ago, in the preface to his own history of the
Norman Kingdom of Sicily, M. Ferdinand Chalandon—a writer,
heaven knows, not normally given to excessive dramatisation—
noted that an unhappy fate seemed to hang over all would-be
historians who tackled the subject; naming no less than three who, as
he delicately put it, had 'prematurely disappeared' before their work
was completed. In 1963, to a writer embarking on his first full-scale
literary venture with an already distinct sensation of having bitten
off more than he could chew, it was hardly an encouraging reminder;
and there have been many moments in the past seven years when the
end of my labours did indeed seem impossibly remote. It is therefore
with more surprise than anything else that I now find that I have
come to the end of my story.

This second volume of the Hauteville saga is self-contained, in the
sense that it presumes the reader either not to have read its predecessor or, if he has, to have forgotten it. It does, however, take up
the tale where *The Normans in the South* left off—at King Roger's
coronation on Christmas Day 1130 in Palermo Cathedral—and
carries it through to that other, blacker Christmas when the most
coruscating crown of Europe was laid, by an English archbishop, on
the head of one of the most loathsome of German Emperors. The
sixty-four short years that separated those two events—less of a span
than we have the right to expect for ourselves—constituted the whole
lifetime of the Kingdom; they also provided the island with its
golden age when, for the first and only time in history, the three
great racial and religious traditions of the Mediterranean littoral
fused under the southern sun and crystallised into that flashing,
endlessly-faceted jewel that was the culture of Norman Sicily.

It is—or at least it should be—above all else the surviving monuments of this culture that draw us to Sicily today; monuments which
miraculously translate the Hautevilles' political achievement into
visual terms and in which Western European, Byzantine and Islamic
styles and techniques effortlessly coalesce in settings of such magical

opulence that the beholder is left dazzled and incredulous. I have therefore done my best to make this book not only an account of people and events but also a guide to these monuments. The most important of them I have described in detail, not in a separate and indigestible chapter but at suitable points in the course of the narrative, so as to relate them as directly as possible to their founders or to the circumstances surrounding their construction. The rest, graded according to the time-honoured star system and furnished with page references where appropriate, I have relegated to a list in the appendix. This, I like to think, records every item of Norman work worthy of the name still surviving in Sicily; it is certainly the most comprehensive one yet to appear in this country.

But the history of Roger's Kingdom is something more than a background to its works of art, however memorable they may be. It is also one of the tragedies of Europe. Had it lasted, had it succeeded in preserving those principles of toleration and understanding to which it owed its existence, had it continued to serve as a focus of intellectual enlightenment in a blinkered and bigoted age and as the cultural and scientific clearing-house of three continents, then ours at least might have been spared much of the suffering that awaited it in the centuries to come, and Sicily might have been the happiest, rather than the most ill-starred, of Mediterranean islands. But it did not last; and this book has had to tell not only of how it flourished, but also of its failure and its fall.

One further point, which I have already made in the introduction to *The Normans in the South*, must I think be re-emphasised here: that this is in no sense a work of scholarship. When I started it I knew no more than anyone else about Sicily or the Middle Ages; and now that I have finished I have no plans to write any more about either subject again. Here, quite simply, is a piece of historical reportage, written for the general public by one of their own number—one whose sole qualifications for the task were curiosity and enthusiasm. I hand over my typescript now with the same hope that I had when I began: that these emotions may prove infectious, and that others may grow, as I have grown, to love—and to lament—that sad, superb, half-forgotten Kingdom, whose glory shone ever more golden as the sun went down.

ACKNOWLEDGEMENTS

MUCH of Chapter 2 of this book was written during a fortnight in June, 1967, when the outbreak of war in the Middle East left me—largely through my own incompetence—stranded in the British Embassy, Khartoum; and I should like to thank Sir Robert and Lady Fowler for the kindness they showed, at an appallingly difficult time for themselves, to an uninvited, unexpected and virtually unknown guest. More thanks wing off to the Languedoc, where Xan and Daphne Fielding saw me so splendidly through Chapter 16. All the other chapters first saw the light in the London Library, of which I seem by now to have become part of the furniture. To Stanley Gillam, Douglas Matthews and every member of the staff—especially those who have to keep calling me down to the telephone—my gratitude is, as always, boundless.

Dr N. P. Brooks of St Salvator's College, St Andrew's, read the book in typescript, saved me several slips and made many invaluable suggestions. Most of these I have accepted; for the few that I have not, I am every bit as grateful. My friend John Parker of the University of York, besides making the substantial indirect contribution listed in the bibliography, also answered several queries about the Orthodox world and solved the Dimitritza problem on p. 342. I also owe a very special debt to Barbarina Daudy, whose astonishing gift of tongues, combined with equally remarkable powers of impromptu translation, saved weeks of my time but cost her untold hours of her own. I can only hope that they and the many others who have given me help and advice at all levels will not feel, on reading the results, that their labours have been altogether in vain.

J. J. N.

PART ONE

MORNING STORMS

THE COST OF THE CROWN

How many and what dreadful shocks and tumults resulted from that great clash when the son of Peter Leoni strove to rise up from the north against Innocent of blessed memory. . . . Did not his fall drag down with it a portion of the stars themselves?

John of Salisbury,
Policraticus, VIII, xxiii

ON Christmas Day 1130 Roger de Hauteville was crowned King of Sicily in Palermo Cathedral. It was a hundred and thirteen years since the first bands of young Norman adventurers had ridden down into the Italian South—ostensibly in response to an appeal for help made by a Lombard nationalist in the Archangel Michael's cave on Monte Gargano, but effectively in search of fame and fortune; sixty-nine since the army of Roger's uncle Robert Guiscard, Duke of Apulia, had first landed on Sicilian soil. Undeniably, progress had been slow: during the same period William the Conqueror had mopped up England in a matter of weeks. But the country William had had to tackle was a well-ordered, centralised state already deeply penetrated by Norman influences, while Robert and his companions had been faced with anarchy—a South Italy torn apart by the con-flicting claims of a Papacy, two Empires, three races and an ever-changing number of principalities, duchies and petty baronies; a Sicily that had languished for two centuries under Saracen domina-tion, where the Greek Christian minority lay helpless as jealous local emirs endlessly squabbled for power.

Bit by bit, the chaos had been resolved. Roger's father Roger I, Great Count of Sicily, had spent the last thirty years of his life weld-ing together the island and its people. With a perception rare for his time, he had seen from the outset that the only hope of success lay in integration. There would be no second-class Sicilians. Everyone, Norman or Italian, Lombard or Greek or Saracen, would have his part to play in the new state. Arabic and Greek, as well as Latin and Norman French, would be official languages. A Greek was appointed Emir of Palermo, a beautiful and resonant title which Roger saw no reason to change; another was given charge of the rapidly growing navy. Control of the exchequer and the mint was placed in the hands of the Saracens. Special Saracen brigades were established in the army, quickly earning a reputation for loyalty and discipline which they were to preserve for well over a century. The mosques remained as crowded as ever they had been, while Christian churches and monasteries, both Latin and Greek—several of them Roger's own foundations—sprang up in increasing numbers throughout the island.

Peace, as always, brought trade. The narrow straits, cleared at last of Saracen pirates, were once again safe for shipping; Palermo and Messina, Catania and Syracuse found themselves thriving *entrepôt* centres on the way to Constantinople and the new Crusader states of the Levant. The result was that by the time the Great Count died in 1101 he had transformed Sicily into a nation, heterogeneous in its races, religions and languages but united in loyalty to its Christian ruler and well on the way to becoming the most brilliant and prosperous state of the Mediterranean, if not of Europe.

Roger II had carried on the work. It suited him perfectly. Born in the South of an Italian mother, educated during his long minority by Greek and Arab tutors, he had grown up in the cosmopolitan atmosphere of tolerance and mutual respect created by his father, and he instinctively understood the complex system of checks and balances on which the internal stability of his country depended. There was little of the Norman knight about him. He possessed none of the warlike attributes which had brought glory to his father and his uncles, and in a single generation had made the name of an obscure Norman baron famous throughout the continent. But of all those Hauteville brothers only one, his father, had developed into a statesman. The rest—even Robert Guiscard himself, for all his genius —were fighters and men of action to the end. Roger II was different.

He disliked war and, apart from a couple of ill-starred expeditions during his youth in which he did not personally participate, had avoided it whenever possible. In appearance a southerner, in temperament an oriental, he had inherited from his Norman forbears nothing but their energy and their ambition, which he combined with a gift for diplomacy entirely his own; and it was these qualities, far more than his prowess on the battlefield, that had enabled him at last to acquire for himself the duchies of Apulia and Calabria and so to reunite the South in a single dominion for the first time since the Guiscard's day.

On a bridge crossing the Sabato river outside the walls of Benevento, soon after sunrise on 22 August 1128, Roger was invested by Pope Honorius II with his triple dukedom; and rose from his knees one of the most powerful of European rulers. He had only one more objective to attain before he could treat as an equal with his fellow-princes abroad and impose his authority on his new South Italian vassals. That objective was a crown; and two years later he got it. Pope Honorius's death early in 1130 led to a dispute over the papal succession, as a result of which two opposing candidates were simultaneously elected to the throne of St Peter. The story of these two elections has already been told[1] and there is no need to repeat it here in detail; suffice it to say that both were highly irregular and that now, as then, it is hard to decide which of the protagonists had the stronger claim. The first, however, who had taken the name of Innocent II, soon had virtually the whole continent behind him; his rival, Anacletus II Pierleoni, holding Rome but little else, turned—like so many of his predecessors in moments of crisis—to the Normans; and so the bargain was struck. Roger promised Anacletus his support; in return, and under papal suzerainty, he became King —of the third largest kingdom in Europe.

The arrangement was, in the short term, even more beneficial to Anacletus than it was to Roger. He should have been in a strong enough position. Uncanonical as his election was, it was no more so than that of his rival, and it certainly reflected the majority view in the Curia; in any free vote by all the cardinals Anacletus would have

[1] *The Normans in the South*, ch. 23, pp. 323–6.

been an easy victor. Even as things were, he had been acclaimed by twenty-one of them. His piety was generally admitted, his energy and ability unquestioned. Rome was still overwhelmingly loyal to him. Why was it, then, that only four months after the wretched Innocent had been forced to flee the city, Anacletus should in his turn have found the ground falling away beneath his feet?

He himself, perhaps, was partly to blame. Although he has undergone so much subsequent vilification that it is now almost impossible to form a clear picture of his character, it is beyond doubt that he was eaten by ambition and totally unscrupulous in the attainment of his ends. For all his reformist background, he had not hesitated to make use of his family's immense wealth to buy support among the aristocracy and people of Rome. There is no reason to believe that he was more corrupt than the majority of his colleagues, but rumours of his bribes had been assiduously spread by his enemies, who supported them with lurid accounts of his spoliation of Church property once Rome was in his power; and they found a ready audience among those in Northern Italy and abroad whose ears were not temporarily deafened by the jingle of Pierleoni gold. He was also handicapped— paradoxically enough—by his tenure of the Holy City, which held him down in the Lateran while Innocent progressed through Europe whipping up support. Yet these were all secondary considerations. There was one other factor which weighed the scales against Anacletus more heavily than all the others put together, and which was ultimately to prove the destruction of all his ambitions and his hopes. That factor was St Bernard of Clairvaux.

St Bernard was now forty years old and far and away the most powerful spiritual force in Europe. To an objective twentieth-century observer, safely out of range of that astonishing personal magnetism with which he effortlessly dominated all those with whom he came in contact, he is not an attractive figure. Tall and haggard, his features clouded by the constant pain that resulted from a lifetime of exaggerated physical austerities, he was consumed by a blazing religious zeal that left him no room for tolerance or moderation. His public life had begun in 1115 when the Abbot of Cîteaux, the Englishman Stephen Harding, had effectively released him from monastic discipline by sending him off to found a daughter house at Clairvaux in Champagne; from that moment on, almost despite himself, his influence spread; and for the last twenty-five years of his life he was constantly on the move, preaching, persuading, arguing, debating, writing innumerable letters and compulsively plunging into the thick of every controversy in which he believed the basic principles of Christianity to be involved.

The papal schism was just such an issue. Bernard declared himself unhesitatingly for Innocent, and from that moment on the die was cast. His reasons, as always, were emotional. Cardinal Aimeri, the papal Chancellor whose intrigues on Innocent's behalf had been directly responsible for the whole dispute, was a close personal friend. Anacletus on the other hand was a product of Cluny, a monastery which Bernard detested on the grounds that it had betrayed its reformist ideals and had succumbed to those very temptations of wealth and worldliness that it had been founded to eradicate. Worse still, he was of Jewish antecedents; as Bernard was later to write to the Emperor Lothair, 'it is to the injury of Christ that the offspring of a Jew should have seized for himself the throne of St Peter'. The question of St Peter's own racial origins does not seem to have occurred to him.

When, in the late summer of 1130, King Louis VI, 'the Fat', of France summoned a Church council at Etampes to advise him which of the two candidates he should support, Bernard was ready to strike. Rightly sensing that any enquiry into the canonicity of the elections themselves might do his cause more harm than good, he stuck firmly to personalities and immediately embarked on a campaign of such vituperation that, in the minds of his audience, a senior and generally respected member of the Sacred College was transformed, almost overnight, into Antichrist. Though no actual record of the proceedings at Etampes has come down to us, one of the abbot's letters dating from this time probably reflects his words accurately enough.

The adherents of Anacletus, he writes, 'have made a covenant with death and a compact with hell. . . . The abomination of desolation is standing in the Holy Place, to gain possession of which he has set fire to the sanctuary of God. He persecutes Innocent and with him all who are innocent. Innocent has fled from his face, for *when the Lion* [a play on the name of Pierleoni] *roars, who shall not be afraid?* He has obeyed the words of the Lord: *When they persecute you in one city, flee unto another*. He has fled, and by the flight that he has endured after the example of the Apostles he has proved himself truly an apostle.'

Nowadays it is hard to believe that this sort of casuistical invective should have been taken seriously, far less that it should have had any lasting effect. Yet Bernard dominated Etampes, and it was thanks to him that the claims of Innocent II received official recognition in France. Henry I of England presented even less difficulty. He too had hesitated at first; Anacletus had been a papal legate at his court and was still a personal friend. Bernard, however, paid him a special visit to discuss the matter and Henry's resistance crumbled. In January 1131 he loaded Innocent with presents and did homage to him in Chartres Cathedral.

There remained the problem of the Empire. Lothair of Supplinburg, King of Germany, was in a difficult position. A strong, proud, stubborn man of sixty, he had begun life as a comparatively inconsequential noble; his election to the monarchy in 1125 had been largely due to the influence of the papal party working closely with Cardinal Aimeri. He should therefore have been favourably disposed towards Innocent. On the other hand Anacletus had recently sent extremely civil letters to himself, his queen, and to the clergy and laity of Germany and Saxony, informing them of how his brother cardinals 'with a wonderful and stupendous unanimity' had raised him to the supreme dignity of the pontificate; and he had followed up the letters by excommunicating Lothair's arch-enemy, Conrad of Hohenstaufen, who was also laying claim to the German throne. Lothair knew that his victory over Conrad could never be assured till he had had himself crowned Emperor in Rome; whatever the claims of the rival Popes he was unwilling to antagonise the one who actually had control of the Holy City. He decided to defer a decision as long as possible, and left Anacletus's letters unanswered.

But he soon found that he could not sit on the fence for long; the situation was developing too fast. Throughout western Europe the Innocentian faction was gathering momentum, and at Etampes it had received yet further impetus. Already by the autumn of 1130 it was strong enough to force Lothair's hand; a council of sixteen German bishops met at Würzburg in October and declared for Innocent; and at the end of March 1131 the latter appeared with full retinue at Liège to receive the King's homage.

Lothair could not go against his bishops; besides, it was plain that Innocent was now the generally accepted Pope. Among all the European princes, there remained to Anacletus only one adherent—Roger of Sicily. This fact alone would have been enough to lose him any imperial support that he might otherwise have enjoyed; for by what right could any Pope, legitimate or otherwise, crown some Norman upstart King over territories which properly belonged to the Empire? Since Roger's coronation there could have been no more serious doubts in Lothair's mind: Innocent it would have to be. And yet—perhaps as much to save his face as for any other reason—he still tried to impose one condition: that the right of investiture of bishops with ring and crozier, lost to the Empire nine years previously, were now restored to himself and his successors.

He had reckoned without the Abbot of Clairvaux. Bernard had accompanied Innocent to Liège; this was just the sort of crisis in which he excelled. Leaping from his seat, he subjected the King to a merciless castigation before the entire assembly, calling upon him then and there to renounce his pretensions and pay unconditional homage to his rightful Pope. As always, his words—or, more probably, the force of his personality behind them—had their effect. This was Lothair's first encounter with Bernard; it is unlikely that he had ever been spoken to in such a way before. He was not lacking in moral fibre, but this time he seems instinctively to have realised that his position was no longer tenable. He gave in. Before the Council broke up he had made his formal submission to Innocent, and had reinforced it with an undertaking that the Pope probably found even more valuable—to lead him, at the head of an imperial German army, to Rome.

Already at the time of his coronation Roger must have been aware of the pressures that were building up against Anacletus and—since he had now irrevocably thrown in his lot with the anti-Pope—against himself. He had taken a gamble and he knew it. His crown might indeed have been a political necessity, but he had paid for it by bringing down upon himself the wrath of half a continent. To some extent this was unavoidable; the appearance of a new power, strong and ambitious, is rarely welcome on the international scene, and Roger had after all set himself up over a land still claimed by both the Western and the Byzantine Empires. It was unfortunate, nevertheless, that at this of all moments he should have had to antagonise not just the temporal forces of Europe but the spiritual as well— particularly when they were represented by such men as Bernard of Clairvaux and Abbot Peter of Cluny. In those first months after the election he would surely have been able to strike a similar bargain with either of the two papal pretenders; how much brighter the future would have looked if it had been Innocent, rather than Anacletus, who had appealed to him for help. As matters stood, Roger must have had an uncomfortable feeling that he had backed the wrong horse.

But Empire and Church, threatening as they might appear, were not the only enemies of the new king. Others, just as dangerous, were considerably nearer to hand. There were the barons, who had already constituted the principal obstacle to order and unity in the peninsula for over a hundred years—since before the Hautevilles were even thought of—and there were the towns. Only in Calabria, where no urban conglomerations of any size or importance existed, were the townsfolk content to accept royal domination. In Campania, the main centres may have been politically less evolved than their northern counterparts where the revival of trade, the loosening of the imperial grip and the beginnings of organised industry had already led to the establishment of those independent mercantile city-states, democratically governed, that were to be so characteristic a feature of later mediaeval Italy; but they too had been ruffled by the breeze of communal self-government, and the variety of forms which this had taken was a significant reflection of the prevailing disunity. In Apulia it was much the same. Bari had become a 'signory', ruled by the nobles of the city under a constitutional prince; Troia had a similar system under its bishop; Molfetta and Trani were communes. None had any wish, if they could avoid it, to be swept up into a disciplined and highly centralised monarchy. It was not long before they were able to make their attitude clear. During his whirlwind progress through the mainland duchies three years before, Roger had occasionally allowed the towns through which he passed, in return for their quick submission, to retain control of their walls and citadels. At the time the arrangement had served its purpose; but he could no longer afford such concessions. From now on his authority, if it were to survive at all, would have to be absolute. In February 1131, he formally requested the citizens of Amalfi to relinquish the command of their own defences and hand over to him the keys of their castle.

And they refused. Their argument that the King was riding rough-shod over the terms on which they had surrendered in 1127 was true but, so far as Roger was concerned, irrelevant. To him this was an act of outright defiance, and one which could not be tolerated. George of Antioch, the young Levantine Greek now on the thres-hold of his career as the most brilliant of Sicilian admirals, was despatched with the fleet to blockade the city from the sea and seize all Amalfitan ships in the roadstead; simultaneously another Greek, the Emir John, approached with an army from the mountains behind. Against such might the beleaguered citizens were powerless. They held out for a time, but when they saw Capri and all the neighbouring strong-points in Sicilian hands they could only surrender.

Twenty-five miles away in Naples, Duke Sergius VII had followed these developments with an anxiety which rapidly gave place to alarm. At one moment he had considered sending help to Amalfi; but when he heard the size of the Sicilian force he hastily changed his mind. And so, as the Abbot of Telese smugly records, the city 'which, since Roman times, had hardly ever been conquered by the sword now submitted to Roger on the strength of a mere report'.[1] At last all the territories bestowed on him by Anacletus the previous September were safely in the hands of the King.

Sailing back to Palermo that summer with three Neapolitan ships as his escort, Roger was suddenly overtaken by a violent tempest. After two days, during which it seemed that he and his crews must perish, he made a vow; if they were spared, then at whatever point they should be brought safely to shore he would build a cathedral to Christ the Saviour. The next day—it was the feast of the Transfigura-

---

[1] Alex. Telese, II, xii.

tion—the wind dropped, and the vessels glided to a quiet anchorage in the bay of Cefalù, under the huge rock that still dominates much of the sea-coast east of Palermo. At one time this rock had sheltered a prosperous little town, the seat of a Greek bishop in Byzantine days; but it had declined in importance during the Saracen occupation and in 1063 it had been sacked and largely destroyed by the Great Count. Now it was for his son to make amends. Stepping ashore, he ordered a chapel to be built near the landing-place in honour of St George, whom he claimed to have seen in a vision during the height of the storm;[1] then he called for measuring-rods and set to work at once to survey a site for his cathedral.

So, at least, runs the legend. Its veracity has been argued by local scholars for a century and more. The sceptics point out that it is attested by none of the local chroniclers—not even by the Abbot of Telese who, besides being Roger's most adulatory biographer, had a particular *penchant* for stories of this kind. The romantics, on the other hand, adduce a contemporary document discovered in the 1880s among the Aragonese archives in Barcelona which, they claim, leaves no further room for doubt.[2] Their case is strong, but not conclusive. All we can know for certain is that on 14 September 1131 Cefalù was once more given a bishop of its own—a Latin one this time—and that already, by that date, the building had begun.

The face of Sicily is changing fast. She is, alas, no more immune than anywhere else in Europe to the attentions of land speculators and property developers, and many are the Arcadian landscapes now ruined by cement-factory or motel. But the island possesses two architectural masterpieces which, viewed from afar as well as in close-up, still have power to catch the breath. The first is the Greek temple of Segesta—the distant prospect of which, however, owes much of its impact to the beauty of the site; one is struck above all by the placing of the building on its eminence, the relation of that

[1] It was not the first time that St George had given moral support to the Normans in moments of crisis; readers of *The Normans in the South* may remember his appearance with Roger's father at the battle of Cerami in 1063.

[2] Rosario Salvo di Pietraganzili, 'La leggenda della tempesta e il voto del Re Ruggiero per la costruzione del Duomo di Cefalù'. In *La Sicilia Artistica ed Archeologica*, vol. II, Palermo, June–July 1888.

eminence to the surrounding hills, the grandeur, the isolation and the silence. This is not to detract from the temple itself; it is superb. But then so are nearly all Greek temples, and one—the fact must be faced—is apt to be very like another.

The second is Cefalù; and Cefalù is unique. Seen first, as it should be, from the coast road to the west,[1] its setting yields nothing to that of Segesta. A gently curving beach fringed with pine and prickly pear leads the eye along to a confusion of roofs, clustered at the far corner of the bay. Above and behind, but still very much a part of the town, rises Roger's cathedral, dominating the houses below as effortlessly as its sisters at Lincoln or Durham. Beyond the cathedral again is the rock that gave the place its name. The ancient Greek inhabitants seem to have seen it as a gigantic head, but it is really more like a pair of great, broad shoulders, four-square and massive, giving the town protection and reassurance. Not so imminent as to be menacing, not so distant as to be incidental, rock merges with town until the two become parts of a single grand design, each complementing the other. And the cathedral forms the link between them.

Such is the first impression. But it is only on arrival in the central piazza that the full splendour of Cefalù is revealed. Now for the second time, but for different reasons, one is astonished by the perfection of its placing. The slope of the rock on which it is built sets it, a little obliquely, on a higher level than the square; it must thus be approached, like the Parthenon, at a slight angle and from below. And, as one approaches, so the realisation grows that here is not just the loveliest Norman exterior in Sicily, but one of the loveliest cathedrals in the world. The façade as we see it, with its twin towers—fraternal rather than identical—and the blind interlaced arcading that runs between them, dates from 1240—a century after Roger's time. By then, that fusion of eastern and western styles so typical of earlier Norman-Sicilian architecture had disappeared; and we are left with a perfect, sunny, southern romanesque, uncluttered but never austere.

So, at least, it seems on the outside. But the great miracle of Cefalù is yet to come. Climb the steps now, pass between two curiously

[1] See plate in *The Normans in the South*.

endearing baroque bishops in stone, cross the inner courtyard to the triple-arched portico—a fifteenth-century accretion, but none the worse for that—and enter the church itself. At first glance it may look a trifle disappointing: the effect of the slender arches—their shape an unmistakable reminder of the proximity of Islam—on the two rows of antique Roman columns is nearly lost under the dead-weight of seventeenth- and eighteenth-century decoration. But soon your eyes forget the sunshine they have left and readjust themselves to the cathedral twilight; they follow the march of the columns towards the sanctuary; from there they are led up, past the high altar and the saints, the angels and the archangels ranged above it; until at last, high in the conch of the great eastern apse, they are met by those of Christ.[1]

He is the Pantocrator, the Ruler of All. His right hand is raised to bless; in his left he carries a book, open at the text beginning 'I am the Light of the World'. It is written in Latin and Greek—and rightly so; for this mosaic, the glory of a Roman church, is itself of the purest Byzantine style and workmanship. Of the master who wrought it we know nothing, except that he was probably summoned by Roger himself from Constantinople and that he was unquestionably a genius. And at Cefalù he produced the most sublime representation of the Pantocrator—perhaps of Christ in any form—in all Christian art. Only one other, at Daphni near Athens, can be said even to rival it; but, near contemporaries though they are, the contrast between the two could hardly be greater. The Christ of Daphni is dark, heavy with menace; the Christ of Cefalù, for all his strength and majesty, has not forgotten that his mission is to redeem. There is nothing soft or syrupy about him; yet the sorrow in his eyes, the openness of his embrace, even the two stray locks of hair blown gently across his forehead, bespeak his mercy and compassion. Byzantine theologians used to insist that religious artists, in their representations of Jesus Christ, should seek to reflect the image of God. It was no small demand; but here, for once, the task has been triumphantly accomplished.

Beneath, his mother stands in prayer. Such is the splendour of her son, the proximity of the four archangels flanking her and the glare

[1] See plate in *The Normans in the South*.

from the window below, that she can easily pass unnoticed: a pity, since if she were standing in isolation amid the gold—as she does, for example, in the apse of Torcello—she too would be hailed as a masterpiece. (The archangels, be it noted, are dressed like Byzantine Emperors, even to the point of carrying the orb and *labarum* of the imperial office.) Further down still are the twelve apostles, less frontal and formalised than so often in eastern iconography, turning a little towards each other as if in conversation. Finally, on each side of the choir, stand two thrones of white marble, studded with Cosmatesque inlays, red and green and gold. One is the bishop's; the other was that of the King.

Here Roger must have sat during his last years, gazing up at the splendour that he had called into being; for an inscription beneath the window records that all these apse mosaics were completed by 1148, six years before his death.[1] He had always conceived of this cathedral as his own personal offering, and had even built himself a palace in the town from which to superintend the building operations.[2] And so it can have come as no surprise to his people when, in April 1145, he designated it as his burial-place, endowing it at the same time with two porphyry sarcophagi—one for his own remains and the other, as he put it, 'for the august memory of my name and the glory of the Church itself'. The sad story of how his wishes were disregarded, so that he now lies not in his own glorious foundation but amid the vacuous pomposities of Palermo Cathedral, will be told later in this book. After eight centuries it would be idle to hope for a change of heart by the authorities; it is hard, nevertheless, to visit Cefalù without putting up a quick, silent prayer that the greatest of the Sicilian kings may one day return to rest in the church which he loved, and where he belongs.

[1] The upper row of mosaics on the walls of the choir, with their inscriptions in Latin instead of Greek, are rather later—presumably the work of local artists in the following century. The same is true of the seraphim on the vaulting above.

[2] Traces of this palace still remain in the so-called *Osterio Magno,* on the corner of the Corso Ruggero and the Via G. Amendola.

2

REVOLT IN THE REGNO

Transalpinati sumus!

Pope Innocent II to the Archbishop of
Ravenna, 16 April 1132

ROGER had weathered one tempest—a fact to which his cathedral at Cefalù was soon rising in superb testimony. But he knew, even before the foundations had been laid, that another, greater storm was gathering fast. Lothair was planning his promised march on Rome, with the dual purpose of establishing Pope Innocent in the chair of St Peter and of having himself crowned Emperor. With the Abbot of Clairvaux, the weight of the western Church and the Kings of England and France behind him, he would probably succeed; and what then was to prevent his leading his army on into Sicilian domains, to rid Europe once and for all of a schismatic Pope and his only champion?

Once in the South, he would find no lack of support. Even more than the towns, the vassals of South Italy had always resented their Hauteville overlords. In the previous century they had been a constant thorn in the flesh of Robert Guiscard, distracting and delaying him in all his operations. But for their perpetual insurrections he would never have taken so long to conquer Sicily; he might even have ended his life as Emperor in Constantinople. Yet Robert had at least been able to exert some degree of authority; under the son and grandson who had succeeded him as Dukes of Apulia the last shreds of that authority were lost and the land had slipped back into chaos. The vassals were free to do as they wished, to fight and to lay waste, to rob and to pillage until, as the Abbot of Telese lamented, a peasant could not even till his own fields in safety.

One thing only united them—a determination to preserve this freedom and to resist any attempt to reestablish a firm and central-ised control. The fact that their suzerain was now no longer a Duke but a King had done nothing to reconcile them to the new order. To be sure, they had no love for the Empire either; but if they had to have a suzerain they liked him to be as far away as possible, and a grizzled old Emperor beyond the Alps was infinitely preferable to a determined and efficient young Hauteville on their doorstep. Almost as soon as the King had returned to Sicily in the summer of 1131 two of the worst of them, Tancred of Conversano and Prince Grimoald of Bari, had stirred up a minor insurrection in Apulia, and by Christ-mas the port of Brindisi was in their hands.

The King was in no particular hurry to bring them to heel. It was his custom to winter in Sicily whenever possible, and Cefalù was doubtless occupying much of his attention. Besides, he loved his wife and family. Queen Elvira, the daughter of Alfonso VI of Castile, had been married to him for fourteen years. We know sadly little about her except that the marriage was a happy one and that she bore her husband seven children, including the four stalwart sons on whom, during his later years, he was so much to rely. The two eldest of these boys, Roger and Tancred, had made one ceremonial appearance in Italy at Melfi in 1129, when they and their father had received the grudging fealty of the Apulian and Calabrian nobles; but for the most part mother and children remained in Sicily, where during recent summers Roger had had little chance of seeing them.

By March 1132, however, he could no longer delay his return to the mainland. It was not only Apulian rebels who claimed his atten-tion; a graver problem was posed by Anacletus, who met him at Salerno to discuss plans for the future. The anti-Pope was growing worried: in preparation for the imperial coming, his rival Innocent had already appeared in North Italy. There was still no immediate danger; so far as anybody knew, Lothair's army had not yet begun to march. But Rome was already alive with rumours and these, fostered by Anacletus's old enemies the Frangipani, were having an unsettling effect on the populace. To make matters worse, the moon —according to Falco, the chronicler of Benevento—had suddenly lost its splendour and turned the colour of blood; no one could call that a good sign. What was needed, Anacletus argued, was a show of strength—a reminder to the Romans that he was still master in their city, and that the King of Sicily was behind him. Roger took the point; two of his leading vassals, Prince Robert of Capua and his own brother-in-law Rainulf, Count of Alife, were immediately despatched with two hundred knights to Rome, with instructions to remain there until further notice.

The gesture, like so many of the King's gestures, was not so altruistic as it looked. Robert of Capua had fought—though admittedly without much determination—with his fellow-nobles to keep Roger out of the South Italian dukedoms a few years before. Later, like the rest, he had capitulated and, in his capacity as leading vassal, had actually laid the crown on the King's head in Palermo Cathedral. But he had never become altogether reconciled to the new regime and Roger was probably glad of the opportunity, in view of the coming crisis, to send him a safe distance away. The Count of Alife was an even trickier character. He had betrayed his brother-in-law more than once before[1] and would undoubtedly do so again if it suited his book. Moreover, his brother Richard, who held in fief the city of Avellino, had recently denied the King's suzerainty and proclaimed himself independent. When Roger had summoned him to order, his reply had been to put out the eyes and split the nostrils of the royal messenger. The King had thereupon seized the disputed territory; but now a further complication ensued. While Rainulf was away in Rome his wife, Roger's half-sister Matilda, deserted him and sought refuge at the court, alleging that her husband's persistent cruelty made any continuation of their married life impossible.

Roger upheld her action, and when Rainulf—in defiance of his orders—left Rome to demand the restitution of both his territorial and his conjugal rights, had replied that though Matilda was of course free to return to him whenever she liked he had no intention of forcing her to do so against her will. Meanwhile she and her son were going back with him to Sicily, and he for his part was obliged to ask Rainulf for the immediate surrender of the lands she had

[1] *The Normans in the South*, pp. 309–18.

brought with her as her dowry—the Caudine valley and all the castles it contained. On the matter of Avellino he was equally unyielding: Rainulf had never raised an eyebrow when his brother had asserted his independence; by failing to defend the rights of his lawful suzerain he had forfeited all claims to the town. One concession only was Roger prepared to make: if the Count and his followers would like to lay their case formally before him at Salerno, he would listen to anything they might have to say.

Rainulf of Alife had no intention of submitting to such treatment, still less of presenting himself cap in hand at Salerno. Instead he approached Robert of Capua—who had also returned unbidden from Rome—and together the two began to lay their plans.

The Apulian rising was quickly suppressed. After a short siege in May 1132 the inhabitants of Bari surrendered Prince Grimoald and his family to Roger, who packed them off as prisoners to Sicily, while Tancred of Conversano bought his liberty only with a promise— which he never kept—to leave for the Holy Land. The whole campaign was over in a month; it was, however, symptomatic of a deeper discontent throughout the South and, more important still, it created a diversion which kept Roger occupied just at that crucial time when Rainulf and Robert were gathering their forces. If he had moved firmly against them the moment they returned from Rome— and their unauthorised departure from the city would have given him pretext enough—he might have saved himself many of the troubles which awaited him in the next few years. But he missed his opportunity. Sure-footed as he was in the conduct of Sicilian affairs, he had still not caught the measure of his vassals on the mainland. Not for the first time, he had underestimated them. He had wounded his brother-in-law in his pride but not in his effective strength, and had succeeded only in turning a potential opponent into a real one. The Count of Alife was now aggrieved and angry—and dangerous, since he could count on the support of the Prince of Capua, still the strongest military force in South Italy after the King.

Robert of Capua had never been particularly distinguished in the past for his moral courage; but rebellion was in the wind, and Lothair and the imperial army could not be long delayed. Besides, was he not

Rainulf's liege-lord? How could he hope to maintain his status as a feudal prince if he lost the confidence of his vassals? With all the energy of which he was capable he threw himself into preparations for a new, nation-wide revolt. By the late spring of 1132 he and Rainulf could boast three thousand knights and perhaps ten times that number of foot-soldiers under arms. And most of the South Italian barons were behind them.

The strength of the opposition took the King by surprise. He had just put down one rising; the last thing he wanted was to find himself faced with another—this time of far more formidable proportions— just when he needed all his energies to deal with the danger from the north. It was his habit never to do battle if he could avoid it; some accommodation might still be possible. In mid-July he sent messengers to the rebels proposing talks. It was no use. The two leaders were adamant. They had been wronged, and there could be no question of negotiations until their wrongs were redressed.

Both armies were by this time gathered near Benevento, and for good reason. Benevento was papal territory. Ever since its citizens had expelled their ruling princes and put themselves under the protection of Pope Leo IX some eighty years before, they had remained loyal subjects of the Holy See, and they now constituted the principal bastion of papal power in South Italy. It was outside the walls of Benevento that Pope Honorius had invested Roger with his dukedom in 1128, and it was from its pontifical palace that Anacletus, two years later, had granted him the crown, pledging him also the city's assistance in time of war. In the present situation this was a significant commitment; but could Roger count on it now?

At first it seemed as if he could. A certain Cardinal Crescentius, Rector of Benevento in Anacletus's name, together with the local Archbishop and a group of the leading citizens, came out to assure the King of their good will; and on hearing from him that he proposed in return to renounce several financial claims on the city, they seem to have had no hesitation in promising him active military help. It was a disastrous mistake; and it lost them, and Roger, the city. During their absence, Robert's agents had been busy; rumours were spreading fast that Crescentius and his friends had sold out to the King of Sicily, and when the terms of the agreement were revealed the Beneventans were horrified. What was the use of being a papal city if they were going to be swept up in internecine squabbles like everyone else? At a general gathering of the entire populace, they made their position clear:

We cannot ally ourselves in this wise with the King, nor can we accept to puff and sweat and exhaust ourselves on long marches with Sicilians and Calabrians and Apulians, all under the blazing sun; for our lines are cast in quiet places, and we were never accustomed to such perilous ways of life.

There is something disarming about such a protestation, but it may not have been quite so naïve as it seems. The citizens of Benevento must surely have known perfectly well that the eyes of Pope Innocent and King Lothair were upon them. When the great confrontation should occur between Pope and anti-Pope, they were still more anxious than everyone else in the South to end up on the winning side. Gentle and peace-loving as they claimed to be, their reception of Crescentius was such that the Cardinal fled back to Roger, having narrowly escaped with his life; meanwhile the wretched Archbishop locked himself, terrified, in the Cathedral.

For the rebels it was a triumph. Prince Robert now had no difficulty in securing promises of friendly neutrality, with free right of passage for his troops through Beneventan territory; and the Archbishop emerged, quaking, from his refuge to witness the solemn swearing of a new treaty between Capua and Benevento—saving always, he was careful to point out, the city's loyalty to the Pope. Just which Pope he had in mind, he did not make altogether clear; his flock seem to have thought it wiser not to ask.

For Roger the loss of Benevento to his enemies came as a severe blow. How serious it might prove in the long term was still an open question, but its immediate effect was to put his own forces in danger. They were dependent on the Beneventans for food and other supplies; and now, suddenly, the good will on which they relied had turned to open hostility. Moreover the Prince of Capua, secure in the knowledge of local support, might at any moment decide to attack. Once again Roger instinctively recoiled, as he nearly always did, from a direct confrontation. He ordered instead that every section of the army should keep a close watch on his standard and be ready to follow it, in any direction, as soon as it moved.

Shortly after nightfall the signal was given, and under cover of darkness the Sicilian army retreated across the mountains to the south. Although technically the manœuvre might have been described as a strategic withdrawal, its circumstances and speed were distinctly suggestive of flight—for dawn broke to find the royalist forces at the foot of Mt Atripalda, just outside Avellino. Twenty miles at night over mountain paths was no small achievement for an army, but the march was not yet over; the King, so Falco tells us, had been revolving thoughts of vengeance in his mind as he rode and was determined to regain the initiative. Thus, instead of making for his mainland capital at Salerno, he swung off to his right towards Nocera—Prince Robert's chief stronghold after Capua itself. A sudden attack might take the town by surprise; and it would with any luck be several days before the insurgents, who would assume that he had returned to Salerno, discovered where he had gone. Once they found out, they would be sure to hasten to the defence of Nocera, taking the quickest—though not the most direct—route via the coastal plain and the valley running between Vesuvius and the Apennine *massif*; but this would mean a crossing of the wide lower reaches of the river Sarno, where there existed only one bridge—an old wooden construction at Scafati, a mile or two away to the west on the road to Pompeii. If this bridge were destroyed, several more days at least would be gained. A party of sappers was despatched forthwith; their work was quickly done and they returned to find the siege of Nocera under way.

It was a brave and imaginative plan, one of which Roger I or Robert Guiscard would have approved. It deserved to work, and it very nearly did. But the rebel forces moved faster than expected. Only five days after the start of the siege, they had completed a makeshift bridge and were encamped opposite the King on the broad plain to the north of the city—Robert of Capua with a thousand knights on the left, Rainulf on the right with another fifteen hundred, split into three separate divisions. Of these, two hundred and fifty were sent up to the walls to divert part of the besieging force; the remainder made ready for battle.

The date was Sunday, 24 July. Roger was reluctant no longer. He had raised the siege of Nocera as soon as he heard of the enemy's crossing of the Sarno and had made his own dispositions. The first wave of the assault force was already drawn up on the field; now, at the King's command, they lowered their lances, spurred their horses to a gallop, and charged. Prince Robert's line crumbled under their impact; the Capuan infantry in the rear, seeing the horsemen bearing down upon them, panicked and fled towards the river. The bridge, so recently and so hastily erected, proved inadequate for their numbers and their speed; hundreds plunged into the water and were drowned.

A second charge of royalists followed with similar effect; but now the Count of Alife, with five hundred of his own knights behind him, swept in from the flank and fell on the attackers. Momentarily they wavered; and before they had time to reform, this onslaught was succeeded by another, and then by yet another as Rainulf's right and left followed his centre—descending on the enemy, as Falco puts it, like a lion that has not eaten for three days.

The tide was turned. Roger, himself now in the thick of the battle, seized a lance and galloped backwards and forwards through his reeling ranks, calling upon them to rally once again around their King. He was too late. His army was in full retreat, and he had no choice but to follow. That same evening he rode into Salerno, blood-stained and exhausted; four knights only were with him. Of the rest some seven hundred, with twenty loyal barons, had been taken prisoner. The others lay dead on the field or, like the bulk of the infantry, had been cut down as they ran. The spoils were immense. Falco admits that he has not the power to describe 'the abundance of gold and of silver, the rich golden vessels, the infinite variety of clothing for men and caparisons for horses, the cuirasses and other accoutrements' that were seized; while Henry, Bishop of St Agatha, who as a staunch champion of Pope Innocent had followed Robert to Nocera, records that the victors found, among the royal archives, the very Bull by which Anacletus had granted Roger his kingdom.[1]

[1] See *J.B.R.G.*, vol. V, *Monumenta Bambergensia*, p. 444.

It was Roger's first major battle, and it had been a disaster. His losses were enormous, his prestige in Italy dangerously shaken. As the news spread across the peninsula the flame of rebellion spread with it, and more and more towns rallied to the Capuan standard. In Benevento a torch-light procession visited all the principal shrines of the city to render thanks, and arrangements were made to receive a representative of Pope Innocent as Rector in place of the unfortunate Crescentius. In Bari, the population rose up again and massacred several of Roger's Saracen guard; at Montepeloso Tancred of Conversano promptly abandoned his crusading preparations and rejoined the revolt. Meanwhile reports were trickling through from Germany that King Lothair had at last got his army together and was even now marching south across the Alps.

And yet, as the King of Sicily set to work at Salerno to rebuild his shattered forces and to strengthen his fleet for the challenges ahead —his command of the sea being now more vital to him than ever— he is said to have impressed all those around him with his cheerfulness and confidence. To some extent this may have been assumed; but not, perhaps, entirely. Heretofore he had always avoided pitched battles. Diplomacy, bribery, prevarication, attrition, siege tactics— at various stages of his career he had used any or all of these rather than meet his enemy in the open field. The withdrawal from Benevento had been a case in point; many of his men would doubtless have preferred to stay and fight rather than make a shameful retreat under cover of darkness, as demoralising as it was undignified; but the long ride through the mountains had given the King plenty of time to search his soul. If he were to still the murmurings of his army and, perhaps, of his own conscience, it had been imperative for him to prove himself worthy of his race and his name. At last, he had gone some way towards doing so. His generalship may have been faulty, the day a disaster; but he had finally discovered, at the age of thirty-six, that when the call to battle came he did not lack courage.

The reports from the north were well-founded. It was nearly a year and a half since Lothair had promised to escort Pope Innocent to Rome. Unrest in Germany had delayed his departure and still prevented him from raising an army on the scale for which he had hoped. He now decided that the key to his domestic problems lay in the earliest possible acquisition of the imperial crown and the prestige it conferred; and so, in August 1132, with his queen Richenza of Nordheim and a force that amounted to little more than an armed escort, he set off over the mountains and into Lombardy.

It proved a disagreeable journey. As the Lombard cities grew every year stronger, richer and more independent, so their resentment of imperial claims increased. The reception which they therefore accorded to this latest claimant varied between coldness and out-and-out hostility—to which was added, when they saw the size of his following, more than a touch of derision. Lothair had to pick his way with care, passing only through those towns in which his unpopularity was least evident and trusting that Innocent, who had already been several months in Italy, would have succeeded in drumming up sufficient local support to enable him at least to enter Rome in style.

He found the Pope waiting for him near Piacenza. Innocent's appeals had not gone entirely unanswered; the imperial army on the last stage of the journey promised to be about two thousand strong. It was still a disappointing figure, but it was no longer shameful. What was principally lacking now was sea support. Pisa and Genoa in particular, the two great maritime republics of the north-west on whose assistance the Pope had relied, could at that moment see no further than the islands of Corsica and Sardinia, over which they had long been squabbling; without their help the imperial forces would stand little chance in the face of a concerted attack. But meanwhile the autumn rains were beginning, the roads rapidly turning to mud; and Lothair decided to postpone his coronation till the following spring. By then, perhaps, the warring cities might be persuaded to settle their differences for the common good.

The fact that they did so was largely due to the Abbot of Clairvaux. He appeared in Italy soon after Christmas; by March he and Innocent together had alternately hectored and flattered the Pisans and Genoese into a truce, and in the following month they were back again at Lothair's camp, ready for the advance on Rome. For a show of strength, the army that now reassembled itself was still sadly unimpressive; but imperial agents reported that Roger was still occupied with his own problems and that there was consequently no fear of serious opposition on the way to the Holy City.

The church of S. Agnese fuori le Mura still stands today, its aspect essentially the same as in the seventh century when it was built; and in front of it, on 30 April 1133, the Emperor-to-be drew up his army for its final entry. For some days already Rome had been in turmoil. Pisan and Genoese ships had sailed up the Tiber and were now lying threateningly under the walls; and their presence, aided by exaggerated rumours of the size of the oncoming German host, had induced many Romans—including the Prefect himself—to make a hurried change of allegiance. Much of the city thus lay open to Lothair and Innocent. They were received at the gates by the Frangipani and Corsi nobles and their minions—who had never wavered in their opposition to Anacletus—and led in triumph to their respective palaces: the King and Queen to Otto III's old imperial residence on the Aventine, the Pope to the Lateran.

But the right bank of the Tiber, with the Castel S. Angelo and St Peter's itself, the traditional setting for imperial coronations, still remained firmly in the hands of Anacletus; and Anacletus was not prepared to give in. Lothair, conscious of his own weakness, proposed negotiations, but the anti-Pope's reply remained the same as it had always been—let the whole question of the disputed election be reopened before an international ecclesiastical tribunal. If such a tribunal, properly constituted, were to declare against him, he would accept its decision. Till then he would stay in Rome where he belonged. Left to himself, Lothair would probably have been ready to accept this suggestion. Anything in his view would have been better than a continued schism in the Papacy; rival Popes might well lead to rival Emperors, and in such an event his own position might be far from secure. But by now he had been joined in Rome by Bernard; and with Bernard at his side there could be no question of compromise. If Anacletus could not be brought to his knees, he must be ignored. And so it was not at St Peter's but at the Lateran that Innocent was reinstalled on the papal throne and there, on 4 June, with as much ceremony and circumstance as he could command, that he crowned Lothair Emperor of the West, and Richenza his Empress.

For the second time in half a century one putative Pope had performed an imperial coronation while another had sat a mile or two away, impotent and fuming. After the previous occasion Gregory VII had been saved only by the arrival, not a moment too soon, of Robert Guiscard at the head of some thirty thousand troops. Anacletus knew that he could expect nothing from that quarter; the King of Sicily, though still his loyal champion, was otherwise engaged. Fortunately, rescue was unnecessary. Powerless the anti-Pope may have been, but he was not in any physical danger. No imperial attack on Trastevere—the right bank—would be possible without control of the two bridges spanning the river at the Tiber Island; and all approaches to these were effectively dominated by the old Theatre of Marcellus, now the principal fortress of the Pierleoni. In the circumstances, the Emperor had neither the strength nor the inclination to take the offensive. Now that his immediate aims were achieved he thought only of returning to Germany as soon as possible. Within a few days of the coronation he and his army were gone; and the Pisan and Genoese ships had slipped back down the river to the open sea.

To Pope Innocent, Lothair's departure was nothing short of calamitous. At once his remaining supporters in the city began to fall away. Only the Frangipani remained loyal; but they could not hold Rome unaided. By July the agents of Anacletus had everywhere resumed their activity, and the gold was beginning to flow freely once again from the inexhaustible Pierleoni coffers. In August poor Innocent found himself forced once again into exile. He slipped unobtrusively from his diocese—just as he had three years before—and made his way, by slow stages, to Pisa and to safety.

Innocent was not the only one to feel betrayed. For the rebels in South Italy too, the news that the Emperor, so long awaited, had now come and gone without lifting a finger to help them must have dashed what slender hopes of victory they had left. Already the last few months had been disastrous. The year 1133 had started well enough with the revolt spreading, under the leadership of Tancred of Conversano, to every corner of Apulia. Even Melfi, the first capital of the Hautevilles, even Venosa, where four of the greatest—including Robert Guiscard himself—lay buried, had declared against their King. But, with the other towns that followed their example, they soon had reason to regret their faithlessness. With the first signs of spring Roger had crossed from Sicily at the head of a new army—and a radically different one. In the past when he had been anxious to win the sympathy and support of the South Italian vassals, he had found that a following wholly or even predominantly composed of Muslims was apt to do his prestige more harm than good; he had therefore used his Saracens sparingly, as little more than a stiffening for his regular troops. Such scruples bothered him no longer. He was desperate, and the Saracens had proved themselves among the loyalest of his subjects, immune alike from subversion by the Norman baronage and excommunication by the Pope. The army that he now landed on Italian soil was in essence a Muslim army, the only remaining way of bringing his Christian vassals to heel.

This altered composition of his fighting force seems to reflect a parallel change in the character of Roger himself. Whichever we read of the two chroniclers who have left us detailed accounts of the ensuing campaign—Falco, the notary of Benevento who hated him or, at the other end of the scale, the sycophantic Alexander of Telese—we are conscious of a new facet of his character, merciless and vengeful. He had always been a master of diplomacy and statecraft, and would remain one till the end of his life; but the events of the past two years had taught him that there are situations where such methods are no longer of any avail; and the battle of Nocera, disastrous though it had been in every other way, had convinced him of his ability to deal with them. No longer, when the occasion demanded it, would he shy away from the shedding of blood.

And so, in the spring and summer of 1133, the Sicilian Saracens fell on rebellious Apulia. Starting with Venosa—for by first assuring himself of the mountain towns of the centre he hoped to cut off Tancred and his rebels from their Capuan allies in the west—the King swept down eastward and southward to the sea, leaving a trail of desolation behind him. None who resisted were spared; many were burnt alive—according, at least, to Falco, who calls God to witness that 'such cruelty to Christian people had never before been known'. Corato, Barletta, Minervino, Matera and other rebel strongholds all fell in their turn, until at last Roger drew up his Saracens before Montepeloso, where Tancred had dug himself in and was awaiting the inevitable siege. With him, notes the Abbot of Telese, were forty knights sent to him by Rainulf of Alife, under the command of a certain Roger of Plenco[1]—'a most courageous soldier but extremely hostile to the King'.

The walls of Montepeloso were no match for the Sicilian siege engines; and after little more than a fortnight, 'with all their trumpets sounding forth and their voices raised in a great shout to heaven', the Saracens burst into the town. Some of the defenders, 'disguised in the vilest garments, lest they should be taken for knights', managed to make their escape, but their leaders were not so lucky. Falco's pen seems to tremble in his hand as he writes:

Then Tancred and the unfortunate Roger [of Plenco] flung down their arms and sought refuge among the darkest and most obscure alleys of the town; but they were sought out, and discovered, and led into the presence of Roger the King. Oh the sorrow, the horror, the weeping! Oh reader, how great would have been your own anguish of heart, had you been present! For the King decreed that Roger should forthwith be hanged by the neck, and that Tancred himself, with his own hand, should pull on the rope. Oh, what crime unspeakable! Tancred, despite his grief, could not but obey the King's command. The whole army was stricken with horror, and called upon God in Heaven to wreak His vengeance upon so great a tyrant and so cruel a man. Next the King ordered that the valiant Tancred should be held a prisoner; we have heard that he was later led captive to Sicily. And then, without further delay, the whole town of Montepeloso, its monasteries and all its citizens, both men and women, with their little ones, were given over to fire and the sword.

After the fall of Montepeloso, Apulian resistance was effectively broken; but Roger's fury was still not assuaged. Now that he had decided to show the mailed fist, he was determined that the lesson should not be lost on any of his subjects. Henceforth, by each and every one, the price of rebellion should be clearly understood. Trani

[1] Falco calls him Roger de Pleuto.

he left a burnt-out shell; at Troia, where a municipal delegation was sent tremblingly out to greet him, he had the five principal magistrates executed on the spot and then razed the city to the ground, dispersing its survivors around the neighbouring villages. Melfi suffered a similar fate; Ascoli fared very little better. At last on 16 October, having destroyed the defences of every important town in Apulia, the King and his Saracens returned to Salerno; on the 19th they took ship for Sicily.

Roger might have no more to fear from Apulia, but there still remained his two Campanian vassals to be brought to heel. Robert of Capua and Rainulf of Alife had hastened to Rome at the first news of Lothair's arrival and had dutifully attended his coronation, doubtless expecting that once the attendant formalities were over he and his army—such as it was—would march south with them against the King of Sicily. They should have stayed where they were; the speed and suddenness of Roger's counter-attack caught them unprepared, separated from their followers at the time they were most needed. Rainulf had returned with all haste, but he seems to have made no serious attempt—unless we include the forty knights under the luckless Roger of Plenco—to stem the tide of the King's advance. Prince Robert was more cautious and more sensible. The events of the previous summer had taught him that, with the forces at present available, not even an overwhelming victory like Nocera could prove decisive in the long term. Roger's power could never be broken without outside assistance, and if that were not forthcoming from the Emperor, then it must be sought elsewhere. Accordingly, in the last week of June, he had left Rome for Pisa; and there, after protracted negotiations, he managed to conclude an agreement by which, in return for three thousand pounds of silver, one hundred Pisan and Genoese vessels would be put at his disposal in March of the following year.

With a fleet of this magnitude sailing against him, Roger's command of the sea would have been seriously imperilled. His enemies might well have risked a full-scale offensive against Messina to block the straits, or even a direct attack on Palermo itself. But he showed no particular concern. In the early spring of 1134 he was back again on the mainland, determined to settle affairs in Italy once and for all. Sweeping up through rebel territory, he met with scarcely any opposition. Reports of his treatment of the Apulian towns in the previous year had long been current in Campania, where the local populations had taken the point, just as he had intended that they should. Wherever his army passed, resistance seemed to crumble; meanwhile the lords of Capua and Alife, strengthened by a thousand Pisan soldiers but still awaiting the bulk of their promised reinforcements from the northern sea-republics, remained on the defensive. Now it was their turn to avoid pitched battles. One after another their castles fell. Even Nocera, scene of Roger's deepest humiliation barely two years before, surrendered as soon as it became clear that Rainulf's attempts to relieve it had failed. The King, as merciful this year as he had been implacable in 1133, took no reprisals; the soldiers of the garrison, once they had sworn an oath of loyalty, were allowed to disperse freely to their homes.

Spring turned to summer, and still the Pisan and Genoese fleets failed to appear. Their presence now was vital, less for strategic reasons than because nothing else could hope to restore the insurgents' morale. Finally a desperate Prince Robert took ship to Pisa, ostensibly to make a last appeal for help but also, one suspects, to save his skin; and Rainulf was left alone to face the oncoming army. The Count of Alife, for all his faults, had never lacked courage. Seeing that a confrontation with his brother-in-law could no longer be avoided, he now mustered all his men in preparation for a final onslaught. But he was too late. The Sicilian agents that Roger had managed to infiltrate into the neighbourhood were open-handed and persuasive; such of the local knights and barons as had remained at his side now suddenly began to fall away. Rainulf was beaten and he knew it. He sent messengers to Roger announcing his unconditional surrender and flung himself on the King's mercy.

Towards the end of June the two met at the village of Lauro, near Avellino. As the Abbot of Telese describes it, it must have been an affecting scene:

Falling on his knees before the King, he [Rainulf] first tried to kiss his feet; but the King raised him up with his own hand and made as if to kiss him in his turn. The Count stopped him, begging him first to cast all anger from him. And the King replied with all his heart, It is cast. Further, said the Count, I ask that thou shouldst henceforth esteem me as I had been thy slave. And the King answered, This will I do. Then the Count spoke once more: Let God himself, he said, be witness of those things which have been spoken between thee and me. Amen, said the King. And at once the King kissed him, and the two were seen to stand for a long time embraced, so that certain of those that were present were seen to be shedding tears for very joy.

Roger was plainly in a very different mood from that in which he had dealt with Tancred of Conversano and the Apulian rebels the year before; and in token of reconciliation he restored to Rainulf his wife and son—the causes, willing or not, of so much of the trouble. They seem to have been happy enough to return home—an indication that Countess Matilda's erstwhile desertion of her husband may have been less straightforward than at first appeared. There were limits, however, to the King's forgiveness. Those lands which had been part of his sister's original dowry remained confiscate; and Rainulf was further required to surrender all the territory he had won since the outbreak of hostilities.

The last enemy was Robert of Capua. He was still, so far as anyone knew, remonstrating with the Pisans for having let him down; and it was at Pisa that a royal messenger now sped to him with Roger's terms: if the Prince returned to Capua before the middle of August and made his submission, he would be confirmed in his possessions, saving only those which the King had captured in the recent fighting. Alternatively, if he preferred to remain absent, his son could be installed on the Capuan throne, with Roger himself acting as Regent on his behalf until the boy became of age. If, however, Robert were to continue in rebellion, his lands would be seized; his principality itself would forfeit its separate identity and revert to the direct control of the Kingdom of Sicily. He could take his choice. Receiving no answer, the King made his formal entry into Capua.

It was, the Abbot of Telese tells us, a great and prosperous city, defended not only by its walls and towers but also by the broad Volturno winding around its base, with scores of little floating water-mills moored along the banks. Now, however, it offered no defence; the King was welcomed in the cathedral with honour and—

if we can accept the Abbot's word for it—with rejoicing. Afterwards he received Duke Sergius of Naples, a faintly ambivalent character in this story, who had always resented Roger's South Italian claims and had made no secret of his sympathy for the insurgents, but who had yet somehow managed to hold himself and his city aloof from any actual fighting. With Capua in the King's hands, Sergius found that he too had no longer any alternative but to come to terms. He too knelt before Roger, and swore him fealty and homage.

The revolt, it seemed, was over. A week or two previously the citizens of Benevento, after yet another internal upheaval, had thrown out Pope Innocent's representatives and declared once again for Anacletus and the King; at last, for the first time in three years, all South Italy was quiet. In each of those three years the autumn had been well advanced before Roger had been able to return home to his family in Palermo; in 1134 he felt free to leave by the end of July.

But if Roger appeared to have solved his problems, for the historian there is still one that remains unanswered. What happened to the reinforcements promised to the rebels by the great maritime city-republics of the north? Negotiations had been completed, prices arranged, dates fixed. The final agreement had been signed at Pisa, in the presence of Pope Innocent himself, the previous February and had been ratified by the rebel barons a week or two later. The hundred ships contracted for, fully manned, were to have arrived in March. Had they done so, the course of events in the summer of 1134 would have taken a very different turn. But they never appeared. What prevented them?

Two of St Bernard's letters, written in 1134 to the Pisans and Genoese respectively, provide us, perhaps, with a significant clue. To the Pisans,[1] characteristically using the Almighty himself as his mouthpiece, Bernard wrote:

He has said to Innocent his anointed, Here let my dwelling be, and I shall bless it. . . . With my support the Pisans shall stand firm under the attacks of the Sicilian tyrant, not shaken by threats, enticed by bribes or hoodwinked by cunning.

To the Genoese,[2] he made himself clearer:

[1] Letter 130.   [2] Letter 129.

I have heard that you have received messengers from Count [*sic*] Roger of Sicily, but I do not know what they brought or with what they returned. To tell the truth, in the words of the poet, *Timeo Danaos et dona ferentes*.[1] If you should find that anyone amongst you has been so depraved as to have held out his hand for filthy lucre, take prompt cognisance of the matter and judge him as an enemy of your good name and as a traitor.

Did the King of Sicily, in the early spring of 1134, bribe the Pisans and the Genoese—and possibly the Venetians as well—to break their commitments and deliberately to delay the help they had promised to Robert of Capua? We shall never be certain. We do know, however, that Sicily, with her unrivalled trading position and financial efficiency, was rich—richer for her size than any other state on the Mediterranean with the possible exception of Venice; and we know too that Roger was a consummate if tortuous diplomatist who always preferred buying off his enemies to fighting them and had long experience in the arts of corruption. St Bernard's suspicions of him may not have been charitable; but it is to be doubted whether they were very far wrong.

[1] I fear the Greeks when they come with gifts. Virgil, *Aeneid*, II, 49.

3

THE IMPERIAL INVASION

So gerieten si an raise　　　　So they embarked on a journey
In das lant ʒe Pulle;　　　　　Into the land of Apulia.
Daʒ was der vursten wille.　　This was the Prince's will.
Der vurste hiez da Ruocher,　The Prince's name was Roger
Den vertraip der chunich Liuther　Whom King Lothair pursued
In Siciliam.　　　　　　　　　To Sicily.

Lothair's *Kaiserchronik*, ll, 17084–89

THE King who sailed back to Palermo in the high summer of 1134 must have been a happy man. Peace and order had been restored to South Italy, and now reigned throughout his kingdom. Though he had not yet managed to prove himself a general worthy of his Hauteville forbears, his courage on the battlefield was no longer in doubt. He was respected in Italy, by friend and foe alike, as he had never been before. The Emperor of Germany had returned across the Alps rather than take up arms against him; the Pope whom he, alone of all the princes of Europe, continued to uphold was still firmly established in Rome. He had done his work well.

But Roger's troubles were not yet over. Soon after his return to Sicily he fell dangerously ill. He recovered, but only to see his wife in her turn struck down, probably by the same infection. The Greek and Arab doctors of Palermo were among the best in the world, and at Salerno the King had at his disposal the foremost medical school of Europe; but their efforts were in vain. Some time during the first week of February 1135, Queen Elvira died. She remains a shadowy figure, this Spanish princess who married Roger—in circumstances unknown to us—when he was twenty-two and shared his life for the next eighteen years. Unlike his mother Adelaide, she seems never to have involved herself in affairs of state; and she certainly never accompanied her husband on his campaigns in the manner of his aunt, the redoubtable and unforgettable Sichelgaita of Salerno. Alexander of Telese notes that she was renowned for her piety and charitable works, but there is no record of any monastic foundations or churches endowed by her; the abbot's words should probably be taken as being little more than the perfunctory tribute expected from friendly chroniclers on the death of a royal personage. The most moving testimony to her remains her husband's reaction to her death. He was broken-hearted. Now he retired with his grief, seeing no one but a few members of his court and *curia* until, as Alexander puts it, not only his subjects far away but even those who lived close to him believed that he had followed his wife to the grave.

Knowledge of his recent illness lent additional strength to this belief, and word of Roger's death spread quickly to the mainland. There could, at such a time, have been no more dangerous rumour. The King's eldest son was barely seventeen, untried in war or statecraft. In the hearts of Rainulf of Alife and of all the erstwhile rebels hope surged anew; they resolved to strike at once. The Pisans, after months of browbeating from Innocent, Bernard and Robert of Capua, no longer malingered, and on 24 April—thirteen months late—their promised fleet, carrying eight thousand men led by Robert himself, dropped anchor in the port of Naples, where Duke Sergius, effortlessly changing sides once again, gave it a warm welcome. News of its arrival decided the waverers. Within days Campania had reverted to its old chaos.

The history of Italy during the Middle Ages—and indeed beyond—is shot through with accounts of inconclusive wars; of tides of battle ebbing and flowing, up the peninsula and then down again, of cities besieged and captured, relieved and recovered, in a dreary struggle that never seems to end. To the historian they are tedious enough; to others they can be insufferable. Readers of this book will therefore be spared the minutiae of the campaigns that were necessary before Roger succeeded once again in establishing his authority.[1] Suffice it here to say that the insurgents soon had

---

[1] Any who yearn for further information can find it, in relentless detail down to the last beleaguered citadel, in the pages of Chalandon.

cause to regret their precipitate action. For the first six weeks, assisted by continuing rumours of the King's death and the absence of any counter-indications from Palermo, they were able to make some minor advances; but Roger's mainland governors and the various garrisons under their command kept a firm grip on the country and blocked any real progress. Then, on 5 June, the Sicilian fleet appeared off Salerno.

It was not just the renewed threat to the tranquillity of his mainland dominions that had roused Roger from the torpor into which his wife's death had sunk him; it was anger. He had never been a choleric man by nature, and even now he seems to have felt no deep resentment against the Prince of Capua. Although by ignoring his call for surrender the previous year Robert had remained a declared rebel, although as a sworn vassal of the King he had violated his oath of fealty, at least he had not compounded his offence by swearing a new oath only a few months before taking up arms again. But with the Count of Alife and the Duke of Naples it was different. Within the past year these two had knelt before Roger, placed their hands in his and pledged their allegiance. Rainulf indeed had gone even further, taking advantage of his kinship with a display of mawkish sentimentality which it must have been nauseating to recall. This was treason at its blackest and most shameless; and it would not be forgiven.

We should remember, in fairness to the Count of Alife, that he may have genuinely believed the stories of the King's death. Brother-in-law or not, however, he knew that he could expect no further mercy. He must play for time. Pope Innocent from his Pisan exile was maintaining the pressure on the northern sea-republics—especially on Genoa, whose men and ships, also promised for 1134, had still not arrived; while beyond the Alps the Abbot of Clairvaux was thundering from every pulpit against the schismatic Pope in Rome and his creature-King, vowing that he would never rest until he had launched a new Crusade against them. Even now, if the rebels could hold out long enough, they might still be saved. With his four hundred remaining followers, Rainulf hurried to Naples. Robert of Capua, ignoring the King's offers of a separate peace, accompanied him; and Duke Sergius, more fearful than either, received them with alacrity and began to prepare his city for a siege.

To the average observer of the South Italian scene in 1135, possibly even to King Roger himself, the events of that summer must have seemed merely a continuation of the struggle for power which had been continuing almost uninterruptedly for the past eight years. In fact, from the moment that the King's three principal Campanian adversaries barricaded themselves in Naples, the whole complexion of that struggle was changed. Hitherto it had been fundamentally an internal, domestic issue, a trial of strength between a King and his vassals. The fact that that King was largely responsible for the continued existence of an Anti-Pope in Rome, and thus for a schism which threw the whole foundation of European political and religious stability into jeopardy, was incidental. No foreign state had actually taken up arms against Roger—unless we count a body of unpunctual and remarkably ineffective Pisan mercenaries—and when Lothair himself had made his long-awaited descent into Italy he had been able to see no further than his own coronation.

The retreat to Naples marks the point at which the leadership of the opposition to Roger passes out of the hands of his vassals and on to the international plane. Pope Innocent and Bernard had long since accepted that Anacletus could never be dislodged from Rome while the King of Sicily remained able to protect him. Clearly, Roger must be eliminated; equally clearly, the Emperor was the man for the job. And St Bernard made sure that Lothair knew it. Towards the end of 1135 we find him writing to the Emperor:

It ill becomes me to exhort men to battle; yet I say to you in all conscience that it is the duty of the champion of the Church to protect her against the madness of schismatics. It is for Caesar to uphold his rightful crown against the machinations of the Sicilian tyrant. For just as it is to the injury of Christ that the offspring of a Jew should have seized for himself the throne of St Peter, so does any man who sets himself up as King in Sicily offend against the Emperor.

At about the same time a similar exhortation, though made for very different reasons, reached Lothair from a less expected quarter.

In Constantinople the Emperor John II Comnenus had been watching developments in South Italy with concern. The Apulian seaports—themselves until less than a century earlier part of the Byzantine theme of Langobardia, to which the Eastern Empire had never renounced its claim—were only some sixty or seventy miles from the imperial territories across the Adriatic; and the rich cities of Dalmatia constituted a temptation to a little gentle freebooting which, in recent years, Sicilian sea-captains had not always been able to resist. Other raids, on the North African coast, had indicated that the King of Sicily would not long be content to remain within his present frontiers and, if not checked, might soon be in a position to close the central Mediterranean at will. There was also some uncertainty about the Principality of Antioch, founded by Roger's cousin Bohemund during the First Crusade. Bohemund's son, Bohemund II, had been killed in battle early in 1130 leaving no male heir, and the King of Sicily had made formal claim to the succession. His South Italian responsibilities had so far prevented him from pursuing it actively; but he could be counted on to revert to the matter as soon as he had the chance, and the last thing the Emperor wanted was to find a Sicilian army digging itself in along his southern frontier. It looked, in short, as if Roger might soon prove himself a thorn in Byzantine flesh every bit as sharp as Robert Guiscard had been half a century before, and John was determined to stop him. In 1135 he sent ambassadors to Lothair with promises of generous financial backing for a campaign to crush the King of Sicily once and for all.

On its way to Germany the Byzantine mission appears to have stopped in Venice to enlist the support of the Republic. Venetian merchants had also been suffering at the hands of Sicilian privateers; already they estimated their losses at forty thousand talents. The Doge was therefore only too glad to help, and promised a Venetian fleet whenever necessary. Meanwhile Venetian envoys joined the Byzantines to give additional strength to the Greek appeal.

They found that Lothair needed little persuading. The situation in Germany had improved over the past two years—thanks largely to the new prestige conferred upon him by the imperial crown—and his Hohenstaufen enemies had been forced into submission. This time he would have no difficulty in raising a respectable army. With it he would be able to reassert his authority in Lombardy and then, entering his South Italian dominions for the first time, mete out to the Hauteville upstart the punishment he deserved. After that he foresaw little trouble from Anacletus. The anti-Pope's last remaining northern stronghold, Milan, had gone over to Innocent in June, and the schism was now confined to the Sicilian Kingdom and to Rome itself. Once Roger were out of the way Anacletus would be left without a single ally and would be obliged to yield. It would be a fitting climax to Lothair's reign. He sent the Bishop of Havelberg off to Constantinople to carry his compliments to John and to inform him that he intended to march against Roger the following year. Then, with something akin to relish, the old Emperor declared a special tax on all Church property—to defray his own share of the costs of the expedition—and began to prepare his army.

For Roger, 1135 had been a bad year. His own illness, his wife's death, the resurgence of trouble in Italy just when law and order seemed to have been re-established—it was enough to make any man want to turn his face to the wall. But the year had at least ended more satisfactorily than it had begun; and the three ringleaders of the revolt, Robert, Rainulf and Sergius, by taking refuge with such unseemly haste behind the walls of Naples, had virtually admitted their inability to carry on the struggle without assistance from outside.

And yet, while there was still hope of this assistance, they refused to surrender. By now Robert of Capua too had lost his last chance of reconciliation. The King's patience was exhausted. A short time before, he had created his eldest son, Roger, Duke of Apulia and his second, Tancred, Prince of Bari, thus dispossessing the rebellious Prince Grimoald. That autumn he invested his third son, Alfonso, with the Principality of Capua in Robert's stead—a ceremony which was shortly afterwards followed by Alfonso's solemn enthronement in Capua Cathedral. The boys were still mere fledglings, Duke Roger only seventeen and Tancred a year or two younger, while Alfonso was barely adolescent. But all three were old enough to play their part in their father's grand design, and in this design there was no longer a place for powerful vassals outside his own family. At the end of 1135, for the first time, every principal South Italian fief was in Hauteville hands.

All through that winter Naples held out. By the spring of 1136 there was serious famine. Falco records that many of the inhabitants, young and old alike, men and women, collapsed and died in the streets. And yet, he adds proudly, the Duke and his followers remained firm, 'preferring to die of hunger than to bare their necks to the power of an evil King'. Fortunately for them, Roger's blockade was never entirely effective; though the besiegers had cut off all access by land, the Sicilian navy never managed to achieve similar success in the sea approaches, with the result that both Robert and Sergius were able on separate occasions to slip away to Pisa for essential supplies. Even so, it is unlikely that Naples could have maintained its morale much longer had not Robert also made a hurried journey to Lothair's court at Speyer and returned, laden with imperial honours, to reveal that the Emperor was already well advanced with his preparations for the relief expedition.

Similar reports had already reached Roger, whose agents had left him with no delusions as to just how strong the imperial army would be. And so he too began to make his preparations, basing them on the assumption that the enemy force would be vastly superior in numbers to anything that he himself could muster. A Sicilian victory through force of arms would be out of the question; he would have to put his faith in guile.

It was high summer before Lothair's army was finally gathered at Würzburg. We have been left no very clear indications of its size, but a list of all the great imperial vassals who were present shows that it must have been on a very different scale from the sad little company that had set off with Lothair to Rome in 1132. In the forefront were Duke Henry the Proud of Bavaria, the Emperor's son-in-law, and Conrad of Hohenstaufen, the old enemy and rival who had now made his submission and whom Lothair had confirmed in the possession of all his lands and honours in return for a promise to participate in the coming campaign. There followed an imposing array of lesser nobles and their retinues, of *Markgrafen* and *Pfalzgrafen, Landgrafen* and *Burggrafen* from all over the Empire, together with an ecclesiastical contingent which included no less than five archbishops, fourteen bishops and an abbot. By the third week of August they were ready to start; and on about the 21st, with Lothair and his Empress at its head, the huge army lumbered off southward towards the Brenner.

The Emperor was no more popular with the Lombard towns than he had been four years earlier, but this time the size of his following commanded respect. Inevitably there were occasions when his men had to draw their swords; but nowhere was progress seriously delayed. Near Cremona his army was swelled by a Milanese detachment; there too he found Robert of Capua waiting for him. Early in February 1137 he reached Bologna, where he split the army into two. He himself proposed to continue through Ravenna to Ancona, and thence to follow the Adriatic coast into Apulia; meanwhile the Duke of Bavaria, with three thousand knights and perhaps twelve thousand infantry, was to press down through Tuscany and the Papal State, if possible re-establishing Innocent in Rome and assuring himself of the monastery of Monte Cassino, before meeting his father-in-law at Bari for Whitsun.

When, in the year 529, St Benedict had chosen a high hill-crest commanding the road between Rome and Naples as the site for the first and greatest of his foundations, he had inadvertently endowed the abbey with a strategic importance which its occupants, over the next fifteen centuries, would more than once have cause to regret. Later, as Monte Cassino grew in power and prestige, its geographical eminence took second place to its political; but for the Normans, ever since their earliest days in the peninsula, the monastery had always represented, both politically and militarily, one of the principal keys to the South. For Roger II, indeed, it was something more—a vital fortress, almost a buffer-state of its own, guarding the frontier which separated his kingdom from papal territory.

The monastery, for its part, had never found its position as a frontier fortress a particularly easy one. When in doubt, however, it had learnt to cast in its lot with the Normans. Thus it had been careful to remain on good terms with Roger's mainland viceroys, and though there had been a brief crisis a few months before when its loyalty had fallen—probably unjustifiably—under suspicion, the new abbot, Rainald, whom it had then been forced to elect was a staunch supporter of the King. When Henry of Bavaria arrived at the foot of the hill towards the middle of April, it was to find the surrounding countryside deliberately laid waste and the gates of the monastery barred against him. Henry had already had a rough passage through Tuscany. Pisa and certain other towns which had always remained loyal to Innocent gave him what help they could; but Florence and Lucca had been subdued only after a stout resistance, and Henry was still occupied with Grosseto when, at the beginning of March, Innocent—probably accompanied by St Bernard—rode out from Pisa to join him.

From the outset Prince and Pontiff seem to have disliked each other intensely. Henry was if anything a stronger and more un-yielding character than his father-in-law. As Prince of the Empire, with every expectation of succeeding to the throne on Lothair's death, he was determined to make no concessions that he might later have cause to regret; as a general with a job to do; and he had no intention of taking orders from the Pope or from anyone else. Matters first came to a head after the capture of Viterbo; an in-demnity of three thousand talents—roughly equivalent to some two thousand pounds of silver—was promptly claimed by Innocent on the grounds that the town lay within the papal frontiers, but was retained by Henry as part of the legitimate spoils of war. Then the Duke decided to by-pass Rome. It was, he maintained, more sensible to crush Roger first and allow Anacletus to collapse through lack of support than to waste time and energy in forcibly expelling him from St Peter's. The logic of this argument was unanswerable and Innocent accepted it; it meant, none the less, a further indefinite extension of his exile—to say nothing of the prospect of a long, hot Apulian summer trailing around in the wake of an imperial army— and it cannot have improved the Pope's temper.

And now, to crown it all, came the trouble at Monte Cassino, with the very fountain-head of western monasticism arrogantly defying not just the imperial army but Innocent himself. Eleven days Henry waited, blocking all access to the monastery and vaguely hoping for some sign that it might be prepared to make terms. But none came.

Its store-houses were well stocked with food, its garrison strong and in good heart; its position, in any case, made it virtually impregnable. The Duke, meanwhile, who had undertaken to join Lothair in Apulia by the end of May, had no time to waste. Swallowing his pride, he sent another messenger up the hill with an offer to negotiate.

Though Abbot Rainald's sympathies lay with Roger his first loyalty was to his monastery, his primary objective to get rid of Henry and his army as soon as possible. When the Duke offered, therefore, to leave Monte Cassino untouched and to confirm him as its abbot, in return only for a small recognisance in gold and an undertaking to fly the imperial banner from the citadel, he readily accepted. Innocent had already excommunicated the monastery for its Anacletan sympathies. His immediate reaction to this new agreement, by which the most venerable religious foundation in Europe—and one, moreover, situated on the very border of the Papal State—was left in the hands of an unrepentant champion of Anacletus and under the imperial rather than the papal colours, is not recorded in any of the chronicles. Perhaps it is just as well.[1]

As Duke Henry led his troops south across the Garigliano he may have congratulated himself on a technical victory, but he cannot have cherished any delusions about its real significance. The imperial flag flying over the monastery might temporarily affect Roger's prestige in the area, but in the absence of a garrison there was nothing to stop its being hauled down the moment the German army had disappeared from sight. At Capua, however, the next stage of his journey, better things awaited him. Immediately on his arrival the two local barons whom Roger had appointed to defend the city transferred their allegiance and opened the gates; and Prince Robert, who had accompanied the army from Cremona onwards, was replaced

[1] According to the *Kaiserchronik*, a long and rambling piece of Bavarian doggerel composed around 1150, the abbey was actually taken by a party of Henry's men, who gained admission by disguising themselves as pilgrims, hiding their swords beneath their robes. But this story, in one form or another, is almost *de rigueur* in mediaeval accounts of monastic sieges—see *The Normans in the South*, pp. 77–8. The only surprising thing is that Bernhardi, the punctilious (if tendentious) biographer of Lothair, should have taken it seriously. (*Lothar von Supplinburg*, pp. 700–1.)

on his old throne. The citizens accepted him willingly enough. The majority had always felt him to be their rightful lord, with a stronger and more ancient claim on their loyalties than the King of Sicily could ever boast; and the remainder, seeing him supported by so large a force, bowed to the inevitable. Robert, it is true, had to pay Henry four thousand talents not to turn his men loose on the city; but at such a price he must have considered his restoration cheap indeed.

Now it was the turn of Benevento. This time the populace stood firm, but were unwise enough to launch what they hoped would be a surprise attack on the imperial camp. It proved a disaster. They fled back to the city; the pursuers passed through the gates on the heels of the pursued; and the following morning—it was Sunday, 23 May—the Beneventans too made their submission, merely stipulating that their city should remain inviolate and that the erstwhile supporters of Anacletus should not be made to suffer. Their conditions were agreed; only Cardinal Crescentius, the Anacletan Rector who had already suffered one expulsion five years before, was seized by an old enemy and delivered over to Innocent, who condemned him to live out the rest of his days in the obscurity of a monastic cell.

Cheered by its successes—though possibly a little disappointed at having been once again cheated of a good day's pillage—Henry's army threaded its way over the mountains into Apulia, joining up with Lothair at Bari just in time to participate in the Whit Sunday thanksgiving. The Emperor indeed had a lot to be thankful for. His progress down the peninsula had been smoother than his son-in-law's. Ravenna had welcomed him. Ancona had resisted but had paid the price. Lothair's savage treatment of it had served as a warning to others and brought out many of the local barons to offer him homage and often material assistance. This pattern had continued as he marched south. The towns tended to be hostile, though after the fate of Ancona they generally managed to commute their hostility into a policy of sullen acceptance; but in the country districts most barons had rallied willingly enough.

Once over the Apulian frontier, the Emperor met with no resistance till he reached the spur of Monte Gargano. There Robert

Guiscard's old castle of Monte Sant' Angelo held out for three days against Conrad of Hohenstaufen and submitted only when Lothair arrived with the main army from Siponto and managed to take it by storm.[1] The anonymous Saxon Annalist, who gives us much the most detailed account of the whole campaign, tells us that Lothair then descended into the cave-shrine, where the whole Norman epic had begun, and 'humbly adored the blessed Archangel Michael'. His humility does not, however, seem to have inhibited him from stripping the shrine of its treasure—the gold and silver, precious stones and vestments presented by Duke Simon of Dalmatia some years before. Nor did it improve his treatment of those who opposed him and later fell into his hands. Mutilations, dismemberments and nose-slittings were the rule; and such was the terror he inspired that, on his return journey through the same region, whole populations were to flee at his approach.

Fortunately for the Apulians he was in a hurry, anxious not to waste time over protracted sieges while he still had only half his army with him. Towns like Troia or Barletta that put up a strong or spirited resistance he simply ignored: they could wait till after his son-in-law had arrived. At Trani, however, it was a different story. No sooner had he reached the town than its inhabitants rose up against the Sicilian garrison—it was probably composed for the most part of Saracens, who were seldom popular in Italy—and destroyed the citadel. A Sicilian relief fleet of thirty-three ships was scattered. The way was clear to Bari.

It was, therefore, a joyful and triumphant German congregation which assembled in the church of St Nicholas at Bari on Whit Sunday, 30 May 1137, to hear a High Mass of Thanksgiving read by the Pope himself.[2] So blessed was the hour that, according to the Saxon Annalist, a great golden crown was seen during the service, slowly descending from heaven over the church; above it

[1] Its ruins still stand today, and very impressive they are.
[2] See plate. This glorious church with its two great western towers, one Lombard, the other semi-oriental, was built to house the remains of St Nicholas of Myra—later metamorphosed into Father Christmas—after they reached Bari in rather dubious circumstances on 9 May 1087. The upper gallery has now been converted into a little museum. It contains, among other things, the huge crown and the enamel portrait of the saint with Roger II, mentioned on p. 458n.

hovered a dove, while from it there swung a smoking censer bearing two lighted candles. This ungainly manifestation seems to have been a little premature, since the Sicilian garrison in the citadel was still holding out; it was another month before it finally surrendered. But in general the Emperor felt he had cause for satisfaction. Between them, he and Duke Henry had made the imperial strength felt over most of South Italy; they had come together, their armies virtually intact, at the appointed time and place; and though they had on several occasions compromised with the opposition when time was pressing they had still not met with a single defeat. The Sicilian on the other hand—they never called him King—had suffered disaster after disaster. His vassals, including members of his own family, had turned against him; so had several of his towns. Garrisons had capitulated without a struggle, a valuable fleet had been put to flight. His arch-enemy Robert of Capua was restored to power and in firm possession of all his domains. And not once since the campaign began had he dared to show his face. Roger, it appeared, was not only a usurper; he was a coward as well.

So must Lothair have reasoned; and yet the situation was not as simple as that. If Roger remained in Sicily, making no effort to halt the imperial advance, it was because he knew that the Emperor was too strong for him; and that he must consequently stick more closely than ever to his old principle and avoid open engagements. He had only one element on his side, but that a vital one—the element of time. Lothair might advance as far as he liked, even up to the straits of Messina—where Roger was confident of being able to hold him; but sooner or later he would be driven back, as so many invading armies had been driven back before, by sickness, the relentless summer heat of Apulia, or the need to reach the Alps before the first snowfalls of the winter made them impassable. There remained a theoretical possibility that the old Emperor might decide to winter in Italy and continue the campaign the following year; but it seemed unlikely. His army would be pressing him to return and he himself would be reluctant to stay too long away from the seat of his power. Certainly no previous imperial expedition had risked a second season. And past experience showed that although such expeditions could have a considerable effect in the short term, the results they achieved seldom lasted for very long after they left. For the time being the only sensible course was to encourage the invaders to extend and exhaust themselves to the limit.

There might also be something to be gained, even at this late stage, by diplomacy. Politically, most of Roger's troubles were due to the fact that his two most powerful enemies, the Emperor and the Pope, were allied against him. If he could only separate them, some settlement might yet be reached. And so—according to the Saxon Annalist—he sent messengers to Lothair with a peace offer; if the Emperor would call a halt and recognise him as King, he for his part would split the Kingdom into two. He would continue to reign in Sicily, but his mainland dominion he would pass to his son, who would hold it forthwith as an imperial fief. In addition he would pay Lothair a substantial war indemnity and send him another son as a hostage.

The proposal was typical of Roger. It sounded reasonable and imaginative, and it would have confirmed the imperial claim on South Italy—which the Normans had tended to forget in the ninety years since Drogo de Hauteville had received his investiture from the Emperor Henry III.[1] In practice it might have meant rather less; Roger had already given his sons mainland fiefs and clearly hoped to leave more and more of the administration in the peninsula to them. The technical suzerainty of the Empire—which in theory existed already—was in any case of little practical value once the Emperor was safely back the other side of the Alps. It would, however, have been a genuine political concession; Roger's offer of his son as hostage would have been a guarantee of his sincerity; and Lothair, had he had only his own interests to consider, would have been well advised to accept an arrangement which, though admittedly less than he hoped to achieve, favoured the Empire and was above all workable.

Unfortunately there were papal interests also at stake; and Pope Innocent was interested in one thing only—the removal, immediately and for ever, of Anacletus from Rome. This was the crucial issue, and Roger's apparent silence on it poses an intriguing problem. Did he really believe that he could draw Lothair into a separate

[1] *The Normans in the South*, p. 74.

peace, and so persuade him to march back to Germany without taking any direct action against the anti-Pope? Or, for the sake of such a peace, was he by now prepared to leave Anacletus to his fate, and awaiting only some later stage in negotiations before overtly saying so? Neither of these possibilities seems likely. Roger was too realistic a statesman to have made the former mistake, too clear-headed an ally to have contemplated the second. But there is a third explanation, which accords far more closely with what we know of his character and with subsequent events. It is that he had no real intention of coming to terms with the Emperor at all—that his purpose was simply to beguile Lothair with as tempting an offer as could safely be made and which only considerations of the papacy would prevent his accepting, thus putting the greatest possible strain on relations between him and the Pope.

And these relations were deteriorating fast. Innocent was not normally a difficult man. Though he came from an ancient and noble family of Rome—the Papareschi—contemporaries like Bishop Arnulf of Lisieux speak of his robust simplicity and the quiet modesty of his manner. He never raised his voice which, we are told, was gentle and pleasant. His private life was without blemish. Before he became Pope he had no enemies, and even afterwards no one was ever able to level any serious accusations against him. Yet behind this rather colourless exterior lay a fundamental stubbornness which, particularly when he had St Bernard at his elbow, made him incapable of compromise. He was determined to be reinstated in Rome before he died, but he was already nearly seventy and time was growing short. Meanwhile the imperial army, during the best part of a year in Italy, had consistently ignored or overridden him. While it wore itself out on cheap triumphs in the remotest corners of the peninsula, he was as far from the throne of St Peter as ever.

We can imagine the Pope speaking, quietly but forcibly, on these lines to Lothair when they met at Bari; and his words doubtless lent additional colour to the stories the Emperor had already heard from his son-in-law about Innocent's attitude at Viterbo, Monte Cassino and elsewhere. But these political and personal differences were themselves only reflections of a more ominous discontent, now making itself felt throughout the camp. The coolness which had long existed between the German army and the papal retinue was developing into open hostility. To some extent this may have been due to a natural antipathy between Teuton and Latin, or between men of the sword and men of the spirit; but there were other, more immediate causes. The climate of Bari is damp and enervating, its summers merciless; malaria was a constant scourge; and the month that the imperial troops were forced to spend besieging the citadel— the longest period that they had stayed in one place since the previous winter—had lost them both their momentum and their morale. Suddenly they seem to have woken up to the pointlessness and inconclusiveness of a campaign against an enemy who refused to come out and fight. If they were ever to force Roger into battle it would mean marching another several hundred miles in almost the opposite direction, passing through barbarous and increasingly hostile country and undertaking a sea crossing which, though short, would in the circumstances be both complicated and dangerous. It would also mean at least another year—and they had been away ten months already—separated from their homes and families. And for what? Just so that a bunch of haughty, endlessly complaining Italians could install themselves in Rome, another two hundred miles away and once again in a different direction, where it was quite obvious that they were not wanted and where there was a perfectly acceptable Pope already.

If Lothair ever in fact intended to march on through Calabria to Sicily—and it is far from certain that he did—this new mood in his army soon dissuaded him. Feudal law laid down precise time limits for the military service due from a vassal to his liege-lord, and not even the Emperor could force his men to go far beyond these limits against their will. After the capitulation of the Bari garrison— whose tenacity he punished by hanging a number of them from gibbets all round the city and flinging the rest into the sea—he decided against any further advance down the coast. Retracing his steps as far as Trani, he turned sharply inland. Perhaps the air of the Apennines would cool his army's temper.

It did nothing of the sort. Nor even, a few days later, did the satisfaction of capturing Melfi, the earliest Hauteville stronghold in Italy, and massacring three hundred of its defenders. By now the imperial camp had been thoroughly permeated by Roger's agents, who were working on the growing disaffection and backing up their arguments with liberal dispensations of Sicilian gold; and they actually succeeded, while the army was still at Melfi, in provoking some of the soldiers to take up arms against the Pope and his Cardinals with the intention of murdering them in cold blood. Lothair heard of the attack just in time; he called for his horse, galloped to the papal tents and somehow managed to restore order before any serious harm had been done. But it was an angry and resentful cavalcade that trailed off once more through the mountains.

At Lagopesole the Emperor called a halt. For a fortnight his army rested while, in the presence of Abbot Rainald and a delegation from Monte Cassino, the whole status of the abbey, including its relations with both Empire and Papacy, was subjected to exhaustive investigation. A full account of what took place—even if we were able to sift truth from falsehood in the distressingly unreliable chronicle of the monastic librarian, Peter the Deacon—need not detain us here; but the conclusions were clear enough. Rainald and his brethren were made to promise 'obedience to Pope Innocent and all his successors canonically elected', and to 'renounce and anathematise all schism and heresy', with particular condemnation for 'the son of Peter Leone, and Roger of Sicily, and all who follow them'. Only then were they received, barefoot, by Innocent and accepted back, with the kiss of peace, into the Church's bosom.

Lothair himself, who had strong feelings about the monastery's imperial status, may have been rather less satisfied than Innocent over the outcome of the Monte Cassino affair. But he could not risk an open breach with the Pope and probably wanted to make some amends for the incident at Melfi. Besides, news had just reached him of far more immediate interest. A Pisan fleet a hundred strong had appeared off the Campanian coast; Ischia, Sorrento and Amalfi had all made their submission. The Pisans had then tried to relieve Naples but, finding the Sicilian blockade too strong for them, had headed south and were now attacking Salerno, Roger's mainland capital.

Eager to give the Pisans every support—and also, one suspects, to be properly represented on the spot in the event of any further quick victories—the Emperor hurriedly despatched Duke Henry, with Rainulf of Alife and a thousand knights, to Salerno. They arrived to find the city already under siege by Robert of Capua, with whose help they had no difficulty in sealing it off completely from the landward side. Meanwhile the Pisans, having commandeered the whole Amalfitan fleet of some three hundred vessels, had been joined by a further eighty from Genoa. Their Sicilian opponents, with only some forty ships in the harbour of Salerno, were hopelessly outnumbered. The siege of Naples, which had now been dragging on for two years, was lifted in order to liberate all available fighting men and ships for the defence of the capital; but against a combined force of such proportions the defenders had little hope and they knew it.

Even now, with his Italian kingdom overrun and its very capital threatened, Roger himself made no move. His attitude, craven as it must have appeared, was in fact the only one possible. To have sailed out from Palermo at the head of a new army of Saracens would have been the action of a hero, but hardly that of a statesman; it would have invited a defeat from which, even if he had survived, he could never have recovered. And so he stayed in Sicily, leaving the defence of Salerno to his local governor—an Englishman, Robert of Selby.

This Robert was the first of a long line of his compatriots who, as the century wore on, were to travel south to take service with the Kings of Sicily. We know nothing of his early life; but in the years since his arrival he had clearly gone a long way towards earning the reputation he was to enjoy ten years later, when a contemporary English historian, John of Hexham, was to describe him as 'the most influential of the King's friends, a man of great wealth and loaded with honours'. He had been appointed governor in Campania only a few months before, and he now proved himself worthy of the King's trust. Salerno, throughout that disastrous summer, had remained unflinchingly loyal to its sovereign. Its garrison of four hundred knights was strong and in good heart; soldiers and citizens together were ready to defend themselves, and for three weeks they fought fiercely and with courage.

Then, on 8 August, the rest of the imperial army appeared over
the mountains to the east, the Emperor himself riding at its head.
Lothair had originally intended to leave the siege to his son-in-
law; but the summer was creeping on, and the unexpected force of
the city's resistance had caused him to change his mind. Events
proved him right. To the Salernitans, his arrival meant two things;
first, that in the face of such reinforcements they themselves could
no longer hope to hold out until the winter, when they had counted
on the Germans to withdraw; and second, that by a quick surrender
to Lothair and a simultaneous request for imperial protection they
might yet escape being sacked and pillaged by the Pisans. These
views, eminently sensible as they were, were fully shared by Robert
of Selby. Summoning the elders of the city, he told them so. He
himself, representing the King over the entire province, could of
course have no part in any capitulation; it would be a matter for
Salerno only. Nevertheless, his advice to them was to lose no time
in sending a deputation to the imperial camp to seek peace and
protection.

The next day it was all over. Lothair, surprised, delighted and
doubtless gratified by this new proof of his prestige, imposed
unusually mild terms. In return for a war indemnity, the lives and
property of all Salernitans were guaranteed; even the four hundred
knights of the garrison were given their freedom. Meanwhile Robert
of Selby, with a small picked force, had withdrawn to the high
citadel above the city—that same so-called *castello normanno* that
had witnessed the stand of Salerno's last independent prince against
Robert Guiscard sixty years before and whose ruins can still be
seen—where he intended to keep the Sicilian banners flying until
the King himself should relieve him. When that moment came, he
would at least find his mainland capital still standing.

The arrangement, in fact, was welcomed by all the parties concerned—except one. The Pisans were furious. Not only had they
looked forward to rich plunder from a captured Salerno; they had
also been relying on this opportunity to annihilate one of their
principal trading competitors for years, perhaps decades, to come.
To the Emperor they had been an indispensable ally, without whom
the city would never have been won; to the Pope they had provided

a refuge for much of the past seven years; and in return they had received nothing. If that was all imperial alliances meant, they would have no more of them. If the Emperor could make a separate peace with his enemies, so could they. One of their ships sped off to Sicily to make terms with Roger; the others turned sulkily home.

Pope Innocent was later to have some moderate success in calming the Pisans down; but to Lothair their defection was of no importance. His campaign was over. He was probably none too sure himself just how much lasting good he had achieved. He had certainly failed to crush the King of Sicily as completely as he had hoped; on the other hand he had equally certainly dealt him a blow from which he must have seemed unlikely to recover. Everything now depended on the arrangements that could be made to govern South Italy and fill the vacuum of power once the imperial army had gone. There were three possible candidates for the Dukedom of Apulia—Sergius of Naples, Robert of Capua and Rainulf of Alife. Sergius and Robert were already powerful princes, and he had no wish to strengthen them still further. The Count of Alife, on the other hand, despite—or perhaps because of—his kinship with Roger, had more reason to fear him than either of the others. Two-faced and slippery as he had shown himself to be on occasions, wherever his own interests were concerned he was brave and determined. Furthermore—though Lothair may not have been consciously aware of the fact—he possessed an insidious, persuasive charm which had in the past won over even Roger himself and to which, more recently, the gruff old Emperor had fallen an easy victim. And so Lothair had made up his mind. Only Rainulf, he had decided, could be trusted to hold the dukedom safe for the Empire. His investiture would be the last official ceremony of the Italian expedition, and would set the seal on the campaign.

But who would perform it? The moment the question arose, the old imperial-papal rivalry flared up again as fiercely as ever. It was no good Lothair protesting that the first Apulian investiture, that of Drogo de Hauteville, had been by the Emperor Henry III ninety years before; Innocent quietly pointed out that Robert Guiscard owed his title to Pope Nicholas II. At last a compromise was reached—a tripartite ceremony, at which Rainulf received his symbolic lance at the hands of Emperor and Pope together, Lothair holding the shaft and Innocent the point. Henry of Bavaria, who had long chafed at what he considered the spineless attitude of his father-in-law towards papal pretensions, was outraged; and many of the German knights agreed with him. But Lothair cared little. He had saved his honour; that was enough. He was old and tired, and he wanted to go home.

As August drew to its close, he started on his way. At Capua, disagreeable news awaited him: Abbot Rainald of Monte Cassino, scarcely a month after his oath at Lagopesole, had been in contact with the agents of the King of Sicily. Innocent, with St Bernard's support, had seized on the opportunity to demonstrate his authority over Monte Cassino and had at once appointed, on his own initiative, a commission of two cardinals and Bernard himself to enquire into the canonicity of the abbot's recent election. It was several days before yet another compromise was patched up. On 17 September, before a joint tribunal consisting of both the Emperor and the papal representatives—including St Bernard who, as always, took it upon himself to be principal spokesman—Rainald's election was pronounced uncanonical. The unfortunate abbot had no choice but to lay down ring and staff on the grave of St Benedict; and Wibald, Abbot of Stavelot, a tough Lorrainer who had accompanied the expedition from the start, was 'elected' in his place. We are not told by what means the monks were induced to accept so obvious an imperial nominee; but with the German army encamped at the foot of the hill they probably had little choice in the matter.

Lothair's health was now failing fast; and to all those around him it was plain that his days were numbered. He himself knew it as well as anyone, but he refused to take to his bed; he was a German, and it was in Germany that he wished to die. Rainulf, Robert of Capua and the Campanian vassals accompanied him as far as Aquino, the border of Norman territory. From there, leaving eight hundred of his knights to help the rebels to maintain themselves after his departure, he took the road to Rome; but before reaching the city he turned off towards Palestrina. For him there could no longer be any question of returning the Pope to St Peter's. At the monastery of Farfa he bade him farewell. Henceforth Innocent would have to fight his own battles.

Though he marched with all the speed of which his dispirited, half-disbanded army was capable, it was mid-November before the Emperor reached the foothills of the Alps. His companions implored him to winter there. The sickness was daily increasing its hold on him; it would be folly, they pointed out, to attempt a crossing of the Brenner so late in the year. But the old man knew that he could not afford to wait. With all the determination of the dying he pressed on, and by the end of the month was descending towards the valley of the Inn. But now his last remaining strength deserted him. At the little village of Breitenwang in the Tyrol he stopped at last; he was carried to a poor peasant's hut; and there, on 3 December 1137, at the age of seventy-two, he died.[1]

[1] Passing recently through Breitenwang and enquiring whether there was any memorial to Lothair, I was directed to a fair-sized house on which was fixed a plaque. It read:

> *Hier starb am 3. Dezember 1137*
> *Lothar II*
> *Deutscher und Römischer Kaiser*
> *in den Armen seines Schwiegersohnes*
> *Heinrich des Stolzen.*
> *In Ehrfurcht gewidmet von*
> *Frederick R. Sims*
> *London und Holzgau.*

4

RECONCILIATION AND RECOGNITION

Thanks be to God who has given victory to the Church. . . . Our sorrow is turned into joy and our mourning into the music of the lute. . . . The useless branch, the rotten limb has been cut off. The wretch who led Israel into sin has been swallowed up by death and thrown down into the belly of hell. May all those like him suffer the same fate!

St Bernard, on the death of Anacletus
(Letter to Abbot Peter of Cluny)

DURING the twelve years since his accession, Lothair of Supplinburg had proved himself to his German subjects a worthy occupant of the imperial throne. Upright, brave and merciful according to the standards of his time, he had brought back peace to a land riven with civil war; jealous as he was of his imperial prerogatives, he was also a genuinely pious man who had worked hard to heal the schism within the Church; and he left his compatriots happier and more prosperous than he had found them. Once south of the Alps, however, he seemed to lose his touch. Italy to him was a strange and foreign land; its people he mistrusted and misunderstood. Ever unable to make up his mind whether his principal task was to restore the rightful Pope or to crush the King of Sicily, he failed in both; and the indecision produced in him a state of general insecurity which led him to veer between uncharacteristic excesses of cruelty on the one hand and dangerous errors of omission on the other.

Above all, he never realised till it was too late that his show of strength through the mainland dominions of the King of Sicily was nothing but a piece of empty shadow-boxing; and that the only way of bringing Roger under control was by exterminating him altogether. Had he thrown all his strength, at the very outset, into an amphibious attack on Palermo, he might—just possibly—have succeeded; but by the time he learnt this lesson his army was in a state of near mutiny, the Pope was becoming more of an antagonist than an ally, and he himself, worn out by his exertions, the South Italian climate and his own swiftly encroaching disease, was a dying man.

It was less than three months after the imperial party left Monte Cassino that the Empress Richenza closed her husband's eyes in death; yet already by that time Roger had regained control of a large part of his territory. There could be no more conclusive justification of his policy over the past year. He was welcomed at Salerno when he arrived there at the beginning of October; and as he swept up through Campania scarcely a hand was lifted against him—though his newly-arrived Saracen regiments left a trail of death and destruction in their wake. Capua suffered worst. Prince Robert was away in Apulia but his city, if we are to believe Falco, was seized as if by a furious tempest and depopulated by fire and the sword. 'The King,' he goes on, 'commanded that the city should be totally despoiled . . . the churches plundered and stripped of their ornaments, the women and even the nuns brought to dishonour.' Falco, as we know, could not have written objectively if he had tried; but even after allowance is made for his hatred of the Normans it seems clear that Roger was bent once again on making an example of the rebel towns, just as he had after the earlier Apulian insurrection. Benevento he spared out of respect for its papal status; Naples too escaped lightly after Duke Sergius, for the second time in three years, had flung himself at Roger's feet and pledged his allegiance. Few adversaries would have forgiven a twofold treason such as this, but Roger was by nature a merciful man; he may have decided that after so long and arduous a siege the Neapolitans had suffered enough.

Had Sergius learnt his lesson? Would he have proved, in the long run, a faithful vassal at last? There is no telling, for within a month he was dead. In the third week of October he accompanied the King to Apulia where Rainulf, determined to defend his new

Dukedom, was busy forging an army. With the eight hundred German knights left him by Lothair, almost as many again culled from various local militias and with infantry in proportion, this amounted to quite a formidable force; Roger might have been better advised to avoid a head-on confrontation. Perhaps his successes in Campania had made him headstrong; possibly his anxiety to have done with this interminable rebellion may have clouded his judgment. His, however, and not Rainulf's, was the decision to do battle —just outside the village of Rignano, at the south-western edge of Monte Gargano where it drops away two thousand feet to the Apulian plain.[1]

His, too, was the responsibility for the defeat that followed. His young son Roger, whom he had invested with the Duchy of Apulia two years previously and who was now fighting his first major action in an effort to regain it, showed himself a worthy scion of the Hautevilles, charging fearlessly into his adversaries and driving one section right back along the road to Siponto. The King, however, had meanwhile decided to lead a second charge. Just what happened we shall never know, but he was utterly routed. Falco gleefully records—though his account is nowhere corroborated —that King Roger himself was the first to flee. He made straight for Salerno, leaving Sergius, thirty-ninth and last Duke of Naples, dead on the battlefield.

At the time of the disaster of Rignano—30 October 1137—the Emperor Lothair had still five weeks to live. We must hope that news of it reached him before he died; it would have given him comfort. And yet, surprisingly, even Rignano did Roger little lasting harm. A few cities of Campania took advantage of his defeat to claim certain concessions which they might not otherwise have been granted, but all stayed loyal; and a day or two after the King's return to Salerno news was brought to him that Abbot Wibald of Monte Cassino, after just a month and a day in office, had fled in

---

[1] The view from Rignano southward over Apulia long ago earned the village its title of *Balcone delle Puglie*. The mediaeval castle into whose ruins many of the houses have been built is more or less contemporary with the events here described.

terror across the Alps. He had paused, it appeared, only long enough to emphasise to his monks that he was leaving for their sake rather than his own—a protestation which they might have been readier to believe had it not been for the King's well-publicised threats to hang him if he remained. From the safety of Corbie, his next abbacy, Wibald was to keep up a steady flow of invective against Roger for the rest of his life; but he never ventured into Italy again. In his place the monks wisely elected one of their own number, a man of staunch pro-Sicilian and Anacletan sympathies; and thenceforth the great abbey, while preserving its technical independence, became to all intents and purposes a part of the Kingdom.

Back once again in Salerno, Roger was able to take stock of the situation. All in all, he was not dissatisfied. His policy of non-involvement, of allowing the German momentum to burn itself out, had been triumphantly vindicated. The Emperor had come and gone; on his arrival he had seemed to carry all before him, but within two months of his departure there was little left to show for his efforts but an Apulian insurrection—of that old, dreary, endemic kind which Roger, his father and his uncles had all had to deal with countless times over the past century and which could, doubtless, be dealt with again. The Kingdom itself was no longer in peril. The toll in money and lives—apart from the losses at Rignano, which need never have happened—had been minimal. Pope Anacletus was still lording it at St Peter's. Yet again, peaceful statesmanship had carried the day over brute force.

On the debit side, however, there was no denying that Roger's prestige had suffered a grave setback. Many of his less far-sighted adherents had been shocked by his passivity, which they had taken for cowardice; and his showing at Rignano, where he had probably hoped to redeem his reputation, had served only to confirm their suspicions. Moreover, though immediate danger had been averted, the undeniable fact remained that none of Roger's basic problems had been solved. The Sicilian crown was still recognised by no one but Anacletus; Robert and Rainulf, those two inveterate rebels, were still at large; while down at the very bed-rock of all the trouble, the Papacy remained divided.

But this last consideration was less disturbing to Roger than to

his enemies—a fact which explains why, some time at the beginning
of November, the hitherto most redoubtable of all those enemies
came personally to call on the King in Salerno. Like all the other
members of Pope Innocent's entourage, St Bernard of Clairvaux
had had a disagreeable summer. His health had long since been
shattered, and seven months spent trailing round the peninsula in
the imperial wake had left him in a state bordering on collapse. He
and Lothair had never liked each other. It was he, far more than the
mild-mannered Innocent, who had been disgusted by the proprie-
torial attitude shown by both the Emperor and Duke Henry towards
South Italy—which even the 'Sicilian tyrant' knew was a papal fief;
and it was he, almost certainly, who had persuaded and encouraged
his master to stand firm—at Lagopesole, Monte Cassino and elsewhere—against imperial pretensions.

When Emperor and Pope had finally parted company at Farfa,
Bernard had hoped to return to Clairvaux for rest. Instead, they had
sent him back to Apulia in the hopes that his prestige might succeed
where their force had failed and that he might be able to bring
Roger to terms. With a reluctance that he did nothing to conceal,
he had turned back, and had actually been present at Rignano, where
he had met Roger for the first time and had tried, unsuccessfully, to
dissuade him from doing battle.[1] After the débâcle, however,
Bernard rightly counted on finding the King in a more amenable
mood. Roger had no desire to perpetuate the schism. His support of
Anacletus, having originally won him his throne, had very nearly
lost it for him again. The situation was very different from what it
had been seven years ago. At that time it had seemed likely that
Anacletus might win an all-out victory; now it was plain that he
could hope for nothing more than to retain the opprobrious title
of anti-Pope, while living for the rest of his life a virtual prisoner
in the Vatican. For as long as Roger continued to support him in
his pigheadedness the Emperor would continue to encourage the
South Italian rebels; and peace would never return to the land.
Naturally the King, to whom the disloyalty of his own vassals was
so constant a preoccupation, felt reluctant to betray his own
suzerain; but there might be other possibilities besides betrayal. At

[1] *Vita Prima,* II, vii.

all events Bernard's visit provided a welcome opportunity for him to pause in the fighting and to talk instead. He badly needed a little time for recovery, and he knew that as a diplomatist he was more than a match for any of his adversaries. He gave the abbot a cordial welcome and readily agreed to look into the whole question of the Papacy again.

His proposal was that the rival Popes should each send three representatives to Salerno to plead their case; and Bernard accepted it. Poor Anacletus must have been horrified at this sign of vacillation on the part of his only ally, but he could hardly refuse. His choice fell on his papal chancellor, Peter of Pisa, and two of his Cardinals, Matthew and Gregory. Innocent also sent his chancellor—that same Cardinal Aimeri who had been largely responsible for the schism in the first place—together with Cardinals Guido of Castello and Gerard of Bologna, later respectively to become Popes Celestine II and Lucius II. The six arrived in Salerno at the end of November.

It was inevitable that Bernard, though technically not even a member of Innocent's delegation, should have done most of the talking. Once again, as at Etampes, he seems to have deliberately ignored the only legitimate subject for discussion—the canonicity of the original elections. This time, however, he did not fall back on invective; the Anacletans present could have defended their master too well and Roger would have been antagonised. Instead, he based his case on strength of numbers. Innocent enjoyed more present support than Anacletus; Innocent, therefore, must be the rightful Pope. It was a shaky thesis by any standards, but such was the fervour with which it was developed that its deficiencies in logic were largely overlooked.

The robe of Christ, which at the time of the Passion neither heathen nor Jew dared to tear, Peter Leoni now rends asunder. There is but one Faith, one Lord, one Baptism. At the time of the Flood there was but one ark. In this eight souls were saved, the rest perished. The Church is a kind of ark. . . . Lately another ark has been built, and as there are two, one must of necessity be false and will surely sink beneath the sea. If Peter Leoni's ark comes from God, then will Innocent's ark be destroyed and with it the Church of the East and the West. France and Germany will perish, the Spaniards and the English and the lands of the barbarians, all will be lost in the depths of the Ocean. The monks of Camaldoli, the Carthusians, the Cluniacs, those of Grandmont and Cîteaux and Prémontré and innumerable others, monks and nuns, all must be drowned in one great whirlpool, down into the deep. The hungry ocean will consume bishops, abbots and other princes of the Church, with millstones tied about their necks.

Of the princes of the world only Roger has entered the ark of Peter; with all the others perished, shall he only be saved? Can it be that the religion of the whole world should perish, and the ambition of Peter Leoni, whose life is so plain to us, should gain for him the Kingdom of Heaven?[1]

As always, the abbot's rhetoric had its effect. It is given to few advocates, in the course of legal proceedings, to win over opposing counsel; and yet, as Bernard rounded off his tirade, it was not the King but Peter of Pisa who advanced towards him to confess his past errors and implore pardon. This public defection of his own chancellor dealt Anacletus a blow only fractionally less severe than if he had been denounced by the King himself; and as the Abbot of Clairvaux stretched out his hand towards the apostate and led him gently but triumphantly away, there can have been few present at the tribunal who did not believe Pope Innocent's cause as good as won.

Roger, by contrast, was unmoved. The longer he could delay his decision, the better; besides, it was not his practice to make concessions without gaining some commensurate advantage in return. Anacletus was, after all, the only authority for his kingship; this would have to be confirmed by Innocent before there could be any question of a change in his allegiance. So too would his son's title to the Duchy of Apulia, of which Rainulf, as Innocent's appointee, would first have to be formally divested. But a public tribunal was no place for negotiations of this sort. On the ninth day the King gave out that he found the issue too complex for him to be able to decide on the spot. He would need to consult his Curia. He therefore proposed that one cardinal from each side should return to Sicily with him. On Christmas Day he would announce his decision.

Bernard did not accompany Roger to Sicily. Instead he returned to Rome with Peter of Pisa. Probably he suspected by now that his attempts to influence the King had failed. Had he still entertained

[1] *Vita Prima*, II, vii.

any serious hopes, it is hard to believe that he would not have followed up what he had begun and pursued his quarry to Palermo. Certainly it seems to have surprised no one when, as he had promised, Roger announced on Christmas Day that he saw no reason to change his previous opinions. He had upheld Anacletus as the true Pope in the past; he would continue to do so in the future.

If, as seems most likely, Roger's answer was prompted by the refusal of Pope Innocent to accept his conditions, Innocent's own attitude was probably governed by developments in Rome. Anacletus never recovered from the loss of Peter of Pisa. As the tormented year of 1137 drew to its close he appeared to be losing his grip on the city, and from November of that year we find Innocent heading his letters with the word *Romae,* in place of his earlier formula *in territorio Romano.* By now the anti-Pope held little more than St Peter's, the Vatican and the Castel S. Angelo, and it was perhaps just as well for him that, on 25 January 1138, he died.[1] His life, at first so promising, had been a sad one. Throughout the eight years that he had occupied the throne of St Peter to which, rightly or wrongly, he believed himself to be entitled, he had suffered—for the most part in silence—the campaign of invective and abuse that his enemies, led by the Abbot of Clairvaux, had ceaselessly waged against him. This campaign, nurtured down the centuries by Catholic apologists and St Bernard's biographers, still persists; in several modern works of reference the name of Anacletus is either vilified or omitted altogether. He deserved better than this. If his early career was stained with simony, it still remains clearer than that of most other pontiffs of his time. If he must take his share of the blame for splitting the Church in two, Pope Innocent and Chancellor Aimeri must each bear at least as large a part. Had events taken a different turn, or had St Bernard been content to occupy himself with the affairs of his abbey and his Order, then Anacletus, with his wisdom, his genuine piety and his diplomatic experience,

[1] Whether the location of his grave was deliberately kept secret by his supporters or whether it was immediately desecrated by those of Innocent we do not know. It has never been found.

might have proved himself an excellent Pope. As things turned out, he maintained an impossibly invidious position with dignity and restraint.

With his death, the schism was effectively at an end. The cardinals who had remained loyal to him did not immediately give up the struggle; in March, possibly with Roger's approval, they elected Cardinal Gregory as his successor under the name of Victor IV.[1] But Gregory's heart was not in it. He had none of the popularity of his predecessor, and the few Romans who at first undertook to give him their support were soon bribed away by Innocent. After a few weeks he could bear the situation no longer. One night in May he slipped out of the Vatican and across the Tiber to St Bernard's lodgings, where he gave himself up; and on 29 May, the Octave of Pentecost, Bernard was able to report to the prior of Clairvaux:

God has given unity to the Church, and peace to the City. . . . The people of Peter Leoni have humbled themselves at the feet of our lord the Pope, and have sworn him faithful homage as his liegemen. So too have those schismatic priests, together with the idol which they set up . . . and there is great gladness among the people.

Neither the death of Anacletus nor the collapse of his faintly ridiculous successor seems to have worried Roger unduly. His continued support for the anti-Pope had not proved the successful bargaining counter for which he had hoped, and the end of the schism certainly cleared the air. Freed now of the commitments that had cast such a blight on the first seven years of his kingship, he saw no point in continuing hostilities with the Holy See. He made public recognition of Innocent as the lawful pontiff, and sent orders to all his subjects to do likewise. Then, his army behind him, he headed for Apulia.

All through the summer and autumn the campaign went on. It must have been a demoralising time for Roger. Once again he swept through the peninsula, sacking and burning wherever he met any

[1] We have only Falco's authority for the suggestion that the King was consulted about this election and approved it. Whatever may be thought about the election of Anacletus, no one could defend the legality of Victor's, based as it was on the vote of a mere handful of schismatic cardinals. And by now Roger had everything to gain from ending the split in the Church.

opposition; yet somehow he could not achieve any real break-through. When he returned to Palermo at the end of the year the greater part of Apulia was still in rebel hands. Meanwhile there had been no word of any kind from Rome—nothing to suggest that Innocent was prepared to contemplate a reconciliation; and the following spring, as Roger was preparing for yet another year of struggle, the Pope showed just how far he was from any such idea. At a Lateran Council on 8 April 1139 he pronounced a renewed sentence of excommunication on the King of Sicily, his sons, and all those of his bishops whom Anacletus had consecrated.

But the end of Roger's nine-year calvary was fast approaching; indeed, it was nearer than any of the protagonists knew. The inconclusiveness of the 1138 campaign had suggested that Rainulf would be able to maintain his position indefinitely in Apulia, and the aggressiveness of the Lateran Council indicated that this confidence was shared in Rome. It was misplaced. Within three weeks of the Council he had fallen sick of a fever at Troia; he was bled unsuccessfully; and on 30 April he died. They buried him in Troia Cathedral.

Falco of Benevento has left us a poignant account of the consternation that spread through all rebel-held Apulia at the news of Rainulf's death: of the wailing of virgins and widows, of old men and children, of the tearing of hair, the lacerations of breasts and cheeks. It all sounds rather exaggerated; and yet we cannot avoid the impression that Rainulf was genuinely loved. For all his faithlessness he was an attractive, quixotic figure, with a charm that neither his friends nor his enemies were ever quite able to resist; in his short rule as Duke he seems to have governed wisely and well. He was a brilliant soldier and a brave one—a good deal braver than Roger, whom he twice defeated on the battlefield. A Norman through and through, in the popular imagination of his compatriots he embodied the knightly ideal in a way that his oriental, devious-minded brother-in-law could never hope to emulate. His weakness lay in his statesmanship; he simply did not see that Roger could never be beaten without long-term support, both political and military, from abroad. It was this blindness that led him—in defiance of his solemn oath, and after the King had shown him a rare degree of mercy—into an enterprise that brought misery and suffer-

ing to the South and laid it open to acts of cruelty by Roger of the
kind which he never committed except when desperate. In short,
the harm that Rainulf did his country was incalculable, and the
sorrow that attended his death was greater than he deserved.

With Rainulf's death the rebellion was officially at an end. Apart
from one or two isolated pockets of resistance which he could
deal with at his leisure—notably Bari and the region round Troia
and Ariano—only one problem remained. In late June Pope Innocent
marched south from Rome with his old ally Robert of Capua. But
Innocent could offer no real threat now. The papal army, by all
accounts, was not particularly large—a thousand knights at the most—
and this time there was every hope that the Pope would be ready
to talk. Indeed, soon after the first reports of his approach, two
cardinals arrived at the Sicilian camp. His Holiness, they reported,
had now reached S. Germano;[1] if Roger would wait upon him there,
he would be received in peace.

Taking his son and his army with him, the King rode off over the
mountains to S. Germano. For a week the negotiations dragged on.
Innocent was apparently quite prepared to recognise the Sicilian
crown, but he demanded in return the reinstatement of the Prince
of Capua. Roger refused. Again and again over the past seven years
he had given Robert the chance to make peace; now his patience
was exhausted. When he saw that the Pope on his side was also
adamant he resolved to waste no more time talking. Giving out that
he had some unfinished business in the Sangro valley, he broke
camp and headed away to the north.

As he must have known they would, Innocent and Robert soon
reopened hostilities and began beating their way towards Capua,
leaving a trail of burning villages and vineyards behind them. Then,
at the little town of Galluccio, they suddenly halted. From a high
position on their left, the Sicilian army was watching them. Innocent
quickly saw the danger and ordered an immediate withdrawal; but he
was too late. While his army was still collecting itself, young Duke
Roger burst out of an ambush with a thousand knights and swept
down into the centre of the papal troops. They broke in disorder.

---

[1] The modern town of Cassino, just below the monastery.

Many were cut down as they fled; countless others were drowned as they tried to cross the Garigliano. Robert of Capua somehow managed to escape, but Pope Innocent was not so lucky. He tried to take refuge, so the legend has it, in the little frescoed chapel of S. Nicola which can still be seen in the church of the Annunziata at Galluccio; but he tried in vain. That evening, 22 July 1139, the Pope and his cardinals, his archives and his treasure, were all in the hands of the King.

Two months before, while Pope Innocent was still assembling his army in Rome, Mount Vesuvius, after nearly a century's quiescence, had burst out in magnificent and terrifying eruption. For a week it had raged, vomiting lava over the neighbouring villages and filling the air with a pervasive reddish dust that darkened the sky over Benevento, Salerno and Capua. No one had doubted that it was a portent, and now at last men knew what it had foretold. The Holy Father himself had been brought low. Here was the greatest humiliation suffered by the Papacy at the hands of the Normans since Duke Humphrey de Hauteville and his brother Robert Guiscard had annihilated the army of Pope Leo IX at Civitate, eighty-six years before.

It was always a mistake for Popes to meet Normans on the battlefield. Just as Leo had had to come to terms with his captors after Civitate, so now Innocent in his turn was forced to bow to the inevitable. At first he refused; the honour and respect with which Roger persisted in treating him seem to have deluded him into believing that he might still be able to impose his own conditions. Only after three days did he finally understand the reality of his situation—and the price of his ransom. On 25 July, at Mignano, Roger was formally confirmed in the Kingdom of Sicily, with the overlordship of all Italy south of the Garigliano. Next, his son Roger was invested with the Duchy of Apulia, and his third son Alfonso with the Principality of Capua. The Pope then said Mass, in the course of which he preached a sermon of enormous length on the subject of peace, and left the church a free man. In the ensuing charter he managed to save a few shreds of the papal honour by presenting the whole thing as being merely a renewal and an extension of Roger's earlier investiture by Honorius II; the King also undertook to pay an annual tribute of six hundred *schifati*.[1] But nothing could disguise the fact that, for the Pope and his party, the treaty of Mignano spelt unconditional surrender.

Writing half a century after these events, the English historian Ralph Niger records in his *Chronica Universalis* that Innocent sealed the treaty by presenting Roger with his mitre; and that the King, having embellished it with gold and precious stones, made it into a crown for himself and his successors. Be that as it may, the two seem to have established a fairly cordial relationship. Together they rode to Benevento, where the Pope was received with such jubilation that, says Falco, it was as if St Peter himself were entering the city; and where, a day or two later in his camp outside the walls, the King received ambassadors from Naples to swear him fidelity and deliver to him the keys of their city.

This submission marked the end of an epoch. For four centuries and more the dukes of Naples had steered their perilous course through the straits and shoals of South Italian politics. Often they had nearly foundered; occasionally even, the Pisans or some other temporary allies had had to take them in tow. Though sailing technically under the Byzantine flag of convenience, they had also in recent years been increasingly obliged to run other colours to the masthead—those of the Western Empire, for example, or even those of the Normans themselves. And yet somehow their ship had always managed to stay afloat. Now it could do so no longer. Naples had suffered three sieges in nine years, and a disastrous famine to boot. Its last duke was dead, the quasi-republican government that had succeeded him an abject failure. The greatness and the glory were gone. When, a few days later, young Duke Roger entered the city to take formal possession in his father's name, he accepted it not as a loyal fief, but as an integral part of the Sicilian Kingdom. The ship had foundered at last.

Only two pockets of resistance remained to be mopped up: the Troia region, where the German rearguard left by Lothair was still

[1] 'The *schifatus* was a convex-shaped Byzantine coin worth, in 1269 at any rate, eight *taris* of gold, i.e. somewhat more than a quarter of an ounce of Sicilian gold; i.e. a *schifatus* had about the same value as an English sovereign.' (Mann, *Lives of the Popes in the Early Middle Ages*, vol. IX, p. 65.)

making trouble, and Bari, whither the last few of the rebel barons had retreated to make a final stand. In the first week of August the King appeared below Troia.[1] The town surrendered on his arrival; since the papal capitulation there seemed no point in continuing the struggle and the citizens, encouraged by reports of the mercy that Roger had shown towards the coastal cities of Apulia, invited him to enter in peace. But now the King revealed, for the first time, how deeply he had felt his brother-in-law's treason. He sent back word that he would accept no surrender from the Troians for so long as Rainulf's body was buried within their walls. His message was received with horror in the city, but Troia's spirit was broken. It had no choice but to comply. Four knights, led by one of the most faithful of Rainulf's old supporters, were given the task of breaking open his tomb. The body was dug up in its shroud, dragged on the King's orders through the streets to the citadel and finally cast into an evil-smelling ditch outside the gates. Soon after this lapse Roger seems to have repented of his inhumanity and, at his son's instigation, to have allowed his old enemy a decent reburial; but although he took no further action against Troia he still refused to enter it. In the remaining fifteen years of his life he never went there again.

It was a still vengeful King who now passed grimly on through Trani—to which his son had accorded remarkably generous terms a few months before—to Bari. No city in Apulia had played him false so often, and its continued resistance, despite the surrender of all its neighbours and the generosity with which they had been treated, had destroyed the last remnants of his patience. After a two-month siege, with famine threatening, the defenders were forced to seek terms. Roger, anxious above all to have done with the rebellion and return to Sicily, agreed to their conditions: there was to be no pillage, and prisoners taken on both sides should be returned unharmed. When he found himself within the walls, however, his vindictiveness again got the better of him. One of his knights, newly released from captivity, reported that he had had an eye put out while he was in prison. It was just the pretext Roger was looking

[1] See plate in *The Normans in the Sun.*

for. Was this not a breach of the agreement that had been made? Judges were summoned from Troia and Trani to join those of Bari in proclaiming the treaty null and void. The rebel Prince, Jaquintus, was delivered up to the King, together with his principal counsellors. All were hanged. Ten other leading citizens were blinded, yet others imprisoned and dispossessed. 'And such was the fear and trembling in the city,' Falco reports, 'that not a single man or woman durst venture out into the streets and squares.'

Even on his return to Salerno the King's anger had not entirely abated. Certain of the Campanian vassals who had been congratulating themselves on having escaped lightly after their part in the uprising suddenly found their lands and property confiscated. Some of these too were imprisoned, the majority exiled 'beyond the mountains'. When, on 5 November, Roger took ship for Sicily, he left a cowed and chastened baronage behind him.

The year 1139 had been the most triumphant of his reign. It had seen the death of his arch-enemy Rainulf and the two petty dynasties of Naples and Bari; and the effective elimination of Robert of Capua who, though he was to pass the rest of his life intriguing against the King, was never again to constitute a serious menace to the Sicilian throne. It had seen the most significant mainland victory for nearly a century, one which effectively wiped out the shame of Rignano two years before. It had seen the pacification of the entire South Italian Kingdom, its utter submission to the King's will, and the disappearance of the last remnants of the German imperial invaders. Finally, it had seen the reconciliation between the Kingdom and the Papacy and the recognition, by the rightful, undisputed Pope, of the Sicilian monarchy. Roger himself had shown courage, diplomacy, statesmanship and—at least until just before the end—mercy; and if in this last virtue he ultimately fell short of his own high standards, his record remains a good deal better than that of most of his contemporaries.

'Thus,' concludes Archbishop Romuald of Salerno, 'Roger, most powerful of Kings, having crushed and destroyed his enemies and betrayers, returned in glory and triumph to Sicily, and held his Kingdom in perfect peace and tranquillity.' It sounds like the ending of a fairy story, and Roger certainly had every cause for satisfaction as he sailed for home. Yet he cannot have been happy. As his conduct at Troia and Bari had shown, he was sick to the heart. The past few years had left him with a legacy of bitterness and disillusion which he would never quite overcome. His generosity had been too often abused, his trust too often betrayed, the great plans he cherished for his Kingdom too often set at nought by the selfish ambitions of the Norman baronage. In Sicily, where there were no great fiefs, men of three religions and four races were living happily at peace and in steadily increasing prosperity; in South Italy he had achieved nothing; his vassals had thwarted him at every turn. He had begun to hate the peninsula. In future he would leave its affairs as far as possible to his sons and devote his attention, as he had never been allowed to devote it in the past, to his island realm.

When, in January 1072, Robert Guiscard and his brother had battered their way into Saracen Palermo, one of their first decisions had been to move the administrative centre of the capital. The Emirs had always ruled from their palace in the district of Al-Khalesa, down by the sea; but they had also maintained an old castle on the higher ground a mile and a half to the west, which had been built some two centuries before to protect the landward approaches. This castle was cooler, quieter, remoter from all the dirt and hubbub of the city; it was also more commandingly situated and more easily defensible in the event of trouble. To the new conquerors that last point was the vital one; no Norman ever felt truly at ease living somewhere that he could not adequately defend in an emergency. Thus the old Saracen fortress, repaired and strengthened, became the seat of the Norman government and, in due course, the palace of the Great Count of Sicily.

Over the years, Roger I and his son had put in hand various far-reaching structural alterations, until little of the original Saracen fabric was left. By 1140 the building was in essence a Norman palace; and though much has inevitably been added during the past eight centuries—*cortiles* and colonnades, loggias and baroque façades, to say nothing of all the ponderous trappings of the Sicilian parliament—much, too, still unmistakably proclaims its Norman origins. The *Torre Pisana*, in particular, at the north end—otherwise

known as the Torre di Santa Ninfa after an early Palermitan virgin
whose immoderate admiration of the Christian martyrs led her to
follow their example—still stands much as Roger must have known
it. Even the copper dome of the local observatory, perched somewhat insensitively on its roof, proves less offensive than one might
expect. The crowning of a romanesque tower with a bulbously
Islamic cupola is a characteristic tendency of Norman-Sicilian
architecture, and the old Palermitan astronomers, whether they
recognised the fact or not, were merely continuing the old tradition.
It is somehow gratifying to learn that it was from this observatory,
on the first evening of the nineteenth century, that they discovered
the first and largest of the asteroids and named it Ceres, after the
patron goddess of the island.

Yet the *Palazzo Reale*, as it is still called, ultimately captures
neither the eye nor the imagination. As an ensemble, it is an architectural hotch-potch which fails to impose any overriding personality; even the *Torre Pisana* seems stilted and uninspired, so that the
casual visitor might be forgiven for turning away with a shrug
to the more immediately photogenic attractions of S. Giovanni
degli Eremiti down the road. Forgiven, but pitied none the less;
for in doing so he would unwittingly have deprived himself of one
of the greatest excitements that Sicily, and perhaps Europe, has to
offer him—his first, unsuspecting discovery of the Palatine Chapel.

As early as 1129, before he became King, Roger had begun to
build his own personal chapel on the first floor of his palace, overlooking the inner courtyard. Work on it had been slow, largely
because his problems on the mainland allowed him only a few months
of each year in which to superintend building operations. But at
last, in the spring of 1140, though still unfinished, the chapel was
ready to enter service; and on Palm Sunday, 28 April, in the presence
of the King and all his leading Sicilian clergy of both the Greek and
Latin rites, it was consecrated, dedicated to St Peter, and formally
granted the privileges appropriate to its palatine status.

Roger had no more love for Byzantium than had any other member
of his family; but both the manner of his upbringing and the
oriental atmosphere in which he lived inclined him towards the
Byzantine concept of monarchy—a mystically-tinged absolutism in

which the monarch, as God's viceroy, lived remote and elevated from his subjects, in a magnificence that reflected his intermediate position between earth and heaven. The art of Norman Sicily, now suddenly bursting into flower, was therefore above all a palace art; and it is fitting that its brightest jewel—*le plus surprenant bijou religieux rêvé par la pensée humaine,* as Maupassant was to describe it[1] seven and a half centuries later—should be the Palatine Chapel at Palermo.[2] It is in this building, with more stunning effect than anywhere else in Sicily, that we see the Siculo-Norman political miracle given visual expression—a seemingly effortless fusion of all that is most brilliant in the Latin, Byzantine and Islamic traditions into a single, harmonious masterpiece.

Its form is in essence that of a western basilica, with a central nave and two side aisles separated from it by rows of antique granite columns, all with richly gilded Corinthian capitals, drawing the eye along to the five steps that lead up to the choir. Western too, though whispering of the South, are the richly ornamented pavements and the coruscating Cosmatesque inlays of the steps, balustrades and lower walls—to say nothing of that immense ambo, proudest of pulpits, studded with gold and malachite and porphyry and flanked by a gigantic Paschal candlestick, a fifteen-foot high bestiary in white marble.[3]

But if we look up now to the mosaics with which the whole chapel glows gold, we are once again brought face to face with Byzantium. Some, alas, of these mosaics, notably those in the upper part of the north wall of the transept, have disappeared; others have been drastically—and in one or two cases disastrously—restored over the centuries. Occasionally, as in the lower half of the central apse and the two side apses, we are confronted with eighteenth-century

---

[1] *La Vie Errante*, Paris, 1890.   [2] See plate.

[3] See plate. This candlestick was almost certainly presented to the chapel by Archbishop Hugh of Palermo when he crowned Roger's son William co-ruler with his father at Easter, 1151. Carved on it, among the angelic supporters of the crucified Christ and roughly at eye-level, a single human figure emerges rather improbably from a palm frond. This figure, wearing a mitre and showing a disturbing resemblance to Mr Punch, was long believed to be a portrait of Roger himself; but since it also bears the papal *pallium,* to which the King was not entitled, it is more likely to represent the donor. (Schramm, *Herrschaftszeichen und Staatssymbolik,* vol. I, p. 80.)

monstrosities which a more enlightened administration would long ago have swept away. The best, however—Christ Pantocrator gazing in benediction from the dome, the circle of angels garlanding him with their wings, the evangelists studious in their squinches— all these are the finest, purest Byzantine, of which any church in Constantinople would have been proud. Over the choir nearly all bear Greek inscriptions, sure testimony of their date and workmanship; by contrast the Virgin in the northern transept,[1] the scenes from the Old Testament in the nave and those from the lives of St Peter and St Paul in the side aisles were added by William I some twenty years later, after his father's death. Here and elsewhere the Latin inscriptions, the preference for Latin saints and certain stylistic attempts to break away from the rigid canons of Byzantine iconography suggest that William was employing native artists—presumably Italian pupils of the original Greek masters. Other Italians, in the later thirteenth century, were responsible for the enthroned Christ on the western wall over the royal dais[2] and the two figures of St Gregory and St Sylvester inside the sanctuary arch, unpardonably introduced in the Angevin period to replace an earlier likeness of Roger himself.

These almost antiphonal responses of Latin and Byzantine, set in so lavish a frame, would alone have earned for the Palatine Chapel a unique place among the religious buildings of the world. But for Roger they were still not enough. Two of the great cultural traditions of his country had been dazzlingly reflected in his new creation, but what of the third? What of the Saracens, the most populous group of all his island subjects, whose loyalty had been unwavering—in marked contrast to that of his Norman compatriots—for more than half a century, whose administrative

[1] Seen from below she is inexplicably off-centre—for which the figure of John the Baptist to the upper left seems an awkward attempt to compensate. From the large window in the north wall, however, she appears in the dead centre of the visible wall space. From this it has been deduced that this window—which communicates with the interior of the palace—was used from about 1160 onwards as a royal box. (For this and much other fascinating detective work on Sicilian mosaics, see Demus, *The Mosaics of Norman Sicily*, London, 1950.)

[2] According to an inscription on the wall of the north aisle, this was restored in the fourteenth century.

efficiency was largely responsible for the prosperity of the Kingdom, and whose artisans and craftsmen were renowned through three continents? Should not their genius also be represented? And so the chapel was further embellished with what is, quite literally, its crowning glory, surely the most unexpected covering to any Christian church on earth—a stalactite ceiling of wood, in the classical Islamic style, as fine as anything to be found in Cairo or Damascus, intricately decorated with the earliest datable group of Arabic paintings in existence.

And figurative paintings at that. By the middle of the twelfth century certain schools of Arabic art had been jockeyed—principally by the Persians, who had never shared their scruples—out of their old abhorrence of the human form, and the tolerant atmosphere of Palermo led them to experiment still further. The details of the paintings are difficult to make out from floor level, but a pair of pocket binoculars will reveal, amid a welter of animal and vegetable ornamentation and Kufic inscriptions in praise of the King, countless delightful little scenes of oriental life and mythology. Some people are riding camels, others killing lions, yet others enjoying picnics with their harems; everywhere, it seems, there is a great deal of eating and drinking going on. Dragons and monsters abound; one man—Sinbad perhaps?—is being carried off on the back of a huge four-legged bird straight out of Hieronymus Bosch.

Yet just as it is the ensemble, rather than the individual details, that makes the real impact on the beholder, so must the Palatine Chapel itself be considered not as the sum of its separate elements but as an integrated whole. It is also a work of profound devotion. No other place of worship radiates such incandescent splendour; no other proclaims with such assurance its origin and purpose. This is a chapel built by a king, for kings to worship in. Yet it is still, above all else, a house of God. The royal dais is raised to the level of the choir, but not to that of the sanctuary. Marble-balustraded, backed with inlays in *opus Alexandrinum* culminating in a huge octagon of porphyry to enhalo the head of the enthroned monarch, it stands at the western end, massive in its majesty. But immediately above it is another throne; this is backed not with marble but with gold; and on it is seated the risen Christ. All the brilliance, all the throbbing colour of this wonderful place, the interplay of verd-antique, ox-blood and cipollino, every inch of it burnished by the million glinting tesserae of the walls, create an atmosphere not of ostentation but of mystery, not of royal pride but of man's humility before his maker. Maupassant chose his metaphor well; entering the Palatine Chapel is like walking into a jewel. And, he might have added, it is a jewel from the crown of heaven.

PART TWO

THE NOONDAY KINGDOM

5

ROGER THE KING

*Ma quando si acquista stati in una provincia disforme di lingua, di costumi e di
ordini, qui sono le difficultà, e qui bisogna avere gran fortuna e grande industria a
tenerli.*

But when territories are acquired in regions where there are differences in
language, customs and laws, then great good fortune and much hard
work are required to hold them.

Machiavelli, *Il Principe*,
Book III

IT is not only to the historian, with all his advantages of hindsight
and detachment, that the year 1140 appears as the watershed of
Roger's reign. The King himself seems to have been fully aware that
after ten years of bitter struggle—years which had brought him
more than his share of disappointments, betrayals and defeats—his
first great task was completed. At last his Kingdom was his own. Of
those vassals who had resisted his authority, the most formidable
were all dead, dispossessed or in exile. Fighting of a somewhat
desultory nature would continue for a few more years yet, notably
in the Abruzzi and Campania, where a clearly-defined border had
yet to be established with the Papal State to the north. But this would
be the primary responsibility of his sons, Roger of Apulia and
Alfonso of Capua; they were old enough now to look after their
own domains. And in any event the overall security of the Kingdom
would no longer hang in the balance.

The way was clear, in fact, for the second stage of Roger's grand
design. The country was united and pacified; now it must be given
a constitution. Eleven years before, at Melfi, he had already imposed
a great oath of fealty on the barons and leading churchmen of South

Italy, setting out the broad outlines of both the political and penal systems by which he intended to govern. But 1129 must have seemed a long time ago. Too much had happened since then—too many oaths broken, too many trusts betrayed. It was better to make a fresh start.

Roger spent much of the first six months of 1140 preparing his new legislation in Palermo. Since it was to apply with equal validity in all parts of the Kingdom, he might well have been content to promulgate it from his capital; but he did not do so. It was on the mainland that his vassals were the strongest, and there that they enjoyed the greatest freedom. On them above all he had to impress the binding force of his royal authority, and of the code of laws through which he meant to exert it. In July he took ship back to Salerno and at the end of the month, after a quick tour of his sons' recent acquisitions in the Abruzzi, rode in state through the mountains to Ariano,[1] where his feudatories had been gathering from all parts of the South.

It is only just over a hundred years ago, in 1856, that the two extant versions of the Assizes of Ariano were discovered—one in the archives of Monte Cassino and the other in the Vatican—and that their importance was first properly understood.[2] Infinitely more far-reaching, both in range and effect, than the oaths sworn at Melfi, they constitute a corpus of law which—though many are borrowed directly from Justinian—yet remains unique in the early Middle Ages, covering as it does every aspect of Roger's rule. Two particular features strike one from the outset. First, as befits so heterogeneous a nation, the King makes it clear that the existing laws of all his subject peoples shall continue in force. Except when there is a direct clash with the new royal ordinances, all the Greeks, Arabs, Jews, Lombards and Normans under his rule are to continue to live, as they have always lived, according to the customs of their fathers.

The second feature, which runs like a *Leitmotiv* throughout the

[1] Now Ariano Irpino.
[2] Both texts are given in Brandileone, *Il diritto romano nelle legi normanne e sueve del Regno di Sicilia*. The Vatican text is probably identical to that published by Roger at Ariano. That of Monte Cassino seems to be an abridgement, though it also contains certain later additions.

work, is the stress on the absolutism of the monarchy, stemming in its turn from the divinely-held power of the King. The law is the will of God; and the King—who alone may make and unmake it and stands alone as its ultimate interpreter—is therefore not only a judge but a priest. To question his decisions, or others taken in his name, is both a sin—sacrilege—and a crime—treason. And treason, *crimen majestatis,* is punishable by death. It extends over a wide and fearful range. It covers, for example, offences and conspiracies not only against the King's person but against any member of his Curia;[1] it includes cowardice in battle, the arming of mobs, the withholding of support from the armies of the King or his allies. No other nation, no other legal code in mediaeval Europe conceived of it in such sweeping terms. But then no other European state, with one exception, cherished so exalted a theory of Kingship. That exception was Byzantium.

Byzantium—here was the key to Roger's whole political philosophy. The feudal system which prevailed in his mainland dominions belonged to Western Europe; the civil service that he had inherited from his father in Palermo and the Sicilian provinces was based largely on Arabic institutions; but the monarchy itself, as he conceived of it and personally embodied it, was Byzantine through and through. The King of Sicily was not, in the manner of his lesser brethren to the north and west, merely the apex of a feudal pyramid. Before his coronation, like the Emperors of ancient Rome and their successors at Constantinople, he had been careful to secure the agreement and the acclamation of his people; but by the ceremony itself he was imbued with a mysterious, charismatic essence which set him above and apart from common humankind. This remoteness Roger was deliberately to foster throughout his life. His biographer Alexander of Telese writes of how, despite the quickness and brilliance of his conversation, 'he would never, in public or in private, allow himself to become too affable or jovial or intimate, lest people should cease to fear him'. And when, three or four years later, we find him, in the course of diplomatic negotiations with

---

[1] The *Curia Regis,* from the reign of Roger II onwards, was the principal organ of central government. Its powers were considerably wider than those of a modern cabinet, since it had important judicial responsibilities, especially in matters of civil law.

Constantinople, demanding recognition as an equal of the Emperor of Byzantium—God's Vice-Regent on earth, Equal of the Apostles—it comes as no surprise.[1]

If this theory, though it is unmistakably and repeatedly implied in the legislation, diplomacy and iconography of the Sicilian Kingdom, is never quite set out in so many words it is probably because of the one overriding practical difficulty which it raised. Just where, in all this, did the Pope fit in? The question was never satisfactorily answered—a failure which does much to explain the curious duality which appears in all Roger's dealings with the Holy See. As a papal vassal he was prepared to do homage to the Pope as his lawful suzerain; as a Christian he was ready to show him all the respect that he considered due; but as King of Sicily, in matters affecting the Church within his own frontiers, he would brook no interference. His hand was admittedly strengthened by the hereditary right of the Apostolic Legation which his father had wrested from Urban II forty-two years before;[2] but, as we shall see, he showed in ecclesiastical affairs a stubbornness and self-will which went far beyond anything that Pope Urban or his successors were ever prepared to contemplate.

Those of the Ariano Assizes which deal specifically with such affairs tend to stress the King's rôle as protector of the Christian Church and of the individual rights and privileges of its representatives. Heretics and apostates—from, not to, Christianity—are to be punished by the loss of civil rights, and there are heavy penalties for simony. At the same time bishops are excused attendance in the public courts, and the lower orders of clergy are granted lesser exemptions according to their rank. All such measures would have found favour in Rome, but—and this point doubtless provoked a very different reaction—all could be countermanded by the King, against whose judgment or decisions there could be no appeal. And so far as Roger was concerned this power—let the Pope make no mistake about it—was derived not through any historic grant of

[1] The fact that Roger styled himself *Rex* rather than *Imperator* in no way weakened this claim. *Rex* was the accepted translation of the Greek *Basileus*; it is also, incidentally, used to describe the Emperor Nero on a mosaic in the Palatine Chapel.

[2] *The Normans in the South,* pp. 273–4.

legatine authority; together with the right to the high canonical insignia—mitre and dalmatic, staff and pastoral ring—which the King wore on appropriate religious occasions, it stemmed directly from God Himself.

Similarly strict control was to be exerted over the feudatories. After ten years of defiance and insurrection they were at last quiescent, but they could not be relied upon to remain so indefinitely. What is interesting about Roger's legislative policy towards them, both at Ariano and later, is his attempt to accommodate an essentially western institution into a predominantly Byzantine political scheme. This meant, in the first place, establishing the maximum degree of separation between Throne and vassalage—a task which was further complicated by the fact that many of the Norman baronial families of Apulia had been in Italy for as long or longer than the Hautevilles and still saw no reason why the grandson of an obscure and impoverished knight of the Cotentin should arrogate to himself powers over them which seemed to exceed those of any other western monarch.

Here was another difficulty that was never entirely overcome, though Roger did his best in the years that followed to lessen its effects by renewing the grant of most of the existing fiefs. Thenceforth his vassals would hold their lands not by virtue of capture or early enfeoffment at the time of the first Norman conquest of Italy in the previous century, but by the King's grace and from the date of their new royal charter. Meanwhile the number, and therefore the power, of the knightly caste was further limited by turning it into what amounted to a closed order, almost like a separate civil service. Assize No. XIX, for example, *De Nova Militia,* lays down categorically that no man can be made a knight or retain his existing knighthood unless he comes of an established knightly family. Other ordinances warn all feudal lords and others—including churchmen— who have authority over townsfolk and villagers to treat them with humanity, and never to demand from them more than what is reasonable and just.

Before leaving Ariano the King announced one further innovation—the introduction, for the first time, of a standard coinage for the whole Kingdom. The unit he had selected was to be called the ducat, named after his Duchy of Apulia, the first of that glinting stream of gold and silver by which, for the next seven centuries, so much of the world's wealth was to be measured. The prototypes, struck in Brindisi, seem to have been of disappointing quality— *magis aereas quam argenteas,* Falco cattily remarks;[1] but they provided a further effective illustration of Roger's theory of Kingship. Typically Byzantine in form, they bear on one side a likeness of the King, enthroned, crowned and robed in full Byzantine regalia, holding in one hand an orb and in the other a long cross with double traverse. Beside him, his hand also on the cross, stands his son Duke Roger of Apulia, in military dress. The reverse of the coin is more significant still. Early Apulian money, minted in the reign of Duke William, invariably bore on the reverse a portrait of St Peter, to denote William's vassalage to the Holy See. Now those days were gone. The new ducats showed not St Peter but Christ Pantocrator. King Roger, they seemed to say, had no need of an intermediary.[2]

Some time in the spring of 1140, King Roger sent his friend the Pope a present of some beams for the roof of St John Lateran— which, like so much else in twelfth-century Rome, was sadly in need of repair. If Innocent took this gesture to mean that he would have no more trouble with the Hautevilles, he was mistaken; it was only a matter of months before the King's two sons, in the course of

---

[1] 'More copper than silver.' The first golden ducats do not appear till 1284— in Venice, where silver ones had been current since 1202.

[2] The contention, doggedly maintained in the eleventh edition of the *Encyclopaedia Britannica*—the most recent edition has dropped the entry altogether—that the ducat owed its name to the inscription on it *Sit tibi, Christe, datus, quem tu regis, iste ducatus* (To thee, O Christ, who rulest this Duchy, be it given) is without foundation. On a small coin there would have been no room for such a legend, even in an abbreviated form. The only inscription on these earliest ducats, apart from the letters identifying the two portraits, consists of the letters AN.R.X.— *anno regni decimo,* i.e. struck in the tenth year of Roger's reign. They constituted a further challenge to the Pope, who naturally counted the years of the Sicilian Kingdom from his own recognition of it at Mignano in 1139. Another coin, worth a third of a ducat, was simultaneously minted at the *zecca* in Palermo. A particularly happy example of Sicilian enlightenment, it bears on the obverse a Latin inscription surrounding a Greek cross, and on the reverse an Arabic one reading 'struck in the city of Sicily [*sic*] in the year 535'—of the Hegira, i.e. 1140 A.D.

what they described as 'restoring' former Apulian or Capuan lands, were pushing up as far as Ceprano in Campania and the Tronto in the northern Abruzzi and making frequent disturbing inroads into papal territories. But the two brothers, one feels, were only flexing their muscles, occupying their time as energetic young Norman knights had always done and were meant to do. They probably enjoyed irritating the Pope, but they showed no real hostility towards him. Their father meanwhile, though allowing his sons a fairly free rein, seems to have been genuinely anxious to improve relations with the Church and to eradicate as far as possible the unpleasant memories of the past decade.

Although Innocent, still smarting from his defeat at Galluccio, was not to be so easily placated, his principal ally had displayed a quite astonishing capacity for *volte-face*. Already at the Salerno tribunal St Bernard seems to have decided that Roger was not the ogre that he had always made him out to be, and set about revising his previous opinions. It comes as something of a surprise to find the man whose diatribes against the 'Sicilian tyrant' had long been famous through every corner of Europe, beginning in 1139 a letter to his old enemy with the words:

Far and wide the fame of your magnificence has spread over the earth; what limits are there untouched by the glory of your name?[1]

The King, though doubtless secretly amused at the suddenness of the change, was always ready to meet his enemies half-way. Soon after Mignano, when the last obstacle to good relations had been swept aside, he wrote to Bernard suggesting that he might pay a

---

[1] Three years later, Bernard's friend and fellow-abbot Peter the Venerable of Cluny, like him an outspoken enemy of Anacletus—and therefore of Roger himself—throughout the years of schism, was to address to 'the glorious and magnificent King of Sicily' an even more impressive testimonial:

Sicily, Calabria and Apulia, regions which before your time were given over to the Saracens, or to dens of brigands and caves of robbers, have now—thanks to God, who aided you in your task—become the home of peace and the refuge of tranquillity, a peaceful and most happy Kingdom, ruled, as it were, by a second Solomon. Would that parts of poor miserable Tuscany might be joined, with their neighbouring provinces, to your Realm!

Book IV, letter 37

personal visit to Sicily to discuss, among other things, a new monastic foundation in the Kingdom. Bernard, still only fifty years old but worn out with exertion, ill-health and his own particular brand of hysterical asceticism, replied with apparently genuine regret that he could not accept Roger's invitation in person; but he at once sent two of his most trusted monks to Palermo to negotiate in his name. They travelled as part of the suite which accompanied Elizabeth, daughter of Count Theobald of Champagne, from France to marry Duke Roger of Apulia in 1140, and arrived in Sicily towards the end of the year. The result was the foundation a short time later of the first Cistercian monastery in the South—almost certainly that of S. Nicola of Filocastro in Calabria.

The site chosen for this monastery may be yet another indication of Roger's policy towards the Church at this time. Though the Cistercians always inclined towards remote and secluded locations for their abbeys, there seems little doubt that St Bernard would have preferred somewhere in Sicily itself—not too far from the capital, where his abbot could keep a watchful eye—and perhaps exert a positive influence—on the ecclesiastical policies of the King. Roger, with the same considerations in mind, would have resisted any such proposals. However sincerely held his religious views, he retained an instinctive mistrust for the large, powerful monasteries of the mainland. Now that he had established a firm control over the Latin Church in Sicily he had no intention of seeing that control weakened by subversion from within. It was typical of him that during his entire reign he should have allowed only one major Latin foundation in Palermo itself—the Benedictine monastery of S. Giovanni degli Eremiti—and that he should have populated it with monks not from obvious sources like Monte Cassino or the great abbey of La Cava outside Salerno but from a small, relatively obscure community of ascetics at Monte Vergine, near Avellino. In taking this step the King made a considerable sacrifice; to have given S. Giovanni, with its superb location next to the royal palace and its huge endowments, to Cistercians or Cluniacs might have seemed a small price to pay for their favour; at once he would have been hailed as one of the most devout and generous monarchs in Christendom. It was a temptation that few Hautevilles—certainly not Robert Guiscard—could have resisted. But Roger was more subtle in his statesmanship. He had suffered too much from the Church of Rome and from St Bernard in particular. This time he was taking no chances.

S. Giovanni degli Eremiti—St John of the Hermits—stands today as little more than an empty shell. Nothing now remains there to suggest that during the most brilliant years of the Norman Kingdom it was the wealthiest and most privileged monastery in all Sicily. It was founded in 1142, and by the charter he granted it six years later Roger decreed that its abbot should serve *ex officio* as chaplain and confessor to the King, with the rank of bishop, and should personally celebrate Mass on all feastdays in the Palatine Chapel. He further laid down that in its cemetery—which still exists in the open court to the south of the church—should be buried all members of the royal family except the Kings themselves and all the senior officials of the court.[1]

The church itself, now deconsecrated, is surprisingly small.[2] It was built on the site of a much earlier mosque, part of which remains to form an extension of the southern transept. But the inside, despite the traces of tile and mosaic and fresco—and even of the stalactite ceiling of the original mosque—holds little interest for the non-expert. The fascination of S. Giovanni is in its exterior. Of all the Norman churches in Sicily it is the most characteristic and the most striking, its five vermilion domes—each standing on a cylindrical drum to give it greater height—bursting out from the surrounding greenery like gigantic pomegranates, in almost audible testimony of the Arab craftsmen who built them. They are not beautiful; but they burn themselves into the memory and remain there, stark and vivid, long after many true masterpieces are forgotten.

A few yards to the north-west there stands a little open cloister,

[1] This last decree was never generally observed. Nearly all the royal family were in fact buried in the chapel of St Mary Magdalen next to the old cathedral. When, forty years later, the cathedral was rebuilt the tombs—which included those of Queens Elvira and Beatrice and of four of Roger's sons, Roger, Tancred, Alfonso and Henry—were transferred to another chapel similarly named. This chapel still stands in the courtyard of the *carabinieri* barracks of S. Giacomo. Of the graves themselves, however, there is no longer any trace. (Deér, *The Dynastic Porphyry Tombs of the Norman Period in Sicily*. Cambridge, Mass., 1959.)
[2] See plate.

with gently poised arcading supported on pairs of slender columns, built half a century later than the church and in perfect contrast to it. Sitting there on a hot afternoon, looking up now at the soaring austerity of the royal palace, now at the aggressively baroque campanile of S. Giorgio in Kemonia, yet always aware of those bulbous oriental cupolas half-hidden behind the palm-trees, one is reminded for the hundredth time that in Sicily Islam is never far away. And it is, perhaps, in the church and cloister of what was once the leading Christian monastery of the Kingdom that its presence is most keenly felt.

The confrontation at S. Giovanni degli Eremiti between Muslim East and Latin West is so striking that the visitor tends to forget the third essential strand of civilisation that made Norman Sicily what it was. In all Palermo there is no longer a single building whose exterior recalls Byzantium. Despite the number of senior Greek officials in the Curia, despite all the Greek scholars and sages whom Roger attracted to the court in the later years of his reign, the capital itself had never boasted an indigenous Greek population of any size. It was, first and foremost, an Arab city, scarcely touched by Byzantine influences in comparison with those regions in which Greek peoples had lived since the days of antiquity—regions such as the Val Demone in eastern Sicily or parts of Calabria, where to this day a Greek dialect is spoken in some of the remoter villages.

And yet, from the time of the Sicilian conquest up to the point we have now reached in this story, the Greeks had played a vital part in the building of the new nation. First, they had kept the balance between Christian and Muslim on which the whole future of Norman Sicily depended. Roger's father the Great Count had encouraged Latin immigration, both ecclesiastical and secular, as far as he dared, but he could not allow too much too quickly for fear of frightening the Greek and Arab communities and turning them against him. Besides, such immigration brought its own dangers. If it had not been kept under rigid control there would have been nothing to stop swarms of swaggering Norman barons from the mainland pouring into Sicily, demanding to be given fiefs in keeping with their rank and station and gradually reducing the island to that chaos which always seemed to follow in their wake.

Without the Greeks, then, the Christian element during those early days might have been swamped altogether. But they also performed another invaluable function. They neatly counterbalanced the claims of the Latin Church, and provided both Count Roger and his son with a powerful bargaining—if not actually blackmailing —counter in their dealings with Rome. It seems in the highest degree improbable that there was any foundation for the rumours, current at the end of the 1090s, that the Great Count was seriously contemplating a conversion to Orthodoxy; but it is a good deal likelier that Roger II, at various moments in his long quarrel with Pope Innocent, may have considered renouncing the pontifical authority altogether in favour of some kind of loose caesaropapism on the Byzantine model. What is certain is that in 1143 the Greek Archimandrite Nilus Doxopatrius of Palermo dedicated to Roger—with the King's full consent—a 'Treatise on the Patriarchal Thrones', arguing that with the transfer of the imperial capital in A.D. 330 and the recognition of Constantinople as the 'New Rome' by the Council of Chalcedon in 451, the Pope had lost his ecclesiastical primacy, which now properly belonged to the Byzantine Patriarch.

But now, as the twelfth century nears its half-way mark, the situation can be seen to have changed. Sicily, first of all, has grown steadily richer; and as her prosperity has increased, so too has her political stability. In contrast to the endemic confusion of the Italian peninsula, the island has become a paragon of just and enlightened government, peaceable and law-abiding, an amalgam of races and languages which seems to give strength rather than weakness; and, as its reputation grows, more and more churchmen and administrators, scholars and merchants and unashamed adventurers are drawn across the sea from England, France and Italy to settle in what must have seemed to many of them a veritable Eldorado, a Kingdom in the sun. Meanwhile the importance of the Greek community has begun to decline. It is inevitable that it should. With no comparable immigration from abroad to sustain it, it is increasingly outnumbered by the Latin. In the prevailing atmosphere of religious toleration and easy coexistence, its value as a bulwark against Islam is negligible. Finally, Roger has now established so firm a control over his Latin Church that he has no longer any need for a counterbalance.

Not that there was any discrimination against the Greeks. In view of the mixed feelings with which the Hautevilles had always regarded the Byzantine Empire—admiration for its institutions and its art, distrust laced with more than a tinge of jealousy in every other field—they might have been excused for treating as second-class citizens a foreign minority whose political and confessional loyalties were openly divided. But they never did so. Roger and his successors continued to support their Greek subjects whenever their support was necessary; they never lost their concern for the welfare of the Greeks, or of their Church. The great and distinguished line of Greek admirals continued throughout the century; at least until the end of Roger's reign the whole fiscal system of Norman Sicily remained in Greek and Arab hands.[1] It was just that the emphasis had shifted. Though from the outset subordinated to the Latin hierarchy, large numbers of Basilian monasteries had sprung up over the past fifty years, notably S. Maria del Patirion near Rossano in Calabria[2]—founded by the Regent Adelaide at the beginning of the century—and its daughter-house, the monastery of the Saviour at Messina, established some thirty years later. But the Saviour, soon to be the chief of all the Greek monasteries in Sicily, was also the last. Henceforth the royal favours would be lavished on the new Latin houses—S. Giovanni degli Eremiti and, later, Maniace and Monreale.

Fortunately the way was still wide open for private patronage; and it is fitting that the sublimest legacy of the Greek Church in all Sicily, the only one that still possesses a beauty comparable to that of the Palatine Chapel and the cathedral of Cefalù, should have been

[1] It is noteworthy that, as Miss Evelyn Jamison points out (*Admiral Eugenius of Sicily*, p. 40), 'No men of Latin culture seem up to this time to have been employed in positions high or low by the central offices of finance'.

[2] Visitors to Rossano are usually content to inspect the Byzantine church of S. Marco and the Archbishop's Palace, home of the justly-famed sixth-century purple codex. They would be well advised to make the short detour to S. Maria, lying up in the hills on the way to the neighbouring town of Corigliano. The monastery buildings are in ruins, but the church itself is still there, with a superb mosaic pavement which alone is worth the visit.

founded, built and endowed by the most brilliant of all the Greeks in the Kingdom's history.

Though the original and rightful name of his church, S. Maria del Ammiraglio, stands as a perpetual monument to its founder, George of Antioch had no need of such memorials to ensure himself a place in history. We first meet him as the gifted young Levantine who, after early service with the Zirid Sultans of Mahdia, transferred his loyalties to Sicily and in 1123 used his perfect Arabic and unrivalled knowledge of the Tunisian coast to score the only victory in Roger's first, ill-fated African expedition.[1] Since then, as commander of the Sicilian navy, he had served his King with distinction on both land and sea, becoming in 1132 the first holder of the proudest title his adopted country had to offer—Emir of Emirs, the high admiral and chief minister of the realm.[2] Despite so distinguished a career, however, his work on the church must not be thought of as the occupation of his declining years, still less of his retirement. In 1143, the year it was endowed, he must have been in his early fifties; within weeks of the endowment he and his fleet were off on another North African adventure, more successful this time; while before he died he was to carry the Sicilian flag to the banks of the Bosphorus itself, returning to Palermo with all the secrets—and many of the leading craftsmen—of the Byzantine silk industry.

But however secure the great admiral may be in his immortality, it still seems a little unfair that the shorter and more usual name for his church should commemorate not him but an infinitely dimmer figure—one Geoffrey de Marturanu, the founder in 1146 of a nearby Benedictine nunnery with which, some three centuries later, George's church was amalgamated. Nor, alas, have the changes been confined to its name. The Martorana—for so, under protest, it must be called from now on—no longer displays any outward sign of its origins. Once, its exterior too was beautiful. On Christmas Day,

[1] *The Normans in the South*, pp. 299–302.
[2] It is perhaps worth recalling in this second volume a point already made in the first, namely that the word *Admiral*, current with minor variations in so many European languages, is derived through Norman Sicily from the Arabic word *Emir*; and in particular from its compound *Emir-al-Bahr*, Ruler of the Sea.

1184, it was visited by the Arab traveller Ibn Jubair on his way back from a pilgrimage to Mecca. He wrote:

We noted a most remarkable façade, which we could not possibly describe and on which we would fain keep silent, since it is the most beautiful work in the world. . . . It has a bell-tower supported on columns of marble, surmounted by a dome resting on further columns. It is one of the most marvellous constructions ever to be seen. May Allah in his mercy and goodness soon honour this building with the sound of the muezzin's call!

Looking at the outside of the Martorana today, one almost wishes that Ibn Jubair's pious supplication had been granted. His co-religionists could hardly have done worse with it than the Christians. The façade itself he would no longer recognise; in sad contrast to that of the adjoining church of S. Cataldo, whose three heavy cupolas unmistakably if somewhat congestedly proclaim it as a Norman building of the mid-twelfth century, this jewel of all Sicilian churches—as opposed to cathedrals or chapels—has been decked out in lugubrious baroque. Only the romanesque bell-tower, domeless since an earthquake in 1726 but still beautifully proportioned, remains to beckon the traveller within.

There, too, all is not as it was. To accommodate the increasing numbers of nuns, a programme of reconstruction and enlargement was undertaken towards the end of the sixteenth century, and all through the seventeenth the grim work went on. The west wall was knocked down, the former atrium and narthex incorporated into the main body of the church. More unforgivable still, the main apse was demolished in 1683 with all its mosaics, to be replaced by a frescoed *capellone,* the hideousness of which all the efforts of nineteenth-century restorers have been powerless to diminish.

Such, then, is the modern Martorana. The eastern extremity is lost, the western bays ought never to have occurred. Miraculously, however, between the two, George's old church has remained, preserving its traditional Byzantine cross-in-square ground-plan and looking still much as it did when it was first consecrated or when, forty-odd years later, it had so alarming an effect on Ibn Jubair:

The walls within are gilded—or rather, they are made from one great piece of gold. There are slabs of coloured marble, the like of which we have never seen, picked out with golden mosaic and surmounted with, as it were, branches of trees in green mosaic. Great suns of gilded glass ranged along the top blaze with a light that dazzled our eyes and caused us such perturbation of the spirit that we implored Allah to preserve us. We learned that the founder, who gave his name to the Church, devoted many quintals of gold to its building, and that he was vizir to the grandfather of this polytheist King.[1]

Like most of those at Cefalù and the best of those in the Palatine Chapel, the mosaics of the Martorana were all the work of a single team of superb artists and craftsmen imported by Roger II from Constantinople and working in Sicily between 1140 and 1155. Unlike either of the other groups, they contain no later additions. All three show a close interrelation; yet each, unbelievably, has a style of its own. Dr Otto Demus, the most eminent living expert on the mosaics of Norman Sicily, has compared them thus:

The mosaicists of Cefalù, confronted with the task of decorating the high commanding apse of a large cathedral, achieved the quiet grandeur which was called for; the artists of the Palatina, who had to decorate a court chapel, expressed themselves in an elaborate and festive style, full of royal splendour, but lacking something of the classic beauty and simplicity of Cefalù. And the workmen who adorned the private foundation of the Admiral adapted themselves to the intimacy of the small church, condensing and simplifying their models and attaining the most perfect charm which can be found in any surviving mediaeval decoration on Italian soil. This quality was not impaired by the fact that they sometimes followed the work of their colleagues in the two royal churches. They gave as it were the quintessence of what was gentle and lovely and intimate in the great art of Comnenian mosaic decoration.[2]

Only the mosaics in the cupola itself strike one as faintly disappointing. Enthroned and depicted at full length, the Pantocrator

[1] Ibn Jubair was writing in the reign of Roger's grandson, William the Good. To devout Muslims all Christians were polytheists. As believers in the Trinity, what else could they be?
[2] *The Mosaics of Norman Sicily.*

has lost much of the majesty that he shows in the Palatine Chapel, to say nothing of Cefalù; and the four archangels beneath him, bending forward in postures which, Dr Demus assures us, are 'without parallel in Byzantine, or indeed in mediaeval art', have bodies so fantastically distorted as to border on the ridiculous. But drop your eyes now to the supporting walls. Look east to the Annunciation, with Gabriel in a slanting swirl of movement, Mary serene with her spindle as the holy dove flutters towards her. Look west to the Presentation in the Temple, the outstretched arms of the infant Saviour on one side and those of St Simeon on the other bridging the entrance to the nave as perfectly as does the great arch they frame. Within its vault, Christ is born and, opposite, the Virgin dies—her soul, like another swaddled child, is carried reverently up by her Son. Lastly, settle in some comfortable corner and look at everything at once while the dark, glowing gold does its work, irradiating the spirit like a soft and gentle fire.

Barely perceptible among that gold, running along the base of the dome beneath the feet of the adoring archangels, you may just discern a narrow wooden frieze. After centuries in darkness, it was only when the restoration work at the end of the last century let the light back into the dome that it was rediscovered and found to bear traces of an inscription—an old Byzantine hymn in honour of the Virgin. Since the Martorana is a Greek church there would be nothing extraordinary about that, but for one fact—the inscription is in Arabic. Why it was translated we shall never know. Perhaps the wooden surround was the work of Arab Christians —Arabs were always the best carpenters—and this was their contribution to the church. But there is another, more intriguing, possibility—that this hymn was the particular favourite of George of Antioch himself, and that he loved it best in the language in which he had heard it first, half a century before, in his Syrian boyhood.

And now, as you leave the original church, running the gauntlet of those simpering cherubs and marzipan madonnas that mark the real dark ages of European religious art, pause for a moment at a western-facing wall on the north side of the nave near the entrance;

and there, in what was probably the narthex of George's building, you will find, glittering wanly in the half-light, his portrait.[1] It is a dedication mosaic, with the admiral, looking old beyond his years and distinctly oriental, prostrating himself before the Virgin. His body has unfortunately been damaged at some period, and the damage compounded by a clumsy restoration which has given him the appearance of a tortoise; but the head is the original work—presumably done from the life—and almost the entire figure of the Virgin has come down to us unscathed. Her right hand is extended towards him, as if to raise him up; and in her left she holds a scroll on which there is written in Greek:

Child, holy Word, do Thou ever preserve from all adversity George, first among the archons, who has raised this my house from its foundations; and grant him the forgiveness of his sins as Thou only, O God, hast power to do.

Across the nave, in the corresponding space on the southern wall, is the Martorana's last and perhaps its greatest treasure—a mosaic portrait of King Roger himself, being symbolically crowned by Christ.[2] There he stands, bending slightly forward, a purely Byzantine figure in his long dalmatic and stole, his crown with jewelled pendants in the manner of Constantinople; even his arms are raised from the elbows in the Greek attitude of prayer. Above his head, great black letters stride across the gold to proclaim him. *POΓΕΡΙΟC PHΞ*, they read, *Rogerios Rex*. This uncompromising use of Greek letters for a Latin word is less curious than it might seem; by Roger's time the normal Greek word for king, *basileus,* was so identified with the Byzantine Emperor that it would have been unthinkable in this context. And yet the simple fact of transliteration makes an impact of its own and—particularly after one has spotted the Arabic inscription on an adjacent pillar—seems to diffuse the whole spirit of Norman Sicily.

This, too, is a portrait from the life; indeed, apart from coins and seals which are too small to give much information and are anyway

---

[1] See plate.   [2] See plate.

mainly symbolical, it is the only surviving likeness of the King which we can safely assume to be authentic.[1] Without it we should have nothing to go on but the evidence of Archbishop Romuald of Salerno, a man with a genius for uninformative description. He writes merely that Roger was tall, corpulent, with a leonine face—whatever that may mean—and a voice that was *subrauca*; hoarse, perhaps or harsh, or just vaguely disagreeable. The mosaic tells us far more. It shows a dark, swarthy man on the brink of middle age, with a full beard and long thick hair flowing to his shoulders. The face itself might be Greek, or it might be Italian; it even has a faintly Semitic cast about it. Anything less like the traditional idea of a Norman knight could scarcely be imagined.

It is always dangerous to read too much of a character into a portrait, particularly when the sitter is already familiar and the portraitist unknown. Dangerous, but irresistible. And even in something so hieratic and formalised as the Martorana mosaic, there are certain inspired touches, certain infinitesimal adjustments and gradations of the tesserae, that bring King Roger to life again before us. Here, surely, is the southerner and the oriental, the ruler of subtle mind and limitless flexibility whose life is spent playing one faction off against another; the statesman to whom diplomacy, however tortuous, is a more natural weapon than the sword, and gold, however corrupting, a more effective currency than blood. Here is the patron of the sciences, the lover of the arts who could stop in the middle of a desperate campaign to admire the beauty of Alife, stronghold of his arch-enemy. Here, finally, is the intellectual who has thought deeply about the science of government and rules with the head and not the heart; the idealist without delusions; the despot,

[1] The only other contemporary portrait to have come down to us—unless we include the figure on the Paschal candlestick in the Palatine Chapel—is on a curious enamel plaque in the church of St Nicholas at Bari. It depicts Roger's coronation by St Nicholas and was probably the origin of the church's one-time claim that he was crowned there and not in Palermo. (His reputed crown, an immense circle of iron and copper more suited to a barrel than a human head, is also displayed there with some pride.) This is not the place to enquire into the origins of the plaque, on which there is an interesting paper by Bertaux which I have listed in the bibliography. The portrait may be from the life, but was more likely copied from another, now lost. The essential physical features appear much the same as on the Martorana mosaic.

by nature just and merciful, who has learned, sadly, that even mercy must sometimes be tempered in the interests of justice.

The Assizes of Ariano set the seal on the Peace. The years before 1140 were the years of storm, when the thunderclouds hung black over the mainland and when Sicily itself, for all its prosperity, was unable altogether to escape their shadow. Afterwards, the sky lightens. It is only in the last fourteen years of Roger's reign that the sun really shines on his Kingdom.

And the Kingdom responds. We have seen how suddenly the art of Norman Sicily, like some rare subtropical orchid after long seasons of germination, at this moment bursts into glory. So, no less spectacularly, does the court of Palermo. Already at the time of his coronation Roger had inherited from his father a civil service, based eclectically on Norman, Greek, Latin and Arab models, which compared favourably with that of any western nation. When he died, he left his successors a governmental machine that was the wonder and envy of Europe. Under the Emir of Emirs and the Curia, two separate land registries—known as divans[1] after their Fatimid prototypes and staffed almost exclusively by Saracens—supervised the gathering of revenues from customs, monopolies and feudal holdings in Sicily and on the mainland. Another branch of the financial administration, the *camera,* was based on the old *fiscus* of the Roman Empire and administered by Greeks; a third followed the model of the Anglo-Norman Exchequer. Provincial government was in the hands of the Chancellors of the Kingdom, the *camerarii,* and below them the local governors—Latin bailiffs, Greek catapans, or Saracen *amil,* selected according to the race and language predominant in their district. To avoid corruption or peculation, the very lowest officials had direct access to the Curia or even, on occasion, to the King himself. Wandering justiciars, magistrates condemned to perpetual circuit, had responsibility for administering the criminal law, with the assistance of varying numbers of *boni homines*—good men and true—both Christian and Muslim, often sitting together in what was in effect the forerunner

[1] From which comes the Italian word *dogana* and, through it, the French *douane.*

of the modern jury. They too had the right to refer appeals to the King when necessary.

The King: always, everywhere, his people were reminded of his presence, his power, his paradoxical combination of accessibility and remoteness. Himself half-way to Heaven, there was no abuse, no miscarriage of justice too insignificant for his attention, if it could not be settled by those empowered to act in his name. However ubiquitous his representatives, however efficient his machine, neither they nor it were ever permitted to come between himself and the day-to-day work of administration, still less to detract from the mystique that surrounded him, that aura of divine majesty on which, he well knew, the cohesion of his Kingdom depended. It was not for nothing that he had been depicted, in the Martorana, as being crowned by Christ himself.

Emirs, seneschals, archons, logothetes, *protonotarii, protonobilissimi*—even the titles of the high palace dignitaries seemed to add to the pervading splendour. Yet it takes more than civil servants, whatever their disguise, to give brilliance to a court; and Roger's court at Palermo was easily the most brilliant of twelfth-century Europe. The King himself was famous for his insatiable intellectual curiosity and his passion for facts. (When, in 1140, he had made his formal entry into Naples, he had astounded the Neapolitans by informing them of the exact length of their land walls—2,363 paces, a figure of which, not perhaps altogether surprisingly, none of them was aware.) With this curiosity went a profound respect for learning, unique among his fellow-princes.[1] By the 1140s he had given a permanent home in Palermo to many of the foremost scholars and scientists, doctors and philosophers, geographers and mathematicians of Europe and the Arab world; and as the years went by he would spend more and more of his time in their company. Outside his immediate family—and he had been many years a widower—it was with them above all that he was able to cast off some of his regality; we are told that whenever any scholar entered the royal presence, Roger would rise from his chair

[1] Henry I of England was admittedly well-educated by the standards of the time—a fact which was considered remarkable enough to earn him the nickname of Beauclerk. But Henry made no effort to form a cultivated court around him, as Roger did.

and move forward to meet him, then take him by the hand and sit him down at his side. During the learned discussions that followed, whether in French, Latin, Greek or Arabic, he seems to have been well able to hold his own.

In mathematics, as in the political sphere, the extent of his learning cannot be described. Nor is there any limit to his knowledge of the sciences, so deeply and wisely has he studied them in every particular. He is responsible for singular innovations and for marvellous inventions, such as no prince has ever before realised.

Those words were written by Abu Abdullah Mohammed al-Edrisi, Roger's close friend and, of all the palace scholars, the one whom he most admired. Edrisi had arrived in Palermo in 1139; he was to remain there during much of his life, for fifteen years heading a commission set up by order of the King to gather geographical information from all quarters, correlate it, record it in orderly form, and so ultimately to produce one compendious work which would contain the sum total of all contemporary knowledge of the physical world. Sicily, standing at the crossroads of three continents, her ports as busy and as cosmopolitan as any in Europe, made an ideal centre from which such a work could be undertaken, and for all those fifteen years scarcely a ship put in at Palermo or Messina, Catania or Syracuse, without those on board being examined as to every place they had ever visited, its climate and its people. Their interrogators in the first instance were most likely to be official agents of the commission; but any traveller who had outstandingly valuable information to impart was liable to find himself conducted forthwith to the royal palace, there to be further cross-questioned by Edrisi or even, on occasion, by Roger himself.

The results of this work, which was completed in January 1154, barely a month before the King's death, were twofold. The first was a huge planisphere of purest silver, weighing no less than four hundred and fifty Roman pounds, on which was engraved 'the configuration of the seven climates with that of the regions, countries, sea-coasts both near and distant, gulfs, seas and watercourses; the location of deserts and of cultivated lands, and their respective distances by normal routes in miles or other known measures; and the designation of ports.' One would give much for this magnificent object to have been preserved; alas, it was to be destroyed during the riots of the following reign, within a few years of its completion.

But the second, and perhaps ultimately the more valuable fruit of Edrisi's labours has come down to us in its entirety. It is a book, properly entitled *The Avocation of a Man Desirous of a Full Knowledge of the Different Countries of the World* but more generally known as *The Book of Roger*; and it is the greatest geographical work of the Middle Ages. On the very first page we read the words:

The earth is round like a sphere, and the waters adhere to it and are maintained on it through natural equilibrium which suffers no variation.

As might be expected, *The Book of Roger* emerges as a combination of hard topographical facts—many of them astonishingly accurate for a work produced three and a half centuries before Columbus— and travellers' tales; but even the latter suggest that they have been subjected to stern critical appraisal. This is, after all, a scientific work, and we are never allowed to forget it; there is no room for tall stories unless they have at least some claim to veracity. But the author, on his side, never loses his sense of wonder, and the book makes fascinating reading.[1] We learn, for example, about the queen of Merida in Spain, who had all her meals floated to her by water, or about the *Chahria* fish of the Black Sea and the unfortunate effect which it has on the local fisherman who catches it in his net.[2] We are told how during the Russian winter the days are so short that there is hardly time to perform all the five obligatory prayers, and how the Norwegians—some of whom are born totally without necks—harvest their corn when it is still green, drying it at their hearths 'since the sun shines very rarely upon them'. Of England we read:

England is set in the Ocean of Darkness. It is a considerable island, whose shape is that of the head of an ostrich, and where there are

[1] There is, so far as I know, no English translation. A French one exists and is listed in the bibliography.
[2] As the French translation puts it, *il entre aussitôt en érection d'une manière inaccoutumée*—whatever that may mean.

flourishing towns, high mountains, great rivers and plains. This country is most fertile; its inhabitants are brave, active and enterprising, but all is in the grip of perpetual winter.

Though Roger's court circle was by no means entirely composed of Arabs like Edrisi, they probably constituted the largest single group; while among the Europeans there were many who had been attracted to Palermo by very reason of its predominantly Arab flavour. There was nothing new in this. Unlike Christianity, Islam had never drawn a distinction between sacred and profane knowledge. During the Dark Ages, when the Church of Rome—following the dire example of Gregory the Great—feared and even actively discouraged secular studies, good Muslims remembered how the Prophet himself had enjoined his Faithful to pursue knowledge all their lives, 'even if the quest led them to China', for 'he who travels in search of learning travels along Allah's path to Paradise'. Muslim civilisation had thus for years been recognised in the West as superior to anything that Christian Europe could boast, especially in the field of mathematics and the physical sciences. Arabic had become the international scientific language *par excellence*. Moreover there were a number of classical works of learning, both Greek and Latin, which had been lost to Christendom through the barbarian invasions or the engulfing tide of Islam and survived only in Arabic translation. By the twelfth century, owing largely to the work of the Sephardic Jews of Spain, some of these were beginning to reappear in western languages; but this did not appreciably diminish the need for any serious student of science to master Arabic for himself.

Yet it was a diabolically difficult language to learn and, in northern Europe at any rate, competent teachers were few. Thus, for half a century and more, men had been travelling to Spain and Sicily, there to unlock, as they hoped, the secrets of the Muslim world—poor clerks, seeking knowledge that would single them out from their fellows and so clear their path to advancement; dreaming alchemists, combing volumes of oriental lore for formulas of the elixir of life or the philosophers' stone; or true scholars like Adelard of Bath, pioneer of Arab studies in England and the greatest name in English science before Robert Grosseteste and Roger Bacon, who came to

Sicily in the first years of the century and was later to restore Euclid's *Elements,* retranslated by him from the Arabic, to the cultural heritage of Europe.

For certain more specialised fields of enquiry these early Arabists continued to gravitate towards Muslim Spain and in particular to the school of Toledo, which had long been the spearhead of the international scientific renaissance. For others, however, Sicily possessed one overwhelming advantage: while culturally still very much part of the Arab world, it also remained in perpetual contact with the Greek East. In the libraries of Palermo, to say nothing of all the Basilian monasteries in the island and in Calabria, scholars could find the Greek originals of works known in Spain only in extracts, or in translations of doubtful accuracy. Nowadays we tend to forget that, until this twelfth-century revival of interest in ancient learning, western Europe was virtually ignorant of Greek; and Roger's Sicily now became the foremost centre of Hellenic studies outside Byzantium itself. But in Byzantium Arabic culture was unknown and mistrusted. Only in Sicily could both civilisations be studied at first hand and employed to explain, complement and cross-fertilise each other. Small wonder, then, that seekers after truth should flock in such numbers to Palermo and that the island should have established itself by mid-century as not only the commercial but also the cultural clearing-house of three continents.

Once again, all this activity was centred on the person of the King. Roger has been accused of being himself uncreative, in contrast to his grandson Frederick II for example, or even to Richard Cœur de Lion, a troubadour poet of considerable ability. It is true that he left no literary compositions of his own; it would have been remarkable if he had, since that marvellous flowering of European vernacular literature that had already begun in Provence had not yet spread further afield. Such poets as flourished in Palermo in his day—and there were many—were nearly all Arabs. Besides, the King's personal preference was for the sciences. Beauty he loved, but splendour too; and one suspects that he did not find it easy in every case to distinguish one from the other. Anyway, he loved knowledge more.

Yet to say that he was not creative is to ignore the fact that without him the unique cultural phenomenon that was twelfth-century Sicily could never have occurred. So diversified a nation needed a guiding hand to give it purpose, to weld its various elements into one. Intellectually as well as politically, Roger provided that hand. In a very real sense, he *was* Sicily. His was the conception, his the incentive; he and only he could have created the favourable climate that was a precondition of all the rest. Enlightened yet always discriminating, he was the first royal patron, focusing the efforts and energies of those around him, never once losing sight of his eternal objective—the greatness and glory of the Kingdom.

6

ENEMIES OF THE REALM

We have captured the fortifications, that is the towers and palaces of the mighty of the City who, together with the Sicilian and the Pope, were preparing to offer resistance to your authority. . . . We pray you therefore to come without delay. . . . The Pope has entrusted his staff and ring, his dalmatic, mitre and sandals to the Sicilian . . . and the Sicilian has given him much money for your hurt and to injure the Roman Empire, which by God's grace is yours.

> Letter from Conrad of Hohenstaufen
> to the Emperor John II Comnenus[1]

ON 24 September 1143 Pope Innocent II died in Rome. He was buried in the Lateran, in that same porphyry sarcophagus that had once held the remains of the Emperor Hadrian; but after a disastrous fire in the early fourteenth century his remains were moved to the church of S. Maria in Trastevere which he himself had rebuilt just before his death. There, self-immortalised in the great apse mosaic, he stares down at us from the conch, his church clutched in his hands, a strangely wistful expression in his sad, tired eyes.

Innocent's long struggle with Anacletus had cost him dear; in those eight years of wandering he had suffered far more than his rival, comfortably entrenched in Rome. Even his allies had proved a mixed blessing. Lothair, once safely crowned, had shown him scant consideration, Henry the Proud still less. Bernard of Clairvaux had been loyal but, deliberately or not, had seemed bent on stealing his thunder at every opportunity. His final triumph had been made possible only by the death of Anacletus; and almost at once it had

---

[1] Quoted by Otto of Freising in *Gesta Friderici I Imperatoris*, I. Translated by C. C. Mierow.

been turned to dust by the rout at Galluccio. He had accepted this humiliation as gracefully as he could—even going so far as to ascribe it to some working of the divine providence for the restoration of peace—and he had made terms with the Sicilian King; but he had been ill repaid. Within a year Roger—emboldened by the years of schism when he had done what he liked and Anacletus had never dared to take issue with him—was acting more arrogantly than ever, creating new dioceses, appointing new bishops, barring the Pope's envoys from entering the Kingdom without his consent and even refusing to allow Latin churchmen in his dominions to obey papal summonses to Rome. Meanwhile his two sons were for ever nibbling away at the southern frontiers of the Papal State, their father never lifting a finger to stop them.

Yet even this was not all. At the very end of his life poor Innocent found himself faced with even more serious problems nearer home. For a century and longer, the inexorable movement towards republican self-government had been gathering momentum among the towns of Italy. In Rome itself successive Popes and the old aristocracy had done their best to save their city from the general contagion, and for a time they had managed to do so; but the recent schism had weakened their hold. Innocent in particular had never enjoyed general popularity; coming from Trastevere he had always been considered one degree less of a Roman than Anacletus, and he was known to be a good deal less generous. When, therefore, they learned that Innocent had made a separate peace with the enemy, the Romans seized the opportunity to denounce the temporal power of the Pope, revive the ancient Senate on the Capitol, and declare a Republic. Innocent resisted as best he could, but he was an old man—probably well over seventy—and the effort was too much for him. A few weeks later he was dead.

On the second day after his death there was held an election which, although somewhat hurried because of conditions in the capital, was nevertheless the first perfectly undisturbed papal election that Rome had seen for eighty-two years. Unfortunately the new Pope was almost as old as his predecessor and equally unable to cope with the problems he had inherited. Consecrated in the name of Celestine II, he was that same Guido of Castello who with St Bernard had pleaded Innocent's cause at Salerno six years before; unlike Bernard, however, he had not been particularly impressed by the King. The Treaty of Mignano had shocked and horrified him, and on his accession he refused to ratify it. Roger, in his eyes, would ever remain a usurper and a tyrant.

It was a foolish stand, and he lived—though only just—to regret it. Roger's chancellor and effective viceroy on the mainland was still that same Robert of Selby who had distinguished himself at Salerno during Lothair's siege. Since then his reputation had grown steadily, and in various directions. John of Salisbury, the English scholar and diplomat, writes of his compatriot that he was

an able administrator and, although without any great learning, extremely shrewd, ready of speech beyond most of the provincials and in eloquence the equal of any, feared by all because of his influence with the Prince, and respected for the elegance of his life—this being the more remarkable in those regions since among the Lombards, who are known to be the most frugal, not to say miserly, of men, he spent prodigiously on sumptuous living and displayed the magnificence characteristic of his nation; for he was an Englishman.[1]

Misers, all too often, tend to associate extravagant living with slackness or indolence. It is unlikely, however, that the Lombards of South Italy ever nurtured so dangerous a delusion in their dealings with Robert of Selby. Almost as soon as the new Pope's decision was announced, the papal city of Benevento found itself under attack by a Sicilian force. The citizens, caught unawares, naturally protested that the privileges granted them in their royal charter were being infringed. Robert arrived in the King's name, strode into the palace and demanded to be shown the document in question. The Beneventans handed it to him. They never saw it again. Furious, they sent their archbishop to complain to the Pope; but scarcely was he outside the city gates than he was taken prisoner. As reports of these developments trickled back to Rome, the Pope saw that

[1] *Policraticus*, VII, ch. 19. John had had personal and, one suspects, embarrassing experience of Robert's hospitality. In a letter written at about this time to the Abbot of La Celle, he ruefully relates how he was persuaded by the chancellor to drink with him 'to my own undoing and the detriment of my health'. (Letter 85.)

he had gone too far. Without any proper army of his own and beset by steadily increasing pressures from the Roman commune, he had no choice but to give in. Soon afterwards, swallowing his pride, he sent Censius Frangipani and Cardinal Octavian of S. Cecilia off to Palermo to discuss terms.

It would be nice to know more about Robert of Selby.[1] The only other story we know about him concerns the efforts of three Campanian churchmen to secure the vacant bishopric of Avella. Each— once again according to John of Salisbury—secretly offered the Chancellor a large sum of money; Robert, apparently nothing loath, bargained hard until he had agreed with each in turn on a splendid price.

A day was appointed for holding the election, solemnly and in due form. But when that day arrived and the archbishops, bishops and many venerable persons had assembled, the chancellor set forth the pretensions of the competitors, described all that had taken place and announced that he was now ready to proceed in accordance with the opinion of the bishops. They condemned all three simoniac competitors; and a poor monk, ignorant of the whole affair, was canonically elected, confirmed and installed. The others were compelled to pay the amounts to which they had bound themselves, down to the very last farthing.[2]

From both these stories it is clear that Robert's administrative methods were as unorthodox as his way of life. He emerges as a far more cheerful and extrovert character than his master, yet the two seem to have had much in common and it is easy to see why the King should have so admired and trusted him. For both, ends counted more than means. Those ends were above all law, order and tranquillity; the peace of the mainland kingdom during these years and the silence of the chroniclers are the best testimonials of how well, thanks largely to Robert of Selby, they were achieved.

The Pope's two representatives, trying to negotiate with Roger in Palermo, were in a weak enough position from the outset. Their

[1] His entry in the *Dictionary of National Biography* must be treated with caution; it is inaccurate in several important respects, particularly where the chronology is concerned.
[2] *Policraticus*, VII, 19.

embarrassment must have been complete when, one day in the middle of March 1144, they arrived in the King's presence to be informed that Pope Celestine was dead and had already been succeeded by Cardinal Gerard of Bologna—henceforth to be known as Lucius II—a moderate man and, it appeared, one of Roger's personal friends.[1] Since their own special powers had expired with Celestine's death, there was no option for them but to muster what dignity they could and to return to Rome; but they took back to Lucius a proposal from the King for an early meeting.

It was held the following June, at Ceprano; and it failed miserably. After a fortnight's abortive negotiations the two sides separated in an atmosphere of disillusion and bitterness. The friendship of which so much had been expected was over. It was the Pope's loss. Had he and his negotiators shown just a little more realism and flexibility, they might have secured a Norman alliance which would have been a match for the commune in Rome. Instead, by bringing upon themselves a new enemy, they were encouraging the old one to make ever more arrogant demands. The 'senators' now began to insist that the Pope surrender all his temporal rights both inside and outside the city and support himself, as the early fathers of the Church had done, on tithes and offerings. Meanwhile, instead of rallying to his assistance, the young Norman princes aided by Robert of Selby had renewed their forays and were penetrating ever deeper into the papal territories.

Within a matter of weeks after leaving Ceprano Lucius was forced

---

[1] There is something of a problem here. Romuald of Salerno tells us of the King's joy at hearing the news, because Lucius was his *compater et amicus*. If, as Chalandon and Bernhardi both maintain—though I can find no contemporary confirmation—this was the same Gerard who had been the pro-Innocentian Rector of Benevento during the schism and subsequently, with his papal predecessor, one of Innocent's delegates to the Salerno tribunal, this friendship would seem a little hard to explain. If we give the word *compater* its usual meaning of godfather, the problem becomes harder still. Mann suggests that the new Pope was in fact godfather to one of Roger's children, but this is equally improbable. Throughout the lifetime of Queen Elvira he seems to have been in Rome or acting as Legate in Germany. Elvira had died in 1135 and the King was not to marry again till 1149; he is hardly likely to have asked a Prince of the Church to stand sponsor to one of his bastards. Conceivably they were fellow-godfathers at some baptism in Salerno, but whose? Duke Roger of Apulia did not marry till 1140.

to sue for peace; and in October—though only after his son Alfonso had been killed in a skirmish—Roger reluctantly agreed to a seven-year truce. But it was too late. As 1144 drew to its close the situation in Rome reached flash-point; fighting between the republicans and the papalists broke out in many parts of the city. In January 1145 we find the Pope writing to Peter of Cluny of how he had been unable to ride from the Lateran to S. Saba on the Aventine for the ordination of the monastery's new abbot. Then, in early February, feeling his back to the wall, he decided to take the offensive. Assisted by his Frangipani allies—to whom he had made over the Circus Maximus as a fortress—he personally led an armed attack on the Capitol. It was a heroic action, but it ended in disaster. A stone flung by one of the defenders struck him on the head; mortally wounded, he was carried by the Frangipani to Gregory the Great's old monastery of St Andrew on the Caelian; and there, on 15 February, he died.

Fifteen years before, almost to the day, Pope Honorius II had breathed his last in that same monastery. His death and the events which followed it had given birth to the Kingdom of Sicily, but they had had dire consequences for Rome. Those consequences, it appeared, were not yet over.

Apart from his unwilling ratification of his sons' truce the previous October, Roger had made no effort to help his old friend—if such Pope Lucius really was—in his distress. At first sight this indifference seems to stand out in unedifying contrast to the attitude of previous Norman leaders—Robert Guiscard, to take but one example, whose memorable march on Rome with twenty thousand followers in 1084 had saved Pope Gregory VII from an equally critical situation, even if he had destroyed a good deal of the city in the process. The Guiscard, however, was answering a call to the aid of his rightful suzerain, from whom he had formally received all his honours and titles at Ceprano four years before. Roger had also gone, at his own request, to Ceprano in the sincere hope—and probably the confident expectation—of a similar investiture. He had asked no more than he had already been granted by Innocent, but he had been rebuffed. He had received nothing at the papal hands, and had done no homage in return. The Pope no longer had any claim on his loyalty.

Besides, Robert Guiscard's spectacular rescue of Gregory from the Castel S. Angelo was more than just his duty as a vassal; it was a political necessity. Had he left the Pope to his fate, he would have also left all the South open to invasion by the Emperor. This time the papal enemy was the Roman populace itself, concerned only with the city and its immediate neighbourhood. The imperial threat, though it still existed, was a good deal less imminent. Lothair's successor, Conrad of Hohenstaufen, had troubles of his own. His election as King of Germany in preference to Henry of Bavaria had set a new spark to the old rivalry between their two houses—that age-long struggle of Welf against Hohenstaufen, Guelph against Ghibelline, that was to stain both Germany and Italy red for centuries to come. Even now, seven years after his accession, Conrad was still hard put to preserve his throne.

Not that Italy had ceased to beckon. An imperial coronation by the Pope could not but strengthen his political position, just as it had strengthened Lothair's before him; and beyond Rome lay Palermo, an even more tempting objective. The thought of that Sicilian bandit, who had now for fifteen years claimed dominion over huge tracts of imperial territory despite repeated efforts to eject him, rankled as much as ever; and Conrad knew perfectly well that the ever-turbulent Welfs would never have been able to maintain their opposition but for the huge subsidies they were receiving from Roger's agents—a fact of which he was doubtless regularly reminded by the bitter little group of South Italian exiles hanging round his court, Robert of Capua, Count Roger of Ariano and Rainulf's brother Richard among them. He had never forgiven Pope Innocent for what he considered a craven betrayal at Mignano, nor St Bernard for having made his own peace with Sicily immediately afterwards; and ever since his accession he had been dreaming of a punitive expedition to the South. It would have to be larger than Lothair's, better organised and better equipped, with a naval force capable of pursuing the war beyond the Straits of Messina if necessary —something, in fact, conceived on a very much grander scale than anything he was capable of mounting by himself, even if his domestic difficulties enabled him to do so. Fortunately he had an ally ready to hand.

The Byzantine Empire also had claims on South Italy; indeed, there may have been old men alive in Bari who still dimly remembered those heroic days, nearly a lifetime ago, when in defiance of Robert Guiscard and the massed Norman army their fellow-citizens had held out for nearly three years in their Emperor's name. Ever since, the restoration of the Italian provinces had loomed large in Greek ambitions. We have seen how as early as 1135 the Emperor John Comnenus had offered Lothair financial assistance against the King of Sicily; it seems likely that a considerable proportion of the expenses of the subsequent expedition was paid for in Byzantine gold. That expedition had failed; but John's determination held firm.

Since then the situation had worsened. When Roger's cousin Bohemund II of Antioch had been killed in 1130 he had left as his only child a two-year-old daughter, Constance; and Roger had laid claim to the throne as the senior surviving member of the House of Hauteville. Five years later he had tried to kidnap the little princess's husband-to-be, Raymond of Poitiers, as he passed through South Italy on his way to join his bride; Raymond had managed to escape only by disguising himself, first as a pilgrim and then as steward of a rich merchant. In 1138 the King had even gone so far as to arrest the Patriarch Radulph of Antioch on a journey to Rome. The Patriarch, whose persuasive charm of manner was in no way affected by a pronounced squint, was soon allowed to proceed; and on his return Roger had treated him very differently, giving him a royal welcome in Palermo and even providing him with an escort of Sicilian ships. Particularly in contrast to his outward journey, it all seemed a little overdone; if Roger really were plotting to seize the throne of Antioch the Patriarch would be a most valuable ally. John Comnenus, who had never trusted either of them, grew ever more suspicious.

During the next few years ambassadors shuttled backwards and forwards between Germany and Constantinople as the two Emperors began to make serious plans for an alliance against their common enemy. Then, in the spring of 1143, John went off on a hunting expedition in the mountains of Cilicia and accidentally scratched himself, between the fourth and little fingers of his right hand, with

a poisoned arrow. At first he ignored the wound, but in the following days the infection spread up his whole arm until, in the words
of a contemporary chronicler, it was swollen to the thickness of his
thigh. His doctors advised amputation, but the Emperor had no
faith in them and refused; and a week or so later he died of blood-
poisoning. His youngest son Manuel who succeeded him was at
first rather better-disposed towards the King of Sicily, and even
toyed with the idea of a marriage alliance; but the negotiations came
to nothing, relations between the two grew worse until they were
finally broken off altogether, and the Sicilian envoys ended up in
prison in Constantinople.

Not, perhaps, altogether without relief, Manuel turned back to
the Western Empire. His father had for some time before his death
been considering another imperial marriage—this time of Manuel
himself, with Conrad's sister-in-law Bertha of Sulzbach—and in
1142 had actually had the proposed bride brought, on approval,
to Constantinople. Manuel's initial reaction to this proposal had
been lukewarm, and his first sight of the German princess had done
little to inflame his ardour; soon, in any case, the minor upheavals
that followed his succession and his brief flirtation with Sicily had
caused the idea to be dropped. But at the end of 1144 he began to
have second thoughts. Conrad for his part was positively enthusiastic. Such a marriage, he wrote, would be a pledge of 'a permanent
alliance of constant friendship'; he himself would be a 'friend of the
Emperor's friends and an enemy of his enemies'—he named no
names, but Manuel would have no difficulty in filling in the blank—
and, if there should ever be any slight to Manuel's honour, he would
come in person to his assistance with all the massed strength of the
German state behind him.

And so the arrangements were made. Bertha, who had been living
for the past four years in forgotten obscurity, now re-emerged into
public view, shed her barbarous Frankish name for the more
euphonious Greek one of Irene, and in January 1146 duly married
the Emperor. He should have made her a splendid husband.
Young, gifted, famous for his dark good looks, he possessed a
gaiety and charm that came as a refreshing contrast after the high-
principled austerity of his father. Whether he was in his palace of

Blachernae or one of the hunting-lodges in which he spent so much of his time, any excuse was good enough for a celebration; while the visit of foreign rulers—particularly from the West—was always a signal for prolonged and elaborate festivities. Unlike most of the older generation of Byzantines he had spent his life in constant contact with the Franks of Outremer, and he genuinely admired western institutions. He introduced knightly tournaments to Constantinople and, being a superb horseman, took part in them himself —an activity that must have shocked many of his more old-fashioned subjects. But there was nothing shallow about him. When he was on campaign all his apparent frivolity fell away and he proved himself a brilliant soldier, tireless and determined. 'In war,' wrote Gibbon, 'he seemed ignorant of peace, in peace he appeared incapable of war.' A skilful diplomat, he also had the imagination and sureness of touch of a born statesman. And yet, through it all, he remained the typical Byzantine intellectual who liked nothing better than to immerse himself for hours in theological arguments of the most speculative kind; and his skill as a physician was, as we shall see, soon to be attested by Conrad of Hohenstaufen himself.

But he never liked Bertha much. As the Greek historian Nicetas Choniates explains,

His wife, a princess from Germany, was less concerned with the embellishment of her body than with that of her spirit; rejecting powder and paint, and leaving to vain women all those adornments which are owed to artifice, she sought only that solid beauty which proceeds from the splendour of virtue. This was the reason why the Emperor, who was of extreme youth, had little inclination for her and did not maintain towards her that fidelity which was her due; although he bestowed great honours upon her, a most exalted throne, a numerous retinue and all else that makes for magnificence and induces the respect and veneration of the people. He also entertained a criminal relationship with his niece, which has left a shameful stain upon his reputation.[1]

It was not in vain that King Roger had built up, over the years, the formidable network of foreign observers and agents that had made him easily the best-informed ruler in the western world. From

[1] *History of the Emperor Manuel Comnenus*, I, ii.

Germany and Constantinople—and, in all probability, from several other places as well—he had been kept constantly posted of all these developments as they occurred; and he had followed them with growing concern. He had had difficulties enough with old Lothair; this time there would be two enemies instead of one, both famous for their skill and courage in battle and both at the height of their powers. Conrad was fifty-three—only two years older than himself—and Manuel not yet out of his twenties. There would also be the Byzantine navy to contend with, and a possible direct attack on Sicily itself. In such an eventuality, could he trust his Greek subjects to stay loyal?

Roger had long been conscious of just such a danger. To avert it he had for years been sending his massive subsidies to the Welfs in Germany, knowing that to keep Conrad fully occupied at home was the best way of discouraging him from any military adventures abroad; and it was with a similar object in view that he had proposed a marriage alliance with Byzantium. Both plans had failed. He had no more diplomatic weapons in his armoury with which he could hope to deflect the two determined Emperors from their intentions. War seemed certain; victory, to say the least, improbable.

He could not know, at the dawn of the year 1146, that he had already been saved twelve months before—saved, paradoxically, by a disaster to Christendom, and one that would soon bring a second, yet greater one in its wake. The first of these twin disasters was the fall of Edessa. The other was to be the Second Crusade.

7

THE SECOND CRUSADE

Now there was in Sicily, among the Muslims of the country, a most learned and wealthy man. The King had much regard for him and showed him great deference, placing him above the priests and monks of his court, so that the Christians of the country accused him of being himself also, in his heart of hearts, a Muslim. One day, when the King was sitting in a belvedere looking out over the sea, a pinnace was seen approaching. Those in the vessel brought news that the Sicilian troops had penetrated into Muslim lands, where they had found much booty and killed several men—in a word, that they had gained great successes. At that moment this Muslim was sitting by the King, and seemed to be asleep; the King said 'Ho, thou! Hast thou not heard what tidings have just been told?' The Muslim replied 'No'. The King repeated, they have told us such and such: 'where was then Mahomet, while these countries and their inhabitants were suffering such treatment?' The Muslim replied, 'He had left them, to be present at the conquest of Edessa. The Faithful have just taken that city.' At these words the Franks who were present began to laugh; but the King said: 'Do not laugh; for, as God is my witness, this man never lies.'

Ibn Al-Athir

In the first years of the Christian era, King Abgar V of Edessa was stricken with leprosy. Having heard reports of recent miraculous occurrences in Palestine, he wrote a letter to Jesus Christ, asking him to come to Edessa to cure him. Jesus declined, but promised to send one of his disciples to heal the King and preach the Gospel to his subjects. With this reply, according to some authorities, he enclosed a portrait of himself, miraculously imprinted on canvas. Later, as good as his word, he arranged with St Thomas to send Thaddeus, one of the Seventy, who accomplished both parts of his mission to the satisfaction of all concerned.

So runs the legend, as told by Eusebius and others; and, as proof of its veracity, the Saviour's letter, written by his own hand in Syriac on parchment, was long exposed to public veneration in the cathedral of Edessa.[1] We know now that Christianity did not in fact reach the city before the end of the second century; but by the middle of the twelfth Edessa could boast other, better authenticated claims to sanctity. It was the site of the earliest recorded Christian church building; it witnessed the first translation into a foreign language—Syriac again—of the Greek New Testament; and one of its later kings, Abgar IX, was, so far as history can tell, the first royal monarch ever to receive Christian baptism.

In more recent times, again, the County of Edessa was the first to be established of all the crusader states of the Levant. It dated from the year 1098 when Baldwin of Boulogne had left the main army of the First Crusade and struck off to the east to found a principality of his own on the banks of the Euphrates. He had not stayed there long; two years later he had succeeded his brother as King of Jerusalem—where, for a short and painful period towards the end of his life, he was destined to become Roger of Sicily's stepfather.[2] But Edessa had continued as a semi-independent state—under the theoretical suzerainty of Jerusalem—until, after a twenty-five-day siege, it fell, on Christmas Eve 1144, to an Arab army under Imad ed-Din Zengi, Atabeg of Mosul.

The news of its fall horrified all Christendom. To the peoples of western Europe, who had seen the initial successes of the First Crusade as an obvious sign of divine favour, it called in question all their comfortably-held opinions. After less than half a century Cross had once again given way to Crescent. How had it happened? Was it not a manifestation of the wrath of God? Travellers to the east had for some time been returning with reports of a widespread degeneracy among the Franks of Outremer. Could it be that they were no longer deemed worthy to guard the Holy Places against the Infidel under the banner of their Redeemer?

Among the Crusaders themselves, long familiarity with these

[1] Subsequently this letter was to find its way to Constantinople, where it disappeared during the revolution of 1185. See ch. XVIII.
[2] *The Normans in the South*, pp. 286–9.

shrines had made possible a more rational approach. To them Edessa had been a vital buffer state, protecting the principalities of Antioch and Tripoli—and through them the Kingdom of Jerusalem itself—from the Danishmends, the Ortoqids and the other warlike Turkish tribes to the north. Luckily these tribes had always been divided against each other, as had the Arab tribes across the eastern mountains; but Zengi, an ambitious politician as well as a brilliant general, was already beginning to unite them behind him and dreaming only of the day when, as the acknowledged champion of Islam, he would deliver Asia once and for all from the Christian invader.

Whatever the Franks may have thought about their spiritual worth, their military weakness was beyond dispute. The first great wave of crusading enthusiasm, culminating in the jubilant capture of Jerusalem in 1099, was now spent. Immigration from the west had slowed to a trickle; of the pilgrims, many still arrived unarmed according to the ancient tradition, and even for those who came prepared to wield a sword a single summer campaign usually proved more than enough. The only permanent standing army—if such it could be called—was formed by the two military orders of the Hospitallers and the Templars; but they alone could not hope to hold out against a concerted offensive under Zengi. Reinforcements were desperately needed; the Pope must declare a Crusade.

Although Edessa had fallen nearly eight weeks before the death of Pope Lucius, his successor Eugenius III had already been over six months on the throne before he received official notification of the disaster. The special embassy that brought it—together with an urgent appeal for help—found him at Viterbo.[1] Eugenius's pontificate had not had an auspicious beginning. His election, held in safe Frangipani territory immediately on the death of the unfortunate Lucius, had been smooth enough; but when he had tried to proceed from the Lateran to St Peter's for his consecration the commune

---

[1] The embassy was led by Hugh, Bishop of Jabala in Syria. According to the historian Otto of Freising who was with the Pope at the time, Hugh also told of a certain John, 'a king and priest who dwells beyond Persia and Armenia in the uttermost east and, with all his people, is a Christian'. A direct descendant of the Magi, he ruled with an emerald sceptre. Thus the legendary Prester John makes his first entrance into recorded history.

had barred his way, and three days later he had fled the city.

The speed of his flight surprised no one; indeed, the only surprising thing about Eugenius was that he should have been elected in the first place. An ex-monk of Clairvaux and disciple of St Bernard, he was a simple character, gentle and retiring—not at all, men thought, the material of which Popes were made. Even Bernard himself, when he heard the news of the election, did not take it well. One might have expected him to be gratified at the raising of the first Cistercian to the Throne of St Peter; instead, obviously nettled at the elevation of one of his 'children' over his head, he made no secret of his disapproval. In a letter addressed collectively to the entire papal Curia, he wrote:

May God forgive you what you have done! . . . You have made the last first, and lo! his last state is more dangerous than the first. . . . What reason or counsel, when the Supreme Pontiff was dead, made you rush upon a mere rustic, lay hands on him in his refuge, wrest from his hands the axe, pick or hoe, and lift him to a throne?[1]

To Eugenius he was equally outspoken:

Thus does the finger of God raise up the poor out of the dust and lift up the beggar from the dunghill, that he may sit with princes and inherit the throne of glory.[2]

It seems an unfortunate choice of metaphor, and it says much for the new Pope's gentleness and patience that he showed no resentment. But Bernard was after all his spiritual father, and besides, Eugenius was no Urban II; he had neither the drive nor the personality to launch a Crusade single-handed. In any case events in Rome made it impossible for him to cross the Alps and, as he put it, to sound the heavenly trumpet of the Gospel in France. In the months to come he was to need his old master as badly as he had ever needed him in his life.

When Pope Eugenius came to consider the princes of the West, he could see only one suitable candidate for the leadership of the new Crusade. Ideally, the honour should have fallen to the western

[1] Letter 237.   [2] Letter 238.

Emperor, but Conrad—as yet only King of the Romans pending his imperial coronation—was still beset with his own difficulties in Germany. When these were solved, he would be more interested in settling the Italian problem than in oriental adventures. King Stephen of England had had a civil war on his hands for six years already. Roger of Sicily was, for any number of reasons, out of the question. The only possible choice was Louis VII of France.

Louis asked nothing better. He was one of Nature's pilgrims. Though still only twenty-four, he had about him an aura of lugubrious piety which made him look and seem older than his years—and irritated to distraction his beautiful and high-spirited young wife, Eleanor of Aquitaine. He was already under a crusading vow, having assumed it from his elder brother Philip after the latter's death in a riding accident some years before. Moreover, his soul was in anguish. In 1143, during a war with Theobald, Count of Champagne, his army had set fire to the little town of Vitry—now Vitry-en-François—on the Marne; and its inhabitants, more than a thousand men, women and children, had been burnt alive in the church where they had taken refuge. Louis had watched the conflagration, but had been powerless to prevent it. Ever since, the memory of that day had weighed him down. The responsibility he knew to be his; nothing less than a Crusade, with its promise of a plenary indulgence for all sins, could be sufficient atonement.

At Christmas 1145 Louis informed his assembled tenants-in-chief of his determination to take the Cross, and implored them to follow him. Odo of Deuil reports that 'the King blazed and shone with the zeal of his faith and his contempt for earthly pleasures and temporal glories, so that his person was an example more persuasive than any speech could be'. It was not, however, persuasive enough. His vassals' reaction was disappointing. They had their responsibilities at home to consider. Besides, the reports they had heard about life in Outremer suggested that their dissolute compatriots had probably brought the disaster on themselves. Let them work out their own salvation. That hard-headed churchman Abbot Suger of St Denis, former guardian and tutor to the King, also turned his face firmly against the proposal. But Louis had made up his mind. If he himself could not fill the hearts and minds of his vassals with crusading fire, he must find someone who could. He wrote to the Pope, accepting his invitation; then, inevitably, he sent for the Abbot of Clairvaux.

To Bernard, who had always taken a lively interest in the affairs of the Holy Land, here was a cause after his own heart; exhausted as he was, broken in health and by now genuinely longing for retirement in the peace of his abbey, he responded to the call with all that extraordinary fervour that had made him, for over a quarter of a century, the dominant spiritual voice in all Christendom. Willingly he agreed to launch the Crusade in France, and to address the assembly that the King had summoned for the following Easter at Vézelay.

At once the magic of his name began to do its work, and as the appointed day approached men and women from every corner of France poured into the little town. Since there were far too many to be packed into the cathedral, a great wooden platform was hastily erected on the hillside. (It stood until 1789, when it was destroyed by the Revolution.) Here, on Palm Sunday morning, 31 March 1146, Bernard appeared before the multitude for one of the most fateful speeches of his life. His body, writes Odo, was so frail that it seemed already to be touched by death. At his side was the King, already displaying on his breast the cross which the Pope had sent him in token of his decision. Together the two mounted the platform; and Bernard began to speak.

The text of the exhortation which followed has not come down to us; but with Bernard it was the manner of his delivery rather than the words themselves that made the real impact on his hearers. All we know is that his voice rang out across the meadow 'like a celestial organ', and that as he spoke the crowd, silent at first, began to cry out for crosses of their own. Bundles of these, cut in rough cloth, had been already prepared for distribution; when the supply was exhausted, the abbot flung off his own robe and began to tear it into strips to make more. Others followed his example, and he and his helpers were still stitching as night fell.

The new Crusaders included men and women[1] from all walks

[1] The legend of a whole female regiment, with Eleanor herself as its titular head, is surprisingly confirmed by the Byzantine chronicler Nicetas Choniates, who reports the appearance in Constantinople of 'a body of women on horseback, dressed and armed like men, completely military in appearance and seemingly braver than Amazons'.

of life—among them many of those vassals whom Louis had failed to rouse from their apathy only three months before. All France, it seemed, had been infused with Bernard's spirit; and it was with pardonable pride that—his earlier resentment against Pope Eugenius now forgotten—he could write to him shortly afterwards:

You have commanded, and I have obeyed . . . I have declared and spoken; and now they [the Crusaders] are multiplied, beyond number. Cities and castles are deserted, and seven women together may scarcely find one man to lay hold on, so many widows are there whose husbands are still living.

It was indeed a remarkable achievement. No one else in Europe could have done it. And yet, as events were soon to tell, it were better had it not been done.

His success at Vézelay acted on St Bernard like a tonic. No longer did he contemplate a return to Clairvaux. Instead he swept through Burgundy, Lorraine and Flanders to Germany, preaching the Crusade to packed churches wherever he went. His line of approach, always direct, was at times alarmingly so. In a letter to the German churchmen he wrote:

If the Lord has called little worms like yourselves to the defence of His heritage, do not conclude that His arm has grown shorter or that His hand has lost its power. . . . What is it, if not a most perfect and direct invention of the Almighty, that he should admit murderers, ravishers, adulterers, perjurors and other criminals for his service and for their salvation?

By autumn Germany too was aflame; and even Conrad, who had at first predictably refused to have any part in the Crusade, repented[1] after a Christmas castigation from Bernard and agreed to take the Cross.

Pope Eugenius received this last news with some alarm. Not for

[1] It may be that Conrad's change of heart was accelerated by a miraculous occurrence two days previously when Bernard, entering the cathedral of Speyer on Christmas Day, had prostrated himself three times to the statue of the Virgin, which had promptly returned his greeting.

the first time, the Abbot of Clairvaux had exceeded his brief. His instructions had been to preach the Crusade in France; no one had said anything about Germany. The Germans and the French were bound to squabble—they always did—and their inevitable jockeyings for position might easily lead to the foundering of the whole enterprise. Besides, the Pope needed Conrad in Italy; how else was he ever to re-establish himself in Rome? But it was too late to change things now. The vows had been taken. Eugenius could hardly start discouraging would-be Crusaders before the movement was even on its way.

In France, meanwhile, Louis VII had flung himself into preparations and had already written to enlist the sympathies of Manuel Comnenus and Roger of Sicily. To Manuel, fond as he was of individual westerners and the western way of life, the prospect of another full-scale incursion of his Empire by undisciplined Frankish armies was disagreeable in the extreme. He knew the problems that the First Crusade had caused his grandfather fifty years before—the descent on Constantinople by hordes of Latin thugs and barbarians, all of them out for what they could get and expecting to be lodged, fed and often even clothed by the Byzantines at no cost to themselves; the swaggering arrogance of their leaders, refusing to do the Emperor homage for their eastern conquests, which all too often had merely substituted one hostile neighbour for another. Admittedly the Danishmend Turks were giving him a lot of trouble just now; it was even conceivable that the new wave of Crusaders might prove better behaved than their predecessors and even turn out to be a long-term blessing; but he doubted it. His reply to Louis was as lukewarm as it could be made without offence. He would provide food and supplies for the Crusading armies, but everything would have to be paid for. And all the leaders would be asked once again to swear their fealty to him as they passed through his Empire.

Writing to the King of Sicily, Louis found himself in a slightly embarrassing position. He himself had formally recognised Roger in 1140 and had no quarrel with him; but he was fully aware that the two Emperors did not share his benevolence. Nor did the Christian rulers in the East. Not only had Roger already made formal claim to Antioch, even trying to lay hands on its present prince, Raymond of

Poitiers, who—to complicate matters further—was the uncle of young Queen Eleanor of France; there was also the unfortunate fact that, by the terms of his mother's marriage with King Baldwin, the Crown of Jerusalem in default of a direct heir should have passed to him. In the event, this contract was later declared null and void; and Baldwin, once he had spent all Adelaide's money, had shipped her unceremoniously back to Palermo. It was an insult that her son had never forgiven, and relations between Sicily and the Crusader states had remained bad. Louis knew that Roger would never be welcome in Outremer and doubted whether he would even consent to go—except as a conqueror.

On the other hand, Roger was now the acknowledged master of the Mediterranean—a position he had further strengthened during the summer of 1146 when, by the capture of the Libyan city of Tripoli, he had effectively sliced the Middle Sea in two. No longer could any ship hope to sail from one end of it to the other without his consent. If, then, the Second Crusade were to succeed, it was essential that the King of Sicily should remain well-disposed; but it was hoped that he would not embarrass everyone by insisting on active personal participation. On the first point Louis was soon reassured. Roger not only declared himself sympathetic to the Crusade; he offered to provide transportation, supplies and, in addition, a considerable force of fighting men to swell the Crusader ranks. On the second, however, his reply was less satisfactory; in the event of this offer being accepted, he himself or one of his sons would willingly lead a Sicilian army to Palestine.

Like most of the King's diplomatic communications, this reply was deeply disingenuous. Roger was just as opposed to the Second Crusade as his father had been to the First. Many of the most distinguished and influential of his subjects were Muslims, whom he understood and whose language he spoke; he liked them, one suspects, a good deal more than the French or the Germans. Furthermore, as we have seen, he had always hated the Frankish states of the Levant. Tolerance was the corner-stone of his kingdom; why should he now support a movement that preached the exact opposite, in a way that would be bound to arouse resentment among an important section of his own people?

485

In reality, he can have had no intention of taking the Cross; not, at least, any further than Antioch. To him the Crusade meant two things only—a means of distracting the two Empires from an attack on Sicily and an opportunity of extending his own influence in the East. But both these objectives would be furthered if he could secure the friendship or support of the King of France, and for this a policy of benevolent neutrality towards the Crusade would not be enough. The situation called for at least some degree of controlled enthusiasm, shown in a line of action that could at any moment be turned from its original aim and redirected against the states of Outremer— or even, if need be, against Constantinople itself.

However, when Roger's envoys formally advanced his proposals to a preliminary conference of the Crusaders held at Etampes early in 1147, King Louis politely declined. His ally Conrad was in any case resolved to take the overland route; even had he not been, the Sicilian offer was impractical. Roger's navy, huge as it was, would not have been adequate to carry the whole crusading force. To have accepted it would have meant dividing the army, putting half of it at the mercy of a notoriously untrustworthy monarch who had already attempted to kidnap the Queen's own uncle on a similar voyage, and leaving the other half to negotiate the long passage through Anatolia—the most perilous part of the whole expedition. They were understandable fears, which might well have been justified in the event; and though Louis's rejection of Sicilian help led to Roger's complete withdrawal from all active participation in the Crusade, his decision was probably a wise one.

St Bernard's uncomplimentary letter to the German clergy quoted earlier in this chapter had been, perhaps, more prophetic than he knew. Largely because of the promise of plenary absolution which accompanied all successful crusading journeys, the crusader armies tended to be even more disreputable than most others in the Middle Ages; and the German host that set off, about twenty thousand strong, from Ratisbon at the end of May 1147 seems to have contained more than its fair share of undesirables, ranging from the occasional religious maniac to the usual collection of footloose ne'er-do-wells and fugitives from justice. Hardly had they entered Byzantine territory than they began pillaging the countryside, raping, ravaging and even murdering as the mood took them. Often the leaders themselves set a poor example to those that followed behind; at Adrianople—now Edirne—Conrad's nephew and second-in-command, the young Duke Frederick of Swabia (better known to history by his subsequent nickname of Barbarossa) burnt down a monastery in reprisal for an attack by local brigands, and slaughtered the perfectly innocent monks. Fighting became ever more frequent between the Crusaders and the Byzantine military escort which Manuel had sent out to keep an eye on them, and when in mid-September the army at last drew up outside the walls of Constantinople—Conrad having indignantly refused the Emperor's request to avoid the capital altogether by crossing directly over the Hellespont into Asia—relations between German and Greek could hardly have been worse.

Even before the populations along the route had recovered from the shock, the French army in its turn appeared on the western horizon. It was a rather smaller force than that of the Germans, and on the whole more seemly. Discipline was better, and the presence of many distinguished ladies—including Queen Eleanor herself—accompanying their husbands doubtless exercised a further moderating influence. Yet even their progress was not altogether smooth. The Balkan peasantry by now showed itself frankly hostile—not surprisingly in view of what it had suffered from the Germans scarcely a month before—and asked ridiculous prices for what little food it had left to sell. Mistrust soon became mutual, and led to sharp practices on both sides. Thus, long before they reached Constantinople, the French had begun to feel considerable resentment against Germans and Greeks alike; and when they finally arrived on 4 October they were scandalised to hear that the Emperor Manuel had chosen that moment to conclude a truce with the Turkish enemy.

Although Louis could not have been expected to appreciate the fact, it was a sensible precaution for Manuel to take. The presence of the French and German armies at the very gates of his capital constituted a far more serious immediate danger than the Turks in Asia. The Emperor knew that in both camps there were extreme elements pressing for a combined western attack on Constantinople; and indeed only a few days later St Bernard's cousin Godfrey, Bishop of Langres, with all 'the un-Christian intolerance of a monk of Clair-vaux',[1] was formally to propose such a course to the King. Only by deliberately spreading reports of a huge Turkish army massing in Anatolia and implying that if the Franks did not make haste to pass through the hostile territory they might never manage to do so at all did Manuel succeed in saving the situation. Meanwhile he flattered Louis—and kept him occupied—with his usual constant round of banquets and lavish entertainments, while arranging passage for the King and his army over into Asia at the earliest possible moment.

As he bade farewell to his unwelcome guests and watched the ferryboats, laden to the gunwales with men and animals, shuttling across the Bosphorus, the Emperor foresaw better than anyone the dangers that awaited the Franks on the second stage of their journey. He himself had only recently returned from an Anatolian campaign; though his stories of the gathering Turkish hordes had been exaggerated, he had now seen the Crusaders for himself and he must have known that their shambling forces, already as lacking in morale as in discipline, would stand little chance of survival if suddenly attacked by the Seljuk cavalry. He had provided them with provisions and guides; he had warned them about the scarcity of water; and he had advised them not to take the direct route through the hinterland but to keep to the coast, which was still under Byzantine control. He could do no more. If, after all these precautions, the Crusaders still persisted in getting themselves slaughtered, they would have only themselves to blame. He, for his part, would be sorry—but not, perhaps, inconsolable.

It cannot have been more than a few days after bidding them farewell that Manuel received two reports, from two very different

---

[1] Sir Steven Runciman, *A History of the Crusades*, vol. II, p. 268. The bishop had formerly been prior of Clairvaux—a fact which led him, according to John of Salisbury, to claim special authority on the grounds that Bernard had committed the King to his counsel. His pomposity was, however, regularly punctured by Bishop Arnulf of Lisieux, worldliest of prelates, who maintained that he was just like the wine of Cyprus—sweet to the taste but lethal unless diluted with water. (*Historia Pontificalis*, ch. xxiv.)

quarters. The first, brought by swift messengers from Asia Minor, informed him that the German army had been taken by surprise by the Turks near Dorylaeum and massacred. Conrad himself had escaped, and had returned to join the French at Nicaea, but nine-tenths of his men now lay dead among the wreckage of their camp.

The second report brought the news that the fleet of King Roger of Sicily was at that very moment sailing against his Empire.

One of the perennial difficulties confronting any historian of the Middle Ages is that the chroniclers on whose works he must rely are so seldom of an analytical turn of mind. They usually give the facts —with varying degrees of accuracy—clearly enough. Questions of cause and motivation, however, they tend to ignore; and there is one such question in particular on which we might wish that they had been more explicit. How serious, in fact, was Roger's attack in 1147 on Byzantium?

Some authorities have maintained that it was very serious indeed —that the operation was timed to coincide with the arrival of the French at Constantinople, and that Roger's original plan was that the Sicilians and French together should then combine to overthrow the Emperor and seize his capital. They even suggest that Manuel had foreknowledge of this plan, which would explain his insistence on oaths of fealty before allowing the Franks to approach. It is an intriguing theory; but there seems to be little evidence for it apart from the conduct of the Bishop of Langres—and even he made no mention, so far as we can tell, of Sicilian help. Had Louis accepted Roger's original offer of transport for himself and his army, might he conceivably have been persuaded to join in a concerted attack on Constantinople before passing on to Palestine, just as the Venetians —to their lasting shame—were to persuade the Franks of the Fourth Crusade fifty-seven years later? Surely not. Louis had no real quarrel with the Byzantines; he was vowed to the Crusade, and he would, one suspects, have vehemently resisted any attempt by the King of Sicily to deflect him from his goal.

If Roger's action is to fit logically into the framework of preceding and following events, it must be looked at in a different light. He was a statesman, not an adventurer. Had he still contemplated a combined operation with the French he would surely have taken far more trouble to ensure that they were sympathetic to his idea. In the circumstances, he had no reason to believe that Louis would help him at all; his envoys had had a noticeably cool reception at Etampes the previous spring. If the Sicilian navy had appeared off Constantinople while the French were there, they might well have found the latter allied with the Greeks against them.

In the event, they did not make for the capital at all. Under the command of George of Antioch, they sailed in the autumn of 1147 from Otranto and headed straight across the Adriatic to Corfu. The island fell without a struggle; Nicetas Choniates tells us that the inhabitants, oppressed by the weight of Byzantine taxation and charmed by the honeyed words of the Greek-Sicilian admiral, welcomed the Normans as deliverers and willingly accepted a garrison of a thousand men.[1] Next, turning southward, the fleet rounded the Peloponnese, leaving further detachments at strategic positions, and sailed up the eastern coast to Euboea. At this point George seems to have decided that he had gone far enough. He turned about, made a quick stab at Athens[2] and then, on reaching the Ionian islands, headed eastward again up the Gulf of Corinth, ravaging the coastal towns as he went. His progress, writes Nicetas, was 'like a sea monster, swallowing everything in its path'.

Of the raiding parties that George sent ashore, one penetrated the hinterland as far as Thebes, centre of the Byzantine silk manufacture. The spoils were considerable. Stocks of rich damasks and bale after bale of brocades were carted back to shore and loaded on to the Sicilian vessels. But the admiral was still not satisfied. A large number of women workers—expert alike in the cultivation of the silkworm and

[1] Otto of Freising maintains that Corfu was taken by the old trick of a bogus funeral procession; but Otto knew little of Byzantine affairs, and variants of the funeral story are too frequent in mediaeval chronicles to encourage much belief. See p. 404n.

[2] The fact that the Norman sack of Athens is mentioned by western chroniclers only has led to some doubt as to whether the city really was raided at this time. The recent American excavations in the Agora have, however, tended to confirm that it was. See K. M. Setton, 'The Archaeology of Mediaeval Athens', in Essays in Medieval Life and Thought, Presented in Honour of Austin Patterson Evans (New York, 1955), p. 251.

its exploitation and almost certainly Jewish[1]—were herded to the ships. They too would be welcomed in Palermo. From Thebes the raiders moved on to Corinth, where—although the Corinthians had received advance warning of their arrival and had fled to the higher citadel of Acrocorinth with everything of value that they possessed— a short siege produced the desired result. The city was pillaged, the relics of St Theodore carried off, and George of Antioch sailed back in triumph, via Corfu, to Sicily.

'By this time,' writes Nicetas, 'the Sicilian vessels were so low in the water with the weight of their plunder that they seemed more like merchantmen than the pirate ships they really were.'[2] He spoke no more than the truth. Thebes, Athens and Corinth were the wealthiest cities in Greece. If this were not piracy, then the word had no meaning. But piracy was not all. Just as George's raids along the North African coast were undertaken less for their own sake than to secure control of the Mediterranean narrows, so his first Greek expedition was a calculated thrust against the western extremities of the Byzantine Empire, launched by Roger as a deliberate act of policy and for impeccable strategic reasons. The Second Crusade, he knew, had not permanently saved Sicily from attack by either Empire; it had merely postponed the day, affording him a year or two of grace in which to prepare his defences. By occupying Corfu and other carefully chosen strongpoints on the Greek mainland, he had deprived Byzantium of the principal bridgehead from which to launch an offensive against South Italy.

That, surely, was the real purpose of the expedition. But if it could provide certain additional benefits, so much the better. The silk-workers proved just such a bonus. It has sometimes been claimed that they were the nucleus around which the celebrated royal silk-mills of Palermo were built up. This theory does them too much honour—though they may well have introduced certain new techniques. Ever since the time of the Omayyads it had been the practice,

[1] The Hebrew traveller Benjamin of Tudela, who visited Thebes about twenty years after George's raid, reported two thousand Jews in the city. 'They are,' he wrote, 'the most skilled artificers in silk and purple cloth throughout Greece.'

[2] Another report, to the effect that the ships were so weighed down with plunder as to be submerged up to the third bank of oars, indicates the degree of caution necessary when dealing with certain imaginative chroniclers.

in all the principal Islamic kingdoms of the East and the West as well as in Constantinople itself, to maintain a silk workshop in or near the palace for the manufacture of robes and vestments for ceremonial court occasions. Sicily was no exception, and the Palermitan silk industry had thus been a thriving concern since the days of the Arabs—from whose language the *Tiraz*, or royal workshop, took its name.[1] Another long-established Muslim custom, however, required the ladies of the *Tiraz*, when not at their looms, to render other more intimate services to the gentlemen of the Court. This tradition too the Normans, eclectic as ever, had appropriated with enthusiasm; and it was not long before the *Tiraz* became a useful, if slightly transparent, cover for the royal harem. As we read of George of Antioch's seizure of the luckless Thebans it is difficult not to wonder which of their two possible functions he had more in mind.

The news of the Sicilian depredations in Greece stung Manuel to a fury. Whatever he himself might have thought about the Crusade, the fact that a so-called Christian country should have taken deliberate advantage of it to launch an attack on his Empire disgusted him; and the knowledge that the admiral concerned was a renegade Greek can hardly have assuaged his wrath. A hundred years before, Apulia had been a rich province of the Byzantine Empire; now it had become nothing but a nest of pirates, a springboard for unprovoked aggression by his enemy. Here was a situation that could not be tolerated. Roger, 'that dragon, threatening to shoot the flames of his anger higher than the crater of Etna . . . that common enemy of all Christians and illegal occupier of the land of Sicily',[2] must be eliminated from the Mediterranean for ever. The West had tried to do so, and had failed miserably. Now it was the turn of Byzantium. Given adequate help and freedom from other military commitments, Manuel believed that he could succeed. Fortunately the crusading armies had passed on. He himself had already concluded a truce with

[1] The best Norman-Sicilian example still extant is Roger II's superb mantle which is now in the Kunsthistorisches Museum at Vienna. It is of red silk, embroidered in gold with a tremendous design of tigers savaging camels. The Arabic inscription around the border identifies it as a product of the *Tiraz* of Palermo, dating from the 528th year of the Hegira—A.D. 1133.

[2] Imperial Edict of February 1148.

the Turks in the spring of 1147, and this he now confirmed and extended. It was essential that every soldier and sailor in the Empire should be free for the grand design that he was planning, a design that might well prove to be the crowning achievement of his life: the restoration of all South Italy and Sicily to the Byzantine fold.

The next problem was to find suitable allies. With France and Germany out of the running, Manuel's thoughts turned to Venice. The Venetians, as he well knew, had long been worried about the growth of Sicilian sea power; they had voluntarily joined the delegation which his father had sent to Lothair to discuss an anti-Sicilian alliance twelve years before. Since then their alarm had increased, and with good reason. No longer could they control the Mediterranean as once they had done; and while the bazaars of Palermo, Catania and Syracuse grew ever busier, so affairs on the Rialto had begun, gently but ominously, to slacken. If now Roger were to consolidate his hold on Corfu and the coast of Epirus, he would be in a position to seal off the Adriatic; and the Venetians might at any moment find themselves under Sicilian blockade.

They bargained a little, of course; no Venetian ever gave anything for nothing. But in March 1148, in return for increased trading privileges in Cyprus, Rhodes and Constantinople, Manuel got what he wanted—the full support of the Venetian fleet for the six months following. The Emperor meanwhile was working feverishly to bring his own navy to readiness; his secretary, John Cinnamus, estimated its strength at five hundred galleys and a thousand transports—a worthy complement to an army of perhaps twenty or thirty thousand men. As its admiral the Emperor appointed his brother-in-law, the Grand Duke Stephen Contostephanus; the army he placed under the Grand Domestic, a Turk named Axuch who had been taken prisoner as a boy fifty years before and had grown up in the imperial palace. Manuel himself would be in overall command.

By April the huge expeditionary force was ready to leave. The ships, refitted and provisioned, lay at anchor in the Marmara; the army waited for the order to march. Then, suddenly, everything went wrong. A South Russian tribe, the Polovtsi or Kumans, swept over the Danube into Byzantine territory; the Venetian fleet was held up by the sudden death of the Doge; a succession of freak summer storms disrupted shipping in the eastern Mediterranean. It was autumn before the two navies met in the southern Adriatic and the joint sea blockade of Corfu began. The land attack, meanwhile, was still further delayed. By the time he had dealt with the Polovtsi it was plain to Manuel that the Pindus mountains would be blocked by snow long before he could get his army across them. Settling it in winter quarters in Macedonia he himself rode on to Thessalonica, where an important guest was awaiting him. Conrad of Hohenstaufen had just returned from the Holy Land.

The Second Crusade had been an ignominious fiasco. Conrad, with such of his Germans as remained after the slaughter at Dorylaeum, had marched on with the French as far as Ephesus, where the army had stopped to celebrate Christmas. There he had fallen gravely ill. Leaving his compatriots to continue the journey without him, he had returned to Constantinople to recover, and there he had stayed as a guest in the imperial palace till March 1148, when the Emperor had put Greek ships at his disposal to carry him to Palestine. The French, meanwhile, though they had fared rather better than the Germans, had had an agonising passage through Anatolia, during which they in their turn had suffered heavily at Turkish hands. Although it was largely the fault of Louis himself, who had ignored Manuel's warnings to keep to the coast, he persisted in attributing almost every encounter with the enemy to Byzantine carelessness or treachery or both, and rapidly built up an almost psychopathic resentment against the Greeks. At last in despair he, his household and as much of his cavalry as could be accommodated had taken ship from Attalia, leaving the rest of the army and pilgrims to struggle on by land as best they might. It had been late in the spring before the remnant of the great host that had set out so confidently the previous year dragged itself miserably into Antioch.

And that was only the beginning of the trouble. The mighty Zengi was dead, but his mantle had passed to his still greater son Nur ed-Din, whose stronghold at Aleppo had now become the focus of Muslim opposition to the Franks. Aleppo should thus have been the Crusaders' first objective, and within days of his arrival in Antioch Louis found himself under considerable pressure from

Prince Raymond to mount an immediate attack on the city. He had refused on the grounds that he must first pray at the Holy Sepulchre; whereat Queen Eleanor, whose affection for her husband had not been increased by the dangers and discomforts of the journey from France and whose relations with Raymond were already suspected of going somewhat beyond those normally recommended for a niece and her uncle, had announced her intention of remaining at Antioch and suing for divorce. She and her husband were distant cousins; the question of consanguinity had been conveniently overlooked at the time of their marriage, but if resurrected could still prove embarrassing—and Eleanor knew it.

Louis, who for all his moroseness was not without spirit in moments of crisis, had ignored his wife's protests and dragged her forcibly off to Jerusalem—though not before he had succeeded in so antagonising Raymond that the latter henceforth refused to play any further part in the Crusade. No one doubted that he had carried off the situation with what dignity he could, but the effect on his reputation, particularly at such a moment, had been unfortunate. He and the tight-lipped Eleanor arrived at the Holy City in May, soon after Conrad; they were welcomed with due ceremony by Queen Mélisende and her son Baldwin III, now eighteen; and there they remained until, on 24 June, all the Crusaders were invited to a huge assembly at Acre to discuss their plan of action. It did not take them long to reach a decision: every man and beast available must be immediately mobilised for a concerted attack on Damascus.

Why Damascus was chosen as the first objective we shall never understand. It was now the only important Arab state in all the Levant to continue hostile to Nur ed-Din; as such it could, and should, have been an invaluable ally to the Franks. By attacking it, they drove it against its will into Nur ed-Din's Muslim confederation and, in doing so, made their own destruction sure. They arrived to find the walls of Damascus strong, the defenders determined. On the second day the besieging army, by yet another of those disastrous decisions which characterised the whole Crusade, moved its camp to an area along the eastern section of the walls, devoid alike of shade and water. The Palestinian barons, already at loggerheads over the future of the city when captured, suddenly lost their nerve and began to urge retreat. There were dark rumours of bribery and treason. Louis and Conrad were shocked and disgusted, but soon they too were made to understand the facts of the situation. To continue the siege would mean not only the passing of Damascus into the hands of Nur ed-Din but also, given the universal breakdown of morale, the almost certain annihilation of their whole army. On 28 July, just five days after the opening of the campaign, they ordered withdrawal.

There is no part of the Syrian desert more shattering to the spirit than that dark-grey, featureless expanse of sand and basalt that lies between Damascus and Tiberias. Retreating across it in the height of the Arabian summer, the remorseless sun and scorching desert wind full in their faces, harried incessantly by mounted Arab archers and leaving a stinking trail of dead men and horses in their wake, the Crusaders must have felt despair heavy upon them. This was the end. Their losses, both in material and in human life, had been immense. They had neither the will nor the wherewithal to continue. Worst of all was the shame. Having travelled for the best part of a year, often in conditions of mortal danger, having suffered agonies of thirst, hunger and sickness and the bitterest extremes of heat and cold, this once-glorious army that had purported to enshrine all the ideals of the Christian West had given up the whole thing after just four days' fighting, having regained not one inch of Muslim territory. Here was the ultimate of humiliations—which neither they nor their enemies would forget.

But for Conrad personally there had emerged from the shambles of the Second Crusade one remarkable result, as happy as it was unexpected. He had formed a deep regard and affection for Manuel Comnenus. When he had fallen ill at Ephesus the previous Christmas the Emperor and his wife had themselves sailed down from Constantinople, picked him up and brought him safely back to the capital; and for the next two months Manuel, who prided himself on his medical skill, had tended him with his own hands and nursed him back to health. Conrad's first passage through Constantinople with his army had not left him with the pleasantest of memories; he was all the more touched at the consideration that he was now being shown. The Emperor, with his intelligence, his charm and his German wife—a sister of Conrad's own—was a perfect host; when his patient was cured he had seized the opportunity to arrange a magnificent series of horse-races and entertainments in his honour, and had finally sent him on his way to Palestine in a Byzantine squadron, together with two thousand horses, all fully equipped, from the imperial stable. Conrad, not surprisingly, had been sorry to leave, and had promised to visit Manuel again on his homeward journey.

And so, the ill-starred Crusade safely in the past, the two monarchs met again at Thessalonica, and Manuel bore Conrad away for his second winter in Constantinople. Their friendship remained unaffected after the six months' separation, and Christmas was marked by a further union of the two imperial houses when, with the utmost pomp and the usual elaborate festivities, Manuel's niece Theodora was married to Conrad's brother Henry of Austria.[1] This year, however, there were serious political problems to be discussed, the most pressing of which was Roger of Sicily. The Byzantines were already at war with him; their navy was at that very moment blockading Corfu and their army was prepared to march just as soon as the melting of the snows made it possible to cross the Pindus. Conrad had not yet opened hostilities, but asked nothing better than to do so. Agreement was quickly reached, and in the first days of 1149 the two rulers undertook, by a treaty of formal alliance, to launch a joint attack on the King of Sicily during that year. Only if one of the parties were struck by grave illness or faced with the imminent danger of losing his throne could this commitment be set aside; even then it would not be cancelled but merely postponed. Sensibly in the circumstances, the treaty also enshrined an understanding about the future of Apulia and Calabria after they had been wrested from Roger's grasp. Both Empires had claimed these territories in the past, and both Manuel and Conrad were anxious to avoid a subsequent wrangle in their division of the spoils. The compromise that they reached did them both credit. Both regions would be made over

---

[1] A slight gloom may have been cast over the proceedings by the horror felt by many Byzantines at the fate of a Greek princess being delivered over to the mercy of Frankish barbarians; Sir Steven Runciman (*History of the Crusades*, vol. II) quotes a poem of condolence addressed to her mother in which she is described as being 'immolated to the beast of the West'.

by Conrad to Byzantium as the belated dowry of his sister-in-law Bertha, now the Empress Irene.

Once future plans had been settled, there was no reason for either of the new allies to linger in Constantinople. In early February they parted—Conrad to Germany and preparations for his new Italian offensive, Manuel back to his army and the siege of Corfu, whence recent reports had not been encouraging. The Sicilian-held citadel rose invulnerable on its high crest in the mountainous north of the island, towering almost perpendicularly above the sea and safely out of range of Byzantine projectiles. The Greeks, wrote Nicetas, seemed to be shooting at the very sky itself, while the defenders could release downpours of arrows and hailstorms of rocks on to those below. (People wondered, he adds rather disarmingly, how the Sicilians had taken possession of it so effortlessly the previous year.) During one of the attacks the Grand Duke Contostephanus was killed and his place taken by Axuch, who had by this time arrived with the land army; but the change of leadership had no effect on the progress of the siege. As the weeks went by it became clear that Corfu could never be taken by storm. The only hope—barring treachery from within—would be to starve out the garrison, who had had a full year in which to provision themselves; and even then the blockade might at any moment be broken by a Sicilian fleet arriving with reinforcements and supplies.

It is a commonplace of warfare that a siege can impose just as great a strain on the morale of the attacking force as on that of the beleaguered garrison. The coming of spring saw the outbreak of serious quarrels between the Greek sailors and their Venetian allies. Axuch did what he could to smooth things over, but failed; and the climax came when the Venetians occupied a neighbouring islet and set fire to a number of Byzantine merchantmen anchored offshore. By some mischance they also managed to gain possession of the imperial flagship, on which they even went so far as to perform an elaborate charade, dressing up an Ethiopian slave in the imperial vestments—Manuel's dark complexion had not gone unnoticed— and staging a mock coronation on the deck, in full view of the Greeks. Whether Manuel was present to witness this monstrous insult against his imperial majesty is not clear; if not, he certainly arrived soon afterwards. He never forgave the Venetians their conduct; for the moment, however, he needed them. A combination of patience, tact and his celebrated charm soon restored a slightly uneasy harmony; the Venetian ships resumed their allotted stations; and the Emperor assumed direct personal command of the siege. There would be time enough, later, for revenge.

Much as he longed to forget his disastrous Crusade, King Louis—unlike Conrad—found himself in no hurry to leave Outremer. The prospect of Easter in Jerusalem doubtless appealed to his piety; and, like so many travellers before and since, he may have been reluctant to exchange the gentle sunshine of a Palestinian winter for the stormy seas and snowbound roads which lay between himself and his own kingdom. He knew, too, that his marriage to Eleanor was past redemption. Once back in Paris he would have to face all the unpleasantness of a divorce and the political repercussions that could not but follow. On and on he stayed, touring the shrines of the Holy Land and reflecting on the perfidy of the Greeks, and in particular of Manuel Comnenus himself, whom he still held responsible for the calamities of his outward journey. Now he understood. A Christian in name only, the Emperor was in reality the foremost enemy and betrayer of Christendom; a secret ally of the infidel, he had opposed the Crusade from its inception and done everything in his power to ensure its failure. Its first task should have been to eliminate him—as Roger of Sicily was very properly attempting to do.

In the spring of 1149, Louis set his face reluctantly for home. This time he and Eleanor had resolved to travel by sea, but had been unwise enough to entrust themselves to Sicilian transport—dangerous craft in which to brave Byzantine waters. Somewhere in the southern Aegean they encountered a Greek fleet—presumably on its way to or from Corfu—which turned at once to attack. Louis managed to escape by hastily running up the French flag; but one of his escort vessels, containing several followers and nearly all his baggage, was captured by the Greeks and borne off in triumph to Constantinople. Queen Eleanor, whose relations with her husband were now such that she was travelling on a separate vessel, narrowly avoided a similar fate; she was rescued by Sicilian warships just in time.

499

Finally, on 29 July 1149, Louis landed in Calabria. There Eleanor joined him, and the pair rode together to Potenza, where Roger was waiting to greet them and where they were to stay as his guests.[1] The two Kings, meeting for the first time, took to each other at once. In the past, as we have seen, their approaches had been inhibited by the dispute of Roger and Raymond of Poitiers, Eleanor's uncle, over the question of Antioch; but since then a new rivalry had arisen—that of Louis and Raymond over the question of Eleanor—and Louis no longer felt constrained. Neither, for that matter, had his recent maritime adventure softened his feelings towards Byzantium; he and Roger may have discovered, during those August days at Potenza, that they had more in common than either had imagined.

After three days their host left them to return to Sicily, and Louis and Eleanor moved on to Tusculum, the nearest town to Rome in which the Pope could safely install himself. Eugenius gave them a suitably royal welcome; politically, for reasons we shall shortly see, he was not particularly encouraging, but for the moment he was less concerned with future military alignments in Europe than with the immediate domestic problems of his guests. A gentle, kind-hearted man, he hated to see people unhappy; and the sight of Louis and Eleanor, oppressed by the double failure of the Crusade and of their marriage, seems to have caused him genuine personal distress. John of Salisbury, who was employed in the Curia at the time, has left us a curiously touching account of the Pope's attempts at a reconciliation:

He commanded, under pain of anathema, that no word should be spoken against their marriage and that it should not be dissolved under any pretext whatever. This ruling plainly delighted the King, for he loved the Queen passionately, in an almost childish way. The Pope made them sleep in the same bed, which he had decked with priceless hangings of his own; and daily during their brief visit he strove by friendly converse to restore the love between them. He heaped gifts upon them; and when the time for their departure came he could not hold back his tears.

[1] Later, in an attempt to bolster Roger's claim to legitimate kingship, the story was put about that Louis had personally re-crowned him during their time together at Potenza. Sheer fabrication though it undoubtedly is, it was to find its way into one of the several interpolations of Romuald of Salerno's chronicle.

Those tears were perhaps made all the more copious by the knowledge that his efforts had been in vain. Had Eugenius known Eleanor
better, he would have seen from the start that her mind was made up
and that neither he nor anyone else could change it. For the time
being, however, she was prepared to keep up appearances, accompanying her husband to Rome where they were cordially received by
the Senate and where Louis prostrated himself as usual at all the
principal shrines; and so back across the Alps to Paris. It was to be
another two and a half years before her marriage was finally dissolved
—St Bernard having persuaded Eugenius to withdraw his early
strictures—on grounds of consanguinity; but she was still young
and only on the threshold of that astonishing career in which, as wife
of one of England's greatest Kings and mother of two of its worst,
she was to influence the course of European history for over half a
century.

The people of Paris received Louis and Eleanor with rejoicing,
and even went so far as to strike medals 'to our unconquered King',
one portraying him in a triumphal chariot with a winged Victory
soaring above, the other illustrating the theme of dead and fugitive
Turks on the banks of the Meander. But they deceived no one.
Elsewhere, men were readier to look facts in the face—though
even then they usually sought to explain or to justify them. Pope
Eugenius, for example, saw in the Crusade a calamity sent by God
as an object-lesson in the transience of terrestrial things. Otto of
Freising points out philosophically that it provided easy opportunities for the acquisition of a martyr's crown. It was left to St Bernard
who, if he did not actually initiate the Crusade, at least gave it its
impetus and its inspiration, to say honestly what he thought. For
him, it was not simply a calamity or even a lesson, but a divine
judgment—one that represented 'so deep an abyss that anyone must
be accounted blessed who is not scandalised thereby'.[1] In passing
this judgment the Almighty had acted, as always, with perfect
justice; but this time, for once, he had left his mercy aside.

In the frantic search for a scapegoat that followed, it was perhaps
inevitable that all fingers save one—Conrad's—should have pointed
to Manuel Comnenus; it was also unfair. The blame for the failure of

[1] *De Consideratione*, II, i.

any military operation can attach only to those directly concerned—those who plan it and those who carry it out. In the Second Crusade, both planning and performance were atrocious. From the start the idea was a bad one. The lasting presence in strength of an alien power in a distant land is possible only when it is acceptable locally; when it is not, its days are numbered. If it cannot maintain itself by its own efforts any attempt at propping it up artificially, especially by military means, is bound to fail. Having decided to mount the attack, the leaders of the West made one mistake after another. They coordinated neither their preparations nor their timing; by a mixture of disingenuousness and sheer political ineptitude they antagonised their most important ally; they arrived too few in numbers and too late; initially indecisive, they eventually settled on a misguided line of action and then lacked the courage to carry it through. They hesitated, retreated, and collapsed.[1]

[1] It is irrelevant, but irresistible, to compare the planning of the Second Crusade with that of the Suez affair eight centuries later.

8

CLIMACTERIC

Our hearts and the hearts of almost all Frenchmen are burning with
devotion for you, and love of your peace; all this we feel particularly in
view of the base, lamentable and unheard-of treachery to our pilgrims of
the Greeks and their detestable King. . . . Rise, and help the people of
God to take their vengeance!

Letter to Roger II from
Abbot Peter of Cluny

THE Crusade had been bad for reputations. Conrad of Hohenstaufen and Louis Capet had been discredited, Manuel Comnenus
had been blamed, Pope Eugenius and St Bernard together had had
to bear the spiritual responsibility. Among the great princes of
Europe in the first rank of power and importance, only Roger of
Sicily had emerged unscathed. And it was Roger who now became
the focal point for all those dissatisfied spirits who called for an
immediate and victorious Third Crusade to wipe out the humiliations
of the Second.

The irony of the situation must have amused him. A Crusader
neither by temperament nor by conviction, he had not scrupled to
take full political advantage of western woolly-mindedness on the last
occasion, and he was quite ready to do so again. For the fate of the
Christians of Outremer he cared not a rap; they deserved all they got.
He himself preferred the Arabs every time. On the other hand,
the Levant tempted him. Was he not the legitimate Prince of
Antioch, perhaps even the rightful King of Jerusalem? More
important still, he had to defend himself against Byzantine attack,
and in such an eventuality opposition would be the best defence.
While Manuel's present unpopularity lasted it would be an easy
matter to turn the weight of any fresh Crusade against him.

Roger therefore willingly accepted his role—improbable as it was —of avenger of the West, and set to work building up his new image. That, above all, was why he had travelled to meet the King of France at Potenza, where he had been assured of Louis's support. His major difficulty, as always, was with Conrad. To the several excellent reasons that the King of the Romans already had for hating him another, perhaps the strongest of all, had now been added— jealousy. Conrad knew that his reputation had been dealt a severe blow by the failure of the Crusade; Roger's—unaccountably and quite unjustifiably—had never been higher. It was the German Emperor, crowned or not, who remained historically and by divine right the sword and shield of western Christendom; and Conrad resented this new usurpation of his imperial prerogatives, as un- pardonable in its way as the seizure of South Italy itself.

St Bernard tried hard to change his attitude, but to no avail. Bernard was a Frenchman, and the French, as far as Conrad was concerned, were almost as bad as the Sicilians; besides, he had painful recollections of the last time he had taken Bernard's advice against his better judgment. Neither was he any more amenable to the argu- ments of Peter of Cluny or Cardinal Theodwine of Porto, one of the most influential voices in the Curia. All these ecclesiastical per- suaders, he knew, were rabidly anti-Byzantine—particularly the Abbot of Clairvaux, who clearly felt responsible for the Crusade and was only too anxious to shuffle as much of the blame as possible off his own shoulders and on to those of the Eastern Emperor. Conrad saw through them all. But Manuel was his friend, and he trusted him. The two were in any case bound by a solemn alliance, which he for his part did not intend to break.

It was not as if Roger had showed the faintest sign of wanting a reconciliation. On the contrary, he had begun a new intrigue with Count Welf of Bavaria, brother of Henry the Proud and Conrad's still-determined rival for the imperial throne. Welf had called in at Palermo on his way home from the Crusade, and Roger had offered him still bigger subsidies than before to organise a confederation of German princes against the Hohenstaufen. This new league threat- ened to be a formidable one, a menace which might well keep Conrad occupied in Germany for some time to come. Once again his plans for a punitive Italian expedition would have to be postponed—but his determination sooner or later to settle scores with the King of Sicily remained stronger than ever.

For Manuel too the year 1149 ended less auspiciously than it had begun. Some time in the late summer Corfu had fallen to him— probably through treachery, since Nicetas tells us that the garrison commander subsequently entered the imperial service; but before the Emperor could follow up his advantage and cross to Italy news was brought to him of a Serbian insurrection, to which the neighbouring Kingdom of Hungary was giving active military support. At about this time too he must also have heard—with particular irritation—of the most recent exploit of George of Antioch who, after the incident with Louis and Eleanor, had taken a fleet of forty ships right up the Hellespont and over the Marmara to the very walls of Constantinople. Thence, after an unsuccessful attempt at a landing, the Sicilians had sailed some distance up the Bosphorus, pillaging several rich villas along the Asiatic shore, and before departing had even fired a few impudent arrows into the grounds of the Imperial Palace.

Roger's capture of Corfu, temporary as it was, had proved a useful holding operation; and the Balkan rising that followed so conveniently after it meant a further postponement of Manuel's own invasion plans. Looking back, one feels that the sequence of events was almost too convenient; could it be, one wonders, that the King of Sicily had indirectly engineered this as well? The chroniclers preserve a discreet silence—perhaps they were not too sure themselves—but it seems probable enough. Roger, whose cousin Busilla had married King Coloman, had always maintained close ties of friendship with the Hungarian throne. If our suspicions are right, then the year 1149 must mark the highest point of his diplomatic virtuosity. Facing the most formidable military alliance that could be conceived in the Middle Ages, that of the Eastern and the Western Empires acting—as they rarely acted in the six and a half centuries of their joint history—in complete concert one with the other, he succeeded in the space of a few months in immobilising both of them. It was a feat comparable to that of his uncle, who in 1084 had actually had the armies of both Empires retreating before him in different directions. But Robert Guiscard had had a force of thirty thousand of his own behind him; Roger had achieved his objective without calling a single Sicilian soldier to arms.

There was another difference too; whereas the Guiscard had had the advantage of papal support, towards Roger Pope Eugenius's attitude remained ambivalent. Naturally he could never forget that Roger was his immediate neighbour to the south, a perennial thorn in the papal flesh, always difficult and on occasion dangerous. On the other hand the King of Sicily now appeared undeniably well-disposed. At the beginning of 1149 he had offered Eugenius both military and financial assistance in his struggle against the Roman commune; and the Pope, seeing the situation in Rome steadily deteriorating and knowing that he could expect no help from Conrad who was still away in the East, had accepted. Thus, thanks to a body of Sicilian troops under Robert of Selby, he had managed to return to the Lateran by the end of the year. Since then, while he still mistrusted Roger's motives, he saw him as a useful ally whom it would be foolish to antagonise without good cause.

And so the Pope wavered; and he was still wavering when in the early summer of 1150 he recived a letter from the King of Sicily with proposals for a meeting. Roger's purpose is clear. An armed conflict between himself and the Empires could not, as it seemed to him, be long delayed. It might be offensive—a new 'Crusade' in which he would lead the forces of the West against the Infidel, represented in the first instance by Manuel Comnenus. For this he would find allies in plenty, though not unless he could first obtain the Pope's blessing. Alternatively there might be a defensive operation. The delaying tactics that he was at present employing to keep his two enemies occupied on home ground could not last for ever. Already Conrad could claim one major victory over Welf, and Manuel was well on the way to restoring the situation in the Balkans. Within a year—perhaps even less—the pair of them might be in a position to launch their two-pronged invasion of his realm. In such an event he would have far fewer allies on whom to rely; and papal support would be still more necessary.

The little town of Ceprano, standing conveniently on the border between the Kingdom of Sicily and the Papal State, had seen respect-

ability bestowed on Robert Guiscard by his investiture at the hands
of Gregory VII seventy years before—a thought which may well
have given Roger some encouragement when, in July 1150, he rode
there to meet Eugenius; for a similar investiture was now his first
and most important objective. To obtain this, the formal recognition
by the Pope of his legitimate sovereignty, he was prepared to concede
much. Nothing else stood between himself and the leadership of
western Europe. His right of appointment of Sicilian bishops, of
refusing admission to papal envoys, even the hereditary privilege of
the Apostolic Legation would have been reasonable prices to pay for
such a reward.

But Ceprano had also witnessed failures. It was, after all, only six
years since Roger and Pope Lucius had separated in disappointment
and bitterness after the breakdown of other negotiations from which
both had stood to gain; and the result of the coming talks with
Lucius's successor was no foregone conclusion. The Pope had just
been obliged once again to leave Rome; a renewed offer of Sicilian
troops might prove a useful sweetener. As against this, Conrad was
now back in Germany, collecting his forces, building up his strength,
and rapidly living down his recent disgrace. If he were contemplating
an early clash, then Eugenius would be unlikely to weaken his hand
—and compromise the papal position—by confirming Roger's
kingship.

And so it proved. The Pope may already have been under pressure
from Conrad; he was certainly being bombarded with letters from
Abbot Wibald of Corbie, a sworn enemy of Roger since the latter
had expelled him from Monte Cassino and now Conrad's closest
ecclesiastical adviser. John of Salisbury, who was probably present
at Ceprano, tells us how Roger made every concession he could;
'but neither his prayers nor his gifts were of any avail'.

Although John is careful to note that King and Pontiff parted on
relatively amicable terms, this new failure to achieve recognition
must have come to Roger as a bitter blow. It could mean one thing
only, that Eugenius had decided to throw in his lot with Conrad;
and this, in its turn, meant that all his own plans for an offensive
coalition against Manuel would have to be abandoned. From the
moment the Ceprano talks ended, he gave up any further attempt to

influence papal policy. Instead, he returned to Sicily to prepare for the coming storm.

He might almost have been relieved, as his ships sailed for Palermo, had he known that he would never set foot on the Italian mainland again.

His tents weep him, and his palaces; the swords and the lances are for him like women mourners. Hearts, no less than garments, are rent with grief. For the arms of the brave have fallen; valiant souls are filled with dread; and the eloquent seek for words in vain.

Thus had the Arab poet Abu ed-Daw lamented the death, on 2 May 1148, of Duke Roger of Apulia, the King of Sicily's eldest son. How he died we do not know; most probably he fell in some skirmish on the northern frontiers of his dukedom, where he had been intermittently engaged for several years. It was a grievous loss. The young Duke—he was only just thirty when he died—had been a Hauteville in the old tradition, a brilliant fighter and capable administrator, fearless in battle and utterly loyal to his father. More and more in the past decade Roger had tended to leave the affairs of the mainland to him—with Robert of Selby holding, perhaps, a watching brief—and he had shown himself a worthy heir to the Sicilian Crown. And now he was dead, the fifth of Roger's and Queen Elvira's six children to die before his father. Tancred, Prince of Bari, had already been nearly ten years in his grave; Alfonso, Prince of Capua and Duke of Naples, had died in 1144 in his early twenties. Another boy, Henry, had not survived his infancy. One only remained, the King's fourth son, William; he inherited the dukedom on his brother's death, and on Easter Day, 1151, Roger had him consecrated and crowned by the Archbishop of Palermo as co-ruler of the Sicilian Kingdom.

To crown a son in the lifetime of his father was no rare thing in the Middle Ages. The practice was regular in Byzantium, where it had been inherited from the earlier days of the Roman Empire; it was also to be followed in England, some twenty years after William's coronation, when King Henry II crowned his own first-born. Its purpose was to ensure the continuity of the royal line and to guard against the possibility of civil strife resulting from a disputed succession. Roger was still only fifty-five; his father had lived to be seventy. There is no suggestion among the contemporary chronicles that he was ill, though it is possible that he had already felt the onset of the disease that was to kill him three years later. Nor could there be any possible doubt about the claim to the throne of the King's only surviving legitimate son. Roger seems, however, to have been genuinely concerned about the succession; otherwise he would hardly have been likely, after fourteen years as a widower, to contract a second marriage in 1149, to a certain Sibyl of Burgundy; and a third, four years later when Sibyl had died in childbed.

Whatever his reasons, he cannot have thought that the news of William's coronation would be well received by the Pope. Technically speaking, he was within his rights; Archbishop Hugh of Palermo, recently promoted from the archbishopric of Capua, had been granted the *pallium* by the Pope, on the grounds that he was one of those 'who presided over the chief cities of certain nations and were therefore privileged by the Papacy to create princes for their own people'.[1] Eugenius had never meant to imply that this grant included the right to perform royal coronations without prior reference to the Holy See, but the phrasing had been unfortunate; and the fact that he himself had given Roger the opportunity to take such a step can only have added to his irritation. It does not seem to have occurred to him that if the King of Sicily did have some good reason for wishing to ensure his son's succession he could hardly—in the light of Eugenius's refusal to grant the investiture himself—have acted otherwise. As far as he was concerned, Sicily and the *Regno* were papal fiefs, of which no disposition could be made without his authority. This authority had once again been flouted. As John of Salisbury confirms, 'he took the news ill, but oppressed as he was by the evils of the time he could offer no resistance'.

If the Pope had ever been in any doubt as to where his best interests lay, he was in doubt no longer. The two special legates

[1] John of Salisbury, *Historia Pontificalis*, chs. 33–4. The *pallium* is a circular band of white wool, shorn from two lambs blessed on St Agnes' Day in the church of S. Agnese fuori le Mura, and marked with six black crosses. It is worn by the Pope across his shoulders and granted by him to Archbishops and Metropolitans, at their petition, to enable them to perform their special functions.

he now sent to Conrad soon showed themselves to be little more than figures of fun;[1] but one point they made abundantly clear. The Emperor-to-be was awaited with impatience in Italy. When he came, for whatever his purpose, he would have the See of St Peter whole-heartedly behind him.

The future of the Kingdom of Sicily had never looked blacker than it did at the start of the year 1152. Conrad of Hohenstaufen was ready to march; Manuel Comnenus, having restored order within his own Empire, was ready to join him. The Venetians had once again pledged their support. The Pope, after long hesitation, had allied himself on their side. And meanwhile the great anti-imperial coalition by which Roger had set so much store had melted away. Louis of France was still in theory an ally; but the death of Abbot Suger the previous year had robbed him of his confidence and, in a large measure, of his freedom of action. Besides, his divorce from Eleanor, now imminent, was occupying his mind to the virtual exclusion of all else. Two years before, at Flochberg, Welf and his friends had sustained a defeat from which they had never recovered. Hungary and Serbia had, for the moment, no more fight left in them.

But just as a few years earlier Roger had been saved from a similar situation by the Second Crusade, so now fate intervened once more to deliver him. On Friday 15 February 1152 King Conrad died at Bamberg. He was the first Emperor-elect in the two centuries since the restoration of the Empire by Otto the Great not to have been crowned at Rome—a failure which somehow seems to symbolise his whole reign. 'A Seneca in council, a Paris in appearance, a Hector in

---

[1] John of Salisbury's description of the papal legates is worth a quotation. 'Jordan [of S. Susanna] used his Carthusian Order as a pretext for his meanness. Ever parsimonious, he wore filthy garments and was austere in speech and demeanour; since like will ever attract like, he had been made chamberlain to the Lord Pope. Octavian [of S. Cecilia, the future Anti-Pope Victor IV], though nobler, easier in manner and more generous, was proud and pompous, a syco-phant of the Germans and a seeker after Roman favour—which he never won. And although the Pope had charged them to act in concert, no sooner had they started out than they began to argue as to which was the greater. . . . Quarrel-ling over everything, they soon made the Church a laughing-stock. . . . Thus it was that complainants converged in swarms upon the papal court, for these two disturbed the churches just as men disturb beehives when they seek to extract the honey from the bees.'

battle',[1] great things had been expected of him; but he died with his promise unfulfilled and his country as divided as always; never an Emperor—just a sad, unlucky King. He was buried in Bamberg Cathedral next to the recently-canonised Emperor Henry II—a distant predecessor who had also, long ago, found the Normans too strong for him.

Otto of Freising, Conrad's half-brother, tells us that the presence at his bedside of certain Italian doctors—probably from the medical school of Salerno—gave rise to inevitable mutterings about Sicilian poison; but though Roger must have welcomed this timely removal of his most dangerous enemy there is no reason to suspect that he was in any way involved. Conrad was fifty-nine and had had a hard life; and mediaeval chroniclers are notoriously reluctant to ascribe to natural causes more deaths than are absolutely necessary. Conrad's mind remained unclouded to the end, and his last injunctions to his nephew and successor, Duke Frederick of Swabia, were to continue the struggle which he had begun until the so-called King of Sicily was finally brought to book. Frederick asked nothing better. Encouraged by the Apulian exiles at the court, he even hoped at one moment to keep to Conrad's original schedule and to march against Roger immediately, picking up his imperial crown on the way. As always, however, the succession brought its own problems, and he soon had to accept a further indefinite postponement. Where foreign adventures were concerned, Conrad's death had left him hamstrung just as Suger's had crippled Louis VII a year before. Sicily had been granted another reprieve.

And these deaths were only the beginning. During the next two years Conrad and Suger were to be followed to their graves by nearly all the great figures who had dominated the European stage over the previous decade. On 8 July 1153 Pope Eugenius died suddenly at Tivoli, and was buried in St Peter's. Though never a great Pope, he had during his papacy revealed a firmness of character which few had suspected at the time of his election. Like so many of his predecessors, he had been forced to spend money freely to buy support

---

[1] This description, by the poet-chronicler Godfrey of Viterbo, is possibly more apt that its author realised. Seneca's position as adviser and confidant of Nero resulted in his suicide; Paris was the lover who ultimately lost; Hector the hero who fled.

among the Romans, yet he personally had always remained incorruptible; his gentleness and unassuming ways had earned him much genuine love and respect of a kind that cannot be bought for gold. Till the day of his death he continued to wear, under his pontifical robes, the coarse white habit of a Cistercian monk; and at his funeral the popular grief was such that, in the words of Bishop Hugh of Ostia, 'one would have believed that he who in death was so honoured on earth was already reigning in Heaven'.[1]

When the news of his death reached Clairvaux, the Abbot himself was failing fast. We have it on Bernard's own authority that by this time he was in constant pain and unable to touch solid food. His hands and feet were swollen with dropsy. Sleep had become impossible. He too seems to have kept his faculties to the end; but on Thursday 20 August, at nine o'clock in the morning, he died at the age of sixty-three. His is a hard character to assess. Modern biographers seem no less susceptible to his magnetism than were his contemporaries; one after another they rhapsodise over his humility, his charity and his general saintliness. For as long as they confine themselves to his spiritual attributes, their encomiums are possibly justified. It is in the political sphere that St Bernard's record becomes, to say the least, questionable. History is full of instances in which ecclesiastics have played valuable and constructive parts in affairs of state; but these men of the Church have nearly always been men of the world as well, realists who have been able to view the great issues of their time with a cool, objective eye. The Abbot of Clairvaux provides a perfect example of what is apt to occur when this condition is not fulfilled. He was that fortunately rare phenomenon, the genuine mystic and ascetic with a compulsion to interfere in politics. His reputation and the sheer force of his personality ensured that he was listened to; his formidable rhetorical gifts and powers of persuasion did the rest.

His weakness was that he was all emotion. He saw the world with the eye of a fanatic, in black and white—the black to be stamped out by any means available, the white to be upheld whatever the price. Scarcely ever in his letters or other writings do we find a trace of

---

[1] Just over seven centuries later, in 1872, he was to be beatified by Pope Pius IX.

logical argument, still less of political understanding. Such a man, raised to a position of virtually limitless influence and prestige, could only cause havoc; and St Bernard's major interventions in the world political scene were, all too often, disastrous. His incitement of Lothair II against Roger of Sicily ended—as it could only have ended—in débacle and was arguably the cause of the old Emperor's death; his launching of the Second Crusade led to the most shameful Christian humiliation of the Middle Ages. Had he lived it would have surprised no one to find him advocating, as his cousin the Bishop of Langres had already advocated, a punitive expedition against Constantinople of the kind which, when it occurred half a century later, was to deal Eastern Christendom so shattering a blow.

Suger, Conrad, Bernard—one by one, the giants were disappearing from the scene. About this time, too, death robbed Sicily of her High Admiral, George of Antioch. The Emir of Emirs has played, it must be admitted, a somewhat shadowy rôle in this story. We have seen him as a young adventurer, as a patron of the arts who has left as his memorial one of his country's loveliest churches, and finally as an elderly buccaneer of courage and *panache*. As an admiral, however, as the man who was for well over a quarter of a century responsible more than any other for the rise of Roger's naval power throughout the Mediterranean, we have done him less than justice. For this the Sicilian records of the time are partly to blame. There exists only one reliable contemporary chronicle covering the second half of George's lifetime—that of Romuald of Salerno; but the Archbishop, not surprisingly, is more concerned with mainland politics than with naval affairs. We are thus obliged to fall back on Arab writers; and while they have left us splendidly detailed reports of the Admiral's seafaring exploits, even they are able to tell us little enough about the man himself.

Yet George of Antioch was the sole architect of Roger II's North African Empire. His capture of Tripoli in 1146—itself the culmination of some ten or fifteen years of regular raids and minor conquests along the coast—had given his master control of the entire littoral as far as Tunis and had consequently marked a turning-point in Roger's African policy. Before it, Sicilian incursions on African soil had all been more or less piratical; henceforth we see authority established on a permanent basis. This authority was not aimed at political domination: Roger was too much of a realist to see such an objective as either possible or even desirable. He was interested only in the economic and strategic advantages to be gained from a North African Empire. Both were immense. By occupying the chief commercial centres of the coast, he could eliminate middlemen; the King's agents, operating at the head of the great caravan routes to the south, with a virtual monopoly of grain and many other commodities as well, were soon able to control a large proportion of the internal trade of the continent. Strategically the position was simpler still: command of the narrow seas between Sicily and Tunis meant mastery of the central Mediterranean.

Only one local ruler of importance continued in power, Prince Hassan of Mahdia. Twenty-three years earlier, at the age of fourteen, after a crushing defeat of the Sicilian navy at the fortress of ad-Dimas,[1] Hassan had been hailed through the length and breadth of the Arab world as a hero of Islam; since then, however, he had voluntarily recognised Roger as his suzerain and had entered into a treaty of alliance which appeared to be to the mutual benefit of both rulers. This happy state of affairs might well have been allowed to continue indefinitely had not the local governor of Gabes in 1147 rebelled against Hassan and offered the city to Roger on condition that he himself were appointed governor. Roger accepted the offer; Hassan, understandably, objected; and the consequent rupture led, in the summer of 1148, to the despatch of two hundred and fifty Sicilian ships under George of Antioch against the port of Mahdia.

Hassan knew that prolonged resistance was impossible. The country was in the grip of a famine and totally dependent on Sicilian corn; Mahdia could not hope to hold out for more than a month at the outside. Calling his people together, he laid the facts before them. Those who preferred to stay and take their chance with the Sicilians might do so; the remainder, with their wives and children and what possessions they could carry, could follow him into voluntary exile.

[1] *The Normans in the South*, pp. 298–302.

It was not till the late afternoon that the Sicilian fleet entered harbour. The few inhabitants who had elected to stay offered no opposition; and the admiral, according to the late twelfth-century historian Ibn al-Athir, found the palace in its normal state. Hassan had taken his crown jewels but had left whole rooms full of other treasures—together, it appears, with a large number of his concubines. 'George put the treasure-rooms under seal; the ladies were all collected in the castle'—after which their fate is unknown.

George's conduct was, as usual, exemplary. After only two hours of pillage—probably the minimum necessary if he were not to find a mutiny on his hands—order in Mahdia was restored. Local citizens were appointed as governors and magistrates; care was taken that no religious susceptibilities were offended; all the fugitives were invited back to the city—beasts of burden were even sent out to help them with their belongings—and offered food and money on their return. The usual *geziah* or poll-tax was insisted upon, but was deliberately kept low. Only poor Hassan seems to have suffered, though not at Sicilian hands; he was ill-advised enough to seek refuge with his cousin, who promptly confined him to an island off the coast where he languished for the next four years. His subjects, however, including the populations of Sfax and Soussa which hastily surrendered in their turn, soon settled down under their new masters; so that five and a half centuries later the North African historian Ibn Abi-Dinar was able to write:

This enemy of Allah restored both the cities of Zawila[1] and Mahdia; he advanced capital for the merchants, did good to the poor, confided the administration of justice to a *qadi* acceptable to the people, and ordered well the government of those cities . . . . Roger consolidated his dominion over the greater part of that region; levied taxes with gentleness and temperance; reconciled the hearts of the people; and governed with justice and humanity.

When George of Antioch died in the year 546 of the Hegira—that is in 1151 or 1152—'beset', so Ibn al-Athir informs us, 'with many diseases, among them piles and the stone', he left three memorials: the church of the Martorana, his beautiful seven-arched bridge over

---

[1] The principal commercial suburb of Mahdia.

the Oreto, and the African Empire. The first two still remain;[1] the third was to last little more than a decade. It was with George that it reached its apogee; perishable as it proved, he left it one of the brightest jewels in the crown of Sicily.

The old admiral's work was completed; yet he died too soon. Had he been spared for another three years he would have survived his master; and the King's subsequent reputation would have escaped its saddest, most baffling and—almost certainly—its most undeserved stain.

The life of King Roger of Sicily ends, as it began, in obscurity. Of his death we know little, save the day it occurred—26 February 1154. As to its cause, Ibn al-Athir speaks of an angina; while from Hugo Falcandus—perhaps the greatest of all the chroniclers of Norman Sicily—who begins his history with the new reign, we have only a single sentence intriguingly ascribing the King's death to 'exhaustion from his immense labours, and the onset of a premature senility through his addiction to the pleasures of the flesh, which he pursued to a point beyond that which physical health requires'. His last two years seem to have been tranquil enough. From both the Eastern and the Western Empires the immediate danger to the Kingdom had been averted, at least temporarily; his son William, already crowned, had assumed some, if not all, of the burdens of state; and Archbishop Romuald of Salerno finds so little to report between the deaths of Conrad and Eugenius and that of Roger himself, that he falls back on a description of the King's country palaces.

In order that none of the joys of land or water should be lacking to him, he caused a great sanctuary for birds and beasts to be built at a place called Favara,[2] which was full of caves and dells; its waters he

---

[1] The Oreto has now been diverted, and George's bridge now spans nothing but mountains of refuse from a nearby gypsy encampment; but it is still known as the Ponte dell' Ammiraglio. On 27 May 1860 it was the scene of the first clash between the Neapolitan forces and Garibaldi's Thousand.

[2] The word comes from the Arabic *Buheira*, meaning a lake. The Favara—also called Maredolce—is a sad place today. The great lake that used to encompass it has dried up, and there are only traces left of the wide courtyard, surrounded with arcades in the oriental style, which was the chief feature of the palace. Just one small wing remains, containing what is left of the chapel, crumbling among the lemon-groves.

stocked with every kind of fish from divers regions; nearby he built a beautiful palace. And certain hills and forests around Palermo he likewise enclosed with walls, and there he made the Parco—a pleasant and delightful spot, shaded with various trees and abounding with deer and goats and wild boar. And here also he raised a palace, to which the water was led in underground pipes from springs whence it flowed ever sweet and clear. And thus the King, being a wise and prudent man, took his pleasure from these places according to the season. In the winter and in Lent he would reside at the Favara, by reason of the great quantity of fish that were to be had there; while in the heat of the summer he would find solace at the Parco where, with a little hunting, he would relieve his mind from the cares and worries of state.

So, at least, runs the Archbishop's account in the earliest extant version of his work. Other, later manuscripts, however, include before the last two sentences a long and sinister interpolation, utterly different both in style and subject from Romuald's bucolic idyll. This tells the story of Roger's treatment of his admiral, Philip of Mahdia. It is not a pleasant episode, and it raises far more questions than it answers; but since it constitutes almost the only clue we have to the internal state of the realm in the twilight of the King's life, it is worth looking at in some detail. We must make of it what we can.

The story as it appears in this curious passage runs, very briefly, as fellows. George of Antioch had been succeeded as Admiral by a certain eunuch, Philip of Mahdia, who had risen through long service in the Curia to be one of Roger's ablest and most trusted ministers. In the summer of 1153 he was despatched with a fleet to Bône on the North African coast, whose ruler had appealed to Roger for aid against an Almohad invasion from the west. Philip captured the city without difficulty, treated it much as his predecessor would have done, and returned triumphantly to Palermo. There, after a hero's welcome, he suddenly found himself thrown into prison on charges of having secretly embraced Islam. Arraigned before the Curia, he initially protested his innocence but finally admitted his guilt. The King then made a tearful speech, pointing out that while he would willingly have pardoned the friend whom he loved any crime committed against his own person, this was an offence against God and could consequently not be forgiven; whereupon the 'counts, justiciars, barons and judges' pronounced sentence of death. Philip was tied to the hoofs of a wild horse and dragged to the palace square, where he was burnt alive.

The manifest improbability of this account, coupled with the fact of its being so obviously a later interpolation in Romuald's manuscript, might almost justify our dismissing it as a complete fabrication. Roger had grown up with Arabs; he spoke their language; he had trusted them, even more than most of his fellow-Normans, all his life. Many of the highest offices in the central government were Muslim-staffed. Both the army and the navy relied on Saracen strength. Commercial prosperity was assured by Arab merchants, treasury and mint were under the control of Arab administrators. Arabic was an official language of the state. Just as his father had turned his back on the First Crusade, so Roger had refrained from playing any active part in the Second. Was it conceivable that he should now publicly impeach his Admiral on religious grounds, opening the way to almost certain confessional strife from which his country might never recover?

Unfortunately, this strange tale cannot be ignored; for it appears, in a slightly different version, in two independent Arab sources—Ibn al-Athir, writing towards the close of the century, and Ibn Khaldun some two hundred years later. These two chroniclers both adduce a second explanation for Philip's fate—the clemency he is alleged to have shown to certain respected citizens of Bône whom he had allowed, with their families, to leave the city after its capture. This reason is plainly no more convincing than the first. Not only does it contradict the version in Romuald's history, which specifically states that Philip returned after his expedition *cum triumpho et gloria*; but it also suggests that he was punished for a policy which, as we have seen, was almost invariably followed in all Roger's North African conquests. Ibn al-Athir even mentions that the citizens concerned were 'virtuous and learned men', a fact which would make Roger's conduct even more inexplicable since we know from several writers, including Ibn al-Athir himself, that Arab intellectuals were his favourite companions.

If, then, we are to accept that the story has some basis of fact, we must look for some other explanation. It must be remembered that

Philip was not simply a Muslim; if, as his name implies, he was of Greek origin— the fact that he was surnamed 'of Mahdia' is no more indicative of his race than were the words 'of Antioch' in the name of his predecessor—it follows that he was also an apostate; and the Sicilian Kingdom, for all its tolerance, had always discouraged apostasy. We know, for example, that members of Count Roger's Saracen regiments were forbidden to receive Christian baptism,[1] and conversions in the other direction were even less popular. In isolation, such a conversion could hardly have been sufficient cause for the vicious treatment that Philip received; but it has been inferred that, in his last years, Roger may have fallen victim—like many other rulers before and since—to some form of religious persecution mania, which might have led him to take violent or unreasoning measures of this kind. The most thorough modern biography[2] suggests that he simply gave in to the Latin clergy, which is known at this time to have been working to diminish Greek influence in the Curia. But both these theories ignore the fact that nearly all the Arab writings—and there are many—which testify so warmly to the King's pro-Muslim sympathies date from after the incident. We need take only one example, the preface to Edrisi's *Book of Roger,* which bears an Arabic date corresponding to mid-January 1154—a few months after Philip's death and only a few weeks before the King's. In this Roger is referred to as 'governing his people with equity and impartiality'; later Edrisi speaks of 'the beauty of his actions, the elevation of his sentiments, the depth of his insight, the sweetness of his character and the justice of his spirit'. Some degree of hyperbole must be permitted to an oriental, writing of his royal friend and patron; but it is hardly likely that a pious Muslim could bring himself to use such terms immediately after so atrocious an *auto da fé.*

The conclusion seems inescapable. If Philip was indeed put to death for either of the reasons given, it can only have been at a time when the King was incapacitated. (The possibility of his absence we can discount. There would almost certainly be a record of it, for one thing; for another, those responsible would never have dared to

---

[1] *The Normans in the South*, pp. 275–6.
[2] Caspar, *Roger II und die Gründung der Normannisch-Sicilischen Monarchie.*

execute such a sentence on Roger's chief minister without first obtaining the royal assent.) We know that two and a half years earlier Roger, while still only in middle age, had had his son crowned as co-ruler; we know too that within months of Philip's condemnation he was dead. Hugo Falcandus's reference to a ' premature senility' might be quoted in support of this theory; alternatively the King may simply have suffered a series of strokes or heart attacks (Ibn al-Athir's 'angina') which gossiping tongues—and none were more venomous than Hugo's—ascribed to his private excesses. There seems, in any event, to have been a waning of his physical and mental faculties, which may well in the end have rendered him incapable of attending to state affairs.

Once this theory is accepted, the tragedy of Philip of Mahdia becomes credible. There remains the problem of why the interpolator of Romuald's history should have taken such pains to involve Roger personally; but his story—which, it is worth noting, contains no suggestion of criticism—seems to date from the very end of the century[1] at a time when, as we shall see, it would have been in the interests not only of the Church of Rome but even of the rulers of Sicily themselves to present the greatest of the Norman Kings rather as a stalwart defender of the Christian faith than as an example of enlightened tolerance; and the two Arab writers might well have echoed them.

Yet even Ibn al-Athir himself betrays a certain lack of conviction; for elsewhere in his history we find another passage in which Roger is portrayed in a very different light. After describing the several Arabic innovations which the King introduced into the Sicilian court ceremonial, he concludes: 'Roger treated the Muslims with honour and respect. He was at his ease with them and protected them always, even against the Franks. Therefore they loved him in return.' From an Arab historian, the King could have asked for no finer epitaph; and it is with these words that his case must ultimately rest.

King Roger was buried in Palermo Cathedral. For nine years already a great porphyry sarcophagus had awaited him in his own

[1] U. Epifanio, whose article (see bibliography) is still, after more than sixty years, the fullest and most detailed study of the affair, tentatively puts the interpolation some half a century later still.

foundation of Cefalù; but during those nine years many things had changed. Palermo had grown in importance as a metropolitan see; Cefalù was only a bishopric and, worse still, one that had been founded by the anti-Pope Anacletus. In the minds of many, and particularly to the Roman Curia, it continued to symbolise Roger's long defiance of papal claims and his determination to be master in his own house. In consequence it was still not recognised in Rome.[1] For many years to come the canons of Cefalù would indignantly assert that Palermo had been chosen only as a temporary resting-place for the King; William, they claimed, had promised that his father's body would be delivered into their care as soon as the status of their cathedral had been properly regulated. But this promise, if indeed it was ever made, was certainly never kept; and the sarcophagus stood empty for sixty years after Roger's death before being itself transferred to Palermo, there in due course to receive the mortal remains of his illustrious grandson, the Emperor Frederick II.[2]

Meanwhile a new tomb, also of porphyry, had been prepared in Palermo for the dead King.[3] The cathedral in which it was erected has been repeatedly—and disastrously—rebuilt over the centuries, but the tomb itself still occupies its original place in the south aisle, where it now stands surrounded by those of his daughter, son-in-law and grandson. Of the four, his is the least ornate, a simple, gabled structure whose only decoration is in the twin supports of white marble, each carved to represent a pair of kneeling youths on whose shoulders the sarcophagus rests, and in the lovely classicising canopy, sparkling with Cosmatesque mosaic, which probably dates from the following century. The tomb has been opened more than once, to reveal Roger's body still dressed in the royal mantle and dalmatic, on its head the tiara with pearl pendants such as we see in the mosaic portrait in the Martorana. It was the King's last gesture towards Byzantium, the Empire he hated but whose concept of monarchy he adopted for his own.

The monarchy: this above all was Roger's gift to Sicily. From his father he had inherited a county; to his son he bequeathed a kingdom

---

[1] Not until 1166 did Pope Alexander III authorise the formal consecration of Bishop Boso of Cefalù, and then only as a suffragan to the Archbishop of Messina.

[2] See p. 750.   [3] See plate.

that embraced not just the island itself and a largely desolate tract of Calabria, but the entire Italian peninsula south-east of a line drawn from the mouth of the Tronto to that of the Garigliano—all the land ever conquered by the Normans in the South. Across the sea it stretched to Malta and Gozo, and then beyond to the whole North African coast, with its hinterland, between Bône and Tripoli. On his sword were engraved the words '*Apulus et Calaber, Siculus mihi servit et Afer*'[1]. It was no more than the literal truth.

But Roger's achievements are not to be measured in terms of territory alone. No one knew better than he that if Sicily were to survive as a European power it must develop into something more than a group of widely differing ethnic, linguistic and religious communities. In the prevailing atmosphere of prosperity and success, these communities had cooperated astonishingly well; but who could tell whether they would maintain their solidarity in a crisis? The Norman baronage had proved itself faithless; what of the rest? If, for example, the island itself had to face a full-scale invasion by the Byzantines, would the Greek community stay loyal? If the Almohads, in the name of Islam, were to launch a counter-attack through North Africa and thence press northward to Sicily, could the Muslims of Syracuse, Agrigento and Catania be trusted to resist them?

Until every one of his people could be persuaded to see himself first and foremost as a subject of the King, these dangers would be very real. This task of persuasion and consolidation could only be a slow, delicate process, spread over several generations; but to it Roger had devoted his life. His father, during the first phase of the Norman-Sicilian state, had concentrated on the problem of reconciling the various elements, previously hostile, to a system of cooperation and interdependence; he himself had taken it a stage further, by giving his subjects a new pride—that of belonging to a great and prosperous nation. Of that nation's greatness, the monarchy must be the living, visible symbol. The very existence of so many laws and languages, of such a variety of religions and customs, called for a strong central authority elevated and remote enough to embrace them all. It was this consideration, quite as much as his

[1] 'The Apulian, Calabrian, Sicilian and African all obey my will.' (Radulph de Diceto, *Opuscula*, vol. II, p. 276.)

innate love of magnificence and his oriental cast of mind, that led Roger to surround himself with an almost mystic splendour which far outshone that of any of his fellow-monarchs of the West.

For with him this splendour was never more than a means to an end. The gold and the jewels, the palaces and the parks, the glinting tesserae and the gorgeous brocades, the great silken canopies held above his head—a custom borrowed from the Fatimid caliphs—on ceremonial occasions, all served a specific purpose: to glorify not Roger himself, but his ideal of what a King should be. And though few sovereigns of his day spent more lavishly, none was more conscious of the value of money. Alexander of Telese notes how he would personally go through all his exchequer accounts, how he never spent anything without making a careful record of the sum involved, how he was as scrupulous in the paying of debts as in their collection. Luxury he loved, as much as any Eastern potentate —it is not for nothing that Michele Amari, greatest of Sicilian Arabists, calls him 'a baptised Sultan'—but his Norman blood saved him from the indolence it so often brings in its train. If he enjoyed— as he had every right to enjoy—the pleasures of kingship, he never shirked its responsibilities; and such was his energy that his friend Edrisi could write in awe that 'he accomplished more in his sleep than others did in their waking day.'

He was only fifty-eight at the time of his death. Had he been granted another fifteen years, his country might have found that national identity which he had laboured so hard to create; had his new young queen borne him a son, the Hauteville dynasty might have survived the century and the whole history of South Europe would have been changed. But such speculations, though intriguing, are also pointless. For a few more years yet Norman Sicily, through a remarkable series of military and diplomatic triumphs, was to increase its influence and prestige from London to Constantinople. Two more Emperors were to be humbled, one more Pope brought to his knees. For a few more years yet the cultural brilliance of the Court of Palermo was to continue undimmed and unparalleled in Europe. But already the internal fabric of the state was showing signs of decay; and with the reign of William the Bad the Kingdom, though still golden in its splendour, embarks on its last, sad decline.

PART THREE

THE LENGTHENING SHADOWS

9

THE NEW GENERATION

King William . . . was handsome of aspect and majestic of presence, corpulent of body, sublime of stature, haughty and greedy for honours; a conqueror on land and sea; in his Kingdom more feared than loved. Though he gave much thought to the acquisition of wealth, he dispensed it with some reluctance. Those who were faithful to him he raised up to riches and honours; those who betrayed him he would condemn to torture, or else banish from the Kingdom. Most punctilious in attending the Holy Office, he held all ecclesiastical persons in the highest respect.

Romuald, Archbishop of Salerno

THE practice of distinguishing reigning monarchs by some characteristic epithet as well as by a bare Roman numeral was never really popular in England. The Unready, the Confessor, the Conqueror and the Lion-Heart are the only four royal sobriquets in our history which will unmistakably identify their bearers. In Europe, however, throughout the Middle Ages and beyond, circlets sparkle round the heads of Drunkards, Stammerers and Devils, of Philosophers, Navigators and Fowlers; of the Handsome and the Bald, the Quarrelsome and the Cruel, the Debonair, the Simple and the Fat. Most intriguing of all, perhaps—though himself uncrowned—was the father of the Byzantine Emperor Romanus I, universally known to his contemporaries as Theophylact the Unbearable. And yet, in the whole limping, simpering, swaggering pageant, two men only have been called upon to carry through eternity the most starkly uncompromising label of them all—the Bad. One was King Charles II of Navarre; the other was King William I of Sicily.

The new King did not altogether deserve his nickname. It was not even given him till some two hundred years after his death—

and was principally due to two misfortunes which he never managed to overcome. The first was his father, Roger II, by whom he was outshone; the second was the principal chronicler of his reign, who vilifies him at every opportunity. The true identity of the author of the *Historia de Regno Sicilie*, though it remains one of the most perplexing enigmas of the Norman Kingdom, lies beyond the scope of this book;[1] we know him only as Hugo Falcandus, which was almost certainly not his name and was indeed only attached to him four centuries later. All we can say is that he was a writer of sophistication and polish, about whom no less an authority than Edward Gibbon could say that 'his narrative is rapid and perspicuous, his style bold and eloquent, his observation keen. He has studied mankind and feels like a man.' Alas, there were two virtues he did not possess. As a man he lacked charity; as a historian, accuracy. His pages are a grisly succession of plots and counterplots, of intrigues and assassinations and poisonings—a tale compared with which the chronicles of the house of Borgia read like an object-lesson in moral rectitude. He sees evil lurking everywhere. There is scarcely an action to which he does not ascribe some sinister motive, scarcely a character who does not emerge as a fiend incarnate. His most lethal venom of all, however, he keeps for the King.

William's appearance, too, was against him. No contemporary portraits survive, apart from those on coins; but a monkish chronicle[2] of the time writes that he was a huge man, 'whose thick black beard lent him a savage and terrible aspect and filled many people with fear'. His physical strength was herculean. He could separate two linked horseshoes with his bare hands; once, we are told, when a fully-laden pack horse stumbled and fell when crossing a bridge, he picked it up unaided and set it on its feet again. Such characteristics must have served him in good stead on the battlefield, where he showed unfailing courage and, to use a cliché of the time, was always to be found where the fighting was thickest; but they can hardly have added to his popularity.

[1] See Notes on the Principal Sources, p. 765.

[2] The *Chronica S. Mariae de Ferraria*, another enigmatic work which, it has been suggested, may be indirectly attributable to the author of Falcandus's history. See Evelyn Jamison, *Admiral Eugenius of Sicily*, pp. 278–97.

If, however, William outstripped his father in physique and military aptitude, he fell far short of him in political ability. Like all the Hautevilles before him, Roger II had always had an immense appetite for work. There was no governmental task to which he could not—and, at one time or another, did not—turn his hand. His son was the reverse. Born with three elder brothers between him and the throne, William had received little of that early training in politics and statecraft that had given Duke Roger, Tancred and Alfonso positions of high responsibility while still in their teens. He had never been groomed for greatness, and when their premature deaths thrust greatness upon him at the age of thirty, it caught him unprepared. Lazy and pleasure-loving, he was to devote the greater part of his time to those occupations with which Roger had only employed his rare hours of relaxation—discussing art and science with the intellectuals whom he kept at the court, or dallying with his women in the palaces which, in the words of one traveller, ringed Palermo like a necklace—the Favara, the Parco, possibly a summer pavilion at Mimnermo,[1] and, later, in his own new and splendid palace of the Zisa. Even more than his father, he was an oriental; the East had entered into his very soul. Married in early youth to Margaret, daughter of King Garcia IV Ramirez of Navarre, he appeared after his succession to take little interest in her or in the four sons she bore him. His life was more like a sultan's than a king's, and his character embodied that same combination of sensuality and fatalism that has stamped so many eastern rulers. He never took a decision if he could avoid it, never tackled a problem if there was the faintest chance that, given long enough, it might solve itself. Once goaded into action, however, he would pursue his objectives with ferocious energy—if only, notes Chalandon a little unkindly, in order to return as quickly as possible to more congenial pursuits.

Unlike his father, then, William tended to leave the day-to-day business of the Kingdom to his ministers, nearly all of them profes-

[1] So, at least, the name appears in the early editions of Falcandus; this, however, is probably a corruption of Minenium, from the original Arabic name of *Al-Menani*. The building—what remains of it—is now known as the Palazzo dell' Uscibene, in the modern village of Altarello. The original structure probably dates back to Saracen times, but the present decoration of sea-shells in stucco is, it need hardly be said, a comparatively recent addition.

sional clerks and civil servants of the middle class who owed their position and advancement to the King alone and whose loyalty was consequently beyond question. Even in their selection he seems to have given himself the minimum of trouble; with only two exceptions that we know of, he simply confirmed the chief functionaries of his father's reign in their existing ranks and offices.

Of these two exceptions one was an Englishman, Thomas Brown. The son or nephew of a certain William Brown, or Le Brun, a clerk in the service of King Henry I, he had come to Sicily in about 1130 when still little more than a boy—probably in the company and as the *protégé* of Robert of Selby. We first hear of him in 1137, and from that time on his name appears regularly in the official documents that have come down to us.[1] Throughout Roger's reign Thomas seems to have enjoyed his confidence and favour; there is even reason to believe that he personally drafted the foundation charter for the Palatine Chapel in 1140. But on William's accession, for reasons unhappily obscure, he lost his high office and returned to England, where he became King's Almoner under Henry II.[2]

Though we cannot be sure, it seems more than probable that Thomas's abrupt departure from Sicily was in fact occasioned not by the King himself but by his new Emir of Emirs, Maio of Bari—whose elevation, besides being the only other important change effected by William in the ranks of his advisers, proved to be one of the most fateful acts of his entire reign. It came as no surprise. Maio had been at least ten years in the royal service and had already reached the rank of Chancellor when William singled him out to succeed the ill-fated Philip of Mahdia in the Kingdom's supreme administrative post. Son of a prosperous oil merchant and judge in Bari, he had received a thorough classical education in his youth and was well able to hold his own in the rarefied intellectual society

---

[1] It is a sign of Thomas's importance—and illustrative too of the polyglot Sicilian administration—that he should figure in the Latin, Greek and Arabic archives. Thus in 1137 we find Roger II granting a charter to the monks of Monte Vergine *per manum magistri Thome capellani regis*; six years later, μάστρο Θωμᾶ τοῦ Βρόννου is named as one of the adjudicators of a boundary dispute; while in 1149 he appears in the disguise of قائد برون, Caïd Brun, a member of the royal Diwan with a secretary called Othman.

[2] *Dialogus de Scaccario*, Stubbs, *Select Charters*, Oxford, 1870.

of the court. He was moreover a discerning patron of the arts and sciences and he has even left us with one work of his own, an 'Exposition of the Lord's Prayer', which, if not an achievement of any outstanding individuality, shows that he was admirably grounded in scholastic philosophy as well as in the works of the early Fathers of the Church. But above all Maio was a statesman; and it was he, rather than his master, who was to shape Sicilian policy for the first six years of the new reign. Stern, pitiless, unswerving in the pursuit of policies which he believed to be justified, he never feared unpopularity—indeed, there were occasions when he seemed deliberately to be courting it. In consequence, though he has been harshly dealt with by Hugo Falcandus and others, there can be no doubt of his political acumen. But for him, William would have been lucky to keep his throne more than a matter of months.

For ten years now the country had enjoyed internal peace, but many of the barons, especially in Apulia, were still unreconciled to the Kingdom; and memories of Roger's savage repression were beginning to fade. Others, who had decided to throw in their lot with the King, had gravitated to the capital in the hopes of obtaining power or preferment but had been disappointed. Roger's mistrust of his compatriots had lasted to the end of his life. These semi-literate Norman barons, arrogant, self-seeking, talking no language but their own, were hopelessly unqualified for positions of responsibility in a highly centralised state; and their record as vassals was not such as to encourage the granting to them of any large fiefs on the island. They had therefore been obliged to watch while Greeks, Italians and Saracens—men often of humble birth, and of races which they considered vastly inferior to their own—rose to eminence and distinction; and, as they watched, so their dissatisfaction grew. Roger, after years of struggle, had ultimately earned their grudging respect; but now that his iron hand had gone, the threat of further trouble could not be far distant; and both William and Maio knew it.

To know it, however, was not to yield to pressure. Maio had been trained by Roger; no one saw more clearly the danger of allowing any part of the Sicilian government to fall into the hands of the feudal aristocracy. He excluded them as mercilessly as ever, drawing his staff from men of his own class and background, the prosperous professional bourgeoisie, both Italian and Arab. Greeks he seems to have been less ready to employ in positions of high authority. Being himself an Italian from the largely Greek city of Bari, he may have been prejudiced against them from childhood; but in Sicily, as we have seen, their influence was now on the wane—Maio's own elevation to an office which had hitherto been a Greek preserve is a case in point, and cannot have increased his popularity among the Greeks of Palermo. Besides, relations with Byzantium were steadily worsening; and it is hardly to be wondered at that, in the circumstances, the Chancellor should have given preference elsewhere.

Meanwhile the immigration of able men from western Europe continued to increase, and with it the power of the Latin Church. Even more than the Norman aristocracy, its hierarchy had yielded to the magnetic pull of Palermo; by the time of William's accession, most of the Sicilian bishops and a good many of the incumbents of mainland sees were in semi-permanent residence at court. This absenteeism was later to reach such scandalous proportions as to require papal intervention; but at the time it aroused little comment and Maio, who saw the Church as one of his principal supports against the baronage, seems if anything to have encouraged it. It also brought to the capital a number of highly capable clerics, among them two more Englishmen destined to play vital parts in Sicilian affairs —Richard Palmer, Bishop-elect of Syracuse, and Walter of the Mill, formerly Archdeacon of Cefalù and later Archbishop of Palermo. But it led to the growth in the Sicilian body politic of an increasingly influential ecclesiastical party which could not fail to do the country harm. By its very nature this party was bound to be intolerant alike of Orthodoxy and Islam, impatient of the whole permissive structure on which the Kingdom was based. Already, in its hounding of Philip of Mahdia, it had dealt that structure its first damaging blow; in succeeding years further blows would follow until Norman Sicily itself, its political and philosophical foundations shattered, collapsed in ruins to the ground.

Thus, when William the Bad received his second coronation at the hands of Archbishop Hugh of Palermo on Easter Sunday, 4 April 1154, the formal acclamation of his assembled vassals might have struck a sensitive ear with a slightly hollow ring. But for the moment the vassals, discontented as they might be, could be kept at least partially under control. The immediate danger to the Kingdom came not from them but from its three old enemies: the Western Empire, Byzantium and the Papacy. It was William's misfortune that his reign should have coincided with the reigns of two Emperors of outstanding ability and the pontificates of the two greatest Popes of the twelfth century. It was his good luck that his enemies—who, united, would have been invincible—mistrusted each other even more than they feared and hated him.

To be sure, they had good reason to do so. The young Frederick Barbarossa, now about thirty-two years old, seemed to his German contemporaries the very nonpareil of Teutonic chivalry. Tall and broad-shouldered, attractive rather than handsome, he had eyes that twinkled so brightly under his thick mop of reddish-brown hair that, according to one chronicler who knew him well,[1] he always seemed on the point of laughter. But beneath this easy-going exterior there lurked a will of steel, an utter dedication to a single objective. 'My wish,' he wrote succinctly to the Pope, 'is to restore to the Roman Empire its ancient greatness and splendour.' It was a conception that left no room for compromise, and, in particular, it ruled out the possibility of any real alliance with Constantinople. Since 1148 Manuel Comnenus had made no secret of the fact that he considered South Italy to be Byzantine territory. Conrad, who knew how much he needed Manuel's friendship, had been prepared to agree to a partition, and on his deathbed he had implored his nephew to pursue the same policy; but to the young Barbarossa such an idea was unthinkable. Barely a year after his accession he had signed a treaty with the Pope at Constance, by the terms of which it was agreed that Byzantium would be allowed no concessions on Italian territory; if its Emperor were to attempt to seize any by force, he would be expelled. The brief honeymoon between the two Empires was at an end.

To Manuel, Conrad's death therefore meant a good deal more than the loss of a friend and ally. Occurring as it did on the eve of the

---

[1] Acerbus Morena, *podestà* of Lodi, who with his father Otto was one of the first lay historians of North Italy.

great campaign that was to restore to Constantinople its long-lost Italian provinces, it also spelt a serious political reverse—just how serious, Frederick's behaviour was soon to show. But though Manuel quickly saw that he could no longer expect any help from the Western Empire, he was unaware of the precise terms of the Treaty of Constance and still believed in the possibility of some sort of Italian partition. One thing only was clear—that whatever he was to regain he would have to fight for. If, as seemed likely, the Germans marched against William of Sicily, it was essential that a strong Byzantine force should be present, ready to protect the legitimate rights of the Eastern Empire. If they did not, then he proposed to take the initiative on his own. When, therefore, in the early summer of 1154, he received ambassadors from Sicily offering, in return for a peace treaty, the restitution of all Greek prisoners and all the spoils from George of Antioch's Theban expedition, he refused outright. Such an offer could only mean that the new King was afraid of an imperial invasion; if he was afraid, he was weak; if he was weak, he would be defeated.

The mutual suspicions that divided the two Empires, together with their common hatred for the Sicilian Kingdom, were fully shared by the Papacy. Eugenius's successor, Anastasius IV, was old and ineffectual, concerned chiefly with his own self-glorification; but he did not last long, and when, in the last days of 1154, his body was laid to rest in the gigantic porphyry sarcophagus that had previously held the remains of the Empress Helena—transferred, on his own orders, to a modest urn in the Ara Coeli a few months previously [1]— he was succeeded by a man of very different calibre: Adrian IV, the only Englishman ever to occupy the Throne of St Peter.

Nicholas Breakspear was born around 1115 at Abbot's Langley in Hertfordshire, at that time a dependency of the monastery of St Albans. While still a student he had moved to France, and later— after a short and not particularly successful period as prior of St Rufus, near Arles—to Rome. There, thanks to his eloquence, ability and outstanding good looks, he had soon caught the attention of Pope Eugenius. Fortunately for him, the Pope was a convinced

[1] The sarcophagus is now in the Sala a Croce Greca of the Vatican Museum. Helena's remains, however, have disappeared without trace.

Anglophile; he once told John of Salisbury that he found the English admirably fitted to perform any task they turned their hand to, and thus to be preferred to all other races—except, he added, when frivolity got the better of them. Frivolity, however, does not seem to have been one of Nicholas's failings. Early in 1152 he was sent as Papal Legate to Norway, there to reorganise the Church throughout Scandinavia. Two years later he was back again in Rome, his mission accomplished with such distinction that, on Anastasius's death the following December, the forceful, energetic Englishman was unanimously elected to succeed him.

It was a wise choice, for energy and force were desperately needed. At the time of Adrian's accession Frederick Barbarossa had already crossed the Alps to his first Italian campaign. On his arrival in Rome he would be sure to demand his imperial coronation; but even if he were to receive it, there was little likelihood that the Pope would ever be able to trust him as an ally. Indeed, with his known absolutist views, Frederick was unlikely to prove anything but a constant anxiety to the Holy See. Another, separate invasion was threatened from the Byzantine East. In the South, William I's Sicily might be going through a critical stage, but was still outwardly as strong and prosperous as ever. Worst of all was the situation in Rome itself. Encouraged by the tractability of Eugenius and Anastasius, the Senate had grown still more arrogant; meanwhile its position had been further reinforced, and the Pope's own spiritual authority dangerously weakened, by the teachings of a monk from Lombardy whose influence, skilfully built up over the past decade, had by now made him the virtual master of Rome.

His name was Arnold of Brescia. In his youth he had studied in the Schools of Paris—probably under Abelard at Notre Dame—where he had been thoroughly imbued with the principles of the new scholasticism, essentially a movement away from the old mystical approach to spiritual matters, and towards a spirit of logical, rationalistic enquiry. To the mediaeval Papacy, radical ideas of this sort would have seemed quite subversive enough; but Arnold combined with them a still more unwelcome feature—a passionate hatred for the temporal power of the Church. For him the State was, and must always be, supreme; the civil law, based on the laws of

Ancient Rome, must prevail over the canon; the Pope, for his part, should divest himself of all worldly pomp, renounce his powers and privileges, and revert to the poverty and simplicity of the early Fathers. Only thus could the Church re-establish contact with the humble masses among its flock. As John of Salisbury wrote:

Arnold himself was frequently to be heard on the Capitol and in various assemblies of the people. He had already publicly denounced the Cardinals, maintaining that their College, beset as it was with pride, avarice, hypocrisy and shame, was not the Church of God but a house of commerce and a den of thieves, men who took the place of the scribes and Pharisees among Christian peoples. Even the Pope himself was other than what he professed; rather than an apostolic shepherd of souls, he was a man of blood who maintained his authority by fire and the sword, a tormenter of churches and oppressor of the innocent, whose only actions were for the gratification of his lust and for the emptying of other men's coffers in order that his own might be filled. . . . There could be no toleration of one who sought only to impose a yoke of servitude on Rome, seat of Empire, fountain of liberty and mistress of the world.[1]

Naturally, the Papacy had fought back. Naturally, too, it had used the Abbot of Clairvaux—to whose unquestioning, unwavering faith Arnold's views were anathema—as its champion. In consequence, as early as 1140 Arnold had been condemned, together with his old master Abelard, at the Council of Sens and had been expelled from France. By 1146, however, he was back in Rome; and the Roman Senate, fired by his blazing piety and recognising in his ideas the spiritual counterpart of its own republican aspirations, had welcomed him with open arms.

Pope Eugenius, another ascetic, possibly out of some secret sympathy for Arnold, had allowed him to return to the capital; and Anastasius, *vieillard pacifique et conciliant* as Chalandon describes him, had turned a deaf ear to his thunderings. But Adrian was of a different stamp. When, on his accession, he found himself confined by Arnold's supporters to St Peter's and the Leonine City, he had at first merely ordered the agitator to leave Rome; but when, predictably, Arnold took no notice and instead allowed his followers to attack and

[1] John of Salisbury, *Historia Pontificalis*.

grievously wound the venerable Cardinal Guido of S. Pudenziana as he was walking down the Via Sacra on his way to the Vatican, the Pope played his trump card. For the first time in the history of Christendom, Rome itself was laid under an interdict.

It was an act of breath-taking courage. A foreigner, who had been Pope for only a few weeks, knew the city and its increasingly xenophobic inhabitants hardly at all and was able to rely on little or no popular support, had dared by a single decree to close all the churches of Rome. Exceptions were made for the baptism of infants and the absolution of the dying; otherwise all ceremonies and sacraments were alike forbidden. No masses could be said, no marriages solemnised; dead bodies might not even be buried in consecrated ground. In the Middle Ages, when religion still constituted an integral part of every man's life, the effect of such a moral blockade was immeasurable. Besides, Easter was approaching. The prospect of the greatest feast of the Christian year passing uncelebrated was bleak enough; without the annual influx of pilgrims, one of the principal sources of the city's revenue, it was bleaker still. For a little while the Romans held out; but by the Wednesday of Holy Week they could bear it no longer and marched on the Capitol. The Senators saw that they were beaten. Arnold and his followers were expelled; the interdict was lifted; the church bells pealed out their message; and on Sunday, as he had always intended to do, Pope Adrian IV celebrated Easter at the Lateran.

Frederick Barbarossa, meanwhile, kept the feast at Pavia, where on the same day he was crowned with the traditional Iron Crown of Lombardy. Like more than one Emperor before him, he had been astonished at the intensity of republican feeling in the cities and towns of North Italy, by their determination to cast off the old feudal obligations in favour of civic independence and communal self-government; and he had considered it his duty—at the cost of some delay to his original plans—to give a further demonstration of imperial strength. Milan, the perennial focus of revolt, was too strong for him, but her ally Tortona had looked an easy victim. The little town had made a heroic stand against the combined forces of the Empire, Pavia and Montferrat; but when, after two months' siege, the wells ran dry and the inhabitants were parched into surrender, they had paid dearly for their heroism. Though their lives were spared, their city had been razed until not one stone was left on another.

After Easter, however, Frederick delayed no longer. His descent through Tuscany was so fast that to the Roman Curia it seemed positively threatening. The fate of Tortona was by now common knowledge throughout Italy; Henry IV's treatment of Gregory VII seventy years before had not been forgotten; and several of the older cardinals could still remember how, in 1111, Henry V had laid hands upon Pope Paschal II in St Peter's itself and held him two months a prisoner until he capitulated. In all the recent reports now circulating about the new King of the Romans, there was nothing to suggest that he would not be fully capable of similar conduct. No wonder the Curia began to feel alarm.

Hurriedly, Adrian sent two of his cardinals north to the imperial camp. They found it at S. Quirico near Siena, and were cordially received. Then, as an earnest of his goodwill, they asked Frederick for help in laying hands on Arnold of Brescia who, after wandering for some weeks round the Campagna, had at last taken refuge with some local barons. Frederick readily agreed; he detested Arnold's radical views almost as much as the Pope himself and welcomed this new opportunity to show his power. Sending a body of troops to the castle in question, he had one of the barons seized and held as a hostage until Arnold himself should be delivered. The fugitive was immediately given up to the papal authorities; and the cardinals, reassured, applied themselves to their next task— to make arrangements for the first, critical interview between Pope and King.

The meeting was fixed for 9 June at Campo Grasso, near Sutri. It began auspiciously enough with Adrian, followed by his bishops and cardinals and escorted by a great company of German barons sent forward by Frederick to greet him, riding in solemn procession to the imperial camp. But now trouble began. At this point, according to custom, the King should have advanced to lead in the Pope's horse by the bridle and to hold the stirrup while its rider dismounted; he did not do so. For a moment Adrian seemed to hesitate. Then, dismounting by himself, he walked slowly across to the throne which had been prepared for him and sat down. Now at last Frederick stepped forward, kissed the Pope's feet and rose to receive the traditional kiss of peace in return; but this time it was Adrian who held back. The King, he pointed out, had denied him a service which, in reverence for the apostles Peter and Paul, his predecessors had always rendered to the Supreme Pontiff. Until this omission was rectified, there could be no kiss of peace.

Frederick objected that it was no part of his duty to act as a papal groom; and all that day and the next the dispute continued. Adrian would not be shaken. He knew that what appeared on the surface to be a minor point of protocol concealed in reality something infinitely more important—a public act of defiance that struck at the very root of the relationship between Empire and Papacy. Against this knowledge explanations and arguments were of no avail. Suddenly and surprisingly, Frederick gave in. He ordered his camp to be moved a little further south, to the neighbourhood of the town of Monterosi; and there, on the morning of 11 June, the events of two days before were restaged. The King advanced to meet the Pope, led in his horse by the bridle for the distance, we are told, of a stone's throw; then, firmly holding the stirrup, he helped him to dismount. Once again Adrian settled himself on the throne that awaited him; the kiss of peace was duly bestowed; and conversations began.

Adrian and Frederick would never entirely trust one another; but the incident had somehow increased their mutual respect and the ensuing discussions seem to have been amicable enough. The terms agreed at Constance were confirmed. Neither party would enter into separate negotiations with William, Manuel or the Roman Senate. Frederick for his part would defend all legitimate papal interests, while Adrian in return would excommunicate all enemies of the Empire who, after three warnings, persisted in their opposition. Reassured of each other's intentions, the two rode on together towards Rome.

From the side of the Papacy there was now no longer any objection to the imperial coronation.[1] This ceremony, on the other hand, had

[1] One chronicler (Helmold, *Chronica Slavorum*) maintains that Frederick had sent ambassadors from Tuscany to Adrian with a formal request for the

not been performed since the establishment of the Roman Commune; how would Rome itself now greet its Emperor-to-be? It was an open question, and Frederick's recent move against Arnold of Brescia had made it more problematical still. But he and Adrian were not kept long in suspense. While they were still some distance from the city they were met by a deputation sent out by the Senate to greet them and to make clear the conditions on which they would be received.

Bishop Otto of Freising, probably an eyewitness, has left us what appears to be a verbatim record of what took place. The dialogue began with a long set speech by the leader of the Roman deputation. Though not by any means hostile, it was bombastic and patronising; it suggested that Rome alone had made Frederick's Empire what it was and that consequently the new Emperor would do well to consider his moral obligations to the city—obligations which apparently included making a sworn guarantee of its future liberty and an *ex gratia* payment of five thousand pounds of gold.

The spokesman was still in full spate when Frederick interrupted him. Speaking, as Otto neatly puts it, 'without preparation but not unprepared'[1], and with 'his usual modest charm of expression', he pointed out that all Rome's ancient glory and traditions had now passed, with the Empire itself, to Germany. He had come not to receive gifts from the Romans but to claim what was rightfully his. Naturally, he would defend Rome as necessary; but he saw no need for formal guarantees and had no intention of giving any. As for gifts of money, he would bestow them as and where he pleased.

Frederick's quiet assurance took the ambassadors off their guard. In reply to enquiries whether they had anything more to say, they could only stammer that they must return to the capital for instructions; with that, they took their leave. As soon as they were gone, Pope and King held an urgent consultation. Adrian, with his experience of the Roman Senate, had no doubt that trouble was to be

coronation; and that they had received the following reply: 'Let him first regain for St Peter the land of Apulia, which William the Sicilian holds by force; then let him come and be crowned by us.' It seems improbable. Adrian was not likely to dispute imperial claims to Apulia at such a time; and he certainly did not insist on this condition at the subsequent negotiations.

[1] *Ex inproviso non inprovise.*

Palermo: the Palatine Chapel from the high altar

Palermo, the Palatine Chapel: ambo and paschal candlestick

Palermo: S. Giovanni degli Eremiti

Palermo, the Martorana: George of Antioch before the Virgin

ΡΟΓΕΡΙΟΣ ΡΗΞ   ΙC   Χ

Palermo, the Martorana: King Roger II crowned by Christ

Palermo Cathedral: tomb of Roger II

Palermo: S. Cataldo (tower of the Martorana at left)

Palermo, Royal Palace: the Pisan Tower

Palermo, the Zisa: interior.

Palermo, Royal Palace: the so-called *Sala di Ruggero*

Monreale: the view to the north-west from the cloister

Monreale: St Thomas Becket

Monreale: William the Good crowned by Christ

Monreale: fountain in the cloister

Monreale – Normans on capital in the cloister

Tancred—the Monkey King—rejoices at the sight of his rival, Roger of Andria, in prison (Peter of Eboli MS.)

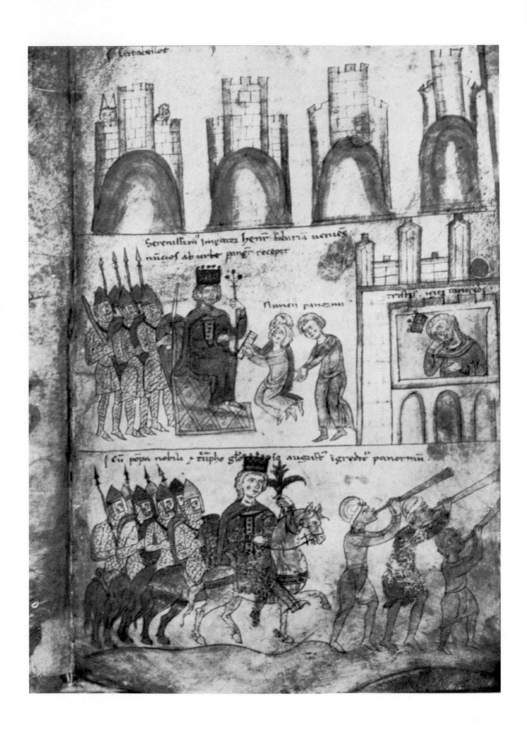

Henry VI receives emissaries from Palermo while Queen Sibylla bewails her fallen crown. Below: Henry makes his triumphal entry into Palermo. (Peter of Eboli MS.)

expected. He advised the immediate despatch of a body of troops, to be accompanied by Cardinal Octavian of Monticelli, to occupy the Leonine City[1] by night and hold it against all adversaries. Even with this precaution, he pointed out, the danger would not be entirely averted. If they wanted to avoid trouble, he and Frederick would have to move quickly.

The date was Friday, 17 June. Such was the urgency of the situation that the two agreed not even to wait for the following Sunday as they would normally have done. Instead, at dawn on Saturday, Frederick rode down from Monte Mario and entered the Leonine City, which his troops had already surrounded, by the Golden Gate near St Peter's. The Pope, who had arrived an hour or two previously, was awaiting him on the steps of the basilica. They entered it together, a throng of German knights following behind. Adrian himself celebrated Mass; and there, over the tomb of the Apostle, he hurriedly girded the sword of St Peter to Frederick's side and laid the imperial crown on his head.

Cardinal Boso Breakspear, Adrian's nephew and biographer, tells us that at this point the German knights thronging St Peter's raised so deafening a cheer that it seemed as though a very thunderbolt had fallen from heaven; but there was no time for any further celebration. As soon as the ceremony was done the Emperor, with the imperial crown still on his head, rode back to his camp outside the walls, his huge retinue following on foot. The Pope meanwhile took refuge in the Vatican to await developments.

It was still only nine o'clock in the morning; and the Senate was assembling on the Capitol to decide how best to prevent the coronation when the news arrived that it had already taken place. Furious to find that they had been outwitted and outmanoeuvred, they sprang to arms; soon a huge mob was pressing across the Ponte S. Angelo into the Leonine City while another, having crossed the river further downstream at the island, advanced northwards through Trastevere. The day was growing hotter. The Germans, tired by their forced march through the night and the excitement of the past few hours,

[1] This comprised that part of Rome on the right bank of the Tiber, including the Vatican, St Peter's and the Castel Sant' Angelo, which was fortified by Pope Leo IV in the ninth century, immediately after the sack of the city by the Saracens.

wanted to relax—to sleep and to celebrate. Instead, they received the
order to prepare at once for battle. Had not their Emperor sworn,
that very morning and before them all, to defend the Church of
Christ? Already its safety was threatened. For the second time that
day Frederick entered Rome, but he wore his coronation robes no
longer. This time he had his armour on.

All afternoon and evening the battle raged between the Emperor
of the Romans and his subjects; night had fallen before the imperial
troops had driven the last of the insurgents back across the bridges.
Losses had been heavy on both sides. For the German casualties we
have no reliable figures; but Otto of Freising reports that among the
Romans almost a thousand were slain or drowned in the Tiber,
and another six hundred taken captive. As for the wounded, he had
given up trying to count them. The Senate had paid a high price for
its arrogance.

And yet, if the Romans had revealed themselves as poor diplomats, they had at least proved brave fighters; and it must be admitted that they had good grounds for resentment. Previous
Emperors arriving for their consecration had been accustomed to
show the city and its institutions at least some marks of respect—
swearing obedience to its laws and submitting themselves to the
votes and acclamations of its people. Frederick had done none of
these things. He had ignored the Romans entirely—and he had done
so at a moment in their history when their Commune had given them
a new sense of civic pride, a new awareness of their past greatness and
the splendour of their heritage. To argue that they had treated him
with singular tactlessness and thus to a large extent brought their
punishment on themselves was neither here nor there; Frederick's
initial treatment of Pope Adrian at Sutri hardly suggested that even
in other circumstances he would have been much more amenable.

The Emperor too had bought his crown dearly. His victory had
not even gained him entrance into the ancient city, for the sun rose
the next morning to show all the Tiber bridges blocked and the
gates of the city barricaded. Neither he nor his army was prepared
for a siege; the heat of the Italian summer, which for a century and a
half had consistently undermined the morale of successive invading
armies, was once again beginning to take its toll with outbreaks of

malaria and dysentery among his men. As Otto feelingly describes it, 'all the air round about became heavy with the mists that rose from the swamps nearby and from the caverns and ruined places about the City: an atmosphere deadly and noxious for mortals to breathe.' The only sensible course was to withdraw, and—since the Vatican was clearly no longer safe for the Papacy—to take Pope and Curia with him. On 19 June he struck camp again and led his army up into the Sabine Hills. A month later he was heading back towards Germany, leaving Adrian powerless at Tivoli.

Although the Pope had been careful, after his first meeting, to allow no open breach with the Emperor, he had good reason to feel resentful. At considerable risk to his own safety he had performed the coronation required of him; he had received little in return. Since leaving Rome he had done his utmost to persuade Frederick to keep to his original plan and march without further ado against William of Sicily; but, though Frederick personally would have been willing enough, his ailing German barons would have none of it. Promises were readily given to return in the near future, when a healthier and more numerous imperial force would bring Romans and Sicilians alike to heel; meanwhile the Pope was left, isolated and in exile, to get on as best he could.

The story of the coronation of Frederick Barbarossa is almost told, but not quite; for, apart from the Emperor who was crowned and the Pope who crowned him, there is a third character who, although he was not even present in Rome on that dreadful day, influenced the course of events as much as either of them. Arnold of Brescia was one of the first of those astonishing popular leaders whom Italy has thrown up at intervals all through her history—fanatics of genius who, by the sheer magic of their personalities, gain absolute and un-questioned domination over their fellow-men. Sometimes, as with Arnold himself or with Savonarola three hundred years later, this domination has a spiritual basis; sometimes, as with Cola di Rienzo, it is inspired by a historic sense of mission; occasionally, as Mussolini showed, it can be political through and through. One characteristic, however, these men have all had in common. All have failed, and have paid for their failure with their lives.

No record exists to tell us exactly when or where Arnold suffered his execution. We know only the manner in which he met his death. Condemned by a spiritual tribunal on charges of heresy and rebellion, he remained firm to the end and walked calmly to the scaffold without a trace of fear; as he knelt to make his last confession, we read that the executioners themselves could not restrain their tears. They hanged him none the less; then they cut him down and burned the body. Finally, in order to ensure that no relics should be left for veneration by the people, they threw the ashes into the Tiber.

For a martyr, misguided or not, there could be no greater honour.

IO

THE GREEK OFFENSIVE

The Emperor Manuel often held that it was an easy matter for him to win over the peoples of the East by gifts of money or by force of arms, but that over those of the West he could never count on gaining a similar advantage; for they are formidable in numbers, indomitable in pride, cruel in character, rich in possessions and inspired by an inveterate hatred for the Empire.

Nicetas Choniates, *History of Manuel Comnenus*, VII, i

OF the many German armies which, in the past century and a half, had marched down into South Italy to restore imperial power in the peninsula, none had ever remained there more than a few months. The Emperors who led them had soon discovered that even if this enervating, pestiferous land were technically theirs, they for their part could never belong to it. Here they would always be strangers, and unwelcome strangers at that; and their men, toiling along in their heavy homespun under a torrid Apulian sky, sickened by the unaccustomed food and plagued, even more than they knew, by the clouds of insects that whined incessantly about their heads, felt much the same. Nearly all, both the leaders and the led, longed for the day when they would once again be able to see a firm mountain barrier rising between themselves and the scene of their sufferings.

Frederick Barbarossa was an exception. He would have been genuinely glad to remain in the South and deal with William of Sicily if he could only have carried his knights with him; but they were resolved to return at once to Germany, and he knew that he must not impose his will too far. This enforced withdrawal saddened and frustrated him; and it can have been little consolation that when he reached Ancona—after the largely gratuitous destruction of

545

Spoleto on the way—he was met by three emissaries from Constantinople, led by the erstwhile governor of Thessalonica, Michael Palaeologus, bringing him rich presents from their master and promising him considerable subsidies if he would change his mind. Frederick kept them waiting some time for his answer; even at this late stage it was worth making one last attempt to inject a little of his own spirit into his followers. But the German barons had had enough; and after a few days the Emperor was obliged to admit to the Greeks that there was nothing he could do.

Palaeologus and his companions were not unduly upset by the news. Strategically it might have been useful to have the German army fighting their battles for them; diplomatically, however, the situation would be very much simpler without the involvement of the Western Empire, particularly as there was by now no shortage of other, more manageable allies closer to hand—King William's rebellious Apulian vassals. They too had put their trust in Frederick and had been disappointed by his hasty departure; but they felt no special ties of loyalty to him any more than to anyone else. Now that he had let them down, they were perfectly ready to accept subsidies and support from Constantinople instead.

All that year, Apulian resistance to the new King of Sicily had been stiffening. This can partly be attributed to the expectation of Frederick Barbarossa's appearance on the scene in what was hoped to be fire and wrath; but much of it was also due to the spirit and determination of a new leader—Robert de Bassonville, Count of Loritello. Robert was the very prototype of the dissatisfied Norman aristocrat. As first cousin of the King—he was the son of Roger II's sister Judith—he considered himself exceptionally qualified for high office; Hugo Falcandus even suggests, with his usual malice, that Roger had considered making him his successor instead of William. Thus he viciously resented the pre-eminence of Maio and the Emir's continued discrimination against the landed nobility. The gift of the distant County of Loritello, which William had bestowed on him at the time of his own accession, had done nothing to mollify him; almost at once, he had begun stirring up discontent among the neighbouring barons. William for his part cherished no delusions about Robert's loyalty. Already in the early spring of 1155, on his first visit to Salerno as King, he had refused to receive him into his presence; and on his return to Sicily soon after Easter he had sent instructions to his Viceroy, Asclettin, to have the Count of Loritello arrested forthwith. Robert, however, had escaped to the Abruzzi, where he had spent the summer gathering his forces—and where he now heard, for the first time, of Michael Palaeologus's arrival in the peninsula.

The two met at Viesti, and at once agreed to join forces. Each was able to provide just what the other lacked. Palaeologus had a fleet of ten ships, seemingly limitless funds and the power to call when necessary on further reinforcements from across the Adriatic. Robert could claim the support of the majority of the local barons, together with the effective control of a considerable length of coast—a vital requirement if the Byzantine lines of communication were to be adequately maintained. By contrast, the royalist army under Asclettin was far away beyond the Apennines—powerless to oppose any swift, surprise strike in northern Apulia.

And so, in the late summer of 1155, Robert of Loritello and Michael Palaeologus struck. Their first attack was directed against Bari. Until its capture by Robert Guiscard in 1071, this city had been the capital of Byzantine Italy and the last Greek stronghold in the peninsula. The majority of its citizens, being Greek, resented the government of Palermo—particularly since Roger had withdrawn several of their ancient privileges after the last Apulian rising—and looked gratefully towards any opportunity of breaking free from it. A group of them opened the gates to the attackers; and though the Sicilian garrison fought bravely from the old citadel and the church of St Nicholas, they were soon obliged to surrender and to watch while the Bariots fell on the citadel—by now the symbol of Sicilian domination—and despite Palaeologus's efforts to stop them, razed it to the ground.

News of the fall of Bari, coupled with a sudden spate of rumours of King William's death—he was indeed seriously ill—shattered the morale of the coastal towns. Trani yielded in its turn; then, despite the heroic efforts of its commander, Count Richard of Andria, the neighbouring port of Giovinazzo. Further south, resistance was still fierce; William of Tyre reports that when the Patriarch of

Jerusalem arrived that autumn in Otranto on his way to visit the Pope, he found the entire region in such turmoil that he was forced to re-embark and make his way by sea up the coast as far as Ancona. But the Greeks and the rebels together continued to gain ground everywhere until, as the winter rains began, the whole of Apulia seemed on the point of collapse.

Now at last, at the beginning of September, Asclettin's royalist army, consisting of some two thousand knights and an unknown but apparently considerable force of infantry, appeared in the field. On their arrival they were joined by Richard of Andria with those of his men who had remained loyal, but the opposition was too strong for them. Hardly had they reached the coast before they found themselves surrounded at Barletta. In a desperate effort to increase his strength, Count Richard broke through the cordon with a body of knights and made a dash for his own territory of Andria, hotly pursued by Robert of Loritello and John Ducas, Michael Palaeologus's principal lieutenant. They caught up with him just as he arrived before the walls. Rather than face a siege, for which he knew that his town was unprepared, Richard turned and gave battle on the spot. At one moment it looked as if he might carry the day; the Greeks' line was broken, and they and their allies retired in disorder. Sheltering, however, behind the long walls of stones which were (and still are) a feature of the region, they managed to reform and return to the charge; and before long the royalists were in full retreat. Count Richard himself, unhorsed by a blow from a flying stone, was finished off by a priest of Trani who, we are told, ripped him open and tore out his entrails. Seeing their lord lying dead, the population of Andria surrendered to Ducas.

The first pitched battle of the new revolt had ended in disaster. For those still loyal to King William, the future looked grim.

From Tivoli first and later from Tusculum, Pope Adrian had followed these developments with satisfaction. Though he had no love for the Greeks, he greatly preferred them to the Sicilians; and it delighted him to see his arch-enemy William, having escaped the vengeance of Barbarossa, finally receiving his deserts. Barely three months before, riding south with Frederick from Sutri to Rome, the

Pope had forsworn any separate diplomatic negotiations with Byzantium, but times had changed; now that the Emperor had defaulted on his own undertakings, Adrian felt once again free to act in whatever way he saw fit. When, therefore, he received a letter from Michael Palaeologus offering him military help against the King of Sicily together with a subsidy of five thousand gold pounds in return for the grant of three coastal towns in Apulia he was interested. He replied that he himself already had troops at his disposal and that he was ready forthwith to embark on the campaign as an ally. On 29 September 1155 he marched south.

It may seem surprising, just a century after the great schism between the Eastern and Western Churches, to find the Emperor of Byzantium putting himself forward as the patron and protector of the Pope of Rome, and the Pope accepting his overtures. It was in fact a policy which had been inaugurated, on the Byzantine side, by John Comnenus as early as 1141; Manuel was merely continuing it and, seeing circumstances so favourable, increasing the pressure. Adrian doubtless recognised in the South Italian situation the opening up of an opportunity that might never recur. He was encouraged, too, by the exiled Apulian vassals who, faced with the possibility of regaining their old fiefs, joyfully agreed to recognise the Pope as their lawful suzerain in return for his support. Already on 9 October, at S. Germano, Prince Robert of Capua, Count Andrew of Rupe Canina and several other Norman barons were reinvested with their hereditary possessions, and before the end of the year all Campania and most of Northern Apulia was in Byzantine or papalist hands.

Michael Palaeologus, mopping up the few pockets of resistance that remained, could congratulate himself on a success greater than he could have dared to hope. In barely six months he had restored Greek power in the peninsula to a point almost equal to that of a hundred and fifty years previously, before the Normans set about the deliberate destruction of the Byzantine theme of Langobardia and seized it for themselves. News had recently been brought to him that his Emperor, encouraged by such rapid progress, was sending out a full-scale expeditionary force to consolidate the position. At this rate it might not be long before all South Italy acknowledged the dominion of Constantinople. William of Sicily would be crushed, his odious Kingdom liquidated. Pope Adrian, seeing the Greeks succeed where the Germans had failed, would be persuaded of the superiority of Byzantine armies and would adjust his policies accordingly; and the great dream of the Comneni—the reunification of the Roman Empire under the aegis of Constantinople—might be realised at last.

Over-confidence is always dangerous; but few impartial observers at the end of 1155 would have held out much hope for the future of the Sicilian monarchy. On the mainland the King's enemies were in control everywhere except in Calabria; and Calabria probably remained loyal only because it had not yet been attacked. It would never be able to resist a determined Byzantine onslaught; if it fell, the rebels and their Greek allies would be only a mile or two from Sicily itself.

And there, on the island, the situation was now equally menacing. From September to Christmas the King lay in Palermo, desperately ill; Maio of Bari, assisted by Archbishop Hugh of Palermo, assumed complete control of the Kingdom. The Emir of Emirs had never been popular, and succeeding reports of one defeat after another on the mainland gave his enemies among the Norman nobility the very opportunity they needed to stir up unrest. He, they murmured, and he alone was responsible for this collapse. It would never have occurred if the Emirate had been bestowed on one of their own number. To have entrusted the supreme executive power in the realm to a Lombard tradesman's son was an act of unpardonable folly. Such a man was bound to be ignored by the proud barons of the peninsula. Even now, with the Sicilian state falling in ruins about his head, he seemed to have no real understanding of the gravity of the situation. He had sent no military reinforcements to Asclettin; he did not even appear worried.

There was only one thing to be done. Maio must be removed. And if his removal should also entail the removal of William himself, then so much the better. The King was already ill; perhaps, with a little help from the right quarter, he might never recover—in which case it would be a relatively easy matter to put the blame on the Emir, the only one of his ministers with unrestricted access to the royal bedchamber. William had already showed himself unfit to govern; how much more satisfactory it would be if the crown were to pass to his three-year-old son. The rightful ruling class could then come into its own, and the Norman barons would regain the power—and the perquisites—to which their birth entitled them.

But the Emir of Emirs kept his nerve. Not even Falcandus, who detested him, can hold back a word of grudging admiration for the way in which, whatever the crisis, he remained cool and unruffled, his face never betraying any sign of his real emotions. This steady refusal to panic—merely to remain, thanks to his spies, always a jump ahead of any plots that might be hatched against him—saved him more than once during that winter. In the twilight world of intrigue and conspiracy, he seems to have been still quietly confident of being able to hold his own. And, before long, his enemies began to agree with him. By the first weeks of 1156 they abandoned their earlier tactics, and adopted instead those which had proved so successful to their fellow-vassals in Apulia. Withdrawing to Butera in the far south of the island, a group of barons under a certain Bartholomew of Garsiliato came out in open rebellion.

At first sight it did not seem a very serious uprising. The insurgents were few in number, their stronghold remote. Nevertheless, this was the first time since the original conquest nearly a century before that a group of Christian vassals on the island of Sicily itself had declared themselves publicly against their ruler; and Maio saw that the time had come for action. Experience on the mainland had shown just how rapidly such revolts could spread. The local population around Butera was largely Arab, and Muslim loyalties must be preserved at all costs. Moreover it looked as if the King, now almost recovered, would have some hard campaigning to do in Italy during the months to come. If so, it was essential that he should have his hands free.

William was still tired after his illness; and he had inherited in full measure his father's preference for diplomatic negotiation over armed force. Remaining himself in Palermo, he therefore sent an emissary to Butera in the person of Everard, Count of Squillace, to treat with the rebels and to ask them why they had taken so drastic a step. Within a few days Everard returned with the answer. They had acted, they claimed, not in defiance of their King but only against the Emir, who with his henchman the Archbishop was plotting to assassinate William and seize the throne for himself. All they asked was that the King should recognise the dangers that threatened him and rid himself of his evil counsellors before it was too late. They themselves would then lay down their arms and come to Palermo to implore his pardon.

William may have been lethargic, but he was not a fool; and he trusted Maio a great deal more than any Norman baron. He took no action, sent no acknowledgement to the rebels' message, and waited for their next move. He did not have to wait long. Towards the end of March, riots broke out in Palermo itself. That they were inspired and financed by the rebels was beyond a doubt; though the anger of the rioters was principally directed against Maio and Archbishop Hugh, there were also loud calls for the release from prison of Simon of Policastro, a young Count who had until recently been Asclettin's right-hand man in Campania but who had since been incarcerated by Maio without trial, on charges of suspected treason.

The appearance of the mob outside his royal palace roused William from his apathy. It was at last borne in on him that there could be no more peace, no more privacy, till the problem was settled. Now that his mind was made up, he moved quickly. To assuage the rioters, he gave orders for the immediate release of Simon of Policastro; then, with Maio at his side but accompanied also by Simon himself as mediator—for he still hoped to avoid bloodshed if possible—he led his army at top speed to Butera.

Perched on a high pinnacle of rock between two steep valleys, Butera was a perfect natural stronghold; and the insurgents were initially resolved to fight hard in its defence. That they did not do so was largely due to the generosity of William's terms and the persuasiveness of Count Simon. He convinced them that the King had no intention of dismissing his counsellors, in whom he had implicit trust, and one of whom was accompanying him at that moment; nevertheless he was disposed, in the circumstances, to show leniency to those who had taken up arms against him. Let them surrender at once; their lives and property would be spared, their liberty preserved; their only punishment would be exile from the Kingdom at the King's pleasure. The rebels accepted the offer. Butera was surrendered, and Sicily was at peace again.

'King William was a man,' wrote Hugo Falcandus, 'who found it hard ever to leave his palace; but once he was obliged to go forth, then—however disinclined to action he had been in the past—he would fling himself, not so much with courage as in a headstrong, even foolhardy spirit, in the face of all dangers.' As ever, Hugo's malice shows through; but it is still possible to detect some faint tinge of admiration in his words, as well as their underlying truth. Now that William had finally embarked on campaign and could look back on one victory already behind him, he had no intention of calling a halt. His health was restored, his blood was up. Spring had come, and spring was the season for campaigning. He was ready to tackle the mainland.

Army and navy met at Messina; this was to be a combined operation, in which the Greeks and their allies were to be attacked simultaneously from land and sea. To Messina also was summoned Asclettin, to explain his lamentable showing over the past months. Asclettin seems to have been an uninspired and somewhat colourless commander (not surprisingly, his previous post having been that of Archdeacon of Catania) and it may well be that other, more serious, charges had been laid against him. Certainly, at Messina, not a single voice was raised in his defence—not even that of Maio, whose creature he was and who had raised him to the Chancellorship in defiance of the King's own wishes. But whether traitor, coward or scapegoat, his goods were confiscated and he himself was cast into prison—where, several years later, he died.

William's treatment of Asclettin epitomised his whole attitude to the coming campaign. This would be in no sense a continuation, however intensified, of last year's pathetic performance. It would be a new operation, offensive rather than defensive, freshly conceived and planned; a blow struck by the combined military and naval power of the Sicilian Kingdom at the enemy's weakest point—the heel of Apulia. In the last days of April, the army crossed to the mainland and set off through Calabria, while the fleet sailed down through the straits and then turned north-east towards Brindisi.

For three weeks already Brindisi had been under siege. The Byzantines, relying as always on bribes and treachery, had managed to gain entrance to the outer town; but the royalist garrison in the citadel was putting up a determined resistance to them and their progress in Apulia had come, at least temporarily, to a stop. It was only the last of several reverses they had suffered in recent months. First, thanks to the increasing arrogance of Michael Palaeologus, they had gradually lost the confidence and goodwill of the Norman rebels until Robert of Loritello had ridden off in disgust. Then Palaeologus himself had died, after a short illness, in Bari. For all his overbearing ways he had been a brilliant leader in the field, and his death had been another blow to his countrymen. His successor John Ducas had eventually got the army moving again and had even achieved a reconciliation with the Count of Loritello; but the old confidence between the allies was never quite restored, the momentum of 1155 never quite regained.

And now news was brought to the Byzantine headquarters that the Sicilians were advancing in formidable numbers and strength, led by King William himself. Once again, the Greeks saw their fellow-fighters begin to fall away. The mercenaries chose, as mercenaries will, the moment of supreme crisis to demand impossible increases in their pay; meeting with a refusal, they disappeared *en masse*. Robert of Loritello deserted for the second time, followed by his own men and most of his compatriots. Ducas, left only with the few troops that he and Palaeologus had brought with them, plus those which had trickled over the Adriatic at various times during the past eight or nine months, found himself impossibly outnumbered.

It was the Sicilian fleet that arrived first, and for another day or two he was able to hold his own. The entrance to Brindisi harbour is by a narrow channel, barely a hundred yards across. Twelve centuries before, Julius Caesar had blocked it to Pompey's ships; and now Ducas, by placing the four vessels at his command in line abreast across its mouth and stationing well-armed detachments of footsoldiers along each bank, followed similar tactics. But when a day or two later William's army appeared to the west, Byzantine hopes were at an end. Attacked simultaneously from the land, the sea and the inner citadel, Ducas could not hope to hold the walls; he and his men were caught, in Cinnamus's words, as in a net.

The battle that followed was short and bloody; the Greek defeat was total. The Sicilian navy had occupied the little islands that circled the harbour entrance and effectively prevented any possibility of escape by sea. Ducas and the other Greek survivors were taken captive. On that one day, 28 May 1156, all that the Byzantines had achieved in Italy over the past year was wiped out as completely as if they had never come.

William treated his Greek prisoners according to the recognised canons of war; but to his own rebellious subjects he was pitiless. This was another lesson he had learnt from his father. Treason, particularly in Apulia where it was endemic, remained the one crime that could not be forgiven. Of those erstwhile insurgents who fell into his hands, only the luckiest were imprisoned. The rest were hanged, blinded or tied about with heavy weights and cast into the sea. It was the first time since his accession that the King had shown himself in Apulia, and he was resolved that the Apulians should not forget it. From Brindisi he moved to Bari. Less than a year before, the Bariots had readily thrown in their lot with the Byzantines; now they too were to pay the price for their disloyalty. Slowly they filed from their homes, to prostrate themselves at the feet of their ruler and to implore his mercy; but their prayers were unavailing. William merely pointed to the pile of rubble where until recently the citadel had stood. 'Just as you had no pity on my house,' he said, 'so now I shall have no pity on yours.' He gave them two clear days in which to salvage their belongings; on the third day Bari was destroyed. Only the Cathedral, the great church of St Nicholas and a few smaller religious buildings were left standing.

'And so it came about that of the mighty capital of Apulia, celebrated for its glory, powerful in its wealth, proud of the nobility of its citizens and admired for the beauty of its architecture by all who saw it, there now lies nothing but a heap of stones.' Thus Hugo Falcandus salutes, a trifle pompously, the city that was a city no more. The Jewish traveller Benjamin of Tudela, writing of it a year or two later, was more succinct: 'From Trani it is a day's journey to Bari, that great city which King William of Sicily destroyed. In consequence of its destruction, neither Jews nor Christians now dwell therein.'

It was the same old lesson—a lesson that the history of South Italy alone should have made self-evident, yet one that the princes of mediaeval Europe seemed to find impossible to absorb: that in distant lands, wherever there existed an organised native opposition, a temporary force could never achieve permanent conquest. Whirlwind campaigns were easy, especially when backed by bribes and generous subsidies to the local malcontents; the difficulties arose when it became necessary to consolidate and maintain the advantage gained. For such a purpose no amount of gold was of any avail. The Normans had succeeded in establishing themselves only because they had arrived as mercenaries, and remained as settlers; even then, the task had taken them the best part of a century. When they embarked on foreign adventures—such as the two invasions of the Byzantine Empire by Robert Guiscard and Bohemund—even they were doomed to failure. In North Africa, admittedly, they fared a little better—though the days of the North African Empire were numbered. But where South Italy was concerned there was no exception to the old rule. Its truth had been demonstrated, unpleasantly, to five of the eight men who had occupied the imperial throne of the West during the past century and a half—most recently to Lothair and Frederick Barbarossa himself. Now it was the turn of the Eastern Empire, and Manuel Comnenus.

But the Greeks and the Bariots were not the only sufferers. As William marched his exultant army westward across the Apennines, his approach caused a general panic among those vassals who had recently returned, in the wake of Pope Adrian, from exile. Some fled back precipitately to the papal court; others like the Count of Loritello escaped to the Abruzzi, where they might be able to carry on a sporadic guerrilla warfare for some time to come. Their leader, however, Prince Robert of Capua, was less fortunate. He too fled, hoping to reach the Papal State; but just as he was crossing the Garigliano into safety he was seized by Count Richard of Aquila and delivered up to the King. By this treachery—for he was one of the Prince of Capua's own vassals and had long been his companion in exile—Count Richard managed to save his own skin. Robert, on the other hand, was sent in chains to Palermo, where his eyes were put out by command of the King.

He was lucky to have escaped with his life—a life which for thirty years he had devoted to subversion and revolt. The chief vassal of the Kingdom, who, in one of his rare bursts of loyalty, had laid the royal crown on the head of Roger II more than a quarter of a century before, the richest and most powerful prince in the *Regno* after the King himself, he might have been the mainstay of the monarchy. He, if anyone, could have brought to the peninsula the stability and peace it so badly needed. But he chose the other course. Twice he had been forced to capitulate; twice he had been offered the King's pardon. It was enough. If the days of the last Prince of Capua ended in darkness, he had only himself to blame.

One lonely figure remained to face the coming storm. All Pope Adrian's allies were gone. Frederick Barbarossa was back in Germany; Michael Palaeologus was dead and his army annihilated; the Norman barons were either in prison or in hiding. Adrian himself, unable to return to Rome since Frederick's coronation, had spent the winter with his court at Benevento. Now, as the Sicilian army drew near, he sent most of his Cardinals away to Campania—mainly for their greater safety but also, perhaps, for another reason. He knew now that he would have to come to terms with William. Die-hard cardinals had wrecked too many potential agreements in the past; if he were to save anything from the disaster, he would need the utmost freedom to negotiate.

As soon as the vanguard of the Sicilian army appeared over the hills, the Pope sent forth his Chancellor, Roland of Siena, with two other cardinals who had remained at Benevento, to greet the King and bid him, in the name of St Peter, to cease from further hostilities.[1] They were received with due courtesy, and formal talks began. The going was not easy. The Sicilian negotiators, led

[1] William of Tyre suggests—and Chalandon, surprisingly, accepts his word without question—that the Sicilians were forced to lay siege to Benevento and starve the Pope out before he would have any dealings with them. For Adrian, anxious now to obtain the best terms he could, such a course would have been ridiculous; and William of Tyre is in any case contradicted by Boso, who was in the city at the time.

by Maio, Archbishop Hugh and Romuald of Salerno, were in a position of strength and drove a hard bargain, but the papal side fought every inch of the way. It was not until 18 June that agreement was finally reached.

The original manuscript of the Treaty of Benevento still exists in the Vatican Secret Archive. It was drawn up by one of Maio's *protégés*, a bright young notary called Matthew of Ajello,[1] and the prevailing mood of victorious exaltation, bordering even on truculence, shows through every line of his neat, crabbed handwriting. The King, we read, 'having defeated and put to flight those enemies, Greek and barbarian, who had infiltrated, not by strength but by treachery, into his Kingdom', had consented to abase himself before the Pope merely in order not to appear ungrateful before the Almighty, from whom he expected continued cooperation in the future. The political terms of the agreement are then set out in detail. William had obtained from the Pope everything he wanted—more than had ever been granted to his father or grandfather. His kingship was recognised not only over Sicily, Apulia, Calabria and the former Principality of Capua, together with Naples, Salerno, Amalfi and all that pertained to them; it was also now formally extended, for the first time, to that whole region of the northern Abruzzi and the Marches which King Roger's elder sons had claimed and fought for during the previous decade. An annual tribute was agreed for all these lands, amounting to the six hundred *schifati* in respect of Apulia and Calabria which had already been settled by Roger and Pope Innocent at Mignano seventeen years before, plus another four hundred for the new territories to the north.

In mainland ecclesiastical affairs William was prepared to be rather more accommodating. Henceforth all disputes within the Church might be submitted to Rome for arbitration; the Pope's consent would be sought for all transfers; he would have free right of consecration and might send legates at will into the *Regno* so long as they did not impose too heavy a burden on the local churches. But where Sicily was concerned, nearly all the King's traditional privileges were preserved. Adrian was obliged to confirm the Apostolic

---

[1] I use the name by which he is generally known. In fact he was from Salerno; Ajello was the county later bestowed on his son by King Tancred.

Legateship, renouncing the right to send special envoys or to hear appeals. He might summon Sicilian clerics to Rome, but they could not obey without first obtaining the King's permission. Ecclesiastical elections were subject to a similar control. Theoretically they were the responsibility of the clergy, proceeding by secret ballot; but they too could be vetoed by the King if the chosen candidate did not meet with his approval.

The instrument by which the Pope accepted these conditions was drafted in equally flowery terms. It is addressed to

William, glorious King of Sicily and dearest son in Christ, most brilliant in wealth and achievement among all the Kings and eminent men of the age, the glory of whose name is borne to the uttermost limits of the earth by the firmness of your justice, the peace which you have restored to your subjects, and the fear which your great deeds have instilled into the hearts of all the enemies of Christ's name.

Even when allowance is made for the traditional literary hyperbole of the time, it is hard to imagine Adrian putting his signature to such a document without a wince of humiliation. He had been Pope only eighteen months, but already he had learnt the bitterness of desertion, betrayal and exile; and even his shoulders were beginning to bow. He appears now in a very different light from that in which we saw him when he placed Rome under an interdict or pitted his will against that of Frederick Barbarossa just twelve short months before.

It was in the church of S. Marciano, on the banks of the river Calore just outside Benevento, that William received at the papal hands the three pennoned lances by which he was invested with his chief dominions—the Kingdom of Sicily first, next the Duchy of Apulia and finally the Principality of Capua. The investitures were sealed by the Kiss of Peace; then, after bestowing appropriate gifts of gold, silver and precious silks on the Pope and all his retinue, he rode back by slow stages through Naples[1] to Salerno. In July he

[1] When he ordered the building of the Castel Capuano (now the Law Courts) and, by enlarging a small island just off the shore, laid the foundation for the future Castel dell'Ovo.

took ship for Sicily, where the ringleaders of the insurrection who had fallen into his hands were now awaiting sentence. One of the captives, Count Geoffrey of Montescaglioso, who had played a prominent part in both the Sicilian and the Apulian revolts, was blinded; many more were imprisoned, including the King's two young nephews William and Tancred, sons of Duke Roger of Apulia; others, if we are to believe Falcandus, were cast into pits full of vipers, while wives and daughters were sent to the harems or forced into prostitution. But there were rewards, too, for those who had given loyal service—in particular Maio's brother Stephen and his Sicilian brother-in-law Simon, the royal seneschal, who were both appointed master captains of Apulia. With his two closest relatives in positions of such authority, the Emir of Emirs thus became more powerful than ever; while William for his part had demonstrated, in a manner that could not possibly be misunderstood, his continuing trust in his chief minister and his contempt for the opinions of those who dared to set themselves up against him.

Later, he would have cause to regret this arrogance. For the moment, however, he was determined to enjoy his triumph, and the humiliation of his enemies, to the full. Not without reason had he caused to be inscribed, around the royal cypher with which the Treaty of Benevento was sealed, the words which his grandfather, the Great Count, had had engraved on his sword in 1063, after the battle of Cerami:

DEXTERA DOMINI FECIT VIRTUTEM;
DEXTERA DOMINI EXALTAVIT ME.[1]

[1] The right hand of God gave me courage;
The right hand of God raised me up.

II

REALIGNMENTS

For I call on the Lord Adrian to witness than no one is more miserable than the Roman Pontiff, nor is any condition more wretched than his. . . . He maintains that the papal throne is studded with thorns, that his mantle bristles with needles so sharp that it oppresses and weighs down the broadest shoulders . . . and that had he not feared to go against the will of God he would never have left his native England.

John of Salisbury, *Policraticus*, VIII, xxiii

THE news of the Apulian *débâcle* was received with horror in Constantinople. The unfortunate Ducas, unable to defend himself from his Palermo prison, made a convenient scapegoat; but though it was he who took much of the blame the ultimate responsibility was clearly the Emperor's, and Manuel was determined to recover his honour. This recovery was made even more necessary the following summer, when a Sicilian fleet of a hundred and sixty-four ships, commanded by Maio's brother Stephen—now promoted Admiral— and carrying nearly ten thousand men, swooped down on the prosperous island of Euboea, sacking and pillaging all the villages and towns along its coasts. From there they sailed on to Almira on the Gulf of Volos, which received similar treatment; and then, if we are to believe Nicetas Choniates, sped up the Hellespont and through the Marmara to Constantinople—where a hail of silver-tipped arrows was loosed upon the imperial palace of Blachernae.[1]

[1] This story bears such a resemblance to that of George of Antioch's similar raid in 1149 that several scholars have suggested that Nicetas is confusing the two. He may be; but surely there is no reason why Stephen should not have been tempted to repeat his predecessor's famous exploit, nor why his sailors should not have felt equally quiver-happy under the palace walls. An odder feature of

And so, some time during the summer of 1157, Manuel Comnenus sent a new emissary to Italy—Alexis, the brilliant young son of his Grand Domestic, Axuch. His ostensible orders were much the same as those given to Michael Palaeologus—to make contact with such rebel barons as were still at liberty, hire mercenaries for a new campaign along the coast, and generally stir up as much disaffection and discord as he could. But he had also been entrusted by his Emperor with a second task; to establish secret contact with Maio and discuss terms for a peace. Until that peace was concluded there could be no cessation of hostilities; the fiercer the fighting, the more favourable to Constantinople William's conditions were likely to be. For a year already, however, it had been growing ever clearer to Manuel Comnenus that the time had come for a radical change in his foreign policy. He now knew that he could never hope to reconquer Apulia by force of arms. His best hope lay in close ties with the Pope, and in trying to play him off against Barbarossa; and since the Treaty of Benevento this must inevitably involve some accommodation with the King of Sicily.

Alexis discharged both parts of his mission with equal success. Within a few months of his arrival he had Robert of Loritello again ravaging Sicilian territory in the north and Andrew of Rupecanina driving down through the Capuan lands and seriously threatening Monte Cassino beneath which, in January 1158, he even defeated a royalist army in pitched battle. Meanwhile, although his support for these operations debarred him from undertaking peace talks in person, he was able to call on the services of the two most distinguished of the Greeks who were still held captive in Palermo, John Ducas and Alexius Bryennius; and through their mediation, some time in the early spring, a secret agreement was concluded. Alexis, having fooled his Apulian supporters into thinking that he was going to fetch more men and supplies, left them in the lurch and

this second account, and one which no other commentator seems to have raised, is the reference by name to Blachernae. This palace stood at the north-west corner of the city; to have reached it, the Sicilians would have had either to launch a land expedition of several miles along the well-defended land walls, or to sail right up the Golden Horn and then scale a steep hill. Here Nicetas surely nods; their target is much more likely to have been the old palace of the Emperors on the Marmara, near Seraglio Point.

slipped off to Constantinople; William, though still understandably suspicious of Byzantine motives, sent off a diplomatic mission to Manuel[1] and returned all his Greek prisoners—except the indispensable ladies from the *Tiraz*; and the Counts of Loritello and Rupecanina, suddenly bereft of funds, had no course but to abandon their new conquests and to ride off in search of another champion.

They found one in Frederick Barbarossa.

*   *   *   *   *

Frederick's relations with the Eastern Empire had deteriorated sharply during the last three years. He had always mistrusted the Greeks; and reports of the Apulian campaign, which he saw as a typically underhand attempt on their part to slip in as soon as his back was turned with the object of snatching away territories which were rightfully his, had alarmed and infuriated him. To add insult to injury, they had set up their headquarters at Ancona, a city which lay under direct imperial control; and had even had the audacity, if reports were true, to forge letters purporting to issue from his chancery, in order to obtain the submission of certain strategic towns. His initial reaction was to break off all relations with Manuel. When, in June 1156, an embassy arrived from Constantinople to discuss his projected marriage to a Byzantine princess (he had divorced his first wife, in somewhat discreditable circumstances, three years before) he refused even to receive it—marrying instead, after the shortest possible preliminaries, the rich and exceedingly attractive Beatrice of Upper Burgundy. Later, when he heard of the Greek defeat at Brindisi, he had relented to the point of resuming formal contacts with his brother-Emperor; but the damage was done and both of them knew it.

Frederick was equally angry with the Pope. Had not Adrian given him a personal undertaking not to enter into any private

---

[1] At the head of this mission went William's sometime tutor and close friend, Henry Aristippus. He returned with a valuable present from the Emperor to the King—a Greek manuscript of Ptolemy's *Almagest*. This tremendous work, a synthesis of all the discoveries and conclusions of Greek astronomers since the science was born, was hitherto known in the West, if at all, only through Arabic translations.

communications with either the Eastern Emperor or the King of Sicily? Was it not a fact, none the less, that he was in constant correspondence with the one, while with the other he had actually signed a treaty of peace and friendship—a treaty, moreover, by which he not only recognised William's claim to a spurious crown but, in ecclesiastical affairs, allowed him privileges more far-reaching even than those enjoyed by the Emperor himself? By what right, in any case, did Adrian so graciously confer imperial territories on others? Did the Empire count for nothing in his eyes? Was there no limit to papal arrogance?

It was not long before his worst suspicions were confirmed. In October 1157 he held an imperial Diet at Besançon. The location had been carefully selected; Besançon was the capital of Upper Burgundy—later to be known as the Franche-Comté—and he was anxious that no effort should be spared to impress his wife's family and his own newly-acquired subjects with the power and magnificence of his Empire. Ambassadors converged on the town from all sides, from France and Italy, from Spain and England—and, of course, from the Pope. The effect of all Frederick's careful arrangements was, however, slightly spoilt when, in the presence of the assembled company, the papal legates read out the letter they had brought with them from their master. Instead of the customary greetings and congratulations that everyone had expected, the Pope had chosen this of all moments to deliver himself of a strongly-worded complaint. It appeared that some time previously the aged Archbishop of Lund, while travelling through imperial territory, had been set upon by bandits, robbed of all he possessed and held to ransom. Such an outrage was in itself serious enough; but, the Pope went on, it was further aggravated by the fact that although the Emperor had already been furnished with full details of all that had occurred, he appeared as yet to have taken no steps to bring to justice those responsible. Turning to more general topics, Adrian began recalling his past favours to the Emperor—reminding him in particular of his coronation at papal hands and adding, more than a little patronisingly, that he hoped at some future date to bestow still further benefices upon him.

Whether the Pope was deliberately intending to assert his feudal overlordship over the Emperor we shall never know. Unfortunately, however, the two words he used, *conferre* and *beneficia,* were both technical terms used in describing the grant of a fief by a suzerain to his vassal. This was more than Frederick could bear. If the letter implied, as it appeared to imply, that he held the Holy Roman Empire by courtesy of the Pope in the same way as any petty baron might hold a few fields in the Campagna, there could be no further dealings between them. The assembled German princes shared his indignation; and when Cardinal Roland, the papal chancellor, blandly replied by enquiring from whom Frederick did hold the Empire if not from the Pope, there was general uproar. Otto of Wittelsbach, Count Palatine of Bavaria, rushed forward, his hand on his sword; only the rapid intervention of the Emperor himself prevented an incident compared with which the misfortunes of the Archbishop of Lund would have seemed trivial indeed. When Adrian heard what had happened he wrote Frederick another letter, this time in rather more soothing terms, protesting that his words had been misinterpreted; and the Emperor accepted his explanation. It is unlikely that he really believed it, but he had no wish for an open breach with the Papacy at a moment when he was about to launch the greatest military operation he had yet undertaken—the subjugation of Lombardy.

The *bagarre* at Besançon, as anyone could have seen, was merely a symptom of a far deeper rift between Pope and Emperor—one which no amount of diplomatic drafting could ever hope to bridge. The days when it had been realistic to speak of the two swords of Christendom were gone—gone since Gregory VII and Henry IV had hurled depositions and anathemas at each other nearly a hundred years before. Never since that time had their respective successors been able to look upon themselves as two different sides of the same coin. Each must now claim the supremacy, and defend it as necessary against the other. When this involved the confrontation of characters as strong as those of Adrian and Frederick, flash-point could never be far off. Yet the root of the trouble lay less in their personalities than in the institutions they represented. While the two of them lived, relations between them—exacerbated by a host of petty slights both real and imagined—became even more strained; but it was only after their deaths that the conflict was to emerge into open war.

If, however, Frederick had put the doctrine of the two swords behind him, there was another eleventh-century concept of Empire which he still stubbornly refused to outgrow. During his first passage through North Italy on the way to his coronation he had been appalled by the spirit of independence and freedom among the Lombard towns, their blatant republicanism and their lack of any respect for his authority. Pressed for time and impatient for the imperial crown, he had delayed there only long enough to make his presence felt and to leave the smoking ruins of Tortona as a mark of his displeasure. Since then he had had plenty of opportunities, notably in Rome itself, to gauge the strength of Italian communal feeling; but he still could not—or would not—understand. For him the Lombards were insubordinate; that was all there was to it. In July 1158, accompanied by the King of Bohemia and a huge army, he crossed the Alps to teach them a lesson.

There is, fortunately, no need for us to follow in any detail the fortunes of Frederick Barbarossa in Lombardy. A few of the towns had remained loyal to him and showed it; a few seized the opportunity offered by the presence of the imperial forces to turn them against their enemies or commercial rivals; others bowed, reed-like, before the storm with every intention of springing up again the moment it was past; one or two even fought magnificently back. But for us the interest of the campaign lies not in the conduct of the individual towns so much as in its effect on that latest and most unexpected newcomer to the Italian scene—the Sicilian-Papal entente.

The Treaty of Benevento proved to be of immeasurably greater significance than either William or Adrian could have known at the time. For the Papacy it inaugurated a new political approach to European problems—one which it was to follow to its own considerable advantage for the next twenty years. Adrian himself, though for some time afterwards he remained strangely hesitant as if unable to adjust to the new pattern, was at last brought to accept what he must always have suspected—that the Emperor was not so much a friend with whom he might occasionally quarrel as an enemy with whom, somehow, he had to live. His concordat with William gave him a powerful new ally and enabled him to adopt a firmer attitude in his dealings with Frederick than could ever otherwise have been possible as the Desançon letter bears witness. It was a tendency that Maio and William were quick to encourage.

In papal circles, so radical a change in policy was bound to meet with opposition at first. Many leading members of the Curia— those, presumably, whom Adrian sent away to Campania before beginning the negotiations—still clung to their imperialist, anti-Sicilian opinions; and the news of the terms agreed had apparently caused almost as much consternation in the Sacred College as in the imperial court. Gradually, however, in the months that followed, opinion swung round in William's favour. There were several reasons. Barbarossa's arrogance was one, as shown at Besançon and confirmed by several other incidents before and since. Besides, the Sicilian alliance was now a *fait accompli*; it was useless to oppose it any longer. William, for his part, seemed sincere enough. On the Pope's recommendation, he had made his peace with Constantinople. He was rich, he was powerful; and, as several of Their Eminences could—if they wished—have testified, he was also generous.

And now, as Frederick Barbarossa set out to sack and ravage the Lombard cities, a great wave of revulsion against the Empire swept down through Italy. With it, too, there was an element of terror. When the Emperor had finished with Lombardy, what was to prevent him from continuing to Tuscany, Umbria, even to Rome itself? Soon, too, Frederick's victims began to appear—the widows and fatherless children, the refugees from the burning towns and devastated villages, the exiled mayors and magistrates; and, inevitably, the conspirators. All were looking, in their separate ways, for a centre of resistance, for some strong power able to focus their aspirations and ideals; liberty against domination, republi-canism against imperialism, Italian against Teuton. And in the alliance forged between an English Pope and a Norman King they found it.

Throughout 1158, Maio had been working to strengthen support for Sicily within the papal Curia—with the invaluable help of Cardinal Roland, Adrian's Chancellor and most trusted associate, who had been the chief architect and was now one of the principal protagonists of the Norman alliance. Together they did their work well. In the spring of 1159 there occurred the first great counterthrust against Frederick that can be directly ascribed to papal-Sicilian instigation. Milan suddenly threw off the imperial authority, and for the next three years the Milanese stoutly defied all the Emperor's efforts to bring them to heel. The following August, representatives of Milan, Crema, Piacenza and Brescia met the Pope at Anagni, a little town situated conveniently near the frontier of the *Regno*. And there, in the presence of envoys from King William—Maio may easily have been there himself—was sworn the initial pact that was to become the nucleus of the great Lombard League. The towns promised that they would have no dealings with the common enemy without papal consent, while the Pope undertook to excommunicate the Emperor after the usual period of forty days. Finally it was agreed by the assembled cardinals that on Adrian's death his successor should be elected only from those present at the conference.

Perhaps it was obvious already that the Pope had not long to live. While still at Anagni he was stricken by a sudden angina, from which he never recovered. He died in the evening of 1 September 1159. His body was taken to Rome, and was laid in the undistinguished third-century sarcophagus in which it still rests and which can still be seen in the crypt of St Peter's. During the course of the demolition of the old basilica in 1607 it was opened; the body of the only English Pope was found entire, dressed in a chasuble of dark-coloured silk. It was described by the archaeologist Grimaldi as being that of 'an undersized man, wearing Turkish slippers on his feet and, on his hand, a ring with a large emerald'.

Adrian's pontificate is hard to assess. To hail him as the greatest Pope since Urban II is not to say very much; he certainly towers above the string of mediocrities who occupied the throne of St Peter during the first half of the century, just as he himself is overshadowed by his magnificent successor. Yet it remains difficult to see how Gregorovius could have written that his nature was always 'as firm and as unyielding as the granite of his tomb'. In the early days it certainly seemed so; but his complete *volte-face* after Benevento, however ultimately beneficial to papal interests, was imposed upon him by force of circumstances, and from that time on he seems to have lost much of the incisiveness that marked his early career. He left the Papacy stronger and more generally respected than he found it, but much of this success was due to its identification with the Lombard League—for which, in turn, he had the diplomacy of Maio of Bari and the wise statesmanship of Cardinal Roland to thank. And he failed utterly to subdue the Roman Senate.

He was Pope for less than five years; but those years were hard and vital for the Papacy, and the strain told on him. Before long his health had begun to fail, and with it his morale. He confided to his compatriot John of Salisbury, who knew him well, that the burden of the Papacy had now become greater than he could bear, and that he often wished that he had never left England. He died, as many Popes had died before him, an embittered exile; and when death came to him, he welcomed it as a friend.

Thus, in the three years separating the Treaty of Benevento from the death of Pope Adrian IV, a curious change occurs in the relative position of King William of Sicily on the European stage. The King himself remains at the still centre of this change. His Sicilian policies, framed and executed by Maio of Bari, continued constant, based as they were on the twin principles of friendship with the Papacy and opposition to the Western Empire. Never did he have any quarrel with the city-states or towns of North Italy, except when they had been bribed or otherwise cajoled into collaboration with his enemies. But, all around him, alignments were shifting. The Papacy, brought to its knees at Benevento, rediscovered a fact that its history over the past hundred years should have made self-evident—that its only hope of survival as a potent political force lay in close alliance with Norman Sicily; Frederick Barbarossa, impressed despite himself by the speed and completeness of William's victories over the Byzantines in Apulia and looking on him with undiminished hatred but new respect, decided on the indefinite postponement of his own punitive expedition into the *Regno*; and, as the supreme paradox, the Lombard towns began to see in the Sicilian monarchy—entrenched in feudalism and more absolutist by far than the Western Empire or any other state of Western Europe— the stalwart defender of their republican ideals, hailing its King as a champion of civic liberty almost before the dust had settled on the ruins of Bari.

But while William and Maio worked for the downfall of one Empire, they were themselves in the process of losing another. North Africa was rapidly slipping away. The rot had begun in the winter of 1155–56, when Sicilian fortunes were at their lowest. At that time the Greeks were sweeping unchecked through Apulia. The Prince of Capua and his followers were seizing back their old patrimonies in Campania and elsewhere. In Sicily itself another band of insurgents was defying the central government from the heights of Butera. Meanwhile there was, living quietly in the capital, an old Sheikh from North Africa named Abu al-Hassan al-Furriani. Some years before, he had been appointed by King Roger as governor of his own city of Sfax, but being already advanced in years he had soon retired in favour of his son, Omar, in pledge of whose good conduct he had himself gone as a voluntary hostage to Palermo. Now, seeing the Kingdom menaced on three fronts and rightly surmising that it could not possibly fight back on a fourth, he wrote secretly to his son proposing an immediate uprising against the Sicilians. He was fully aware, he said, that he himself would probably pay for it with his life, but that was of no great moment; he was an old man, and for such a cause he would be happy to die.

Omar did as he was bid. On 25 February 1156 the native population of Sfax rose up and massacred every Christian in the city. William, hearing the news, at once sent over an ambassador to demand the governor's surrender; if he did not give himself up immediately, his father's life would be forfeit. On his arrival, however, the ambassador was stopped at the gates; and the next morning he was met by a long funeral procession following a coffin. With it came a message from Omar. It read: 'He who is being buried today is my father. I remain in my palace to mourn his death. Do with him as you will.' The ambassador returned to Palermo to report, and old

Abu al-Hassan, praising Allah with his last breath, was led to the gallows on the banks of the Oreto and hanged.[1]

But the collapse of William's North African Empire had begun. The islands of Djerba and Kerkenna followed where Sfax had led, and some time during the year 553 of the Hegira—between 2 February 1158 and 22 January 1159—the signal was given for revolt in Tripoli itself. By the middle of 1159 only Mahdia, with its suburb of Zawila, was left in Sicilian hands. Thither had flocked all William's remaining Christian subjects in Africa, arriving in such numbers that a new Archbishop had to be installed to minister to them all. His ministry was short-lived. Already three years previously the local Muslims had made one attempt to take over the city, failing only because of the opportune arrival of a Sicilian fleet; now the Almohads themselves appeared in strength under their leader Abd al-Moumen firmly resolved to eradicate the last traces of Christian domination from the continent. Mahdia was ringed by land and sea, and on 20 July the siege began.

For the first few weeks, morale in the beleaguered city remained high. There was a garrison of three thousand men, provisions were plentiful and no one doubted that a fleet would soon be on its way from Palermo with relief. Sure enough, on 8 September there it was—no less than a hundred and sixty Sicilian vessels, hastily recalled from a raiding expedition to the Balearics, under the command—surprisingly, in the circumstances—of King William's chief eunuch, a converted Muslim from Djerba who had been baptised in the name of Peter. The situation appeared to be saved; Abd al-Moumen, horrified at the size of the navy now bearing down upon him, even ordered sixty of his own ships to be beached so that, if the forthcoming battle went against him, he and his men should at least have some means of escape.

He need not have worried. Hardly, it seems, had battle been joined outside the harbour mouth when Peter's flagship suddenly turned about and made with all speed for the open sea; and the others followed. The Almohads, taking full advantage of their good

---

[1] This story is told by no less than three of the principal Arab sources for Norman Sicily—Ibn al-Athir, At-Tigani and Ibn Khaldun, the last two writing as late as the fourteenth century. The heroism of the two Al-Furriani was not, it seems, quickly forgotten.

fortune, set off in pursuit and captured seven or eight of the Sicilian vessels before returning jubilantly to port.

What had happened? Hugo Falcandus, who can always be trusted to interpret everyone's actions in the unkindest possible light, has no doubts on the matter. Peter, he points out, was, 'like all the eunuchs of the palace, only in name and dress a Christian, and a Saracen at heart'. It followed that his retreat must have been due not to incapacity or cowardice, but to treachery pure and simple. The other chroniclers are more charitable; they make no suggestion of any betrayal, and at-Tigani even quotes an eye-witness account by a certain Ibn Saddad, according to whom the Sicilian fleet had been scattered by a gale and was attacked by the Muslims before it had time to reform. This, or some similar catastrophe, seems to have been the true explanation; for nowhere do we find any record of disciplinary action taken against Peter on his return to Palermo. On the contrary, he had a long and distinguished political career before him. Clearly he was no George of Antioch; but there is no evidence, apart from Falcandus's unsupported testimony, that he acted with dishonour.

The same, alas, cannot be said for the Sicilian government. The garrison held out bravely for another six months, confidently awaiting another relief expedition; none came. At last, when supplies were running so low that the men had begun eating their horses, they sent Abd al-Moumen an offer. Let him allow one or two of their number to go to Palermo and ascertain, once and for all, whether any further help could be expected; if the answer was negative, the garrison commander would surrender the city forthwith. The request was granted. The emissaries left, and soon afterwards returned with the sad and, to the Christian community of Mahdia, almost unbelievable news: in Palermo, North Africa was already considered lost. It had quite simply been written off. On 11 January 1160 Mahdia surrendered. The garrison were given safe conduct, with arms and baggage, back to Sicily.

Falcandus, it is hardly necessary to add, suggests that the Almohad leader was in contact with the palace eunuchs in Palermo and already knew in advance of William's decision. This theory, like so many others from the same pen, can probably be discounted; but there remains another more important and more intriguing question. Why did William and Maio let North Africa go so easily? In their European policy they had proved—once the King had shaken off his initial inertia—vigorous, energetic and imaginative. How could they now watch, impassively, while the North African Empire crumbled before their eyes? It was not, after all, only during the siege of Mahdia that this apathy had come upon them; there indeed they had made at least some attempt to fight back. But what of Sfax and Djerba, of Kerkenna and Tripoli? In none of these places had there been more than a token resistance, if that. In 1156, admittedly, the Sicilian forces were fully extended on other, more important fronts; but by 1160 there were no enemies to occupy them elsewhere, and still there was no sign of any counter-offensive—any move, even, military or diplomatic—to regain their former possessions. What held them back?

These questions also occurred to William's subjects at home, many of whom lost no time in blaming Maio for the loss of the overseas empire; and the Emir of Emirs became more unpopular than ever. But in fact, when we look back over these years, his apparently feeble attitude is shown in its proper light and becomes comprehensible. He was playing for higher stakes. By now the pattern of Italian politics had become infinitely more complex and more challenging than in the days of Roger II and George of Antioch, when the African territories had been conquered. Suddenly there had appeared a chance of gaining the moral leadership of all Italy in its emerging struggle against German imperial power; and moral leadership today could mean political leadership tomorrow.

To achieve it, however, Sicily must have freedom of action. With two Empires, a Papacy and an endless number of independent and semi-independent city-states to deal with, to say nothing of an endemic revolutionary situation within her own borders, she could not afford to indulge in enterprises and adventures outside her logical sphere of influence. And, as Maio was intelligent enough to understand, North Africa was well outside. To recover it would mean not just the despatch of an expeditionary force, the siege and capture of a city or two. It would mean the forcible subjection of a whole people and the breaking of a great power—for the Almohads, with an Empire which already extended from the Atlantic to the frontiers of Egypt and from Andalusia to the southern limits of the Sahara, could have held their own against virtually any European army or armies that might have been thrown into the field against them.

The old principle still held good—expeditionary forces could make conquests, but they could not hold them. The fact had been proved time and time again; to it, Sicily owed her continued existence as a nation. Those who forgot it paid dearly for their forgetfulness. Maio of Bari had no intention of falling into the same error himself.

MURDER

This Maio was a very monster; indeed, it would be impossible to find vermin more loathsome, more pernicious or more damaging to the Kingdom. His character was capable of any baseness, and his eloquence was equal to his character. Great was his facility for pretence or dissimulation at will. He was, in addition, much given to debauchery, for ever seeking to bring noble matrons and virgins to his bed; the more unstained their virtue, the more ardently did he strive to possess them.

Hugo Falcandus

WILLIAM had slipped back into his old ways. It might have been expected that his crushing defeat of the Byzantines, and the three ensuing years of intense diplomatic activity during which his star rose higher and higher in the European firmament, would have given him a taste for politics, or at least have tempted him to prove himself as gifted a statesman as he had a general. They did neither. No sooner had he returned to Sicily in July 1156 and passed sentence on those who had taken up arms against him than he once more abandoned himself to a life of pleasure. The old attractions of palace and park, of bower and bedchamber, were too strong. For the next six years he never once visited the mainland, seldom even setting foot outside Palermo and its immediate neighbourhood. The handling of state affairs, both domestic and foreign, he placed as before in the capable hands of Maio of Bari.

Maio's power was now at its zenith. Not only was this Apulian merchant's son the effective ruler of the Kingdom; he was rapidly becoming, thanks to the success of his foreign policies, one of the most influential statesmen in Europe.¹ The baronial party, both on the mainland and in Sicily, resented him more than ever. More than ever they found themselves outcasts, obliged to stand impotently by while the government of the Kingdom became, as they saw it, the exclusive preserve of two separate groups, the one detested, the other despised: first, the Emir's family and henchmen, men like Stephen and Simon, the Master Captains in Apulia; like Archbishop Hugh of Palermo, or like the young Salernitan notary Matthew of Ajello who had drafted the Treaty of Benevento and was obviously being groomed by Maio as his eventual successor; second, the palace eunuchs—almost all of them, like that Peter who had cut such a sorry figure against the Almohad fleet, being baptised Saracens and thus politically as well as physically suspect in the eyes of their enemies.

It was small wonder, in such conditions, that the air of Palermo was heavy with rumours. Men whispered that the Emir was scheming to seize the crown for himself—indeed that he had already appropriated several items of the regalia, which he had been showing off to his friends. He had had no difficulty in laying his hands on such treasures; they were passed to him by the Queen, whose infatuation for him was well known. Others made even more scandalous assertions—that he had revived his plans to do away with the King, and that he had already bribed the Pope, through the agency of Matthew of Ajello, to give him his blessing as William's successor.

Where rumours were so rife, conspiracies were bound to follow. In Palermo, Maio's ubiquitous agents and informers were usually able to nip them in the bud; but the mainland provided would-be plotters with opportunities in plenty and here, some time towards the end of 1159, a group of dissatisfied nobles evolved a scheme to

¹ He was also beginning to build the church of S. Cataldo, immediately west of the Martorana (see plate). With its three high cupolas and honeycomb windows, this church looks, from the outside, as Islamic as S. Giovanni degli Eremiti. Like S. Giovanni, too, its interior is now stripped of all decoration—though the floor and the altar are both original and quietly remarkable in their way. S. Cataldo is, incidentally—with the possible exception of the lovely little SS. Trinità di Delia just outside Castelvetrano—the last Norman Sicilian church in which the Arabic influence is apparent. Henceforth every new Latin church to be built also looked like one.

rid Sicily for ever of the Emir and his whole hated clan. Surprisingly, this group seems not to have included William's own two principal enemies to date; Robert of Loritello and Andrew of Rupecanina were certainly in sympathy with their aims, but preferred to devote their energies to more active warfare along the northern borders of the *Regno*. The leaders of the present conspiracy were, on the whole, less notable figures—barons of the second rank like Richard of Aquila, Roger of Acerra and Bohemund of Tarsia, Count of Manopello. Among them, however, one name stands out, a name we shall meet on several occasions in the story of the coming years— Gilbert, Queen Margaret's cousin, who had recently arrived at court and been sent almost at once to South Italy with the title of Count of Gravina.

Unlike most of the previous conspiracies that had so plagued the peninsula for a century and more, this one had as its object not insurrection but murder. Maio of Bari was to be assassinated. But by whom? There could be no possibility of entrusting the task to hired killers; the Emir was too important, his spies too well-informed. The blow must be struck by one of the parties to the plot, one who knew Maio and could approach him easily, without arousing his suspicions. Thus the choice fell on a young aristocrat, Matthew Bonnellus.

Though Bonnellus bore no title and was therefore not, strictly speaking, a member of the nobility, he came from one of the oldest Norman families in the South. He was brave, he was handsome and, with his vast estates on both sides of the straits of Messina, he was also extremely rich. It had thus been no surprise to anyone when Maio—who, for all his mistrust of the aristocracy, was like everyone in those days something of a snob and who certainly knew a good *parti* when he saw one—had given him preferment at the court and had singled him out as a prospective son-in-law. Shortly afterwards, reports of baronial unrest had arrived from Calabria; and Bonnellus, who had important family connections in the region, had been the obvious emissary to send on a mission of diplomatic pacification. It was, arguably, the greatest mistake of Maio's career. Loving the young man, as Falcandus puts it, like his own son, he seems to have seriously overestimated his intelligence and his fundamental reliability. Once on the mainland, Bonnellus proved unable to resist the pressures which were put on him, notably those exerted by the ravishingly beautiful Countess Clementia of Catanzaro. Within days he too was on the side of the conspirators, sworn to destroy his benefactor; in return for which service he was promised the hand in marriage not of a little Bariot *bourgeoise* but of Clementia herself, the richest and most influential heiress in Calabria.[1]

One of the dangers of being a dictator—as Maio by now effectively was—is that it becomes progressively harder to believe unpalatable truths. Repeated warnings from his brother Stephen had no effect on him. At last he was presented with incontrovertible evidence of the plot, complete with the names of all the principal conspirators with Matthew Bonnellus at the head of the list; but even then the arrival of a single letter from Matthew, announcing that his mission had been successfully completed and asking, as a reward, that his longed-for marriage to Maio's daughter should be brought forward in date, was enough to soothe away all the latter's fears. Reassured, he flung himself into arrangements for the wedding; while his intended son-in-law, now back in Palermo, quietly busied himself with a very different set of plans.

On St Martin's Eve, 10 November 1160, he was ready. And, writes Falcandus,

. . . as the sun went down and the twilight began to fall, you might have seen the whole city alive with vague and sudden rumours, with the citizens moving about hither and thither in groups, anxiously enquiring of each other what was that about to happen that was causing such consternation. Others, with their heads bowed but their ears ever alert for news, were meeting together in the squares and the piazzas, all expressing contradictory opinions. Most of them seemed to think that the King was coming that night, at

[1] At this point in the story, Chalandon falls victim to one of his mercifully rare flights of romantic imagination. He suggests that Matthew Bonnellus's mission to Calabria was arranged by Maio in order to put a stop to the love affair he was already having with the Countess Clementia—whom he describes as the natural daughter of Roger II—in Palermo. As his authority for this story he cites Falcandus; but Falcandus says no such thing. It is in fact highly improbable that Matthew ever met Clementia in Palermo, since she lived permanently in Calabria. Neither is there any reason to doubt her being the perfectly legitimate daughter of Count Raymond of Catanzaro.

Maio's instigation, to the Archbishop's palace, and that there, in that very street, he was to be slain.

They were wrong only in the choice of victim; it was not William but his Emir of Emirs who was calling on Archbishop Hugh that night, and who would not live to see the morning. Whether Hugh was himself an accomplice we cannot tell; Falcandus of course maintains that he was. In any case, soon after Maio's arrival, Matthew Bonnellus silently stationed his men along the Via Coperta, which connected the Archbishop's palace with the Emir's own house. He himself took up a position near the Porta S. Agata, where the street suddenly narrowed before splitting into three. There, in the shadows, he settled down to wait.

At length the palace doors opened and Maio emerged. He was deep in conversation with the Archbishop of Messina and followed by a small escort. Still unconscious of the enemies that surrounded them, they began to move down the Via Coperta; but before they had reached the Porta S. Agata they were accosted by two frightened figures—the notary Matthew of Ajello and the chamberlain Adenulf, who had somehow discovered what was afoot and had hastened to warn their master of the danger. Maio stopped in his tracks and gave orders that Bonnellus should be brought to him at once; but he was too late. The assassin, hearing his name called, leaped from his hiding-place and flung himself forward with drawn sword.

It was all over quite quickly. Maio did his best to defend himself, but his escort had already melted away. He was surrounded and struck down; and his attackers disappeared into the night. Matthew the notary, who had already risked his life to avert the ambush, was also caught in the *mêlée*; gravely wounded, he just managed to scramble away to safety. Meanwhile the body of Sicily's last Emir of Emirs, slashed and lacerated by a dozen sword-thrusts, lay lifeless against the wall where it had fallen.

But not for long. Hearing the tumult, the inhabitants of the nearby houses had hurried to the scene, and within minutes the news was all over Palermo. From every corner of the city men poured into the Via Coperta. Some, according to Falcandus, refused to believe that the blood-soaked corpse at their feet could be that of the great and formidable Emir under whose iron rule they had suffered for nearly seven years; but the majority knew that there could be no mistake and made no effort to conceal their joy. They hurled the body into the centre of the street, kicked it, spat on it; the hair and beard they tore out in handfuls. At last, tiring of the sport, they paused; but they did not disperse. After the violence and brutality of the past hour, what had begun as a curious, faintly apprehensive crowd had been transformed into a wild, vindictive mob. It clamoured for more blood, more destruction. Suddenly it turned and surged away down the street, leaving the former object of its wrath an obscene and shapeless bundle in the dust.

Away in his private apartments on the first floor of the royal palace, the King had heard the shouting, and had soon afterwards received from his Master of the Horse a detailed account of what had happened. As always in a real crisis, William had acted quickly and decisively—so quickly, indeed, that when the mob reached Maio's house they found it already protected by a detachment of the royal guard, the Emir's wife and family having been escorted to the palace for their safety. Other detachments had been sent out to patrol every quarter of the city; it was essential that the rioters should not get out of hand before the King had decided on his future course of action.

But what should this course be? William needed no Emir of Emirs to tell him that his position was both delicate and dangerous. Not only, as he himself put it, had he lost his right hand; he was threatened with the loss of his neck. He was aware that the great mass of his subjects, Muslim and Christian, proletariat as well as aristocracy, had hated Maio and were firmly on the side of Matthew Bonnellus; he knew too just how empty were many of their protestations of loyalty to himself. If he were to yield to his distracted Queen's entreaties by taking firm action against Maio's murderers, he might unleash a general uprising which he would be unable to quell. Regretfully, he saw that he had no choice but to come to terms with the assassins. One day, when his position was more assured, he would punish them as they deserved. For the moment he must hide his anger, dissemble as best he could, and welcome them as his deliverers.

The following morning, 11 November, the King summoned to his presence his old friend and former tutor Henry, Archdeacon of Catania—usually known as Henry Aristippus—and appointed him head of an interim administration. Almost certainly a Norman by birth despite his Greek nickname, Henry was above all a scholar and a scientist. The range of his interests can be judged from the works he translated into his beautiful Latin—two Platonic dialogues, the *Meno* and the *Phaedo*, the fourth book of Aristotle's *Meteorologica*, the *Lives of the Philosophers* by Diogenes Laertius and the *Opuscula* of St Gregory Nazianzen. In addition he was an enthusiastic astronomer and, thanks to the proximity of Mt Etna, an intrepid vulcanologist. He was hard-working and utterly trustworthy; but he was neither an administrator nor a statesman. William seems to have chosen him as much for his gentle, conciliatory character and his knowledge of languages as for any other reason. He deliberately refrained from investing him with Maio's titles—Aristippus became neither Emir of Emirs nor even Chancellor—but he did give his old tutor two lieutenants to help him in his task. One was Count Sylvester of Marsico, a middle-aged aristocrat distantly related to the royal family. His appointment was obviously intended as a sop to Bonnellus and his friends—of whom, though the King could not have known it, Sylvester may even have been an accomplice.[1] The other was considerably more important: Richard Palmer, Bishop-elect of Syracuse, that learned and almost obsessively ambitious Englishman who was destined to remain for the next thirty years one of the leading figures of the political and religious hierarchy of Sicily.

Although two members of this triumvirate had been on friendly terms with Maio in the past they also accepted the necessity of reaching some sort of accommodation with Bonnellus, whose responsibility for the murder was now common knowledge. The

---

[1] One of his first actions on Maio's death was to secure the Emir's property in Palermo for himself—including the church of S. Cataldo, in which his daughter Matilda is buried.

first policy that they adopted, politically expedient as it may have been, therefore redounds to the credit of none of them, and still less to that of William himself—the deliberate and systematic blackening of the Emir's character to the point where his assassin could be shown as the saviour of the country. To his wife and children, already kept in the palace for their protection, the official attitude changed. Gradually they came to realise that they were no longer in care, but in custody. Maio's son was arrested and imprisoned, as was also his chief eunuch; under torture, the two were said to have revealed a whole series of embezzlements and extortions. The worst of those rumours that had so long been circulating were now, it seemed, confirmed.

Once the ground had been suitably prepared William could no longer put off the grant of his royal pardon. Immediately after the murder Matthew Bonnellus had fled with his friends to his castle of Caccamo;[1] thither now arrived royal emissaries, to assure him that the King wished him well, and that he might return without danger to the capital. Though it is unlikely that Bonnellus ever trusted William an inch, recent events had left him in no doubt of his own personal popularity. He accepted the King's invitation. A few days before, he and his men had fled from Palermo at full gallop, under cover of darkness. Now they rode back in triumph. And so, reports Falcandus,

as Bonnellus entered the city, a great crowd swarmed out to greet him, numbering as many men as women; and they accompanied him with immense rejoicing to the gates of the palace. There he was welcomed graciously by the King, and once more received back fully into the royal favour. . . . Thus, by this celebrated deed, he won the love and admiration of the nobility and the common people alike. . . . Meanwhile in Sicily, and especially in Palermo, all the people claimed with one accord that if any man should attempt to do him harm, he should be adjudged a public enemy; and that they would even take up arms against the King himself if he should ever try to exact a penalty for the Emir's death.

[1] This castle, rebuilt and restored but undeniably impressive, still stands on the western slopes of Mt Calogero some seven miles from Termini Imerese. Within, visitors are still shown the Salone della Congiura, in which Bonnellus and his fellow conspirators are said to have held their councils.

Even when we allow for Falcandus's exaggeration, it is clear that as 1161 opened Matthew Bonnellus had become one of the most powerful figures in the Kingdom. But that wave of popularity that had carried him so superbly forward on its crest was soon to break. William, increasingly irritated by the young man's arrogance and encouraged by the Queen to assert his strength and authority, began to recover his nerve. Dissimulation never came easily to him. His true feelings towards the murderer of his friend and counsellor grew daily more evident. Then, one day, he demanded of Bonnellus the payment of duty on his dead father's estate amounting to sixty thousand *taris*—a debt that Maio had deliberately overlooked for the sake of his prospective son-in-law.

The debt was paid: but the incident was a warning. Bonnellus did not underestimate the Queen's influence over her husband; nor that of the palace eunuchs, all creatures of Maio, whom he knew to be urging the King to avenge their old master. He had seen sinister figures loitering around the gates of his house in Palermo, he knew that palace agents were watching him and following his every movement; and he could not escape the conclusion that his life was in danger.

Ever since the Emir's death, Matthew had been under pressure from his associates to move against the King; but he had always held back. To deliver Sicily from a detested tyrant was one thing; to lay hand's on the Lord's anointed was quite another, and he was far from certain of how William's subjects would react. Such a move might lose him all the popularity, and with it all the power, that he was now enjoying. Slowly, however, he began to see that his counsellors had been right. The King, too, must go.

Yet even now Matthew shrank from the idea of regicide. The important thing was to remove William from the seat of power. Once he were safely out of the way there would be plenty of time to decide what to do with him. And as long as he suffered no violence and his little son Roger were enthroned in his stead, royalist opinion should be manageable. Moreover there were at present in Palermo two men of undoubted Hauteville blood who had never concealed their dislike of the King and who could be relied upon to give open support to his removal. The first was his half-brother Simon, Roger II's illegitimate son, who had borne him an understandable grudge ever since William had refused to allow him to keep the Principality of Taranto, with which Roger had invested him in 1148, on the grounds that it was too important a fief to go to a bastard. The second was his nephew Count Tancred of Lecce, natural son of Duke Roger, who in consequence of the part he had played in the Apulian revolt, had spent the last five years in the palace dungeons.

It was perhaps the thought of Tancred that suggested to the conspirators the basic idea for their plot. To seize the person of the King was no easy task. He seldom appeared in public; of his two principal residences, the Favara was set in the middle of a lake, while the royal palace in Palermo was still in essence the Norman fortress that the two Rogers had made it. Furthermore its exterior was patrolled by a special guard, three hundred strong, commanded by a castellan known for his absolute incorruptibility and loyalty to his sovereign. Beneath the south-west corner of that same building, however, was the political prison, which the upheavals of the recent years and the repressive policies of Maio of Bari had kept filled to capacity. If all its inmates could be simultaneously released they might, as it were, storm the building from within.

Fortunately for Bonnellus and his friends, the palace official directly responsible for the safety of the prisoners proved open to persuasion; sweetened by an enormous bribe and, doubtless, the promise of advancement to some position of higher authority under the new regime, he readily agreed not only to liberate them at a pre-arranged signal but also to supply them with arms. The prisoners were alerted, and their duties explained to them. When all had been arranged, Matthew rode off to another of his castles, at Mistretta, away in the Nébrodi mountains some miles to the south-east of Cefalù. Here, it seems, he proposed to hold William till the King's ultimate fate could be decided; he now set about preparing it for its royal prisoner and putting its defences in readiness to withstand an attack. He told his associates that he would be back in Palermo shortly, and in any case well before the day appointed for the *coup*; on no account were they to take any action until his return.

Had he been a little older and wiser, he would have known that in any military or paramilitary operation one of the first duties of a leader, particularly during the crucial period immediately before the action, is to keep contact at all times with his men. Away at Mistretta there was no means of reaching him in an emergency; and now, suddenly, an emergency arose. The scheme was indiscreetly revealed to a local knight who proved loyal to the King; from that moment on, the plotters were no longer safe. There was no time to be lost waiting for Bonnellus; the only hope lay in putting their plan into operation at once, before they were themselves arrested.

On the morning of 9 March 1161, at about the third hour after sunrise, the signal was given. The dungeons were flung open, the prisoners snatched the weapons that had been laid out ready for them and hurried to let in the conspirators by the side door where they were waiting. Then, led by the princes Simon and Tancred who knew the palace well, they ran to the large room in the Pisan Tower where they knew the King would be holding his regular morning conference with Henry Aristippus. William was taken utterly by surprise. Seeing that flight was impossible, he dived for the window and began shouting for help; but hardly had the first cry left his lips when he was seized bodily and dragged away. Two of the plotters, William of Lesina and Robert of Bova, the first described by Falcandus as 'a most atrocious man'—*vir atrocissimus*—the second 'famous for his cruelty', now advanced threateningly upon him with drawn swords; only the intervention of a third, Richard of Mandra, saved his life. Meanwhile another group made straight for the Queen's apartments and arrested Margaret and her two sons.

As soon as the royal family had been safely secured, the pillage began. The palace was a veritable treasure-house, and the intruders went through it like locusts. The collections of gold and jewels so lovingly amassed by Roger and William over the past forty years were ransacked. Nothing portable was left behind. The precious pots and vases, with everything else that could do duty as a container, were filled with coins from the coffers and carried off, as were all the royal and ecclesiastical vestments from the *Tiraz*. Saddest of all perhaps, Edrisi's great silver planisphere, despite its immense weight, disappeared never to be seen again. A fire was lit in the courtyard, and nearly all the government records, including the entire registry of fiefs and the services due for them, were hurled on to the flames. Meanwhile all those eunuchs who could not make good their escape were put to the sword; the harem—left undefended—was broken into, its inmates dragged screaming away or violated on the spot.

The massacre of the eunuchs introduced a new and sinister element into the situation. The aristocratic party had long objected to what it considered the disproportionate influence of Muslims at the court, and the initial success of the *coup* seems to have released a pent-up hatred of the whole Islamic community. Suddenly, no Saracen was safe. Even those working innocently in the *diwan*, the mint and other public offices had to flee for their lives; several of the Muslim artists and sages whom William, like his father, accommodated permanently in the palace—among them one of the most distinguished Arabic poets of his day, Yahya ibn at-Tifashi—were hunted down and killed; while down in the lower part of the city a Christian mob descended on the bazaar, forcing all the Arab merchants and shopkeepers, who since the African defeats of 1159–60 had been forbidden by law to carry arms, to retreat to the specifically Muslim quarter of the town where the narrow streets gave them the protection they needed.

By now a still larger crowd had gathered in the great square before the palace. Swept by conflicting and contradictory rumours, its prevailing mood was still one of bewilderment. The King was dead; he was alive; he was a prisoner; he was free; it was a Saracen plot to seize power; it was a Christian one to purge the government of Muslim influence. Within the building, however, the ringleaders knew that this atmosphere of uncertainty could not last. Sooner or later, popular feeling must crystallise; and on the form it eventually took the success of the entire *coup* would depend. It was not enough to curry the favour of the mob by flinging an occasional handful of coins out of the palace windows. The time had come for a public declaration of policy and intent. It was therefore announced that William's eldest son Roger had formally succeeded his father on the Sicilian throne, and that he would be crowned in the Cathedral within a very few days—just as soon, in fact, as Matthew Bonnellus returned to Palermo. Meanwhile the little boy, now nine years old, was mounted on a horse and solemnly paraded through the streets of the capital, and the people were invited to acclaim their new King.

Their reaction does not seem to have been enthusiastic; and when the procession was repeated on the following morning, an acute observer might have noticed that even those accompanying the young prince were looking a trifle uncomfortable. Before long the whole city knew why. The conspirators, their ranks now swollen by a number of senior government and church officials who had since pledged their support, were themselves in open conflict. A growing body of opinion was now turning against the idea of a child king, and was favouring instead the succession of Simon, Roger's bastard son.

For the moment there was deadlock, and the leaders of the revolt decided to leave the issue open until the return of Bonnellus. It was a fatal mistake. Any political *coup*, if it is to succeed, must be swift and certain. Momentum is everything. The people must be presented with a *fait accompli*; there can be no half-way pauses and changes of direction. Thus a second vital rule was broken, and King William's throne was saved. The royalists seized the opportunity to regroup themselves; their agents went to work in the streets and taverns, spreading rumours unfavourable to Bonnellus and his party and everywhere finding ready listeners. The conduct of the insurgents and in particular the sack of the palace had had a deplorable effect. All respectable citizens had been revolted by the bloodshed and the violence, and shocked by the indiscriminate looting of riches which might one day be needed for the defence of the Kingdom. Little by little public opinion began to harden; sympathy grew for the captive King; and the conspirators suddenly awoke to find all Sicily united against them.

Their last hope lay in Matthew Bonnellus. By his absence he had avoided any direct responsibility for what had occurred; if he could be brought back quickly enough, the magic of his name and prestige might yet save the day. Two of the leaders rode off at top speed to Mistretta to fetch him. They were too late. Scarcely had they left Palermo when a group of high ecclesiastics, whose loyalty to the King had never wavered, took an initiative of their own. They were led by the Archbishops Romuald of Salerno and Robert of Messina,

Bishop Tristan of Mazara and Richard Palmer, the Bishop-elect of
Syracuse. None of them had been particular friends of Maio, but
they had no wish to see their own considerable influence at court
destroyed by the aristocrats. They also genuinely deplored the offer
of violence to an anointed King. On Saturday 11 March they called
on the people of Palermo to storm the palace and rescue their
sovereign; and the people responded.

The rebels soon saw that against such numbers resistance was
hopeless. To gain time, they tried to negotiate, pointing out that
Bonnellus would soon return and that once he resumed control all
the present misunderstandings would be resolved. It was no use.
The name had lost its magic. Meanwhile those defending the walls
reported that they could not hold out much longer; if the building
were taken by storm, it would be a miracle if any of them escaped
with their lives. They were beaten. Running to the captive King, they
fell on their knees before him and implored his pardon.

William was saved—in theory; but he was not yet out of danger.
Physically he remained in the power of his enemies, to whom he was
an invaluable hostage. They were desperate, and if they thought they
had nothing to lose they might yet carry him with them to destruction. Walking slowly to a window of the Pisan Tower[1], he showed
himself to the crowd gathered below. Immediately a great cry went
up, a demand for the palace gates to be opened and vengeance taken
on the traitors; but William raised his hand for silence. His subjects,
he said, had given him more than adequate proof of their loyalty and
affection. He would ask them now simply to lay down their arms and
to disperse quietly to their homes, allowing free egress from the
palace to all those still within, to whom he had granted his royal
pardon. The crowd obediently withdrew; the rebels slipped out and
fled back to Caccamo.

Only after they had gone did Romuald and his fellow-churchmen
enter the King's chamber. From the window, shortly before, William
had spoken bravely and well; but they found him now in a state of

[1] See plate. Falcandus claims that it was from the neighbouring Gioaria that
William addressed the throng, in which case he almost certainly spoke from
the window of what is now known as the *Sala di Ruggero*. (See pp. 601–2.) But
Romuald of Salerno, who was an eye-witness, is categorical on the subject,
and we must accept his word.

near-collapse, sobbing uncontrollably. After the events of the past three days, such emotion would in any case have been easy enough to understand; but the real tragedy, they now learned, had occurred at the moment of his salvation. During the last assault on the palace his little son and heir Roger, who had been in the room with him, had been struck in the eye by a stray arrow, and now lay dying. This final shock had been too much; William's spirit was broken.[1] With difficulty the bishops persuaded him to descend to the great hall beneath, where a numerous delegation of his subjects, heedless of his earlier injunction, was waiting to congratulate him on his escape. He appeared before them but still could not trust himself to speak. All he could do was stammer a few words into the ear of Richard Palmer— 'a man of great learning and eloquence' as Falcandus reminds us— who relayed them in the King's name to the assembled company. It was a strangely humble speech, in which William admitted his past wrongs, acknowledged that his recent sufferings were not undeserved and promised to revoke certain recent decrees which had caused resentment. As an earnest of his good intentions, the local customs dues levied on all foodstuffs brought into the city were abolished from that moment.

Whether this last idea was the King's or Palmer's, it suited the occasion perfectly. William was cheered to the echo. Henceforth, at least in Palermo, his position was re-established, his popularity assured.

But, though the rebellion had failed, the rebels were still free and under arms; and from the castle of Caccamo to which they had retreated there came no word of surrender. Militarily, the King remained vulnerable. He had no forces in the capital except the three hundred men of the palace garrison; they had been singularly ineffectual during the past few days and were no longer to be relied upon. He therefore summoned the bulk of the army and the fleet from Messina; meanwhile, playing for time, he sent an ostensibly friendly

[1] Falcandus, leaping at the chance of pinning a new atrocity on to his old enemy, admits the arrow wound but suggests that little Roger was in fact kicked to death by his father, in a rage at what he considered to be the boy's earlier disloyalty: a suggestion so improbable that one wonders whether it could ever have been taken seriously.

message to Matthew Bonnellus, now himself back at Caccamo, asking why he was giving asylum to enemies of the Crown.

Matthew's reply was an interesting one. He began by assuring the King that he was himself quite unconnected with the last uprising. It was true, however, that the insurgents were his friends and colleagues; how then could he possibly refuse them shelter? They had done what they did out of sheer despair, only because there was no other way of obtaining redress for the wrongs that they, with all other members of the nobility, were obliged to suffer. To cite but one example, they could no longer even marry off their daughters without prior permission of the Curia; and this permission was often so long in coming that many a lady had to wait for a husband till she was long past child-bearing age, while others were condemned to perpetual virginity.[1] In short, there could be no reconciliation between King and aristocracy until William agreed to restore the old customs and usages introduced by Robert Guiscard and Roger I in the preceding century.

Once again Matthew had miscalculated. This was no time for arrogance. His reply infuriated the King. If, William protested, the nobles had first laid down their arms and then come to him as suppliants, he would have listened sympathetically to their grievances; as it was, he would willingly sacrifice his kingdom or even face death itself rather than give in to threats. Negotiations were immediately broken off; he had nothing more to say.

The rebels had badly overplayed their hand. Bonnellus saw that his only hope was to strike again—and to strike quickly, before the expected reinforcements could arrive from Messina. Suddenly and without warning he and his men swooped down from Caccamo to a point near Favara, only a mile or two from Palermo itself, and from there spread out to occupy all the approach roads to the capital. It was a bold and well-executed plan. The Palermitans, taken by surprise and without adequate provisions or defences, began to panic; and if Matthew had pressed his advantage home and marched straight into the city this second attempt might well have proved

---

[1] This grievance was prompted by something more than paternal compassion; Bonnellus apparently forbore to add the real reason for the nobles' indignation— the fact that if they died childless their estates reverted to the Crown.

successful. Instead, at the critical moment, he hesitated. As he did so
the first ships from Messina appeared in the harbour; soldiers were
hurriedly disembarked and posted in key positions; other loyal
detachments arrived from the interior of the island to join them; and
the rebels, now hopelessly outnumbered, retreated once again to
Caccamo.

This time they were ready to talk reasonably; and the terms which
William was prepared to offer proved more generous than any of
them had a right to expect. There were no executions, no imprison-
ments. Most of the leaders elected to go into exile, including Simon,
Tancred and William of the Principate—another distant cousin of the
King—to whom passage was offered in Sicilian ships as far as
Terracina. Several were sent on forced pilgrimages to Jerusalem.
Richard of Mandra on the other hand—who, on that first fateful
morning, had shielded his sovereign's body with his own—received
a free pardon. As for Matthew Bonnellus, the driving force behind
three *coups* within six months, he too was granted a pardon and
summoned back to the court, where William once again received
him with every show of friendliness and favour.

Why, at such a moment, did the King show himself so astonishingly merciful? Only five years before, after an insurrection no whit
more serious than that which was just over, he had embarked on an
orgy of hanging, drowning and blinding, filling his prisons with
those lucky enough to escape anything worse, leaving the smouldering ruins of what had once been Bari as an example of the fate which
awaited any city in his dominion that dared set itself up against him.
How can it be that, after three days of terror from which he had
narrowly escaped with his life, we find him pronouncing no more
fearful sentences than those of comfortable exile, and receiving back
with open arms the traitor who had come nearer than any other in
the Kingdom's history to toppling the Sicilian throne?

The first, short answer is that although the insurgents had failed
in both their attempts to seize power, they had still not surrendered.
The fortress of Caccamo was commandingly situated and strongly
defended, and if Matthew had resolved to stand firm it might well
have held out for a year or more. Just what effect this would have
had on the general morale in Palermo is hard to assess, but the terror

caused by the recent blockade suggested that it might be serious; and William could not risk any more major disturbances in the capital. Only by the total cessation of hostilities and the speedy dislodging of his enemy from Caccamo could tranquillity be restored. But Matthew would not surrender unless he were sure of a pardon. In such a case it would hardly be possible to make an example of his followers.

It was lucky for William that the young man was as conceited as he was foolish. Otherwise he could never have been persuaded, as he apparently was, that his prestige was still such as to make him at once indispensable and invulnerable. But when at last he swallowed the bait and stood, truculent as ever, once more before his sovereign, William must have known that Matthew Bonnellus was finished. Victim of his own vanity, he would never make trouble again. He was to enjoy a few more weeks of liberty, swaggering about Palermo and boasting of his power over the King; but when, towards the end of April, new revolts broke out in central Sicily and on the mainland, William decided to have done with him once and for all.

The arrest itself presented no problems. Matthew was simply summoned to the palace. Despite several secret warnings he still believed his position unshakable, and obeyed without hesitation. Once there, he was seized by the guards and hustled away to what Falcandus is at pains to describe as a particularly revolting dungeon —not, this time, in the palace itself (William never made the same mistake twice) but in the adjacent fortress, usually known by its Arabic name of al-Halka, the Ring.

The civil disturbances that followed seem to have been little more than a formality. Since his return to Palermo Matthew had worked hard to keep his image bright, and on hearing of his capture his agents in the town lost no time in mobilising support for a popular demonstration. But the citizens' hearts were not in it. They were tired of unrest and upheaval, and were discouraged almost before they began. Both the palace and the Halka had been put under close guard; a rather desultory attempt to burn down the gates was easily frustrated; and, writes Falcandus,

seeing that they could achieve nothing, the people . . . suffered a sudden change of heart—preferring, as is characteristic of the Sicilians, to bow to the needs of the moment rather than to maintain any constant faith. And as many as had formerly cried out for the liberation of Bonnellus now took pains to make it clear that they had never been among those who sought his friendship.

Among the King's supporters only one casualty is recorded—Adenulf, the royal chamberlain, who was set upon and stabbed to death by one of Bonnellus's knights. The rebel side, however, was less fortunate; William's mood of clemency was past. Few of those who now fell into his hands escaped death or multilation. And Matthew himself, blinded and hamstrung, was left to languish in his dungeon cell—in which, not long afterwards, he died.

13

THE END OF A REIGN

Civis obit, inquit, multum majoribus impar
Nosse modum juris, sed in hoc tamen utilis aevo.
Gone is a citizen [he said] who though no peer
Of those who disciplined the state of yore . . .
Yet in this age irreverent of law
Has played a noble part.

[Tr. E. Ridley]

From Cato's funeral oration on Pompey, as given by Lucan, *Pharsalia*, Book IX; quoted, according to Hugo Falcandus, by the Bishop-elect of Syracuse on the death of William I.

THE revolts in the Sicilian heartland and in Apulia were serious but short-lived. In the former, the danger lay not so much in any direct threat to the safety of the King as in the ominously confessional turn which events had taken. The two nobles primarily responsible, Tancred of Lecce and Roger Sclavo, had left Caccamo just in time and withdrawn to the south of the island, taking Piazza[1] and Butera and deliberately stirring up the local Lombard[2] communities

[1] Now more generally known as Piazza Armerina—a name derived from the fortified camp—*castrum armorum*—built by the Great Count Roger I on the nearby Piano Armerino. As a town it is now best known for the ruins of a third-century imperial Roman villa, the so-called *Villa del Casale*, probably destroyed by William in 1161 and rediscovered only in quite recent years. The floor-mosaics of this palace have justly made it one of the most popular tourist attractions of all Sicily. Visitors to Piazza should not, however, overlook the lovely little priory of S. Andrea, a mile or two away to the north. It was built in 1096 by Simon, Count of Butera, cousin of Roger II through his mother Adelaide and probably—though Chalandon does not accept this—the natural father of Roger Sclavo.

[2] The past half-century had seen an enormous growth in the Lombard colonies originally introduced into Sicily by Roger I. Apart from Piazza and Butera, their principal centres were Randazzo, Nicosia, Capizzi, Aidone and Maniace. La Lumia, writing just a century ago, noted that the inhabitants of these areas still spoke a dialect more akin to those of North Italy than to normal Sicilian.

against the Muslim peasantry. The terror spread as far as Catania and Syracuse. In many areas the Saracens escaped massacre only by disguising themselves as Christians and taking flight; even when order had been re-established, few returned to their former homes.

On the mainland, too, the pot was back on the boil. Robert of Loritello, never inactive for long, had driven down into the Basilicata—the instep of Italy—as far as Taranto and Oriolo; Andrew of Rupecanina was raising a similar revolt in Campania; Salerno, disloyal for the first time, had joined the insurgents; and now even Calabria, in the past the most reliable of all the King's dominions, had been aroused by the Countess Clementia—perhaps in revenge for William's treatment of her lover—and was taking up arms against him. Only a few barons in the entire peninsula had remained loyal— men like Bohemund of Manopello and the Queen's cousin Gilbert of Gravina who, despite their complicity in the plot against Maio, had recently been restored to favour.

But however desperate things might become on the mainland, Sicilian problems must be dealt with first; William could only appeal to Gilbert to hold the situation there as best he could with such forces as were already available, while he himself marched against Tancred and Roger Sclavo. By the end of April he was in the field. Piazza, after a few weeks' siege, was sacked and levelled to the ground. Butera, his next objective, presented a more formidable challenge. The rebels, hoping that the troubles beyond the straits might at any moment force the King to raise the siege, fought with determination—even consulting astrologers to determine the most favourable occasions for sorties and counter-attacks. Since William was able, through his own astrologers, to predict the precise moments they would choose and make his dispositions accordingly, this method seems to have done more harm than good; nevertheless, winter was already closing in before shortage of food, combined with growing discontent on the part of the civilian population, persuaded them to surrender the town in return for their own safe conduct into exile. William accepted their terms and let them go; but on the town that had betrayed him twice in five years he had no pity. By Christmas the proud pinnacle where once Butera had stood bore nothing but a heap of smouldering ruins.

After a pause in Palermo to keep the feast and to prepare for the coming campaign, the King crossed to the mainland early the follow-following March. As he pressed up through Calabria, the Countess Clementia and her family had retreated to their fortress of Taverna, up in the mountains due north of Catanzaro. They too fought hard, releasing quantitites of heavy barrels studded with spikes which trundled down the steep escarpments into the ranks of the besiegers, causing heavy and hideous casualties; but William's second assault was successful. The Countess's two uncles were executed; she and her mother were taken prisoner and sent back to an unknown fate in Palermo.

Henceforth, as on his previous campaign, the opposition seemed to disintegrate at William's approach. He himself showed no mercy. When his Great Chamberlain, the eunuch Johar, was caught in the act of absconding with the royal seals, he had him drowned on the spot. At Taranto, which capitulated after the shortest of struggles, he hanged all the supporters of Robert of Loritello that he could find— though Robert himself had already fled to join Frederick Barbarossa in Lombardy. Up through Apulia, across the mountains into Campania, everywhere it was the same story—quick surrenders followed by hangings, blindings and mutilations, occasionally commuted to the payment by a whole town or district of 'redemption money'—a compulsory imposition which, though it frequently ruined those upon whom it fell for many years to come, did much to replenish the King's own ransacked treasury.

Some time in the summer he reached Salerno. Many of the elders of the city who had identified themselves with the revolt had disappeared; but the remainder came out to greet their King with every protestation of affection and loyalty. William would not listen; he refused point-blank even to enter the city. His betrayal by his own capital was the ultimate treason, and it demanded the ultimate penalty. And indeed Salerno would undoubtedly have suffered the same fate as Bari half a dozen years before had it not been for the intervention of two powerful protectors. The first was its patron saint, St Matthew, who according to Archbishop Romuald suddenly sent out of a clear and cloudless noonday sky a tempest of such fury as to uproot the tents of the entire army, including William's own, in their camp outside the walls. Thus, it seems, was the King persuaded of the divine displeasure that he would incur if any harm came to the city. The second advocate was the saint's namesake and a native son of Salerno, Matthew the Notary, who persuaded Sylvester of Marsico and Richard Palmer to intercede on behalf of his birthplace.

The combined efforts of the two Matthews had their effect. William contented himself with ordering a purge of all unreliable elements and hanging all those who were found guilty of conspiring against him. Salerno was saved.

But though the immediate danger was over, the damage done could never be entirely repaired. When, in the late summer of 1162, William returned to Sicily, it was to find the island tormented and terrorised by confessional hatreds on a scale unprecedented in its history. He had left it in a hurry, knowing full well that many of those who had taken part in the Sicilian uprisings had not yet been brought to justice; and he had entrusted the task of tracking them down, together with the government of Palermo itself, to one of the palace Caïds,[1] a baptised eunuch called Martin. It had been a disastrous choice. Martin had narrowly escaped with his life when the rebels had stormed the palace in the previous year; his brother had been killed in the massacre that followed; and ever since that day he had nurtured a deep loathing for all Christians. Thus, on William's departure for the mainland the previous March, a veritable reign of terror had begun. Everywhere, those who had at any time plotted or even spoken against the King or his ministers were hunted down, and many an old score between Muslim and Christian must have been settled by a timely denunciation to the public investigators. Those on whom suspicion fell were subjected to various forms of trial by ordeal which, since survival was usually equated with guilt, could be relied upon to eliminate all undesirables, however tenuous the case against them. The local authorities, ordered to institute purges in all areas under their control, were too frightened to disobey. Redemption money was levied even in those towns and districts which had

---

[1] Caïd, the Arabic word for master or leader, was the title given to the Muslim or originally Muslim administrative officials of the palace. In the Latin chronicles it usually takes the form of *gaitus* or *gaytus*.

never wavered in their loyalty. Thus order was restored and the state
coffers refilled—but at a heavy price. The respect which, despite
every upheaval, the bulk of the local populations had felt for the
central government was hereafter tinged with a new, unhealthy fear;
and the harmony which the two Rogers had worked so hard to
create between their Christian and their Muslim subjects was destroyed for ever.

Among the victims was Henry Aristippus. Falcandus claims
that he had been party to the last plot and had forfeited any
hope of a pardon by abducting certain ladies of the harem for his own
delectation; considering Henry's age and record, it is hard to say
which of the two charges is the more improbable. There is another,
far simpler explanation for his downfall. He was a gentle scholar,
suddenly swept up into a world of plot and counter-plot, of court
intrigue at its most violent and vicious. His position in such a world
was bound to make him enemies; and when it was time for those
enemies to overthrow him they did so without a qualm, using
weapons he did not understand and against which he had no defence.
And so William's oldest friend and staunchest supporter shared the
same fate as his bitterest and most unscrupulous adversary; like
Matthew Bonnellus, Henry Aristippus ended his career in a dungeon
cell, and never knew freedom again.

The crisis was past. In the space of a single year William had
suffered the loss of his most trusted counsellor, murdered in a public
street; of his own son and heir, shot by an insurgent's arrow before
his very eyes; of much of his country's wealth and nearly all his
personal possessions; and, not least, of his reputation and his self-
respect. He had survived two major attempts to dethrone him—
one of which had very nearly succeeded and had resulted in his being
held a captive, with his family, in hourly expectation of death—only
to find both his island and his mainland Kingdom in a state of open
revolt. Here, surely, was the ultimate vindication of Maio's policies,
however unpopular they may have been; one short year after the
Emir's death, Sicily must have seemed on the point of disintegration.
Yet only one more year had sufficed for William to restore his
authority, together with a large part of his finances; and by the time

he returned to Palermo his grip on his country was firmer and more assured than ever it had been. A few months later, the prisoners in the palace dungeons made one more attempt at a mass escape as in 1161; they failed, and the King closed down the palace prison for ever. With that single exception, his reign was never again troubled with sedition or revolt.

William was still young—a little over forty. He had shown himself to be a man of courage and strength, when these qualities were indispensable. But now that he could afford to relax he once more cut himself off from all the cares of kingship, leaving the government in the hands of a new triumvirate in which Henry Aristippus was replaced by the notary Matthew of Ajello, and old Count Sylvester—who died at about this time—by Caïd Peter, that same slightly colourless eunuch who had made such an indifferent showing at Mahdia but who had now been promoted to the rank of Great Chamberlain of the Palace. Only one member remained unchanged—Richard Palmer, the still unconsecrated Bishop of Syracuse. Together, the three represented a wide cross-section of the King's subjects: the Italian-Lombard bourgeoisie, the Muslim bureaucracy and the Latin Church. Only two groups were pointedly omitted—the Greeks and the Norman aristocracy, who had if anything even less say in the government than before. But the importance of the Greeks was declining fast; and as for the Norman aristocracy, it had only itself to blame.

And so William, 'having given strict orders to his ministers to tell him nothing that might disturb his peace of mind'—as the reader may suspect, we have to rely largely on Falcandus for such knowledge as we have of this period—relapsed once again into his private world of ease and pleasure. But not altogether into idleness; 'for,' writes Romuald of Salerno, 'in those days, King William built near Palermo a palace of considerable height, constructed with superb artifice, which he called the Zisa;[1] and he surrounded it with beautiful fruit-bearing trees and pleasant gardens, and with divers watercourses and fish-pools he rendered it delectable.'

The neighbourhood of the Zisa—out beyond the Porta Nuova to

---

[1] The word comes from the Arabic *aziz*, or magnificent. The earliest versions of Romuald's chronicle wrongly transcribe it as *Lisa*.

the north-west of the city—is now a good deal less salubrious than it was eight centuries ago; and those centuries have also taken their toll of the building itself. Recently, however, it has been carefully restored and it remains, after the Royal Palace, the most splendid of all the Norman secular buildings left to us. The exterior is, undeniably, somewhat forbidding; in the twelfth century palaces were still designed to do duty as fortresses should the occasion require, and William's experiences over the past few years were not such as to encourage him to make an exception. Though the little square towers at each end and the gently recessed blind arches do something to lighten the structure, the general effect at first sight is more awesome than attractive; and the crenellations along the roof, cut into the original entablature during the fifteenth or sixteenth century and making nonsense of the great Arabic inscription that formerly ran the length of the façade, hardly improve matters.

But step now into the central hall of the palace. At once you are in a different world.[1] Nowhere does Norman Sicily speak more persuasively of the Orient; nowhere else on all the island is that specifically Islamic talent for creating quiet havens of shade and coolness in the summer heat so dazzlingly displayed. The ceiling is high and honeycombed, the three inner walls set with deep niches, roofed in their turn with those tumbling stalactites so dear to Saracen architects. All around, zig-zagging in and out of the niches, runs a frieze of marble and multi-coloured mosaic, broadening out in the centre of the back wall into three medallions in which, against a background of exquisite decorative arabesques, confronted archers are busy shooting birds out of a tree, while two pairs of peacocks peck dates, with studied unconcern, from conveniently stunted palms. It takes no great effort of the imagination to picture the King in this lovely room, taking his ease with his wise men or his concubines, and gazing out into his sunlit garden, while from a fountain in the wall comes the soothing plash of water, trickling down a marble incline into an ornamental channel and thence to the vivarium outside.

But William never saw the Zisa completed. The finishing touches were left to his son; and it was William II who was to sum up what the building meant to him in the second magnificent

[1] See plate.

Arabic inscription, raised in white stucco round the entrance arch.[1]

Here, as oft as thou shalt wish, shalt thou see the loveliest possession of this Kingdom, the most splendid of the world and of the seas.
The mountains, their peaks flushed with the colour of narcissus . . .
Thou shalt see the great King of his century in his beautiful dwelling-place, a house of joy and splendour which suits him well.
This is the earthly paradise that opens to the view; this King is the *Musta'iz*;[2] this palace the *Aziz*.

Despite the restoration much remains to be done, both to the Zisa itself and to its surroundings, before it can once again live up to this description. The neglect of centuries cannot be repaired overnight, and an air of desolation still lingers over the bleak expanse where once the songbirds sang and the fish leaped lazily in the pools.

From this gentle afternoon of William's reign only one more monument remains—though it too may have been completed after his death. It is a room on the second floor of the royal palace, nowadays irritatingly and misleadingly known as the *Sala di Ruggero*;[3] a small room that could almost have been described as unassuming were it not for the mosaics with which its vault and upper walls are so sumptuously encrusted. Like those of the Zisa—the only other secular mosaics that have come down to us from Norman days[4]— they are decorative rather than devotional; and the emotions they evoke are those of sheer pleasure. Here are scenes of the country-

[1] The central part of this inscription was destroyed when the original high arch was removed and replaced by the lower one which appears, surmounted by a French window, in so many of the older photographs. Now the original proportions have been restored; but the missing words are lost for ever.

[2] *The Glorious One.* The title was used only by William II, hence the dating of the inscription.

[3] See plate.

[4] I do not count the few odd traces still clinging to the walls of the *Sala degli Armigeri* in another section of the palace. This hall, forty-five feet high and topped by a stalactite ceiling of considerably greater interest than the mosaic, forms part of the Torre Pisana, and probably served as a guardroom for the Tesoro nearby. It is not normally open to the public, but enthusiasts should have no difficulty in obtaining permission to visit it from the office of the Soprintendenza ai Monumenti on the first floor.

side and the chase, Byzantine in their formal symmetry but Sicilian in their joyful portrayal of palms and orange-trees, and all radiant with a liveliness and humour that is wholly of the west. Here once more are the date-gobbling peacocks and the myopic archers, but now they have been joined by a pair of centaurs and a host of other fauna both probable and improbable, many of them with expressions on their faces that seem almost human—leopards consumed with guilt and suspicion, other peacocks frankly shocked, lions self-conscious, and two burly stags, affronted in both senses of the word, glowering at each other in innocent unawareness of the horrid fate that awaits them in the rear.

We have no documentary evidence to tell us about these mosaics, nothing but their style—and in particular their affinity with those of the Zisa—to help us to date them. No matter. What really counts in this enchanting room, this gorgeous bestiary in blue and green and gold, is the way it speaks to us, like the Zisa but far more loudly and clearly, of the happier and more carefree side of Norman Sicilian life; reminding us how, despite all the intrigues and conspiracies and rebellions that fill so many of these pages, the sun still shone through the forest and men still looked on the world around them, and laughed, and were grateful.

William the Bad ended his reign as he had begun it, leaving all the responsibilities of state to others while he enjoyed all the privileges himself. There is no suggestion that his conscience ever troubled him; not even the appalling earthquake of 4 February 1163 which shook all eastern Sicily, virtually destroying Catania and causing a large section of Messina to crumble into the sea, seems to have worried him unduly. After all, the western end of the island where he lived remained unaffected. In Palermo, the walls of the Palatine Chapel were still further enriched with mosaic and marble;[1] the Zisa rose ever higher; the harem, the library and the game parks were constantly enriched for his pleasure. For him it should have been a happy time.

But it did not last. In March 1166 the King was stricken with a violent dysentery, accompanied by fever. Doctors were summoned,

[1] See p. 435.

among them Archbishop Romuald, who had probably attended the famous medical school at Salerno during his youth and who certainly enjoyed a high reputation as a physician. Later, to explain his lack of success, Romuald was to claim that his royal patient refused to accept many of the medicaments prescribed for him. In any event, after languishing for two months, rallying and relapsing by turns, William died on 7 May 1166, at about three o'clock in the afternoon. He was forty-six years old.

Even Hugo Falcandus, who loathed the late King and who, as we know, never hesitated to adjust historical truth to his own purposes, has to admit that William the Bad was genuinely mourned. The citizens of Palermo, he writes,

dressed themselves in black garments, and remained in this sombre apparel for three days. And throughout that time all the ladies, the noble matrons and especially the Saracen women—to whom the King's death had caused unimaginable grief—paraded day and night in sackcloth about the streets, their hair all undone, while before them went a great multitude of handmaidens, singing sad threnodies to the sound of tambourines till the whole city rang with their lamentations.

Despite energetic demands by the canons of Cefalù—where Roger's two great porphyry sarcophagi still awaited worthy occupants—it was agreed that William should be buried in Palermo; not even with his father in the cathedral, but more privately in the Palatine Chapel. No preparations had been made for an elaborate tomb; the body was laid in a relatively modest receptacle and consigned to the Chapel crypt.[1] Twice since then it has been disturbed. The first time was barely twenty years after the King's death, when it was transferred to its existing sarcophagus—of porphyry, like his father's—and its present position in the sanctuary of Monreale Cathedral. The second was in 1811 when, after a serious fire in the building, the sarcophagus was opened. William's corpse was found to be in a remarkable state of preservation, the pale face still covered with that thick beard that had struck such terror into the hearts of his more timorous subjects.

[1] The place where it rested was rediscovered during the restorations of 1921 and can still be seen today.

He had not been a good king. Despite his formidable appearance, he seems to have had little real confidence in himself. To some extent this was natural. To follow Roger II on the throne of Sicily would have been a daunting enough prospect for anyone; William had received no training for kingship until he was thirty, and if Roger had had a low opinion of his fourth son's capabilities—as there is good reason to believe that he did—he is unlikely to have concealed the fact. It is hardly surprising, then, that William should have tried to conceal his insecurity behind that fearsome exterior, and to pass off his shortcomings as an administrator with elaborate demonstrations of indifference. It may also be more than coincidental that he tended to shy away from those very aspects of statecraft—finance, diplomacy and legislation—that had so fascinated his father. Only where he felt that he could compete with Roger on equal terms could he prove to the world that he too was a Hauteville. Thus he too could build magnificently; and, above all, he could fight. He was a better soldier than his father had ever been, and he knew it. When he was besieged in his own palace, bereft of friends or counsellors, he had revealed himself as what he so often was—a hesitant, frightened man; but once he was in the field, his army behind him, he was transformed. And when the final crisis came, it was his courage and military skill that saved the Kingdom.

This very contrast, however, is typical of him. Throughout his life he remained unsteady and mercurial—a consequence, perhaps, of that same lack of self-reliance that was his most fatal weakness. Long periods of the profoundest lethargy would be interrupted with bursts of frantic, almost hysterical activity. He could be cruel to the point of savagery at one moment, almost unbelievably merciful the next. His attitude to Matthew Bonnellus, hostile and welcoming by turns —to say nothing of his shameful treatment of Henry Aristippus— shows how pathetically easily he could be swayed by his changing moods, or by the counsels of those around him. Lacking any real equilibrium himself, he proved incapable of maintaining all those delicate political balances on which the safety of his realm depended —between himself and his subjects, nobility and bourgeoisie, Christian and Muslim.

And yet—William the Bad? The epithet still rings false. There was nothing evil about him. In no sense was he a wicked man;[1] and, if the above analysis is correct, it would suggest that his reluctance to face up to so many of his political responsibilities was due not only to his natural indolence but also to a genuine conviction that there were others around him better qualified for the task. It might also mean that William, far from being the careless hedonist that Falcandus depicts, was in fact a profoundly unhappy man who saw in every new palace and pleasure merely another temporary refuge for his troubled spirit. Perhaps William the Sad might have been a more accurate description. We shall never know. Of the only two important contemporary chroniclers of his reign, one is accurate but maddeningly sketchy, the other brilliant but hopelessly unreliable. In the absence of any further evidence we can only return a verdict of Not Proven, and leave one of the most enigmatic characters in the history of Norman Sicily to his rest.

[1] There is still a Sicilian popular tradition to the effect that William called in all the gold and silver coinage of the kingdom and replaced it with copper, keeping the proceeds for himself. No contemporary records suggest anything of the kind. Certain measures may well have been taken to restore the economy after 1161, but not even Falcandus accuses the King of deliberately impoverishing his subjects for his own profit.

PART FOUR

SUNSET

14

THE COUNSELLORS OF UNWISDOM

For although both peoples, Apulians and Sicilians, are faithless, unreliable and given to every kind of villainy, yet are the Sicilians more cunning in dissimulation and in the concealment of their true motives, beguiling those whom they hate with honeyed words and gentle flattery in order to do them greater hurt by taking them unawares.

Hugo Falcandus

LEGALLY, there was no problem over the succession. The dying King had made it clear that he wished the crown to pass to his elder surviving son, William; and that the younger, Henry, must be content with the principality of Capua. Since William was still only twelve years old, his mother Queen Margaret was to act as Regent, with the continued help of Richard Palmer, Caïd Peter and Matthew of Ajello. It all seemed straightforward enough.

The three advisers, however, were not so sure. Long minorities under a woman regent were always dangerous; the prestige of the Crown had not altogether recovered from the events of 1161; there might easily be a movement by the aristocracy in favour of the dead King's illegitimate brother Simon. Young William, after all, had never been associated with the throne during his father's lifetime; he had not even been created Duke of Apulia, the traditional title for the heir apparent. Such were their misgivings that they had even persuaded Margaret to delay the announcement of her husband's death while preparations were made for the coronation, and to proceed with the ceremony as soon as the three-day period of mourning was over.

They need not have bothered. On the day appointed for his coronation—which was also the day of his first public appearance—

young William immediately won all hearts. Unlike his father, the
boy started off with one supreme advantage: he was quite outstandingly good-looking. When, in Palermo Cathedral, Romuald of
Salerno anointed him with the holy oil and laid the Crown of Sicily
on his head, and when, later, he rode in state through the city to
the Royal Palace, the golden circlet still gleaming on the long fair
hair inherited from his Viking forbears, his subjects—whatever their
race, creed or political affiliation—could not contain their joy.
Fresh-faced but solemn—he was still a few weeks short of his thirteenth birthday—he seemed to combine the innocence of a child with
a gravity beyond his years. Loyalty was suddenly in the air. Even
Hugo Falcandus, describing the scene, permits himself one of his
rare bursts of charity:

Though always of surpassing beauty, on that day he appeared—by
what means I cannot tell—more beautiful than ever before. . . . And
so he gained the love and favour of all, to the point where even those
whose hatred of his father had been bitter and who had resolved
never more to owe any allegiance to his heirs and successors were
claiming that the first man to harbour evil designs against him would
have passed beyond the bounds of all common humanity. It was
enough, they said, that he who was responsible for their ills should
have been taken from their midst; an innocent boy should not be
blamed for the tyrannies of his father. For truly the child was of such
beauty that it would be impossible to allow of an equal, far less of a
superior.

On the same day, as a further indication that this was indeed the
beginning of a new era for the Kingdom, Queen Margaret declared
a general amnesty, opened all the prisons and restored all confiscated
lands to their former owners. More significant still, she also abolished
redemption money, the most unpopular of all her late husband's
impositions, by means of which many cities and towns of the mainland were still being bled white for having dared, five years before, to
rise up against him.

It was an auspicious start; but Margaret knew that she would be
hard put to maintain her advantage. For one thing, she had grave
doubts about her present triumvirate of advisers. She was a strong-
willed woman, at thirty-eight still in the prime of life, and they were

probably inclined to be overbearing in their attitude towards her, insufficiently mindful of her superior authority; but what made them in the last resort unacceptable was the fact that as former counsellors and nominees of William I they were all irremediably identified with the previous regime. Clearly they would have to go; but who was to take their place?

Among the aristocracy there were countless barons only too eager —and, doubtless, in several cases confidently expecting—to assume the positions of power they had so long coveted; Margaret, however, recoiled at the prospect. Again and again these nobles had shown how shallow their real loyalties were. It was they, and they alone, who had taken up arms against her husband and had held her and her children prisoner; to admit them now to the inner councils of government would lead to a proliferation of feudal estates in Sicily until the island became as unmanageable as Apulia and Campania had always been. This in turn would be bound to sharpen the already smouldering confessional animosities; and the result, sooner or later, would be a *coup* against herself and her son, against which they would have little if any defence. Fortunately since the fall of Matthew Bonnellus the aristocratic party had been without an effective leader and seemed to have lost much of its cohesion. For the time being it constituted no real threat. Margaret could afford to look elsewhere.

There was always the Church—but what a Church it had become. Like so many high ecclesiastics of the Middle Ages, the bishops and archbishops of the Sicilian Kingdom were a worldly lot, more politicians than prelates, many of them never going near their dioceses[1] but remaining permanently at the court in Palermo, endlessly meddling, bickering, squabbling and intriguing against each other. Of them all, by far the ablest and most influential was Richard Palmer—whose absenteeism was such that he was not consecrated Bishop of Syracuse till 1169, fourteen years after his election to the see. He had been largely responsible for the bishops' initiative that had saved William I in 1161 from the hands of the

---

[1] This practice soon became such a scandal that Pope Alexander III had to pass a decree in 1176 requiring Sicilian bishops who had spent seven years or more at court to return to their posts.

insurgents, as a result of which he had become the late King's closest adviser. He was, however, universally disliked for his arrogance and haughtiness; and his rapid advancement had not endeared him to his colleagues, particularly since he made no secret of the fact that he had his eye firmly fixed on the greatest of all prizes for a Sicilian church-man—the vacant archbishopric of Palermo.

But Richard Palmer was not the only contender. Romuald of Salerno, the present primate, was another obvious possibility; so too was Bishop Tristan of Mazara. Then there was Roger, Archbishop of Reggio, in the description of whom Falcandus finds the top of his form:

Already on the brink of old age, he was tall and so excessively thin that he appeared to be eaten away from the inside. His voice was weak as a whistle. His face—and indeed his whole body—was pale and yet somehow tinged with blackness, making him look more like a corpse than a man; and his external aspect well indicated the charac-ter within. He counted no labour difficult if there were hope of gain therefrom; and he would willingly endure hunger and thirst beyond the limits of human tolerance in order to save money. Never happy at his own table, he was never sad at those of others, and would frequently spend whole days without food, waiting to be invited to dinner.

One of the Archbishop's most frequent hosts was Gentile, the Bishop of Agrigento, felicitously described by Chalandon as a *prélat aventureux et vagabond*, who had originally come to Sicily as an ambassador from King Geza of Hungary and then decided to stay on. Gentile, as Falcandus informs us with some relish, made no secret of his *penchant* for debauchery, and profited by his sumptuous and vaguely orgiastic banquets to start a serious whispering campaign against Palmer with the intention of blocking his candidature. His complaints about the Bishop-elect's foreign origins must have sounded a little strange in the circumstances, but he had rather more success when he persuaded Matthew of Ajello that Palmer was plotting his assassination; Matthew was with difficulty restrained from getting his own knife in first.[1]

[1] Although, as the above paragraphs make clear, pressure of affairs in Palermo normally prevented these clerics from paying any but the most fleeting visits to

One other candidate remained for the coveted archbishopric. At the time he must have seemed something of an outsider, since he could not even boast episcopal rank. He also was an Englishman, whose various orthographical disguises—Ophamilus or Offamiglio to name but two—represent nothing more than desperate Sicilian attempts to deal phonetically with his perfectly ordinary English name, Walter of the Mill. First brought to Sicily as tutor to the royal children, he had been successively appointed Archdeacon of Cefalù, then Dean of Agrigento. Now he was one of the canons of the Palatine Chapel, where he was proving himself even more unscrupulous and ambitious than the compatriot whose career he was working so hard to undermine. Only he, of all the rivals, was to attain his objective. For reasons which we shall presently see, he had to wait for it another three years; but for a quarter of a century after that he was destined to occupy the highest political and ecclesiastical posts in the realm, building the present cathedral and becoming almost certainly the only Englishman in history regularly to sign himself *Emir and Archbishop*. As such, he will play an important—and ultimately disastrous—part in the closing chapters of this story.

The aristocracy, then, was dangerous and of doubtful loyalty; the hierarchy self-seeking and—so far as the personalities of its principal members were concerned—distinctly unattractive. That left only one other significant group—the palace officials and civil servants, headed by the eunuch Caïd Peter and the Grand Protonotary, Matthew of Ajello. Even by eunuch standards, Peter was an uninspiring character; but he too had proved his devotion to the King and his family in 1161, and his administrative efficiency was beyond question. Matthew for his part was at least as able; he had recently completed the herculean task—which no one but he could possibly have

their dioceses, several seem to have tried to make amends by magnificent donations and endowments. Thus Romuald of Salerno is responsible for the superb marble and mosaic ambo in his cathedral (originally founded, it will be remembered, by Robert Guiscard) and Richard Palmer for the glass and mosaics—what is left of them—at Syracuse. The cathedral treasury of Agrigento possesses a very fine Byzantine portable altar, which is certainly of the twelfth century and may well have been a gift from Gentile. Despite his proclivities, however, we cannot alas connect him with the other pride of the Agrigento collection—a handwritten letter from the Devil which is preserved, very properly, in the archives.

accomplished—of recompiling, largely from memory, a comprehensive register of lands and fiefs to replace that which had been destroyed in the insurrection. Like Richard Palmer, however, he had one of those dominating characters that Queen Margaret instinctively mistrusted. He was furthermore obsessed with the idea of being appointed Emir of Emirs—a rank and title which had remained in abeyance since the death of Maio of Bari—and was consequently for ever immersed in intrigues of his own, besides giving himself the airs and graces of a *grand seigneur* and using his steadily increasing wealth to build a noble church in the city as George of Antioch and Maio had done before him.[1] Of the pair, the Queen much preferred Peter. He was not the ideal solution—the nobles, in particular, hated and despised him—but he seemed relatively free of personal ambition and was less of an intriguer than most of his fellows. In any case he would be able to hold the Kingdom together while she found someone more suitable. To the fury of Matthew and of Richard Palmer, she promoted him over their heads—thus putting the effective direction of the Sicilian Kingdom, now one of the richest and most influential powers in Christian Europe, in the hands of a Muslim eunuch.

But she had also made another decision. To govern the realm as it needed to be governed and to preserve it for her son, she had to have someone who was not only firm and capable but disinterested and, above all, uncommitted. He must also be someone who spoke her language and whom she found personally sympathetic. In all Sicily, it appeared, no such paragon existed. Very well, she would look elsewhere. New situations called for new men to handle them. Secretly, she wrote a long letter to her cousin[2] Rothrud, Archbishop

---

[1] Though Matthew's church, known as the Magione, was badly damaged during the second world war, it has been sensitively restored and is well worth a visit. With its three apses, its blind and interlaced arcading and the lovely cloister that adjoins it, it provides an excellent example of later Norman-Sicilian architecture, shorn of all obvious Arabic influences. With the fall of the Norman Kingdom at the end of the century, the church and neighbouring convent were given over to the military order of the Teutonic Knights, traces of whose occupancy are still visible. Most guidebooks, incidentally, give the date of the original construction as 1150; in fact it was almost certainly begun a good decade later, and finished during Queen Margaret's regency.

[2] Not her uncle, as Chalandon maintains—see genealogical table on p. 756.

of Rouen, explaining her situation and suggesting that he might send some member of their family out to Palermo to help her. Two names she mentioned in particular: Rothrud's brother Robert of Newburgh or, failing him, another cousin—Stephen du Perche.

That the Queen's anxieties for the future were justified, the next few months were all too clearly to show. On the other hand her confidence, such as it was, in Caïd Peter's abilities proved to have been misplaced. By the middle of the summer Sicily was in chaos. With all the various factions jockeying ever more frenziedly for position, the plots more plentiful, the intrigues still thicker than before, no proper government was possible; and Peter, a civil servant rather than a statesman, was incapable of imposing his will on an unruly and discontented people. To have done so at that time would have needed a man of infinitely greater stature—a Maio of Bari at the least. And even Maio had succumbed in the end.

Typical of those who sought to fish in these troubled waters was the Queen's cousin, Gilbert.[1] Some clue to his character may be seen in the haste with which, on his arrival in Sicily a few years before, he had been placated with the County of Gravina and packed off to Apulia—where, as we have seen, he had later become involved in the conspiracy against Maio. On the late King's death and his cousin's assumption of the Regency he had hurried back to the capital and, with the covert support of Richard Palmer, had soon become the focus of the opposition to Caïd Peter, complaining publicly that Sicily was being run by slaves and eunuchs and constantly pressing Margaret to appoint him her chief minister in Peter's stead. The Queen, with understandable reluctance, had at last offered him a seat on the council, but Gilbert had indignantly refused—in the course of a hideous scene in which, if Falcandus is to be believed, he berated Margaret for having put him on the same level as a slave,

---

[1] I have not been able to trace Gilbert's relationship with the Queen. Chalandon says that he had arrived from Spain, but gives no references to support this theory; from his name and from subsequent events it seems to me far likelier that he was one of the French side of the family—possibly a son or grandson of a sibling of Margaret of Laigle, the Queen's mother. (See genealogical table, p. 756.) La Lumia accepts him as a Frenchman and even on one occasion refers to him as Stephen's nephew—surely most improbable.

threatened her with a nation-wide revolution, and left her in tears.

But the aristocratic faction had found in the Count of Gravina the mouthpiece they had long been seeking, and as they grew daily more threatening the Queen and Peter recognised that some voice in the council chamber could no longer be denied them. With Gilbert still persisting in his refusal, they therefore nominated one of the army leaders, that same Richard of Mandra who had protected William I with his own body during the 1161 insurrection—whom, in order to give him equal rank with her odious cousin, Margaret now created Count of Molise. This appointment was more than Gilbert could stand. He did his best to conceal his anger; but henceforth he began to plot seriously against the eunuch's life.

It was not long before Peter's agents brought him word of what was going on. At first he merely strengthened his bodyguard; but finally, with Maio's fate constantly at the back of his mind, his nerve failed him. A ship was secretly fitted out in the harbour; and one dark night, taking with him a few fellow-eunuchs and a large quantity of money, Peter slipped back to those shores whence, long ago, he had come. On his return to Tunis he resumed his former name of Ahmed, the religion of his fathers and, ultimately, his original profession; for we later find him commander of Caliph Yusuf's Moroccan fleet, in which capacity he is said to have fought with great distinction against the Christians.[1] After what he had suffered from them in Palermo, this should cause us no surprise; perhaps, as Falcandus maintained, he was ever a Saracen at heart.

Peter's defection came as a blow to Margaret, and also as a severe embarrassment. She vigorously denied allegations that he had absconded with any of the royal treasure, but she could not muffle the triumphant crowings of Gilbert of Gravina. What other conduct could ever have been expected of a Muslim slave, he demanded; had not Peter already once betrayed his country—at Mahdia seven years before? The only wonder was that he had not long ago introduced his Almohad friends into the palace, to make off with the rest of the treasure and, in all probability, with the King as well. Richard of

[1] These details of Peter's subsequent career are given us by Ibn Khaldun (*B.A.S.,* II, pp. 166 and 238). He refers to him as Ahmed es-Sikeli; from the chronological and other details he gives of the flight from Sicily there can be no doubt that Ahmed and Peter are one and the same. (See p. 666.)

Molise, who chanced to be present, could restrain himself no longer and sprang to the defence of his former patron, pointing out that Peter was no slave—he had been formally enfranchised by William I —and that his departure was solely due to the Count of Gravina's notorious intrigues against him. If any man called him traitor, then he—Richard—would be prepared to settle the matter once and for all by single combat.

Somehow the two were separated before any violence was done, but the incident was enough to convince the Queen that her cousin could no longer be permitted to remain in the capital. On the pretext that Frederick Barbarossa was said to be preparing another expedition to the south, she confirmed Gilbert as Catapan of Apulia and Campania and invited him forthwith to return to the mainland and prepare the army for war. The Count had no delusions as to the real reason for his departure; seeing, however, that in the present state of affairs there was no future for him in Palermo he accepted the charge and, still fuming, took his leave.

With Gilbert of Gravina out of the way, Margaret must have felt some measure of relief; but in other respects the situation was little easier than before. Fortunately she still had one counsellor whom she liked and could trust—Richard of Molise, who had now taken Peter's place as chief minister in the Council. Though Richard had little political experience and was inclined to be intemperate and headstrong, he was completely loyal and, says Falcandus, was greatly feared by all—a useful attribute at such a time. But, he too was powerless to stop the decline. Perhaps because he was held in greater respect than Peter he also failed to draw as much popular criticism on himself, with the result that Margaret found herself increasingly blamed for the state of the realm. Already her popularity—based largely on the amnesty she had declared and by the remission of redemption money, but tinged also with the admiration due to the mother of so beautiful a son—had vanished away. Nowadays, in the street, men were openly grumbling and gossiping about 'the Spanish woman',[1] and even looking nostalgically back to the bad old days of her husband's reign.

[1] Just as, six centuries later, Marie Antoinette was to be known as '*l'Autrichienne*' in the streets of Paris.

And now, at the worst possible moment—which was in itself typical of him—there arrived in Palermo another of the Queen's more disreputable relations. Gilbert had been bad enough; the new-comer was more unattractive still. Not only the timing of his arrival but everything about him seemed inept and tactless—even his birth. In theory at least, he was Margaret's brother; Falcandus on the other hand is at pains to point out that it was common knowledge—and admitted as such even by the gang of Navarrese adventurers whom the young man had brought with him—that King Garcia had never accepted him as a son, believing him to be the child of one of his wife's prodigious collection of lovers. Then there was his name, Rodrigo, which sounded so barbarous and indeed ridiculous to Sicilian ears that his sister at once made him change it to Henry. Finally we have Falcandus's description of his appearance, character and way of life.

This Henry was short in stature; his beard was extremely thin, his complexion unpleasantly swarthy. He was imprudent and of poor conversation, a man who had no interests but dice and gaming, no wants but a partner to play against and plenty of money to lose; he would spend wildly, with neither forethought nor consideration. Having passed some little time in Palermo, during which by his immoderate spending he had soon squandered the immense sums given him by the Queen, he announced his intention of crossing to Apulia; but on his arrival at Messina he at once fell in with many fellows of the kind he found congenial. Now this city, which is largely given over to foreigners, predators and pirates, harbours almost every kind of man within its walls: persons expert in every villainy, acquainted with every vice, men who esteem nothing illicit which lies within their power to achieve. Thus he was soon sur-rounded by thieves, pirates, buffoons, yes-men and criminals of all descriptions, carousing by day and spending whole nights gambling. When these things reached the ears of the Queen, she wrote him a severe reprimand, ordering him to cross the straits without delay. And so, though hardly able to tear himself away, he took his comrades' advice and set off for Apulia.

Soon after his arrival in Sicily, Margaret had given up her original idea of marrying him off to an illegitimate daughter of Roger II, and had instead bestowed upon him the County of Montescaglioso—just as she had given Gilbert that of Gravina—with the deliberate object of keeping him as far as possible from the capital. When at last she received word of his safe arrival in his fief, she may ruefully have reflected that he had already done just about all the damage he could. If so, she was soon to discover that she was wrong; but not before the advent of yet a third member of her family, as different from the other two as it was possible to imagine and distinctly more promising.

When Archbishop Rothrud of Rouen received his cousin Margaret's appeal for help, he acted swiftly. His brother, Robert of Newburgh, seems to have had little inclination to involve himself in Sicilian affairs; but Margaret's other suggestion, young Stephen du Perche, was immediately attracted to the idea. The invitation reached him just in time, as he was on the point of setting out, with a suite of no less than thirty-seven, for the Holy Land. When he left France, this was still his ultimate objective; but he saw no reason not to stop off for a few months in Palermo on his way.

After a short stay in Apulia with Gilbert—who presumably gave him a highly tendentious account of the Sicilian political scene—Stephen arrived in Palermo towards the end of the summer, to an enthusiastic, even effusive, welcome from Queen Margaret. One of the first things that struck the Palermitans about him was his extreme youth. He can have been only in his early twenties at most, while the fact that Falcandus and William of Tyre describe him with the words *puer* and *adolescens*—this in an age when men were often leading armies before they were out of their teens—suggests that he may have been even younger. Such a supposition, on the other hand, raises a new problem. Rothrud II, Count of Perche, whom Margaret referred to as his father, is known to have died in 1143; if Stephen were in fact his son, he could not in September 1166 be less than twenty-two—a little old for boyhood or adolescence. But we also know that soon after Rothrud's death his widow was married again, this time to Robert of Dreux, brother of Louis VII—who, in a letter to his fellow-ruler William II, was later to refer to Stephen as *caro et sanguis noster*, 'our own flesh and blood'. It has therefore been argued that Stephen was not of the family of Perche at all, but a nephew of the French King. If he were, however, why did he not say so and take advantage of the fact, and why is it mentioned by none of the contemporary chroniclers? As Chalandon character- istically puts it, *l'on ne peut pas sortir du domaine de l'hypothèse*; the question must remain unresolved.[1]

Man or boy, Stephen seems to have appeared to the Queen just the person she needed to support her in her tribulations; and she in turn had little difficulty in persuading him, with promises of power, riches and honours for himself and his companions, to postpone his pilgrimage indefinitely and to share with her the government of the realm. From the outset he seemed able and energetic; just as im- portant—and even rarer in Sicily—he proved personally incorrupt- ible. Margaret was delighted with him. In November 1166, scarcely two months after his arrival in Palermo, she appointed him Chan- cellor.

The news of the appointment, as might have been expected, called forth a storm of protest. It was now over a century since the Normans had invaded the island, thirty-six years since the founding of the Kingdom. The Sicilians were beginning to feel themselves a nation, and to resent seeing more and more of the senior—and most pro- fitable—positions in the land being given to foreign newcomers. Matthew of Ajello, it now appeared, was not the only one in the palace to have had his eye on the Chancellorship. Besides, while the office remained vacant its revenues had been divided among the members of the inner council. Stephen's appointment thus not only blighted their hopes; it reduced their incomes too.

Nor was it the new Chancellor alone who aroused such feelings. He had arrived, it will be remembered, with an entourage of thirty- seven; in the months that followed others came out from France to

[1] A genealogical table showing the two possible relationships between Queen Margaret and Stephen du Perche will be found on p. 756. The theory of Stephen's royal parentage was first put forward, by Bréquigny, as long ago as 1780 (*Mémoires de l'Académie des Inscriptions*, vol. XLI). It is strongly contested by La Lumia, while Chalandon, as we have seen, sits firmly on the fence. My own opinion, for what it is worth, is that Stephen was what he purported to be—a younger son of the Count of Perche—and that the phrase of Louis VII must be dismissed as a figure of speech, not too far-fetched in the circumstances. It seems in any case unlikely that he would have been made both Chancellor and Archbishop if he had not been at least in his twenties—hardly more than boy- hood for the two highest posts in the kingdom.

join him: and before long the court and many sections of the administration seemed more French than Sicilian. It was perhaps natural that the young man should prefer to surround himself with people he knew, whose native language he understood; but it was natural too that those who suffered by the change should resent it, the more so since many of his friends—especially those who had received Sicilian fiefs—behaved with curious tactlessness, treating the country folk around them as a subject race and everywhere imposing French habits and customs without regard for local susceptibilities.

On the other hand, Stephen was a genuine idealist. He may have lacked sensitivity and finesse, but he sincerely wished to make Sicily a better place and lost no time in instituting the reforms he considered necessary. He turned his attention first to the notaries—thus antagonising Matthew of Ajello, the Protonotary, of one of whose relations he made a public example; then, in rapid succession, he dealt with judges, local officials and castellans, clamping down on injustice wherever he saw it. 'He never,' says Falcandus, 'allowed powerful men to oppress their subjects, nor ever feigned to overlook any injury done to the poor. In such a way his fame quickly spread throughout the Kingdom . . . so that men looked on him as a heaven-sent angel of consolation who had brought back the Golden Age.'

Even when we make due allowance for exaggeration, tendentious reporting and the sad scarcity of reliable source material, it is hard to avoid the conclusion that Margaret was initially justified in her decision to bring in an outsider to govern the Kingdom. Reforms were obviously overdue; and in the prevailing atmosphere of discord and mistrust it would have been virtually impossible for any Sicilian—whether by birth or by long-term adoption—to bring them about. Stephen, impartial and uncommitted, was in a position to do so, and because he did not lack moral courage he succeeded. But in the process, however much favour he gained with the masses, it was inevitable that he should have made himself hated by his Sicilian subordinates; and though his preference for Frenchmen around him may have gratuitously provided additional grounds for resentment, his own presence and power in the land would have been more than enough to ensure his lasting unpopularity.

And was this unpopularity so bad a thing? Nothing unites a people like a common enemy, and in a country so torn by factional strife any unifying force, even an oppressive and corrupt tyranny, might have had an ultimately beneficial effect. Stephen was neither oppressive nor corrupt; he was simply disliked. And it is at least arguable that the greatest benefit he conferred on the Kingdom lay not in any of his administrative reforms but in the solidarity he gave to his opponents, reminding them that they were above all Sicilians, and Sicilians with a job to do—to rid their country of foreign intruders.

Just how successfully they did it will be told in a later chapter. Meanwhile there appeared on the horizon another intruder, compared with whom Stephen du Perche and his friends must have seemed petty irritations indeed. Within weeks of their coming to power, news reached Palermo that the Emperor was once again on the march.

15

THE SECOND SCHISM

Quid facis insane   patrie mors, Octaviane!
Cur presumpsisti   tunicam dividere Christi?
Jamjam pulvis eris; modo vivis, cras morieris.

(Octavian, by what aberration
Do you seek to bring Rome to damnation?
How were you ever enticed
So to sever the tunic of Christ?
You too will be dust by and by;
As you lived, so tomorrow you'll die.)

                              Britto, a pamphleteer of Rome

WHEN, at the close of the year 1166, Frederick Barbarossa led his immense army southward on the new campaign, he had before him three distinct objectives. First, he intended to liquidate the unofficial Byzantine outpost at Ancona; next, he would march against the Pope in Rome, whom he was resolved to replace on the throne of St Peter by an anti-Pope of his own choosing; finally, as always, there was the Norman Kingdom of Sicily to be smashed. Separate as these three targets were, the reasons which led the Emperor to attack them were closely interrelated; to understand them, however, we must cast a quick retrospective glance at the progress of the imperial-papal duel during the seven years since the death of Pope Adrian—and, in particular, at the melancholy farce which had attended the election of his successor.

It may be remembered how, just before Adrian died, the assembled cardinals of the pro-Sicilian party gathered at Anagni had agreed to elect as the next pope one of their own number—their leader, Cardinal Roland, being the obvious favourite. Since this group

623

constituted some two-thirds of the electoral college, there was reason to hope that the election might pass off smoothly enough—as indeed it might have but for the presence in the pro-imperialist opposition of Cardinal Octavian of S. Cecilia. This prelate has already made two brief and faintly ludicrous appearances in our story—the first when, as a papal emissary to Roger II, he had to be told by Roger himself of the Pope's death and the consequent expiry of his own special powers, and the second when, on a similar mission to Conrad of Hohenstaufen, his behaviour earned him the ridicule of John of Salisbury.[1] But never in his long and inglorious career can he have made such an exhibition of himself as on this occasion.[2]

On 5 September 1159, the day after Adrian's body had been laid to rest in the crypt of St Peter's, about thirty cardinals assembled in conclave behind the high altar of the basilica;[3] two days later, all but three of them had cast their votes for Cardinal Roland, who was therefore declared to have been elected—a declaration, be it noted, perfectly in accordance with canon law. The scarlet mantle of the Papacy was brought forward and Roland, after the customary display of reluctance, bent his head to receive it. Suddenly Octavian dived at him, snatched the mantle and tried to don it himself. A scuffle followed, during which he lost it again; but his chaplain instantly produced another—presumably brought along for just such an eventuality—which Octavian this time managed to put on, unfortunately back to front, before anyone could stop him.

There followed a scene of scarcely believable confusion. Wrenching himself free from the furious supporters of Roland who were trying to tear the mantle forcibly from his back, Octavian—whose frantic efforts to turn it right way round had resulted only in getting the fringes tangled round his neck—made a dash for the papal throne,

[1] See pp. 470 and 510n.

[2] I have taken the following account from Gerhoh of Reichensburg (*De Investigatione Antichristi*, i. 53), whose version is not only the fullest but also—in the opinion of at least one authority (Mann)—'more likely to be impartial than any of the others'. Impartiality, however, is a rare virtue among historians of the twelfth century; and it is only fair to add that among writers of more imperialist sympathies Octavian also has his champions.

[3] By the end there may have been only twenty-nine; according to Arnulf of Lisieux (*Ep. ad cardinales*, Migne, vol. 201, col. 41) Bishop Imarus of Tusculum, a renowned epicure, left early because he refused to miss his dinner.

sat in it and proclaimed himself Pope Victor IV.[1] He then charged off through St Peter's until he found a group of minor clergy, whom he ordered to give him their acclamation—which, seeing the doors suddenly burst open and a band of armed cut-throats swarming into the church, they hastily did. Temporarily at least, the opposition was silenced; Roland and his adherents slipped out while they could and took a hasty refuge in St Peter's tower, a fortified corner of the Vatican which was safe in the hands of Cardinal Boso. Meanwhile, with the cut-throats looking on, Octavian was enthroned a little more formally than on the previous occasion and escorted in triumph to the Lateran—having been at some pains, we are told, to adjust his dress before leaving.

However undignified in its execution, the *coup* could now be seen to have been thoroughly and efficiently planned in advance—and on a scale that left no doubt that the Empire must have been actively implicated. Octavian himself had long been known as an imperial sympathiser and his election was immediately recognised by Frederick's two ambassadors in Rome, who at the same time declared a vigorous war on Roland. Once again they opened their coffers, and German gold flowed freely into the purses and pockets of all those Romans—nobles, senators, bourgeoisie or rabble—who would openly proclaim their allegiance to Victor IV. Meanwhile Roland and his faithful cardinals remained blockaded in St Peter's tower.

But almost at once Octavian—or Victor, as we must now call him—saw his support begin to dwindle. The story of his behaviour at the election was by now common knowledge in the city and, we may be sure, had lost nothing in the telling; everywhere, the Romans were turning towards Roland as their lawfully-elected Pope. A mob had formed around St Peter's tower and was now angrily clamouring for his release. After a week he had to be removed to a place of greater security in Trastevere, but they only clamoured the louder. In the street, Victor was hooted at and reviled; lines of doggerel were chanted mockingly at him as he passed. On the night of 16 September he could bear it no longer and fled from Rome; and on the following day the rightful Pontiff was led back into the capital amid general rejoicing.

[1] Strangely, it was the second time this title had been chosen by an anti-Pope. See p. 425.

But Roland knew that he could not stay. The imperial ambassadors were still in Rome, where they still had limitless money to spend. Victor's family, too, the Crescentii, was among the richest and most powerful in the city. Pausing only to assemble an appropriate retinue, on 20 September the Pope travelled south to Ninfa, then a thriving little town under the sway of his friends the Frangipani; and there, in the church of S. Maria Maggiore, he at last received formal consecration as Alexander III[1]. One of his first acts, predictably, was to excommunicate the anti-Pope—who soon afterwards and equally predictably excommunicated him in return. For the second time in thirty years, the Church of Rome was in schism.

The election of his old friend Cardinal Roland to the Papacy had been the last major diplomatic triumph for Maio of Bari; but the fact that it proved an even greater blessing to the Kingdom of Sicily than Maio had ever dreamed was due, paradoxically, to Frederick Barbarossa himself. Had Frederick bowed to the inevitable and accepted Alexander as the rightful Pope he undoubtedly was, there is no reason why the two should not have reached some accommodation; instead, at the Council of Pavia in February 1160, he formally recognised the ludicrous Victor, thereby forcing Alexander—whose claim was soon accepted by all the other rulers of Europe—into even closer alliance with William I and saddling himself with a new series of vain and useless obligations which were to cripple him politically for the best part of twenty years. But for these obligations he would almost certainly have been able to take advantage of the Sicilian crisis of 1161–62 as we know he planned to do;[2] and the Norman Kingdom of Sicily might have ended even sooner and more tragically than it did.

It was that crisis that decided Alexander to take positive action against the Emperor. To be sure, he had excommunicated Frederick

[1] The town of Ninfa was sacked and destroyed in 1382, since when it has lain in ruins. By then, however, it had been acquired by the Caetani family, to whom it still belongs; and since 1922 they have turned the site into one of the loveliest and most romantic gardens in all Italy.

[2] Treaties signed by Frederick with Genoa and Pisa during the early summer of 1162 made his intention clear. In both of them he seems to consider his conquest of Sicily a foregone conclusion.

as early as March 1160—after Pavia he had had little choice—and absolved all imperial subjects from their allegiance; until the end of the following year, however, he had divided his time—apart from one short and unsuccessful attempt to re-establish himself in Rome—between Terracina and Anagni, two papal cities conveniently close to the borders of the Sicilian Kingdom, to which he looked both for his physical protection and for the financial subsidies he so desperately needed. The events of 1161, starting with the Palermo insurrection and ending with the whole of South Italy up in arms against the King, changed all that. The Pope saw that William of Sicily could no longer be relied upon in an emergency; other allies were needed. Leaving Terracina on a Sicilian ship in the last days of 1161, he landed in April near Montpellier.

For the next three and a half years, Alexander was to live in exile in France—mostly at Sens, where Peter Abelard had been crushed by the oratory of St Bernard almost a quarter of a century before—working to form a great European League comprising England, France, Sicily, Hungary, Venice, the Lombard towns and Byzantium, against Frederick Barbarossa. He failed, as he was bound to fail. Long conversations with the kings of England and France resulted in broad measures of agreement, cordial expressions of support and —more important still—further heavy subsidies; but no alliance. Henry II in particular he found impossible to trust. In the early days of the schism he had been a firm friend; as early as 1160 Arnulf of Lisieux had reported that while the King 'received all Alexander's communications with respect, he would not so much as touch Octavian's letters with his hands, but would take hold of them with a piece of stick and throw them behind his back as far as he could'. But in 1163 his difficulties with Thomas Becket had begun, and in the following year his promulgation of the Constitutions of Clarendon—deliberately designed to strengthen his hold over the English Church at the expense of the Pope—had caused a distinct chill in Anglo-Papal relations.

William of Sicily too had made difficulties. Alexander had no firmer friend, Barbarossa no more convinced opponent. William was on excellent terms with England, France, Hungary and the Lombard towns, and would willingly have reached some sort of agreement with Venice. But Byzantium was another matter. In 1158, at the insistence of Pope Adrian, he had made his peace with Manuel Comnenus—and a generous peace at that, considering how soundly he had trounced him only two years before. Even at the time, however, he had known that it could not last; the Byzantines showed no signs of giving up their long-term ambitions in Italy. Subsequent developments had proved him right. Within a year or two Manuel was building up his position again, not only in his old headquarters at Ancona but in all the main towns of Lombardy, to say nothing of Genoa and Pisa; everywhere his agents were busy, encouraging anti-imperial feeling and dispensing subsidies with a generous hand. Insofar as this policy was directed against Barbarossa it was no doubt to be welcomed, but William had had enough experience of the Greeks to know that their presence anywhere west of the Adriatic was, directly or indirectly, a threat to Sicily. Besides, if Manuel's intentions were honourable, why was he still giving shelter to Sicilian rebels? He was no better than Frederick. William replied to the Pope's overtures in the only way he could—that he would never, at any price, voluntarily allow Byzantine troops on his territory.

But Alexander's disappointment at his diplomatic failure must have been forgotten when, early in 1165, he received an invitation from the Roman Senate to return to the city. His rival, the anti-Pope Victor, who had also been forced to spend the last years in exile, had died the year before in pain and poverty at Lucca, where he had been keeping alive on the proceeds of not very successful brigandage and where the local hierarchy would not even allow him burial within the walls. Frederick, stubborn as ever, had immediately given his blessing to the 'election', by his two tame schismatic cardinals, of a successor under the name of Paschal III; but the action had earned him and his anti-Pope nothing but scorn, and it may well have been the ensuing wave of resentment and disgust at the absurdity of the schism and the pig-headedness of the Emperor that had at last brought the Romans to their senses. Besides, the pilgrim trade had dried up. Without a Pope, mediaeval Rome lost its *raison d'être*.

For all that, the homecoming was not an easy one. Frederick did everything he could to prevent it, even hiring pirates to waylay the papal convoy on the high seas. Next he sent another army into Italy, which established the wretched Paschal at Viterbo and ravaged all the Roman Campagna until Gilbert of Gravina, at last justifying his existence, appeared with a Sicilian force and drove it back into Tuscany. But somehow Alexander defeated all these machinations. In order to escape the Pisan, Genoese and Provençal ships that he knew were lying in wait for him he took a roundabout route and landed, in September 1165, at Messina. William I did not come to greet him; by that time he had retired so completely into seclusion that not even the Roman Pontiff himself could bring him out. But he sent orders that his honoured guest should be treated as a 'lord and father', and furnished with all the money and troops he needed; and on 23 November the Pope reached Rome where, escorted by senators, nobles, clergy and people, all bearing olive branches in their hands, he rode in state to the Lateran.

Although at the time of Alexander's visit King William had only a few more months to live, this was not the last instance of his generosity towards the Pope whose closest ally he had never ceased to be. On his death-bed he sent Alexander a further gift of forty thousand florins, the better to continue his struggle against the Emperor.[1] The gesture was not altruistic, nor was it merely a selfish attempt to purchase divine favour in the life to come. It was the dying King's last recognition of political reality; William knew that if Pope Alexander did not emerge victorious from that struggle, the Kingdom of Sicily could not long survive.

Frederick Barbarossa's army crossed the plain of Lombardy early in 1167; then it split into two parts. The smaller was jointly commanded by the Archbishop of Cologne, Rainald of Dassel—who was also imperial Chancellor and the Emperor's right hand—and by another warlike ecclesiastic, Archbishop Christian of Mainz. Their orders were to march down the peninsula towards Rome, enforcing the imperial authority as they went, and to open up a safe road to the city for the anti-Pope Paschal, still sitting nervously in Tuscany. On their way they were to stop at Pisa, there to secure the services

[1] John of Salisbury's letter 145 (to Bartholomew, Bishop of Exeter).

of its fleet for the moment when, later in the year, the whole weight of the Empire was to be flung against Sicily. Meanwhile Frederick himself, with the bulk of his army, pressed on across the peninsula towards Ancona, the nucleus of Byzantine influence in Italy.

Frederick was, if anything, even angrier with the Greek Emperor than with Pope Alexander. For well over a decade Manuel Comnenus had been stirring up trouble in Venice and Lombardy. His agents treated Ancona—a city standing squarely within the territory of the Western Empire—as if it were a Byzantine colony. More irritating still, he had recently tried to take advantage of the papal schism by putting himself forward as a protector of Alexander. He seemed to forget that he was himself a schismatic. He would be reminded—forcibly—of this and of many other things as well once the German army reached Ancona.

Barbarossa would have been more enraged still had he understood the full extent of his fellow-Emperor's ambitions; for Manuel had seen in the schism nothing less than a chance of realising his father's old dream—the reunion of the Christian Church under the Pope of Rome in return for that of the Roman Empire under the Emperor at Constantinople. Frederick's recent behaviour had persuaded him that the time was now ripe for a direct approach; and some time in the spring of 1167—possibly at the very moment that the imperial troops were marching on Ancona—a Byzantine ambassador in the person of the *sebastos* Jordan, son of Prince Robert of Capua, arrived in Rome to offer Alexander men and money 'sufficient', as he put it, 'to reduce all Italy to papal obedience' if he would endorse the scheme.

Manuel was fully aware that at this of all moments the Pope could not antagonise the King of Sicily; and he had no delusions about the Sicilian view of his interference in Italian affairs. But even this problem, he believed, might be soluble. Though he had now been married for six years to his second wife, the fabulously beautiful Mary of Antioch, their marriage was still childless; the heir to the Empire remained his daughter by Bertha-Irene, a girl named Maria now fifteen years old.[1] Though she was theoretically betrothed

[1] Bertha-Irene had died of a sudden fever in 1060. Manuel had given her a splendid funeral and had her buried in the church of the Pantocrator; but he had married Mary within a year.

to Prince Béla of Hungary, he now proposed that she should be given in marriage to young William of Sicily; once the boy found himself heir apparent to the throne of Constantinople, he would see Byzantine ambitions in a very different light. It was a bold and imaginative proposal, and Manuel had had it formally put to the Queen Regent immediately after her husband's death. So far, however, the Sicilians had expressed only a cautious interest, and the Emperor was still awaiting a definite reply.[1]

All this, we must assume, was unknown to Frederick Barbarossa as he marched towards Ancona. But his dislike of the Greeks was already more than enough to give him enthusiasm for the task before him, and as soon as his army had dug itself in the siege of the city began. The inhabitants put up a spirited resistance. Their defences were strong and in good order, and they were determined not to be deprived of an association that was bringing so much wealth to them all. Luck, too, was on their side. First the Emperor was diverted by the appearance further down the coast of a Sicilian force under Gilbert of Gravina; soon after his return he received news which caused him to raise the siege altogether and leave at once for Rome. The Anconans were saved.

The Romans, on the other hand, were as good as lost. On Whit Monday, 29 May, just outside Tusculum, their large but undisciplined army had attacked the Germans and Tusculans under Christian of Mainz, and, though outnumbering them many times over, had been utterly shattered. Out of a total estimated at some thirty thousand, barely a third had escaped. Before the last survivors had left the field, imperial messengers were already speeding to Frederick with the news. Rome itself, they reported, was still holding out, but failing massive reinforcements it could not last long; still less could it hope to resist a new German attack at full strength. When he heard the news, the Emperor was jubilant. With Rome ripe for the plucking, what did Ancona matter? He could deal with the Greeks later.

Although the troops under Archbishop Christian had now been swollen by the local militias of several neighbouring towns, all

[1] For a fuller discussion of this proposal—which, if it had been accepted, would quite possibly have changed the course of history—see J. S. F. Parker, 'The attempted Byzantine Alliance with the Sicilian Norman Kingdom, 1166–1167', Papers of the British School at Rome, vol. XXIV, 1955.

eager for revenge after years of Roman arrogance and oppression, Rome itself was still fighting hard. The Emperor's arrival, however, sealed the fate of the Leonine City.[1] A single savage onslaught smashed the gates; the Germans poured in, only to find an unexpected inner fortress—St Peter's basilica itself, ringed with strong-points and hastily-dug trenches. For eight more days, we are told by an eyewitness, Acerbus Morena, it held out against every attack; it was only when the besiegers set fire to the forecourt, destroying first the great portico so carefully restored by Innocent II, then the lovely little mosaic-covered oratory of S. Maria in Turri, and finally hacking down the huge portals of the basilica itself, that the defending garrison surrendered. Never had there been such a desecration of the holiest shrine of Europe. Even in the ninth century, the Saracen pirates had contented themselves with tearing the silver panels from the doors; they had never penetrated the building. This time, according to another contemporary,[2] the invaders left the marble pavements of the nave strewn with dead and dying, the high altar itself stained with blood. And this time the outrage was the work not of infidel barbarians but of the Emperor of western Christendom.

It was on 29 July 1167 that St Peter's fell. On the following day, at that same high altar, the anti-Pope Paschal celebrated Mass and then invested Frederick with the golden circlet of the Roman *Patricius*—a deliberate gesture of defiance to the Senate and People of Rome. Two days later still, he officiated at the imperial coronation of the Empress Beatrice, with her husband—whom Pope Adrian had crowned twelve years previously—standing by. That day marked the summit of Frederick's career. He had brought the Romans to their knees, imposing on them terms which, though moderate enough, should ensure their docility in the future. He had placed his own Pope on the Throne of St Peter. North Italy he had already subdued; and now, with the imperial strength still undiminished and the Pisan ships already moored along the Tiber quays, he was ready to mop up the Kingdom of Sicily. He foresaw no difficulties. The Sicilians were governed—if that was the word—by a woman, a child and, he understood, some Frenchman who was little more than a child himself. Soon they would all three be grovelling before

[1] See p. 541n.   [2] Otto of St Blaise.

him, and the ambition that had been gnawing away at him for fifteen
years would be fulfilled at last.

Poor Frederick—he could not have foreseen the catastrophe that
was so soon to overtake him, one that in less than a single week was to
destroy his proud army in a way that no earthly foe could ever have
matched. On that memorable first of August, the skies had been
clear and the sun had blazed down on his triumph. Then, on the
second, a huge black cloud suddenly obscured the valley by Monte
Mario; heavy rain began to fall, followed immediately by a still and
oppressive heat. On the third came pestilence. It struck the imperial
camp with a swiftness and a force such as never before was known;
and where it struck, more often than not, it killed. Within a matter
of days, it was no longer possible to bury all the dead; and the growing piles of corpses, swollen and putrefying in the heat of a Roman
August, made their own grim contribution to the sickness and the
pervading horror. Frederick, by now in despair, seeing the flower
of his army dead or dying around him, had no choice but to strike
his camp; and by the second week of August, 'like a tower in flames'
as John of Salisbury describes him, he and his silent, spectral procession were dragging themselves back through Tuscany. The plague
went with them. Rainald of Dassel, his Chancellor-Archbishop,
succumbed on the fourteenth,[1] so, at about the same time, did
Frederick of Rotenburg, son of Conrad III and thus the Emperor's
first cousin, who had been responsible for the destruction of the
doors of St Peter's; so, did Bishop Daniel of Prague, Acerbus Morena
the historian and more than two thousand others.

And even now the nightmare was not over. Full reports of the
plague had already spread through Lombardy, and the Germans
arrived to find town after town closed against them. At last, and with
considerable difficulty, they reached the imperial headquarters
at Pavia; and there Frederick was forced to halt, watching in
impotent despair when, on 1 December, no less than fifteen of the
leading cities of the region formed themselves into the greater
Lombard League, the foundations of which had been laid at

---

[1] So convinced were his followers—on what grounds it is hard to say—that
Rainald had been a saint, that they boiled his body until there was nothing left
but the bones, which they took back as relics to Germany.

Anagni eight years before. It was his crowning humiliation; such was his Italian subjects' contempt for him that they had not even bothered to wait until he was back over the Alps before making their ultimate gesture of defiance. And indeed, when the spring at last came and the snows began to melt, he saw that even this last lap of his homeward journey would be a problem; all the mountain passes were now controlled by his enemies and closed alike to himself and his shattered army. It was secretly, shamefully and in the guise of a servant that the Emperor of the West finally regained his native land.

But, it may be asked, while Frederick Barbarossa was tasting his triumph and his disaster, what had happened to his old enemy the Pope? Alexander had first taken refuge with his Frangipani friends in the Cartularia tower near the Colosseum. Serious as the situation was, he seems to have thought that he might still be able somehow to maintain himself in the capital; and when two Sicilian galleys sailed up the Tiber with further massive subsidies from Queen Margaret, he had actually refused their captains' offer to carry him away to safety. It was a noble decision but, as he soon saw, an unwise one. The Romans, fickle as ever, turned against him. Disguised as a pilgrim, he had embarked in a small boat just as the Pisans were arriving and slipped down the river to freedom. Landing at Gaeta, he had then made his way via Terracina to Benevento —where, ultimately, his loyal cardinals joined him. He had escaped not a moment too soon. If he had fallen into the Emperor's hands, it would have been the end of his active pontificate; even if he had somehow avoided capture, he would probably have perished in the epidemic which, it need hardly be said, did not confine itself to the imperial army but raged through Rome until the Tiber was thick with corpses. The Almighty, perhaps, had been on his side after all.

Such was certainly the view of the papal supporters. God-fearing men everywhere, and in Germany perhaps most of all, saw in that dreadful visitation on Barbarossa the hand of the exterminating angel—not only a just retribution for his crimes, but also a proof of the rightness of Alexander's cause. The Pope's popularity soared, and with it his prestige. The Lombard cities made him patron and chief of their new League and even invited him—though he did not accept—to take up residence among them. Meanwhile they founded a new city between Pavia and Asti and named it Alessandria in his honour.

In Rome, the anti-Pope Paschal had meanwhile lost what derisory support he had ever had. No longer did he dare even to set foot outside the melancholy tower of Stephen Theobald, the only place in the city where he felt safe. His health too was failing fast, and everyone knew that he had not long to live. In such circumstances it would have been a simple matter for Alexander to return to the Lateran; but he refused. He had come to hate Rome, and he despised the Romans for their faithlessness and venality. Three times in eight years they had welcomed him to their city; three times, through intimidation or bribery, they had turned against him and driven him into exile. He had no wish to go through it all again. Benevento, Terracina, Anagni—there were plenty of other places from which, as he knew from previous experience, the business of the Papacy could be transacted with efficiency and despatch, free from the intrigues and the ceaseless violence of the Eternal City. He preferred to remain where he was.

It was eleven years before he saw Rome again.

16

THE FAVOURITE'S FALL

... for that land devours its inhabitants.

Peter of Blois, Letter 90

THE exterminating angel that had wrought such havoc and destruction on the army of Frederick Barbarossa must have appeared, in Sicilian eyes, a messenger of deliverance. In the century and a half that had elapsed since the Normans first arrived in the peninsula, South Italy had faced the threat of imperial invasion more times than its inhabitants cared to remember; but never could the danger have loomed more large than in that agonising summer of 1167. Then, suddenly, it was past. Expenses, largely in the form of papal subventions, had admittedly been heavy; but the actual losses—apart from a few stragglers in Gilbert of Gravina's army who had failed to retreat fast enough south of Ancona—had been nil. The Kingdom was safe again—at least from the outside.

In the capital, Stephen du Perche remained at the centre of power, still beloved by the faceless masses but more and more hated by those upon whom, had he but realised it, his survival depended— a hatred which had grown even more bitter after that day in the early autumn when the Queen, while retaining him as her Chancellor, had also had him elected by the complaisant canons of Palermo to the vacant archbishopric of the city. It was an extraordinary step— one in which both Margaret and Stephen demonstrated yet again their strange imperviousness to the sensibilities of those around them. The young man had never been intended for the Church; he had been ordained—by Romuald of Salerno, with one can imagine what reluctance—only a few days before. Richard Palmer in particular had made no secret of his disgust. And it was not only Romuald and Richard who felt the appointment as a personal affront. From the moment Stephen took his seat on the Archbishop's throne in Palermo Cathedral and the choir shattered the sullen silence with the *Te Deum*, the entire ecclesiastical party became his enemy.

Once more, plots against the Chancellor began to proliferate, just as they had proliferated against Maio and Caïd Peter, until Stephen saw that he could now trust no one outside his French entourage. Among the Sicilians, all were now suspect—even the palace eunuchs, even Matthew of Ajello himself, who had made no secret of his hostility ever since the business of the notaries. One day Stephen, hoping to obtain material proof of Matthew's sinister intentions, arranged with a crony, Robert of Bellême, to waylay a messenger travelling between the protonotary and his brother, the Bishop of Catania, and to bring him whatever letters the man was found to be carrying. Robert's ambush failed; the messenger escaped and reported the whole incident to his master, who was understandably furious—so much so that when Robert died shortly afterwards in somewhat sinister circumstances Matthew immediately fell under the suspicion of having had him murdered. This suspicion was increased at the ensuing enquiry, when a certain doctor, known to be a close friend of Matthew's and a fellow-Salernitan to boot, was revealed as having introduced himself into Robert's house with a curious medicament which he described as a simple rose syrup, but which another witness testified to have burnt all the skin off his hand. Though the doctor was found guilty and imprisoned, he never confessed. Nothing was ever proved against Matthew; but his relations with Stephen became worse than ever.

Some time during the summer of 1167, Queen Margaret's wastrel brother Henry of Montescaglioso had returned to Palermo. Once again, the circumstances of his arrival were typical of him. On reaching Apulia the year before, he had allowed himself to be persuaded by a group of discontented vassals that this ostracism to a remote fief was an insult to his royal dignity, and that his proper place was at his sister's side in the capital, in the seat at that time still occupied by Count Richard of Molise. Count Richard, they explained, was nothing but an upstart opportunist who had wormed himself into Margaret's favour—and, most likely, into her bed—in the cold-blooded pursuit of his own ends. Henry's only honourable course was therefore to go to Palermo and demand his dismissal, thus simultaneously vindicating his own and his sister's honour. It was a task in which they would be happy to assist.

When, however, Henry arrived in Sicily a few months later with his followers, both Spanish and Apulian, it was only to discover what everyone else in the Kingdom had known long ago—that Richard had already surrendered his position to Stephen du Perche. Though he probably knew little enough of Stephen, it must have been immediately clear to him that he could not object to a blood relation in the same way as he had objected to a local *parvenu* like the Count of Molise. On the contrary, this new appointment might prove very much to his advantage—if he played his cards right.

The Chancellor, meanwhile, played his own very cleverly indeed. From what he had been told of Henry, it seemed likely that a few promises and a fair measure of flattery would be all that was needed to render him harmless. Once he himself were won over, there would be nothing to fear from his hangers-on. And so it proved. Stephen, whose career throughout his short life shows that he must have possessed considerable charm, exerted it to the full. In next to no time Henry was one of his cousin's most enthusiastic supporters. The Apulian discontents were disgusted to see their former leader riding everywhere at the Chancellor's side, even accompanying him to the baths, and generally behaving as if the city belonged to him. Beaten, they had no course open to them but to return to their lands—which, not long afterwards, they did.

So, for some months, Henry basked; but he was too unstable—or perhaps simply too gullible—to remain quiet for long. The weakness of his character, his conceit and his close kinship with the Regent made him the perfect tool for intriguers and, as the summer wore on, more and more of them began to murmur in his ear how disgraceful it was that the Queen's cousin should rank above her brother, how instead of calling on the Chancellor, Henry should insist that Stephen should call on him—how iniquitous it was, in fact, that Stephen du Perche rather than Henry of Montescaglioso should hold the reins of power in Sicily.

At first, Falcandus tells us, Henry would reply that he had had no practice in the art of government, and that in any case he spoke no French, an indispensable language at the court. He was therefore perfectly content to leave state affairs in the hands of his good friend Stephen, who was after all a wise and prudent man, admirably qualified by his noble birth to occupy his high office. Soon, however, the murmurs took on a new note, with more than a tinge of scorn. How could the Count of Montescaglioso continue on such friendly terms with the Chancellor in view of the latter's notorious relationship with the Queen? Was he publicly pandering to their ignoble and incestuous desires? Or was he still feigning ignorance of what was going on under his nose? Surely he could not be so crass and supine—the words are Falcandus's own—as to be genuinely unaware of what was now the talk of the city?

Whether there was any foundation for these rumours we shall never know. Falcandus speaks elsewhere of how the Queen would be seen 'devouring the Chancellor with her eyes'. Margaret was still under forty and is said to have been beautiful;[1] she had been largely ignored by her late husband, and it would perhaps have been surprising if she had not formed some sort of attachment to a young and handsome man of high birth, intelligence and marked ability who was, incidentally, one of the few people in Sicily whom she could trust. Even if there had been no such attachment, gossip on the subject would have been unavoidable. In any event, Henry was convinced. He became morose; where hitherto he had sought Stephen's company probably a good deal more often than the Chancellor found necessary or agreeable, now he began to avoid him. More ominous still, he took advantage of his free *entrée* into the palace to recount to the King the stories he had heard about his

[1] La Lumia describes her as *bella ancora, superba, leggiera*—but gives no references. His beautifully-written book on William II's reign, though now just a century old, remains the standard work for the period; occasionally, however, he allows his romantic imagination to cloud his scholarship.

mother, in an attempt—not very successful, as it turned out—to cause a rift between them.

The Count of Montescaglioso seems to have had no thought of concealing his altered feelings from his benefactors, and Stephen soon saw that—incredible as it might appear—he had overestimated his cousin; Henry was even more unreliable than he had supposed. His faithlessness had, on the other hand, served one useful purpose: it had indicated, more surely than any number of agents' reports could have done, that another conspiracy was in the wind and that the Count was a party to it. A few secret enquiries—and Henry could have been followed by a dozen spies without ever being aware of the fact—were enough to confirm the Chancellor's suspicions. He resolved to strike.

But could he? One of his bitterest enemies among the palace eunuchs, the Great Chamberlain Caïd Richard, had control of the royal guard and could certainly not be relied upon in the event of trouble. Indeed, one of the inevitable results of a successful *coup* by the Chancellor would have to be the arrest and probably the imprisonment of all the senior Muslims of the court, including the baptised Caïds; a step which, in the present circumstances, might easily provoke a general rising among the Islamic population of the capital. If then he were to forestall his enemies with a sudden swoop of his own, he would be well advised to do it elsewhere than in Palermo. Fortunately it had already been agreed that young William should make his first official visit to the mainland in the following year. On the pretext of making the necessary arrangements, it was accordingly announced that the whole court would move for the winter to Messina.

Hugo Falcandus's description of Messina has already been quoted. The second city of Sicily, with a harbour as busy if not busier than that of Palermo itself, it enjoyed, like all great ports, an agreeably *louche* reputation. For Stephen, however, it had one overriding advantage: it was a purely Christian city. Ibn Jubair, visiting it some twenty years later, noted that it seemed 'full to overflowing with the adorers of the Cross' and that 'it was thanks only to the handful of Muslim menials and servants that a traveller from the Islamic lands was not treated like some wild beast'. The population was in fact largely Greek, with a generous admixture of Italians and Lombards; none had ever shown any dissatisfaction with the present regime. Another point in the city's favour was its proximity to the mainland; and Stephen now wrote secretly to his cousin Gilbert, with whom he had been on excellent terms ever since his visit to Gravina the previous year, asking him to hurry to Messina, bringing with him as many soldiers as he safely could without arousing suspicions or causing alarm.

Meanwhile, in court circles, news of the coming move had been received with almost general consternation. Except, we may imagine, for Henry of Montescaglioso, who never understood much of what was going on and probably looked forward to a reunion with his witty Messinan companions, those who planned the Chancellor's overthrow recognised at once how much, in a strange city where they could not rely on any popular support for their action, their strategic position would be weakened. The high ecclesiastics, in particular, were horrified. They knew that they would have to go —anyone who did not would be sure to suffer from the intrigues of the others the moment his back was turned—but they were loath to leave their sumptuous Palermitan palaces in order to pass the winter in rented accommodation which threatened to be both cold and uncomfortable, and to venture their cossetted persons on the rough mountain tracks which, at this time of year, might well be washed away altogether.[1] Here, to be fair, they had a point; the rains that autumn proved the heaviest in living memory. But Stephen was firm. Letters were sent under royal seal to all the local authorities on the route, ordering them to look to the state of the roads throughout the region under their control, widening or levelling them wherever necessary and preparing them in all respects for the passage of the King. A day or two before the date fixed for the departure the skies cleared, and on 15 December[2] William and his family set out in state for Messina, his courtiers and churchmen riding morosely behind.

[1] Until the middle of the last century the road from Palermo to Messina was still so bad that travellers normally went by sea from one city to the other.

[2] Falcandus gives the date as 15 November, but this is probably a copyist's mistake. See Chalandon, II, p. 331n. Romuald of Salerno expressly states that it was around Christmas.

Messina greeted its King with joy, and William settled with his mother into the royal palace—'rising white as a dove,' wrote Ibn Jubair, 'from the water's edge, a building in which a great number of pages and young girls find employment'. Meanwhile Stephen du Perche, well-meaning as always—but conscious too that he might need their support in a crisis—made a genuine effort to endear himself to the local inhabitants, even restoring to them privileges that they had been formerly granted by Roger II but since lost. Try as he might, however, he could not hold their affection for long. Within a month, the arrogance and high-handedness of his entourage had made the French hated throughout the city and alienated even those who, on their arrival, had been the most favourably disposed towards them.

In these circumstances the long-discussed plot against the Chancellor's life which—owing largely to the inanity of the Count of Montescaglioso—had till now remained somehow inchoate and formless, suddenly began to take shape. Though there had never been any shortage of adherents, their numbers were now further increased by certain Calabrian vassals, whom the King's arrival had attracted across the straits; but participation was by no means confined to the noble faction. Several court officials, among them Matthew of Ajello and Caïd Richard, were heavily implicated; while the hierarchy was represented by that old voluptuary Gentile of Agrigento—who only a few weeks before had insisted on swearing his faith to Stephen in an oath of quite unnecessary length and almost baroque pomposity. The whole weakness of the conspiracy, in fact, lay in its size. The agreed plan, which was simply to strike Stephen down on a given morning as he was leaving his palace, needed no very large group to implement it. What it did demand was secrecy; and it was the inability of the conspirators to preserve this one essential that led to their undoing.

The member responsible, it need hardly be recorded, was Henry of Montescaglioso. For some reason we shall never understand, he blurted out full details of the plot to a local judge, who at once passed them on to the Chancellor. Stephen acted with equal swiftness, pausing only to tell the King and his mother what he proposed to do and then summoning, in the Regent's name, an immediate council of the whole court, including all the bishops, nobles and justiciars at that time in Messina. As soon as it was assembled, Gilbert of Gravina was to have his men surround the palace; those of the clerks known to be loyal were discreetly advised to carry daggers or short swords concealed about their persons. The Chancellor himself, when he entered the council chamber, was wearing a coat of mail under his state robes.

As soon as the meeting opened, the Count of Montescaglioso rose to his feet and launched into a passionate if incoherent diatribe, in which pride and self-pity were uneasily combined. He was, he confessed, heavily in debt—a fact which nobody had any difficulty in believing—the revenues of his fief being nowhere near adequate to maintain the scale of living to which he was accustomed and, by his rank, entitled. As uncle to the King, he therefore laid formal claim to the Principality of Taranto—with which Roger II had invested his bastard son Simon but which William I had taken back—or, failing that, all the lands and properties which Simon had formerly possessed in Sicily.

His outburst, for which such a gathering clearly offered neither a suitable time nor place, seems to have been deliberately intended to provoke bad feeling in the chamber. The Chancellor would be certain to refuse; Henry or one of his supporters would protest, as offensively as possible; and the ensuing uproar would provide an ideal opportunity for the assassination. At this point, however, things took a different turn. Scarcely had Henry finished speaking when Gilbert of Gravina leaped up and delivered, before the assembled company, not so much a reply as a blistering indictment of the Count of Montescaglioso, his character and his misdeeds. Had Henry ever comported himself with a minimum of dignity or decency, Gilbert pointed out, he might long ago have been freely offered what he was now demanding with menaces; instead, he had dissipated huge sums in the pursuit of immorality and vice; he had oppressed his feudatories and inflicted unspeakable outrages upon them; he had done his best to poison relations between the King and his mother, suggesting to Margaret that her son was plotting her overthrow while simultaneously vilifying her to William, and all the time insinuating that he himself should be entrusted with the government of the Kingdom. Let Henry deny it if he dared; both King and Queen were present to hear him. Finally, thundered the Count of Gravina, let him confess to them and to the entire assembly the evil which he had been plotting against the Chancellor for that very day, thus revealing himself as 'a perturber of the Kingdom, against the King's majesty contumacious and rebellious; one who, saving the royal mercy, deserved to lose not only all the lands he already possessed, but his own miserable life as well'.

Taken utterly by surprise and paralysed with fear, Henry could only bluster. He was quickly cut short. A witness was called—the very judge to whom he had confided his plans only a day or two before, and whose evidence now settled the matter. The Count relapsed into silence; and when he heard the Chancellor ordering his arrest and detention in the castle of Reggio he made no objection.

The news spread quickly through Messina, and with it the usual crop of rumours. In the house only recently vacated by the Count of Montescaglioso his Spanish henchmen prepared for armed resistance. But Stephen was ready. Gilbert's men were still stationed around the palace and at other strategic points in the town; and now heralds were despatched through all the streets and squares announcing that every Spaniard had twenty-four hours to leave Sicily. Henry's men, who had not expected to escape so easily, accepted without hesitation; many Calabrians who had been involved in the conspiracy also elected to leave while the going was good. Unfortunately, it proved rather less good than they had hoped. Bands of Greek brigands from Messina pursued the fugitives before they were able to cross the straits and stripped them of all they possessed —including, so Falcandus assures us, their clothes; so that the majority of them, left with no protection against the winter snows, perished miserably in the mountains.

Though several of his advisers recommended the hanging or mutilation of all concerned in the plot, the Chancellor refused to listen. He had a natural dislike of violence; moreover, the sheer numbers of the conspirators argued against any such savage measures. Only one or two of the ringleaders followed Henry of Montescaglioso into prison; the rest, like the Bishop of Agrigento—who had been stricken with a convenient indisposition on the very day of the *débâcle*—were allowed to slip away. There was only one notable and undeserving sufferer—Richard, Count of Molise. Although he had had good reason to dislike Stephen du Perche, having been supplanted by him in power, he had almost certainly taken no part in the conspiracy; but he was hated by Gilbert of Gravina, who had not forgotten the circumstances of his own dismissal from Palermo some eighteen months before and was determined to have his revenge. He now had the unfortunate Count arraigned on a charge of illegal tenure of his lands; the accusation was upheld on a technicality and the estates in question were confiscated. Richard protested, loudly and with vehemence, against the sentence; and his enemies pounced. That sentence, they crowed, was passed in the name of the King. To question it was, by Sicilian law, tantamount to sacrilege. The poor Count was dragged before an ecclesiastical court composed of such bishops and archbishops as were still in the neighbourhood, found guilty and imprisoned at Taormina.

Bluff, impulsive, not too intelligent, innocent alike of malice or guile, there is something likeable about Richard of Molise—and, in the fetid atmosphere of lies and subterfuge in which he lived and which emerges with such sickening vividness from the pages of Falcandus—something refreshing. Twice, admittedly, he was himself involved in conspiracies; but on the first occasion, the moment he saw his King in danger, he had sprung forward to shield him with his own body; while on the second, as we shall see, he could hardly have behaved otherwise than he did. Never did he deliberately strive for advancement or personal gain; he accepted high office when it came his way, laying it down again when required to do so without complaint or resentment. A sheep among wolves, the only wonder is that he lasted for so long.

When Stephen du Perche returned to Palermo with the King and the Regent towards the end of March 1168, it was to find that he had indeed been too lenient with his adversaries. In particular, he had feigned to overlook the complicity in Count Henry's plot of the two most powerful palace officials, the Grand Protonotary Matthew of Ajello and the Great Chamberlain, Caïd Richard—trusting, presumably, that they would congratulate themselves on a lucky escape and keep well away from sedition in future. He had miscalculated badly. Matthew and Richard knew that the Chancellor could not possibly be ignorant of the part they had played; sooner or later he was bound to strike, and the blow would fall none the less heavily for being deferred. Immediately after Henry's arrest they had therefore hurried back to the capital with the Bishop of Agrigento to plan one more attempt. There, with a population already hostile to Stephen and no Gilbert of Gravina to contend with, their task promised to be easier. By the time the Chancellor returned with the rest of the court, all would be in readiness. He would be given no chance even to discover what had been going on in his absence; they would move too quickly. Within a day or two of his arrival—on Palm Sunday to be precise—he would be dead.

But Stephen was better informed than they thought. After eighteen months in Sicily he had developed a keen nose for plots, and his first action on reaching Palermo was to throw Matthew and several of his accomplices into prison. Fears of a Muslim rising dissuaded him from doing the same to Caïd Richard, whom he placed instead under close surveillance. The Bishop of Agrigento fled hastily to his diocese but, on the arrival of a royal justiciar to arrest him, his flock handed him over with every appearance of relief. He was taken under guard to the fortress of S. Marco d'Alunzio—the first Norman castle ever built on Sicilian soil which, having once been a Hauteville residence, was probably not too uncomfortable—there to be kept in indefinite detention.

Now at last the Chancellor might have been forgiven for believing that all was well, and that he would henceforth be able to resume the normal tasks of government free from the constant necessity of looking over his shoulder or behind the arras. But cut off as he was, by the barriers of language and his own eminence, from the Sicilian population, he seems to have had no idea of the strength of anti-French feeling. Nowhere was this more true than in Messina, where memories of the insults and abuses suffered during the past winter were still fresh and where, after so many encouraging rumours, the news of the failure of Count Henry's plot had been received with gloom and despondency. The Messinans had no need of conspirators or demagogues to rouse them to action; among the Greek

majority in particular, the atmosphere was already explosive enough.
All it needed was a spark, and that spark was provided, ironically,
by the Chancellor-Archbishop's own Master of the Household, a
canon of Chartres Cathedral named Odo Quarrel.

Odo had been one of the original party who had arrived in Sicily
with Stephen in the autumn of 1166. Though he never seems to have
considered making a permanent home for himself in the island, he
had promised to remain for two years while his friend found his feet.
He sounds, from Falcandus's description, like one of the worst of
the lot:

He was neither cultivated nor even prudent in the ordering of civil
affairs; but was of such cupidity and greed that he would seize on to
any method by which he might extort money; he measured friendship not by virtue or faithfulness but only by the value of the gifts
which he hoped to receive.

By Easter 1168 Odo was in Messina preparing for his departure.
His time had in theory another six months to run, but the Regent
had asked him to leave rather earlier so that he could escort Henry
of Montescaglioso back to Spain—she having decided, rather than
keeping her brother indefinitely in prison, to send him home with a
bribe of a thousand gold pieces in return for a promise never to
return to Sicily. Despite exhortations from Palermo, however,
Odo's preparations were extremely slow—chiefly, Falcandus maintains, because he had discovered a splendid new way of augmenting
his income and was now making a small fortune by levying his own
harbour dues on all ships that passed through the straits on their
way to Palestine. This practice, as may be imagined, had not endeared him to the people of Messina; and when, one evening, some
of his domestics became involved in a tavern brawl with a party of
Greeks, what began as a minor disturbance soon developed into a
riot. The news was brought to Odo, who immediately summoned
the governor of the city[1] and ordered him to arrest all the Greeks

[1] In Latin, *stratigotus*. These officials, as their name suggests, were formerly
confined to the Greek-speaking areas of the Kingdom; but in later years they
crop up elsewhere as well. Their duties are hard to define, since they seem to have
varied from place to place. In Messina, a largely Greek city, the *stratigotus* was
the highest civil authority.

concerned. The governor protested, then—fearing Odo's influence in high places—reluctantly agreed; but no sooner did he appear on the scene and make his purpose known than he was met by a volley of stones and forced to retire. By nightfall Messina was under mob rule. Old rumours were reborn, new ones sprang up. Stephen du Perche, it was whispered, had already married the Regent; he had killed the young King; he planned to seize the throne; once he had done so, he would dispossess all Greeks, dividing their property among the French and Latins; the true purpose of Odo Quarrel's journey was to fetch the Chancellor's brother from Normandy, so that he could be married to Roger II's posthumous daughter Constance, now a child of fourteen.

But by now Odo can have had little thought of returning to Sicily for any reason whatever—if indeed he ever managed to leave it alive. He barricaded himself into his house and waited, terrified, for developments. Meanwhile a crowd of Messinans hurried to the harbour, commandeered seven galleys and crossed the straits to Reggio where the Count of Montescaglioso was imprisoned. Once there, they had no difficulty in persuading the local population to make common cause with them, march on the citadel and insist on the Count's immediate release. Their arrival took the local garrison by surprise; outnumbered many times over, it soon capitulated and handed over its prisoner.

Henry of Montescaglioso had never been renowned for his intelligence, but he was quick to seize an opportunity. On his return to Messina, his first thought was to assure himself of Odo Quarrel—and in particular of the immense treasure which the canon was known to be taking back with him to France. A notary was called and instructed to make a complete inventory of all the gold and silver, jewels and silks in his house and have them stored in a place of safety; Henry then ordered Odo to be transferred from the royal palace, where he had hoped to find a safe refuge from the mob, to the old fortress overlooking the harbour. At this point, however, the Messinans objected. They still did not altogether trust their chosen leader—he was, after all, well known in certain sections of the town—and they suspected, probably with good reason, that he might at any moment start negotiating with Stephen du Perche, using his quivering captive as a bargaining counter. Their leaders went straight to Henry and demanded that Odo be surrendered to them for punishment; the Count hesitated, but dared not refuse.

Odo Quarrel was an unattractive character; he was also a stupid one, who by his stupidity brought about not just his own downfall but that of all his recently arrived compatriots in Sicily. But he did not deserve the fate that awaited him. Stripped naked and tied backwards on a donkey, he was led through the streets under a hail of stones. When he reached the gates some citizen, whether deputed for the task or acting on a sudden impulse we do not know, stepped forward and plunged a long Pisan knife into his neck, licking the blade afterwards as a final gesture of hatred and contempt. The mob then fell on its victim, stabbing the lifeless body again and again in its fury, cutting off the head, impaling it on a lance and parading it through the city. Finally they flung it into the public sewer, from which it was later recovered and secretly buried.

Odo's end was but a beginning. The following morning, when dawn broke over Messina, there was not a Frenchman left alive.

Away in Palermo, Stephen du Perche began to see that he was faced no longer with a local uprising, but with a rapidly spreading rebellion. Messengers were now arriving daily at the capital, and the news they brought grew daily more ominous. The rebels had taken Rometta, an important vantage-point commanding the Palermo–Messina road; they had swept down the coast to Taormina, attacking the citadel and releasing Richard of Molise; the Bishop of Cefalù had declared openly in their favour, and where the bishop led, other ecclesiastics would be sure to follow. There were no reports as yet of any further incidents on the mainland, but the recent events at Reggio were a clear enough indication that the fire of revolt could jump the straits whenever necessary.

The Chancellor's first reaction was to mobilise an army and march against Messina. Many of the regular detachments, he knew, might be of doubtful loyalty; but the Lombard colonies round Etna—who had no special love for the Greeks—had offered on their own initiative to put twenty thousand men into the field against them,

and with such a nucleus it should be possible to build up a reasonably effective striking force. But there were delays. The fifteen-year-
old King, in his first recorded political intervention, counselled
postponement of the campaign until the stars should be in a more
favourable conjunction—a poor augury for his future statecraft.
And now Stephen himself, in the gravest crisis of his short career,
hesitated. Should he, as his French friends advocated, remain with
the King and the Regent in Palermo where, in an atmosphere now
more highly charged than ever, his life was once again in peril? Or
should he follow the advice of Ansald, the palace castellan, leave the
capital and organise resistance from some distant stronghold, where
William and Margaret could later join him?

Had Stephen known that Matthew of Ajello in his prison cell had
already arranged for his assassination, it might have helped him to
make up his mind. Using Constantine, Ansald's deputy, as his
intermediary, Matthew had had no difficulty in making contact with
his friends among the domestics of the palace and persuading them
to do the deed. His plan, like its two predecessors, was simple;
Stephen was to be struck down on a given morning as he entered
the building, at a point between the first and second gates where he
would have little room to defend himself.

The Chancellor, alerted in time, remained in his house. His non-
appearance, however, was an unmistakable sign that the alarm had
been given, and warned his enemies that they must act again quickly
if they wished to save their own lives. Fortunately for them, Ansald
the castellan was ill; confined to his room on an upper floor of the
palace, he had left his deputy Constantine in command. The latter
at once summoned the sergeants-at-arms and ordered them to go
through the city, calling on the whole population to unite in preventing the Chancellor from making a getaway with the royal treasure.
Whether Constantine really believed in this last possibility is open to
doubt; but his appeal had the desired effect. Ever since the first reports from Messina, excitement in Palermo had been growing;
Matthew's agents had fanned it yet higher; Christian and Saracen
alike were now avid for the chance of avenging themselves on the
foreigners they loathed, while in the stews and alleys of the town
bands of ruffians were already preparing for the looting that would

surely follow. Now, as the sergeants spread their message, men everywhere snatched up their swords and streamed into the streets. Within the hour the Chancellor's house was under siege.

At the first sign of disturbance Stephen had been joined by a number of his followers. They put up a brave defence, but their task was hopeless. Outside, the crowd was growing larger and more menacing every moment; its numbers had now been swelled, as the defenders saw to their horror, by the archers of the royal guard. Such troops as had remained faithful, fewer in number than the aggressors and probably no better armed, were unable to force their way through to the beleaguered building—which itself, being the official residence of the Archbishop of Palermo, was ill equipped to withstand a siege. It had, however, one advantage—a narrow corridor linking it directly with the cathedral. To Stephen and his companions, desperate now, this corridor represented their one slender chance of escape. Down it they sped, leaving a few knights behind to cover their retreat, thence through the great church to the bell-tower. Here at last was something they could defend; here, at any rate, they would be safe for a little longer.

In the general tumult that had spread through the city it had been an easy matter for Matthew of Ajello and Caïd Richard to escape and to place themselves once more at the head of the rebellion. Now, calling out the royal trumpeters, they had them blow a fanfare outside the archbishop's palace where the mob, unaware of Stephen's flight, was still hammering at the doors. It was a brilliant move. To all who heard it, the sound could mean one thing only—that the King was behind the insurgents. Those who were already in the streets found new enthusiasm and redoubled their efforts; many who had remained in their homes—often through uncertainty as to where their duty lay—hurried out to join them. Meanwhile someone, probably Matthew himself, had remembered the little corridor—seeing it not so much as an escape route for the besieged but as a means of infiltrating the palace from the rear. At once there was a rush to the cathedral. Stephen's men had locked and bolted every entrance, but faggots were brought up and soon the great wooden doors themselves were aflame. The crowd burst in, overwhelmed the few brave swordsmen who tried to turn them back, and, without giving a thought to the bell-tower, poured down the corridor into the palace.

Only when the entire building had been ransacked—and, we may imagine, stripped bare by looters—did it dawn on the mob leaders where Stephen must have gone. Back to the bell-tower they ran; but its winding stair was narrow, its defenders fighting for their lives. The few hot-heads who ventured up soon reappeared, streaming with blood. There was a pause. Some were for burning the whole tower down; others held that a stone building would be better attacked by a siege engine; yet others proposed undermining the foundations. They were still arguing when darkness fell. Enough had happened for one day; it was agreed that, however the tower was to be attacked, the operation was better left till the morrow.

But Matthew of Ajello was growing anxious. The building, he knew, was strong—stronger than most of its would-be assailants seemed to think. Stephen and his friends would have carried provisions with them from the palace; once settled in, they might easily be able to hold out for a week or more—a good deal longer, probably, than the mob's enthusiasm. The King, also, presented a problem. He was showing signs of unexpected spirit. Already he had demanded to be allowed to ride out and face his subjects, calling upon them to lay down their arms and return to their homes; and Matthew, strong as his position was, had had a hard time restraining him. The boy's popularity in the city was as great as ever; once he managed to make his true sympathies known, support for the rebellion would dwindle rapidly.

And so Matthew and his associates decided to offer the Chancellor terms. Emissaries were sent to the tower with their offer. Stephen and all those of his compatriots who wished to accompany him would be taken in Sicilian galleys to Palestine; the rest would be given free passage back to France. As for those Sicilians who had supported him, there would be no reprisals taken against either their persons or their property. Such mercenaries as he had employed would be allowed to continue in service with the King if they so wished; otherwise they might leave the country unhindered. The agreement would be guaranteed by Richard Palmer, Bishop John of Malta,

Romuald of Salerno and Matthew himself. In the circumstances, they could hardly have been more generous. Stephen accepted.

It remained only to get the Chancellor and his friends out of Sicily as soon as possible. A suitable vessel was found, and all that night the loading and provisioning went on until, by the following morning, it was ready to sail. To avoid incident, the party was embarked a little distance from the capital, near the modern suburb of Mondello; but just as the ship was about to weigh anchor, a commotion broke out on the quay. The canons of the cathedral had suddenly remembered that they had failed to obtain from Stephen an instrument of resignation from his archbishopric; without such a document they would be unable to elect his successor. At first Stephen—whose mood by now cannot have been of the best— refused to give it; only when he heard the mutterings of those present and saw their hands tightening on their swords did he understand how they had interpreted his refusal—as a sign that he secretly intended to return to Sicily and seize power once more. Then he relented—probably in genuine horror that anyone should think him willing, in any circumstances, to set foot again in a land which he had sincerely tried to serve and by which he had been so shamefully repaid.

Poor Stephen: he was to do so sooner than he knew. Hardly was his galley out of the harbour than it proved totally unseaworthy. Whether it had been sabotaged or not we shall never know; but by the time it reached Licata, half-way along the south-west coast of the island, it could go no further. The local population was openly hostile; it was only with the utmost reluctance that Stephen was allowed to land at all, and then for a period not exceeding three days. In so short a time repairs were out of the question; it was in another vessel, bought at his own expense from some Genoese merchants he found in the harbour, that he finally reached the Holy Land.

Into the two years since he had left France, Stephen du Perche had packed a lifetime of experience. He had attained the highest ranks, both civil and ecclesiastical, in one of the three greatest kingdoms of Europe, he had risen from layman to metropolitan archbishop, he had won the respect of some, the detestation of many—and, probably, the love of a queen. He had learned much—about power and the abuses of power, about the art of government; about loyalty, friendship and fear. But about Sicily he had learned nothing. He never understood that the nation's strength, if not its very survival, depended upon the maintenance of its unity; and that since it was by nature heterogeneous and fissile, that unity must be imposed from above. Because of this incomprehension, he failed; and the fact that in the end he accidentally and involuntarily united his enemies against him in no way diminishes his failure.

It might be said that he was unlucky, and perhaps he was; unlucky in that he came to Sicily at a moment when the island was more demoralised than it had been at any time since the Normans first landed on its soil; unlucky in his companions, for whose arrogance and boorishness he was inevitably blamed; unlucky, even, in his age and inexperience—for it is all too easy to forget that at the time of his inglorious departure he was still in his early or middle twenties. Yet even at the end Fortune had cast on him one thin, watery smile; if the ship's captain had elected, on setting sail, to head east instead of west, taking the more direct route through the straits rather than the longer one via Trapani, his vessel might have been forced to put in not at Licata but at Messina instead. Had it done so, the Sicilian adventure of Stephen du Perche might have had a different and still unhappier end.

Of the thirty-seven Frenchmen who had accompanied Stephen to Sicily, two only were still alive when the time came to depart. One was a certain Roger, 'learned, industrious and modest', who now makes his first and last appearance in our story. The other was Peter of Blois, one of the foremost scholars of his day. Peter had studied the humanities at Tours, theology at Paris, and law at Bologna; soon after his return to France, he had been selected by Rothrud of Rouen to go to Sicily as tutor—with Walter of the Mill—to the young King. It was a position that was bound to excite the envy of the court, and his enemies had never stopped trying to get rid of him, twice offering him the see of Rossano and once even the archbishopric of Naples; but he had always refused. Despite a highly-developed sense of his own importance, he was neither grasping nor ambitious; and though intellectuals no longer enjoyed the same pre-eminence as in the two previous reigns, learning was still respected in Palermo more than in any other contemporary court of Europe. He had had no desire to leave.

But the events of the summer of 1168 changed all that. When the crisis came, Peter was lucky enough to be ill in bed, under the expert care of Romuald of Salerno; but when, on his recovery, the King explained that the expulsion of all Frenchmen did not apply to him and pleaded with him to remain, Peter showed himself as firmly determined to depart as he had previously been to stay. As he wrote later to his brother, he 'would not be persuaded by gifts, or promises, or rewards'. A Genoese ship was about to leave for France with the last forty of Stephen's friends on board; Peter insisted on taking it; and before long he was congratulating himself on having exchanged the bitter wines of Sicily for the rich and mellow vintages of his native Loire. Three or four years later his old friend Richard Palmer wrote to him suggesting that he might like to revisit his old friends. Peter's reply speaks for itself:

Sicily drags us down by her very air; she drags us down too by the malice of her people, so that to me she seems odious and scarcely habitable. The distempers of her climate render her abominable to me, as does the frequent and poisonous dissemination by whose immense power our people in their heedless simplicity are constantly endangered. Who, I ask, can live in safety in a place where, leaving aside all other afflictions, the very mountains continually vomit infernal flame and fetid sulphur? For there beyond doubt is the gate of hell . . . where men are taken from the earth and descend living into the regions of Satan.

Your people err in the meagreness of their diets; for they live on so much celery and fennel that it constitutes almost all their sustenance; and this generates a humour which putrefies the body and brings it to the extremes of sickness and even death.

To this I would add that, just as it is written in books of science that all island peoples are in general unworthy of trust, so the inhabitants of Sicily are false friends and, in secret, the most abandoned betrayers. . . .

To you in Sicily, most beloved father, I shall not return. England shall cherish me, an old man, as she cherished you, a child.[1] Rather

---

[1] She did so rather well, and for some forty years. Peter became Archdeacon, first of Bath and then of London, before he died early in the following century.

is it for you to leave that mountainous, monstrous land and return to
the sweetness of your native air. . . . Flee, father, from those flam-
mivomitous mountains, and look on the land of Etna with suspicion,
lest the infernal regions greet you on your death.

As the ships disappeared over the horizon, bearing first Stephen du
Perche and his reluctant fellow-pilgrims and then Peter of Blois with
his home-bound compatriots, Queen Margaret must have been near
despair. She had staked everything on these Frenchmen, and she had
lost. With her son William still only fifteen, her own regency had
another three years to run; but her reputation, both political and
moral, was ruined. The last sad champion of the departed order, the
'Spanish woman' was now neither feared nor resented; she was
simply ignored.

No longer, even, could she choose her own advisers. All three
principal factions—the nobles, the Church and the palace—had had
enough of her friends and relations, and were resolved that neither
she nor they should have any more say in the conduct of affairs.
Scarcely had she recovered from the shock of the revolution when
she found a self-styled and self-constituted council of *familiares*
already in existence—a coalition of the three groups that would have
been unthinkable only two years before. The aristocracy was
represented by Richard of Molise and Roger of Geraci, the first
baron to join the Messinan revolt; from the Church there were
Archbishop Romuald, Bishops John of Malta, Richard Palmer of
Syracuse, Gentile of Agrigento (now released from prison) and
Walter of the Mill; while palace interests were assured by Caïd
Richard and, of course, Matthew of Ajello. For a short time this
Council also included Henry of Montescaglioso, who had returned
from Messina in quite unnecessary pomp with a fleet of twenty-four
ships, doubtless taking full credit for the success of the revolution and
infuriating everyone by his smugness. But Henry was the one issue
on which Margaret and the council found themselves in agreement.
The absence of his name from any subsequent documents suggests that
he soon accepted his sister's bribes and returned, at long last, to Spain.

One only of the Queen's family now remained to be dealt with;
and among the council's first pronouncements was a sentence of
banishment on Gilbert of Gravina. He, his wife and his son, Bert-

rand of Andria, dispossessed of their lands but promised safe conduct from the Kingdom, followed Stephen du Perche to the Holy Land; and Sicily, with an almost audible sign of relief, settled down to govern herself alone once more.

For Margaret, Gilbert's removal must have been the ultimate humiliation. She had had her differences with him in the past, but he had shown himself a good friend to Stephen and, in the last resort, to herself as well. Now that it was his turn to face expulsion, and by a government of which she remained the titular head, she was powerless to help him. Meanwhile the whole Kingdom saw her impotence, and rejoiced. In her anger and frustration, however, Margaret gave continued proof of her total unfitness to govern. After the events of the past few months she might have been expected to have learnt some sort of a lesson. Had she collaborated with the council, she might even have managed to regain some of her lost influence. Instead, she sought to obstruct them at every turn. They had been the enemies of Stephen; for this reason alone, she could never be a friend of theirs. More than ever one suspects that between the Queen and her Chancellor there had existed something more than a working partnership and a family tie.

And still, unbelievably, Margaret seems to have cherished a hope that Stephen might one day return. His departure had left the archbishopric of Palermo once again vacant, and after the usual intrigues the choice of the canons had at last been forcibly directed towards Walter of the Mill.[1] From Margaret's point of view it would not have been a bad appointment. Walter had served as her son's tutor for several years. He was less hidebound than Romuald, less overbearing than Richard Palmer, less disreputable than Gentile and younger, probably, than any of them. But he was not Stephen; and so she turned her face against him, protesting that her cousin was still the rightful archbishop—his renunciation having been extracted only under duress—and sending an appeal to Pope Alexander, persuasively backed with seven hundred ounces of gold, that he should refuse to ratify Walter's election.

---

[1] The circumstances of his elevation are not recorded. Falcandus, however, refers to Walter as having succeeded to the archbishopric 'less by election than by violent intrusion', so we may fear the worst.

Not content with badgering the Pope, the Queen had also written to the second most respected churchman in Europe—Thomas Becket, Archbishop of Canterbury, now in exile in France. From the very beginning, some five years before, of Thomas's quarrel with King Henry, both protagonists had looked to Sicily for support—the King as a potential intermediary with Pope Alexander, the archbishop as a possible place of refuge for himself or his friends. As time went on, the Sicilians had found their position more and more embarrassing. Emotionally, there had been much sympathy for Becket. Richard Palmer was a regular correspondent of his and Walter of the Mill, another compatriot, seems to have been similarly well-disposed, together with most other members of the hierarchy; while Stephen du Perche, high-minded, religious and suddenly to his surprise a fellow-archbishop, had always championed Becket's cause. On the other hand, as Matthew of Ajello had been quick to point out, King Henry was fighting, just as Roger I and II had fought, to free his country of papal interference in civil affairs; the privileges he was now demanding were in many respects a good deal more modest than those which Sicily had enjoyed for decades. It hardly became the government in Palermo to take a sanctimonious line against him.

It had therefore been agreed to remain as far as possible on the sidelines of the dispute; but Sicily had soon emerged as a favourite centre for all those friends and relations of the exiled archbishop for whom England was no longer safe. Thus, when Stephen and his associates were expelled, the Regent in her despair had felt justified in writing to Becket also, asking him to use whatever influence he could to bring about their return. It was a patently forlorn hope, but Thomas did his best. Soon afterwards we find him replying to Margaret:

Though we have never met[1] . . . we owe you a debt of gratitude; and we render our heartiest thanks for the generosity which you have shown to our fellow-exiles and kinsfolk, those poor ones in Christ, who have fled to your lands from him that persecutes them and

[1] In fact Thomas may have known Margaret's family quite well. The constant companion of his youth, Richer de Laigle, was almost certainly a relation of her mother's.

have there found consolation. . . . So, as the first fruits of our devotion, have we used our good offices with the most Christian King [Louis VII] to second your prayers, as you may know by the requests that he has made to our dear friend the King of Sicily.[1]

In a letter written about the same time to Richard Palmer, Thomas is still more explicit. After similar expressions of thanks, he goes on to say:

There is one other request, which I will whisper in your ear and which I hope you will grant me; and that is that you will do your utmost with the King and Queen to obtain the recall to Sicily of that noble man Stephen, Elect of Palermo; both for reasons which shall at present be nameless and also because by doing so you will earn the lasting gratitude of the King of France and his entire Realm.[2]

We can be perfectly sure that Palmer took no action on this request, which Thomas would probably never have made if he had had a better understanding of the circumstances. Meanwhile Queen Margaret's near-hysterical refusal to accept the political reality of her favourite's expulsion, combined with Stephen's own last-minute reluctance to surrender his see, made the council more determined than ever to have the new archbishop enthroned as quickly as possible. A mission left at once for the papal court to offer Alexander, in return for his early approval, a yet larger sum than that by which Margaret had hoped to pursuade him to refuse. After a seemly interval for consideration the Pope notified his agreement—keeping both bribes. On 28 September, in the presence of the King and court, Walter of the Mill received his consecration in Palermo Cathedral.[3]

After this last reverse, Margaret seems to have lost heart. She made little or no further effort to maintain her authority. Her name continues to figure on the occasional deed or diploma until her son's

---

[1] Letter 192.
[2] Letter 150.
[3] When he heard the news, Peter of Blois wrote Walter a splendidly two-edged letter of congratulation—worthy of St Bernard himself—begging him to thank Providence for having raised him up to his present glory from the 'contemptible poverty' and the 'dust of destitution' whence he had begun. (Letter 66.) As joint tutors to the young King, one suspects that the two may not have been the very best of friends.

coming of age in 1171; she then retires, probably with considerable relief, into obscurity. Of these twilight years of her life, one monument only remains—the church of S. Maria di Maniace, built on the site of the Byzantine general George Maniakes's victory over the Saracens in 1040.[1] According to legend, Maniakes had already raised a castle there, in whose chapel he had placed a portrait of the Virgin said to have been painted by St Luke himself; and it was the better to house this treasure that Margaret in 1174 endowed a great Byzantine abbey on the same spot.[2] We can only hope that her interest in this new foundation did something to brighten the last lonely decade of her life. She lived on until 1183, when she died at the age of fifty-five.

But she never saw Stephen again. For the end of his story we have to look not in any Sicilian chronicle but in that of William of Tyre, the historian of Outremer. 'The following summer,' he writes:

. . . a certain nobleman, Stephen, Chancellor of the King of Sicily and elected to the Church of Palermo, a young man, handsome and of excellent character, brother of the noble Rothrud, Count of Perche, was expelled from the Kingdom as a result of the intrigues and conspiracies of the Prince of that country; to the great regret of the King, still a child, and of his mother, who had not the strength to put down these troubles. Stephen was hard pressed to escape from the snares of his enemies; but he succeeded, with a small number of persons, and landed in our Kingdom.

A short while after, he was seized with a serious malady, and died. He was buried with honour at Jerusalem, in the chapter-house of the Temple of the Lord.

[1] See *The Normans in the South*, p. 54 n.
[2] The remains of this abbey now form part of the Brontë estate, which was given in 1799 by Ferdinand III of Naples to Lord Nelson and is now the property of Lord Bridport, the descendant of Nelson's niece Charlotte. Of the church itself, the three apses were destroyed in the famous earthquake of 1693, but much of the rest is as Margaret left it—notably the splendid doorway with its fantastically carved capitals and most of the wooden roof. Also preserved is the Virgin's portrait, now on the altar—beside which, incidentally, stands a marble figure which may well represent Queen Margaret herself.

17

THE ENGLISH MARRIAGE

Ora conosce come s'innamora
Lo ciel del giusto rege, ed al sembiante
Del suo fulgor lo fa vedere ancora.

Dante, Paradiso, XX

Now knows he how the righteous king compels
The love of heaven, and the consciousness
Thereof his glorious semblance yet forthtells.

Tr. Bickersteth

QUEEN MARGARET'S relief at laying down the burdens of state
was fully shared by her subjects. Though her regency had lasted only
five years it must have seemed to them like an eternity; and they
looked gratefully and hopefully towards the tall, fair-haired youth
who, some time during the summer of 1171, formally took the
government of Sicily into his hands.

Not that they knew much about him. His beauty, to be sure, was
famous; he had preserved it intact through his adolescence, and the
boy who had seemed like an angel on the day of his coronation now
at eighteen reminded people more of a young god. The rest was
largely rumour. He was said to be a studious lad, who read and
spoke all the languages of his kingdom, including Arabic; mild-
mannered and gentle, given neither to those brooding silences nor
to those sudden outbursts of rage that had rendered his father so
formidable; deeply religious, yet tolerant of faiths other than his own.
Ibn Jubair recounts with approval one of the best-known stories
about him—how, during the 1169 earthquake, he had reassured the
staff of the palace, Muslim and Christian, with the words, 'Let each of
you pray to the God he adores; he who has faith in his God will

feel peace in his heart.' His statecraft and political judgment were still untried, but this was more an advantage than anything else; having heretofore been kept well away from public affairs, he was safe from blame for any of the disasters his mother had brought upon the Kingdom.

If, in the years immediately following William's assumption of power, Sicily had once again fallen victim to the political instability that had so blighted her past history, there is no telling how long her new young ruler would have maintained his people's love. It was his good fortune that there should have now begun, simultaneously with his majority, a period of peace and security which was soon to become identified with his reign. This much-needed *détente* was not of William's making; though he was never himself to lead an army in the field, he had a disastrous predilection for foreign military adventures and ultimately proved more bellicose than either his father or his grandfather before him. But those adventures, costly as they might be in lives and money, scarcely even ruffled the surface of domestic life in his own realm. Thus it was he, both during his lifetime and posthumously, who took the credit for this new tranquillity; thus too, in later years, men looked back on the Indian summer—for such it turned out to be—of the Sicilian Kingdom, thought of their last legitimate Norman King who looked so glorious and who died so young, and gave him in gratitude the name by which he is still known—William the Good.

Nothing bears more persuasive testimony to this change of atmosphere than the fact that, for the first five years of William's majority, the greater part of Sicilian diplomatic activity in Europe was taken up with the relatively pleasant task of finding him a wife. This was not a new issue. Sicily's domestic upheavals never seemed to have much effect on her international reputation, and it had long been evident that when the time came there would be no shortage of prospective brides; indeed there was not a ruler in Europe who would not have been proud to have the young King as a son-in-law. First in the field, as we have seen, had been Manuel Comnenus; since his daughter would probably have brought the whole Empire of the East as her dowry, Queen Margaret and her advisers might well have accepted the proposal on the spot. But they had refused to be hurried,

and the field was still open when, some time in 1168, King Henry II
of England suggested his third and youngest daughter, Joanna.

To all Sicilians of Norman or English origin, such an alliance must
have seemed even more attractive than the Byzantine proposal.
Links between the two kingdoms had been forming ever since
Roger's day. The English scholars, churchmen and administrators
whose names have already appeared in these pages constitute only a
small fraction of the total;[1] and by the 1160s there were few important
Norman families in either country who could not claim members
in both.[2] Henry himself, whose French dominions alone covered
considerably more territory than those of Louis VII, was beyond
question the most powerful king in Europe. Moreover, though
Joanna was still little more than a baby—she had been born in 1165
—he seemed genuinely keen for the match. There was, admittedly,
the problem of Thomas Becket. Had Stephen du Perche remained in
Sicily the obstacle would have been almost insuperable, but once he
was out of the way it no longer seemed quite so serious. He and
Thomas were known to have been on excellent terms, and some of his
own unpopularity may have rubbed off on to his friend. Meanwhile
Matthew of Ajello, now Vice-Chancellor of the Kingdom and at the
height of his power,[3] was a constant champion of Henry's cause. It
was almost certainly on his advice that, early in 1170, Count Robert
of Loritello and Richard Palmer of Syracuse set off to discuss the
whole question with the Pope at Anagni.

It was a curious choice of delegates. Robert, after years of rebellion

---

[1] Apart from Richard Palmer and Walter of the Mill, there were at least two
other English prelates in the Kingdom during William II's reign—Hubert of
Middlesex, Archbishop of Conza in Campania, and Walter's brother Bartholomew who succeeded Gentile as Bishop of Agrigento. This latter see had in
fact listed a certain John of Lincoln among its canons as early as 1127, while the
name of Richard of Hereford appears among those of Palermo in 1158.

[2] In the contemporary *Lai des Deux Amants* by Marie de France, the Princess of
Pitres on the Seine confides to her lover that

> *En Salerne ai une parente,*
> *Riche femme, mut ad grant rente*

to whom she sends him that he may build up his strength before returning to
win her hand by carrying her bodily over a steep mountain.

[3] After Stephen's departure the office of Chancellor had been allowed to lapse
—just as that of Emir of Emirs had lapsed after the death of Maio.

which had on several occasions nearly cost him his life, had been recalled from exile only the year before, when his former fiefs had been restored to him. He was, however, a cousin of the King and his rank gave the mission a status it would otherwise have lacked. The name of Richard Palmer, at one time perhaps Becket's most trusted friend in Sicily, comes as still more of a surprise—just as it did to Thomas himself when he heard it. The archbishop's own explanation for what he considered a betrayal—that King Henry had won Palmer over to his side with the promise of the bishopric of Lincoln[1] —somehow seems hard to accept. Richard had recently and at long last been consecrated at Syracuse, which had been declared a metropolitan see, under the direct authority of the Pope; he had received his *pallium*[2] shortly afterwards. There is no conceivable reason why he should have wished to exchange Syracuse for Lincoln at such a moment, and certainly he never did so. It is much more likely that, as an Anglo-Norman who had settled in Sicily, he favoured the proposed alliance and was simply anxious to smooth its path all he could; as far as the Becket issue was concerned, he probably saw himself more as a mediator than anything else.

Alexander raised no objection to the marriage, and after the news came of Henry's reconciliation with Thomas in the summer of 1170, the last uncertainties must have been swept away. Then, at nightfall on 29 December, came the archbishop's murder. A dark pall hung over England. Henry's continental subjects were placed under an interdict; the King himself was forbidden to enter any church until such time as the Pope saw fit to absolve him. All Europe was horror-stricken; to the Sicilians, little Joanna suddenly seemed a less desirable bride. Negotiations were broken off abruptly and, once again, the hunt for a Queen began.

Three months later, in March 1171, Manuel Comnenus offered William his daughter Maria for the second time. The princess no longer possessed quite the attractions of five years before; in the interim her stepmother had given birth to a son, Alexius, and the succession to the Byzantine throne was again assured. But she was still an Emperor's daughter, her dowry would be worthy of her

[1] Confided in a letter to Humbald, Bishop of Ostia, in 1169.
[2] See p. 509n.

rank and the marriage would, with any luck, put a stop to her father's eternal meddling in Italian affairs.[1] The offer was accepted, and it was agreed that Maria should arrive in Apulia the following spring.

On the appointed day William, accompanied by his twelve-year-old brother Prince Henry of Capua, Walter of the Mill and Matthew of Ajello, was waiting at Taranto to greet his bride. She did not appear. On the next day there was still no sign of her, nor on the next. After a week of waiting, the King decided to make the pilgrimage to Monte Gargano and the cave of the Archangel Michael. That would take him another ten days at least; Maria would surely have arrived by the time he returned. But when on 12 May he was back on the coast at Barletta, it was to learn that there was still no news. Clearly the girl was not coming; the Greeks had deceived him. Angry and humiliated, he started for home. Still worse misfortunes were to come. The royal party had intended to pass through Capua, where young Henry was to be formally invested with his Principality; shortly before they reached the city, the boy came down with a raging fever. He was hurried to Salerno and thence by ship to Sicily; but when William followed a few weeks later, his brother was dead.[2]

Why had Manuel changed his mind at the last moment, incurring the lasting bitterness of Sicily's young King? He never, so far as we know, apologised or explained, and his motives remain a mystery. The most probable answer is that Frederick Barbarossa had begun bidding for Maria's hand on behalf of his own son; but to us the incident of the bride that never was is important for one reason only; it explains the resentment against Constantinople that was to smoulder in William's heart for the rest of his life—a resentment that was to cost both Sicily and Byzantium dear in the years to come.

What made this snub from Constantinople still more galling to the

[1] In the past three years or so Manuel had sent handsome contributions for the rebuilding of Milan, destroyed by Frederick in 1162; poured, as one chronicler put it, 'a river of gold' into Ancona; and married his niece to one of the Frangipani to assure himself of support in Rome.

[2] According to an old tradition, perpetuated by several of the more venerable historians of Sicily, Prince Henry at his death was betrothed to a daughter of King Malcolm of Scotland. There is no truth in this story. King Malcolm IV, who reigned from 1153 to 1165, not only died unmarried and without issue, but was known during his lifetime as the Virgin King.

King of Sicily was the fact that he was already beginning to envisage an important role for himself in the eastern Mediterranean. Though without any personal appetite or aptitude for military activity, he cherished immense political ambitions which soared far beyond the existing boundaries of his realm. The mere thought of how his father had thrown away his North African possessions—almost without a struggle—was enough to rouse his anger; he preferred to look upon himself as a successor to his grandfather Roger and to Robert Guiscard, as a young scion of the Hautevilles whose destiny it was to win for Sicily a new and glorious overseas empire.

For the time being, at least, there could be no question of reconquering the territories along the North African coast. The Almohads were now supreme; thanks to their brilliant admiral Ahmed es-Sikeli (the Sicilian)—our old friend Caïd Peter[1]—they had built up a fleet of their own which, if not the equal of William's, might still prove a dangerous adversary. They were also in a position, if so inclined, to stir up trouble among the Sicilian Muslims, by no means all of whom had forgotten the terrors of recent years. Fortunately the Almohads remained well-disposed towards their northern neighbour; trade was flourishing, and their leader, Abu-Yakub Yusuf, was anxious to keep his hands free for his projected conquest of Spain—an enterprise which was ultimately to lead to his death. William, headstrong as he was, had no wish to make trouble in that quarter.[2]

His expansionist dreams would have to be directed elsewhere; and he was consequently more than a little intrigued to receive, some time during 1173, a letter from Amalric, the Frankish King of Jerusalem. It appeared that the Fatimids of Egypt, incensed by the abolition of their Cairo Caliphate the previous year, had decided to rise in rebellion against their overlord Nur ed-Din, King of Syria, and his local vizier, Saladin. Knowing that the whole question of Christian survival in the Levant depended in the last resort on Muslim disunity, Amalric had undertaken to give the Egyptians all the help he could; he was now canvassing the princes of the West for support.

[1] See p. 616.

[2] It was not until 1181, however, that William was to conclude a formal treaty of peace with the Almohads—which he sealed, according to the historian Abdul-Wahid al-Marrakeshi, by sending Abu-Yakub a ruby the size and shape of a horseshoe.

It was just the kind of opening that William was looking for; an opportunity to make his name in the East, to show the rulers of Outremer—and Manuel Comnenus too, for that matter—that a new Christian leader, and one to be seriously reckoned with, had emerged on the Mediterranean stage.[1] He responded with enthusiasm. Command of the expedition was given to his first cousin Tancred, Count of Lecce, bastard son of Duke Roger of Apulia, now long since forgiven for his part in the *coup* against William I in 1161; and on an appointed day in the last week of July 1174 a massive Sicilian fleet appeared off Alexandria—two hundred ships, if the Arab chroniclers can be believed, carrying a total of thirty thousand men, including fifteen hundred knights; another thirty-six vessels for the horses, forty for stores and provisions, and six for siege materials.

Had King Amalric seen this huge force, he would doubtless have been as impressed as William had hoped. But King Amalric was dead —of dysentery, just a fortnight before the Sicilians' arrival. And his death meant that there was no Frankish contingent from Jerusalem waiting to join forces with them. Nor was this the only unpleasant surprise in store. Saladin had already uncovered the plot against him and had crucified the ringleaders. There would be no revolt after all. Tancred and his men disembarked to find themselves on hostile territory, utterly unsupported. Almost at once the Alexandrians, who had previously retreated within their walls, burst out again, set fire to the Sicilian siege engines and followed up with a night attack that threw the invaders into total confusion. By now Saladin, apprised of the landings by carrier pigeon, was hurrying up from Cairo at the head of an army. He need not have troubled. Long before he arrived Tancred had given the order to re-embark and the Sicilian ships had disappeared over the horizon, leaving behind them three hundred knights whose retreat had been cut off and who, after heroic but hopeless resistence, were taken prisoner.

To give him his due, William had inherited all his grandfather's resilience. He does not seem to have been particularly cast down by the disaster, and showed it by sending, for the next few summers,

[1] Another Arab historian, al-Maqrisi, claims that a Sicilian fleet had already been sent to the Levant in 1169, to assist in the Frankish siege of Damietta. But no other source confirms this, and extracts from one of Saladin's letters quoted by Abu-Shama strongly imply that no Sicilian ships were present on that occasion.

annual raiding parties to harry the Egyptian coast. But none of these operations was of any real political importance; in the Crusader states of the Levant they passed virtually unnoticed. And they certainly did not obscure the plain fact that William II's first foreign adventure had ended in catastrophe.

The murder of Thomas Becket, deeply as it had shocked all Christian consciences, had no lasting effect on Anglo-Papal relations. At Avranches on 21 May 1172, having performed a public penance and given various promises for the future—some of which he actually kept—Henry II received his absolution; thenceforth, with his abrasive archbishop no longer there to complicate matters, his reconciliation with the Pope was complete. Where Alexander led, the states of Europe were quick to follow; and it was not long before Henry found his diplomatic position stronger than at any time in the previous decade.

William of Sicily, having attained his majority, was among the first of his fellow-rulers to re-establish contact, and for the next few years the two Kings maintained a cordial if rather spasmodic correspondence. Curiously, however, neither seems to have liked to resurrect the marriage proposal—not even after the Byzantine fiasco of 1172, when William was once more on the lookout for a wife. When at last the idea was raised again, it came not from William or Henry but from a more august source than either—Pope Alexander himself.

For Alexander was growing uneasy. Sicily was still his most important ally against Frederick Barbarossa, and it was vital for him that this alliance should be maintained. An ill-advised marriage, however, could destroy it overnight. There had already been one bad moment in 1173 when Barbarossa, to everyone's surprise, had offered William one of his own daughters—a proposal which, if accepted, would have delivered up all South Italy to imperial control and left the Papacy surrounded. Fortunately the King had turned it down; but the very thought of such an eventuality and its consequences had been enough to stir the Pope to action. The Sicilian marriage, he had decided, was too important to be left to chance. He himself would have to intervene.

The alacrity with which both Kings responded to Alexander's new overtures makes it even more surprising that they had not reopened the discussions on their own initiative; and early in 1176 three specially accredited Sicilian ambassadors, the Bishops-Elect of Troia and Capaccio and the Royal Justiciar Florian of Camerota, left Palermo to make a formal request on behalf of their sovereign for Joanna's hand. On their way they were joined by Archbishop Rothrud of Rouen, and at Whitsuntide they presented themselves before the King in London. Henry received them warmly. Although for form's sake he had to summon a council of prelates and nobles to consider the question, their unanimous agreement was a foregone conclusion. But before the betrothal could be announced there remained one further—and potentially embarrassing—preliminary; William had sensibly stipulated that he would enter into no formal commitment without some assurance as to the physical attractions of his bride. The ambassadors therefore proceeded to Winchester, where Joanna was living with her mother Eleanor—held captive by the King since her involvement in her sons' rebellion three years before—'to see', in the words of a contemporary chronicler,[1] 'whether she would be pleasing to them'. Fortunately, she was. 'When they looked upon her beauty,' he continues, 'they were delighted beyond measure.' Back to Palermo hurried the Bishop of Troia with an English embassy led by John, Bishop of Norwich, bearing letters signifying the King's consent to the match; his colleagues meanwhile stayed in England until Joanna should be ready to leave.

Though she was still only ten years old, Henry was determined that his daughter should travel in a state appropriate to her rank and the occasion. To the Bishop of Winchester he entrusted the task of engaging a suitable household and preparing her wardrobe, while he himself ordered seven ships to be made ready to carry the party safely across the Channel. In mid-August he held a special court at Winchester where he showered the Sicilian ambassadors with presents of gold and silver, clothes, cups and horses, and formally surrendered

[1] Roger of Hoveden, whose authorship of the *Gesta Regis Henrici Secundi*—formerly known by the name of Abbot Benedict of Peterborough—has now been established by Lady Stenton (*English Historical Review*, October 1953.)

Joanna to their care. Then, accompanied also by her uncle, Henry's natural brother Hameline Plantagenet, the Archbishops of Canterbury and Rouen and the Bishop of Evreux, the little princess rode off to Southampton and, on 26 August, set sail for Normandy. Her passage through France was smooth; her eldest brother Henry escorted her as far as Poitiers, where her second brother Richard took over, conducting her safely through his own Duchy of Aquitaine and the tributary County of Toulouse to the port of St Gilles.

At St Gilles Joanna was greeted in King William's name by Richard Palmer and the Archbishop of Capua. Twenty-five of the King's ships were waiting in the harbour; henceforth the princess's safety was in Sicilian hands. But it was the second week in November, and the winter gales had begun in earnest. The news may already have reached the party that, not long before, two other vessels escorting the Bishop of Norwich back from Messina had foundered, with the loss of all the presents William was sending to his prospective father-in-law; in any event it was decided not to risk the open sea at such a time, but to sail along the coast, keeping as close inshore as possible. Even this journey seems to have been uncomfortable enough; six weeks later the fleet was still no further than Naples, and poor Joanna was suffering so severely from sea-sickness that it was decided to remain there over Christmas, giving her a chance to recover her strength—and, perhaps, her looks. She would then complete the journey overland.

Early in the New Year the party was off again, following the coast road through Campania and Calabria, then across the straits to Messina and on to Cefalù; at last, on the night of 2 February 1177, they reached Palermo. William was waiting at the gates to welcome his bride. She was mounted on one of his royal palfreys, and escorted by her husband-to-be to the palace which had been prepared for herself and her household—probably the Zisa—through streets so brightly illuminated that, in the words of the same chronicler, 'it might have been thought that the city itself was on fire, and the stars in the heavens could scarcely be seen for the brilliance of the lights'. Eleven days later, on St Valentine's Eve, they were married and garlanded with flowers; and immediately afterwards Joanna, her long hair flowing down over her shoulders, knelt in the Palatine

Chapel before her countryman Walter of the Mill, now Archbishop of Palermo, as he anointed and crowned her Queen of Sicily.

At the time of her coronation, the young Queen was barely eleven, her husband twenty-three. Yet despite the difference in ages the marriage was, so far as we can tell, an ideally happy one. There was no language problem; Joanna, born in France and educated largely at the abbey of Fontevrault, was by her upbringing far more French than English, and Norman French was still the everyday language of the Sicilian court. Her new subjects, too, took her to their hearts and seemed to identify her, as they had her husband, with those radiant, tranquil years when the Kingdom, finally at peace with the world and with itself, prospered and was happy.

They were quite right to do so; for within a few months of the marriage there occurred in Venice an event which was to put an end to hostilities between William and his most formidable adversary for the rest of the latter's life. On 29 May of the previous year, at Legnano just outside Milan, Frederick Barbarossa had suffered at the hands of the Lombard League the most crushing defeat of his career; and while the Milanese had celebrated their triumph by carving a series of suitable bas-reliefs on the Porta Romana,[1] imperial ambassadors had sought out Pope Alexander at Anagni, negotiating the terms of a treaty that would bring an end to the seventeen-year schism and peace to Italy. At last the broad outlines of the agreement emerged; and it was duly arranged to hold, in July 1177, a great conference in Venice—to be attended by the Pope, representatives of both the League and the King of Sicily, and ultimately, when all their deliberations were concluded, by the Emperor himself.

The two envoys chosen by William were Count Roger of Andria and—fortunately for posterity—Archbishop Romuald of Salerno, who has left us a remarkably detailed account (for him) of all that took place. On the morning of 24 July, he reports, the Pope went early

[1] Or fairly suitable. In his book *Italian Sculptors*, quoted by Augustus Hare, C. C. Perkins refers to two carved portraits of Frederick and his Empress, 'one of which is a hideous caricature, the other too grossly obscene for description'. The Porta Romana was demolished in the eighteenth century; but what is left of it—including Frederick's bas-relief—has been incorporated in a reconstruction now to be seen in the Castello museum.

to St Mark's and despatched a delegation of cardinals to the Lido, where, at the church of St Nicholas, Frederick was waiting. There the Emperor solemnly abjured his anti-Pope and made formal acknowledgement of Alexander as rightful pontiff, while the cardinals in return lifted his long excommunication. Now at last he could be admitted to the Republic, to which he was escorted with great pomp by the Doge in person, the Patriarch of Venice and the cardinals. Landing at the Piazzetta, he proceeded on foot between the two high masts from which flew the banners of St Mark, to the front of the great basilica where Alexander, enthroned and in full pontificals, waited to receive him. Romuald goes on:

As he approached the Pope, he was touched by the Holy Spirit; venerating God in Alexander, he flung aside his imperial mantle and prostrated himself at full length on the ground before him. But the Pope, with tears in his eyes, gently raised him up, kissed him and gave him his blessing, while the assembled Germans lifted up their voices in a *Te Deum*. Then, taking him by the right hand, the Pope led him into the church for a further benediction, after which the Emperor retired with his following to the Doge's Palace.[1]

The treaty of Venice marks the culmination of Alexander's pontificate. After all the sufferings and humiliations he had had to endure, through eighteen years of schism and ten of exile, and in the face of the unremitting hostility of one of the most redoubtable figures ever to wear the imperial crown, here at last was his reward. By now well over seventy, he had lived to see the Emperor's recognition not only of himself as legitimate Pope but of all the temporal rights of the Papacy over the city of Rome—those same rights that Frederick had so arrogantly claimed for the Empire at the time of his coronation. The fifteen-year peace that Barbarossa had signed with Sicily meant the end of those fears of imperial encirclement that had in the past

[1] In the atrium of St Mark's, immediately in front of the central doorway, a small lozenge of red and white marble still indicates the place of the Emperor's abasement. 'The Venetian legends say that the Emperor, facing Alexander on this very spot, agreed to apologise to St Peter but not to the Pope, and that Alexander replied sternly: "To Peter *and* the Pope." ' (James Morris, *Venice.*) It is a nice story, but it hardly accords with Romuald's version; and Romuald, as a highly-placed eyewitness, should have known.

so tormented the papal Curia; while the six-year truce concluded
with the Lombard League was, it was agreed, only a preliminary to
the formal acknowledgement by the Empire of the Lombard
cities' independence. It was a triumph—greater far than that which
Pope Gregory had scored over Henry IV exactly a century before;
but to the faithful who rejoiced with the old Pope at Venice during
those sweltering summer days it was also a tribute to the wisdom and
firmness with which he had steered the Church through one of the
most troubled times of her history.

Even now the troubles were not quite over. It was a further year
before first one anti-Pope and then another made their submission
to him; even then, the Roman Senate remained so hostile that in the
summer of 1179 Alexander left Rome for the last time. He had never
liked the city, never trusted its people; to him, all through his life, it
had been enemy country. And when, after his death at Civita
Castellana on the last day of August 1181, his body was brought
back to the Lateran, the Romans proved him right. Not four
years before, they had welcomed him back from exile to the sound
of trumpets and with hymns of thanksgiving; now, as his funeral
cortège entered the city the senseless populace, not content with
flinging curses on Alexander's name, threw mud and stones at
the bier that carried his corpse, scarcely suffering it to be buried in
the basilica.[1]

The thing that struck people most about Alexander's successor,
Lucius III, was his immense age. Such little evidence as we have
suggests that he had been born in the previous century; if so, he
would have already have been in his eighties when he ascended the
throne of St Peter. '*Vir grandaevus*' is how William of Tyre describes him, adding—perhaps a trifle bitchily—'*et modice litteratus*'.[2]
The Treaty of Venice had absolved him, during his four-year
pontificate, from the necessity of paying much attention to Sicilian
affairs; and his principal contribution was a Bull, dated 5 February

---

[1] It was, all the same; but the original tomb has, alas, gone and has been
replaced by a nasty baroque affair, erected in 1660 by his namesake and enthusiastic admirer, Alexander VII.
[2] 'A very old man, and—up to a point—cultured'.

1183, granting the status of an archbishopric to William II's new foundation—the abbey and cathedral of Monreale.[1]

William had been working on this huge project for the past nine years. In 1174, so runs the legend, the Virgin Mary had appeared to him while he was resting from the hunt in his royal deer-park just outside Palermo, had revealed the location of a hoard of treasure secretly buried there by his father, and had commanded him to unearth it and devote it to some pious purpose. The story doubtless served to justify the astronomical sums of money that the King was to lavish on Monreale in the years to come—just as variants of it have done for so many other expensive foundations over the centuries. William's real motives, however, were more complex. Deeply religious by nature, he was unquestionably sincere in wishing to raise up some mighty edifice to the glory of God; and the hero-worship that he had always felt for his grandfather, the founder of Cefalù and S. Giovanni degli Eremiti and the builder of the Palatine Chapel, must have further strengthened his determination. If the church he was to build served also as a monument to himself, then so much the better.

But the considerations that led him to press on so hurriedly with the work were more political than personal. From the moment he had assumed power he had been aware—and Matthew of Ajello had constantly reminded him—of the growing influence of Walter of the Mill. As Archbishop of Palermo Walter had by now managed to unite nearly all the leading barons and prelates behind him in a reactionary, feudalist party that, if it were allowed to develop unchecked, boded ill for the Kingdom. Even in ecclesiastical affairs he was pursuing a dangerous course. The upheavals of the Regency had given the Sicilian Church the opportunity to assert itself independently not just of the Pope—there was nothing new in that—but of the King as well; and this tendency Walter was doing everything he could to encourage. His power in the land was already second only

[1] There can be no clearer indication of the change that had come about in Sicilian-Papal relations since the days of King Roger. He would never for a moment have tolerated such interference in what he would have considered the domestic affairs of his kingdom. A legend exists to the effect that Pope Lucius actually visited Monreale for its consecration; but this is certainly untrue.

to William's own; and William knew that he must curb it while there was still time.

But how could he do so? Only by creating a new archbishopric as near as possible to Palermo, whose incumbent would be equal in rank to Walter himself and could serve as a direct link between Crown and Papacy. This in turn raised another problem: Archbishops were normally elected by the Church hierarchy, and the hierarchy was under Walter's control. Thus it was that William and his Vice-Chancellor decided on a further refinement to their plan. The new foundation must be a Benedictine abbey, run on strictly Cluniac lines, whose abbot would automatically receive archiepiscopal rank and could be consecrated by any other prelate he might choose, subject only to the King's approval.

Such a scheme, it need hardly be said, could not fail to meet with furious and determined opposition from Walter of the Mill. William and Matthew seem to have managed to conceal their plan for the new archbishopric till 1175, but after that they had to fight every step of the way. They might indeed have failed altogether if it had not been for two factors. One was that by a fantastically lucky chance there still stood, in the grounds of the new abbey, the little chapel of Hagia Kyriaka[1] which had been the official see of the Greek Metropolitan of Palermo during the Arab domination. This enabled the champions of Monreale to claim that in establishing the archbishopric there they were merely continuing a venerable tradition. The second factor was the support given to the plan by Pope Alexander, who from 1174 onwards issued a series of Bulls emphasising the exceptional character of the proposed foundation. Against such artillery even Walter was powerless. He was forced to stand by while several churches and parishes were removed from his archdiocese and transferred to that of Monreale; and, in the spring of 1176, having grudgingly agreed to the exemption of its first abbot from his jurisdiction, he watched in impotent fury as a hundred monks from La Cava arrived in Palermo on their way to colonise the new monastery.

[1] 'The name does not refer to a saint but characterises the church as the Sunday Church, in contrast to the former cathedral of Palermo which under the Arabs was the Friday Mosque of the town.' (O. Demus, *The Mosaics of Norman Sicily*.)

It was therefore probably as much in the nature of a counter-attack as anything else that in 1179 Walter began his own building programme—a completely new cathedral for Palermo itself. But however rich he was himself, and however unscrupulous his methods of extracting money from others, he could not hope to rival Monreale; and when William announced that he wished this latest royal foundation, rather than Cefalù or Palermo, to be the burial-place of the Hauteville dynasty, it can only have been a further blow to the Archbishop's hopes. Palermo Cathedral, by the time he finished it, must have been a credit to himself and to the city—very unlike the sad travesty we see today; but it could not begin, any more than it can now, to stand comparison with one of the most sumptuously magnificent religious buildings in the world.

Sumptuous and magnificent, certainly; yet from the start it must be admitted that Monreale, considered as a whole, is more impressive than beautiful. It lacks the gem-like perfection of the Palatine Chapel, the Byzantine mystery of the Martorana, the sheer magic that streams down from the great Pantocrator at Cefalù. Its impact is principally due to its size and its splendour. But this impact, like the cathedral itself, is colossal.

As so often in the churches of Norman Sicily, the exterior is un-promising. Except for the eastern apses and the north-west view from the cloister,[1] it has been radically changed since William's day. The long north colonnade was clamped on by the Gagini family in the sixteenth century, the west porch by someone else in the eighteenth. This latter addition in particular need not cause us much distress, since it screens some of that original decoration of interlaced blind arches in reddish lava (Gothic now and ornate, with none of the rounded purity of Cefalù), the full unpleasantness of which can still be experienced by anyone walking along to the east end. This vacuous doodling, especially when contrasted with the simple statement of the south-west tower, illustrates better than any words just how great was the loss to European architecture when Roman-esque began to decline.

Before entering the building, it is worth taking a close look at its

[1] See plate.

two sets of bronze doors. Those in the north porch are the work of
Barisanus of Trani and date from 1179, while the main doors at the
west end were made by Bonannus of Pisa in 1186.[1] Apart from their
considerable intrinsic beauty, these doors are interesting for two
reasons. First, they are Italian. Throughout the eleventh and early
twelfth centuries, such craftsmanship was virtually a monopoly of
Byzantium; to mention only those shrines which have a place in our
story, the cathedrals of Amalfi and Salerno and the cave at Monte
S. Angelo all possess Byzantine doors of outstanding quality,[2] in all
of which the Greek masters have followed their usual practice of
engraving their designs on the metal and then picking them out with
silver thread—or, occasionally, enamel. By the latter half of the twelfth
century, however, the Italians had not only adopted Byzantine
techniques but were rapidly improving on them and trying their
hand at real bas-reliefs; and the second point of interest about the
Monreale doors is in the opportunity they give us to compare the
progress of the two leading bronzeworkers of their day towards the
evolution of that specifically Italian style that was to reach its apogee
with Ghiberti two centuries later. As is only to be expected, Barisanus,
whose life had been spent in southern Italy where Greek influence
was strongest—and who had already been responsible for the cathedral doors at Ravello as well as those of his home town of Trani—is
the less evolved of the two; his techniques may be western, but
his designs—the hieratic saints, the oriental archers, the descent
into Hell and the deposition from the Cross—are still the designs of
Byzantium. Bonannus, by contrast, though possibly less fine an
artist, is a westerner through and through; his biblical scenes are as
earthy and naturalistic as any twelfth-century religious art can be.

Unlike the outer façade, the interior of the cathedral remains
essentially as it always was—apart from the roof over the nave, which
had to be replaced after a fire in 1811. Most of the obvious features of
the Palatine Chapel are there—the polychrome marble inlays of the
floor and lower walls, the antique cipollino columns, the superb

[1] See plate.
[2] Those of Monte S. Angelo were the cause of angry demonstrations as
recently as March 1964, when the local inhabitants refused to allow them to be
removed to Athens for the Byzantine Exhibition held later that year. (*The Times*,
4 and 6 March 1964.)

Cosmati work fringing the dado with its line of palmettes, the ambo, the altar-rail, the thrones. And yet the atmosphere is utterly different. It is not simply the difference between a chapel and a cathedral; rather does it stem from the fact that the architecture of Monreale is fundamentally undistinguished. West of the apse, the vast expanses of wall are flat and unarticulated; one longs in vain for a niche or a buttress—anything to break this relentless uniformity. Thus, while the Palatine Chapel throbs, about Monreale there is always something dry and a little lifeless.

It is redeemed by its mosaics; for this building is above all a picture-gallery, and to this function every architectural feature has been subordinated. There they glitter in all their vastness, covering the better part of two acres of wall space. Perhaps by reason of their very quantity, it has been the fashion in recent years to decry these mosaics, to suggest that they are somehow a little crude in comparison with those in the other churches of Norman Sicily. They are nothing of the kind. The gigantic Christ Pantocrator in the central apse—his arms outstretched as if to embrace the entire congregation, his right hand alone more than six feet high—cannot admittedly be classed with his counterpart at Cefalù; few works of art can. He is none the less superb. For the rest, although so immense a work must inevitably show some variations in quality, the general standard both of design and of execution remains astonishingly high.

This fact becomes all the more remarkable when we remember that the entire group was completed in the space of five or six years, and quite possibly less—between 1183 and the end of the decade. The leading authority on the subject, Professor Demus, therefore deduces that the artists were Greeks, since 'only at Byzantium could [William] find an organised workshop able to finish the enormous task in so short a time';[1] and indeed the upper half of the apse, with its Greek inscriptions and the hieratic formalisation of the figures, is Byzantine in its very essence. But where the anecdotal mosaics are concerned the attribution is surprising; for they show a fluidity of expression and invention which is hard to reconcile with the stylised rigidity that still characterised most Greek art of the twelfth century. Look, for example, at the south wall of the transept, and in particular at the

[1] *The Mosaics of Norman Sicily*, p. 148.

three pictures that form the lowest row—the Washing of the Feet, the Agony in the Garden, the Betrayal. The iconography is impeccably Byzantine; but the relaxed attitudes, the swirling draperies, the movement and the rhythm of the drawing have developed as far beyond the styles of the Palatine Chapel or the Martorana as have Bonannus's doors from those of Barisanus. And this development is surely Italian. Christian art as we know it was born on the banks of the Bosphorus, and for nearly a thousand years Constantinople continued to point the way forward—evolving in the process the only idiom that has completely succeeded in translating Christian spiritual values into plastic terms. Then, with the end of the twelfth century, Italy began to take the lead. It is another hundred and fifty years before we find, in the church of the Chora in Constantinople,[1] purely Greek mosaics executed with the dynamism and *panache* of those at Monreale.

Wandering slowly through the cathedral, one might be forgiven for supposing that these endless mosaics tell every Bible story, from Genesis to the Acts of the Apostles, in strip cartoon. So indeed they very nearly do; and the visitor, once he has gazed his fill at the Pantocrator, might easily pass over the figures of the saints below and turn at once to more narrative material. But this would be a pity, for he would be missing one of the few real iconographical surprises Monreale has to offer—the second figure to the right of the central window. There is no problem of identification; in conformity with the usual canons of the time, the name runs down each side of the halo for all to read: SCS. THOMAS CANTUR. Whether or not it bears any physical resemblance to the martyred archbishop we cannot tell; mosaic portraits of saints are seldom known for their fidelity to the originals.[2] It remains, however, the earliest certain representation of

[1] Nowadays better known by its Turkish name of Kariye Cami.

[2] See plate. It certainly gives no hint of the only one of Thomas's distinguishing characteristics of which we can be absolutely sure—his remarkable height. This was first mentioned by his own chaplain, William Fitzstephen, and again in a fifteenth-century manuscript at Lambeth Palace (306 f. 203) where, under the general heading 'The Longitude of Men Folowynge', Thomas is described as being 'vij fote save a ynche'. The most telling evidence of all, however, is provided by the saint's own vestments, still displayed in the cathedral treasury at Sens. 'On the feast of St Thomas till very recently, they were worn for that

Thomas Becket known to us, dating from less than a generation after his death.[1]

At first sight, this seemingly gratuitous distinction accorded to a saint by the son-in-law of his arch-enemy strikes one as a little strange—and even in rather doubtful taste. We know from other sources, however, that Queen Joanna always held Thomas in particular veneration, and it may well be that she encouraged her husband to commemorate him in this way. What better means, after all, could she have had of making her own personal atonement for her father's conduct? A closer look at Thomas's fellow-saints around the apse lends still more weight to this theory. The first pair, immediately to the left and right of the window, are two early Popes, Clement I and Sylvester, both long-time exiles and defenders of the temporal and spiritual primacy of Rome.[2] Next, opposite Thomas, comes St Peter of Alexandria, another prelate who fought for the Church against temporal encroachment and returned from exile to face martyrdom. Beyond them stand the protomartyrs Stephen and Lawrence, who died for the same cause. Finally, facing the nave, we find two other canonised archbishops—Martin, always a favourite among the Benedictines, and Nicholas of Bari, one of the chief patrons of the Norman Kingdom. The conclusion seems inescapable; the choice of figures for the apse not only symbolises the principles for which Monreale stood from the moment of its foundation; it is also a deliberate tribute to one of those depicted: England's most recent—and already most beloved—saint and martyr.

Above the thrones, on each side of the main eastern arch, stands

one day by the officiating priest. The tallest priest was always selected—and, even then, it was necessary to pin them up.' (Dean Stanley, *Memorials of Canterbury*, 1855.)

[1] A curious little reliquary of Becket in the form of a gold pendant, now in the New York Metropolitan Museum of Art, bears the inscription ISTUD REGINE MARGARETE SICULORUM TRANSMITTIT PRESUL RAINAUDUS BATONIORUS, surrounding the engraved figures of the Queen and a prelate in the act of benediction. Since Margaret died in 1183 this must very slightly antedate the mosaic. But is the prelate Rainaud or Thomas? There is no means of knowing. (*Bulletin of the Metropolitan Museum of Art*, vol. XXIII, pp. 78–9.)

[2] Clement, according to tradition, was martyred under Trajan; Sylvester is credited with having baptised Constantine the Great and having received the legendary Donation.

William himself; on the left receiving his crown at the hands of Christ,[1] on the right offering his church into those of the Virgin. Judged as mosaics they are not particularly good; they cannot be compared with the corresponding pair in the Martorana. But this time there can be no real doubt that the two portraits are as lifelike as the artist could make them. After all we have heard of William's beauty, that round face, fair scrubby beard and slightly vacant expression come as a faint disappointment; for a man only just into his thirties, one had hoped for something more impressive. But perhaps he has been done less than justice.

He was even unluckier in his tomb. Following his plan of making Monreale the St Denis of Sicily, William had interred Queen Margaret there after her death in 1183, shortly afterwards transferring his father's remains from the Palatine Chapel and those of his two brothers Roger and Henry from Palermo Cathedral and the chapel of St Mary Magdalene. But when William himself died in 1189, Walter of the Mill quickly intervened and ordered the sarcophagus brought at once to his own new cathedral, now almost completed. After a long and acrimonious struggle between the two archbishops, the King's body was finally laid to rest in Monreale as he had wished; but the sarcophagus was retained in Palermo and has since disappeared. Its eventual replacement, carved in white marble and donated nearly four hundred years later, in 1575, by Archbishop Lodovico de Torres, is as unsuited to a Norman king as anything that could be imagined, and contrasts sadly with the great porphyry tomb of William the Bad, standing four-square and magnificent on its marble pedestal nearby.[2]

Staggering as Monreale is, there is something gloomy about its grandeur. Perhaps it is the lacklustre quality of the gold, which gives it none of the Martorana's glowing radiance, nor any of the joyous sparkle of the Palatine Chapel. It is too big, too impersonal. After half an hour or so one is grateful to emerge once again into the sunshine.

[1] See plate.

[2] The tombs of Margaret and her two sons, set against the north wall of the sanctuary, were refurbished in the last century and are worth only a cursory glance. Of greater interest is the altar of St Louis of France, who died of the plague while crusading in Tunisia in 1270 and whose heart and other internal organs are here preserved.

And, above all, into the cloister. Here at last is the splendour without the gloom. Here, too, is the only touch of Saracen influence to be found at Monreale—the slim, arabising arches, a hundred and four of them, supported by pairs of slender columns, some carved, some inlaid with that same glorious Cosmati-work in marble and mosaic that is such a feature of the interior. In the south-west corner they have been extended to make a fountain, Arabic again, but in a form unique to the cloisters of Norman Sicily.[1] (There is a similar one at Cefalù.) The effect of the whole is that of radiant, yet tranquil beauty—more formal than the exquisite miniature at S. Giovanni degli Eremiti, but a place none the less where life seems good and the brethren of Monreale must have found serenity as well as shade. And this is not all; for the capitals of the columns, each one an individual triumph of design and invention, together constitute a *tour de force* of romanesque stone-carving unequalled in Sicily.[2] Their variation is endless—biblical stories (including a marvellous Annunciation in the north-east corner), scenes of daily life, the harvest, the battlefield and the chase, subjects contemporary and antique, Christian and pagan; even—on the south wall, two pairs of columns along from the fountain—a sacrifice to Mithras. Finally, on the west, the eighth capital from the south end translates into stone what we have already seen in its mosaic form: William the Good, beardless now, presents his new cathedral to the Mother of God. The last and greatest religious foundation of Norman Sicily is offered and accepted.

[1] See plate.   [2] See plate.

18

AGAINST ANDRONICUS

The King's palaces are strung around the hills that encircle the city, like pearls around the throat of a woman. And in their gardens and courts he takes his ease. How many palaces and buildings, watch-towers and belvederes he has—may they soon be taken from him!—how many monasteries he has endowed with rich lands, how many churches with crosses of gold and silver! . . .

Now, as we hear, the King intends to send his fleet to Constantinople. . . . But Allah, who is glorious and all-powerful, will throw him back in confusion, showing him the iniquity of his way and sending tempests to destroy him. For as Allah wills, so can He perform.

Ibn Jubair

A KINGDOM in the sun, prosperous and peaceful; youth, good looks, and limitless wealth; the love of his subjects and of a beautiful young Queen; with such gifts as these, William II must have appeared to his contemporaries—even to his fellow-princes—as a man upon whom the gods had always smiled. And so, up to a point, they had. Three blessings only they withheld from him: first, a long life; second, a son and heir; third, a modicum of political wisdom. Had he been granted any one of these, his kingdom might have been spared the sadness that lay in store for it. As he lacked all three, Sicily was doomed. And it was William the Good, all unconscious of what he was doing and with the best will in the world, who wrought her destruction.

Frederick Barbarossa had long been turning over in his mind the possibility of a Sicilian marriage alliance. As long ago as 1173, when William was still looking for a suitable bride, the Emperor had proposed one of his daughters; he may not have been altogether surprised, in the circumstances prevailing at the time, when his offer was rejected out of hand. A decade later, however, the situation was very different. The Treaty of Venice had brought about a striking *volte-face* in imperial policy. Frederick, having at last understood that his North Italian enemies could never be overcome by force, had adopted new tactics of friendship, negotiation and compromise; and they had served him well. After the death of Alexander III, relations between the Lombard cities and the Papacy had once again become strained; and the Emperor had had no difficulty in concluding a treaty with the League, signed at Constance in 1183, allowing the cities full liberty to elect their own leaders and enact their own laws, in return for recognising his own overall sovereignty. As a result of these concessions the League lost its cohesion, and Frederick found his position in North Italy stronger than ever. With the Papacy correspondingly weaker, there seemed a possibility that a renewed approach to the Sicilians might have a better reception. Some time during the winter of 1183-84, imperial ambassadors arrived in Palermo with his proposal—nothing less than the marriage of his son and heir, Henry, with Princess Constance of Sicily.

It seems, in retrospect, incredible that William and his advisers should have contemplated the idea for a moment. Constance, the posthumous daughter of Roger II—she was in fact a year younger than her nephew the King—was heiress-presumptive to the realm. If she were to marry Henry and William were to die childless, Sicily would fall into the Emperor's lap, its separate existence at an end. Admittedly, there was plenty of time yet for Joanna to bear children; in 1184 she was still only eighteen, her husband thirty. But life in the twelfth century was even more uncertain than it is today, infant mortality was high, and to take such a risk before the succession was properly assured would be, by any standards, an act of almost criminal folly.[1]

[1] A contemporary chronicler, Robert of Torigni, writes of how he has heard from certain people that Joanna did indeed bear a son, Bohemund, in 1182, and that his father invested him immediately after his baptism with the Duchy of Apulia. If this were true, it might go some way towards explaining William's agreement to the imperial marriage, particularly if the child were still alive at the time. But in that case why is Robert—who, as Abbot of Mont St Michel, was hardly well placed to report on Sicilian affairs—the only chronicler who thought the event worth mentioning? Richard of S. Germano, our best source for this last period of the Kingdom and one of William's own subjects, laments Joanna's barrenness in his very first paragraph.

In Palermo there were plenty of counsellors to suggest as much. Matthew of Ajello in particular, who like most South Italians of his time had been brought up on ghoulish tales of the havoc wrought by successive imperial invasions and who looked upon all Germans as potential despoilers of his homeland, spoke out violently against the proposal; and few Sicilians relished the prospect of surrendering their independence to a distant and in their eyes barbarous Empire that had always been the traditional enemy of their country. Walter of the Mill, however, took the opposite view. His reasons are not altogether clear. One authority, Richard of S. Germano, asserts that he did so purely to spite Matthew—an unworthy motive, perhaps, but one which, knowing the bitterness that existed between them, we cannot quite discount. Chalandon, more charitably inclined, suggests that as an Englishman Walter saw the situation more dispassionately than his fellows and considered imperial domination a lesser evil than the civil war which in his eyes may have been the only alternative.

But was it? Could not Constance have married any other husband, reigned in her own right, then passed the crown in the fullness of time to a legitimate son? Possibly. But whatever may have been the Archbishop's motives, there was a further consideration in William's own mind when he came to make his decision—a single, overriding reason why, for the next few years, he needed to be sure of the goodwill of the Western Empire; and why, in the summer of 1184, to the horrified dismay of the large majority of his subjects, he gave his consent to the betrothal.

He was preparing to march, as Robert Guiscard had marched just a hundred years before, against Byzantium.

On 24 September 1180 Manuel Comnenus had died in Constantinople after a long illness. He was buried in the church of the Pantocrator; next to his tomb was placed the red stone slab on which Christ's body had been embalmed, and which Manuel himself had carried on his shoulders from the harbour when it had arrived from Ephesus some years before. He had not been a good Emperor. Over-ambitious abroad, over-prodigal at home, in his thirty-eight years on the throne he had managed to drain his Empire of almost all its

resources, leaving it in a state of economic near-collapse from which
it never properly recovered. During his lifetime, by the brilliance of
his personality, the splendour of his court and the lavishness of his
entertainments, the world had been deceived into thinking that
Byzantium was still the force it had always been; after his death,
disillusion was swift and cruel.

The successor to the throne was Manuel's only legitimate son
Alexius, now eleven years old. He was an unimpressive, unattractive child. According to Nicetas Choniates, who was imperial
secretary under Manuel and who has left us one of the most reliable
and—with that of Psellus—the most entertaining histories of mediaeval Byzantium, 'this young prince was so puffed up with vanity
and pride, so destitute of inner light and ability as to be incapable
of the simplest task. . . . He passed his entire life at play or the chase,
and contracted several habits of pronounced viciousness.' Meanwhile his mother, Mary of Antioch, governed as Regent in his stead.
As the first Latin ever to rule in Constantinople, she started off at a
serious disadvantage. Her husband's love of the West and his
introduction of western institutions into Byzantine life had always
been resented by his subjects; in particular, they had hated seeing the
greater part of the Empire's trade falling into the hands of the
Italian and Frankish merchants who thronged the business centre
of the city. They now feared—and with good reason—still further
extensions to these merchants of their trading rights and privileges;
and they were more worried still when Mary took as her principal
adviser another character of extreme pro-western sympathies—
Manuel's nephew, the *protosebastos* Alexius, uncle of the Queen of
Jerusalem. Before long it was generally believed that her adviser
was also her lover, though from Nicetas's description it is not easy
to see what the Empress—whose beauty was famous throughout
Christendom—saw in him:

He was accustomed to spend the greater part of the day in bed,
keeping the curtains drawn lest he should ever see the sunlight. . . .
Whenever the sun appeared he would seek the darkness, just as wild
beasts do; also he took much pleasure in rubbing his decaying teeth,
putting new ones in the place of those that had fallen out through
old age.

As the dissatisfaction grew, various conspiracies began to take shape for Mary's overthrow; notably one by her step-daughter Maria—that same princess whose hand her father had twice offered to William of Sicily. The plot was discovered; with her husband Rainier of Montferrat and her other associates, Maria barely had time to flee to St Sophia and barricade herself in. But the Empress-Regent was not prepared to respect any rights of sanctuary; the imperial guard was despatched with orders to seize the conspirators; and the great church was saved from desecration only through the mediation of the Patriarch himself. This incident deeply shocked the Byzantines, and the subsequent exile of the Patriarch to a monastery for his part in the affair made the regime more unpopular than ever—unnecessarily too, since such was the state of public indignation against her that Mary never dared to punish her step-daughter. Nor, later, did she lift a finger when the people of Constantinople marched *en masse* to the Patriarch's monastery and led him back in triumph to the capital. The whole matter, in fact, could scarcely have been handled worse.

This first *coup* had, none the less, failed; but there followed a threat from another of the Emperor's relatives—a man this time, and one of a very different calibre. Andronicus Comnenus was a unique phenomenon. Nowhere else in the pages of Byzantine history do we find so extraordinary a character; perhaps his cousin Manuel comes closest; but next to him, even Manuel is outshone. And nowhere else, certainly, do we find such a career. The story of Andronicus Comnenus does not read like history at all; it reads like a historical novel that has gone too far.

In 1182, when Andronicus first enters this story, he was already sixty-four years old, but looking nearer forty. Over six feet tall and in magnificent physical condition, he had preserved the good looks, the intellect, the conversational charm and wit, the elegance and the sheer *panache* that, together with the fame of his almost legendary exploits in bed and battlefield, had won him an unrivalled reputation as a Don Juan. The list of his conquests was endless, that of the scandals in which he had been involved very little shorter. Three in particular had roused the Emperor to fury. The first was when Andronicus carried on a flagrant affair with his cousin—and Manuel's niece—the Princess Eudoxia Comnena, effectively answering criticism by pointing out that 'subjects should always follow their master's example, and two pieces from the same factory normally prove equally acceptable'—a clear allusion to the Emperor's relationship with another niece, Eudoxia's sister Theodora, for whom he was well known to cherish an affection that went well beyond the avuncular. Some years later, Andronicus had deserted his military command in Cilicia with the deliberate intention of seducing the lovely Philippa of Antioch. Once again he must have known there would be serious repercussions; Philippa was the sister not only of the reigning prince, Bohemund III, but of Manuel's own wife, the Empress Mary. But this, as far as Andronicus was concerned, merely lent additional spice to the game. Though he was then forty-eight and his quarry just twenty, his serenades beneath her window proved irresistible. Within a few days she had capitulated.

His conquest once made, Andronicus did not remain long to enjoy it. Manuel, outraged, ordered his immediate recall; Prince Bohemund also made it clear that he had no intention of tolerating such a scandal. Possibly, too, the young princess's charms may have proved disappointing. In any case Andronicus left hurriedly for Palestine to put himself at the disposal of King Amalric; and there, at Acre, he met for the first time another of his cousins—Queen Theodora, the twenty-one-year-old widow of Amalric's predecessor on the throne of Jerusalem, Baldwin III. She became the love of his life. Soon afterwards, when Andronicus moved to his new fief of Beirut—recently given him by Amalric as a reward for his services—Theodora joined him. Consanguinity forbade their marriage, but the two lived there together in open sin until Beirut in its turn grew too hot for them.

After a long spell of wandering through the Muslim East they finally settled down at Colonea, just beyond the eastern frontier of the Empire, subsisting happily on such money as they had been able to bring with them, supplemented by the proceeds of a certain amount of mild brigandage; and their idyll was only brought to an end when Theodora and their two small sons were captured by the Duke of Trebizond and sent back to Constantinople. Andronicus, agonised by their loss, hurried back to the capital and immediately gave himself up, flinging himself histrionically at the Emperor's feet and promising anything if only his mistress and his children could be returned to him. Manuel showed his usual generosity. Clearly a *ménage* at once so irregular and so prominent could not be allowed in Constantinople; but Andronicus and Theodora were given a pleasant castle on the Black Sea coast where they might live in honourable exile—and, it was hoped, peaceful retirement.

But it was not to be. Andronicus had always had his eye on the imperial crown and when, after Manuel's death, reports reached him of the growing unrest against the Empress Regent he needed little persuading that his opportunity had come at last. Unlike Mary of Antioch—'the foreigner', as her subjects scornfully called her—he was a true Comnenus. He had energy, determination and ability; more important still at such a moment, his romantic past had lent him a popular appeal unmatched in the Empire. In August 1182 he marched on the capital. The old magic was as strong as ever. In a scene inescapably reminiscent of Napoleon's return from Elba, the troops sent out to block his advance refused to fight; their general, Andronicus Angelus, surrendered and joined him[1]—an example followed soon afterwards by the admiral commanding the imperial fleet in the Bosphorus. As he progressed, the people flocked from their houses to cheer him on his way; soon the road was lined with his supporters. Even before he crossed the straits, rebellion had broken out in Constantinople; and with it exploded all that pent-up hatred of the Latins that the last two years had done so much to increase. What followed was a massacre—the massacre of virtually all the Latins in the city—women, children, the old and infirm, even the sick from the hospitals, as the whole quarter in which they lived was burnt and pillaged. The Protosebastos was found cowering in the palace, too frightened even to try to escape; he was thrown into the dungeons and later, on Andronicus's orders, blinded;[2] the young

---

[1] It was typical of Andronicus Comnenus that he should have had a joke ready when Angelus came over to his colours. 'See,' he is said to have remarked, 'it is just as the Gospel says: "I shall send my *Angel*, who shall prepare the way before thee." ' The Gospel in fact says no such thing; but Andronicus was not a man to quibble over niceties.

[2] Though not before he had recovered his nerve and lodged a formal complaint that his English guards were not allowing him enough sleep.

Emperor and his mother were taken to the imperial villa of the Philopation to await their cousin's pleasure.

Their fate was worse than either of them could have feared. Andronicus's triumph had brought out the other side of his character —a degree of cruelty and brutality that few had even suspected, unredeemed by a shred of compassion, or scruple, or moral sense. Though all-powerful, he was not yet Emperor; and so, methodically and in cold blood, he set about eliminating all those who stood between himself and the throne. Princess Maria and her husband were the first to go; their deaths were sudden and mysterious, but no one doubted poison. Then it was the turn of the Empress herself. Her thirteen-year-old son was forced to sign her death-warrant with his own hand, and she was strangled in her cell. In September 1182 Andronicus was crowned co-Emperor; two months later the boy Alexius met his own death by the bowstring and his body was flung into the Bosphorus.

'Thus,' wrote Nicetas, 'in the imperial garden, all the trees were felled.' Only one more formality remained. For the last three years of his short life, Alexius had been betrothed to Agnes of France, the second daughter of Louis VII by his third wife Alix of Champagne. Owing to their extreme youth—at the time of their engagement Alexius was eleven, Agnes barely ten—the marriage itself had never taken place; but the little princess was already installed at Constantinople, where she had been rebaptised in the more seemly Byzantine name of Anna and was treated with all the respect due to a future Empress. And so indeed she proved. Before 1182 was out the new Emperor, now sixty-four, had married the twelve-year-old princess—and, if at least one modern authority is to be believed— consummated the marriage.[1]

No reign could have begun less auspiciously; yet in many ways Andronicus did more good to the Empire than Manuel had ever done. He attacked all administrative abuses, wherever he found them and in whatever form. The tragedy was that as he gradually eliminated

[1] Diehl, *Figures Byzantines,* vol. II, which includes scholarly but highly readable short biographies of both Andronicus and Agnes. What became of Theodora is unknown. She may have died; but she was still relatively young and it is more probable that she was packed off to end her days in a convent.

corruption from the government machine, so he himself grew more and more corrupted by the exercise of his power. Violence and brute force seemed to be his only weapons; his legitimate campaign against the military aristocracy rapidly deteriorated into a succession of blood-baths and indiscriminate slaughter. According to one report,

he left the vines of Brusa weighed down, not with grapes but with the corpses of those whom he had hanged; and he forbade any man to cut them down for burial, for he wished them to dry in the sun and then to sway and flutter as the wind took them, like the scarecrows that are hung in the orchards to frighten the birds.

But it was Andronicus himself who was afraid— both for his own skin and for his Empire. His popularity was gone; the saviour of his country had revealed himself a monster. The air was once again thick with sedition and revolt; conspiracies were springing up, hydra-headed, in the capital and the provinces alike. Traitors were everywhere. Those who fell into the hands of the Emperor were tortured to death—often in his presence and by his own hand—but many others escaped to the West, where they could be sure of a ready welcome for, as Andronicus was well aware, the West had not forgotten the massacre of 1182. He also understood, all too clearly, the implications of the Treaty of Venice. For a long time now, Byzantium had had two principal enemies in Europe: the Western Empire and the Kingdom of Sicily, the Hohenstaufen and the Hauteville, both equally determined to block the Greeks from realising their legitimate claims in South Italy. While these two had remained at loggerheads Constantinople had had no cause for alarm; but now they were friends, and soon they might be allies. In that event, Andronicus had an unpleasant suspicion in which direction they would march; and when, in the autumn of 1184, there was announced at Augsburg the betrothal of Constance of Sicily to Henry of Hohenstaufen, his alarm was not diminished.

Early in January 1185 the Arab traveller Ibn Jubair was in Trapani, having just taken passage on a Genoese ship to return to his native Spain. A day or two before he was due to depart, an order arrived from the government in Palermo: the harbour was closed to all outgoing traffic till further notice. A great war fleet was being made ready. No other vessel might leave until it was safely on its way.

The same order had been simultaneously circulated to all the ports of Sicily—a security embargo on an unprecedented scale. Even within the island, few people seemed to know exactly what was happening. In Trapani, Ibn Jubair reports, everyone had their own idea about the fleet, its size, purpose and destination. Some said it was bound for Alexandria, to avenge the fiasco of 1174; others suspected an attempt on Majorca—a favourite target for Sicilian raiders in recent years. There were also, inevitably, many who maintained that the expedition would be against Constantinople. In the past year hardly a ship had arrived from the East without its quota of blood-curdling reports concerning Andronicus's latest atrocities; and it was now widely rumoured that among the increasing number of Byzantines taking refuge in Sicily was a mysterious youth claiming to be Alexius II, the rightful Emperor. If, as men said, this youth had actually been received by the King and had convinced him of the truth of his story, what was more natural than that William the Good should launch an expedition to re-establish him on his throne?

These last years of William's reign are sadly undocumented. Archbishop Romuald of Salerno had died in 1181; and with his death we lose the last of the great chroniclers of Norman Sicily. We shall therefore never know whether such a claimant did in fact present himself at the court in Palermo. There is nothing inherently improbable in the idea. *Coups d'état* of the kind Andronicus had achieved in Constantinople normally produce a pretender or two; Robert Guiscard had unearthed one to strengthen his hand before his own Byzantine adventure in 1081, and Metropolitan Eustathius of Thessalonica—of whom we shall be hearing more before long— assumes that a pseudo-Alexius was wandering through northern Greece shortly after the time of which Ibn Jubair was writing. But whether the rumour was true or false, we know for a fact that William did not lack encouragement for his enterprise: one of Manuel Comnenus's nephews—maddeningly, also called Alexius— had recently escaped to Sicily and had been received at the Court, since when he had been urgently pressing William to march to Constantinople and overthrow the usurper.

Throughout the winter of 1184 85 the King was at Messina. True to his normal practice, he had no intention of himself participating in the campaign, but he had taken personal charge of preparations. Though he naturally admitted it to no one, his ultimate objective was nothing less than to gain for himself the crown of Byzantium; and he was determined that the force he sent out to attain it should be worthy of such a prize—stronger, both on land and sea, than any other ever to have sailed from Sicilian shores. And so it was. By the time it was ready to start, the fleet—commanded once again by his cousin Tancred of Lecce—is said to have comprised between two and three hundred vessels and to have carried some eighty thousand men, including five thousand knights and a special detachment of mounted archers. This huge land army was placed under the joint leadership of Tancred's brother-in-law Count Richard of Acerra and a certain Baldwin, of whom virtually nothing is known apart from an intriguing passage by Nicetas:

Although of mediocre birth, he was much beloved of the King and was appointed general of the army by virtue of his long experience of military affairs. He liked to compare himself with Alexander the Great, not only because his stomach was covered—as was Alexander's—with so much hair that it seemed to sprout wings, but because he had done even greater deeds and in an even shorter time —and moreover, without bloodshed.

The expedition sailed from Messina on 11 June 1185 and headed straight for Durazzo. Although William's attempt to seal all Sicilian ports had not been entirely successful—Ibn Jubair's Genoese captains had had little difficulty in bribing their way out of Trapani— his security precautions seem to have had some effect; it is hard to see how Andronicus could otherwise have been caught so unprepared. As we know, he had long mistrusted western intentions, and he must have been aware that Durazzo, as his Empire's largest Adriatic port and the starting point from which the main imperial road—the old Roman *Via Egnatia*—ran eastward across Macedonia and Thrace to Constantinople, was the obvious if not the only possible Sicilian bridgehead. Yet he had made little effort either to strengthen the city's fortifications or to provision it for a siege.

When he did at last receive reports of the impending attack he quickly sent one of his most experienced generals, John Branas, to take charge of the situation; but Branas arrived at Durazzo only a day or two before the Sicilian fleet, too late to accomplish anything of value.

When Durazzo had fallen to Norman arms a century before, it had been only after a long and glorious battle, fought heroically on both sides; a battle in which the Byzantine army had been led by the Emperor himself, the Norman by the two outstanding warriors of their age, Robert Guiscard and his son Bohemund; in which the Lombard Sichelgaita had proved herself the equal in courage of both her husband and her stepson; in which the stalwart axe-swinging Englishmen of the Varangian Guard had perished to the last man.[1] This time it was a very different story. Branas, knowing that he had no chance, surrendered without a struggle. By 24 June, less than a fortnight after the fleet had sailed out of Messina, Durazzo had surrendered.

The subsequent march across the Balkan peninsula was swift and uneventful. Not a single attempt was made to block the invaders' progress. On 6 August the entire land force was encamped outside the walls of Thessalonica; on the fifteenth the fleet, having sailed round the Peloponnese, took up its position in the roadstead; and the siege began.

Thessalonica was a thriving and properous city, with fifteen hundred years of history already behind it and a Christian tradition going back to St Paul. As a naval base it dominated the Aegean; as a commercial centre it vied with Constantinople itself, even surpassing it during the annual trade fair in October, when merchants from all over Europe gathered there to do business with their Arab, Jewish and Armenian colleagues from Africa and the Levant.[2] Thanks to this fair the city also boasted a permanent European mercantile community living in its own quarter just inside the walls.

[1] See *The Normans in the South,* pp. 231–3.

[2] The fair has continued, intermittently, until the present day. Thessalonica maintained its predominantly Jewish character throughout Ottoman times and up to the second world war, when its entire Sephardic population of some fifty thousand was deported to Poland, never to return.

Largely composed of Italians, it was to prove of more than a little value to the besiegers during the days that followed.

Yet the principal blame for the disaster that overtook Thessalonica in the summer of 1185 must lie not with any foreigner but with its own military governor, David Comnenus. Although he had strict instructions from the Emperor to attack the enemy at every opportunity and with all his strength,[1] and although—unlike Branas at Durazzo—he had had plenty of time to prepare his defences and lay in provisions, he had done neither. Within days of the beginning of the siege his archers had run out of arrows; soon there were not even any more stones for the catapults. Worse still, it soon became clear that he had failed to check the water cisterns, several of which were found—too late—to be leaking. Yet at no time did David Comnenus betray the slightest sign of shame or discomfiture. Nicetas Choniates, who probably knew him personally, writes:

Weaker than a woman, more timid than a deer, he was content just to look at the enemy, rather than to make any effort to repulse him. If ever the garrison showed itself eager to make a sortie he would forbid it, like a hunter who holds back his hounds. He was never seen to carry arms, or to wear a helmet or cuirass. . . . And while the enemy battering-rams made the walls tremble so that the masonry was crashing everywhere to the ground, he would laugh at the noise and, seeking out the safest corner available, would say to those around him, 'Just listen to the old lady—how noisy she is!' Thus he would refer to the largest of their siege-machines.

Nicetas was not himself at Thessalonica during those dreadful days; his account of them, however, is based on the best possible authority—that of the city's Metropolitan Archbishop, Eustathius. Though a Homeric scholar of repute, Eustathius was no stylist;[2] neither, as a good Greek patriot, did he ever try to conceal his own hatred of the Latins, whom—with good reason in his case—he

[1] Andronicus's orders were 'to see that the city was preserved and, far from being afraid of the Italians, to leap on them, bite them and prick them. Those were his own exact words, though I believe that only he knew precisely what he meant. Those who liked to joke about such things gave them a most unseemly interpretation—which I have no intention of repeating here.' (Nicetas.)

[2] Unless, perhaps, he was too much of one. Even Chalandon, whose own prose style can hardly be described as compulsive, speaks with feeling of what he calls '*l'ennui que cause sa rhétorique ampoulée*'.

considered no better than savages. But his *History of the Latin Cap-ture of Thessalonica*, turgid and tendentious as it is, remains the only eye-witness account we have of the siege and its aftermath. The story it tells is not a pretty one.

Even had it been adequately prepared and defended, it is unlikely that Thessalonica could have held out very long against so furious and many-sided an attack as that which the Sicilians now launched upon it. The garrison resisted as bravely as its commander per-mitted, but before long the eastern bastions began to crumble. Meanwhile, on the western side, a group of German mercenaries within the city was being bribed to open the gates. On 24 August, from both sides simultaneously, the Sicilian troops poured into the second city of the Byzantine Empire.

So huge an army must have contained hundreds of soldiers of Greek extraction; hundreds more, from Apulia and Calabria as well as from the island of Sicily itself, must have grown up near Greek communities, been familiar with their customs and religious trad-itions, even spoken a few words of their language. It would have been pleasant to record that these men had exerted a moderating influence on their less enlightened comrades; but they did nothing of the kind—or, if they tried, they failed. The Sicilian soldiery gave itself up to an orgy of savagery and violence unparalleled in Thessa-lonica since Theodosius the Great had massacred seven thousand of its citizens in the Hippodrome eight centuries before. It is perhaps more than coincidental that Eustathius puts the number of Greek civilian dead on this present occasion at the same figure; but even the Norman commanders estimated it at five thousand, so he may not be very far out. And murder was not all; women and children were seized and violated, houses fired and pillaged, churches dese-crated and destroyed. This last series of outrages was surprising. In the history of Norman Sicily we find very few cases of sacrilege and profanation, none on such a scale as this. Even the Greeks, for all their poor opinion of Latin behaviour, were as astonished as they were horrified. Nicetas admits as much:

These barbarians carried their violence to the very foot of the altars, in the presence of the holy images. . . . It was thought strange that they should wish to destroy our icons, using them as fuel for the fires on which they cooked. More criminal still, they would dance upon the altars, before which the angels themselves trembled, and sing profane songs. Then they would piss all over the church, flooding the floors with urine.

Some degree of pillage had been inevitable and expected—the recognised reward to an army after a successful siege, and one which the Greeks would not have hesitated to claim for themselves had the roles been reversed. But these atrocities were something different, and Baldwin took firm measures at once. The city had been entered during the early hours of the morning; by noon he had managed to restore a semblance of order. But then the logistical problems began. Thessalonica was not equipped to cope with a sudden influx of eighty thousand men. Such food as there was tended to disappear down Sicilian gullets, and the local population soon found itself half-starved. The disposal of the dead presented further difficulties. It was several days before the task was completed, and long before that the August heat had done its work. An epidemic ensued which, aggravated by overcrowding—and, Eustathius maintains, the immoderate consumption of new wine—killed off some three thousand of the occupying army and an unknown number of the local inhabitants.

From the start, too, there were serious confessional troubles. The Latins took over many of the local churches for their own use, but this did not stop certain elements of the soldiery from bursting into those that had remained in Greek hands, interrupting the services and howling down the officiating priests. A still more dangerous incident occurred when a group of Sicilians, suddenly startled by the sound of urgent, rhythmic hammering, took it to be a signal for insurrection and rushed to arms. Only just in time was it explained to them that the noise they had heard was simply that of the *semantron*, the wooden plank by which the Orthodox faithful were normally summoned to their devotions.[1]

[1] The beating of the *semantron* is of considerable symbolic significance. The Church represents, as we know, the ark of salvation; and the monk who balances the six-foot plank on his shoulder and raps his tattoo on it with a little wooden hammer is echoing the sound of Noah's tools, summoning the chosen to join

Within a week or so some uneasy kind of *modus vivendi* had been established. Baldwin, conceited as he may have been, showed himself a tactful commander and Eustathius, though technically a prisoner, seems to have done much to prevent unnecessary friction. His flock, for their part, soon began to discover—as peoples under occupation are apt to do—that there was money to be made out of these foreigners who had so little understanding of real prices and values. Before long we find him lamenting the ease with which the ladies of Thessalonica were wont to yield to the Sicilian soldiery. But the atmosphere in and around the city remained explosive, and it must have been a relief to Greek and Sicilian alike when the army drew itself up once more in line of battle and, leaving only a small garrison behind, headed off to the east.

By this time Andronicus had despatched no less than five separate armies to Thessalonica to block the Sicilian advance. Had they been united under a single able commander they might have saved the city; this fragmentation of his forces seems to be yet another indication of the Emperor's growing instability. As it was, all five retreated to the hills to the north of the road whence, apparently hypnotised, they watched the Sicilian advance. Baldwin's vanguard had thus pressed as far as Mosynopolis, nearly half-way to the capital, when there occurred an event that changed the entire situation—completely and, as far as Sicily was concerned, disastrously. The people of the capital rose up against Andronicus Comnenus and murdered him.

In Constantinople as elsewhere, the news from Thessalonica had brought the inhabitants to the verge of panic. Andronicus's reactions were typical of his contradictory nature. On the one hand he took firm action to repair and strengthen the city's defences. The state of the walls was carefully checked, houses built too closely against them were destroyed wherever it was considered that they might provide a means of entry for a besieging army; a fleet of a hundred ships was hastily mobilised and victualled. Though this

him. In Ottoman times, when the ringing of church bells was forbidden, the *semantron* continued in regular use. It is rarely heard nowadays, except on Mount Athos—where it remains the rule—and in a few isolated rural monasteries.

was less than half the size of the Sicilian naval force—now reported to be fast approaching—in the confined waters of the Marmara and the Bosphorus it might still serve its purpose.

But at other moments and in other respects the Emperor seemed totally indifferent to the emergency, drawing back further and further into his private world of pleasure. In the three years since his accession his life had grown steadily more depraved.

He would have liked to emulate Hercules, who lay with all the fifty daughters of Thyestes in a single night;[1] but he was nevertheless obliged to resort to artifice as a means of strengthening his nerves, rubbing himself with a certain balm to increase his vigour. He also ate regularly of a fish known as the *scincus*, which is caught in the river Nile and is not dissimilar to the crocodile; and which, though abhorred by many, is most effective in the quickening of lust.

By now, too, he was developing a persecution mania that led him to new extremes of cruelty. A day on which he ordered no one's death, writes Nicetas, was for him a day wasted; 'men and women lived only in anxiety and sorrow, and even the night afforded no rest, since their sleep was troubled by hideous dreams and by the ghastly phantoms of those whom he had massacred.' Constantinople was living through a reign of terror as fearful as any in its long, dark history—a terror which reached its culmination in September 1185, with the issue of a decree ordering the execution of all prisoners and exiles, together with their entire families, on charges of complicity with the Norman-Sicilian invaders.

Fortunately for the Empire, revolution came just in time to avert the tragedy. The spark was fired when the Emperor's cousin, Isaac Angelus, a normally inoffensive nobleman who had incurred Andronicus's displeasure when a soothsayer had identified him as successor to the throne, leaped on the imperial henchman who had been sent to arrest him and ran him through with his sword. Then, riding at full gallop to St Sophia, he proudly announced to all present what he had done. The news spread; crowds began to

---

[1] Nicetas nods here. The patriarch concerned was not Thyestes but Thespius. This thirteenth labour of Hercules must surely have been the most arduous of the lot, but its success rate was remarkable: all the girls produced male children, in many cases twins.

collect, among them Isaac's uncle John Ducas and many others who, though they had had no part in the crime, knew that in the present atmosphere of suspicion they would be unable to dissociate themselves from it. Therefore, says Nicetas, 'seeing that they would be taken, and having the image of death graven in their souls, they appealed to all the people to rally to their aid'.

And the people responded. The next morning, having spent the night in a torchlit St Sophia, they ran through the city calling every householder to arms. The prisons were broken open, the prisoners joined forces with their deliverers. Meanwhile, in the great church, Isaac Angelus was proclaimed Emperor.

One of the vergers climbed on a ladder above the High Altar and took down the crown of Constantine to place it on his head. Isaac showed reluctance to accept it—not for reasons of modesty nor because of any indifference towards the imperial diadem but because he feared that so audacious an enterprise might cost him his life. Ducas, on the other hand, stepped forward at once, and taking off his cap presented his own bald head, which shone like the full moon, to receive the crown. But the assembled people cried out loudly that they had suffered too much misery from the grizzled head of Andronicus, and that they would have no more senile or decrepit Emperors, least of all one with a long beard divided in two like a pitchfork.

When the news of the revolution had reached Andronicus on his country estate of Meludion, he had returned to the capital confident in his ability to reassert his control. Going straight to the Great Palace at the mouth of the Golden Horn he had ordered his guard to loose its arrows on the mob, and finding the soldiers slow to obey had seized a bow and begun furiously shooting on his own account. Then, suddenly, he understood. Throwing off his purple buskins, he covered his head with a little pointed bonnet 'such as the barbarians wear'; and hastily embarking his child-wife Agnes-Anna and his favourite concubine Maraptica—'an excellent flautist, with whom he was besottedly in love'—on to a waiting galley, he fled with them up the Bosphorus.

Simultaneously the mob burst into the Great Palace, falling on everything of value that it contained. Twelve hundred pounds of gold bullion alone, and three thousand of silver, were carried off, and jewels and works of art without number. Not even the imperial chapel was spared: icons were stripped from the walls, chalices snatched from the altar. And the most venerable treasure of all—the reliquary containing the letter written by Jesus Christ in his own hand to King Abgar of Edessa[1]—disappeared, never to be seen again.

The Emperor, Agnes-Anna and Maraptica were soon caught. The ladies, who behaved throughout with dignity and courage, were spared; but Andronicus, bound and fettered and with a heavy chain about his neck, was brought before Isaac for punishment. His hand was cut off and he was thrown into prison; then, after several days without food or water, he was blinded in one eye and brought forth on a scrawny camel to face the fury of his erstwhile subjects. They had suffered much from him, but nothing could excuse the brutality they now showed. As Nicetas remarks:

Everything that was lowest and most contemptible in the mob seemed to combine. . . . They beat him, stoned him, goaded him with spikes, pelted him with filth. A woman of the streets poured a bucket of boiling water on his head. . . . Then, dragging him from the camel, they hung him up by his feet. He endured all these torments and many others that I cannot describe, with incredible fortitude, speaking no other word among this demented crowd of his persecutors, but *O Lord, have pity on me; why dost thou trample on a poor reed that is already quite broken?* . . . At last, after much agony, he died, carrying his remaining hand to his mouth; which, in the opinion of some, he did that he might suck the blood that flowed from one of his wounds.

It is tempting to go on about Andronicus Comnenus—a figure, as Eustathius of Thessalonica observed, so full of contradictions that he can with equal justice be extravagantly praised or bitterly condemned; a colossus who possessed every gift save that of moderation, and who died as dramatically as he had lived; a hero and a villain, a preserver and a destroyer, a paragon and a warning. He has his place in this book, however, only in so far as his fortunes affect those of the Kingdom of Sicily; and just as his rise to power gave William II his pretext to march against Byzantium, so his fall was to bring about the Sicilian defeat.

[1] See p. 477.

Isaac Angelus, when at last he accepted the crown, inherited a desperate situation. At Mosynopolis, the invaders' advance column was less than two hundred miles from Constantinople; their fleet, meanwhile, was already in the Marmara, awaiting the army's arrival before launching its attack. Immediately on his accession, he sent Baldwin an offer of peace; when it was refused, he did what Andronicus should have done months before—appointed the ablest of his generals, Alexius Branas, to the overall command of all five armies, sending him the most massive reinforcements the Empire could provide. The effect was instantaneous; the Greeks were infused with new spirit. They saw too their enemy grown overconfident; no longer expecting resistance, the Sicilian soldiers had dropped their guard and relaxed their discipline. Carefully selecting his place and his moment, Branas swooped down upon them, routed them completely and pursued them all the way back to the main camp at Amphipolis.

It was, wrote Nicetas, a visible manifestation of the Divine Power.

Those men who, but a short while before, had threatened to overturn the very mountains, were as astonished as if they had been struck by lightning. The Romans,[1] on the other hand, no longer having any commerce with fear, burned with the desire to fall upon them, just as an eagle falls upon a feeble bird.

At Dimitritza,[2] just outside Amphipolis on the banks of the river Strymon, Baldwin at last consented to discuss peace. Why he did so remains a mystery. The defeat at Mosynopolis had not affected the main body of his army, encamped in good order around him. He

[1] The Byzantines always so described themselves, seeing their Empire as the unbroken continuation of that of ancient Rome. The word *Romiòs* is still used by their descendants today—on occasion. See Patrick Leigh-Fermor's brilliant essay on the subject in *Roumeli*, London, 1966.

[2] I have had some trouble over Dimitritza. This is the version given by Nicetas Choniates (Δημητρίτζα) but there is no trace of any place of such a name along the Strymon. Chalandon calls it Demetiza, then adds in brackets (without giving his authority) the obviously Turkish word Demechissar. If he is right in so doing, it is tempting to see this word as a corruption of Demir-Hisar, i.e. Iron Fort; in which case we must be talking about the modern Greek town of Siderókastron, which today stands just where Dimitritza might have been expected to be.

still held Thessalonica. Though the new Emperor in Constantinople was not senile as his predecessor had been, he was not in his first youth; and his claim to the throne was certainly weaker than that of Andronicus or of the pretender Alexius, who had accompanied the army all the way from Messina and was seldom far from Baldwin's side. But winter was approaching, and the autumn rains in Thrace fall heavy and chill. To an army that had counted on spending Christmas in Constantinople, Mosynopolis had probably proved more demoralising than its strategic importance deserved.

Alternatively, Baldwin may have had a darker purpose. The Greeks certainly claimed that he did. On the pretext that he intended to take advantage of the peace negotiations to catch them in their turn unprepared, they decided to strike first—'awaiting,' Nicetas himself assures us, 'neither the sound of the trumpets nor the orders of their commander'. Baldwin's army was taken unawares. His men resisted as best they could, then turned and fled. Some were cut down as they ran; many more were drowned as they tried to cross the Strymon, now swift and swollen from the rains; yet others, including both the Sicilian generals, Baldwin and Richard of Acerra, were taken prisoner, as was Alexius Comnenus, whom Isaac subsequently blinded for his treachery. Those who escaped found their way back to Thessalonica, where some managed to pick up ships to return them to Sicily. Since, however, the bulk of the Sicilian fleet was still lying off Constantinople waiting for the land army to arrive, the majority were not so lucky. The Thessalonians rose up against them, taking a full and bloody revenge for all that they had suffered three months before. Of the titanic army which had set out so confidently in the summer, it was a poor shadow that now dragged itself back through the icy mountain passes to Durazzo.

Byzantium was saved. Isaac Angelus would, however, have done well to take the Sicilian invasion as a warning. There were other western eyes fixed covetously on his Empire. Only twenty years later Constantinople was to face another attack, ludicrously known to history as the Fourth Crusade. Then too, Norman adventurers would be playing their part, and this time they would be victorious.

For William of Sicily, this destruction of the greatest army he or any of his predecessors had ever sent into the field spelt the end of his Byzantine ambitions. But he was not yet ready to admit himself beaten. His fleet under Tancred of Lecce, after seventeen days' waiting in the Marmara, had returned unscathed; and the following spring he sent it off to Cyprus, where another member of the Comnenus family, Isaac, had seized power and, in defiance of his namesake in Constantinople, had proclaimed himself Emperor. Although this histrionic gesture was to result in the permanent loss of the island to the Byzantine Empire, neither it nor the indecisive and somewhat desultory struggle that followed it need concern us here—except in one particular. It is in Cyprus that we first hear of the fleet's new commander Margaritus of Brindisi, the last great admiral of Norman Sicily, whose brilliance and courage were to do much to restore his country's military reputation and to shed a few last rays of glory over a doomed Kingdom.

The squabble over Cyprus gave Margaritus little opportunity to show his qualities. To appear at his best advantage he needed a greater challenge and a wider conflict. Neither was long in coming. In the autumn of 1187 he was summoned back to Sicily, ordered to refit his ships in haste and then to sail, at the earliest possible date, for Palestine. William had at last forgotten his differences with Byzantium; there were graver matters on hand. On Friday 2 October the Muslim armies under Saladin had retaken Jerusalem. The whole future of Christianity in the Holy Land hung in the balance.

19

THE RESPLENDENT SHADOW

Vos matrone nobiles	Ye noble matrons,
Virgines laudabiles	Most excellent virgins,
Olim delectabiles	Once so full of joy,
Nunc estote flebiles . . .	Now is the time for tears . . .
Iacet regnum desolatum	Desolate lies the Kingdom,
Dissolutum et turbatum,	Torn asunder and in disarray,
Sicque venientibus	Lying open to the enemies
Cunctis patet hostibus	Approaching from all sides;
Est ob hoc dolendum	A cause for weeping
Et plangendum	And for lamentation
Omnibus . . .	By all people . . .
Rex Guilielmus	William the King
Abiit non obiit.	Has departed, not died.
Rex ille magnificus	Glorious he was,
Pacificus	And a bringer of peace,
Cujus vita placuit	Whose life was pleasing
Deo et hominibus.	To God and to men.

Contemporary dirge quoted by Richard of S. Germano

EARLY in August 1185, while his still unvanquished army was battering on against the walls of Thessalonica, William of Sicily had escorted his aunt Constance across the sea to Salerno on the first stage of her bridal journey; and on the 28th of the same month, just four days after those walls had crumbled, Constance was delivered into the care of Frederick Barbarossa's special emissaries, waiting at Rieti. Thence, followed by a retinue of five hundred pack-horses and mules laden with a dowry appropriate to a future Empress who was also the wealthiest heiress in Europe, she travelled by easy stages to Milan.

The marriage was to take place in the ancient capital of Lombardy at the request of the Milanese themselves. To them the bride's name had a special significance; for it was at Constance, only two years previously, that Frederick had recognised the claims of the Lombard cities to self-government. What more fitting gesture could there be to mark the ending of their long struggle than to select the greatest of those cities for the marriage of his son?

Twenty-three years before, the Emperor had sacked Milan and left it a pile of rubble. He now returned to find a proud new city already risen on the ruins of the old. Only the cathedral was not yet rebuilt; fortunately, however, the imperial soldiery had spared the loveliest and most venerable of the city's churches, the fourth-century basilica of S. Ambrogio.[1] Long abandoned as a place of worship, S. Ambrogio had in recent years been doing service as a granary; it was now hastily refurbished and before its high altar, on 27 January 1186, Henry and Constance were declared man and wife. The ceremony was immediately followed by another, in which the couple were both crowned by the Patriarch of Aquileia with the iron crown of Lombardy.

Brides, by their very nature, have always provided a rich field for speculation and gossip—royal or imperial ones most of all. But few have ever caught the imagination of their subjects as Constance did. Not that there was anything particularly romantic about her: she was tall and fair-haired and, according to at least one source,[2] beautiful; but at thirty-one she was also eleven years older than her husband— by the standards of her day, a middle-aged woman. What intrigued people was her power, her wealth, and above all the mysterious seclusion in which she was said to have passed her early life, a seclusion which quickly gave rise to the rumour that she had actually taken the veil in her youth and had left the cloister only when reasons of state gave her no alternative. This theory was to gain more and more credence as the years went by; little more than

---

[1] S. Ambrogio is still there, and still the most beautiful building in Milan. It was founded by St Ambrose in A.D. 386, and despite a good deal of subsequent reconstruction—notably after the bombing of August 1943—still looks substantially the same as on the day of Constance's marriage. Visitors are implored not to miss the little fifth-century chapel of S. Vittore in Ciel d'Oro, refulgent with contemporary mosaic, tucked away in the south-east corner.

[2] Godfrey of Viterbo.

a century later Dante was even to allow her a place in Paradise—though admittedly in the lowest heaven—on the strength of it.[1]

But whatever Constance's new subjects thought about the marriage, for the Papacy it spelt disaster. Ever since the days of Robert Guiscard, when the Normans in the South had first become a force to be reckoned with, the thought of any alliance—let alone a union—between its two mighty neighbours had been a recurrent papal nightmare. Now that the Lombard cities had gained their independence, the danger of encirclement might seem a little less fearsome than before; but the cities still acknowledged the Emperor as their suzerain, their relations with Rome were strained, and they might even serve to increase the potential pressure if they had a mind to do so. In such an event the Papacy—which even in the days of the Sicilian alliance had often been hard put to hold its own—would be cracked like a nut.

The aged Pope Lucius was dead.[2] His successor, Urban III, seeing that there was nothing further to be done, had bowed gracefully to the inevitable and had even sent legates to Milan to represent him at the ceremony. He had not, however, been told about the

> [1] *Sorella fu, e così le fu tolta*
> *Di capo l'ombra delle sacre bende.*
> *Ma poi che pur al mondo fu rivolta*
> *Contra suo grado e contra buona usanza,*
> *Non fu dal vel del cor già mai disciolta.*
> *Quest' è la luce della gran Costanza*
> *Che del secondo vento di Soave*
> *Generò il terzo e l'ultima possanza.*

> She too a nun, her brows were forced to part
> With the o'ershadowing coif she held so dear.
> Yet, when against her will—and though to thwart
> That will was sin—she found herself re-cast
> Upon the world, she stayed still veiled in heart.
> This light is the great Constance: from one blast,
> The second Swabian, did she generate
> The third imperial whirlwind, and the last.
> (Tr. Bickersteth)
> *Paradiso*, iii, 113–2

[2] He died at Verona and was buried in the cathedral. In 1879 a great storm blew down part of the apse on to his tomb, smashing its sixteenth-century cover and revealing the original stone, bearing a portrait of the Pope in high relief and a neat but pointless inscription not worth transcribing here. It has now been built into the wall of the little chapel to St Agatha.

plans for the coronation, news of which threw him into a fury. To crown a son in his father's lifetime was always a dangerous precedent in papal eyes, since any strengthening of the hereditary principle in the imperial succession could only weaken the Pope's own influence; moreover, the coronation of the Lombard Kings was tradtionally the privilege of the Archbishop of Milan—a post which Urban himself had held before his election to the Papacy and which he had never technically given up.

The Patriarch was excommunicated for his presumption; and from that moment, in the words of a contemporary, Arnold of Lübeck, 'the quarrel between the Emperor and the Pope became open, and great trouble arose in the Church of God'. After Frederick returned to Germany, leaving Italy at the mercy of his son, the situation grew even worse; Henry soon showed that he understood no argument save that of violence. Open warfare soon broke out, the King of Lombardy at one moment even going so far as to cut off the nose of a high-ranking papal official. Ten years after the Treaty of Venice, it seemed as if breaking-point had once again been reached; the Pope's patience was exhausted and the Roman Emperor once again faced the prospect of excommunication.

That he escaped it was due neither to himself nor to Urban, but to Saladin. In mid-October 1187, as the Bull of Excommunication lay on the Pope's table ready for signature, a Genoese mission arrived at the papal court with the news of the fall of Jersusalem. Urban was old and ill, and the shock was more than he could bear. On 20 October, at Ferrara, he died of a broken heart.

As usual, the West reacted to the sad tidings from Outremer with genuine emotion but too late. To most Europeans, the Crusader states of the Levant were remote to the point of unreality—exotic, privileged outposts of Christendom in which austerity alternated with sybaritic luxury, where *douceur* and danger walked hand in hand; magnificent in their way, but somehow more suited to the lays of troubadour romance than to the damp and unheroic struggle that was the common lot at home. Even to the well-informed, Levantine politics were hard to follow, the names largely unpronounceable, the news when it did arrive hopelessly distorted and out of date.

Only when disaster had actually struck did they spring, with exclamations of mingled rage and horror, to their swords.

So it had been forty years before, when news of the fall of Edessa and the fire of St Bernard's oratory had quickened the pulse of the continent and launched the ludicrous fiasco that was the Second Crusade. And so it was now. To any dispassionate observer, European or Levantine, who had followed the march of events for the past fifteen years, the capture of Jerusalem must have seemed inevitable. On the Muslim side there had been the steady rise of Saladin, a leader of genius who had vowed to recover the holy city for his faith; on the Christian, nothing but the sad spectacle of the three remaining Frankish states of Jerusalem, Tripoli and Antioch, all governed by mediocrities and torn apart by internal struggles for power. Jerusalem itself was further burdened, throughout the crucial period of Saladin's ascendancy, by the corresponding decline of its leper King, Baldwin IV. When he came to the throne in 1174 at the age of thirteen, the disease was already upon him; eleven years later he was dead. Not surprisingly, he left no issue. At the one moment when wise and resolute leadership was essential if the kingdom were to be saved, the crown of Jerusalem devolved upon his nephew, a child of eight.

The death of this new infant king, Baldwin V, in the following year might have been considered a blessing in disguise; but the opportunity of finding a true leader was thrown away and the throne passed to his stepfather, Guy of Lusignan, a weak, querulous figure with a record of incapacity which fully merited the scorn in which he was held by most of his compatriots. Jerusalem was thus in a state bordering on civil war when, in May 1187, Saladin declared his long-awaited *jihad* and crossed the Jordan into Frankish territory. Under the miserable Guy, the Christian defeat was assured. On 3 July, he led the largest army his kingdom had ever assembled across the Galilean mountains towards Tiberias, where Saladin was laying siege to the castle. After a long day's march in the most torrid season of the year, they were forced to camp on a waterless plateau; and the next day, exhausted by the heat and half-mad with thirst, beneath a little double-summited hill known as the Horns of Hattin, they were surrounded by the Muslim army and cut to pieces.

It only remained for the Saracens to mop up the isolated Christian fortresses one by one. Tiberias fell on the day after Hattin; Acre followed; Nablus, Jaffa, Sidon and Beirut capitulated in quick succession. Wheeling south, Saladin took Ascalon by storm and received the surrender of Gaza without a struggle. Now he was ready for Jerusalem. The defenders of the Holy City resisted heroically for twelve days; but on 2 October, with the walls already breached by Muslim sappers, they knew that the end was near. Their leader, Balian of Ibelin—King Guy having been taken prisoner after Hattin —went personally to Saladin to discuss terms for surrender.

Saladin, who knew and liked Balian, was neither bloodthirsty nor vindictive; and after some negotiation he agreed that every Christian in Jerusalem should be allowed to redeem himself by payment of the appropriate ransom. Of the twenty thousand poor who had no means of raising the money, seven thousand would be freed on payment of a lump sum by the various Christian authorities. That same day the conqueror led his army into the city; and for the first time in eighty-eight years, on the anniversary of the day on which Mohammed was carried in his sleep from Jerusalem to paradise, his green banners fluttered over the Temple area from which he had been gathered up, and the sacred imprint of his foot was once again exposed to the adoration of the Faithful.

Everywhere, order was preserved. There was no murder, no bloodshed, no looting. Thirteen thousand poor, for whom ransom money could not be raised, remained in the city; but Saladin's brother and lieutenant, al-Adil, asked for a thousand of them as a reward for his services and immediately set them free. Another seven hundred were given to the Patriarch, and five hundred to Balian of Ibelin; then Saladin himself spontaneously liberated all the old, all the husbands whose wives had been ransomed and finally all the widows and children. Few Christians ultimately found their way to slavery. This was not the first time that Saladin had shown that magnanimity for which he would soon be famous through East and West alike;[1] but never before had he done so on

[1] Four years before, when he laid siege to the castle of Kerak during the wedding celebrations of its heir, Humphrey of Toron, to Princess Isabella of Jerusalem, he had carefully enquired which tower contained the bridal chamber and had given orders that it was to be left undisturbed.

such a scale. His restraint was the more remarkable in that he had not forgotten the dreadful story of 1099, when the conquering Franks had marked their entry into the city by slaughtering every Muslim within its walls and burning all the Jews alive in the main synagogue. The Christians, for their part, had not forgotten it either; and they could not fail to be struck by the contrast. Saladin might be their arch-enemy; but he had set them an example of chivalry which was to have an effect on the whole of the Third Crusade—an example which was to remain ever before them in the months to come.

The new Pope, Gregory VIII, lost no time in calling upon Christendom to take the Cross; and of the princes of Europe, William of Sicily was the first to respond. The fall of Jerusalem had shocked and troubled him deeply; he dressed himself in sackcloth and went into retreat for four days. Then he despatched Margaritus to Palestine, himself settling down to compose careful letters to his fellow-rulers, pressing them to devote all their energies and resources to the coming Crusade, as he himself planned to do.

It would be naïve to suppose that William's motives in this were purely idealistic. Pious he was, but not so pious that he could not scent another opportunity of realising his old dream of eastern expansion. After all, there were precedents enough in his own family. In the First Crusade the Guiscard's son Bohemund had carved out for himself the Principality of Antioch; in the Second, his own grandfather Roger had emerged with an enormously enhanced reputation—and incidentally, a good deal richer—without stirring from Palermo. Might he himself not now turn the Third to equally good account? The time had come to take his rightful place among the councils of the West. In his letters to the other kings he was careful to stress the advantages of the sea route to the Levant over the long land journey across the Balkans and the treacherous passes of Anatolia. Henry II in England, Philip Augustus in France and Frederick Barbarossa in Germany were all encouraged to break their journey in Sicily, with promises of additional reinforcements and supplies if they did so.

Diplomatically William was in a strong position. Alone of European monarchs, he had a contingent already in the field. His admiral Margaritus commanded a fleet of only sixty ships and some two hundred knights, but all through 1188 and 1189, when for most of the time he represented virtually the only organised resistance to the Saracens, he kept up a steady patrol of the coast which, thanks largely to his admirable intelligence system, proved effective out of all proportion to its strength. Time and again when Saladin's forces arrived at a port that was still in Christian hands, they found that Margaritus had forestalled them. In July 1188 news of the Admiral's arrival off Tripoli caused Saladin to raise the siege of Krak des Chevaliers and decided him against any attack on the city itself. The Saracens were similarly deflected at Marqab and Latakia, and again at Tyre. It was small wonder that during those two years the dashing young admiral, now popularly known as 'the new Neptune', acquired a legendary reputation throughout Christendom. His renown might have been yet greater and his command infinitely further extended had the Sicilians ever been able to raise the mighty army of which their King had dreamed; but suddenly his hopes of crusading glory were dashed. On 18 November 1189 William II died, aged thirty-six, at Palermo.

Of all the Hauteville rulers of Sicily, William the Good is the most nebulous and the most elusive. We know nothing of the circumstances of his death except that it seems to have been non-violent —Peter of Eboli's manuscript contains a picture of the King, surrounded by his doctors and attendants, dying peacefully in his bed —and about his life, short as it was, we are scarcely better informed. Hardly ever in his thirty-six years do we see him clearly face to face. There is a moment on the day of his coronation, when Falcandus gives us a brief glimpse of him riding through the streets of Palermo in the bright morning of his youth and beauty; another, even more fleeting, at the time of his marriage. For the rest we are thrown back on legend, or inference, or hearsay. It is sometimes hard to remember that he ruled over Sicily for eighteen years and occupied the throne for almost a quarter of a century; we are conscious only of a dim, if faintly resplendent, shadow that passes fleetingly over a few pages of history and is gone.

Yet William was regretted as few European princes have ever
been, and far beyond the confines of his kingdom. Among the Franks
of Outremer he had already gained, thanks to Margaritus, the renown he had always longed for, and his death was seen as a further
disaster to the Christian cause. In Sicily and South Italy, the grief of
his subjects was universal and profound. It was not so much that
they feared the future—though many of them did so, and with good
reason; the overriding feeling was regret for the past, for the peace
and tranquillity that had marked his reign but might not survive it.
As the Archbishop of Reggio recalled in his memorial address:

In this land a man might lay down his head under the trees, or under
the open sky, knowing himself to be as safe as if he were in his own
bed at home; here the forests and the rivers and the sunlit meadows
were no less hospitable than the walled cities; and the royal bounty
extended over all, ever-generous and inexhaustible.

But he spoke, let it be noted, in the past tense.

The orations and encomiums, the threnodies and the laments, to say
nothing of the whole labyrinth of legend that grew up around the
name of William the Good and still keeps it fresh eight centuries
later in Sicilian folklore, would have been more appropriate to a
Charlemagne or an Alfred than to the last and weakest of Roger's
legitimate line. If few rulers have achieved so enviable a reputation
none, surely, have deserved it less. True, the reorganisation of the
government machine after the departure of Stephen du Perche may
have allowed rather more scope to the feudal nobility than they had
formerly enjoyed; certain of them, men like Robert of Loritello or
Tancred of Lecce, were able to find an outlet for their ambitions in
the King's service rather than in battling vainly against him. But
be that as it may, what really kept the Kingdom's internal peace
through William's majority was neither his wisdom nor his statesmanship; rather was it a general revulsion on the part of the potential discontents against the unceasing violence of former years. The
history of their land from its beginnings had been an almost uninterrupted saga of rebellion and revolt; and what, men suddenly
asked themselves, had any of the rebels ever gained by their activities?
How many had escaped death, or mutilation, or a prison cell? Was

it not better to accept the Hauteville domination as the political reality it was, and to concentrate instead on amassing the largest possible share of the ever-increasing national wealth? Suddenly, rebellion was no longer in the air; and for this William can take little enough of the credit.

Meanwhile, on the debit side, he has a lot to answer for. His reign did nothing to strengthen his country; instead it marked a return to the most dangerous and irresponsible foreign policy that any state can pursue—that of land-grabbing for its own sake, without consideration for political consequences. The fact that all William's attempts in this direction were ignominious failures, that time and again he emptied the national coffers on enterprises that brought him nothing but defeat and humiliation, can hardly serve as an excuse; nor can it be claimed that he was merely reverting to the policies of Robert Guiscard. Robert was an adventurer whose achievement was to create a dominion out of chaos; William was an anointed sovereign of an influential and prosperous kingdom, with moral duties to his subjects and to his fellow-rulers. One might, perhaps, have had a little more sympathy for him if, like the Guiscard, he had led his troops in person on these escapades; but he never ventured beyond the point of departure. To others would be left the ungrateful task of trying to satisfy their master's ambitions; he himself would withdraw once again to his harem and his pleasure-domes, and await results.[1]

On such a record alone William II must stand condemned; but that is not all. He must also bear the blame for the most disastrous decision of the whole Sicilian epic—his agreement to Constance's marriage. He knew that if he died childless the throne would be hers; and he had been married long enough to understand that

[1] Two of these pleasure-domes have lasted to the present day and are—just—worth a visit. The first and more important is the Cuba. Once set in an ornamental lake within the royal park—its main entrance is half-way up the wall—it later became a cavalry stable for the Neapolitan army and now stands in the middle of a gloomy barracks at No. 94, Corso Calatafimi. Noble but now sadly neglected, its walls defaced with painted goalposts, one finds it hard to believe that this pavilion in its heyday provided the setting for one of Boccaccio's stories (Day 5, No. 6). Not far off, in the garden of Cav. di Napoli at No. 375, stands another, smaller kiosk, the Cubula; and on the east front of the Villa Napoli a line of arcading marks the remnants of yet a third, the Cuba Soprana.

Joanna might well fail to bear him a son. True, he could always put her away and take another wife; but who was to say that his second marriage would be any more fruitful than the first? Meanwhile Constance was the Kingdom; and by giving her to Henry of Hohenstaufen he sealed the death warrant of Norman Sicily.

Handsome is—for monarchs even more than for their subjects—as handsome does. Youth, beauty and piety are not enough, and the record of the last legitimate Hauteville king is not an edifying one. Apart from Monreale—a monument to himself as much as to his God—he can be credited with only one real achievement: the fact that by his promptness in sending help to the Levant at the very start of the Third Crusade he was able, through the brilliance of Margaritus of Brindisi, to save Tripoli and Tyre, temporarily, for the Christian cause. As to the rest, he is revealed as irresponsible, vainglorious and grasping, lacking even the rudiments of statesmanship and quite possibly a coward into the bargain. His sobriquet is thus more misleading even than his father's before him. William the Bad was not so bad; William the Good was far, far worse. And for those who like to see a connection between sanctity in life and incorruptibility in death, this judgment was given a macabre confirmation when, in 1811, their two sarcophagi were opened. In contrast to the body of William the Bad, almost perfectly preserved, of William the Good there remained only a skull, a collection of bones covered with a silken shroud, and a lock of reddish hair.

20

THE THREE KINGS

Behold, an ape is crowned!

Peter of Eboli

SHORTLY before the Princess Constance left the territory of her future kingdom, her nephew had called a great assembly of his chief vassals at Troia and made them swear fealty to her as his heir and eventual successor. But not even William can have been foolish enough to imagine that her succession would be unopposed. Whatever his own feelings on the subject, the fact remained that to the immense majority of his people the Western Empire had always been the most persistent and dangerous of enemies. In South Italy, to which it had never renounced its claim, few could remember how often in the past two centuries one Emperor after another had descended into the peninsula to claim his due; but every town and village had its stories of the atrocities wrought by the imperial soldiery. In Sicily, where there had been no such invasions, the prevailing emotion was not so much fear as contempt—the contempt of a highly cultivated and intellectually arrogant society for the one European culture of which it had no experience or understanding. This attitude seems to have been already prevalent in the days of King Roger;[1] and forty years later we find Hugo Falcandus writing to Peter, church treasurer of Palermo, of the terror felt by Sicilian children at the sound of 'the harsh stridencies of that barbarian tongue'.

This is not to say that Constance was left entirely without supporters. Walter of the Mill, for one, had backed her marriage from

---

[1] 'All foreigners were more or less welcome in his domain, except men of the Kingdom of Germany, whom he was unwilling to have among his subjects; for he distrusted that people and could not endure their barbarous ways.' John of Salisbury, *Historia Pontificalis*, ch. XXXII. Tr. Chibnall.

the outset, and apart from the anarchy-loving barons on the mainland there were plenty of fatalists who, even if they had originally deplored the idea, now accepted it as an accomplished fact. Nothing, such men reasoned, could now prevent Henry from coming to Sicily to claim his wife's throne; better surely that he should come in peace and friendship than in power and wrath. But in these early days the legitimist party was small; its leader, Walter of the Mill, had only a few months to live; and it was in any case almost immediately overshadowed by two other factions, bitterly opposed to Constance, which had sprung up even before William's death was announced. One of these called for the succession to the throne of Roger, Count of Andria; the other favoured Tancred of Lecce. Both candidates had important qualities to recommend them. Separately and together—they had fought side by side against the imperial forces in 1176 and gained an impressive if ultimately insignificant victory—they could boast outstanding military records. Tancred had commanded the Sicilian fleet in William's two principal foreign expeditions; though both of these had ended in disaster, no blame had attached to him personally. Roger had for his part also won diplomatic distinction as one of the leading negotiators of the Treaty of Venice. He was now Great Chamberlain of the Kingdom, a widely admired and respected figure.

But whereas the Count of Andria's claim to the blood royal was tenuous to say the least,[1] Tancred's was undeniable: he was the illegitimate son of Duke Roger of Apulia by Emma, daughter of Count Achard of Lecce. He was small, and villainously ugly. That arch-polemicist Peter of Eboli, who hated him, hexametrically describes him as an *embrion infelix, et detestabile monstrum* and depicts him, both in verse and in his accompanying illustrations, as a monkey.[2] But like so many small men, Tancred was energetic, able and determined; his youthful disloyalty to William I had been forgotten; and he had recently been appointed Grand Constable and Master Justiciar of Apulia. Above all, he had as his champion Matthew of Ajello. Matthew was by now an old

[1] La Lumia, p. 344, refers to him as the great-grandson of Drogo de Hauteville and thus second cousin to the dead King; but I can find no corroboration and the lineage looks distinctly uncertain.
[2] See plate.

man, tormented by gout,[1] who had long contemplated retirement and had even, a dozen years before enrolled himself as a lay brother in the Basilian monastery of the Saviour at Messina. But his love of power had proved too strong for him; and he and Walter of the Mill together, despite their mutual loathing, had continued to stand as what Richard of S. Germano was later to describe as 'the two firmest columns of the Kingdom'. Now one of those columns was showing signs of collapse; but Matthew remained as firm as ever. A genuine Sicilian patriot, he never disguised his revulsion at the Hohenstaufen marriage; and before King William's body was cold he had flung all his energies, his political expertise and his considerable financial resources into the campaign to secure Tancred's succession.

The struggle was hard and bitter. The nobility and their hangers-on were overwhelmingly in favour of Roger of Andria; the bourgeoisie and populace preferred Tancred. Neither side pulled its punches and on at least one occasion the rival factions fought it out in the streets of Palermo. But Matthew knew of certain irregularities in the Count of Andria's private life, and used his knowledge to disastrous effect. He also had no difficulty in obtaining support from Pope Clement III—who, he rightly guessed, would jump at any chance of preventing the union of his two formidable neighbours.

Thus it was that some time in the first weeks of 1190 Tancred of Lecce received the crown of Sicily, at the hands of Archbishop Walter of the Mill who appears to have resigned himself, if only temporarily, to the inevitable. Tancred's first act was to appoint Matthew of Ajello Chancellor of the Kingdom—an office that had lain vacant since the departure of Stephen du Perche. Nothing, he knew, would give the old man greater pleasure or bind him more closely to the throne; besides, his support would be still more necessary in the future. There was desperate fighting ahead for them all if the Kingdom were to survive.

Strangely enough, the first challenge to the new King's authority came from neither of the two factions he had just defeated. It revealed,

[1] Which Peter of Eboli, in a masterpiece of sustained invective, claims that he sought to alleviate by bathing his feet in the blood of slaughtered children.

however, another still more ominous rift in the structure of the state —a growing antagonism between the Christian and the Muslim sectors of the population. Hardly had Tancred assumed power when inter-confessional strife broke out in the capital. The trouble seems to have been started by the Christians, who took advantage of the disorder following William's death to attack the Arab quarter of Palermo. In the ensuing affray several Muslims lost their lives; many others, fearing a general massacre, fled to the hills where they managed to take possession of several castles, and where they were gradually joined by increasing numbers of their co-religionists. Before long Tancred saw that he had a full-scale insurrection on his hands.

Tension between the two communities had naturally been height-ened by the news of the fall of Jerusalem and the subsequent preparations for the Crusade; but the true causes of the revolt lay deeper in the Sicilian past. For half a century and more the steady immigration of Christians from northern and western Europe, un-matched by any corresponding movements of Greeks or Muslims, had led to the dangerous strengthening of the Latin element at the expense of the others. Intolerance was bound to follow. Ever since the anti-Muslim riots that followed the *coup* against William the Bad in 1161 the situation seems to have been progressively deterio-rating. Here is Ibn Jubair, reporting from Palermo at the end of 1184:

The Muslims of this city preserve the remaining evidence of their faith. They keep in repair the greater number of their mosques, and come to prayers at the call of the muezzin. . . . They do not congre-gate for the Friday service, since the *khutbah*[1] is forbidden. On feast-days only may they recite it with intercessions for the Abbasid Caliphs. They have a *qadi* to whom they refer their law-suits, and a cathedral mosque where, in this holy month [of Ramadan] they assemble under its lamps. . . . But in general these Muslims do not mix with their brethren under infidel patronage, and enjoy no security for their goods, their women, or their children.

In the royal palace itself, although it was almost entirely staffed by Muslims, the actual practice of Islam seems to have been tolerated

---

[1] The sermon delivered on Fridays at the time of the midday prayer.

only when it was conducted in private. Ibn Jubair tells of an interview in Messina with one of the leading eunuchs of the court:

He had first looked about his audience-room, and then, in self-protection, dismissed those servants about him whom he suspected. . . . 'You can boldly display your faith in Islam,' he said, '. . . but we must conceal our faith and, fearful of our lives, must adhere to the worship of God and the discharge of our religious duties in secret. We are bound in the possession of an infidel who has placed on our necks the noose of bondage.'

Apart from the specifically religious issue, the prevailing attitude of the Sicilian Christians towards their Muslim fellow-subjects by the end of the century is inescapably reminiscent of that shown by the British sahibs towards the people of India in the heyday of the Raj:

Their King, William, . . . has much confidence in Muslims—who all, or nearly all, concealing their faith, yet hold firm to the Muslim divine law. He relies on them for his affairs, and the most important matters, even the supervisor of his kitchen being a Muslim; and he keeps a band of black Muslim slaves commanded by a leader chosen from amongst them. His ministers and chamberlains he appoints from his pages, of whom he has a great number and who are his public officials and are described as his courtiers. In them shines the splendour of his realm for the magnificent clothing and fiery horses they display; and there is none of them but has his retinue, his servants, and his followers.

Thus, in scarcely more than a generation, the status of the Muslims of Sicily had declined from that of a universally respected, learned and immensely able sector of the population to the level at the worst of menials and at the best of privileged purveyors of local colour. Their women might set the fashions which Christian women were happy to follow; Ibn Jubair notes with wonder how on Christmas Day 1184 the latter 'all went forth in robes of gold-embroidered silk, wrapped in elegant cloaks, concealed by coloured veils and shod with gilt slippers . . . bearing all the adornments of Muslim women, including jewellery, henna on the fingers and perfumes.' The King himself might read and write Arabic, and murmur oriental endearments to his Muslim handmaidens and concubines.[1] Yet it was all a far cry from the ideals of the two Rogers. The betrayal of those ideals by their successors was probably unwitting, possibly inevitable, certainly catastrophic. And it was, perhaps, more than fortuitous that the final breakdown of the confessional interdependence on which Norman Sicily had been founded should have coincided with the extinction of the Kingdom itself.

The first year of his reign was a particularly hard one for King Tancred. The Muslim insurrection grew—one chronicler puts the numbers involved as high as a hundred thousand—and though he managed to confine it to the west of the island it was not till the end of 1190 that order was restored. Meanwhile, on the mainland, his enemies were gathering fast. The adherents of Roger of Andria, who included nearly all the principal barons of Apulia and Campania, had been outraged by Tancred's election, and had no intention of recognising him as their lawful sovereign. In this they were joined by the legitimists, who genuinely championed Constance and Henry, and by the fatalists—this last group by now increasing rapidly as the news spread of Henry's preparations to march. By spring much of the peninsula was in open revolt. Roger of Andria had gathered all the malcontents under his banner; and in May a small German army under Henry of Kalden crossed the frontier near Rieti and descended the Adriatic coast into Apulia.

But Tancred too had acted fast. The Muslim insurrection and his own shaky political position made it unwise for him to leave Sicily, or even to despatch any substantial body of troops; but he had sent his wife's brother, Count Richard of Acerra, a large sum of money with which to raise an army locally and, if need be, abroad. Richard had risen splendidly to the occasion. That summer he successfully prevented the forces of the Count of Andria and Henry of Kalden from joining up with the rebels of Campania—where Capua and Aversa had already declared against Tancred—and held the position until September when, for reasons unknown, the German army withdrew

[1] 'One of the strangest things told us by Yahya ibn Fityan, the embroiderer, who embroidered in gold the King's clothes, was that the Frankish Christian women who came to his palace became Muslims, converted by these handmaidens. All this they kept secret from their King.' (Ibn Jubair.)

once again into imperial territory. He then pursued the demoralised rebels back into Apulia where, during a swift and triumphant campaign, he ambushed the Count of Andria and took him prisoner.[1]

As 1190 ended it was clear that, thanks in a large measure to his brother-in-law, Tancred had won the first round. An imperial expedition sent against him had proved abortive, the rebels both in Sicily and on the mainland had been forced into submission. His two principal enemies within the Kingdom were both in their graves—Roger of Andria, whom he had had executed for his part in the rebellion, and Walter of the Mill who had died of natural causes earlier in the year, to be succeeded by his brother Bartholomew as Archbishop of Palermo.

It would be pleasant to be able to write a friendly word or two about a compatriot who played so prominent and prolonged a part in the history of his adopted country. The inescapable fact is, however, that of all the Englishmen whose names have from time to time appeared in these pages, it was Walter of the Mill who exerted the most baleful influence on the Kingdom. He was not, so far as one can tell, a wicked man; but he was the very prototype of those prelates, vain and ambitious and worldly, who were such a feature of mediaeval Europe. It is impossible to like him. In his quarter of a century as Archbishop and chief minister to William II, there is no evidence of his having taken a single constructive step to improve the Sicilian position or to advance Sicilian fortunes. When the crisis arose over Constance's marriage his influence, allied with that of Matthew of Ajello, could almost certainly have secured William's rejection of the imperial proposals. Instead, he encouraged his master to give away the Kingdom. Time-server as he was, he did not hesitate soon afterwards to lay the crown on Tancred's head; but even this did not stop him from resuming his intrigues against the new King within weeks, if not days, of the coronation.

Thus, in the absence of any more attractive achievement, Walter's chief memorial must be his cathedral of Palermo, where his tomb may still be seen in the crypt. Though the building is curiously appropriate to its founder—imposing in a messy sort of way, pompous, grandiloquent, yet vacuous and fundamentally hypocritical

[1] Plate 28.   [2] Plate 30.

—Walter cannot really be blamed for its present appearance; it has been reworked and restored so often that even the exterior allows us only a few glimpses of the original conception—the east end with its apse decorations uncomfortably reminiscent of Monreale, and the long range of windows along the south wall above the side aisles. Even here, nothing seems particularly distinguished; for the most part, the fourteenth-century work somehow contrives to look like a nineteenth-century *pastiche*. But the crowning desecration, literally and figuratively, on the outside and within, took place in the eighteenth century when the Florentine architect Fernando Fuga clapped on a ludicrous and totally unrelated dome, hacked away the side walls to make fourteen chapels, removed the wooden roof and replaced it with inferior vaulting, then whitewashed the whole thing—the apse mosaics had already been torn down two centuries earlier—and baroqued it up beyond recognition. Today, the kindest thing to do about Palermo Cathedral would be to ignore it—were it not for the royal tombs. But the time to speak of these has not yet come.

Walter of the Mill left one other building in the capital, and a much more satisfying one it is. The church of Santo Spirito, built for the Cistercians a decade or so before the cathedral, has miraculously escaped the attentions of restorers and improvers and retains all the austere, uncluttered purity of Norman architecture at its best. Its fame rests, however, less on its beauty than on its historical associations; for it was outside Santo Spirito, just before the evening service on 31 March 1282, that a sergeant of the Angevin army of occupation insulted a Sicilian woman, was stabbed to death by her husband and so, unwittingly, sparked off that triumphantly successful rebellion by the Sicilians against their overlord Charles of Anjou that was ever afterwards to be known as the Sicilian Vespers. Thus, of the two foundations of an English archbishop, one was destined to witness, with the coronation of Henry and Constance, the most abject betrayal of Sicily by her own people; and the other, a century later, the proudest upsurge of popular patriotism in all her history.

King William's proposals to his fellow-monarchs that they should use Sicily as an assembly-point for their crusading forces had not

1 Plate 31.

passed altogether unheeded. Frederick Barbarossa, despite what must have been fairly painful recollections of his journey to Palestine more than forty years before, had resolved once again to take the land route—a decision that was shortly to cost him his life; but Philip Augustus had accepted the invitation, and so had the new King of England—Richard I, Cœur de Lion.

In the high summer of 1190 these two Kings and their armies met together at Vézelay—a choice of meeting place that might have seemed to some people another ominous precedent. They were to set off on the journey together less for reasons of companionship than because neither trusted the other an inch; and indeed no pair could have been more unlike. The King of France was still only twenty-five; but he was already a widower and apart from a shock of wild, uncontrollable hair there was nothing youthful about him. His ten years on the throne of France had given him unusual wisdom and experience for one so young, making him permanently suspicious, and teaching him to conceal his thoughts and emotions behind a veil of taciturn moroseness. Never handsome, he had now lost the sight of one eye so that his face looked somehow asymmetrical. He lacked courage on the battlefield and charm in society; he was, in a word, a thoroughly unattractive man and he knew it. But beneath his drab exterior there lay a searching intelligence, coupled with a strong sense of both the moral and political responsibilities of kingship. It was easy to underestimate him. It was also unwise.

Yet whatever his hidden qualities, Philip Augustus cannot have looked upon his fellow-ruler without envy. Richard had succeeded his father Henry II in July 1189, just a year before. At thirty-three, he was now in his prime. Though his health was often poor, his superb physique and volcanic energy gave the impression of a man to whom illness was unknown. His good looks were famous, his powers of leadership no less so, his personal bravery already a legend through two continents. From his mother Eleanor he had inherited the Poitevin love of literature and poetry, and to many people he himself must have seemed like some glittering figure from the troubadour romances he loved so much. Only one element was lacking to complete the picture: however sweetly Richard might sing of the joys and pains of love, he had left no trail of betrayed or broken-hearted damozels behind him. But if his tastes ran in other directions they never appreciably affected that shining reputation, burnished as his breastplate, that remained with him till the day of his death.

Those who knew Richard better, on the other hand, soon became aware of other, less admirable sides to his character. Even more impetuous and hot-tempered than the father he had so hated, he altogether lacked that capacity for sustained administrative effort that had enabled Henry II, for all his faults, to weld England almost single-handed into a nation. His ambition was boundless and, nearly always, destructive. Himself incapable of love, he could be faithless, disloyal, even treacherous, in the pursuit of his ends. No English king had fought harder or more unscrupulously for the throne; none was readier to ignore the responsibilities of kingship for the sake of personal glory. In the nine years of life left to him, the total time he was to spend in England was just two months.

The hills round Vézelay, wrote an eyewitness, were so spread with tents and pavilions that the fields looked like a great and multi-coloured city. The two Kings solemnly reaffirmed their crusading vows and sealed a further treaty of alliance; then, followed by their respective armies and a huge multitude of pilgrims, they moved off together to the south. It was only at Lyons, where the collapse of the bridge across the Rhône under the weight of the crowds was interpreted as a bad augury for the future, that French and English parted company; Philip turned south-east towards Genoa, where his navy was awaiting him, while Richard continued down the Rhône valley to meet the English fleet at Marseilles. They had agreed to join forces again at Messina, whence their combined army would sail for the Holy Land.

Philip arrived first, on 14 September, and Richard nine days later. Nothing was more typical of the two men than the manner of their disembarkation:

When the King of France was known to be entering the port of Messina, the natives of every age and sex rushed forth to see so famous a King; but he, content with a single ship, entered the port of the citadel privately, so that those who awaited him along the shore saw this as a proof of his weakness; such a man, they said, was not likely to be the performer of any great matter, shrinking in such fashion from the eye of his fellows. . . .

But when Richard was about to land, the people rushed down in crowds towards the beach; and behold, from a distance the sea seemed cleft with innumerable oars, and the loud voices of the trumpets and the horns sounded clear and shrill over the water. Approaching nearer, the galleys could be seen rowing in order, emblazoned with divers coats of arms, and with pennons and banners innumerable floating from the points of the spears. The beaks of the vessels were painted with the devices of the knights they bore, and glittered with the rays reflected from the shields. The sea was boiling with the multitude of oars, the air trembling with the blasts of the trumpets and the tumultuous shouts of the delighted crowds. The magnificent King, loftier and more splendid than all his train, stood erect on the prow, as one expecting alike to see and be seen. . . . And as the trumpets rang out with discordant yet harmonious sounds, the people whispered together: 'He is indeed worthy of empire; he is rightly made King over peoples and kingdoms; what we heard of him at a distance falls far short of what we now see.'[1]

Not all of Richard's admirers on that memorable day may have been aware that that superb figure had preferred, through fear of seasickness, to take the land route down the peninsula; and that this mighty landfall was in fact the culmination of a sea journey that had brought him only a mile or two across the straits. Fewer still could have guessed that, for all the golden splendour of his arrival, Richard was in a black and dangerous mood. It was not the fact that a few days previously, passing through Mileto, he had been caught in the act of appropriating a hawk from a peasant's cottage and narrowly escaped death at the hands of the owner and his friends; it was not even the discovery, on landing at Messina, that the royal palace in the centre of the city had already been placed at the disposal of the King of France and that he himself had been allotted more modest quarters outside the walls. Neither of these misfortunes can have improved his temper, but this time there was more at stake than a simple matter of *amour-propre*.

The truth was that he bore a deep grudge against Tancred. Though William the Good had died intestate, he seems at some stage to have

---

[1] *Itinerary of Richard I.*

promised his father-in-law Henry an important legacy that included a twelve-foot golden table, a silken tent big enough to hold two hundred men, a quantity of gold plate and several additional ships, fully provisioned, for the Crusade. Now, with both William and Henry dead, Tancred was refusing to honour the promise. Then there was Joanna. As he rode south through Italy, Richard had heard unpleasant stories of how his sister was being treated by the new King of Sicily; it seemed that Tancred, knowing her to be a partisan of Constance and fearing her influence in the Kingdom, was keeping the young Queen under distraint and wrongfully withholding the revenues of the County of Monte S. Angelo which she had received as part of her marriage settlement. From Salerno her brother had already sent word to Tancred calling for satisfaction on both these points and adding, for good measure, a demand that Joanna should also be presented with the golden throne that was, he claimed, her traditional right as a Norman queen. The tone of his letter was threatening, and clearly implied that once in Sicily with his army and navy he had no intention of continuing his journey until he had received satisfaction.

How far these complaints were justified it is not easy to say. Richard's subsequent behaviour suggests that he saw Sicily as a potential new jewel in his own crown and that he was already on the lookout for any excuse to make trouble. On the other hand he was genuinely fond of Joanna, and there seems little doubt that her freedom had been in some degree restricted. Tancred, in any case, was seriously alarmed. He had too much on his plate to risk hostilities in yet another quarter, and his first reaction was to get his unwelcome guest away from the island as soon as possible. If this meant making concessions, then concessions there would have to be.

Richard did not have to wait long for results. Only five days after his arrival at Messina he was joined there by Joanna herself, now once more at complete liberty and the richer by one million *taris*, given her by Tancred in compensation for her other losses. It was a generous offer; but Richard was not to be bought off so easily. Coldly rejecting Philip Augustus's well-intended attempts at mediation, on 30 September he set off furiously across the straits to occupy the inoffensive little town of Bagnara on the Calabrian coast. There, in an abbey founded by Count Roger a century before, he settled Joanna under the protection of a strong garrison. Returning to Messina he then fell on the city's own most venerable religious foundation, the Basilian monastery of the Saviour, magnificently sited on the long promontory across the harbour from the town. The monks were forcibly and unceremoniously evicted; and Richard's army moved into its new barracks.

By this time the 'long-tailed Englishmen,' as the Messinans called them, had made themselves thoroughly unpopular. It was many years since any Sicilian city had been called upon to accommodate a foreign army, and the predominantly Greek population of Messina had already been scandalised by their barbarous conduct. Their free and easy ways with the local women, in particular, were not what might have been expected of men who called themselves pilgrims and bore the Cross of Christ on their shoulders. The occupation of the monastery of the Saviour came as the final outrage, and on 3 October serious rioting broke out. Fearing—with good reason— that the King of England might seize the opportunity of taking possession of their city and even, as many maintained, of the whole island, the Messinans rushed to the gates and bolted them; others barred the harbour entrance. Preliminary attempts by the English to force an entry failed; but no one believed that they could be held in check for long. The sun set that evening on an anxious city.

Early the following day Philip Augustus appeared at Richard's headquarters outside the walls. He was accompanied by Hugh, Duke of Burgundy, the Count of Poitiers and the other leaders of the French army, together with a similarly high-ranking Sicilian delegation—the military governor, Jordan du Pin, several notables of the city including Admiral Margaritus, and the archbishops of Monreale, Reggio and of Messina itself; this last none other than Richard Palmer, transferred from Syracuse some years before. It is unlikely that Palmer's words carried any special weight with the King—who, except in the technical sense, was no more English than any other of those present and scarcely even spoke the language—but the ensuing discussions went surprisingly well. The parties seemed on the point of agreement when suddenly the noise of further tumult was heard.

A crowd of Messinans, gathered outside the building, were shouting imprecations against the English and their King.

Richard seized his sword and ran from the hall; summoning his troops, he gave the order for an immediate attack. This time the Messinans were taken by surprise. The English soldiers burst into the city, ravaging and plundering it as they went. Within hours, 'in less time than it took a priest to say matins,'[1] Messina was in flames; only the area around the royal palace, where Philip was quartered, was left undamaged. Margaritus and his fellow-notables narrowly escaped with their lives, leaving their houses in ruins behind them.

All the gold and silver, and whatsoever precious thing was found, became the property of the victors. They set fire to the enemy's galleys and burnt them to ashes, lest any citizens should escape and recover strength to resist. The victors also carried off their noblest women. And lo! when it was done, the French suddenly beheld the ensigns and standards of King Richard floating above the walls of the city; at which the King of France was so mortified that he conceived that hatred against King Richard that lasted all his life.

The author of the *Itinerary of Richard I* goes on to explain how Philip insisted, and Richard finally agreed, that the French banners should be flown alongside the English; he does not mention how the citizens of Messina felt about this new insult to their pride. And there were further humiliations in store for them. Not only did Richard demand hostages as a guarantee of their future good conduct; he also caused to be built, on a hill just outside the city, an immense castle of wood—to which, with typical arrogance, he gave the name Mategrifon, 'curb on the Greeks'. Just whom, the Messinans must have asked themselves, was the King of England supposed to be fighting? Did he intend to remain indefinitely in Sicily? It seemed a curious way to conduct a Crusade.

To Philip Augustus, the incident over the flags seemed to confirm his worst suspicions. Within a fortnight of his arrival as an honoured guest, Richard was in undisputed control of the second city of the

---

[1] *Plus tost eurent il pris Meschines*
C'uns prestres n'ad dit ses matines.
            Estoire de la Guerre Sainte

island; and the King of Sicily, though not far distant at Catania, had made not the slightest effort to oppose him. To Catania therefore Philip now despatched his cousin the Duke of Burgundy, charging him to warn Tancred of the gravity of the situation and to offer the support of the French army if Richard were to press his claims any further.

Tancred needed no warning—from the French King or from anyone else. He was well aware of the danger of leaving Messina in Richard's hands. But a new idea was now taking shape in his brain. He had the long-term future to consider, and he knew that in the final reckoning Henry of Hohenstaufen was a greater menace than Richard would ever be. Sooner or later Henry would invade, and when he did he would find plenty of support in Apulia and elsewhere. If Tancred were to resist him successfully he too would need allies; and for this purpose the English would be preferable to the French. Crude and uncivilised they might be—and their King, for all his glamorous reputation, was as bad as any of them; but Richard with his Welf connections—his sister Matilda had married Henry the Lion of Saxony—had no love for the Hohenstaufen. Philip, on the other hand, had been on excellent terms with Frederick Barbarossa; if the Germans were to invade now, while the Crusaders were still in Sicily, French sympathies would be to say the least uncertain. Tancred therefore returned the Duke of Burgundy to his master with suitably lavish presents but not much else, and sent his own most trusted envoy—Richard, the elder son of old Matthew of Ajello— to negotiate direct with the King of England at Messina.

This time the financial inducements offered were more than the King could resist. Tancred could not return to Joanna her county of Monte S. Angelo; its position on his north-east frontier was of too much stategic importance at such a moment. But he was prepared to grant her twenty thousand ounces of gold in compensation, over and above the million *taris* she had already received, while to her brother he offered another twenty thousand in lieu of the lost legacy. It was further agreed that Richard's nephew and heir, the three-year-old Duke Arthur of Brittany, should forthwith be betrothed to one of Tancred's daughters. In return Richard promised to give the King of Sicily full military assistance for as long as he and his men should remain within the Kingdom, and undertook to restore to its rightful owners all the plunder he had taken during the disturbances of the previous month. On 11 November, with due ceremony, the resulting treaty was signed at Messina.

The reaction of Philip Augustus to this sudden *rapprochement* between his two fellow-monarchs can well be imagined. As usual, however, he concealed his resentment. Outwardly his relations with Richard remained cordial. The two of them had plenty to discuss before they set off again. Rules of conduct must be drawn up for soldiers and pilgrims alike; there were endless logistical problems still unsolved; it was vital, too, that they should reach agreement in advance about the distribution of conquests and the division of spoils. On all these matters Richard proved surprisingly amenable; on one point only, unconnected with the Crusade, did he refuse to be moved. It concerned the French King's sister Alice, who had been sent to England more than twenty years before as a bride for one of Henry II's sons. She had been offered to Richard who, predictably, would have nothing to do with her; but instead of returning her to France Henry had kept her at his court, later making her his own mistress and, almost certainly, the mother of his child. Now Henry was dead and Alice, at thirty, was still in England and as far away from marriage as ever.

Philip was in no way concerned for her happiness; he had never lifted a finger to help his other, even more pathetic sister Agnes-Anna of Byzantium, twice widowed in hideous circumstances before she was sixteen. But this treatment of a Princess of France was an insult which he could not allow to pass. He found Richard just as adamant as Henry had been. Not only did he refuse once again, point-blank, to consider marrying Alice himself; he had the effrontery to try to justify his attitude on the grounds of her besmirched reputation. Here indeed was a test of Philip's *sang-froid*; and when Richard went on to inform him that his mother Eleanor was at that very moment on her way to Sicily with another bride, the Princess Berengaria of Navarre, relations between the two monarchs came near breaking point. It was probably more to keep up appearances than for any other reason that Philip accepted Richard's invitation to the great banquet at Mategrifon that was held on

Christmas Day; but he may have been consoled by the reflection that most of the Sicilian notables also present had had a similar struggle with their consciences.

On 3 March 1191 the King of England rode down in state to Catania to call on the King of Sicily. The two reaffirmed their friendship and exchanged presents—five galleys and four horse transports for Richard who, according to at least two authorities, gave Tancred in return a still more precious token of his affection— King Arthur's own sword, Excalibur itself, which had been found, only a few weeks before, lying beside the old King's body at Glastonbury.[1] The meeting over, the two returned together as far as Taormina, where a disgruntled Philip was waiting. A new crisis was narrowly averted when Tancred, for reasons which can only be guessed, showed Richard the letters he had been sent by the King of France the previous October, warning him of English machinations; but by the end of the month the allies were again reconciled and relations seem to have been comparatively cordial all round when, on 30 March, Philip sailed with his army for Palestine.

He had timed his departure well; or, perhaps more likely, it was Eleanor and Berengaria who had timed their arrival. Scarcely had the French fleet disappeared over the horizon when their own convoy dropped anchor in the harbour. It was forty-four years since the old Queen had last seen Sicily, calling on Roger II at Palermo on her journey from the Holy Land. On this second visit she had hoped to witness the marriage of her favourite son to the wife she had chosen for him; but Lent had begun, and a Lenten marriage was out of the question. Despite a recent prohibition of women from going on the Crusade, it was therefore decided that Berengaria should accompany her future husband to the East. Young Queen Joanna, who could obviously not be left in the island, would make a perfect

---

[1] *Le ray Richard saunz plus à ly a redonez*
La meyllur espeye ke unkes fu forgez.
Ço fu Kaliburne, dount Arthur le senez
Sei solait guyer en gueres et en mellez.

So writes Peter of Langtoft in his curious brand of Yorkshire French, echoing Roger of Hoveden a century earlier. But since the so-called grave of Arthur was discovered only at the beginning of 1191, Excalibur would have needed all its magic properties to reach Sicily by early March.

chaperon for her. Once everything was settled, Eleanor saw no reason to delay any longer. After only three days in Messina, with that energy for which she was famous all over Europe—she was now sixty-nine and had been travelling uninterruptedly for over three months—she left again for England.

The day after bidding her mother goodbye for the last time, Joanna herself set off with Berengaria for the Holy Land. Richard had put at their disposal one of his heavy *dromons*; it was slower than a galley but a good deal more comfortable, and it had plenty of room for the ladies' attendants and their enormous quantities of baggage. He himself remained another week, organising the embarkation of his army and the demolition of Mategrifon. Finally, on 10 April, he too sailed away. The Messinans cannot have been sorry to see the last of him.

But their King did not share their relief. Certainly Sicily might be a happier and more peaceful place without Richard's turbulent presence—but only for as long as Henry of Hohenstaufen delayed his invasion. Had Richard been able to stay a little longer, his help would have been invaluable, perhaps even decisive. He could not be blamed for leaving when he did; his presence was urgently needed in Palestine—where, four years after Hattin, the situation was now desperate—and his crusading oath took precedence over all other commitments. None the less, his departure shattered Tancred's greatest single hope of saving his country from the imperial clutches. Now, when the crisis came, he would have to face it alone. He could not know that that crisis was less than three weeks away.

21

NIGHTFALL

O Singer of Persephone!
In the dim meadows desolate
Dost thou remember Sicily?

Wilde, Theocritus

IF Henry of Hohenstaufen had been able to follow his original plan of campaign, he would have left Germany in November 1190 and almost certainly arrived in Sicily before the departure of the English troops. His failure to do so was principally due to a report that reached him just as he was setting out. On 10 June his father, Frederick Barbarossa, after a long and arduous journey across Anatolia, had led his army out of the last of the Taurus valleys and on to the flat coastal plain. The heat was sweltering and the little river Calycadnus[1] that ran past the town of Seleucia to the sea must have been a welcome sight. Frederick spurred his horse towards it, leaving his men to follow. He was never seen alive again. Whether he dismounted to drink and was swept off his feet by the current, whether his horse slipped in the mud and threw him, whether the shock of falling into the icy mountain water was too much for his tired old body—he was nearing seventy—remains unknown. He was rescued, but too late. The bulk of his army reached the river to find their Emperor lying dead on the bank.

His son Henry, with two crowns to claim instead of one, was still more anxious to leave for the South as soon as possible. Internal problems following his father's death kept him occupied for some weeks; fortunately the winter was mild, the Alpine passes still open.

[1] In modern Turkish Seleucia has become Silifke, while the Calycadnus is now less euphoniously known as the Göksu.

By January he and his army were safely across. Then, after a month spent strengthening his position in Lombardy and securing the assistance of a fleet from Pisa, he headed towards Rome where Pope Clement III was expecting him.

But before Henry could reach the city Pope Clement was dead. Hurriedly—for the imperial troops were fast approaching—the Sacred College met in conclave and selected as his successor the Cardinal-deacon of S. Maria in Cosmedin, Hyacinthus Bobo. It seemed, in the circumstances, a curious choice. The new Pope was of illustrious birth—his brother Ursus was founder of the Orsini family—and could boast a long and distinguished ecclesiastical record, having stoutly defended Peter Abelard against St Bernard at Sens more than fifty years before. But he was now eighty-five—hardly, one might have thought, the man to handle the overbearing young Henry during a crisis that threatened the position of the Church almost as much as it did that of the Kingdom of Sicily. There is every indication that he shared this view himself; only the proximity of the German army, together with widespread fears of another schism if there were any delay in the election, at length persuaded him to accept the tiara. A cardinal since 1144, it was only on Holy Saturday, 13 April 1191, that he was ordained priest; on the following day, Easter Sunday, he was enthroned at St Peter's as Pope Celestine III; and on the 15th, as the first formal action of his pontificate, he crowned Henry and Constance Emperor and Empress of the West.

With his experience of half a century in the papal service, no one knew better than Celestine the dangers of allowing the Empire to annex the Kingdom of Sicily. In the circumstances, however, he could hardly insist on an undertaking from the new Emperor to advance no further to the south; and such attempts as he did make to dissuade Henry from pursuing his plans were, as might have been expected, poorly received. On 29 April, just a fortnight after his coronation—*papa prohibente et contradicente* as Richard of S. Germano puts it—Barbarossa's son led his army across the Garigliano and into Sicilian territory.

Within the limits of his possibilities, Tancred was ready for him. The defection of so many of his mainland vassals had prevented him from raising an army capable of defeating the imperial forces in the field; he therefore wisely concentrated on building up his defences in those areas on whose support he could rely—in Sicily itself, in his own territory around the heel of Apulia and, above all, in the larger towns on both sides of the peninsula where the bourgeoisie, republican as they might be, far preferred a King to an Emperor and readily accepted the privileges, charters and indemnities he promised them. Meanwhile he sent Richard of Acerra north, at the head of as large a force as he could muster, to stiffen local resistance.

At first Richard made little progress. He probably knew that any attempt to secure the loyalties of the lands along the northern frontier would be doomed to failure and, like Tancred, focused his energies where he felt they would be most effective. Thus, in the first weeks of the invasion, Henry carried all before him. One town after another opened its gates; more and more of the local barons joined the imperial ranks. From Monte Cassino to Venafro, thence to Teano—nowhere was there a sign of opposition. Even Capua, once the most jealously independent of the cities of Campania, now welcomed the Germans as they approached, its archbishop giving orders for the Hohenstaufen standard to be hoisted on the ramparts. At Aversa, the first Norman fief in all Italy, it was the same story; Salerno, King Roger's mainland capital, did not even await the arrival of the imperial troops before writing to assure Henry of its loyalty—simultaneously inviting Constance to spend the hot summer months in her father's old palace. Only when the Emperor reached Naples was he brought to a halt.

In the half-century during which it had formed part of the Norman Kingdom, Naples had grown and prospered. It was now a rich trading port numbering some forty thousand inhabitants, including an important Jewish community and commercial colonies from Pisa, Amalfi and Ravello. Recently, to encourage their loyalist sympathies, Tancred had accorded to the Neapolitans a whole series of grants and privileges. Richard of Acerra had therefore wisely selected the city as his headquarters. Its defences were in good order—Tancred had had them repaired the year before at his own expense—its granaries and storehouses full. When the Emperor appeared with his army beneath its walls, the citizens were ready for him.

The ensuing siege was not, from their point of view, a particularly arduous one. Thanks to the incessant harrying of the Pisan ships by the Sicilian fleet under Margaritus, Henry never managed properly to control the harbour approaches, and the defenders continued to receive reinforcements and supplies. On the landward side the walls took a heavy battering; the Count of Acerra was wounded and temporarily replaced as commander by Matthew of Ajello's second son Nicholas, now Archbishop of Salerno, who had deliberately left his flock a few weeks previously in protest at their disloyalty. But the defences held firm; and it became clear, as the summer dragged on, that it was the besiegers rather than the besieged who were beginning to feel the strain.

Looking back—as we can now do, for the end is near—over the whole chequered history of the Normans in the South, we might well be forgiven for seeing it as an almost unrelieved saga of treachery and betrayal. Only one of their allies had never let them down: the heat of the southern summer. Again and again it had saved them from successive waves of imperial invaders, from that distant day in 1022 when Henry the Holy had withdrawn in despair from the siege of Troia to now, the best part of two centuries later, when his namesake, seeing his forces decimated by malaria, dysentery and wholesale defections and eventually himself falling seriously ill, recognised that he too must turn his army homeward while there was still time.

It was on 24 August that Henry gave the order to raise the siege of Naples, and within a day or two the imperial host, still impressive but now noticeably smaller and slower than it had been a few weeks before, had trailed off northward over the hills. The Neapolitans watched them go with satisfaction. They knew, however, that to Henry this withdrawal was nothing more than an irritating reverse; it meant delay, but not defeat. He had posted imperial garrisons in all the most important towns and cities and, in order that there should be no possible doubts about his future intentions, had arranged to leave Constance in Salerno till his return.

Here, however, he made a serious mistake. He did not understand the temper of the South, and it obviously never struck him that news of his retreat, combined with fears of Tancred's vengeance at their disloyalty, would, within days of his own departure, reduce the Salernitans to panic. In their frantic search for a scapegoat, a Salernitan mob attacked the palace in which Constance was staying and would probably have killed her had not Tancred's nephew, a certain Elias of Gesualdo, appeared on the scene just in time and taken her into protective custody, sending her on at the earliest opportunity to the King in Messina.

To Tancred the capture of the Empress must have seemed like a godsend. He had been much heartened by the news of Henry's departure, but he knew that the battle was still scarcely joined. Henry might have found the going harder than he had expected, but his army had not been routed—it had not even been opposed in the open field—and much of northern Campania, including Monte Cassino, remained under his control. The first round, though less disastrous than Tancred had feared, could at best be said to have ended in a draw; and prospects for the second were not particularly bright.

Not, at least, until Constance appeared. But now the situation was suddenly altered; the most valuable diplomatic hostage that Tancred could ever have hoped for had fallen into his lap. No longer was he obliged to wait in impotent suspense till Henry should choose to invade his territory again: he was in a position to negotiate. Meanwhile, as a further encouragement to him, Pope Celestine was showing unmistakable signs of friendship. Even while the siege of Naples was still in progress, the Pope had gone behind the Emperor's back and negotiated with Henry the Lion; and four months later, in December, he excommunicated the whole monastery of Monte Cassino as a punishment for having espoused the imperial cause. Monte Cassino still maintained its opposition to Tancred, but there could no longer be any question where the Pope's own sympathies lay.

Sympathy, however, did not mean endorsement. To any pope, too powerful a Sicily was every bit as dangerous as too powerful an Empire. Safety, as always, lay in holding the balance between them. What was required was mediation; and if in the course of that mediation the Pope were to incline towards the Sicilian point of view, he saw no reason why he should not extract concessions in return.

Tancred's popular support was reduced, in particular, by his still shaky legal position; a papal investiture confirming his right to the crown would be of immense value to his cause—if he were prepared to pay for it.

Which of the two took the initiative, and when, is no longer known; but discussions through intermediaries must have been going on during the spring and summer of 1192 for when Tancred, fresh from a successful punitive expedition against his rebellious vassals in the Abruzzi, met the papal envoys at Gravina in June, the main terms of a treaty had already been agreed. They were simple enough in their way, and they obtained for the King the investiture he wanted; but they involved the surrender of all those special rights over the ecclesiastical administration in the island of Sicily that had been secured with such difficulty by Roger I and II and re-negotiated by William the Bad at Benevento in 1156.[1] Henceforth the Sicilian clergy would be entitled, in just the same way as their main-land brethren, to appeal to Rome in cases of supposed injustice. The Pope might send his special envoys to Sicily whenever he liked and not only when the King asked for them. Elections to the hier-archy would no longer be subject to royal approval.

Seeing the Latin Church in Sicily placed, for the first time in its history, under full papal control, Pope Celestine could justifiably con-gratulate himself on a diplomatic *coup* of some magnitude. It was not often that Popes had got the better of Normans in negotiations of that sort. Tancred, however, had not been disposed to argue. He had his back to the wall. The privileges he had surrendered seemed to belong to a happier and more spacious age; they were a small enough price to pay for legitimacy.

But, though he did not yet know it, he had also lost something else—something far more valuable to him at that moment than any number of ecclesiastical sanctions. Pope Celestine, undeterred by Henry's reception of his last proposals, still cherished the hope that one day, through his mediation, King and Emperor might be reconciled; and he had therefore pressed Tancred as a gesture of goodwill to deliver Constance into his care. Chalandon, with un-accustomed heat, condemns the Pope's advice as *détestable*; it was

[1] See pp. 557–9.

certainly ill-conceived, and its effect was disastrous. Tancred, not wishing to antagonise the Pope at such a time, reluctantly complied. The Empress was entrusted to a special escort that included several cardinals, and set off for Rome.

Had she gone by sea, all might have been well; but the land route passed through territory still under Henry's control, and the inevitable happened. When the party reached the frontier at Ceprano it ran into a group of imperial knights. Constance at once placed herself under their protection. The cardinals objected, but were ignored. They returned empty-handed to Rome while the Empress, carefully avoiding the city, hastened back over the Alps to her husband.

Tancred had been robbed of his trump card. He was not to be dealt another.

During the last weeks of 1192 Joanna Plantagenet called at Palermo on her way back from Palestine—accompanied by her sister-in-law Berengaria, now Queen of England since her marriage to Richard at Limassol in Cyprus some eighteen months before. The fact that she chose to do so suggests that, whatever her brother may have pretended, she had not been too badly treated by Tancred after her husband's death; she certainly bore him no grudge, and Tancred and his wife Sibylla gave the two young queens a suitably royal welcome. A week or two later they sailed on again, Berengaria to welcome widowhood in France, Joanna towards a second marriage.[1] She seems to have been delighted with her reception, in a Palermo that must have appeared outwardly unchanged from the days when she and her godlike young husband had reigned over Norman Sicily at its loveliest and most peaceful. One hopes that she understood how fortunate she was to have known it at such a time—or even to have found, on her return, her old realm still in existence at all.

[1] She had had a narrow escape in Palestine when Richard, for reasons more diplomatic than humane, had tried to marry her off to Saladin's brother al-Adil. Her second husband was in fact to prove much more to her taste—Count Raymond VI of Toulouse, whom she was to marry as his fourth wife in 1196. They were happy together, but not for long. Three years later, when still not quite thirty-four, Joanna died in childbirth, having been received on her death-bed into the religious order of Fontevrault—where she lies buried, with her father, mother and brother.

For if, that summer, Henry VI had led a second expedition to the South as he had intended to do, better equipped than its predecessor and provided with adequate naval support, it is unlikely that Tancred, even with the help of Margaritus and his fleet, would have been able to hold out. The long peace that had marked the reign and made the reputation of William the Good was now over; after twenty-five years anarchy had returned; already the mainland had lapsed once again into chaos. Not a road was safe, scarcely a baron could be trusted; in such conditions organised resistance to an invader was well-nigh impossible. But Henry had not marched. The Welfs, transparently supported by Pope Celestine, were making too much trouble for him at home. The best he had been able to do was to send a relatively meagre force under Berthold of Künsberg to hold the situation until conditions became more favourable to his purpose. Norman Sicily was granted a stay of execution.

But it was still fighting for its life. Though Tancred had spent nine months continuously on campaign up and down the peninsula, he had returned to Sicily in the autumn with little to show for his efforts and more convinced than ever that without active help from abroad the days of his Kingdom were numbered. Much of the winter he spent concluding negotiations with the Byzantine Emperor Isaac Angelus, as a result of which he was soon able to announce the betrothal of his elder son Roger—whom he had duly created Duke of Apulia some time before—to the Emperor's daughter Irene.

The wedding was celebrated the following spring, at Brindisi. It served little practical purpose. Isaac could provide the King of Sicily with a daughter-in-law, but he was too busy with his own troubles to furnish anything else. Duke Roger was dead by the end of the year; his young wife was left, disconsolate and alone, in Palermo. Meanwhile King Richard of England, who might otherwise have been ready to help, had been captured by one of Henry's vassals on his return journey from Palestine and was now languishing in a German castle. Sicily's only ally remained Pope Celestine; but the Pope was hamstrung by an openly imperialist Roman Senate, and had no army. He was also eighty-seven.

Tancred fought on alone. Still there was no sign of the Emperor, but even without him the situation was deteriorating; the royalist troops might recapture a few towns and castles here and there, but they could make no real headway. Monte Cassino in particular proved as impregnable as it always had, still shamelessly flying the imperial standard from its tower. Then, in the late summer, Tancred fell ill. He continued as long as he could, but the sickness increased until he was forced to return to Sicily. All winter long he lay in Palermo, growing steadily weaker; and on 20 February 1194 he died.

Now there was no hope left. With Tancred of Lecce Sicily had lost her last effective champion. Of all the Norman kings, he was the most selfless and the most tragic. In happier times he would never have sought the crown; nor, when it was thrust upon him, did he ever have an opportunity to savour the delights of kingship. His four years on the throne were years of unremitting strife—against the Empire above all, but also against his fellow-Sicilians, Christian and Muslim, who were too egotistical or too blind to understand the enormity of the crisis that faced them. Seeing it himself with such terrible clarity, he strove to turn it aside by every means within his power, military and diplomatic, overt and clandestine. Had he lived, he might even have succeeded—though the odds were heavily against him. Dying as he did in early middle age, he is remembered in Sicily—when he is remembered at all—as a mediocrity and a failure, or even as the misshapen ogre of the imperial propagandists. It is an unfair judgment. Tancred lacked, perhaps, the greatness of his proudest forbears; but with his persistence, his courage and—most of all—his political vision, he surely proved himself a not unworthy successor.

To the ever-superstitious subjects of the crumbling Kingdom, the deaths of both King Tancred and his heir within a few weeks of each other seemed yet another sign from heaven that the Hautevilles had run their race and that Henry of Hohenstaufen must now prevail. The fact that Tancred's only other son, William, was still a child and that Sicily, at the time of her greatest trial, was once more to be entrusted to the care of a woman Regent appeared only additional, unnecessary confirmation of the divine will. The dark clouds of defeatism that had long been gathering over the *Regno* now spread to

the capital itself as Queen Sibylla, still in the first paralysing numb-
ness of her widowhood, took the reins of government into her tired,
reluctant hands.

She had no illusions. To her as to her husband, the crown had
never been anything but a burden, and she knew as well as anyone
that the task before her was impossible. If Tancred with all his energy
and courage had ultimately failed to unite his people against the
oncoming menace, how could she and her little son hope to succeed?
She herself was without political ability or understanding; the one
adviser on whom she might have relied, old Matthew of Ajello, had
died the previous year. His two sons, Richard and Nicholas, the latter
now Archbishop of Salerno, remained loyal and capable enough in
their way; but neither could hope to match the experience or prestige
of their father. Her third chief adviser was Archbishop Bartholomew
of Palermo, brother and successor of Walter of the Mill. She did not
trust him, and she was almost certainly right. All she could do was to
wait for the blow to fall—and, meanwhile, to try to keep her head.

She did not have long to wait. Henry VI, his domestic problems
settled, was now once again directing all his energies towards the
conquest of Sicily. He was not in any particular hurry; time was on
his side, and there was no point in risking any repetition of the
Naples disaster of three years before. Then he had been let down by
inadequate naval support; thanks to Margaritus, the Pisan fleet had
been rendered useless and the Genoese, arriving only after the
imperial retreat had begun, had narrowly escaped total destruction.
This time he would be properly prepared. Margaritus would find
himself faced not only by Pisans and Genoese, but by fifty fully-
equipped galleys from the one source, perhaps, that he least expected
—King Richard of England.

It was not really Richard's fault; he had had little choice. On 4
February 1194—less than two and a half weeks before Tancred's
death—he had at last obtained his release from captivity; but Henry
had made him pay dearly for his freedom. To the original ransom
figure of a hundred thousand silver marks he had added another fifty
thousand, to be used specifically for the Sicilian expedition, together
with the fifty galleys and the services of two hundred knights for not
less than a year. As a final piece of gratuitous humiliation, the

743

Emperor had forced his prisoner to do homage to him for the Kingdom of England itself.

For the moment, however, it was the ships that mattered. Henry expected little serious opposition from Tancred's army—and none at all in Campania where his garrisons, aided by the reinforcements brought in by Berthold of Künsberg, had been steadily extending their authority since Tancred's death. Everything depended on his power at sea. Towards the end of May he crossed the Splügen pass into Italy and spent Whitsun in Milan. A week or two later he was in Genoa and then in Pisa, making sure of his ships and planning every detail of the coming campaign. The dates were fixed; and on 23 August the combined fleets under the overall command of the Steward of the Empire, Markward of Anweiler, appeared in the bay of Naples. They found the city open to them. The Neapolitans, who only three years before had defied the imperial army to do its worst and had soon afterwards triumphantly watched it go limping back to Germany, had this time capitulated even before the enemy had arrived. With Tancred's death, the last remaining shreds of South Italian morale were gone.

Henry did not even bother to stop at Naples. He went straight on to Salerno, where he had an old score to settle. Three years before, the Salernitans had betrayed him. They had made their submission, had offered his wife their hospitality and then, at the first reports of an imperial retreat, had turned against her and delivered her up to her enemies. The Emperor was not the man to let such treachery go unpunished. Fear of his vengeance, rather than courage or feelings of loyalty towards their King, at first led the Salernitans to resist, but they could not do so for long. Their city was taken by storm and given over to merciless pillage. Such of the population as escaped massacre had their property confiscated and were sent into exile. The walls were reduced to rubble; by then there was little left for them to enclose.

If any example was necessary of the treatment to be expected by towns that sought to resist the German advance, Salerno provided it. With two heroic exceptions—Spinazzola and Policoro—which suffered a similar fate, Henry's authority was accepted everywhere without question. His ensuing march through the South was less of a campaign than a triumphal progress; even the cities of Apulia, long the focus of anti-imperial feeling, accepted the inevitable, Siponto, Trani, Barletta, Bari, Giovinazzo and Molfetta, each in turn opened its gates to the conqueror. In Calabria it was the same story. At the end of October Henry VI, now master of the mainland, crossed the straits of Messina. For the first time in well over a century, a hostile invading army was encamped on Sicilian soil.

The navy had arrived several weeks earlier, and the Emperor disembarked to find Messina already an occupied city. So too—despite serious differences between the Pisans and Genoese which were resolved only after a full-scale naval battle fought by their respective fleets—were Catania and Syracuse. Everywhere, the central administration was breaking down; the island was in a state of growing confusion. Once Henry had established his bridgeheads, it was clear that no real opposition could be organised against him. Queen Sibylla did her best; whatever her other faults, she did not lack courage. The boy King and his three small sisters she sent off to comparative safety in the fortress of Caltabellotta,[1] near Sciacca on the south-west coast; then she attempted to rally a last-ditch resistance. It was no use. The citadel overlooking the port was commanded by Margaritus; he too was eager to hold out till the end. But the fatalism that had paralysed the capital had now spread to the garrison. They laid down their arms. Margaritus could not continue the struggle single-handed. While the Queen Regent, seeing that her cause was lost, fled with the Archbishop of Palermo and his brother to join her children at Caltabellotta, he remained to negotiate the final surrender.

Henry, meanwhile, advanced on Palermo. A few miles outside the walls, at Favara, he was received by a group of leading citizens to assure him of the city's submission and future fidelity.[2] In return he issued strict orders, immediately relayed throughout the army, that there should be no pillage or licentiousness. Palermo was his king-

---

[1] A single tower of this castle—where, incidentally, the peace was signed in 1302 that brought to an end the war of the Sicilian Vespers—still rises from a pinnacle above the town, commanding one of the most stunning views in all Sicily. Below, the Chiesa Madre is also worth a visit; it was erected by Count Roger I when he captured Caltabellotta in 1090.

[2] See plate.

dom's capital, and was to be treated as such; at all times the strictest discipline was to be maintained. His promise given, he rode through the gates and made his solemn entry into the city.

Thus, on 20 November 1194, the rule of the Hautevilles in Palermo was brought to an end. It had begun nearly a century and a quarter before, when Robert Guiscard, with his brother Roger and his magnificent wife Sichelgaita riding behind him, had led an exhausted but exultant army into the city. They had fought with tenacity and courage—qualities that had been matched in full measure by the defenders; and in the soldierly admiration felt by each side for a worthy adversary was born the mutual respect and understanding that lay at the root of the Norman-Sicilian miracle. The result had been the happiest and most glorious chapter of the island's history. Now that chapter was closed—with the surrender of a demoralised people to an invader whom they feared too much to fight and who felt for them, in return, a contempt which he made little effort to conceal.

On Christmas Day, 1194, the Emperor Henry VI of Hohenstaufen was crowned King of Sicily in Palermo Cathedral. In places of honour before him, to witness his triumph and their own humiliation, sat Sibylla and her children, among them the sad little William III, who after a ten-month reign, was now King no longer. So far, they had been treated well. Instead of attacking Caltabellotta—which he could have quickly subdued—Henry had offered them reasonable, even generous, terms, under which William was to receive not only his father's county of Lecce but also the principality of Taranto. Sibylla had accepted, and had returned with her family to the capital. Now, as she watched the crown of Sicily—that crown that had brought so much misery to her husband, her son and herself during the past five years—slowly lowered on to Henry's head, it is hard to imagine her feeling any emotion but that of profound relief.

If so, however, it was premature—and short-lived. Four days later, the atmosphere suddenly changed. A conspiracy to assassinate the Emperor had, it was claimed, been uncovered in the nick of time. Sibylla, her children and a large number of leading Sicilians who had been summoned to Palermo for the coronation—among them

Margaritus of Brindisi, Archbishop Nicholas of Salerno and his brother Richard, Counts Roger of Avellino and Richard of Acerra, even Princess Irene, the bewildered Byzantine widow of the last Duke of Apulia—were accused of complicity in the plot, and sent off under close guard to captivity in Germany.

How much truth, if any, was there in these charges? Several chroniclers, particularly those writing in Italy such as Richard of S. Germano, categorically deny that there was ever a plot at all; for them the whole story was merely a pretext by which Henry could rid his new kingdom of all undesirable and potentially subversive elements. The idea is not impossible; no one who has followed the course of the Emperor's stormy career can doubt that he would have been fully capable of such conduct had it suited him. But if not out of character with Henry himself, it still runs contrary to the whole policy which we find him pursuing towards his new kingdom. Everywhere except in Salerno—where he had good reason for resentment —we find him in a merciful and conciliatory mood, a phenomenon rare enough, where he was concerned, to be in itself remarkable; and it is unlikely that he would have switched overnight from conciliation to repression without good reason. What is in the highest degree improbable is that, given the unpopularity of the Germans and the Sicilian *penchant* for intrigue, the possibility of a *coup d'état* was never at this time considered. If one was actually planned, several of those arrested would certainly have been involved, or at any rate aware of what was going on. They were lucky in that case to escape a more unpleasant punishment.

Or some of them were. Others proved less fortunate than they had supposed. Two or three years later, following further insurrections in Sicily and on the mainland, many of these prisoners were blinded by order of the Emperor—despite the fact that having been in captivity since 1194 they could have played no part in the more recent disturbances. By then, with the whole Kingdom trembling under a reign of terror more violent than anything known under the Normans, few of its subjects can have cherished any illusions about the disaster that had befallen them.

But the story of Sicily after the Hautevilles are gone has no part in this book. It remains only to record the fate, in so far as we know it, of the last pale representatives of that extraordinary clan that had burst forth so dazzlingly across three continents, only to peter out in less than two centuries with the spectacle of a sad, frightened woman and her children. Sibylla, after five years or so of tolerable captivity with her three daughters in the convent of Hohenburg in Alsace, was eventually released to live out her remaining days in the obscurity she should never have left. Her daughter-in-law Irene, on the other hand, had a very different future awaiting her. In May 1197 she married Henry's brother, Philip of Swabia, and the following year became in her turn Empress of the West.

As for William III himself, his end remains a mystery. According to one theory he too was blinded and castrated in a German prison by order of Henry VI; another story—which does not necessarily contradict the first—relates that he was set free and became a monk. The only fact of which we can be reasonably sure is that, captive or cloistered, he did not long survive. Before the turn of the century he was dead, still hardly out of his boyhood—but the time and place of his death are unrecorded.

And what, finally, of Constance? We have heard nothing of her since her escape from the papal escort and her hasty return to Germany in 1191. She—through no fault of her own—was the cause of her country's suffering, the ultimate justification for her husband's seizure of the Sicilian throne. Theoretically, where Sicily was concerned, she was the true monarch; Henry was merely her consort. Many people must have wondered why, when he invaded the Kingdom for the second time in the summer of 1194, his wife was no longer at his side; or why, on Christmas Day in Palermo, it was Henry alone who knelt at the altar for his coronation.

But there was a reason, and a good one. At the age of forty, and after nearly nine years of marriage, Constance was expecting a child. She did not put off her journey to Sicily on that account; but she travelled more slowly and in her own time, starting out a month or two after her husband and moving by easy stages down the peninsula. Even so, for a woman of her age and in her condition, it was a dangerous undertaking. The days and weeks of being shaken and jolted over the rough tracks of Lombardy and the Marches took their toll; and when she reached the little town of Jesi, not far from Ancona, she felt the pains of childbirth upon her.

Ever since the beginning of her pregnancy, Constance had had one fixed idea. She knew that both her enemies and Henry's, on both sides of the Alps, would do everything they could to discredit the birth, citing her age and the long years of her barrenness to claim that the child she was to bear could not really be hers; and she was determined that on this question at least there should be no possible room for doubt. She therefore had a large tent erected in the market square of Jesi, to which free entrance was allowed to any matron of the town who wished to witness the birth; and on the feast of St Stephen, 26 December, the day after her husband had received the Sicilian crown in Palermo Cathedral, the Empress brought forth her only son. A day or two later she showed herself in public in the same square, proudly suckling the child at her breast. The Hauteville spirit was not quite dead after all.

In the following century it was to appear again, in a new guise but more refulgently than ever, when that son—Frederick—grew to manhood. Though history may remember him as Emperor of the West, he himself never forgot that he was also King of Sicily, the grandson not only of Barbarossa but of Roger II as well. He showed it in the splendour of his court, in his lions and his leopards and his peacocks, in the Italian and Arabic poets he loved, in his classicising architecture and his Apulian hunting-lodges, and above all in that insatiable artistic and intellectual curiosity that was to make him the first of Renaissance princes two hundred years before his time, earning him the appellation of *Stupor Mundi,* the Wonder of the World. He showed it too in 1215, when he brought to Palermo the two huge porphyry sarcophagi that his grandfather had installed seventy years before at Cefalù.

Two other sarcophagi, of similar material but vastly inferior quality, already stood in Walter of the Mill's cathedral. One was that of Roger II, specially prepared for him in the capital when he had been denied burial in his own foundation;[1] the other was that which Constance had had made for her husband after his sudden death at Messina in 1197. This latter receptacle, however, was of poor

[1] See pp. 520–1.

workmanship—closer inspection shows it to have been glued together from fourteen separate parts—and Frederick seems to have thought it unworthy of his father. He therefore transferred Henry's corpse, still overlaid by the long tresses of fair hair cut off by his widow in her grief, to one of those from Cefalù, replacing it with the body of Constance, who had survived her husband by little more than a year; the fourth sarcophagus—that which Roger had originally intended for his own remains—Frederick kept for himself.[1] In it he was duly laid after his death in 1250; but he was not long to retain sole occupancy. In the fourteenth century the tomb was opened to receive two more bodies—those of the feeble-minded Peter II of Aragon and an unknown woman.

Father, daughter, son-in-law, grandson—a natural enough group, one might think, for a family burial. And yet, in those massive sepulchres, silent under their canopies of marble and mosaic, the four lie uneasily together—the architect of the Norman Kingdom and its destroyer, the unwilling cause of the collapse and its ultimate beneficiary. Nor do any of them really belong. Henry, by the time he died at the age of thirty-two, was detested and feared throughout Sicily; Constance was seen—unfairly but understandably—as having betrayed her homeland. Roger, to be sure, was loved; but he belongs at Cefalù, where he had always wished to lie and where the setting is worthy of him. Even Frederick, who was only twenty when he ordered his tomb, would probably have later preferred a different resting-place—in Capua perhaps, or Jerusalem, or, best of all, on some lonely hilltop under the wide Apulian sky. But Frederick's story, superb and tragic as it is, belongs elsewhere; ours is done.

Sixty-four years is a short life for a kingdom; and indeed Sicily might have been saved had William II—his sobriquet is better forgotten—shown himself either sensible or fertile. Instead, to serve the interests of a vain, aggressive ambition, he made a present of it to its oldest and most persistent enemy—an enemy against whom every one of his predecessors from the days of Robert Guiscard onwards had successively fought to defend it. Thus, when the

---

[1] Such, at least, are the conclusions drawn, after brilliant detective work, by J. Déer. (*The Dynastic Porphyry Tombs of the Norman Period in Sicily.*)

Kingdom fell, it was not even properly defeated; it was thrown away.

And yet, even if Henry VI had never marched to claim his inheritance, it could not have lasted for long. A monarchy so absolute, so centralised, as that created by the two Rogers must depend for its survival on the personality of the monarch; and the decline of the Kingdom only reflects the decline of the Hautevilles themselves. As each generation gave way to the next, it was as though the cold Norman steel were slowly softening, the rich Norman blood growing thinner and more sluggish under the Sicilian sun. At last, with Tancred, saved by his bastardy from the oriental effeteness of the court at Palermo, the old vigour returned. But it was too late. Sicily was lost.

Perhaps, from the start, it carried within itself the seeds of its own destruction. It was too heterogeneous, too eclectic, too cosmopolitan. It failed—indeed, it hardly tried—to develop any national traditions of its own. Patriotism is an overrated and potentially dangerous emotion, but it is indispensable to a nation fighting for its life; and when the crisis came, there was not enough of it to carry the Kingdom through. Norman and Lombard, Greek and Saracen, Italian and Jew —Sicily had proved that for as long as they enjoyed an enlightened and impartial government, they could happily coexist; they could not coalesce.

Yet, if the Kingdom died the victim of its ideals, those ideals were surely worth dying for. Inevitably in the last years, with the slow sickening of the body politic, the status of the religious and racial minorities began to decline. But nations should be judged on their achievements rather than on their lapses, and to the very end Norman Sicily stood forth in Europe—and indeed in the whole bigoted mediaeval world—as an example of tolerance and enlightenment, a lesson in the respect that every man should feel for those whose blood and beliefs happen to differ from his own. Europe, alas, was ungrateful and the Kingdom perished; but not before it had been rewarded by a sunburst of brilliance and beauty that blazes undimmed down the centuries and still speaks its message as clearly as ever. That message is to be read in the Palatine Chapel, when the great Islamic roof seems itself to glow gold with the reflected radiance of Byzantium; in the swell of the five crimson cupolas above the little cloister of St

John of the Hermits; in a little garden outside Castelvetrano, where SS. Trinità di Delia stands lonely and immaculate in the afternoon sun; in the all-embracing Pantocrators of Monreale and Cefalù; and in the swirling Arabic calligraphy of George of Antioch's childhood hymn to the Virgin as it twines mistily round the dome of the Martorana while, far below, Latin fuses with Greek in another, simpler inscription, proud and unadorned: ROGERIOS REX.

GENEALOGICAL TREES

MAPS

APPENDIX: The Norman Monuments of Sicily

BIBLIOGRAPHY

THE HOUSE OF HAUTEVILLE

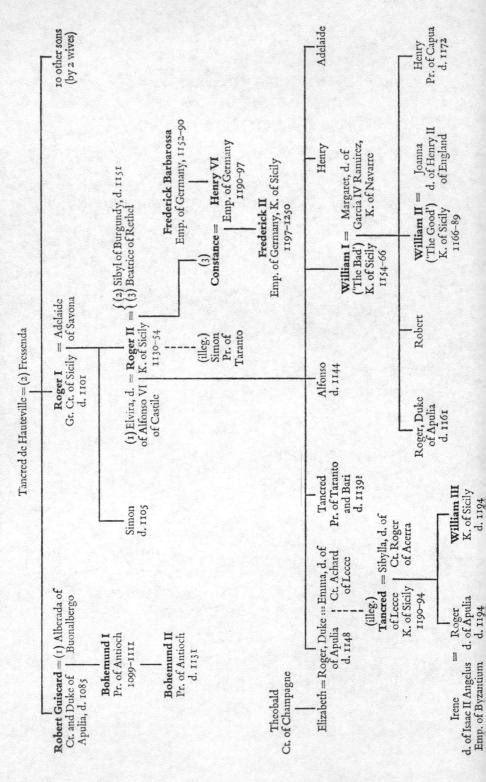

THE HOUSES OF NAVARRE AND PERCHE

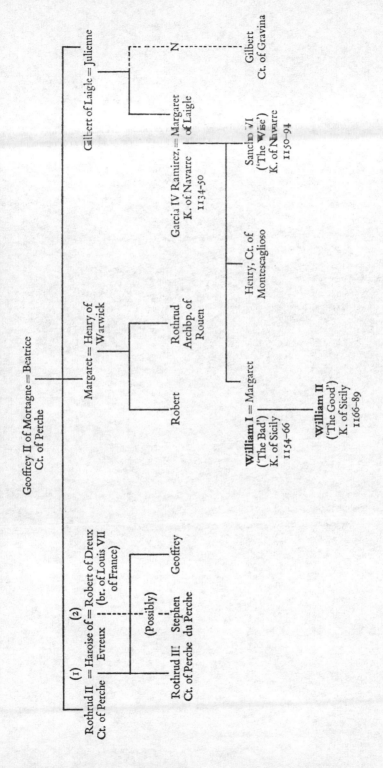

Geoffrey II of Mortagne = Beatrice
Ct. of Perche

(1)   (2)

Rothrud II = Haroise of = Robert of Dreux   Margaret = Henry of   Gilbert of Laigle = Julienne
Ct. of Perche   Evreux   (br. of Louis VII   Warwick
                          of France)

                    (Possibly)   N

Rothrud III Stephen   Geoffrey   Robert   Rothrud   Garcia IV Ramirez, = Margaret   Gilbert
Ct. of Perche du Perche   Archbp. of   K. of Navarre   of Laigle   Ct. of Gravina
                                                 Rouen   1134-50

                                        William I = Margaret   Henry, Ct. of   Sancho VI
                                        ('The Bad')   Montescaglioso   ('The Wise')
                                        K. of Sicily   K. of Navarre
                                        1154-66   1150-94

                                        William II
                                        ('The Good')
                                        K. of Sicily
                                        1166-89

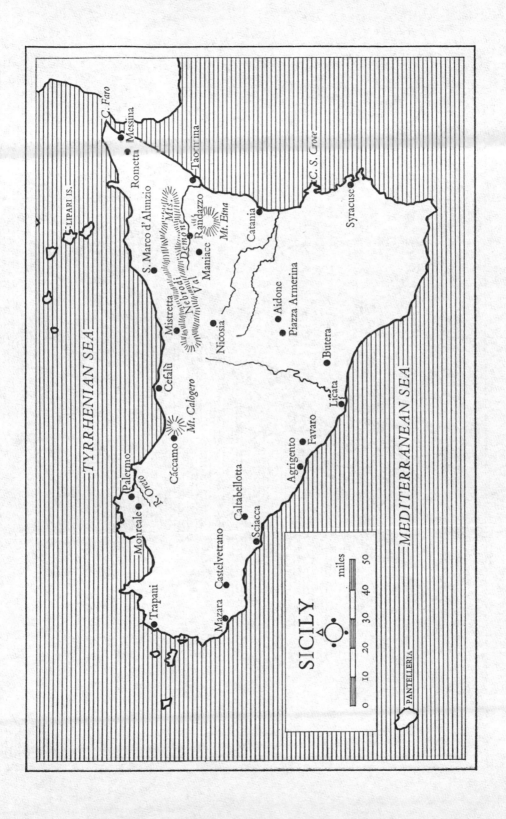

SICILY

miles

0 10 20 30 40 50

TYRRHENIAN SEA

MEDITERRANEAN SEA

LIPARI IS.

C. Faro
Messina
Rometta
Taormina
C. S. Croce
S. Marco d'Alunzio
Mts. Demone
Randazzo
Mt. Etna
Maniace
Catania
Mistretta
Nebrodi
Val
Syracuse
Aidone
Piazza Armerina
Nicosia
Butera
Cefalù
Licata
Mt. Calogero
Cáccamo
Favaro
Agrigento
Palermo
R. Oreto
Monreale
Caltabellotta
Sciacca
Castelvetrano
Mazara
Trapani

PANTELLERIA

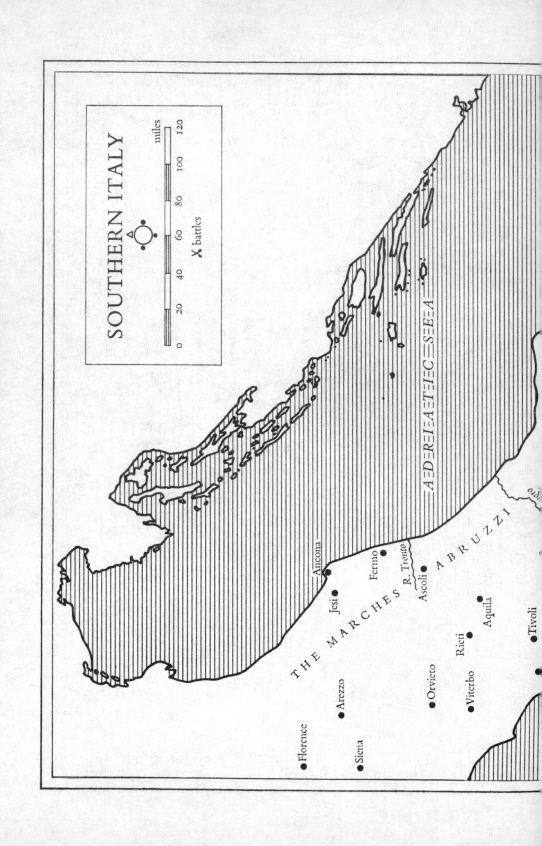

SOUTHERN ITALY

X battles

miles
0   20   40   60   80   100   120

A D R I A T I C   S E A

Ancona

Jesi
Fermo
R. Tronto
Ascoli
ABRUZZI
Aquila
Tivoli

THE MARCHES

Arezzo
Orvieto
Ricti
Viterbo

Florence
Siena

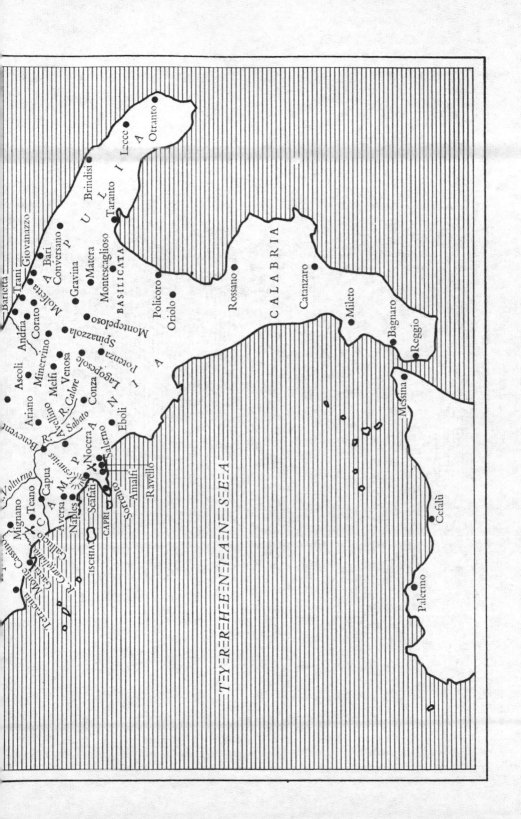

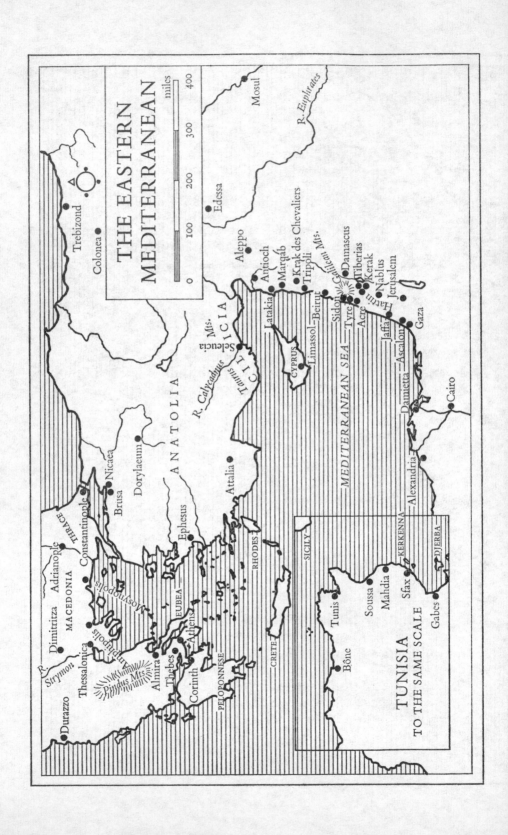

THE EASTERN
MEDITERRANEAN

miles

0   100   200   300   400

Mosul

R. Euphrates

Edessa

Trebizond
Colonea

Aleppo
Antioch
Marqab
Krak des Chevaliers
Tripoli
Damascus
Tiberias
Kerak
Nablus
Jerusalem
Gaza
Latakia
Beirut
Sidon
Tyre
Acre
Hattin
Jaffa
Ascalon
Damietta

Galilean Mts.

Seleucia
Tarsus Mts.
CILICIA
R. Calycadnus
Mts.

ANATOLIA

Nicaea
Brusa
Dorylaeum
Ephesus
Attalia

Limassol
CYPRUS

MEDITERRANEAN SEA

Alexandria
Cairo

Constantinople
Adrianople
THRACE
MACEDONIA
Mosynopolis
Dimitritza
R. Strymon
Thessalonica
Amphipolis
Pindus Mts.
Almira
Thebes
Athens
Corinth
EUBEA
Durazzo
PELOPONNESE
RHODES
CRETE

SICILY
KERKENNA
DJERBA

Soussa
Mahdia
Sfax
Tunis
Gabes
Bône

TUNISIA
TO THE SAME SCALE

Appendix

THE NORMAN MONUMENTS OF SICILY

A complete list of all the Norman buildings still extant in Sicily is not easy to draw up. Hardly any of them has escaped the attention of restorers or rebuilders at some time or another, often to the point where—as in the outside of the Martorana or the inside of Palermo Cathedral—the original character has been completely lost. I have also ruefully to admit that there remain a few places on the list which I have not visited myself. Usually the invaluable guidebook of the *Touring Club d'Italia* has been able to help me out, but in one or two cases I have had to rely on sketchier and less authoritative accounts. For the sake of completeness, too, I have added four items —identified with a question mark—which may be wholly or partly of Norman origin but can only be classified as doubtful. For the remainder I have adopted the following categories:

***The loveliest and best. Worth going to Sicily to see.
 **Memorable.
  *Buildings which have on the whole retained their original appearance and character.
Unstarred—Buildings which have been largely restored or rebuilt. They may be beautiful, but are no longer essentially Norman in feeling.

?AIDONE S. Maria la Cava.

?AIDONE Torre di S. Michele.

ALTARELLO See Palermo.

*ALTAVILLA MÍLICIA S. Michele, known as the Chiesazza. The ruins of a small church built by Robert Guiscard in 1077, about 25 km from Palermo, just off the main coast road to Cefalù. Below it the little *Ponte Saraceno* may go back to the Arab occupation.

*ALTOFONTE Formerly the Parco (see p. 157). The royal palace has gone, but the little chapel behind the *Chiesa Madre* is still standing, though restored.

*BURGIO S. Maria di Rifesi.

*CALTABELLOTTA The *Chiesa Madre* and the castle tower. (See p. 385n.)

*CALTANISSETTA The Badia di S. Spirito was consecrated in 1153; the frescoes are of the fourteenth and fifteenth centuries.

**CASTELVETRANO The little twelfth-century church of the SS. Trinità di Delia is a gem—the perfect fusion of Arab and Byzantine. About two miles outside the town to the west.

CATANIA Of the basically baroque cathedral, only the Norman apses of black lava withstood the earthquakes of 1169 and 1693. The best view of them is from the courtyard of the seminary behind the cathedral (Via Vittorio Emmanuele). Inside, the two Norman chapels, the Cappella della Vergine and the Cappella del Crocifisso, are barely recognisable.

***CEFALÙ CATHEDRAL Though much of the inside is now distressingly baroque, the outside is exquisite and the great apse mosaic the most sublime masterpiece Sicily has to offer. (See pp. 13–15.)

CEFALÙ The Osterio Magno; a few remains of Roger II's palace, on the corner of the Corso Ruggero and the Via G. Amendola.

?ERICE S. Ippolito.

**FORZA D'AGRÒ A few kilometres outside the town, SS. Pietro e Paolo is one of the most important Basilian churches on the island. The inscription over the west door dates it to 1171–72.

*FRAZZANÒ The Basilian abbey of S. Filippo di Fragalà was built by Count Roger I in the late eleventh century.

*GRATTERI S. Giorgio.

ITÁLA S. Pietro.

*MANIACE S. Maria di Maniace. (See p. 300.)

*MAZARA Ruins of Roger I's castle, 1073.

*MAZARA S. Nicolò Regale, or S. Nicolicchio, twelfth century.

*MAZARA Just outside the town to the east is the church of the Madonna dell' Alto or S. Maria delle Giummare, built in 1103 by a daughter of Roger I.

MAZARA In the cathedral, begun by Roger I in 1073, traces of Norman work can still be seen in the apse.

*MESSINA The church of the Annunziata dei Catalani is beautiful, though now so restored as to be virtually rebuilt. Parts of the apse are original.

*MESSINA The Cathedral is aptly described by Christopher Kininmonth as 'a post-war reconstruction of the post-earthquake reconstruction of the Norman original'. Little, if any, of the original work remains; but it merits inclusion in this list since it is a purely Norman church and a very beautiful one, and tells the visitor as much about Norman-Sicilian architecture as anything on the island. The sculptured slab from Richard Palmer's tomb has, unaccountably, survived almost intact.

?MESSINA La Badiazza.

*MILI S PIETRO The little church of S. Maria was founded for Basilian monks by Roger I in 1082. Here, too, Roger's bastard son Jordan was buried in 1091. (See *The Normans in the South*, p. 281 n.)

***MONREALE Cathedral and Cloister. (See pp. 316–22.)

*MONREALE The twelfth-century *Castellaccio* stands on the summit of Monte Caputo and commands a sensational view of the Conca d'Oro.

*MONREALE Remains of William II's palace can be seen in the courtyard of the seminary at No. 1, Via Arcivescovado.

***PALERMO In the Royal Palace (the exterior of which, gloomy as it is, merits two stars on its own account) are to be found two of the most stunningly beautiful things in Sicily; the Palatine Chapel and the so-called *Sala di Ruggero*. (See pp. 72–7 and 241–2 respectively.)

***PALERMO S. Maria dell' Ammiraglio, popularly known as the Martorana. (See pp. 93–9.)

**PALERMO S. Giovanni degli Eremiti. (See pp. 88–90.)

**PALERMO S. Spirito, the church of the Vespers. (See p. 363.)

**PALERMO The Royal tombs of Roger II, Henry VI, Constance and Frederick II in the cathedral. (See pp. 389–90.)

*PALERMO S. Giovanni dei Lebbrosi, one of the earliest Norman churches on the island. (See *The Normans in the South*, p. 178 n.)

*PALERMO S. Cataldo. (See p. 216n.)

*PALMERO The Cathedral. (See pp. 362–3.)

*PALERMO SS. Trinità (La Magione). (See p. 254n.)

*PALERMO The Zisa. (See pp. 239–41.)

*PALERMO The Cuba, Cubula and Cuba Soprana. (See p. 354n.)

*PALERMO The Ponte del Ammiraglio. (See pp. 155–6.)

*PALERMO S. Cristina, another foundation of Walter of the Mill.

*PALERMO La Maddalena, a twelfth-century church in the court-yard of the Carabinieri barracks next to the Porta Nuova.

*PALERMO S. Maria della Speranza.

*PALERMO The Castello della Favara, otherwise known as Maredolce. (See pp. 156–7.)

PALERMO The Cappella dell' Incoronata behind the Cathedral.

PALERMO In the suburb of Altarello, the Palazzo dell' Uscibene was formerly the royal hunting-lodge of Mimnermo. (See p. 169.)

PALERMO For the sake of completeness, a brief mention should be made of the remains of some Norman work in the tower of the Palazzo Conte Federico. Pedants might also include a house known as the Casa Martorana and one in the Via Protonotaro; but both of these were badly damaged during the last war and hardly anything remains of the mediaeval structure.

*PATERNÒ The Castello was built by Roger I in 1073. It has been much restored but is still worth a visit. Ask at the Municipio for the keys.

PATTI The cathedral is of Norman origin, though there is little enough to show for it now—except the tomb of Roger II's mother Queen Adelaide. (See *The Normans in the South*, p. 289 n.)

*PIAZZA ARMERINA The priory of S. Andrea, a few kilometres outside the town, was founded in 1096 by Simon, Count of Butera, cousin of Roger II. The frescoes are of the fifteenth century. (See p. 234n.)

*S. FRATELLO S. Alfio.

*S. MARCO D'ALUNZIO The church in the Badia Grande di SS. Salvatore was founded in 1176 by Queen Margaret, wife of William I.

*SCIACCA S. Nicolò.

SCIACCA Of the Cathedral, the three apses of the east end are Norman.

SCIACCA S. Maria della Giummare, though today no more than an agreeable hotch-potch, still retains traces of its Norman origins.

SYRACUSE The extraordinary cathedral contains a little Norman work, just as it contains a little of everything else.

TROINA The bell-tower of the Chiesa Matrice.

BIBLIOGRAPHY

NOTES ON THE PRINCIPAL SOURCES

Falco of Benevento

Member of one of the leading families of Benevento, a palace notary and scribe, Falco wrote a retrospective history of his own city and South Italy as a whole between 1102 and 1139. It is of interest not only for its own qualities—it is reliable, methodical, vivid, and contains much of which its author was an eyewitness—but also because it reflects the opinions of a Lombard patriot, for whom the Normans were little better than a bunch of uncivilised brigands. An Italian translation exists and is listed in the bibliography.

Alexander of Telese

Alexander, Abbot of the monastery of S. Salvatore near Telese, wrote his chronicle at the request of Matilda of Alife, half-sister of Roger II. Though ostensibly a biography of Roger, the first part is sketchy in the extreme; we are told nothing about Adelaide's regency and the account becomes interesting only from 1127, with the events leading up to the establishment of the Sicilian Kingdom. From that point until 1136, when Alexander abruptly breaks off, he becomes a valuable source—though allowance must be made for his extreme tendentiousness. For him Roger was divinely appointed to bring peace and order to the South, after meting out just punishment for earlier iniquities. Despite his cloth, the Abbot has little respect for the Pope, and even chides Honorius II for his 'insolence'. There is an Italian translation listed below.

Romuald of Salerno

Romuald Guarna, a member of the old Salernitan nobility, was archbishop of his native city from 1153 until his death in 1181. Throughout this time he played a leading rôle in the political life of the Kingdom, both in Sicily and on the mainland, in domestic and foreign affairs. He was one of the negotiators of the Treaty of Benevento; later he was implicated in the plot against Maio of Bari and was largely responsible for the rescue of William I during the 1161 uprising. Under William II—whose coronation he performed—he represented Sicily at the signing of the Treaty of Venice. His *Chronicon sive Annales*, which begins with the Creation and continues till 1178, is one of the most important sources in existence for the period covered by this book. It would have been more valuable still if Romuald had only been more impartial and less discreet. As it is, he consistently exaggerates his own part in the events he records and minimises that of others. Matters in which he is not directly involved—or those in which he or his friends do not show to particular advantage—he tends to leave out altogether. The work has never been translated into English or French; an Italian translation is listed below.

Hugo Falcandus

Everything, as Chalandon points out, that relates to Falcandus is a mystery; even his name is in doubt. The most distinguished living English scholar of the period, Miss Evelyn Jamison, has cogently argued—in a book listed below—that he is to be identified with Eugenius, a politician and scholar who was appointed Admiral of the Kingdom in 1190. The *Liber de Regno Sicilie* covers only the period from 1154 to 1169. It has little to say of Sicilian foreign policy; but as a picture of the social life and the political intrigues of Palermo during a particularly troubled time, it is a masterpiece. The author needs no more than a couple of lines to transform a name into a character; his eye for the significant detail is unerring. In the art of making his story live, none of the other sources with whom we have had to deal can hold a candle to him—except, perhaps, Amatus of Monte Cassino; but whereas Amatus is a *naif*, Falcandus is a polished and sophisticated man of letters. His great defect is his tendentiousness, and his bitter, almost universal contempt for those around him. For him, every man is a villain; for every action, the worst motives are unfailingly ascribed. Just how accurate he is we have no means of telling; checks are seldom possible, since no other chronicle covers the period in anything like such detail. But he certainly makes splendid reading. It seems almost incredible that a writer who has been compared to Tacitus and Thucydides should never have been translated into English or French; the only version I have been able to find is del Re's Italian one, written in so convoluted a style that Falcandus's elegant Latin is often easier to read.

Peter of Eboli

Peter of Eboli's long poem, the *Carmen de Rebus Siculis,* gives us a detailed account of the last days of the Sicilian Kingdom, from the death of William the Good to the arrival of Henry VI. As with Falcandus, his reliability as a historian is diminished by his hatred—in this case for Tancred of Lecce, his family and his adherents. His facts can all too seldom be checked against other sources, and when they can they are not always found to be accurate. On the other hand he appears to have lived at the court of Henry VI, so that he must have been better placed than most people to see what went on. Here is another work that cries out for a good modern translation; for the moment, none exists. When it appears—as some day it must—we can only hope that it will include reproductions of the delightful and often brilliantly witty drawings with which Peter has embellished his text. Four of them are reproduced in this book.

I. ORIGINAL SOURCES

1. Collections of Sources

(The abbreviations used elsewhere in this bibliography and in the footnotes follow each entry in parentheses.)

AMARI, M. *Biblioteca Arabo-Sicula*. Versione Italiana. 2 vols. Turin and Rome, 1880–81. (*B.A.S.*)

Archivio Storico Siciliano. (*A.S.S.*)

BOUQUET, M. *et al. Recueil des historiens des Gaules et de la France*. 23 vols. Paris, 1738–1876. New Series, Paris, 1899– (in progress). (*R.H.F.*)

CARUSO, G. B. *Bibliotheca Historica Regni Siciliae*. 2 vols. Palermo, 1723. (*C.B.H.*)

Corpus Scriptorum Historiae Byzantinae. Bonn, 1828–97. (*C.S.H.B.*)

GRAEVIUS, J. C. *Thesaurus antiquitatum et historiarum Italiae, Neapolis, Siciliae, Sardiniae, Corsicae, Melitae, atque adj. terrarum insularumque*. 10 vols. in 45 fol. Leyden, 1704–25. (Vol. X, which is so called only in the general index, is that specifically relative to Sicily and has 15 parts.) (*G.T.A.*)

GUIZOT, F. *Collection des Mémoires Relatifs à l'Histoire de France*. 29 vols. Paris, 1823–27. (*G.M.H.F.*)

JAFFÉ, P. *Bibliotheca Rerum Germanicarum*. 6 vols. Berlin, 1864–73. (*J.B.R.G.*)

—— *Regesta Pontificum Romanorum ab cond. Eccl. ad a. 1198*. 2nd edn., 2 vols. Leipzig, 1885–88. (*J.R.P.R.*)

Liber Pontificalis, ed. L. Duchesne. 2 vols. Paris, 1886–92. (*L.P.*)

MIGNE, J. P. *Patrologia Latina*. 221 vols. Paris, 1844–55. (*M.P.L.*)

Monumenta Bambergensa, ed. Jaffé. *J.B.R.G.*, vol. V.

Monumenta Germaniae Historica, ed. G. H. Pertz, T. Mommsen *et al*. Hanover, 1826– (in progress). (*M.G.H.*)

Monumenta Gregoriana, ed. Jaffé. *J.B.R.G.*, vol. II.

MURATORI, L. A. *Rerum Italicarum Scriptores*. 25 vols in 28. Milan, 1723–51. New Series, ed. G. Carducci and V. Fiorini. Città di Castello—Bologna, 1900– (in progress). (*R.I.S.*)

RE, G. DEL *Cronisti e Scrittori Sincroni della Dominazione Normanna nel Regno di Puglia e Sicilia*. 2 vols. Naples, 1845, 1868. (*R.C.S.S.*)

Recueil des Historiens des Croisades. Publ. Académie des Inscriptions et Belles Lettres. Paris, 1841–1906. *Historiens Occidentaux*, 5 vols. (*R.H.C.Occ.*) *Historiens Orientaux*, 5 vols. (*R.H.C.Or.*)

STUBBS, W. *Select Charters*. Oxford, 1870. (*S.C.*)

WATTERICH, J. M. *Pontificum Romanorum qui fuerunt inde ab exeunte saeculo IX usque finem saeculi XIII vitae ab aequalibus conscriptae*. 2 vols. Leipzig, 1862. (*W.P.R.*)

2. *Individual Sources*

ABU SHAMA, Shihab ed-Din Abdul-Rahman ibn Ismail, *Book of the Two Gardens*. Extracts, with French tr., in *R.H.C.Or.*, vols IV–V.

AL-EDRISI, Abu Abdullah Mohammed, *Géographie d'Edrisi*, tr. A. Jaubert. 2 vols. Paris, 1836. (Vols V and VI of *Recueil de Voyages et de Mémoires*, published by the Société de Géographie.)

ALEXANDER OF TELESE *Rogerii Regis Siciliae Rerum Gestarum Libri IV*. In *R.C.S.S.*, vol. II (with Italian tr.).

AL-MAQRISI *Histoire d'Egypte*. French tr. by E. Blochet. Paris, 1908.

AL-MARRAKESHI *Histoire des Almohades*. French tr. by E. Fagnan. Algiers, 1893.

AMBROISE *L'Estoire de la Guerre Sainte*. Ed. and tr. into modern French by Gaston Paris. Paris, 1897. English tr. and notes by M. J. Hubert and J. L. La Monte. New York, 1941.

Annales Barenses. In *M.G.H. Scriptores*, vol. V.

Annales Beneventani. In *M.G.H. Scriptores*, vol. III.

Annales Casinenses. In *M.G.H. Scriptores*, vol. XIX.

ANNALISTA SAXO In *M.G.H. Scriptores*, vol. VI.

ANONYMUS VATICANUS *Historia Sicula*. In *R.I.S.*, vol. VIII.

ARNOLD OF LUBECK *Chronica Slavorum*. Ed. Lappenburg. In *M.G.H. Scriptores*, vol. XXI.

ARNULF OF LISIEUX *Letters*. In *M.P.L.*, vol. 201.

—— *Tractatus de Schismate orto post Honorii II Papae decessum*. In *M.P.L.*, vol. 201.

BECKET, ST THOMAS *Epistolae*. In *M.P.L.*, vol. 190. See also in *Materials for the History of Becket*, ed. J. C. Robertson, vols. V–VII. (Rolls Series, 67, 1875–85).

BENEDICT OF PETERBOROUGH *Chronicle of the Reigns of Henry II and Richard I, transcribed by the order of B. of P*. Ed. Stubbs, Rolls Series, vol. 49, London 1867. (Now established as the work of Roger of Hoveden, *q.v.*)

BENJAMIN OF TUDELA *Itinerary*. Tr. with notes by M. N. Adler. London, 1907.

BERNARD OF CLAIRVAUX, ST *Vita Prima* and *Acta*. In *M.P.L.*, vol. 185.

—— *Life and Works*. Ed. J. Mabillon; tr. with notes by S. J. Eales. Vols. I–IV, London, 1889–96.

BERNARD OF CLAIRVAUX *Epistolae*. In *M.P.L.*, vol. 182. English tr. by B. Scott James, London, 1953.

BOSO *Vita Adriani*. (Incorporated in the *Liber Censuum*.) In *L.P.*, vol. II.
—— *Vita Alexandri*. In *L.P.*, vol. II.

CINNAMUS, JOHN 'Ἐπιτομή. In *C.S.H.B.*, ed. Meineke, with Latin tr.

DANTE, *The Divine Comedy*, translated by G. Bickersteth, Oxford, 1965.

DICETO, RADULPHUS DE *Opera Historica*. In *M.G.H. Scriptores*, vol. XXVII. (Also Rolls Series, 68, i and ii.)

EUSTATHIUS OF THESSALONICA *De Thessalonica a Latinis capta, a. 1185*. Ed. Bekker. In *C.S.H.B.* German tr. by H. Hunger, Vienna, 1955.

FALCANDUS, HUGO *Historia*, or *Liber de Regno Sicilie*, with *Epistola ad Petrum Panormitane Ecclesie Thesauriarium*. Ed. Siragusa, Rome 1897. In *R.C.S.S.*, vol. I with Italian tr.

FALCO OF BENEVENTO *Chronicon*. In *R.C.S.S.*, vol. I, with Italian tr.

GERHOH OF REICHENSBURG. *De Investigatione Antichristi*. In *M.G.H.*, *Libelli de Lite Imperatorum et Pontificum Saeculis XI et XII*. Vol. III. Hanover, 1897.

Gesta Henrici II et Ricardi I. Ed. Liebermann. In *M.G.H. Scriptores*, vol. XXVII.

GODFREY OF VITERBO *Pantheon, Gesta Friderici*, and *Gesta Henrici VI Imperatoris*. Ed. Waitz. In *M.G.H. Scriptores*, vol. XXII.

HELMOLD *Chronica Slavorum*. In *M.G.H. Scriptores*, vol. XXI.

Historia Welforum Weingartensis. Ed. Weiland. In *M.G.H. Scriptores*, vol. XXI.

IBN ABI DINAR *Kitab al-Munis*. Ed. with Italian tr. by M. Amari. In *B.A.S.*

IBN AL-ATHIR *Kamel al Tawarikh*. Ed. with Italian tr. by M. Amari. In *B.A.S.*

IBN JUBAIR *The Travels of Ibn Jubair*. Tr. R. J. C. Broadhurst. London, 1952.

IBN KHALDUN *Kitab al Ibr*. Italian tr. of relevant passages by M. Amari in *B.A.S.*

Ignoti Monachi Cisterciensis S. Mariae de Ferraria Chronica. Ed. Gaudenzi. Società Napoletana di Storia Patria; *Monumenti Storici, Seria Prima, Cronache*. Naples, 1888.

INNOCENT II, POPE *Epistolae*. In *M.P.L.*, vol. 179.

Itinerarium Peregrinorum et Gesta Regis Ricardi. Ed. Stubbs. Rolls Series, 38, i. London, 1864.

JOHN OF HEXHAM *Historia*. In *M.G.H. Scriptores*, vol. XXVII. English tr. by J. Stevenson in *The Church Historians of England*, vol. IV, i. London, 1856.

JOHN OF SALISBURY *Historia Pontificalis*. Ed. with tr. by M. Chibnall. London, 1956.

JOHN OF SALISBURY *Policraticus*. In *M.P.L.*, vol. 199; also ed. with notes by C. C. I. Webb, 2 vols. Oxford, 1909. Partial tr. by J. Dickinson, New York, 1927, and J. B. Pike, Minneapolis, 1938.

—— *Letters*. Ed. with tr. by W. J. Millor, S. J., and H. E. Butler. Vol. I, London, 1955.

Kaiserchronik. In *M.G.H.*, *Deutsche Chroniken*, vol. I.

LANGTOFT, PETER OF. *Chronicle*. Ed. Wright, with English tr. 2 vols. London, 1868.

MORENA, OTTO and ACERBUS *Geschichtswerk des Otto Morena und seiner Fortsetzer über die Taten Friedrichs I in der Lombardei*. Ed. F. Güterbock. In *M.G.H. Scriptores*, New Series, vol. VII.

NICETAS CHONIATES *Historia*. In *C.S.H.B.* French tr. by Cousin in *Histoire de Constantinople*, vol. V. Paris, 1685.

NIGER, RADULPHUS *Chronica Universalis*. In *M.G.H. Scriptores*, vol. XXVII.

ODO OF DEUIL *De Profectione Ludovici VII in Orientem*. Ed. Waquet. Paris, 1949.

ORDERICUS VITALIS *The Ecclesiastical History of England and Normandy*. Tr. with notes by T. Forester. 4 vols. London, 1854.

OTTO OF FREISING *Chronica, sive historia de duabus civitatibus*. In *M.G.H. Scriptores*, vol. XX. English tr. by C. C. Mierow, New York, 1928.

—— *Gesta Friderici Imperatoris, cum continuatione Rahewini*. Ed. Wilmans. In *M.G.H. Scriptores*, vol. XX. English tr. by C. C. Mierow, New York, 1953.

OTTO OF ST BLAISE *Chronica*. In *M.G.H. Scriptores*, in usum scholarum, 1912.

PETER OF BLOIS *Epistolae*. In *M.P.L.*, vol. 207.

PETER THE VENERABLE OF CLUNY *Epistolae*. In *M.P.L.* vol. 189.

PETER THE DEACON *Chronicon Monasterii Casinensis*. Ed. W. Wattenbach. In *M.G.H. Scriptores*, vol. VII of *M.P.L.*, vol. 173.

PETER OF EBOLI *Carmen de Rebus Siculis*. In *R.I.S.*, vol. XXXI, i, 1904.

RADEWIN, RAGEWIN, RAHEWIN See OTTO OF FREISING.

RICHARD FITZNIGEL *Dialogus de Scaccario*. In *S.C.*

RICHARD OF S. GERMANO *Chronicon Regni Siciliae*. In *R.I.S.*, vol. VII.

ROBERT OF TORIGNI *Chronicle*. Ed. Delisle. Société de l'Histoire de Normandie, Rouen, 1873.

ROGER OF HOVEDEN *Annals*. Tr. H. T. Riley. 2 vols. London, 1853. (See also BENEDICT OF PETERBOROUGH)

ROMUALD OF SALERNO *Chronicon*. In *R.I.S.*, vol. VII. Italian tr. in *R.C.S.S.*

Rouleaux de Cluny ed. Huillard-Bréholles. In *Notices et Extraits des Manuscrits de la Bibliothèque Impériale*, vol. XXI. Paris, 1868.

WIBALD OF STAVELOT *Epistolae*. In *J.B.R.G.* vol. I—*Monumenta Corbeiensia*.

II. MODERN WORKS

AMARI, M. *Epigrafi Arabiche di Sicilia, tradotte e illustrate.* Palermo, 1875–85.

BELOCH, J. *Bevölkerungsgeschichte Italiens*, vol. I. Berlin and Leipzig, 1937.

BERAUD-VILLARS, J. *Les Normands en Méditerranée.* Paris, 1951.

BERNHARDI, W. *Lothar von Supplinburg. (Jahrbücher der Deutschen Geschichte.)* Leipzig, 1879.

—— *Konrad III. (Jahrbücher der Deutschen Geschichte.)* 2 vols. Leipzig, 1883.

BERTAUX, E. *L'Art dans l'Italie Méridionale.* Paris, 1903.

—— 'L'Email de St Nicholas de Bari'. In Fondation E. Piot, *Monuments et Mémoires*, pub. by the Académie des Inscriptions, vol. VI, 1899.

BOECKLER, A. *Die Bronzetüren des Bonanus von Pisa und des Barisanus von Trani.* Berlin, 1953.

BIAGI, L. *Palermo.* Istituto Italiano d'Arti Grafiche, Bergamo, 1929.

BLOCH, H. 'The Schism of Anacletus II and the Glanfeuil Forgeries of Peter the Deacon of Monte Cassino', *Traditio,* vol. VIII, 1952. (Fordham University.)

BRANDILEONE, F. *Il Diritto Romano nelle Legge Normanne e Sueve del Regno di Sicilia.* Turin, 1884.

BREQUIGNY, L. DE 'Mémoire sur Etienne, chancelier de Sicile', *Mémoires de l'Académie des Inscriptions*, vol. XLI, Paris, 1780.

BUFFIER, C. *Historie de l'origine du Royaume de Sicile et de Naples, contenant les avantures et les conquestes des princes normands qui l'ont établi.* 2 vols. Paris, 1701.

Cambridge Medieval History 8 vols. Cambridge, 1911–36.

CARAVALE, M. *Il Regno Normanno di Sicilia.* Rome, 1966.

CARINI, I. *Una pergamena sulla fondazione del Duomo di Cefalù.* In *A.S.S.,* New Series, vol. VII, 1883.

CASPAR, E. *Roger II und die Gründung der Normannisch-sicilischen Monarchie.* Innsbruck, 1904.

CERONE, F. *L'Opera politica e militare di Ruggero II in Africa ed in Oriente.* Catania, 1913.

CHALANDON, F. *Jean II Comnène et Manuel I Comnène.* (Vol. II of *Etudes sur l'Empire Byzantin au XIe. et au XIIe. siècles*). 2 vols. Paris, 1912. Republished New York, 1960.

—— *Histoire de la Domination Normande en Italie et en Sicile.* 2 vols. Paris, 1907. Republished New York, 1960.

COHN, W. *Die Geschichte der Normannisch-sicilischen Flotte unter der Regierung Rogers I und Rogers II 1060–1154.* Breslau, 1910.

CONIGLIO, G. *Amalfi e il commercio amalfitano.* Nuova Rivista Storica 28/9, 1944/5.

CURTIS, E. *Roger of Sicily.* New York, 1912.

DEER, J. *The Dynastic Porphyry Tombs of the Norman Period in Sicily,* tr.

G. A. Gillhoff. Dumbarton Oaks Studies No. V, Cambridge, Mass., 1959.

DEER, J. *Der Kaiserornat Friedrichs II*. Berne, 1952.

DEMUS, O. *The Mosaics of Norman Sicily*. London, 1950.

Dictionary of National Biography.

Dictionnaire de Théologie Catholique ed. Vacant and Mangenot. 9 vols in 15. Paris, 1926–50.

Dictionnaire d'Histoire et de Géographie Ecclésiastiques ed. Baudrillart. Paris. (In progress.)

DIEHL, C. *Figures Byzantines*. 2 vols. Paris, 1906–8.

DOUGLAS, D. C. *The Norman Achievement*, London, 1969.

Enciclopedia Italiana.

Encyclopaedia Britannica 11th edn.

Encyclopaedia of Islam London and Leyden, 1913–38. (New edn. now in progress).

EPIFANIO, U. *Ruggero II e Filippo di Al Mahdiah*. In *A.S.S.*, New Series, vol. XXX.

GABRIELI, F. 'Arabi di Sicilia e Arabi di Spagna', *Al-Andalus*, XV, 1950.
—— *Storia e civiltà musulmana*. Naples, 1947.

GALASSO, G. *Il commercio amalfitano nel periodo normanno*. Studi in onore di Riccardo Filangieri, I, Naples, 1959.

GAROFALO, A. *Tabularium Regiae ac Imperialis Capellae Collegiatae Divi Petri in Regio Panormitano Palatio*. Palermo, 1835.

GARUFI, C. A. *Per la storia dei monasteri di Sicilia del tempo normanno*. *Archivio Storico per la Sicilia*, VI, 1940.

GIBBON, E. *Decline and Fall of the Roman Empire*, ed. J. B. Bury. 7 vols. London, 1896.

GIUNTA, F. *Bizantini e Bizantinismo nella Sicilia Normanna*, Palermo, 1950.

GREGOROVIUS, F. *History of the City of Rome in the Middle Ages*, tr. A. Hamilton. 8 vols in 13. London, 1894–1902.

GREEN, M. A. E. *Lives of the Princesses of England*, vol. I. London, 1849.

HARE, AUGUSTUS. *Cities of Southern Italy and Sicily*. London, 1883.

HARTWIG, O. *Re Guglielmo e il suo grande ammiraglio Majone di Bari*. In *Archivio Storico per le provincie napoletane*, VIII, Naples, 1883.

HASKINS, C. H. *Norman Institutions, 1035–1189*. Harvard Historical Studies, 24. Cambridge, Mass., 1913.
—— 'England and Sicily in the twelfth century', *English Historical Review*, July and October, 1911.

HOLTZMANN, W. *Papst-, Kaiser- und Normannenurkunden aus Unteritalien:* in *Quellen und Forschungen aus italienischen Archiven und Bibliotheken*, 35, 36. Rome, 1955.

HUILLARD-BREHOLLES, J. L. A. *Recherches sur les Monuments et l'Histoire des Normands et de la Maison de Souabe dans l'Italie méridionale.* Paris, 1844.

INVEGES, A. *Annali della Felice Città di Palermo.* 3 vols. Palermo, 1651.

JAMISON, E. 'The Sicilian-Norman Kingdom in the Mind of Anglo-Norman Contemporaries', *British Academy papers,* XXIV, 1938.

—— 'The Norman Administration of Apulia and Capua, especially under Roger II and William I, 1127–66', *Papers of the British School at Rome,* VI, 1913.

—— *Admiral Eugenius of Sicily, his life and work, and the authorship of the Epistola ad Petrum and the Historia Hugonis Falcandi Siculi.* London, 1957. (Reviewed by L. T. White, *q.v.*)

KANTOROWICZ, E. *Frederick the Second,* tr. E. O. Lorimer, London, 1931.

KEHR, K. A. *Die Urkunden der Normannisch-sicilischen Könige.* Innsbruck, 1902.

KEHR, P. *Italia Pontificia,* vol. VIII. Berlin, 1935.

KEHR, P. 'Die Belehnungen der Süditalienischen Normannenfürsten durch die Päpste, 1059–1192', *Abhandlungen der preussischen Akademie der Wissenschaften,* Phil.-hist. K1., 1934, No. 1.

KELLY, A. *Eleanor of Aquitaine and the Four Kings.* Cambridge, Mass., 1950.

KININMONTH, C. *Sicily.* Travellers' Guides. London, 1965.

KITZINGER, E. *I Mosaici di Monreale,* tr. F. Bonajuto. Palermo, 1960.

KNIGHT, H. GALLY *The Normans in Sicily.* London, 1838.

KRÖNIG, W. *Il Duomo di Monreale e l'Architettura Normanna in Sicilia.* Palermo, 1965.

LA LUMIA, I. *Storia della Sicilia sotto Guglielmo il Buono.* Florence, 1867.

—— *Studi di Storia Siciliana.* 2 vols. Palermo, 1870.

LAMMA, P. *Comneni e Staufer. Ricerche sui Rapporti fra Bisanzio e l'Occidente nel Secolo XII.* Rome, 1955.

LOPEZ, R. S. See SETTON, K. M.

MACK SMITH, D. *Medieval Sicily.* (Vol. II of *A History of Sicily.*) London, 1968.

MANN, H. K. *The Lives of the Popes in the Middle Ages.* Vols. 6–12. London, 1910–15.

MARONGIU, A. 'A Model State in the Middle Ages: the Norman and Swabian Kingdom of Sicily', *Comparative Studies in Society and History,* vol. VI, 1963–4. (See also STRAYER, J. R.)

—— 'Lo Spirito della Monarchia Normanna di Sicilia nell' allocuzione di Ruggero II ai suoi grandi', *Archivio Storico Siciliano,* Ser. 3–4, 1950–51.

MENAGER, L. R. *Amiratus—Αμηρᾶς—L'Emirat et les origines de l' Amirauté (XIe.-XIIe. s.).* Paris, 1960.

MASSON, G. *The Companion Guide to Rome.* London, 1965.

MEO, A. DI *Annali Critico-Diplomatici del Regno di Napoli della Mezzana Età.* 12 vols. Naples, 1795–1819.

MICHAUD, J. F. *Histoire des Croisades.* 10 vols in 5. Brussels, 1841.

MONNERET DE VILLARD, U. *Le Pitture Musulmane al Soffitto della Cappella Palatina di Palermo.* Rome, 1950.

MONTI, G. M. *L'Espansione Mediterranea del Mezzogiorno d'Italia e della Sicilia.* Bologna, 1942.

—— *L'Italia e le Crociate in Terra Santa.* Naples, 1940.

MOR, C. G. 'Roger II et les assemblées du royaume normand dans l'Italie méridionale', *Revue Historique de Droit Français et Etranger.* Sér. 4, 36, 1958.

MUNZ, P. *Frederick Barbarossa, A Study in Medieval Politics.* London, 1969.

NATALE, F. *Avviamento allo studio del medio evo siciliano.* Pub. by the Istituto di Storia Medioevale e Moderna dell' Università di Messina, fasc. 2. Florence, 1959.

New Catholic Encyclopaedia. Washington, 1967.

NIESE, H. *Die Gesetzgebung der normannischen Dynastie im 'Regnum Siciliae'.* Halle, 1910.

OSTROGORSKY, G. *History of the Byzantine State,* tr. J. M. Hussey. Oxford, 1956.

PALMAROCCHI, R. *L'Abbazia di Montecassino e la Conquista Normanna.* Rome, 1913.

PARKER, J. S. F. 'The attempted Byzantine alliance with the Sicilian Norman Kingdom, 1166–7', in *Essays Presented to Miss E. Jamison. Papers of the British School at Rome,* XXIV, 1955.

PEPE, G. *I Normanni in Italia Meridionale, 1166–1194.* Bari, 1964.

PIETRAGANZILI, R. S. DI 'Gli osteri di Cefalù', *Sicilia Artistica ed Archeologica,* Palermo, July 1887.

—— 'La Leggenda della tempesta e il voto del Re Ruggero per la costruzione del Duomo di Cefalù', *Sicilia Artistica ed Archeologica,* Palermo, June–July, 1888.

PIRRO, R. *Sicilia Sacra.* In *G.T.A.,* vol. X, ii, iii.

PONTIERI, E. *Tra i Normanni nell' Italia Meridionale.* Revised edn., Naples, 1964.

PROLOGO, A. DI G. *Le Carte chi si conservano nello Archivio del Capitolo Metropolitano della Città di Trani (Dal IX secolo fino all' anno 1266).* Barletta, 1877.

RASSOW, P. *Zum byzantinisch-normannischen Krieg 1147–9: Mitteilungen des österreichischen Instituts für Geschichtsforschung,* 62, 1954.

RENAN, E. *Vingt Jours en Sicile.* In *Mélanges d'Histoire et de Voyages.* Paris, 1878.

RUNCIMAN, S. *History of the Crusades.* 3 vols. Cambridge, 1954.

SCHRAMM, P. E. *Herrschaftszeichen und Staatssymbolik: Beiträge zu ihrer Geschichte vom 3. bis zum 16. Jahrhundert.* 3 vols. Stuttgart, 1954.

SETTON, K. M. (editor-in-chief) *A History of the Crusades.* See in particular sections by R. S. Lopez and H. Wieruszowski. 2nd edn. by University of Wisconsin Press, vols. I and II, 1969.

SIRAGUSA, G. B. *Il Regno di Guglielmo I in Sicilia.* 2nd edn. Palermo, 1929.

STEFANO, A. DE *La Cultura in Sicilia nel periodo normanno.* 1932.

STEFANO, G. DI *Monumenti della Sicilia normanna.* Palermo, 1955.

STRAYER, J. R. Comment on A. Marongiù's article 'A Model State in the Middle Ages' (*q.v.*). *Comparative Studies in Society and History,* vol. VI, 1963–64.

TESTA, F. *De Vita, et rebus gestis Gulielmi II Siciliae Regis libri quatuor.* With Italian tr. by S. Sinesio. Monreale, 1769.

TOECHE, T. *Kaiser Heinrich VI.* (*Jahrbücher der deutschen Geschichte.*) Leipzig, 1867.

TOSTI, L. *Storia della Badia di Monte-Cassino.* 3 vols. Naples, 1842.

TOURING CLUB ITALIANO. *Sicilia.* (Regional Guide.) Milan, 1953.

VACANDARD, E. *Vie de St Bernard, Abbé de Clairvaux.* 2 vols. Paris, 1895.

VALENTI, F. *Il Palazzo Reale Normanno.* Bolletino d'Arte, IV, 1924–25.

VASILIEV, A. A. *History of the Byzantine Empire, 324–1453.* Oxford, 1952.

WHITE, L. T. *Latin Monasticism in Norman Sicily.* Pub. 31 (Monograph 13), Medieval Academy of America. Cambridge, Mass., 1938.

—— Review of *Admiral Eugenius of Sicily* by E. Jamison (*q.v.*). *American Historical Review,* 63, 1957–58.

WIERUSZOWSKI, H. 'Roger II of Sicily, Rex-Tyrannus, in twelfth-century political thought', *Speculum,* 38, 1963. See also SETTON, K. M.

WILLIAMS, W. *St Bernard of Clairvaux.* Manchester, 1953.

775

INDEX

779

781

Falcandus (*cont'd*)
546, 551, 553, 555, 560, 572, 575, 577–8, 582–3, 585, 588n., 589, 592, 594, 598–9, 603, 605, 609–10, 612, 615–19, 621, 639, 644–5, 647, 657, 712, 716, 766

Falco of Benevento, 306–7, 312, 315, 340, 377, 382–3, 388–9, 401, 418–19, 425n., 426, 429, 431, 446, 765

Farfa, 416, 421

Farò, Cape, 136–7, 139

Fatimids, 523, 666

Favara, 516–17, 529, 584, 745, 764

Fermò, March of, 218

Ferrara, 708

First Crusade, 268, 276–8, 284–7, 289

Flochberg, 510

Florence, 105, 122, 403

Florian of Camerota, Royal Justiciar, 669

Foggia, 3

Fontevrault, 677, 740n.

Formosus, Bishop of Porto, 98

Fortore, river, 90–1, 96, 156

Forza d'Agrò, 762

Francis of Assisi, St, 5

Frangipani family, 324–6, 377, 386–7, 471, 479, 626, 634, 665n.

Frangipani, Cencius, 314, 324, 469–70

Frazzano, 143, 762

Frederick I Barbarossa, Western Emperor, 487, 511; character and appearance, 533–4; first Italian campaign and coronation, 535, 537–43, 545–6, 548–9, 556–7, 559; relations with papacy, 562–7; second Italian campaign, 566–9; and papal schism, 622–9; third Italian campaign, 623, 629–34, 636; submits to Pope at Venice, 671–3; marries son Henry to Constance of Sicily, 683–4, 705–6, 708; on Third Crusade, 711, 724; other references, 665, 668, 730, 749

Frederick II of Hohenstaufen, Western Emperor, xiii, 464, 521, 749–50

Frederick of Lorraine, Cardinal *see* Stephen IX, Pope

Frederick of Rotenburg, 633

Fressenda de Hauteville, 39

Fuga, Fernando, 723

Furriani, Abu al-Hassan al-, 570–1

Furriani, Omar al-, 570, 571n.

Gabes, 295, 514

Gaeta, 11, 21, 36, 88–9, 109, 634

Gaimar IV, Prince of Salerno, 16–17, 21–2, 32–3, 35

Gaimar V, Prince of Salerno, 41–3, 45, 47–9, 62, 66–7, 70–2, 74–6, 79, 82–4, 86–8, 108

Gaimar, brother of Gisulf II of Salerno, 212

Gaitelgrima, Duchess of Apulia, 307

Galeria, 122, 124–5

Gallipoli, 107, 260

Galluccio, 427–8, 447, 467

Garcia IV Ramirez, King of Navarre, 529, 618

Gargano *see* Monte Gargano

Garibaldi, Giuseppe, 516n.

Garigliano, river, 19, 22–3, 404, 428, 522, 556, 735

Gaza, 710

Gebhard, Bishop of Eichstätt *see* Victor II, Pope

Genoa, 277, 290, 327, 385–7, 390–1, 393, 397, 412, 626n., 628–9, 725, 743–5

Gentile, Bishop of Agrigento, 612, 613n., 642, 644–6, 656–7

Geoffrey of Andria, 311

Geoffrey of Conversano, the elder, 164–5, 168, 182, 217

Geoffrey of Conversano, the younger, 317–18

Geoffrey de Hauteville, son of Tancred, 39, 107, 198–9

Geoffrey de Hauteville, son of Roger I, 281

Geoffrey, Count of Montescaglioso, 560

George of Antioch, 292–3, 299, 301–2, 310, 317, 371, 453–7, 490–2, 505, 513, 515–17, 534, 561n., 752

Gerace, 132, 149–51, 254

Gerard of Bologna, Cardinal *see* Lucius II, Pope

Gerhoh of Reichensburg, 624

Geza II, King of Hungary, 612

Giato (S. Giuseppe Iato), 253

Gibbon, Edward, 6, 67, 89, 109n., 117, 119, 247, 248

Gilbert, Norman leader: killed at Cannae, 20

Gilbert, Count of Gravina, 577, 595, 615–19, 629, 631, 636, 641, 643–6, 656–7

Henry of Kalden, 721
Henry, Count of Montescaglioso, 618–19, 637–44, 646–9, 656
Herman, son of Rainulf II of Avisa, 79
Herman, son of Humphrey de Hauteville, 180, 194, 235–6
Hildebrand, Archdeacon *see* Gregory VII, Pope
Hohenburg, 748
Honorius II, Pope, 308–18, 322, 324–7, 365, 380, 428, 471, 765
Honorius II, anti-Pope, 159, 341
Hugh, Duke of Burgundy, 728, 730
Hugh of Este, 217
Hugh, Bishop of Jabala, 479
Hugh of Jersey, 253
Hugh, Archbishop of Lyons, 237, 261, 264–5
Hugh, Bishop of Ostia, 512
Hugh, Archbishop of Palermo, 434n., 508–9, 550, 552, 558, 576, 579
Humbert de Hauteville, 40
Humbert of Mourmoutiers, Cardinal, 99–105, 119, 122
Humphrey de Hauteville, Count of Apulia, 39–40, 75, 79, 87, 90, 92–3, 95, 107–8, 164, 247, 428

Ibn Abi-Dinar, 515
Ibn al-Athir, 135, 277, 296, 477, 516, 518, 520, 571n.
Ibn Hamdis of Syracuse, 252, 290
Ibn Hamud, Emir of Enna, 260–1
Ibn Haukal, 177
Ibn al-Hawas, 133, 135–8, 141–5, 160, 164, 166, 260
Ibn Jubair, 454–5, 640, 642, 661, 683, 691–3, 719–20, 721n.
Ibn Khaldun, 518, 520, 571n., 616n.
Ibn at-Timnah, Emir of Syracuse, 133, 135–6, 138, 141–2, 144, 145, 148, 151, 155, 160, 176
Imarus, Bishop of Tusculum, 624n.
Inn, river, 416
Innocent II, Pope, 325–8, 363, 365–70, 376–7, 381, 383–7, 393, 396–8, 400, 402–4, 406, 408–9, 411, 413–16, 421–9, 431, 446–7, 451, 466–8, 471–2, 632
Irene, Duchess of Apulia, later Western Empress, 741, 747–8
Isaac I Comnenus, Byzantine Emperor, 229, 704

Isaac II Angelus, Byzantine Emperor, 699–704, 741
Ischia, 411
Itála, 762
Ithaca, 245

Jaffa, 710
Jaquintus, Prince of Bari, 431
Jericho (Orikos), 246
Jerusalem, 9, 86, 182, 245, 284, 286–9, 293–4, 478–9, 485, 495, 499, 503, 660, 666–7, 704, 708–11, 719
Jesi, 749
Jews, 23n., 323
Joanna of England, Queen of Sicily, 663–4, 669–71, 680, 684, 715, 727–8, 730, 732–3, 740
Jocelin of Molfetta, Duke of Corinth, 164, 171–2
Johar, Great Chamberlain, 596
John XIX, Pope, 33, 73
John II Comnenus, Byzantine Emperor, 399–400, 466, 473–4, 549
John Ducas, 548, 554–5, 562, 700
John, Emir, 371
John, Abbot of Fécamp, 82
John of Hexham, 412
John, Bishop of Malta, 652, 656
John, Bishop of Norwich, 669–70
John the Orphanotrophos, 46, 48, 57, 63–4, 99
John, Prester, 479n.
John of Salisbury, 363, 468–9, 488n., 500, 507, 509, 510n., 535–6, 561, 569, 624, 629, 633, 716n.
John, Bishop of Trani, 99–100
Jordan, Count of Atiano, 306, 309
Jordan I, Prince of Capua, 214–18, 224, 235, 237, 259, 262–5, 269
Jordan, natural son of Roger I, 252, 254–7, 280–1
Jordan, Cardinal of S. Susanna, 510
Jordan du Pin, 728–9
Jordan, *tebastos*, 630
Judith of Evreux, wife of Roger I, 146–7, 151–4, 156, 176, 192, 278
Judith, daughter of Roger I, 546
Justinian I, Byzantine Emperor, 11, 51

Kairouan, 47, 133
Kaiserchronik, 395, 404n.
Kastoria, 233, 235, 254
Kerkenna, 571, 573

Nicotera, 255, 296–7, 300
Niger, Ralph (Radulphus), 429
Nijmegen, 26
Nilus, St, 53n.
Nilus Doxopatrius, Archimandrite, 451
Ninfa, 626
Nocera, 382–3, 388, 390–1
Norbert of Magdeburg, 328
Noto, 257, 260, 269
Nur ed-Din, Emir of Aleppo, King of Syria, 494–6, 666
Nusco, 666

Ochrid, 232
Octavian of S. Cecilia, Cardinal see Victor IV, anti-Pope
Octavian of Monticelli, Cardinal, 541
Odo of Deuil, 481–2
Odo, Bishop of Ostia see Urban II, Pope
Ofanto, river, 19, 61, 156
Offamiglio, Ophamilus see Walter of the Mill
Olivento, river, 60–1, 156
Ordericus Vitalis, 37n., 250–1, 281–2, 293n., 307n.
Oreto, river, 161n., 177–9, 516, 571
Oria, 107, 138, 162, 260
Orikos, 246
Oriolo, 595
Ortoqids, 479
Ostrovo, 65
Otranto, 11, 27, 107, 175, 227, 234–5, 246–7, 260, 312, 490, 548
Otto I ('the Great'), Western Emperor, 13, 124
Otto II, Western Emperor, 5, 13
Otto III, Western Emperor, 5, 13
Otto, Bishop of Freising, 466, 479n., 490n., 501, 511, 540, 542–3
Otto of St Blaise, 632n.
Otto of Wittelsbach, Count of Bavaria, 565

Palaeologus, George, 229–32
Palaeologus, Michael, 466, 546–9, 554, 557, 562
Palatine Chapel, Palermo, 433–7, 444n., 449, 452, 455–6, 458n., 530, 602–3, 613, 670–1, 677–9, 681, 751, 763
Palazzo Reale, Palermo see Royal Palace
Palermo, 51–3, 156, 161–4, 166–7, 174–85, 189–91, 229, 259, 269, 271, 276, 283, 289, 291, 299, 306, 312, 330–1;

Cathedral, 363, 375, 378, 449n., 520–1, 610, 613, 637, 651, 659, 676, 681, 722–3, 746, 749, 761, 763
Palestrina, 80, 415
Palmer, Richard, Bishop of Syracuse, later Archbishop of Messina, 532, 581, 588–9, 597, 599, 609, 611–12, 613n., 614–15, 637, 652, 655–9, 670, 728, 763
Pandulf III, Prince of Capua, 21–3, 25–9, 32–6, 38, 40–3, 47, 70–1, 74–6, 88, 127
Pandulf IV, Prince of Capua, 108–10
Pandulf, Count of Teano, 29, 31, 34–5, 87, 89
Pantelleria, 298
Pantheon, Rome, 266
Papareschi, 409
Parco, 517, 529, 761
Paris, 499, 501
Pascal II, Pope, 293–4, 303–5, 321, 323, 340, 538
Paschal III, anti-Pope, 628–9, 632, 635
Pateranos, Stephen, 170–1
Paternò, 143, 764
Patti, 289, 764
Paul IV, Pope, 323
Pavia, 10, 29, 537, 626–7, 633, 635
Perenos, Duke of Durazzo, 164, 169, 175
Peter II, King of Aragon, 750
Peter, Archbishop of Amalfi, 89, 101–5
Peter of Blois, 636, 654–6, 659n.
Peter, Caïd (Ahmed es-Sikeli), 571–2, 576, 599, 609, 613–17, 666
Peter ('the Venerable'), Abbot of Cluny, 328, 370, 417, 447, 471, 503–4
Peter Damian, St, 340, 411
Peter the Deacon, 340, 411
Peter of Eboli, 712, 716–18, 766–7
Peter of Langtoft, 732n.
Peter of Pisa, 422–4
Peter of Trani, 194, 217
Petralia, 147–8, 164
Philip, 257
Philip I, King of France, 278, 285
Philip Augustus, King of France, 711, 724–32
Philip, brother of Louis VII, 481
Philip of Mahdia, 517–20, 530, 532
Philip of Swabia, Western Emperor, 748
Philippa, Princess of Antioch, 688

ance, 69–70, 364; early years in Italy, 75–9; trickery, 77–8; marriage to Alberada, 78–9; at Civitate, 90, 92–3; succeeds Humphrey 107–8; differences with Roger, 113–15; marriage to Sichelgaita, 116–18; papal investiture at Melfi, 126–31; first Sicilian campaign, 131–46, 363; Latinisation of Calabria, 147, 192; quarrel with Roger, 147–51; second Sicilian campaign, 162–3; trouble in Apulia, 164–8; siege of Bari, 168–73, 472, 547; capture of Palermo, 174–85, 432, 746; restores order in Apulia, 193–5; illness, 195–6; relations with Gregory VII, 197–204, 387; wooed by Henry IV and Gregory, 207–9; capture of Salerno, 209–13, 413; breach with Gregory, 214–18; investiture at Ceprano, 218–19, 262, 507; first Byzantine expedition, 222–33, 253–4, 399, 556, 685, 692, 694; return to Italy and march on Rome, 234–42, 254–5, 428; escorts Gregory to Salerno, 242–3; second Byzantine expedition, 243–5, 556; death and burial, 245–50, 388; trouble with S. Italian vassals, 376; other references, 258–60, 322, 382, 405–6, 414, 449, 471, 473, 506, 590, 613n., 714

Robert of Bellême, 637
Robert of Bova, 585
Robert of Dreux, 619
Robert de Grantmesnil, Abbot of St Evroul, 146–7, 319n.
Robert of Grantmesnil, 319
Robert, Count of Loritello, 198–9, 214–15, 546–7, 554, 556, 562–3, 577, 595–6, 663–4, 713
Robert, Archbishop of Messina, 579, 587–8
Robert of Montescaglioso, 164
Robert of Newburgh, 615, 619
Robert of Selby, 412–13, 468–9, 470, 506, 508, 530
Robert de Sourval, 254
Robert of Torigni, 684n.
Robert, Bishop of Troina and Messina, 272–3
Rocca d'Asino, 255, 257
Roger I de Hauteville, Great Count of Sicily: beginnings, 112–14; Calabrian famine, 114–15; first Sicilian cam-

paign, 131–46; marriage to Judith of Evreux, 146–7; quarrel with Robert Guiscard, 147–51; besieged in Troina, 151–4; slow progress through Sicily, 155–68; besieges Bari, 171–3; capture of Palermo, 174–85, 372, 432, 746; consolidation in Sicily, 189–93; supports Robert Guiscard in Italy, 236–7; gives home to Helena, 251; concludes conquest of Sicily, 252–61, 269; government in Sicily, 269–70, 363–4, 450–1, 590, 739; relations with Rome, 270–4; policy towards Saracens, 274–7, 294, 485, 518–19; death, family and achievements, 278–81, 283, 509; other references, 40, 54n., 106, 382, 485, 521–2, 560, 594n., 658, 728, 745n., 762–4

Roger II de Hauteville, King of Sicily: birth, 281; becomes Count of Sicily, 282; childhood, 282; knighted, 283; character, 284, 297–8; claim to Jerusalem, 280, 287, 289; early years of power, 290–4; attacks on Gabes and Mahdia, 294–302; first Apulian expedition, 305–7; wins Duchy of Apulia, 307–15; establishes authority in Apulia, 316–19; summons court at Melfi, 319–22; receives submission of Capua, 322–3; negotiates for crown, 328–30; coronation, 330–1, 363; background, 364–5; in papal schism, 365, 369–70; consolidates on mainland, 371; founds Cefalù, 371–5; 1132 revolt, 376–84; 1133 revolt, 388–90; 1134 revolt, 390–4; 1135 revolt, 395–9; invests sons, 400; and Lothair's 1137 invasion, 401–5, 407–15; pacification of Regno, 418–32; rebuilds Royal Palace, 432–3; founds Palatine Chapel, 433–5; Assizes of Ariano, 441–6; reconciliation with Rome, 446–9; founds S. Giovanni degli Eremiti, 448–50; attitude to Greek community, 450–2; portrait in Martorana, 457–9; character, 443, 458–9, 464–5, 523; administration, 459–60; patronage of art and learning, 460–5; relations with papacy, 367–72; relations with two empires, 467–72; attitude to Second Crusade, 477–8, 481, 484–6; attacks Greece, 489–93; meeting with Louis VII and

S. Maria in Turri, Rome, 272
St Mark's, Venice, 672
S. Martino d'Agri, 147
S. Nicandro, 108
St Nicholas, Bari, 406, 458n., 547, 555
S. Nicola of Filocastro, Calabria, 448
S. Paolo di Civitate, 96
St Peter's, Rome, 73, 80, 95, 236, 241, 243, 266, 326, 386, 403, 424, 479, 511, 536, 538, 541, 568, 624–5, 632–3
S. Quirico, 538
S. Salvatore, Messina, 452, 718, 728
S. Spirito, Palermo, 723, 763
SS. Trinita di Delia, Castelvetrano, Palermo, 576n., 752, 762
Sala di Ruggero, Royal Palace, Palermo, 588n., 601–2, 763
Saladin, Sultan, 666–7, 704, 708–12
Salerno, 16–17, 27–30, 38, 43, 84, 86–8, 108–9, 116, 201, 210–14, 215, 218, 220, 243, 259, 264–5, 273–4, 303, 307–11, 319, 330, 377, 379, 382–4, 390, 395, 397, 411–13, 418–22, 428, 431, 447–8, 468, 511, 547, 558–9, 595–7, 603, 665, 677, 705, 736–8, 744–7; Cathedral, 212, 243, 263n., 303–4, 307
Salso, river, 184
Sangro, river, 427
Saracen troops, 368–9, 412, 418
Sardinia, 385
Sarno, river, 382–3
Sarule of Genzano, 79
Saviour, Monastery of the *see* S. Salvatore, Messina
Saxon Annalist, 406, 408
Scafati, 382
Scalea, 114–15, 117
Sciacca, 745, 764
Scilla, 132
Sclavo, Roger, 594–5
Scribla, 76–7
Segesta, 372–3
Seleucia (Silifke), 734
Seljuks, 165, 168, 171, 200, 284
Senate, Roman, 467, 470, 501, 536–7, 539–42, 569, 628, 632, 673, 741
Sens, 536, 627, 679n., 735
Sergius, Duke of Amalfi, 201
Sergius IV, Duke of Naples, 34–8
Sergius VII, Duke of Naples, 371, 393, 396–8, 400–1, 414, 418–19
Serlo de Hauteville, the elder, 39, 136

Serlo de Hauteville, the younger, 136, 156–7, 183–4, 189
Sfax, 515, 570–1, 573
Sibyl of Burgundy, Queen of Sicily, 509
Sibylla of Acerra, Queen of Sicily, 740, 742–3, 745–6, 748
Sichelgaita of Salerno, Duchess of Apulia, 116–18, 146, 153, 183, 195–7, 201, 210, 217, 231–2, 245–7, 249–51, 258–9, 396, 694, 746
Sicilian Vespers, 723, 745
Sidon, 710
Simeto, river, 143
Simon, Count of Butera, 594n., 764
Simon, Duke of Dalmatia, 406
Simon, Count of Policastro, 552
Simon, Prince of Taranto, 584–5, 587, 591, 609, 643
Simon, royal seneschal, 560, 576
Simon, son of Roger I, 281–2
Siponto, 4, 67, 90, 406, 419, 745
Skleros, Romanus, 64
Sorrento, 38, 88, 411
Soussa, 514
Speyer, 401, 483
Spinazzola, 744
Splugen pass, 744
Spoleto, 10, 90, 546
Squillace, 76, 115, 132n., 175
Staina, river, 91
Stephen, King of England, 481
Stephen IX, Pope (*formerly* Frederick of Lorraine), 89, 101–5, 110–11, 117, 120–2, 124
Stephen, Byzantine admiral, 48, 55, 63, 560–1, 576, 578
Stephen du Perche, 615, 619–22, 631, 638–9, 641–2, 644–6, 648, 650–6, 658, 660, 663, 713, 718
Stethatus, Nicetas, 103
Stilo, 13
Strymon, river, 702–3
Studion monastery, 64, 103
Suger, Abbot of St Denis, 481, 510–11, 513
Sutri, 74, 538, 542, 548
Sylvester III, Pope, 73–4
Sylvester, Count of Marsico, 581, 597, 599
Syracuse, 52, 54–5, 66, 98, 133, 183, 252–9, 271, 281, 291, 364, 461, 493, 522, 595, 611, 613n., 664, 745, 764

READ MORE IN PENGUIN

In every corner of the world, on every subject under the sun, Penguin represents quality and variety – the very best in publishing today.

For complete information about books available from Penguin – including Puffins, Penguin Classics and Arkana – and how to order them, write to us at the appropriate address below. Please note that for copyright reasons the selection of books varies from country to country.

In the United Kingdom: Please write to *Dept. JC, Penguin Books Ltd, FREEPOST, West Drayton, Middlesex UB7 0BR*

If you have any difficulty in obtaining a title, please send your order with the correct money, plus ten per cent for postage and packaging, to *PO Box No. 11, West Drayton, Middlesex UB7 0BR*

In the United States: Please write to *Penguin USA Inc., 375 Hudson Street, New York, NY 10014*

In Canada: Please write to *Penguin Books Canada Ltd, 10 Alcorn Avenue, Suite 300, Toronto, Ontario M4V 3B2*

In Australia: Please write to *Penguin Books Australia Ltd, 487 Maroondah Highway, Ringwood, Victoria 3134*

In New Zealand: Please write to *Penguin Books (NZ) Ltd,182–190 Wairau Road, Private Bag, Takapuna, Auckland 9*

In India: Please write to *Penguin Books India Pvt Ltd, 706 Eros Apartments, 56 Nehru Place, New Delhi 110 019*

In the Netherlands: Please write to *Penguin Books Netherlands B.V., Keizersgracht 231 NL–1016 DV Amsterdam*

In Germany: Please write to *Penguin Books Deutschland GmbH, Friedrichstrasse 10–12, W–6000 Frankfurt/Main 1*

In Spain: Please write to *Penguin Books S. A., C. San Bernardo 117–6° E–28015 Madrid*

In Italy: Please write to *Penguin Italia s.r.l., Via Felice Casati 20, I–20124 Milano*

In France: Please write to *Penguin France S. A., 17 rue Lejeune, F–31000 Toulouse*

In Japan: Please write to *Penguin Books Japan, Ishikiribashi Building, 2–5–4, Suido, Tokyo 112*

In Greece: Please write to *Penguin Hellas Ltd, Dimocritou 3, GR–106 71 Athens*

In South Africa: Please write to *Longman Penguin Southern Africa (Pty) Ltd, Private Bag X08, Bertsham 2013*

BY THE SAME AUTHOR

Byzantium: The Early Centuries

In this exciting narrative history, John Julius Norwich tells of the five formative centuries of an empire that would enthral the western world for more than eleven hundred years. 'He is brilliant ... He writes like the most cultivated modern diplomat attached by a freak of time to the Byzantine court, with intimate knowledge, tactful judgement and a consciousness of the surviving monuments' – *Independent*

A History of Venice

John Julius Norwich's loving and scholarly portrayal of 'the most beautiful and magical of cities'. 'As a historian Lord Norwich knows what matters. As a writer he has a taste for beauty, a love of language and an enlivening wit ... He contrives, as no English writer has done before, to sustain a continuous interest in that crowded history' – Hugh Trevor-Roper

Christmas Crackers

Over the past ten years John Julius Norwich has sent out commonplace selections of prose and poetry to his friends at Christmas. Collected here in one volume are these Crackers; from contributors as diverse as Confucius and W. S. Gilbert, on subjects as varied as love, the longest palindrome, and the French, German and Russian versions of *Jabberwocky*. 'A bouquet of individually picked flowers culled by a master gardener, and arranged in a manner that would get him first prize in any literary flower shower' – Bernard Levin in *The Times*

also published:

Byzantium: The Apogee
More Christmas Crackers